ON CONTEMPORARY LITERA-TURE contains critical essays on the major aspects of contemporary, post-World War II literature. Its purpose is to provide students of today's writing with the most useful criticism of the major movements and writers. These essays provide not just an off-hand evaluation or a single critical insight but a thorough understanding and illumination of, in some essays, a large area of literature and, in others, of all of a writer's work. By judiciously selecting chapters of books and essays in magazines and by commissioning original critical essays where none in print were satisfactory, Richard Kostelanetz, we believe, has put together the most comprehensive and perceptive book available on today's literature.

RICHARD KOSTELANETZ is a prolific young American critic. Editor of *The New American Arts* (1964), he writes particularly on contemporary fiction and theater, and also on criticism and culture, for a wide variety of journals, ranging from weeklies to quarterlies, both here and abroad.

ON CONTEMPORARY LITERATURE

An anthology of critical essays
on the major movements and writers
of contemporary literature

Edited, with an introductory essay,

by RICHARD KOSTELANETZ

An Avon Book

This book is especially for
S. FOSTER DAMON
JUAN LOPEZ-MORILLAS
WILLIAM C. McLOUGHLIN
DENNIS H. WRONG,
with my admiration and gratitude.

AVON BOOKS
a division of
The Hearst Corporation
959 Eighth Avenue
New York 19, N. Y. 10019

Acknowledgements

Gore Vidal, "Ladders to Heaven," reprinted and abridged from *New World Writing #4*, by permission of Gore Vidal. Copyright, 1954, by New American Library.

Ihab H. Hassan, "The Character of Post-War Fiction in America," reprinted from *English Journal* (January, 1962), by permission of the National Council of Teachers of English and Ihab H. Hassan. Copyright, 1962, by the National Council of Teachers.

John Gassner, "New American Playwrights: Williams, Miller and Others," reprinted and abridged from *The Theatre in Our Times* by John Gassner, by permission of Crown Publishers, Inc. Copyright, 1954, by the author.

Leslie A. Fiedler, "Class War in British Literature," reprinted from *Esquire* (April, 1958), Copyright © 1958 by Esquire, Inc., by permission of *Esquire* Magazine, Revised by permission of the author.

A. Alvarez, "English Poetry Today," *Commentary* (September, 1961), copyright by The American Jewish Committee, reprinted and abridged by permission of A. Alvarez, Penguin Books and *Commentary*.

John Russell Taylor, "British Drama of the Fifties," reprinted from *World Theatre*, official organ of the l'Institut International du Theatre, by permission of the author and Francois Mennes. Revised by permission of the author.

Henri Peyre, "Trends in the Contemporary French Novel," reprinted from *New French Writing* (New York, 1961), edited by Georges Borchardt, by permission of the publisher. Copyright, 1961, by Criterion Books, Inc.

Jean Paris, "The New French Poetry," reprinted, revised, and translated from *The American Society French Legion of Honor Magazine* (1960), by permission of the author.

Sergio Pacifici, "Italian Novels of the Fifties," reprinted from *Books Abroad*, XXXVI, No. 3 (Summer, 1962), by permission of *Books Abroad* and the author.

Sergio Pacifici, "Something Old and Something New," reprinted from *Yale French Studies*, No. 21, copyright 1958, *Yale French Studies*, with revisions by permission of the author and *Yale French Studies*.

Andrew Field, "A Literature Appears," copyright, 1964, by Andrew Field, by permission of the author.

Martin Esslin, "The Theatre of the Absurd," reprinted from the *Tulane Drama Review* (1961), copyright by the *Tulane Drama Review* and Martin Esslin.

Alfred Kazin, "Good-By to James Agee," reprinted from *Contemporaries* by Alfred Kazin, by permission of Little, Brown and Co., Atlantic Monthly Press and *The New York Times*. Copyright, 1957, by *The New York Times*.

Richard Kostelanetz, "Edward Albee," extracted from "The Art of Total No," *Contact* (October-November, 1963), by permission of *Contact* and the author.

Norman Podhoretz, "In Defense of a Maltreated Best Seller," reprinted from *Show: The Magazine of the Arts* (October, 1962), by permission of Norman Podhoretz.

Leslie A. Fiedler, "John Barth: An Eccentric Genius," reprinted with permission from *The New Leader* of February 13, 1961.

Kenneth Rexroth, "The Point Is Irrelevance," reprinted and abridged by permission from *The Nation*, December 7, 1957.

Maurice Blanchot, "Where Now? Who Now?", reprinted and abridged from *Evergreen Review #7*, as translated from *Le livre à venir* by Maurice Blanchot, copyright by Editions Gallimard, by permission of Editions Gallimard and the author. The translation, copyright, 1957, by Grove Press, reprinted by permission of Grove Press.

Jacques Guicharnaud, "Existence on Stage," reprinted with omission of footnotes by permission of Yale University Press from *Modern French Theatre*, by Jacques Guicharnaud. Copyright, 1961, by Yale University Press.

v

Leslie A. Fiedler, "Saul Bellow," reprinted from *Prairie Schooner* (Autumn, 1957), by permission of the University of Nebraska Press and the author.

Jack Ludwig's pages on Saul Bellow, extracted from a longer essay on *Recent American Novelists*, copyright, 1962, by permission of the University of Minnesota Press.

Stanley Edgar Hyman, "Anthony Burgess," reprinted from the afterword to *The Clockwork Orange* by permission of W. W. Norton and Stanley Edgar Hyman. Copyright, 1963, by W. W. Norton and Co.

S. Beynon John, "Albert Camus," reprinted from *Modern Languages*, Vol. XXXVI, No. 1 (December, 1954), pp. 13-18, by permission of *Modern Languages*.

Norman Podhoretz, "Solitary or Solidary?", reprinted from *The New Yorker* (March 29, 1958), by permission of Norman Podhoretz. Copyright © 1958 by The New Yorker, Inc.

John Unterecker, "The Protean World of Lawrence Durrell," copyright, 1964, by John Unterecker, adapted from a section of his *Lawrence Durrell*, Columbia University Press, 1964. Reprinted by permission of the author.

Frank Kermode, "William Golding," reprinted from *International Literary Annual #3* (London, 1961), by permission of John Calder, Ltd.

Frank Kermode, "Postscript, 1964" to William Golding, reprinted from *The New York Review of Books* (April 30, 1964), by permission of the author. Copyright © 1964 by New York Review, Inc.

Shimon Wincelberg, "A Deadly Serious Lunacy," reprinted with permission from *The New Leader* of May 14, 1962.

Richard Schechner, "The Inner and Outer Reality," abridged and reprinted from the *Tulane Drama Review* (Spring, 1963), copyright, 1963, by *Tulane Drama Review*, by permission of *Tulane Drama Review* and Richard Schechner.

Walter Allen, "Her Early Novels," from the book *The Modern Novel* by Walter Allen. Copyright © 1964 by Walter Allen. Slightly adapted and reprinted by permission of E. P. Dutton & Co., Inc., and J. M. Dent Ltd.

Robert Taubman, "Free Women," reprinted from *The New Statesman* (April 20, 1962) with the permission of Robert Taubman and *The New Statesman*.

Randall Jarrell, "From the Kingdom of Necessity," reprinted by permission from *The Nation*, January 18, 1947.

John Hollander, "Robert Lowell's New Book," reprinted from *Poetry* (October, 1959), by permission of the author. Copyright, 1959, by *Poetry*.

Walter Allen, "The Masterpiece of the Forties," from the book *The Modern Novel* by Walter Allen. Copyright © 1964 by Walter Allen. Slightly adapted and reprinted by permission of E. P. Dutton & Co., Inc., and J. M. Dent Ltd.

Alfred Kazin, "The Magic and the Dread," reprinted from *Contemporaries*, by Alfred Kazin, by permission of Little, Brown and Co., Atlantic Monthly Press. Copyright, 1958, by Alfred Kazin.

Stanley Edgar Hyman, "A New Life for a Good Man," reprinted by permission from *The New Leader*, October 2, 1961.

R. W. B. Lewis, "Alberto Moravia: Eros and Existence," reprinted from *The Picaresque Saint*, by R. W. B. Lewis, copyright © 1956, 1958, by the author, by permission of J. B. Lippincott Company.

Francis Hope, "The Novels of Iris Murdoch," reprinted from *The London Magazine* (August, 1961), copyright by *The London Magazine*, by permission of Francis Hope.

Andrew Field, "The Defenseless Luzhin," reprinted from *The New Leader* (September, 1964), by permission of Andrew Field and *The New Leader*. Copyright, 1964, by the American Labor Conference on International Affairs, Inc.

John Hollander, "The Perilous Magic of Nymphets," reprinted from *Partisan Review* (Summer, 1956), copyright by *Partisan Review*, by permission of *Partisan Review* and John Hollander.

Frank O'Hara, "About Zhivago and His Poems," reprinted, with a revision, from *Evergreen Review #7*, copyright, 1959, by Grove Press, by permission of Frank O'Hara.

Stanley Edgar Hyman, "The Goddess and the Schlemihl," reprinted by permission from *The New Leader*, March 18, 1963. Revised by permission of the author.

Roland Barthes, "Robbe-Grillet Today," reprinted from the preface to *Les Romans de Robbe-Grillet*, by Bruce Morrissette, published 1963 by Éditions de Minuit, by permission of Éditions de Minuit. Translation copyright, 1964, by Avon Book Division, The Hearst Corporation.

Stanley Edgar Hyman, "A Novelist of Great Promise," reprinted with permission from *The New Leader* of June 11, 1962.

Donald Barr, "Saints, Pilgrims and Artists," reprinted from *The Commonweal*, Vol. 67, No. 4, for October 25, 1957, by permission of *The Commonweal*.

Anne Kostelanetz, "Manifesto for a New New French Novel," reprinted from *The Massachusetts Review* (Winter, 1964), by permission of The Massachusetts Review, Inc., and the author.

Anne Kostelanetz, "Postscript, 1964" to Nathalie Sarraute, reprinted with revisions from "A Velvet Clawing for the Modish," *Book Week* (Feb. 9, 1964), by permission of the author and the New York Herald Tribune, Inc. Copyright © 1964, by the New York Herald Tribune, Inc.

William Barrett, "Jean-Paul Sartre," reprinted from *Irrational Man*, copyright © 1958, by William Barrett, by permission of Doubleday and Co., Inc.

Irving Howe, "Demonic Fiction of a Yiddish 'Modernist,'" reprinted from *Commentary* (October, 1960), by permission of *Commentary*. Copyright, 1960, by The American Jewish Committee.

Stanley Edgar Hyman, "The Yiddish Hawthorne," reprinted with permission from *The New Leader* of July 28, 1962.

Renata Adler, "Muriel Spark," a revision reprinted from *The Village Voice* (September, 1963), copyright, 1963, by The Village Voice, Inc., by permission of *The Village Voice* and Renata Adler.

Ihab H. Hassan, "Encounter With Necessity," reprinted with omission of footnotes from *Radical Innocence,* by Ihab H. Hassan, copyright, 1961, by Princeton University Press, by permission of the publisher.

William York Tindall, "The Poetry of Dylan Thomas," reprinted from *The American Scholar,* Volume XVII, Number 4, Autumn, 1948, copyright © 1948 by the United Chapters of Phi Beta Kappa, by permission of the publisher.

Eric Bentley, "The Meaning of Robert Penn Warren's Novels," revised and reprinted from *Kenyon Review* (Summer, 1948), by permission of *Kenyon Review* and the author.

Acknowledgements of Quotations
(Listed in the order they appear in the book.)

From J. M. Cohen's translation of Rafael Alberti's *Castigos,* reprinted from *The Creative Experiment* by C. M. Bowra, by permission of Grove Press.

From T. S. Eliot, "The Fire Sermon," *The Waste Land,* reprinted by permission of Harcourt, Brace and World, Inc.

From Jerome Rothenberg's translation of Paul Celan's "Death Fugue," reprinted from *The Fifties #3* © 1959 by The Fifties Press, by permission of The Sixties Press.

From Samuel Beckett, "Dieppe," reprinted from *Poems in English,* by permission of Grove Press.

From Nicanor Parra, "The Soliloquy of the Individual," reprinted from *Anti-Poems,* copyright © 1959 by Nicanor Parra, by permission of City Lights Books.

Philip Larkin, "At Grass" and "To the Daughter of a Friend," reprinted by permission of Marvell Press.

From Donald Davie, "Remembering the Thirties," reprinted from *New and Selected Poems,* by Donald Davie, by permission of Wesleyan University Press. Copyright © 1955 by Donald Davie.

Ted Hughes, "A Dream of Horses," reprinted from *Lupercal* by permission of Faber and Faber, Ltd., and Harper and Row, Publishers, Inc.

From William Golding, *The Spire,* reprinted by permission of Harcourt, Brace and World, Inc.

From Robert Lowell, *Lord Weary's Castle,* reprinted by permission of Harcourt, Brace and World, Inc.

From Robert Lowell, *Life Studies,* reprinted by permission of Farrar, Straus and Company, Inc. Copyright 1956, 1959, by Robert Lowell.

From Norman Mailer, *The Deer Park,* reprinted by permission of G. P. Putnam's Sons, Inc. Copyright 1955 by Norman Mailer.

From Avrahm Yarmolinsky's translation of Boris Pasternak's poetry, excerpts taken from *An Anthology of Russian Verse,* published by the Vintage Russian Library, copyright 1965 by Avrahm Yarmolinsky, reprinted by permission of the translator.

From Max Hayward and Manya Harari's translation of Boris Pasternak, *Doctor Zhivago,* copyright © by Pantheon Books, Inc., reprinted by permission of the publisher.

From Bernard Guilbert Guerney's translation of "The Poems of Yuri Zhivago," in Boris Pasternak, *Doctor Zhivago,* reprinted by permission of Pantheon Books, Inc.

From James Purdy, *Malcolm,* copyright 1959 by James Purdy; and *The Nephew,* copyright 1960 by James Purdy; reprinted by permission of Farrar, Straus and Company, Inc.

From John Berryman; *Homage to Mistress Bradstreet,* copyright 1956 by John Berryman; and *77 Dream Songs,* copyright 1959, 1962, 1963, 1964 by John Berryman; reprinted by permission of Farrar, Straus and Company.

From John Berryman, "Dream Song: Columbus Day," reprinted from *Encounter* (Oct., 1962) by permission of the author.

From Theodore Roethke, "The Bat," copyright 1938, 1939 by Theodore Roethke; and "Open House," copyright 1941 by Theodore Roethke, from *Words for the Wind,* reprinted by permission of Doubleday & Co., Inc.

Theodore Roethke, "The Moment," "The Geranium," copyright 1963 by Beatrice Roethke as administratrix of the estate of Theodore Roethke, reprinted by permission of Mrs. Roethke. Originally published in, respectively, *The New Yorker* and *Partisan Review.*

Selections from *The Planetarium* and *The Golden Fruits* by Nathalie Sarraute, copyright by George Braziller, Inc., reprinted by permission of the publisher.

From *Lie Down in Darkness* by William Styron, copyright 1951 by the author, reprinted by permission of Bobbs-Merrill, Inc.

Preface

This book contains critical essays on the most important aspects of contemporary literature. The coverage is limited to writers whose major work appeared after the end of World War II. Thus, of those who wrote both before and after, Robert Penn Warren and Jean-Paul Sartre are included, but William Carlos Williams and St. Jean Perse, whose major phases preceded the war, are not. In Boris Pasternak's case, the decision was more difficult, and here I was motivated by my own compelling admiration for *Doctor Zhivago* (1957) and a sense that for American readers this novel will always be more important than his early poetry. In selecting the writers to be covered, I relied largely on my own taste for writing that engages the present with an originality, a coherence, and a radical form of perception and that, moreover, embodies the traditional values of literature such as emotional fidelity, thematic reasonance, a unity of vision, a realized integration of elements and a propitious use of language. Yet my prejudices were tempered by an awareness of the reader's interests. This, in turn, explains and rationalizes why several English and American writers of somewhat lesser achievement receive individual essays, while Europeans of comparable value do not. For this reason, in the bibliographies following the survey essays on the various areas of European literature, I have listed—for all but French—the important essays in English on the neglected individual figures. On grounds of space, the scope of the book is limited to the literatures of the United States, Canada and Europe.

The purpose of *On Contemporary Literature* is to provide students of today's literature with the most helpful general criticism of the major movements and writers. Since the best criticism of this sort, I have found, does not exist in one place, it had to be collected from a variety of sources. My function as the editor was to piece together, as one would a jigsaw puzzle, the best possible book of criticism of contemporary literature. By "criticism," I mean not an off-hand evaluation, but a thorough understanding that comes when the critic wrings order from his taste and perceptions, offering us not just a critical insight into one book but an illumination of a writer's work and, sometimes, a large area of literature. In general, there has been exceedingly little criticism of this sort, and that is the major reason why so many of the pieces were commissioned especially for publication here.

To suit the overall purpose, the essays tend to vary in style, method and approach. In the surveys of the major national literatures and, in one case, an international style, the critic defines and evaluates the work of the individual writers and identifies various large lines of interest. For essays on the specific authors, I have tended to choose analytical studies for writers whose works are not particularly difficult, such as Moravia and Ellison; and for more difficult authors, such as Sarraute and Burgess, I have favored introductory pieces. All but one of the essays focus upon the writer's creative work. For the section on Jean-Paul Sartre, I picked an essay that identified and analyzed Sartre's key overarching ideas.

Most of the essays, I hope, fulfill the two-fold task of good general criticism: they both introduce and explain a writer's work. To readers unfamiliar with a writer's books, the essay on him should convey a sense of his style, his themes, his major preoccupations, his successes and his failures, and his achievement in the perspective of contemporary literature. For those who already know a writer's work, these essays will, I trust, provide and stimulate a deeper understanding of what they have read. These essays should not only prove interesting in themselves but should lead the reader back to contemporary literature itself.

Like every anthologist, I am indebted to many people for their co-operation—editors, agents and writers who gave me permission to use essays under their control and, in some cases, who accepted my requests for changes, as well as several translators who guided me through unfamiliar languages. I would like especially to thank the critics who wrote essays especially for this volume—Joseph P. Bauke, Jonathan Cott, Harris Dienstfrey, Manuel Duran, Raymond Federman, Andrew Field, Ellin Horowitz, Henri Peyre, John Unterecker, and George Woodcock. For other favors, my gratitude goes to my parents Ethel and Boris Kostelanetz, Douglas MacLeod, Carol and Thomas Mather, Peter Mayer, Dorothy Tidaback, Charles H. Watts and, above all, my wife Anne.   Richard Kostelanetz
New York, New York
May 14, 1964

CONTENTS

Contemporary Literature
BY RICHARD KOSTELANETZ

Despite scattered opinion to the contrary, there exists, I am convinced, a contemporary literature that is worth our most serious attention. Not only does this Post–World War II writing offer a wide spectrum of numerous important works, but several recent writers, such as Samuel Beckett, Albert Camus, Ralph Ellison, Jean Genet, Alberto Moravia, and Jean-Paul Sartre, have produced some of the most significant literature of the twentieth century. Like their predecessors, the great moderns of forty years ago, the best contemporary writers critically engage the continuous upheavals in both society and literary form that define the culture of the twentieth century. Though their style and subjects are as pertinent as the morning news, their purposes remain as traditional as writing itself. Through literature, they strive to understand the radical nature of the present, both in its content and form, and to show how the eternal in man and the legacy of history fare in the world today. To do this, they have largely resisted the efforts of conservative critics to make them toe the line of the "rules" for their art. Rather, contemporary writers, particularly the best of them, continue to reject forms and subjects they feel are archaic and to create original vehicles to carry their awareness of the unprecedented modern situation. The best of this recent literature, because of its pertinence, excellence and difficulty, merits the most conscientious analysis and delicate appreciation a critic can give.

Like the masters of all twentieth century art, contemporary writers express their oppressive awareness of the predicament of the times. Though man has achieved extraordinary material and technological progress, the greatest literature of the past forty-five years tells us over and over again that the quality of his life has not improved apace, for he is the victim, rather than the beneficiary, of the advances of history. In depicting modern life, individual writers choose to concentrate upon various aspects of the total situation. Albert Camus and Jean-Paul Sartre emphasize that modern man, alienated from society, is free from consciousness of moral responsibility, and Saul Bellow and Boris Pasternak insist that the institutions of modern society inevitably frustrate human wants. Totalitarian methods of control, so George Orwell and Norman Mailer tell us, infiltrate democratic societies as well as dictatorial, and more recently Anthony Burgess sees that life in our time is so horrendously violent that the lone individual can do little to defend himself against its unexpected onslaughts. Alberto Moravia and others dramatize that true human relations are made impossible both by biological needs and the selfishness of man isolated in mass society; and Eugene Ionesco and Samuel Beckett demonstrate that contemporary man, who has neither a universally accepted explanation for the mysteries nor an ethical system universally observed, faces an existence which is fundamentally absurd. James Purdy and Ralph Ellison emphasize that although man is terribly alone and incapable of overcoming his isolation, he still asserts his right to exist. Many of these themes, it is true, characterized the major writings of forty years ago. The rootlessness and *anomie* of twentieth century man were, of course, felt and explored by Eliot and Joyce as well as by Mann and Kafka, all profoundly aware of the contagious malaise of the age.

However, this literary image of the modern world has recently undergone a slight, but perceptible, shift. A comparison of the major themes of T. S. Eliot and Samuel Beckett, both among the most eminent and most representative writers of their respective generations, illustrates this change. In *The Waste Land*, Eliot emphasized intellectual disillusion and despair, historical disintegration from stability into anarchy, and the decline of religious faith. In his portrait of the modern situation, he generally opposes the present to the past. Beckett, however, discards all sense of linear history in order to focus upon the eternity of individual isolation. He suggests that man is doomed to recognize that systematic beliefs and concerted actions are impotent before the metaphysical absurdity that has always been his fate. Unlike Eliot, whose pessimism was so thorough he could envision redemption only in a *return* to the past, Beckett believes in the ontological indomitableness of the human spirit. In his recent novel, entitled with the pun *Comment C'est* (How It Is, or To Begin), Beckett's Pim, the prototypical man, struggles through limbo, crawling *forward* at an excruciatingly slow pace, his face always down in the mud. Despite all obstacles and with no discernible reason for being or going on, Pim continues to move.

The shift in emphasis from Eliot to Beckett epitomizes other changes in literature's view of man's existence. For one contrast, what separates the best contemporaries from the generation of Faulkner and Hemingway is the former's refusal to let their sensitive protagonists escape into death. Bellow's Tommy Wilhelm, Ellison's Invisible Man, the narrator of Jean Genet's prose, J. D. Salinger's Holden Caulfield, Michael Butor's Jacques Revel, Günter Grass's insane narrator, and Sartre's Roquentin are all faced with the possibility of death, but their awareness of their possible extinction only inspires them to draw strength from their deepest sources of resilience and to salvage their lives. This refusal to retreat into history or death signifies, I think, that the best writers *accept* modern existence, with all its horror and absurdity, as an incontrovertible fact. From this straight-forward acceptance comes a more affirmative attitude, albeit very tentative, towards man's destiny. Despite the most adverse of situations, despite incessant failures and indignities, and despite an oppressive sense of impotence, humankind in recent writing continues to crave life, even a partial existence in a cave or in limbo, to affirm at all costs the passionate desire merely to exist.

Likewise, writers today observe the modern decay from a different perspective. Whereas Eliot and Mann, as ultimate authorial voices, seem aloof from the modern chaos, the voices of, say, Beckett, William Burroughs, Ellison and Genet are clearly in the midst of it; not even the privileges of literature afford an outpost of retreat. This transition emerges from these passages of poetry. The first is a translation from the Spanish of Rafael Alberti's *Castigos* (*Punishments*) of 1929:

> I did not know that the doors changed their places,
> That souls could blush at their bodies,
> Nor that at the end of a tunnel light brought death.
>
> (Trans. J. M. Cohen)

The same alienation and despair are expressed in these famous lines from "The Fire Sermon" section of *The Waste Land:*

> I can connect
> Nothing with nothing.

In both passages, the narrator is an outsider, supposedly a more sensitive being, cut off from the world around him. In recent poems by the Frenchman Jean Laude, the Rumanian Paul Celan and Samuel Beckett, the narrator makes his own predicament that of Everyman:

> The words sink in the sand. Surrounded by eggs, the numbers rot and the pendulum goes wild in the dead zone where the body of a new day takes form. Everything is a sign. On the ground strewn with bodies, clenched hands point in opposite directions, but I am the crossroad, the confluence where threats find their source.
>
> (Jean Laude, trans. Jean Paris)

In his "Todesfuge" (Death Fugue), one of the greatest contemporary poems, Paul Celan, a Rumanian-born Jew who lives in Paris and writes in German, makes "black milk" his symbol for the quality of life after the atrocities of Hitler:

> Black milk of morning we drink you at dusk
> we drink you at noontime and dawntime we drink
>   you at night
> we drink and drink . . . .
>
> (Trans. Jerome Rothenberg)

The following passage is from "Dieppe," which Beckett first wrote in French and then translated into English:

> What would I do without this world fearless
>   incurious

where to be lasts but an instant where every
  instant
spills in the void of ignorance of having been
without this wave where in the end
body and shadow together are engulfed.

In Beckett's poetry, as in his later fiction and much other recent writing, there is in essence no difference between the experiences of the narrator and the world at large.

Contemporaries eschew the historical and religious contrasts that were plentiful in the literature of the 1920's and 1930's. In an earlier time, the protagonist of Hemingway's "A Clean Well-Lighted Place" substituted "nada" for every important word in the Lord's Prayer, a symbolic way of saying that for him each of these phrases means "nothing." Beckett's protagonists, in contrast, have moved beyond nothingness, which depends upon an awareness of possible significance, to a further point, which we call absurdity. "For to know nothing is nothing, not to want to know anything likewise, but to be beyond knowing anything," concludes Beckett's Molloy, "it is then the true division begins, of twenty-two by seven for example, and the pages fill with the true ciphers at last." Since twenty-two divided by seven, or Pi, produces a number without final limits, an indefinite answer, it, along with permutations that signify that all is possible and nothing meaningful, becomes Beckett's paradigm for an existence "beyond knowing anything." Through vignettes and symbolic musings like these, Beckett demonstrates that the first mark of the more extreme condition of absurdity is the recognition that traditional codes of value are not just meaningless but that they are so irrelevant as to be forgotten. In this respect, the symbolic likenesses of decaying tradition, such as falling church steeples, dirty rivers, decrepit mansions, dissonant music, and ineffectual men of the cloth—so abundant in the writings of a generation ago—are largely absent from major contemporary works. The literary careers of Joyce and Eliot themselves foreshadowed this change. In their early works, they used mythological and historical parallels to contrast the present with the past, or the probable past; however, in their later work, they largely omitted such comparisons. In *Finnegans Wake*, Joyce sees human history as circular—the book

xx   *Contemporary Literature*

ends with the same sentence with which it began; and
Eliot turned from modern life to the ahistorical purity
of traditional religion.

Following the most important writers since 1920, the
crucial contemporaries have continued the revolt against
literary realism in favor of more imaginative ways of
rendering human existence. The realist writer, exemplified
by Emile Zola, believed he could best evoke reality
through the accumulation of accurate details, as though
his point would not be convincing unless it was supported
by verifiable data; and though this tradition has influenced
writers as diverse in talent, intelligence and seriousness as
C. P. Snow and Herman Wouk, Vasco Pratolini and
Françoise Sagan, Philip Roth and Augus Wilson, it is
distinctly separate from the dominant tradition of modern
narrative literature. Rather, the key recent writers attempt
to describe a large group of people or even the modern
human condition by isolating the *essence* of its existence
in one collection of people or, sometimes, one man.
Through a sensitive portrait of the resonant microcosm,
they illuminate the macrocosm. In early modern literature,
Joyce's Leopold Bloom took on universal dimensions, as
did Thomas Mann's sanitarium in *The Magic Mountain*.
In contemporary writing, just as Orwell's Winston Smith
represents Every Englishman confronting a society that
suppresses his humanity and the plague of Camus' Oran
represents the sickness of modern life, so Vladimir and
Estragon in their waiting for Godot take on the dimension
of modern man confronting a world without discernible
meaning, and Joseph Heller's Yossarian, *un homme moyen
sensuel,* recognizes there is today no justification for violence and death.

In addition to adopting, with slight modification, their
predecessors' picture of the world, most of today's significant writers have absorbed the major stylistic revolutions
of modern literature by employing the advances of their
elders for their own purposes. As Joyce in *Finnegans Wake*
coined a new prose, a blend of many languages, to express
his particular message about the universality of the basic
familial pattern, so Anthony Burgess devised "Nadsat," an
English heavily infused with Russian, to enrich his fictional
vision of life in the near future. Exemplifying the same
fusion of language and content, the eloquent repetitions

that flood Samuel Beckett's prose evoke his special sense of life, as the adjectiveless, unmetaphoric prose of Alain Robbe-Grillet matches his emotionless, super-objective view of the human scene. Following Henry James and Faulkner, contemporary writers as different as J. D. Salinger and Doris Lessing, as Nathalie Sarraute and Lawrence Durrell, have shifted the narrative voice from one character to another to reveal more of the situation than we would learn from just a single point-of-view. Likewise, just as poets from Rimbaud to Theodore Roethke have tried to depict the depths of the human unconscious, so novelists from Henry James to the present have attempted to penetrate and describe the subtleties of consciousness and modes of perception, an effort developed by Marcel Proust and Virginia Woolf and continued by Jean-Paul Sartre in *Nausea* and, with especial success, by Nathalie Sarraute in *The Planetarium*. Here the voices are not characters in the traditional sense but participating consciousnesses spinning free and deflecting like objects in a planetarium.

Intrinsic in this is the desire to capture time and objects not as they are in natural fact but as we actually perceive them. To achieve this experiential fidelity, contemporary novelists often discard conventional methods of describing time and space. Instead, they create a fiction in which the original technique itself, rather than what it describes, becomes the center of interest. In confronting this kind of work, then, the reader first must perceive the writer's particular style rather than, as he did with conventional fiction, first comprehending the natures of the various characters.

Just as composers, dancers and painters exhibit the modern impulse to explore the possibilities of their arts, so writers have pursued several paths of experiments which have increased the possibilities of literary reality and our range of perception. One line leads towards a fiction where time ceases to have any existential significance for its characters, as in Beckett's last novels; or where time, individually and thus subjectively perceived, becomes the central issue in the novel, a preoccupation mastered by Faulkner in *The Sound and the Fury* and continued by Claude Simon in his several novels and Lawrence Durrell in *The Alexandria Quartet*.

Similarly, whereas we once witnessed the characters

and the scene emerge from pertinent details, now some novelists have pushed the visual content of fiction to two opposite extremes. First, through an excess of visual facts, as in the fiction of Alain Robbe-Grillet, the narrator's eye becomes a movie camera that is obligated to report all that it sees. At the other limit, the author compresses his visual material, painting a character with a single idiosyncratic detail; and to evoke his presence later in the novel, the writer needs only to mention that essential detail. This device was used successfully by F. Scott Fitzgerald and Nathanael West in the twenties and thirties, and James Purdy and John Hawkes have employed it more recently. Likewise, playwrights from Strindberg to Genet have tried to invert and distort our normal perceptions of illusion and reality, often, as in Pirandello, making the ambiguous relation between the two the central issue of a play.

For all these reasons, form in all modern literature, pre-Second World War as well as post, tends to be, in Joseph Frank's incisive dichotomy, spatial rather than narrative, or lyric rather than dramatic. That is, what ties a book together is not its developing action, which focuses our interest on what happens next; but its vision, which is generally conveyed by resonant images, by fragmented characterizations, by telling juxtapositions, by a disordered arrangement of the scenes and by haphazard glimpses into human states of consciousness and mood. All these elements, if the literary work is successful, coalesce into a coherent whole which we perceive as we see a painting— visually, at once, rather than temporally, in time. To effect this change, modern writers have eliminated certain devices and patterns which have been the skeletal bones of traditional narrative literature—expository structure, climaxes, turning points, and symmetrical plot.

Therefore, with spatial form comes a distortion of traditional lines of emphasis. The sort of small aspect that might be of secondary interest in a traditional work can, in a modern piece, take on a special symbolic significance. In classic modern works, examples include the birds and trees of Yeats' poetry, Benjy's wrong turn around the village circle at the end of *The Sound and the Fury,* and the soap and potted meat in Joyce's *Ulysses;* in recent literature, writers continue to infuse significance into the seemingly trivial—the sucking of stones in Beckett's *Molloy,* the tin drum in Günter Grass's novel, and the contents of the Invisible Man's suitcase. Our interest in these books comes from recognizing the important details, discovering their significance, and piecing them together into a whole.

Contemporary poets, too, have accepted the modern revolutions. First, the spatial organization of long poems as diverse as Alexander Blok's "The Twelve" and Eliot's *The Waste Land* has been also employed in recent long poems, such as Yves Bonnefoy's *Douve* and Kenneth Koch's *Ko,* and, as before, in most major short poems. From this follows the destruction of traditional syntax in favor of other systems for structuring the lines of poetry, a change that occurred in all the languages of poetry early in the twentieth century. In place of traditional connectives, poets today depend upon nongrammatical kinds of relations, such as the repetition of emotional states, patterns of images, suggestive contrasts, a consistent range of suggestion, and a coherent symbolic or metaphoric dimension, to unify their poems. Recent poetry does not directly tell or argue but rather evokes and suggests; likewise, it presents not a clear, sequential development but one that is distorted, multiple and ambiguous. To put it another way, modern poets have shifted away from a poetry of concrete images and relations as well as an easily identifiable meaning to a more abstract poetry in which relations are tenuous and elliptical, comparisons more often implied than stated, and, in more extreme cases, both intention and final meaning sometimes undiscernible. Such poetry has a compositional logic of its own; and by reading and rereading the poem, particularly concentrating on its vital elements, one can discern an organizing principle in what at first and even second glance seems chaos. As Joseph Frank put it, "The meaning relationship is completed only by the simultaneous perception in space of word-groups that have no comprehensible relation to each other when read consecutively in time." In prose, the most ambitious and interesting experiment in this direction is Michel Butor's travelogue of America, *Mobile* (1962); in theatre, Beckett's *Play* (1963) exhibits a similar achievement. They are, perhaps, the forerunners of a thoroughly spatial novel and drama.

In addition to assimilating the key formal developments

of modern literature, contemporaries have added their
own lines to the chart of literary possibility. Since, after
Hitler, after the extermination of captive peoples and the
bombing of civilian cities in World War II, after the fact
of atomic war and the threat of a thermonuclear war
that could end all human history, the world *felt* considerably different from an earlier generation, post-war writers
recognized the need first to understand precisely how life
today is different and then to devise new forms that could
match their awareness. Since Ionesco, so he said, felt
that, "Cut off from his religious, metaphysical and tran-
scendental roots, man is lost; all his actions become senseless, absurd, useless," he was forced to reject the going
theatrical guidelines in order to find an absurd form, one
heavily imbued with nonsensical and ludicrous images,
that would match the disorder and madness he saw around
him. The idea of human life as absurd had, of course,
been espoused by earlier writers; but where the characters
of Camus' and Sartre's plays argue about it or discover
it in the course of action, Pinter's and Ionesco's people
present it in absurd language, absurd situations, and absurd
conflicts until the vision of absurdity encompasses both
the detail and the totality. Just as Ionesco's lecturer in
The Chairs when assigned to deliver Ultimate Truth speaks
gibberish, so Pinter's dumbwaiter, which is man's only
contact with the Mysterious Above, sends down incomprehensible messages. This literature embodies the most
representative form of contemporary writing; and to
judge by the widespread admiration for the plays of
Ionesco, Beckett, Pinter, N. F. Simpson, Jack Gelber and
the fiction of Heller and John Barth, readers today find
in absurd literature a most thoroughly appropriate image
of the contemporary predicament.

After absurdity, the second most pertinent trend in
contemporary writing includes those writers who with an
unprecedented force have uncompromisingly damned the
events of recent history, the worth of conventional ideas
of normalcy, and the pretense that modern man has progressed from the savages. True, these themes permeated
most modern literature, but what distinctly separates the
contemporaries from the earlier writers is the intensity,
both in style and vision, of the works that embody these
themes. In dealing with the Nazi atrocities, André Schwarz-

Bart in *The Last of the Just* ties the extermination of European Jewry, particularly the death of "the just men," to the disintegration of all modern life, all told in a prose that sings hysteria on every page; in the same way, the protagonist of Elie Wiesel's *Night,* written in French by an Israeli, evokes the incredible horror of a Nazi concentration camp, while Paul Celan captures in "The Death Fugue" the tone of the mechanized humanity that performed such horrors. In these works, the ferocious strength of the writer's negation makes earlier works of protest seem faintly tame.

Throughout modern literature, the image of the modern world as hell is evoked likewise with a violence and intensity equally unprecedented. The unrelieved terror and depravity of William Burroughs' *Naked Lunch* strikes me as more frightening than Celine's visions, for Burroughs succeeds in repudiating Celine's boast that only he could sustain intense negation for the length of a novel. This kind of extreme dissent illuminates a wide variety of contemporary works—the novels of the Spaniard Camile José Cela; the poetry of Allen Ginsberg; in a slightly different guise, the plays (not the novels) of Jean Genet; Anthony Burgess' best fiction; and Ralph Ellison's *Invisible Man.* Perhaps the final touch to this theme of denial is provided by the closing lines of the "Soliloquy of the Individual," a stunning history of mankind by the Chilean poet, Nicanor Parra:

> Perhaps I'd better return to that valley,
> To that rock which once was home,
> And start to engrave again,
> From end to beginning,
> The world in reverse.

> (Trans. Jorge Elliott)

Just as negative modern writers have often, but not always, achieved comedy in the ferociousness of their rejection, so absurd writers accomplish the same fusion by creating terror at the heart of their comedy. In this respect, too, contemporary literature contrasts with earlier modern. If the dominant tone of the most penetrating works of Eliot and Hemingway is a humorless despair, Beckett, again the epitome, creates an air of tragi-comic finality—

under each moment of terror lies the joke of our existence and under each joke a grim terror. More specifically, the writer may start with a comic sequence that eventually takes on the dimensions of terror, as Joseph Heller or Ionesco do; or he may open with an image of terror that eventually becomes funny, as in, say, James Purdy's *Malcolm* or William Burroughs' *Naked Lunch*.

In contrast to writers who indirectly engage the contemporary situation, others demonstrate a retreat into the most private kind of experiences, particularly man's perception of himself, nature and others; the writers who pursue this path generally employ rather traditional forms. This response to the present, perhaps better understood as an anti-response, presupposes a distinct contradiction between modern life and the "art" of literature and, it follows, the feeling that the purity of the second must be salvaged from the terrors of the first. This retreat defines the work of two important poets: Theodore Roethke, whose "Words for the Wind" opens "Love, love, a lily's my care," and René Char, whose characteristic moment is, "The stride of the girl / Has caressed the lane / Has passed through the gate." In fiction, the comparable response characterizes most of the recent American gothic novelists ranging from Flannery O'Connor to Truman Capote, the work of the English "New University Wits," the novels of Françoise Sagan and their imitations—in general, books by novelists who cultivate an accuracy of detail rather than a pervasive and resonant vision. Retreat into private perception is probably the privilege of the poet; but such an inclination in novelists, though their talents and techniques may be prodigious and fine, produces essentially minor works, for his books will lack the scope and urgent contemporaneousness that are the prime characteristics of truly significant contemporary writing. The major authors of our time have looked unflinchingly at our condition; and out of its anti-poetic ugliness, they have fashioned works of an original, compelling and relevant form, a literature illuminating and more profound than "beautiful," which at its best perceives some of the contemporary reality that evades our limited perspective.

Just as it is naive to condemn contemporary writers for having too bleak a view of the human condition or for presenting their vision in too difficult a form, it is useless,

I think, to speak, as is often done, of absurd theatre as "anti-theatre" and, say, the objectivist French novel as "anti-fiction." Both are simply new forms of each genre. Neither repudiates all the conventions of that genre as much as the "anti" prefix suggests. Rather, each draws selectively upon certain trends in each genre (Martin Esslin has traced the genealogy of absurd theatre; the new novel has a comparable one); and in using the tradition with discrimination, the author fuses the possibilities of the genre with his awareness of the specialness of the present.

While the literature of the last twenty years has included several great works which are important to us today, I do not think literary historians of the future will look upon 1944–1964 as comparable to the twenty years between the First and Second Wars, which witnessed the appearance of the best writings of Eliot, Yeats, Joyce, Mann, Proust, and Faulkner. Nonetheless, it is foolish to write off, as some pessimistic critics have done, the past twenty years as insignificant, for in that time appeared the flowering of the absurd theatre, the beginnings of the absurd novel, a variety of propitious experiments in fiction, the development of the first substantially modernist British theatre, the major works of Sartre, Camus and Beckett, Pasternak's great novel, the poetry of John Berryman, Yves Bonnefoy and Robert Lowell, Moravia's psychologically incisive fiction, and the novels of Ralph Ellison, Alain Robbe-Grillet, and Saul Bellow. Moreover, through the efforts of those who have refused to accept the "rules" of literature and, instead, seem to follow Claude Levi-Strauss' dictum that, "Truth lies in the progressive expansion of meaning," the range of what is possible in literature has continued to enlarge, so that the young and unborn will be able to confront a greater variety of usable forms and viable attitudes than has ever been available in the past.

Ladders To Heaven
BY GORE VIDAL

Much of the despondency and apparent confusion in the
world of peripheral letters today derives partly from the
nervous, bloody age in which we live and partly from that
hunger for the absolute which, in our own immediate experience, delivered two intelligent, ancient countries into
the hands of barbarous tyrants, while in our own nation
the terror of being man alone, unsupported by a general
religious belief and undirected by a gaudy central authority,
has reduced many intellectuals either to bleak nihilism or,
worse, to the acceptance of some external authority like the
absolutism of Rome, or of Aristotle, of Marx or of the
Freudians. One is reminded forcibly of Flaubert's comment
nearly a century ago: "The melancholy of the ancients
seems to me deeper than that of the moderns who all more
or less assume an immortality on the far side of the black
pit. For the ancients the black pit was infinity itself; their
dreams take shape and pass against a background of unchanging ebony. No cries, no struggles, only the fixity of
the pensive gaze. The gods being dead and Christ not yet
born there was between Cicero and Marcus Aurelius one
unique moment in which there was man."

Our own age is one of man alone but there are still cries,
still struggles against our condition, against the knowledge
that our works and days have value only in the human
scale; and those who most clearly remember the secure
authority of other times, the ordered universe, the im-
mutable moral hierarchies, are the ones who most protest
the black pit. While it is perfectly true that any instant in
human history is one of transition, ours, more than most,
seems to be marked by a startling variety of conflicting
absolutes, none sufficiently great at this moment to impose

itself upon the majority whose lives are acted out within
that unhuman universe which some still prefer to fill with
a vast man-like shadow containing stars while others behold
only a luminous dust which *is* the stars, and us as well.
This division between those who recognize the unhumanity
of creation and those who protest the unchanging ebony
sets the tone of our literature, with the imaginative writers
inclining (in their different ways) to the first view and
their critics to the second. The sense of man not being king
of creation (nor even the work of a king of creation) is
the burden, directly and indirectly, of modern literature.
For the writers there is no reality for man except in his
relations with his own kind. Much of the stuff of earlier
centuries like fate, high tragedy, the interventions of *deus
ex machina,* have been discarded as brave but antique conceptions which, though often engaging as literary devices,
hardly seem applicable in a world where kings and com-
moners occupy the same sinking boat.

Those of our writers who might yet enjoy the appellation
"affirmative" are the ones who intensely devote themselves
to the dramas within the boat, the encompassing cold sea
ignored in the passions of the human moment. Most of
the worst and a number of the best writers belong to this
category. The key words here are "love" and "compassion,"
and though, like most such devices, they have grown indistinct with use one can still see them at work, and marvelously so, in the novels of Carson McCullers and certain
(though not all) of the plays of Tennessee Williams.
Christopher Isherwood once said that to his mind the
finest single line in modern letters was: "I have always
depended upon the kindness of strangers," from *A Streetcar Named Desire.* At such moments, in such works, the
human drama becomes so unbearably intense that time and
the sea are blotted out and only the human beings are
illuminated as they cease through the high magic of art
and love to be mere residents in a time which stops and become, instead, archetypes, elemental figures like those wild
gods our ancestors peopled heaven with.

Then there are the writers to whom neither sea nor boat
exists. They have accepted some huge fantasy wherein they
need never drown, where death is life and the doings of
human beings on a social and ethical level are of much
consequence to some brooding source of creation who dis-

penses his justice along strictly party lines at the end of a gloomy day. To this category belong such talented writers as Graham Greene and Evelyn Waugh. In theory, speculation has ended for them; dogma supports them in all things. Yet it is odd to find that the tone of their works differs very little from that of the other mariners adrift: they are, if anything, perhaps a bit more lugubrious since for them is not the principality of this world.

And, finally, there are those who see human lives as the lunatic workings of compulsive animals no sooner born than dead, no sooner dead than replaced by similar creatures born of that proliferating seed which too will die. Paul Bowles is a striking example of this sort of writer as he coolly creates nightmare visions in which his specimens struggle and drown in fantasy, in madness, in death. His short stories with their plain lines of monochromatic prose exploit extreme situations with a chilling resourcefulness; he says, in short, "Let it sink; let us drown."

Carson McCullers, Paul Bowles, Tennessee Williams are, at this moment at least, the three most important creative writers in the United States. Each, in his different way, is engaged in the task of truth-saying (as opposed to saying the truth, which is not possible this side of revelation); they have gone further into the rich interior of the human drama than any of their immediate predecessors with the possible exception of William Faulkner, much of whose recent work has unfortunately resembled bad translations from Pindar. On a social level, the hostility shown these essential artists is more significant than their occasional worldly successes for it is traditional that he who attempts to define man's condition demoralizes the majority, whether relativist or absolutist: we do not want ever to hear that we will die but that *first* we must live and those ways of living which are the fullest, the most intense are the very ones which social man traditionally dreads, summoning all his superstition and malice to combat strangers and lovers, his eternal victims.

The obsessive concern with sexuality which informs most contemporary writing is not entirely the result of a wish *épater le bourgeois* but, more, the reflection of a serious battle between the society man has constructed so illogically and confusedly and the nature of the human being which needs a considerably fuller expression sexually and emotionally than either the economics or morality of this time will permit. The sea is close; two will often find the interval between awareness and death more meaningful than one alone. Yet while ours is a society where mass-murder and violence are perfectly ordinary and their expression in the most popular novels, the most widely read comic books, is accepted with aplomb, any love between two people which does not conform is vehemently attacked.

A few years ago the reviewers were overwhelmed with admiration for an ill-written war novel which contained nearly every sadistic act a wounded adolescent mind could conceive. The reviewers were much excited by the viciousness and the violence of the episodes and, though the story was patently incredible (as any soldier could have told them), they justified their delight by viewing soberly its social aspects which, of course, were absurd. The same publishing season produced Tennessee Williams' first novel, *The Roman Spring of Mrs. Stone,* a delicate, elegiac work which, though slight, was certainly that season's one significant work. The reviewers, and even the critics, who had so reveled in the bad writing, the exciting sadism of the war book, turned bitterly upon the Williams novel, using against it all the epithets which should have been used to describe the moment's idol: degenerate, vicious, decadent . . . and why? Because Williams had, with some sympathy, described an aging actress who turns to sexuality in order to stop the aimless "drift of her days," a situation which is hardly unique. Unfortunately, our morality has become so dangerously confused that acts of love which do not conform with ancient law are considered wicked while acts of violence and degradation are accepted with a secret delight. One should never be startled by the political state of our world since its chronic mass-murders are, finally, only a reflection of the private dreams of absolutists which the militantly mediocre are usually quick to render actual, in life as well as in art.

Mr. Malcolm Cowley has complained that writers no longer handle some of the more interesting social relationships of man, that there is no good stock market novel, no Balzacian concern among the better writers with economic motive. His point is valid. The public range of the novel has been narrowed; it would be good to have well-written accounts of the way we live now, yet our important writers eschew, almost deliberately it would seem, the kind of book which provided not only Trollope but Tolstoi with so much power. Mr. Cowley catches quite well the tone of the second-rate good writers (a phenomenon peculiar to this moment . . . it seems as if the whole generation writes well, though not often to any point); they are concerned with the small scale and goodness as exemplified by characters resembling the actress Shirley Booth holding out valiantly against villainous forces, usually represented by someone in business. But Mr. Cowley does not mention the novelist from whom these apotheosis-in-the-kitchen writers derive: Carson McCullers who, using the small scale, the relations of human beings at their most ordinary, transcends her milieu and shows, in bright glimpses, the potentiality which exists in even the most banal of human relationships . . . the "we" as opposed to the meager "I."

Or, again, in Tennessee Williams' remarkable play *Camino Real,* though the world is shown in a nightmare glass—a vision of those already drowned—there are still moments of private triumphs . . . in Kilroy's love with (not for) the gypsy's daughter and in Lord Byron's proud departure through the gate to *terra incognita,* his last words a reproach and an exhortation: "Make voyages! Make voyages!"

And, finally, most starkly, we have a deliberate act of murder, Gide's *l'acte gratuite,* which occurs at the end of Paul Bowles's *Let It Come Down.* Here the faceless, directionless protagonist, in a sudden storm of rage against his life, all life, commits a murder without reason or passion and in this one terrible moment (similar perhaps to that of a nation gone to war) he at last finds "a place in the world, a definite status, a precise relationship with the rest of men. Even if it had to be one of open hostility, it was his, created by him." In each of these three writers man acts, through love, through hate, through despair. Though the act in each is different, the common emotion is sufficiently intense to dispel, for a time at least, the knowledge of that cold drowning which awaits us all.

The malady of civilized man is his knowledge of death. The good artist, like the wise man, addresses himself to life and invests with his private vision the deeds and thoughts of men. The creation of a work of art, like an act of love, is our one small "yes" at the center of a vast "no."

The lesser writers whose works do not impress Mr. Cowley despite their correctness possess the same vision as those of the major writers but their power of illusion is not so great and their magic is only fitful: too often their creatures are only automatons acted upon; though they may shed light on interesting aspects of ordinary life they do not, in the best sense, illuminate, flood with brilliance, our strange estate.

Among the distinguished second rank of younger writers there is much virtuosity, and potentiality. The coolly observant short stories of Louis Auchincloss provide wise social comment of the sort which the Cowleys should genuinely admire but never seem to read in their haste to generalize. Eudora Welty fashions a subtle line and Jean Stafford, though currently obsessed with literary interior decoration, has in such stories as "The Echo and the Nemesis" displayed a genius which makes all the more irritating her recent catalogues of bric-a-brac, actual and symbolic. John Kelly, whose two novels have been oddly neglected, has created a perverse, bravura world like nothing else in our literature, while the late John Horne Burns, out of fashion for some years, was a brilliant satirist in a time when satire is necessary but difficult to write since to attack successfully one must have a complacent enemy, and though there are numerous villains today, none is entirely complacent.

The serious writers have been attacked by the reviewers for their contempt of narrative and their neglect to fashion "real live characters" (which means familiar stereotypes from Victorian fiction masquerading in contemporary clothes). The reviewers have recognized that a good deal of writing now being done doesn't resemble anything they are used to (although in almost a century there has been a royal line of which they are ignorant . . . from *The Temptation of Saint Anthony* to *The Golden Bowl* to *Mrs. Dalloway*); they still feel most at home with *The Newcomes* or, if they came to maturity in the twenties, with *The Sun Also Rises*. When the technique of a play like *Camino Real* seems bizarre and difficult to follow for those accustomed to the imitators of Ibsen, there must be a genuine reason for the change in technique, other than the author's presumed perversity. The change from the exterior to the interior world which has been taking place in literature for at least a century is due not only to a general dissatisfaction with the limitations of naturalism but also to the rise of a new medium, the movies, which, when properly exploited, are infinitely superior to the novel, and to the naturalistic play, in the rendering of straight narrative. . . .

. . . For the present, however, the tone of the contemporary novel, though not cheerful, is precise. Man is on his own. In certain human actions, in love, in violence, he can communicate with others, touch and be touched, act and in the act forget his fate. The scale is often small. Kings are neglected because, to relativists, all men are the same in eternity; or, rather, their crisis is the same. The concern in modern letters is with that crisis which defines the prospect.

In general, the novelists have rejected authority, parting with their cousins-germane the serious critics. To the creative man religious dogma and political doctrine, when stated in ultimate terms, represent the last enemy, the protean Lucifer in our race's bloody progress. The artist speaks from that awareness of life, that secret knowledge of life *and* death which it is the perennial task of absolutists to obscure and to distort, to shape, if possible, to *their* own tidy ends.

The interior drama at its most bitterly human comes into sharp focus in the writings of Williams and McCullers and there are signs that other writers, in their different ways, undismayed by the hostility of the absolutists, may soon provide us with some strength in these last days before the sure if temporary victory of that authoritarian society which, thanks to science, now has every weapon with which to make even the most inspired lover of freedom conform to the official madness.

The Character of Post-War Fiction in America
BY IHAB H. HASSAN

Contemporary American fiction is sometimes noted to be dismissed by critics who seem to have lost their youth in the golden age of Faulkner and Hemingway. At other times, it is noticed merely to document the sociological imagination of our time, as if literature were a nice footnote to our mass culture. People somehow expect the fad to pass, the dust to settle, so that the objects of our critical admiration may be finally certified, so that our judgments may escape the sin of error. Why take a chance on a fleeting fashion? As if fashions did not hold the enigma of our time!

My first statement, obviously, is a judgment and a plea. The contemporary novel—and it is of the novel that I mainly speak—has energy and persuasion. It deserves from us a response equally patient and passionate. It deserves, above all, to be read.

There was a moment, I think, right after the Second World War when everyone sensed a bracing quality in the climate of literature. There was a promise of intensity, a new and troubled kind of awareness, a feeling that a new world had been born in catastrophe and that it required to be expressed in ways unlike the old ways. The old ways, to be sure, had been radical in their formal experiments, in the freedom writers took with time and space, consciousness and metaphor. But the experiments of one generation can become the pieties of the next. Language had been stretched to its limit—as in *Finnegans Wake*. It was now time not to retrench but to discover characters or styles, a new vision, to describe the new experience. The dislocation of time, after all, may not be the most radical thing in a world where science, with the approval of the State, does so every hour!

The intensity which people discerned in fiction after the last war—particularly in "war novels"—has not entirely vanished; it has been merely threatened by a powerful cliché. This is the cliché that our literature is a literature of conformity. It is not. Our literature is a literature of *opposition*. America is still, as Van Wyck Brooks claimed fifty years ago, "a vast Sargasso Sea," and there are all manners of living things drifting in it. Nor is heresy, as one might be led to believe, the privilege of few critics alone. Heresy and heterodoxy make vital a great part of our fiction. Where others see conformity, I sense protest unto anarchy.

For one thing, naturalism and symbolism, comedy and tragedy, picaresque and romance, even surrealism, crowd into the form of the recent novel. They jostle and jangle in Styron's *Lie Down in Darkness,* Swados' *Out Went the Candle,* Ellison's *Invisible Man,* Salinger's *The Catcher in the Rye,* Bellow's *Henderson the Rain King,* Purdy's *Malcolm,* and Hawkes' *The Lime Twig.* The fusion of modes in contemporary fiction—a subject to which I must later return—does not prove that ours is a generation of cool or silent writers. Fusion does not always mean confusion.

It is also misleading, I think, to speak in obituary tones of the death of manners in the novel. Henry James, to be sure, is no longer with us except as a rare spirit, and Jane Austen, who never immigrated to America anyway, has been laid to rest for some years. But the crucial fact about manners in recent fiction is that in becoming more diverse, they have also become more fragmentary. This is not to say that manners—the way gestures body forth the hum or buzz or whatever sound implications are reputed to make in a culture—have disappeared. (It would be more accurate to claim that society itself has vanished.) This is rather to say that the Jewish society of Bernard Malamud may be as incomprehensible to the Southern characters of Flannery O'Connor as the hipster gang of Jack Kerouac may be bewildering to the Yankee protagonists of John Cheever. Better then to say that manners and gestures have not died but that they are there to betoken the death of a coherent society.

There are, we see, pockets of resistance in American

culture, and Bible, hibachi, and marijuana belts of manners in it too. America, despite our cars, fashion models,
and supermarkets, is not entirely the septic, air-conditioned
dream Europeans dream it is. It is still possible, for
instance, to draw some distinctions between the wide
agrarian valleys of the South and the dense industrial cities
of the North. The two most active centers of contemporary
fiction in America are situated in the Gentile rural South
of Carson McCullers, Flannery O'Connor, Truman Capote,
and William Styron, and the Jewish urban North of Saul
Bellow, J. D. Salinger, Bernard Malamud, Harvey Swados,
and Philip Roth. It may very well be that the Southern
novelist and the Jewish writer have both emerged from
the tragic underground of our culture as the true spokesmen of mid-century America.

The most meaningful expression of diversity in our
culture, however, is encountered in the huge discrepancy
between its dominant and opposing images. Compare—if
you can!—the cellophane world implied by the Miss
America contests in Atlantic City with the nightmare of
junk and homosexuality which emerges, say, from William
Burroughs' *The Naked Lunch*. Yet it is this dialectic between the normative and dissenting selves of our society,
irrespective of mode, manners, or locale, that gives our
literature its particular character.

The normative image of our culture can be projected in
a series of preposterous or unctuous clichés. It is the
image of an organization man who forgoes the ulcerous
rewards of executive suite, pottering about a house with
a cracked picture window looking into the crack of another picture window, and viewing with apathy the coming
caesars of our imperial state, the hidden persuaders and
clowns of commerce of Madison Avenue, and the explod-
ing metropolis on whose far fringes our Quiet American
has found his corner of Shangri-La. In this other-directed
paradise, where everyone is another to someone else and
nothing to himself, the American Adam obviously can
have no knowledge of evil, except perhaps that which is
vicariously rendered on his stereophonic set by Eartha
Kitt: "I wanna be evil—I wanna be bad," thus fulfilling
his manifest destiny in the republic of consumers united
under God.

In this orgiastic technological phantasy in which our

lives are led for us, it is all too easy to assume that basic human needs are altered or radically modified. Culture itself retreats from the unreality of its surface image, and literature, which plumbs the depths of culture, recognizes at least two other levels on which basic needs can be acknowledged or realized.

The first level of reaction against the normative image of culture harbors values still powerless to be born. It is the level on which the temporary and temporizing search for privacy and disaffiliation is conducted. Richard Frede's inadequate novel of college life, *Entry E,* Sloan Wilson's best-seller, *The Man in the Grey Flannel Suit,* express and criticize the impulse to affirm a kind of passive or epicurean sanity in a world of insane bustle. The reaction of privacy, however, has proven too mawkish for our most serious writers. Disaffiliation, these writers conclude, is simply not enough. Crime, or that saintliness which is the other face of crime, is perhaps the only way to keep up with the Joneses in these days of affluence and obsolescence.

Dissent from the ballyhoo and lunacies of a mass society finds, in consequence, a more compelling means of expression on a second and more fundamental level of responses to culture. On that level, the search for *love* and for *freedom* continues with radical intensity. The search for love brings men to the threshold of religious experience—Zen or Buddhist thought, Christian mysticism, the I-Thou encounter so vividly explored by Martin Buber—and the search for freedom ends, sometimes, in crime or anarchy, the burden of the hipster, the plight of the "White Negro" which Mailer expounded with eloquence and vigor. The two quests start from different points—they often meet in the idea of the holy-goof, the criminal-lover, the rebel-victim.

So far, I have overemphasized, perhaps, the diversity in the background and underground of contemporary fiction. Diversity, however, is for the radical mind akin to disorder. Our quest for order requires that we discover some controlling image of recent fiction in America. I find such an image in the figure of the hero of fiction, or rather, its typical anti-hero.

The central and controlling image of recent fiction is that of the rebel-victim. He is an actor but also a sufferer. Almost always, he is an outsider, an initiate never confirmed in his initiation, an anarchist and clown, a Faust and Christ compounded in grotesque or ironic measures. The poles of crime and sainthood define the range of his particular fate, which is his character. Nihilism, frenzied self-affirmation, psychopathy constitute the limit towards which one type of hero tends. Martyrdom, immolation, defeat constitute the other limit which a different type of hero approaches. More often, however, both elements of rebellion and victimization are conjoined in the quixotic figure of what R. W. B. Lewis has called the picaresque saint: Bellow's Henderson, Salinger's Caulfield, Capote's Holly Golightly, Purdy's Malcolm. They are conjoined, too, in the figure of the grotesque who is perhaps the true, ironic symbol of man in this century: Flannery O'Connor's Hazel Motes, in *Wise Blood,* Carson McCuller's Miss Amelia, in *The Ballad of the Sad Café,* or even Ralph Ellison's Invisible Man in the novel by that name. For in the grotesque, the distortion of physical forms corresponds to that perversion of mental states which is the malady of the age. Of this, the Mugwumps of Burroughs' *The Naked Lunch* are the ghoulish example.

The figure of the rebel-victim, we see, incarnates the eternal dialectic between the primary Yes and everlasting No. He is man's answer that he conform or abolish himself. There is, perhaps, a mixture of Prometheus, Job, and Sisyphus in him. Compounding the ambiguities of initiation prefigured in *The Adventures of Huckleberry Finn* with the spiteful dissent of Dostoyevsky's *Notes from the Underground,* the new hero mediates the contradictions of American culture by offering himself, in passive or demonic fashion, as scapegoat. His function is to create those values whose absence from our society is the cause of his predicament and ours. It is fatuous, therefore, to say that recent fiction is devoid of values. The "ethic" which the new hero projects is inductive; it is defined existentially by his actions and even more by his passions. This accounts for the shifts and evasions, the ironies and ambiguities, the self-made quality, of his morality. Still, in a post-individual era, the rebel-victim is perhaps one of the last exemplars of a vanishing conception of man. A grotesque effigy to the rule of chaos, this half-demonic and half-quixotic creature still placates darkness with the light of human pride, agony, or derision. In this, he does not differ greatly from the ancient heroes and scapegoats of myth. His true design, however, is to fashion some unity where none can obtain save in the momentary repose of artifice. Art, we see, seems to persist in its romantic role as ironic redeemer of life. Yet our age is also a post-romantic age, and the emergent role of art may be an aspiration to complex silence. When the new will of literature finally becomes clear, we may discover it to be a religious will, born under the shadow of nihilism, yet dedicated to some mode of life, earthly or utopian, that transcends the facts of our existence.

I may have given the impression that the rebel-victim, in our time, is indeed the hero with a thousand faces. I should now like to view some of the particular faces—or are they grimaces?—which he presents in fiction. The novels I shall cite as examples are, I believe, among the remarkable works of the last two decades.

First: The hero as a child who may stand for truth or Edenic innocence, and is victimized, as in Jean Stafford's *The Mountain Lion*, or Truman Capote's *Other Voices, Other Rooms*, or James Purdy's *63 Dream Place*, by an ideal that society can never sanction or recognize. Innocence, it seems, can only reveal its face in perverse guises, and childhood recalls the demon world as few adults can safely remember.

Second: The lonely adolescent or youth, exposing the corrupt adult world, as in Salinger's *The Catcher in the Rye* and Purdy's *Malcolm;* or destroyed by a regressive search for an Oedipal relation, as in Styron's *Lie Down in Darkness* or Swados' *Out Went the Candle*. In no case is full initiation granted. Even in Jean Stafford's *Boston Adventure*, Carson McCullers' *The Member of the Wedding*, or Herlihy's *All Fall Down*, dramatic emphasis is on loss, the pain and bitterness of growth, the fall from uneasy grace.

Third: The lover caught in the impossible web woven by instincts and institutions around him. Adultery is usually the focus of the action, as in Nemerov's *Federigo*, Buechner's *A Long Day's Dying*, or Macauley's *The Disguises of Love*. A more desperate version of the lover is the homosexual, as seen in Vidal's *The City and the Pillar* or Baldwin's *Giovanni's Room*. In time of organization, Eros is utterly disorganized.

Fourth: The Negro in search of the eternal, elusive identity which white men refuse to grant him or themselves, shadow boxing with shadows, as in Ellison's *Invisible Man* or Baldwin's *Go Tell It on the Mountain*. The cellar to which Ellison's hero repairs is the very underground of our culture where issues can be seen finally starkly, unembellished by reason or piety.

Fifth: The Jew engaged with Gentiles in a harrowing dialogue of reciprocal guilt and ironic self-betrayals, as in Bellow's *The Victim* and Malamud's *The Assistant*. The limits of responsibility, the dignity of suffering, the price of failure—these define the ironic meaning of redemption.

Sixth: The grotesque, sometimes a hellbent seeker of godliness, as in O'Connor's *Wise Blood* and *The Violent Bear It Away*, sometimes a freakish and crippled saint, as in McCullers' *The Heart Is a Lonely Hunter*.

Seventh: The underdog, most often a hapless soldier, victim of the awesome powers of regimentation in war or peace, as in Mailer's *The Naked and the Dead*, Jones' *From Here to Eternity*, and George Garrett's *Which Ones Are the Enemy?*

Eighth: The disinherited American, uprooted from his civilization yet finding no roots in the primitive African setting which witnesses, in Bowles' *The Sheltering Sky* and *Let It Come Down*, his violent end with cosmic indifference.

Ninth: The comic picaro, traveling through a crowded life with verve, and sustained by a gift of hope, but never finding for himself a home, except in the mythical territory ahead. Bellow's *The Adventures of Augie March* and Capote's *Breakfast at Tiffany's* are examples of this, and so is Joseph Heller's "hilarious" *Catch-22*.

Tenth and last: The hipster, the holy-goof, in search of kicks and revelation, gunning his cars into the American night or straining for an apocalyptic orgasm at a tea party, as in Kerouac's *On the Road*, or Holmes' *Go*. Variations of the hipster may be found in Donleavy's *The Ginger Man*, the "carnies" of Gold's *The Man Who Was Not With It*, and of course in William Burroughs' shocking book, *The Naked Lunch*. What the heroes of all these works share is the condition of extreme alienation, the status of the marginal man.

These are a few, twisted faces of the contemporary hero.

The mask he wears, however, is usually frozen into the same grimace, which is neither comic nor exactly tragic.

Masks are a kind of form, and it is appropriate for us to ask: Given the character of the rebel-victim, what form does his destiny assume in the novel? The form of fiction is the pattern of the hero's existential encounter with experience. The encounter, as we have seen, tends to be destructive. It is delimited by outrage and defiance. Its true nature, however, can be most accurately described by referring to the assumptions neither of comedy nor of tragedy, nor yet of romance, but to those of irony.

In his *Anatomy of Criticism,* Northrop Frye has elucidated these assumptions in a way pertinent to recent fiction. Irony selects from the tragic situation the element of absurdity, the demonic vision, the sense of isolation; it takes from comedy the unlawful or quixotic motive, the savagery which is the other face of play, and the grotesque scapegoat rituals of comic expiation; and from romance it adopts the quest motif, turning it into a study of self-deception, and the dream of wish-fulfillment, transforming it into a nightmare. Irony, the mythos of winter, is the form to which other literary forms tend when disintegration overtakes them. It is, nevertheless, preeminently suited to the needs of the present situation. Irony, in fact, is the basic principle of the form which dominates our fiction. It is the literary correlative of the existential ethic; it implies distance, ambiguity, the interplay of views. It is the form of containment, a self-created pattern of contradictions, the union of the terrible and the ludicrous. Irony is all the certainty we can allow ourselves where uncertainties prevail. Yet irony also commits itself to that which it criticizes. It is, at bottom, not the form of negation but rather the stark shape of hope when death and absurdity are finally recognized. A good many structural and stylistic elements—the function of time, the handling of point of view, the nature of imagery in the contemporary novel—derive from these general assumptions of irony. "Comic" novels like Cheever's *The Wapshot Chronicle* or Nabokov's *Lolita,* tragic books like Styron's *Lie Down in Darkness* or Hawkes' *The Lime Twig,* "picaresques" like Salinger's *The Catcher in the Rye* or Bellow's *Henderson the Rain King,* "romances" like Capote's *The Grass Harp* or Kerouac's *The Dharma Bums,* "gothic" tales like Mc-

Cullers' *The Ballad of the Sad Café* or O'Connor's *Wise Blood*, "allegories" like Mailer's *Barbary Shore* or Buechner's *A Long Day's Dying* or Hawkes' *The Cannibal*, "satiric fantasies" like Terry Southern's *The Magic Christian*, and "morality novels" like John Updike's *Rabbit, Run*, all share an ironic sense of dreadfulness, and manifest that fusion of genres and modes, that ambiguity of tone and attitude, which is characteristic of the age.

Forms may outlast the ravages of time, but critics really have no business with eternity. It is, after all, the confluence of gifted authors at a particular moment that gives the moment its character. The literary stock market, to be sure, vacillates from day to day, and the crystal ball in which future reputations are revealed remains a blank, lucent space for me. Still, there are novelists whose achievement has engaged our interest over the years; their impact on the contemporary scene, I feel, has force, promise, and magnitude. I should like to mention ten of these. Five have been inclined to explore tighter and more nervous fictional forms. Their works, in fact, have tended to be compact. The other five make fuller use of the mixed resources of the novel. Their books have tended to be crowded and long. Each in his particular way remains unique.

Carson McCullers is perhaps the oldest novelist in the first group. Her conception of grotesques seeking to transcend their spiritual isolation in love—witness her best work, *The Ballad of the Sad Café*—is one of the central facts of our time. With her, the Southern tradition of the Gothic novel is refined into a poetic sensibility which has not escaped either imitation or misuse.

Truman Capote, though he does not like to be labelled a Southerner, has moved from the haunted dream of *Other Voices, Other Rooms* to the daylight romance of *The Grass Harp*, and, most recently, to the zany story of Holly, in *Breakfast at Tiffany's*. The precision of his idiom should not prejudice us against the stubbornness with which he defends the complex and infrangible values of the imagination. For Capote remains, above all, a devotee of the *word*, and it is that devotion which permits him to roam the fabulous underside of consciousness with steady tread.

Bernard Malamud has a tough, sardonic, and deeply

compassionate vision. The obscurities which mar his first
novel, *The Natural,* are absent from his second book, *The
Assistant.* Few writers can transform pain into responsibility with the quiet, steady glow Malamud can give to
language. The refuge he sometimes takes in Jewish irony
defines his basic commitment—and limits its scope.

Salinger's *The Catcher in the Rye* is perhaps the classic
of post-war fiction. It is both mature and adolescent in the
best manner of the American tradition. A virtuoso of the
short story too—"For Esmé, With Love and Squalor"—
Salinger penetrates in his prose to the elusive center where
love and squalor silently meet. His latest novelettes,
"Zooey" and "Seymour: An Introduction," make an attempt to break down the form, re-creating it in the shape
of parody and autobiography. His Glass family has become a myth by which the actualities of American life
may be gauged, criticized, and—as few critics seem to
realize—even upheld.

The last novelist in this arbitrary group is one who has
been much neglected. John Hawkes has written five novels
to date, bringing satire and surrealism to bear on the
shocking realities of our time. *The Cannibal* may be the
most profound novel written about the last war. And *The
Lime Twig* reveals a nightmare world of evil that is miti-
gated only by a unique style that reclaims man from the
absurdity of his condition.

In the second group, Ralph Ellison, like Salinger, rests
his high reputation on a single novel, *Invisible Man.* It is
a rich, passionate, and original book, and it shows an
energy of *mind* comparable only to Bellow's. The shifting
perspective in which Ellison reveals the Negro is unparalleled even by Faulkner.

William Styron, another Southerner who does not like
to limit himself to the assumptions of Southern fiction, has
written a brilliant and powerful first novel, *Lie Down in
Darkness.* His novelette about the Marine Corps, *The Long
March,* is notable, and his most recent book, *Set This
House on Fire,* reminds us that existential fiction has become as indigenous to America as it is to Europe.

The most extreme and ambitious talent of our time is
perhaps Norman Mailer. It is a mistake, I think, to define
his achievement by his first novel, *The Naked and the
Dead.* His essay, "The White Negro," gives to anger the

dignity of a metaphysical principle. And the lurid imperfections of *Barbary Shore* and *The Deer Park* are the
source, I feel, of the controlled violence in *Advertisements
for Myself*. Power, demonic, instinctual, and human, is
the crucible into which Mailer's values are cast, burnt out
of their dross, and re-fashioned.

Saul Bellow, no doubt, seems to many the most impressive novelist since the war. He writes in the great intelligent
tradition of fiction, concerning himself with freedom—the
way things are and the way they can be—in its irreducible
forms and manifold disguises. His versatility is evident in
the difference between such earlier novels as *Dangling
Man* and *The Victim* and the torrential narratives of *Augie
March* and *Henderson the Rain King*. But it may well be
that his finest work is a novelette, *Seize the Day*.

Finally, there is Vladimir Nabokov, who writes in three
languages with an antic and subversive disposition, pressing language to create illusions and subvert realities, and
pressing it again to strike at the cunning core of reality.
Pnin, Invitation to a Beheading, and *Laughter in the Dark*
are not as widely known as the notorious *Lolita*. Yet all
writhe into life under the touch of grim or ironic comedy,
and they show that in our time language may parody itself
into some form of metaphysical play, leaving the mirror
of art unblemished by any image.

The names and titles I have been dropping freely are
an admission that, in the end, the best thing a critic can
do is point back to such literary works as call attention to
themselves. The spectacle before us is not a bland or
shabby spectacle. There are novelists—Flannery O'Connor,
James Purdy, John Updike, Philip Roth, James Baldwin,
Frederick Buechner, William Burroughs, Terry Southern
—who deserve more attention than I have been able to
give them in this hurried profile of our fiction. No summary is possible without a fiat of the critical will.

In conclusion, however, I take my cue from a dark, rich,
and exasperating book, Lawrence's *Studies in Classic
American Literature*. Lawrence claims that the American,
the "homunculus of the new era," is nothing but a sort
of "recreant European." Perhaps one had better say that
the "recreant European" is the rebel-victim of American
literature, the Man from Underground in the soul of
Huck Finn, a figure unique and indigenous, radical and

innocent, troubled with memory and haunted by hope. The figure is acquainted with anarchy; it insists on the extreme imperatives of the Self; it acknowledges neither death nor the end of man. Hence the energy of the contemporary novel which is the energy of opposition.

New American Playwrights: Williams, Miller and Others
BY JOHN GASSNER

If one had to report to Europeans on new American playwrights after the Second World War* what would one say? Like every other national theatre, the American stage after World War II had to be tested, to a degree, by the caliber of its new playwrights, and several of these had revealed a striving toward something more valuable—considerably more valuable—than play-carpentry. Two of the newcomers, Tennessee Williams and Arthur Miller, actually and deservedly aroused interest abroad.

Tennessee Williams, who was born in the South in 1911, made a first impression on the stage with his memory-play *The Glass Menagerie* in the spring of 1945, when he was no longer an unseasoned young writer, having had a Theatre Guild production five years earlier that was retired in Boston. Born four years after Williams, in New York City, Arthur Miller achieved importance in our theatre two years after the production of *The Glass Menagerie*, with *All My Sons*. He, too, had gone through the experience of a Broadway production with *The Man Who Had All the Luck*, which expired after a short run in 1944. Miller, whose talent belongs primarily to the theatre, actually established himself first as a novelist in 1945, with the successful publication of *Focus*, a novel about anti-semitism. He first impressed Broadway in January, 1947, with the taut dramaturgy and moral passion of *All My Sons*.

Within two years, then, the two young writers were equally in the limelight, and before long it was difficult to decide who was the more important of the two. Williams, after giving the theatre the mild dramatization of a D. H. Lawrence story *You Touched Me* in 1946, pro-

*This essay was written in 1954; more recent dramatists are mentioned elsewhere in this book.

ceeded to overwhelm Broadway again with *A Streetcar Named Desire,* which opened in New York on December 3, 1947. And Miller made an equally strong, if not actually stronger, impression with *Death of a Salesman,* fifteen months later. The two pieces found large and enthusiastic audiences, and subsequently reached an even larger public in generally faithful film versions. Miller followed *Death of a Salesman* with a tendentious version of *An Enemy of the People,* and started work on *The Crucible,* one of the two outstanding plays of the 1952–53 season. Williams provided *Summer and Smoke* in the fall of 1948 and *The Rose Tattoo* in 1951. The former, which resembled *A Streetcar Named Desire* in some respects, was a failure when first produced, but became the most acclaimed production of 1952 when staged in the arena theatre of Circle-in-the-Square. And turning to symbolism on a grand scale, Williams expanded an early one-act play of his into the *Camino Real* over which New York buzzed with controversy in 1953.

Between them, the young man from the North and the young man from the South have virtually encompassed the range of modern dramatic art and style, and that is what might interest the European observer especially. Miller represents the social realism that has characterized a large percentage of modern playwriting since Ibsen's middle period; Williams, the effort to transcend realism that started in Europe with the neoromantic and symbolist reaction against Naturalism. Miller uses lean colloquial prose; Williams writes musically, poetically, and imagistically charged dialogue. Miller exemplifies the theatre of the common man and of more or less collective issues; Williams, the perennial avant-garde theatre of subjectivity and private sensibility.

II

Miller, whose descent from Ibsen can be clearly traced, was rightly designated by Harold Clurman as a dispenser of moral jurisprudence. In *All My Sons,* the conflict between self-interest and social responsibility is developed as a drama of hidden guilt, discovery, and retribution in the manner of *Pillars of Society,* a play which we associate with Ibsen's early technique of intrigue in the manner of

Scribe. We don't think well of this kind of contrived dramaturgy, of course, but we draw a sharper line between it and the method employed in Ibsen's later plays, from *A Doll's House* and *Ghosts* to *John Gabriel Borkman,* than is warranted. The difference is essentially one of degree, or, perhaps, of tone. It comes down to a question of whether the work is one of calculation for the sake of the plot or for the sake of idea, irony, or some other interest intended to stimulate rather than befuddle and thrill the playgoer. An incriminating letter brought to light in the third act of *All My Sons,* when it could just as well have been discovered earlier, calls attention to plot machinery. Adventitious occurrences in Ibsen's *Pillars of Society* belong to the same order of contrivance. The burning down of the orphanage in *Ghosts* shortly after Pastor Manders refused to insure the charitable edifice out of conventional piety calls attention to irony. An irony compounded by the fact that the orphanage was intended as a memorial to Mrs. Alving's amorously roving husband! And compounded further as a means of representing the destruction of the entire façade of the Pastor's beliefs and Mrs. Alving's conventional life. The superiority of *Ghosts* to either *Pillars of Society* or *All My Sons* is obvious.

Still, we must realize, too, that the plot contrivance of *All My Sons* (or of Miss Hellman's *Watch on the Rhine, The Little Foxes,* or even *Another Part of the Forest*) does not exist as something isolated from other interests served up by the playwright. In a typical "well-made play" intended to be nothing more than audience-catching theatre, whether it be Scribe's *Verre d'Eau* intrigue in the court of Queen Anne or the latest melodrama, the plot contrivance serves only the plot. In the atypical "well-made play," *Pillars of Society* or *All My Sons* (or a Hellman play), the plot contrivance serves something else than the plot. The argument, the idea, or the author's passion for something *beyond theatre* dominates our interest. We must grant, of course, that the contrivance is esthetically meretricious, since the author has reached out for an easy, obvious way of getting on with his play or idea and resolving it. He has been guilty of distinguishing between means and ends, whereas in every artistic enterprise means and ends or content and form should be truly identical. Nevertheless, we must allow the work a place on the foothills of creative art—as a flawed work that nonetheless has merit. And that is precisely the case when audiences and critics, to whom some intelligence is granted by all but fledgling intellectuals, respond to the work, as they did to *All My Sons,* with excitement and a considerable measure of respect.

Nor is it just the "idea" that commands this respect. In a play such as *All My Sons,* there are elements beyond both plot and idea that engage our interest. Characters are brought to life, an atmosphere or mood is evoked, an environment is presented; and insight into how people feel and think or rationalize is present. The texture and actual aliveness of *All My Sons* consists of the reality of family life observed by Miller; of the reality of Miller's Joe Keller, depicted as a shrewd "little man" with a feeling for family and a sense of cleverly concealed desperation; of Keller's wife, presented as the affectionate "little woman" for whom issues of right and wrong or guilt and retribution are secondary to keeping life going with creature comforts and amiable personal relationships; of the ambivalences of Keller's surviving son, whose filial loyalty is being severely tested when he must inform against his father. In addition, Miller made reality out of the neighborliness of suburban neighbors, and out of various other details, down to a blasted little tree in a cramped backyard which is symbolic of the Keller family's narrow way of life, normal intellectual-moral range, and questionable moral situation. Miller, in short, *created* his play rather than merely contrived it. He presented life, as well as argument, on the stage.

Miller's argument could not, however, be slighted either; it had passion and principle. The war-profiteer Joe Keller, who had caused the death of a number of aviators by supplying the government with defective airplane parts, was depicted by Miller as a "little man" rather than as a stereotyped capitalistic villain. Keller justified his conduct on the grounds that he was preserving his small business for his sons. But the crime is exposed by his own son, and the malefactor, stripped of his sentimental defenses, kills himself. The categorical imperative operates here in a manner that recalls the relentless dramaturgy of the Scandinavian master. Narrow practicality is morally bankrupt and has criminal consequences in the case of Miller's

"Consul Bernick," Joe Keller. The latter's paternal love and devotion to his family's welfare are exposed as disguised manifestations of egotism, since he endeavored to secure his sons' interests at the expense of other men's sons. Miller wages war against "Gyntism," whatever its form or its self-justification.

Miller's later slighting reference to his "well-made play" as a conventional exercise should not mislead us into believing that *All My Sons* is completely atypical of his dramatic method. In essential matters, he followed the same course of closely demonstrating his social philosophy when he wrote *Death of a Salesman*. He moved the dramatic action freely from one stage area to the other without making any attempt to set the scene realistically. He combined the realistic technique with the expressionistic, weaving a complex pattern of present and past events, of immediate tensions and recollected crises. But he rooted his imaginatively conceived scenes in common reality; the characters and the background were always recognizably middle-class. The composition of the play held present and past events in a vise of dramatic logic as a misguided man, bitterly disappointed in his life and in his hopes for a favorite son, moved from despair to suicide within twenty-four hours. The man's memories and hallucinations moved erratically over time and space, but they were tied tightly together by his immediate tensions and conflicts.

There was, it is true, no "well-made play" kind of intrigue or crime detection in this chronicle of Willy Loman, the mentally distressed sixty-year-old salesman whose life and errors are weighed in the balance of fate. All the discoveries in this drama are essentially self-discoveries by Willy Loman and the son he miseducated. Yet the play was charged with suspense, since Miller was trying a man for his faults and follies. The fact that Willy Loman shared these with a great many ordinary men, a fact that gave *Death of a Salesman* a good deal of its meaning, was not allowed to exempt him from judgment. Miller scrupulously prepared a trap for his main character, and the trap was nothing less than Willy's entire misspent life of hollow success-worship, false values, and chronic inability to face the truth. Ignoring the importance of integrity and achievement, Willy naïvely thought that popularity gained by windy charm constituted a successful way of life. He acted on this belief, blustered about it, and indoctrinated his children with it. But the verdict of reality is ultimately against this deluded man, and Miller, accepting this verdict as essentially just, renders it strictly. The hour of reckoning arrives inexorably in this drama. "Gyntism" is exposed and punished in *Death of a Salesman* even more relentlessly than in *All My Sons,* in spite of Miller's great compassion for a broken man who had never intended to harm anyone.

Miller has generally been applauded for the balance he maintained between pity and justice. The only non-dramaturgic question that has been seriously raised is whether his misguided salesman is worthy of tragic treatment, and the point is rather well taken. It should not be overworked, however. For very obviously the play is not a tragedy in the grand manner, and Miller did not intend it to be one. He defined his play as the tragedy of a common man rather than of an exceptional hero. Where we can part company with the author is in feeling that his Willy Loman is *too* common. Miller intended to affirm the tragic dignity of an "average" man's refusal to relinquish his ideal of himself as an indispensable and admired person, an independent individual, and the father of a son who has a bright future in spite of objective evidence to the contrary. Miller's *ordinary* hero is *extraordinary* in the passionate manner in which he lives and dies for his dream. Is that dream worthy? We balk at this point to a degree which varies with our background and sense of values.

Whether or not *Death of a Salesman* entirely sustains itself as a tragedy, it expresses a sympathetic and heroic view of realities that reveal a good deal of the life and struggles of a by no means negligible stratum of American —and not only American—society in our times. The very dichotomy of the argument is characteristic of this reality. Willy is a victim, but also a fool. Society, with its over-publicized materialistic values and vulgar view of success, pumped him full of notions. But not all men, not even the suburban neighbor "Uncle Charlie," a character who has no towering mind or aspirations, succumb to this nonsense of success as "show" and glib talk and a state of being "well liked." The point is, of course, that Willy did succumb, and that there are many Willys, as average New

York audiences readily believed. This is part of Willy's misfortune. But Willy is also an employee, who has become superannuated. He is ready for the scrap-heap, a fate to which he could not have resigned himself easily, given his character, even if he could have drawn old-age benefits or a pension, any more than Othello could have resigned himself to possessing a wife who is not above suspicion. (Iago could, to a degree. But that is one of the many differences between Iago and Othello.) In other words, Willy is a "social problem" as a discarded employee, and a "human problem" as a personality too big in his feelings and necessary pretensions to be merely a case history soluble by social legislation. The play is both sociological and non-sociological and at least oriented toward "tragedy."

Without continuing this line of inquiry, we can say that Miller, for whatever reasons we wish to ascribe to the author, split his play between *social causation* and *individual responsibility* for Willy's fate. Which causation stands out for us depends upon our bias. Both communist critics and their communism-obsessed antagonists focused on the social causation. The former complained that Miller obscured the social issue. And he certainly did lessen the importance of social causation by making Willy's folly responsible for his fiasco. Others could complain, and with some justice, that Miller had carried over a left-wing animus from the social theatre of the thirties in presenting Willy as a callously discharged and helpless employee when it was evident that Willy had made a mess of life quite independently. And in *Partisan Review,* Eleanor Clark went so far as to accuse the author of a disingenuous effort to cover up "leftist" tracks by exposing Willy's personal follies and allocating to him a personal responsibility for his misfortunes when, according to her, Miller actually sought to indict capitalist society. Many of us, myself included, however, are inclined to contend that Miller placed the *personal causation* in the foreground of the play. The most obvious proof is that Uncle Charlie, the small businessman, succeeds as a human being in the play, although his life and values have been made thoroughly "middle-class" by Miller. There is nothing in the play to indicate that Willy's choice of a career as a salesman was a social or economic necessity rather than truly a necessity of his nature or of his illusions, granted the existence of a milieu favorable to the latter. The dichotomy of Miller's presentation of Willy's plight is undoubtedly in the play. It is not necessarily a virtue, for it causes some confusion in our attitude toward Willy and in our perception of his situation. Yet the dichotomy is not necessarily as egregious a flaw in *Death of a Salesman* as some critics claim. The dichotomy is actually present in the life and destiny that Miller's Willy exemplifies.

There is a failure in tragic art in the treatment. No doubt of it, for Willy never arrives at tragic insight; he even rejects the insight of his son Biff. But could he have arrived at this insight, which amounts to realizing his (and Biff's) littleness, without losing the heroism—confused and morally intellectually limited though it be!—that gives him some stature? Willy, as characterized by Miller, is constitutionally incapable of giving up his dream. That is his tragedy. It nominates him for the select company of those passionate souls that Edith Hamilton calls the only tragic characters of literature. Whether we are willing actually to elect him to that company is debatable. We can divide sharply on that question, and in casting our vote for or against his election we only reveal ourselves. We reveal our bias, our conditioning, our values, moral or esthetic, or both. And at this point our argument arrives at an impasse, for we arrive at the "dead end" of what we ourselves are, and to expect us to change our vote is to expect us to change ourselves.

III

Without possessing Miller's socially directed attitude, Williams, too, has been concerned with the dream-mechanisms of unfortunate characters who try to create and preserve ideal images of themselves. Like Miller, he regards their delusions with compassionate interest as pathetic defenses against the frustration or shipwreck of their lives. In fact, he is able to create a tracery of fantasy for them with much greater subtlety and grace than Miller, although he is vulnerable to the temptations of bohemian preciosity, as Miller is not. His portraits of women who cannot face reality are masterful. Unlike Miller, however, Williams gives primacy to the psychologically rather than socially relevant facts of each situation. This is the case even in *The Glass Menagerie,* in which an important factor is the economic distress of a family during the depression period. No particular affirmation has ruled Williams' plays; he has been content to remain a tender chronicler of failure, and he has not evinced any desire to prove social causation even when he has made reference to it. The primary factors in all his produced plays, except perhaps *Camino Real,* have been instinct and sensibility. Moreover, if Williams has evinced one paramount conviction it is a belief in the power of the libido to both animate and destroy a human being. In this respect, Williams reveals his kinship to D. H. Lawrence, whom he has admired to the point of imitation. Only in *The Glass Menagerie,* among the full-length plays, does sex play a secondary part, and there we encounter a world of pre-adult innocence (even in the case of Amanda, the mother steeped in her girlish past) which entails failure. There is no particular social passion in his work.

Williams has a bohemian writer's "art for art's sake" passion. It appears to be his only passion, as well as his only faith—the faith of a *fin de siècle* or "Décadent" writer with whom Europeans are considerably more familiar than Americans. The interest of the French in *A Streetcar Named Desire* and *The Rose Tattoo,* which they have acclaimed as a great play, might be explained on the basis that *décadence* is a powerful literary tradition of late nineteenth and twentieth century France. His "estheticism," which has made him unusual and fascinating in the American theatre, has been his main limitation as dramatist, in my opinion, ever since I started following his career in 1940 when Miss Theresa Helburn and I gave him a Bureau of New Plays scholarship.

The essence of bohemianism is preoccupation with the artist's singularity or specialness, which is often the same thing as a sense of alienation defensively exaggerated into exhibitionistic defiance. Williams held this tendency in check and transmuted it into objective observation while writing his dramas of emotionally bankrupted women whom he honestly set down as neurotics. He did not do so in the first produced full-length play *Battle of Angels* in 1940; and his latest play *Camino Real,* produced in 1953, is completely grounded in the cult of alienation, for which "symbolism" has been the favorite technique. These plays romanticize the childlike or "wild" individual. He is a Cajun Robin Hood of sex and artist *manqué* in *Battle of Angels* and an American, "Kilroy," sort of innocent or naif in *Camino Real*. Significantly, the hero of *Camino Real* shares the stage with Casanova, Mlle. Gautier, Byron, and Don Quixote, all literary figures associated with defiance of convention and with romance.

Williams' estheticism, with which the realistic details of his plays exist in a dramatically effective fusion, translates itself in other ways, too. The overdelicateness and fastidiousness of Blanche DuBois form a sharp contrast to her circumstances and her compulsive incontinence; and it is altogether apparent that Williams loves her over-refinement as much as he exposes it. The brute masculinity of Stanley Kowalski also unduly fascinates Williams at the same time that he deplores it. (Kowalski, too, is a "wild" man!) Williams' ambivalence in the play has made playgoers fluctuate between a feeling that Stan Kowalski gives Blanche what she deserves and a sense of outrage when he rapes her during his wife's stay in the hospital, where she has given birth to his child. Different actors may vary the emphasis, but the objective line of action (Kowalski has a right to resent Blanche, but is brutish, and Blanche is both annoying and pathetic) betrays the author's ambivalence. It produces a provocative, but also damaging, ambiguity in the play; damaging to the point of preventing *Streetcar* from attaining tragic magnificence. Another ambivalence appears in *The Rose Tattoo*. There is a sharp contrast here between the erotic obsessiveness of the heroine, who is herself divided between sensuality and concern for her daughter's virtue, and the almost asexual purity of Williams' treatment of the love of the daughter and a young sailor.

A close study of "texture" such as the New Critics of the Ranson-Tate-Brooks school employ so efficiently would, indeed, reveal numerous instances of "ambiguity" and ambivalence on which to base analysis, evaluation, and speculation. I am sure that if Williams had been an English or Irish poet instead of an American playwright who has succeeded on Broadway (how injudicious of him!), he would have already been put through the New Critics' wringer. The results would have been fascinating, if not necessarily as conclusive as the New Critics would have believed, for Williams, like every other professional playwright, has had to consider and yield to many objective facts of stage production essentially unrelated to the subjectivity of the author. Williams' fondness for atmospheric and musical effects is transparent, and his consciousness of dramatic and theatrical form makes him a deliberately "theatricalist" playwright. The theatricalism of *Camino Real* is an extreme example of his concern with non-realistic formal devices. A glance at the stage contrivances he prescribed for the staging of *The Glass Menagerie* (they appear in the published version, but were discarded in part by Eddie Dowling, the director of the Broadway production), reveals a bias for theatrical ingenuity and stylization even in this relatively modest piece of playwriting. Actually, the most affecting scenes of *The Glass Menagerie* are written with sensitive realism. Here and elsewhere, Williams is most convincing when he writes without trying too hard to play the symbolist and the gymnast of theatrical effects. No American or living European playwright is his equal when he modestly confines himself to a realistic rendering of non-allegorical, non-literary characters who belong to a real rather than a poetic environment. But it is apparent that he puts a premium both on literariness and on "art theatre" virtuosity in the use of the theatre's physical facilities. He also likes to play with symbols, to use literary allusions, and like the Pound-Eliot disciples, to embellish the programs and published versions of his books with epigraphs (from Hart Crane and other "alienated" writers). He is Broadway's most dedicated avant-gardist.

Williams' work has been popularly called "poetic realism." It edges over into *theatricalist realism* because he tends toward the symbolist school of writing, and whenever symbolism has to be given physical equivalents it becomes theatricalism. Had he devoted himself solely to poetry he would have been a "symbolist." Fortunately he did not, for he would have been a distinctly minor, perhaps only barely tolerable, lyric poet. The theatre has compelled him to objectify experience, which he can do very well.

Realism still proves highly efficacious and rewarding in the modern drama, and that Williams has known this to be the case is apparent. But he has a theatrical imagination and likes to use it. Williams, moreover, has been suspicious of realism, no doubt because he has seen so much degenerate realism in the form of commonplace playwriting. Probably, too, he has confused realism with naturalism to such a degree that he would have been pleased to do without the realistic technique and style entirely if he had been less strongly ruled by his talent for observation and his emotional closeness to his early environment in the South. He has himself edged over into naturalism from time to time. He did so, for example, in the one-act play *The Lady of Larkspur Lotion* and in the rape scene of *Streetcar*. Naturalism pushes realism over the edge of moderation and good taste and becomes a sensational exploitation of sordid behavior and circumstances. Bohemianism tends to succumb to naturalism even while favoring estheticism, for the bohemian artist is fascinated with "raw life," which he idealizes precisely because he feels more or less alienated from life itself. Sensational pictures of reality satisfy the craving for self-assertion and the desire to defy convention and bait the bourgeois or the Babbitt. In his best scenes and plays, however, Williams has managed realism without excess and with considerable insight, sympathy, and accurate observation. He has treated the lost and the damned with understanding and pity, and has also revealed a capacity for humor compounded of a tolerant feeling for human failure and shrewd awareness of bizarre and unrealistic behavior on the part of his characters.

Williams' symbolist tendencies are often controlled by the requirements of his realistic observation and analysis. He is particularly successful when he uses atmosphere and employs music expressively. Except in *Camino Real*, among his produced full-length plays, he never allows the atmosphere to thin out into a symbolist fog. He may overstress symbolism when he resorts to the civic statue of "Eternity" to signify Alma's virginal idealism or "soulfulness" in *Summer and Smoke*, since these traits are more than sufficiently stressed in action and characterization. But the "symbol" is put to effectively ironic use when it is at the foot of this statue that Alma ultimately renounces her purity. The skeleton, or "anatomy," hanging in her lover's office contrasts "body"—that is, the wild young doctor's physical desire for her—with "soul," or Alma's revulsion against sexuality. This symbol is employed too obviously. But it furnishes the occasion for a strong dramatic scene between the two characters. In *Streetcar*, Blanche DuBois, the former belle of a Southern plantation reduced to prostitution, has a mania for covering electric bulbs with colored lampshades, a habit that validly expresses her desire to soften reality. The morbidly shy Laura of *The Glass Menagerie* collects glass figurines and occupies herself with them. They represent her own fragile girlhood, but they also fit realistically into the portrait of Laura the lame girl who lacks friends, and the glass animals serve the play admirably and naturally in her scene with the ably drawn gentleman caller. When in that scene her little glass unicorn falls to the ground and loses the horn that made it unique, the event signifies to the girl her wish to become a normal young woman. It would be absurd to ask for a more natural and delicately written episode than this delicately managed revelation—that is, for a more discreetly managed "symbolism."

Except in *Camino Real*, in fact, the underlying fascination of Williams' work, as distinct from its more obvious interest to playgoers, has come from contrasts between realistic and symbolist writing; and from contrasts, too, between the reality of characters and environment, on one hand, and the theatrical deployment of his material, on the other. It may be that this is what casual commentators mean when they refer to him as a "poetic" realist, for they do not, obviously, mean that he writes formal poetry in the plays or that he confines his playwriting to evoking mere nuances *à la* Maeterlinck.

After 1949 Miller and Williams acquired three gifted colleagues. One of these is William Inge, a young writer from the Mid-Western states, whose *Come Back, Little Sheba*, produced in 1950, presented the stalemate of a sensitive alcoholic and his love-starved wife. Mr. Inge's authentic dialogue, economy of means, and ability to make uncommonly revealing drama out of common life have inspired high hopes for him. Mr. Inge was an admirer of Williams' early work. The other two recruits, Truman Capote and Carson McCullers, are Southerners. They received encouragement from Williams, and, like him, they present Southern backgrounds in their plays. Both first attained prominence as novelists, and their respective plays, *The Grass Harp* and *The Member of the Wedding,* were dramatizations of their own work. But the dramatizations were made by themselves and revealed talent for the theatre. *The Grass Harp* had extreme inadequacies and made innocence indistinguishable from idiocy. But this drama about some of life's innocents, who upset the conventions by trying to live in a tree, possessed unusual delicacy and poetic feeling. *The Member of the Wedding,* produced in 1950, was an even more delicately conceived play and was entirely successful. Instead of making a young girl's adolescence the springboard for a conventional plot, Mrs. McCullers gave us a sensitive study of the awkward age of growing out of childhood and groping toward womanhood. Her play became a little drama of life itself—of life's irrational course (in the fate of the girl's little playmate who dies of meningitis), of vague hopes and keenly felt disappointments, and of the essential loneliness of children and adults.

A simple term that may be used conveniently to define a small trend in American playwriting is "poetry of theatre." By this I mean a tendency on the part of writers to use the dramatic medium sensitively and imaginatively without actually writing their dialogue in verse, and without relinquishing their hold on common reality. This style of playwriting, which may also be called a species of "poetic realism," is present even in *Come Back, Little Sheba,* in which the author deals with commonplace characters and facts. (It was present again in Inge's *Picnic,* with some notable, if not always tasteful, assistance from Joshua Logan who directed the Broadway production.) In Inge's first Broadway production, the poetic component was an atmosphere of uneasy quiescence before and after the explosive second act in which the alcoholic man became violent.

Atmosphere was the very essence of Mrs. McCullers' *The Member of the Wedding,* where conventional dramatic action was largely replaced by vignettes representing the temporary companionship of a bewildered girl, an imaginative little boy, and a patient Negro nurse. Atmosphere, moreover, attained symbolic value in Capote's *The Grass Harp*, since the tree-house in which the main characters spent a night represented satisfaction of their desire for freedom and self-realization. The huge tree, which spread across the stage, overshadowed the people below it, making the world of small-town conventions appear small and insignificant. The tree was a visible symbol of the innocents' dream, which was also conveyed expressively by exquisite music composed for the play by Virgil Thompson.

Even Arthur Miller, the social and moral realist, moved toward a poetic form of theatre with *Death of a Salesman,* requiring expressive stage lighting and music, shuttling back and forth between present reality and dreamlike reminiscence, and employing fantasy and symbolism in the case of Willy Loman's shadowy brother Ben, who represents Willy's obsession with "success." In an earlier unproduced tragedy about the Spanish conquest of Mexico, *Montezuma,* Miller wrote a thoroughly poetic drama removed from contemporary life, if related to it by implication. And in *The Crucible,* he did the same thing, once more attempting to write tragedy on a more transparently heroic level than Willy Loman's drama. In *The Crucible,* as well as in *Montezuma,* Miller found an epic subject and tried to give the central character of his Salem witch-hunt history some heroic elevation. The need to write tragedy has been very much present in this playwright's mind. So has the need to write dramatic poetry when the context of the play justifies it. Although he has not yet proved himself a poet in words and may never be able to, he has already sought out those areas of subject matter and those possibilities of theatrical expressiveness that point in the direction of poetic drama. A tension exists in his work between the moral passion and political idealism that propel him toward social drama and the desire of a formative artist to rise to visions of human grandeur, however difficult the ascent.

We may conclude, then, that some of our new playwrights have been striving for maximum dramatic expressiveness short of actually writing distinguished dramatic verse. They have endeavored to give their playwriting a variety of levels of interest by using the theatre's resources poetically even when the life they have represented is externally commonplace and its milieu is prosaic.

Class War in British Literature
BY LESLIE A. FIEDLER

During the past four or five years,* there has been the
sense in England that something painful at least, perhaps
critical, is occurring in the world of literature. Cries of
rage are heard, mingled with shouts of triumph; insults
meet counterinsults, and everyone seems astonished that
it has all come to *matter* so much. Certainly, there has been
nothing like it since the thirties, when Auden and Spender
and the other wild boys came down from Oxford crying
the names of Freud and Marx and Kierkegaard as battle
slogans. But the excitement of the thirties was confined almost entirely to poetry, while the new changes affect the
novel, prose drama and criticism as well; and, oddly
enough, the survivors of the earlier literary breakthrough
are among those who cry out most loudly against the
newer writers.

For an American such recent developments have a special meaning. Over the last twenty-five years, there has
been little in English literature which has deeply moved
us by seeming itself to move out of impulses anything
like our own. Dylan Thomas, to be sure, proved an import
article successful beyond belief; but in general, British
writing has threatened to become merely exotic—more
foreign to us and less relevant than the fiction, say, of
France or Italy.

Now, however, distant sounds of pain and elation begin
to reach us; and even before we have read the verse or the
novels which inspire them, we realize that at last new
writers have arrived on the English scene capable of giving
offense as only the truly new gives offense. The correspondence columns of *The Spectator, The New Statesman* and
The Observer are kept full; and we learn that there are

*This essay was written in 1958.

even public debates on the new movement, special discussions in the theatre following the production of certain new plays.

The young have not only, it appears, managed to please themselves (which is simple enough), but to displease the elder statesmen of their literature, critics pledged to a dishearteningly broad range of tolerance. Unlike most of our own younger writers, the British ones have succeeded in appearing shockingly impossible! Literary rebels of the thirties, retired from their rebellion or grown confirmed in it, have looked to the young for the kind of rebellion which they themselves once provided—and have found, of course, only a rebellion against their own.

Everyone in England is aware that, with the close of the last war and the election of a Socialist government, a cultural as well as a political era has closed; and some at least are equally aware that the death of certain literary magazines (*Criterion, Horizon*—even *Scrutiny*, which represented an almost official opposition to the official literary orthodoxy) has signaled the disappearance of a kind of literature and of the taste which sustained it. To the young, something else, much more disconcerting, has become clear, too: that the literary revolt of the thirties did not make any really basic changes in the values which have informed British art since before World War I.

Auden and Spender, Day Lewis and MacNeice had extended, even strained those values, but had not fundamentally broken through them; and the poets of the forties had disrupted them no more than had their predecessors. T. S. Eliot could welcome Stephen Spender as cordially as Spender could hail Dylan Thomas; and all of them, everyone from E. M. Forster to W. H. Auden, came to tea with Virginia Woolf, whose husband could remember lunching with the Empress Eugénie.

It is this which offends (rightly or wrongly scarcely matters) the newer English writers, who are resolved to break at last out of a world of taste which has been, it seems to them, too long confined to the circumference of a tea table. It is, of course, possible that certain of them will be lured into the orbit of the witty and charming self-perpetuating society that they began by attacking; but in general that society is doomed. Already there are young men willing to write the sort of frank review of a

dull and repetitious volume of verse by Edith Sitwell that
no one would have written earlier; because (though it
was possible, indeed expected, to comment on that dullness and repetitiveness in private malicious gossip) one
did not publicly attack a member of the official first family
of the arts.

The new writers are, in short, not *gentlemen* like their
forerunners; if born to that status, they flee from it guiltily;
if lucky enough to be sons of factory workers or furniture
dealers, they exult in their origins. The ideal of the gentleman they associate with what they call (like its other
enemies before them) "Bloomsbury." What "Bloomsbury"
was historically, even the question of whether in fact it
existed at all, does not matter; it has become a *myth,* a
handy label for a hated world. In the minds of the new
writers, "Bloomsbury" means quite simply a society
pledged before all else to an ideal of elegant style in conversation, art, life itself; a society in which the liberal
and aristocratic are subtly blended; an international society
bounded in England by Oxford and Cambridge on the one
side and London on the other, but existing, too, in colonies
at Cagne-sur-mer or on Capri or Ischia.

In "Bloomsbury," all that had seemed "new thought"
at the end of the nineteenth century had been grafted onto
the grace and wit of an upper bohemia invented in the
days of Oscar Wilde. Its origins indicate its hospitality to
the politer forms of homosexuality and Marxism, and perhaps suggest why it has also welcomed the new economics
of Keynes or admired such conventions of avant-garde
literature as stream of consciousness.

Members of this world (it is more loosely organized than
the term "Bloomsbury" perhaps suggests) know at one
and the same time that they must fight to defend a far from
ignoble ideal of life; and that they are doomed—that the
world of television and Public Health Service and the disappearance of servants is more congenial to their enemies
than to them. Their resistance is already half a surrender;
yet the newer writers feel this resistance as a "conspiracy"
against youth and art. At least they choose to describe it
so. Young writers tend everywhere to classify those who
do not admire them in McCarthyite terms, finding it easier
to believe in a behind-the-scenes plot than in a simple
difference of taste; and identifying themselves so totally

with the main development of literature that they cannot distinguish an attack on any one of them from an assault on the whole future of art.

From this side of the Atlantic, it is obvious that the struggle is not between "gangs," plotting and counter-plotting, but between classes trapped in a common plight in a world of transition. Ultimately it is a conflict between two worlds: the class world of the past and the declassed world to come—from our point of view, between a world very different from ours and one which becomes ever more like it. The special irony of the situation lies, of course, in the fact that the defenders of the caste system of "Bloomsbury" are, in large part, declared proponents of the "classless society," and that *politically* they have always worked to undercut the order which maintains them.

It must be embarrassing for them now to discover themselves on the barricades in a literary class war, attacked by the kind of scholarship boy they themselves have sponsored. They had dreamed, I suppose, of the intellectuals in the New Order adopting their values and imitating their literary manners as individual lower-class writers had done for so many decades. The new writers are, however, no longer V. S. Pritchetts, eager to assimilate culturally to a level of society into which they have not been born. They are no more impressed by his example than they are by the fact that writers they regard as superseded still function; that Leonard Woolf, for instance, still attacks and rejoins, and, in a certain sense, *writes better than any of them*. The latter is one of their chief grievances against him. They no longer aspire to the canons of taste he and Pritchett variously represent. Clumsy and sullen and defensive as young outsiders always tend to be, they make of their clumsiness and sullenness and defensiveness their definition; they will neither be bullied into adapting nor flattered into assimilating.

In the Welfare State, whether under Conservative or Labor rule, they find nothing to encourage the courtliness and grace once considered the hallmarks of literature as well as the adornments of conversation in a salon. For an older generation, the drabness of contemporary society is tempered by an awareness that it is they who have made it; for the young it is simply a world they did not make, someone else's utopia. They are its awkward and diffident offspring, to whom it is, despite its faults, merely *home*. When they challenge the codes and values which survive from an earlier state of affairs, they do not raise their voices with the vehemence of those who fought "Bloomsbury" in its palmier days. Unlike D. H. Lawrence or Wyndham Lewis or even F. R. Leavis, the young are not driven to shrillness and paranoia in the fight against what seems invulnerable. Chiefly, they *laugh*. They are angry enough at the deepest level, in earnest all the way through; yet their typical response is the horse laugh. For, in a way, they know what they do not like to confess: that they have already won a victory (a victory not entirely satisfactory) by being born at the right time, by being now rather thirtyish than somewhere near forty or fifty.

Rather typically, they have no journal of their own to celebrate this victory, no special publication to say precisely what it is that is being born out of the collapse of older values. It is not only that journals are these days too expensive for any except the middle-aged, well-heeled or at least well-known to sponsoring foundations; it is in the very nature of the new literary revolution that it should make itself known through the back door of journalism. There are, indeed, two new magazines in England, *The London Magazine* and *Encounter* (the latter, of course, only in part literary); but these are edited by survivors of the thirties, John Lehman and Stephen Spender, the latter a favorite whipping boy of the new writers.

To be sure, Lehman and Spender print the newer writers along with older ones and between editorials deploring their aims; for it is their code to be eclectic and tolerant. What is wanted, however, is precisely a partisan magazine, strident and narrow, to speak for what has come to be called the "Movement." Meanwhile, the only forum of the new young is the back pages of news magazines and papers, particularly *The Spectator*. Members of the Movement have consistently been book reviewers for that journal, and a leading article which appeared in its pages in the fall of 1954 comes close to being a manifesto for the group. Its poets have been published in a series of slim pamphlets, sold for ninepence and published under the title of Fantasy Poets by the Oxford Poetry Society. In addition, of course, there have been individual volumes of criticism, verse and fiction; and some of the latter have even become best sellers, one at least (Kingsley Amis' *Lucky Jim*) being translated into a movie.

Typically again, however, the real introduction of the Movement to a larger public came through one of the newer mass media which distinguish its special world. John Wain, novelist, poet, critic and teacher of literature, was entrusted in 1953 with a literary program called *First Reading* that was being broadcast over the Third Programme of the B.B.C. He used the occasion to present the ideas behind the Movement and to introduce over the air the work of several writers now counted among what their detractors call the Angry Young Men. A nasty review in *The New Statesman* by Hugh Massingham attacked Wain's "maggoty and bureaucratic" style, and unleashed a controversy which drew letters to their editor for weeks. Before the first furor died down, various major literary figures from Graham Greene to V. S. Pritchett had put themselves on record (chiefly against), and a kind of definition of the Movement began to take shape.

That many of the new writers are "bad" writers, inept, over-serious, heavily magisterial, has been evident from the first. What became clear only in the event was that they were not just bad, but bad in a special way—a strategical and perhaps necessary one. Certainly, it was not only their ineptness which enraged their foes; it was their program of which that ineptness was improbably a part.

But what is that program? It is not easy to say; indeed, there has been a growing tendency recently to deny that any Movement exists at all. Deep within the British mind, there lurks a profound embarrassment at being caught out in so seemingly ideological a position; "Movements" are for the French! Yet it is undeniable that certain new writers are linked together in their own awareness and that of the larger reading public. There are the novelists John Wain (who wrote *Hurry on Down* and *Living in the Present*), Kingsley Amis (author of *Lucky Jim* and *That Uncertain Feeling*) and Iris Murdoch (who has three novels: *Under the Net, Flight from the Enchanter* and *The Sand Castle*). Amis has come to seem in most ways an epitome of the group, his first protagonist Lucky Jim and his own person blending into a composite portrait of the Angry Young Joker at Work and Play. Miss Murdoch, a teacher of philosophy at Oxford, seems often only loosely associated with the others; and her latest book rather turned away from their typical themes and tone in an (unsuccessful!) attempt to show she could compete with the older school of writers on their own home grounds.

John Wain is the spokesman for the group of which Amis is the embodiment. It is not only that Wain is more seriously polemical than Amis, but also that he sums up in himself almost all aspects of the Movement as well—a pattern typical to many of its members of turning indifferently from genre to genre. A poet like Amis himself, Donald Davie, Elizabeth Jennings and Philip Larkin, Wain is also a critic like Al Alvarez and Lawrence Lerner. Drama is the one field he has not yet tried; and here the new values have been represented chiefly by John Osborne, whose *Look Back in Anger* was successfully played in New York, after annoying critics and intriguing playgoers in London.

Wain is also (more accurately, has been until recently) a teacher of literature; and in this respect, too, he is not unusual. The Movement is largely academic; at least its members are teachers in the lower ranks and in the remoter colleges. Here he and his colleagues are not unlike many of our contemporary American writers, though quite different from such earlier rebels against "Bloomsbury" as D. H. Lawrence. Imagine Lawrence settling down to a lifetime of lecturing on Metaphysical poetry at a university in, say, Leeds! Like their authors, the protagonists of the new novels are teachers, and their conflicts are fought out in terms of teaching jobs won or lost.

It would be wrong, however, to think of these writers as sitting securely behind the walls of a traditional British university. They cluster rather in the provincial universities (the "redbrick" schools founded during the nineteenth century in the grimmer industrial cities of England), whose faculties are drawn more and more from sons of working-class and lower-middle-class parents, seeking security and worrying not about the quality of the port but about the availability of baby sitters. The new British writer finds himself in a college, that is to say, when the colleges are well on the way to becoming merely other centers for the status-hungry.

It is easier to say what the new writers are against than

to define what they are for. In general they are against the alliance of high culture, fashion, Fabian socialism and homosexuality which has been described earlier; but this begins to seem more and more like being against the Holy Roman Empire, for "Bloomsbury," whatever life it may once have possessed, is now dying. The novels of the Movement are, in this sense, weapons in a class war which is already over. Yet the fight must still go on—if not against the fact, against certain illusions which survive it. What the new writers satirize is the tendency in themselves to pretend to the standards of an upper class which no longer has roots or function, the tendency in their more insecure colleagues to turn themselves into parodies of artists in a (lovely, after all!) world which they have destroyed in the act of entering.

The poets of the thirties, who had seemed to challenge but had ended by adapting themselves to the values of "Bloomsbury," irk them especially. They are less appalled by the defection of Guy Burgess to Moscow than they are by the fact that Stephen Spender can sit at peace with E. M. Forster. They refer contemptuously to the "hygienic Marxist-Freudian" approach of Auden and his followers, and comment wryly on their desire to be "one with a vaguely conceived People." Charles Lumley, protagonist of John Wain's *Living in the Present,* doubtless speaks for his author as well as himself when he boasts that he had been "right to despise them [the intellectuals of the thirties] for their idiotic attempt to look through two telescopes at the same time: one fashioned of German psychology and pointed at themselves, the other of Russian economics and directed at the English working class."

Part of the problem arises because the Marxist intellectuals became the schoolmasters of the newer generations, generations to which, therefore, the obsessive social concerns of the earlier period took on the peculiar irreality of classroom "history." Donald Davie puts it succinctly in a poem which has infuriated certain survivors of the thirties:

> *The Anschluss, Guernica—all the names*
> *At which those poets thrilled, or were afraid,*
> *For me mean schools and schoolmasters and games;*
> *And in the process someone is betrayed.*

Not only the social concerns, but even more the religious impulses of their elders baffle and bore the new writers. When Kingsley Amis, invited to comment on Colin Wilson (one pretentious young man exaggeratedly praised by his elders, though quite out of tune with his contemporaries), asks who the hell is Kierkegaard, this is in part a pose; but it is also the reflection of a fundamental indifference to any religious thinkers and a furious contempt for the more fashionable ones. The atheist existentialists are scarcely more congenial to the new young than the believers; though Iris Murdoch has written a sympathetic book on Sartre, John Wain expresses a more typical response: "he was English enough to feel a savage contempt for modish philosophers who went about preaching a profitable brand of nihilism, blandly informing their fellow creatures that they were already in hell. . . ." The philistine tone, the half-information are both revelatory; but *"English* enough" is the critical phrase; for the young writers have turned inward to domestic concern and home-grown virtues, turning away from all internationalisms, whether of chic or Marxism.

The literary enthusiasms of their predecessors seem to the newer writers as alien as their other allegiances. John Donne, Gerard Manley Hopkins, the French symbolists, the "revolutionists of the word" associated with *transition* —these they reject as they reject the guarded irony of tone with which the poets of the thirties played their literary games. Davie's poem comments on this, too:

> They played the fool, not to appear as fools
> In time's long glass. A deprecating air
> Disarmed, they thought, the jests of later schools;
> Yet irony itself is doctrinaire . . .

For the thirties, the new writers have, I think, a certain residue of respect—at least the sense that there one finds foes worthy of engaging. The forties, on the other hand, apparently strike them as thoroughly despicable; and perhaps the strongest charge they have to make against the surviving upper-class Marxists is that they were taken in by later fads; that they cooperated in the "canonization of Dylan Thomas" and of the turgid Romanticism for which he stood. To many of the new young, Thomas has come to

seem the apotheosis of the False Poet: operatic, sodden, all
shapeless dithyrambics and professional Welshness. Though
they are domestic, the new writers are not parochial; and
local color offends them as much as internationalism.

A character shamelessly drawn from Thomas plays the
role of "a dirty little sod" in Amis' *That Uncertain Feeling,* and a professional Scots bard, equally drunk and
devoted to chasing women, makes a similar appearance in
Wain's *Living in the Present.* The writers of the Movement like to claim they have their own anti-Thomas (R. S.
Thomas, author of *Song of the Year's Turning*), an Angli-
can clergyman who believes that poetry should be read
to oneself, heard with the inner ear.

What most disturbs them is finally not Dylan Thomas
himself so much as his *cult;* for the latter seems to them to
sum up all they hate in intellectual pretentiousness and
faddism. They are driven by a rage against ladies' literary
societies, chamber-music groups, recorder concerts, amateur dramatics, academic flummery—any kind of culture-
mongering. At their worst, they list toward a true middlebrow (and English) sort of anti-intellectualism, not unlike
that which motivated George Orwell, who is one of their
models. It must be said frankly that philistinism is a part
of their artistic program, a New Philistinism, to be sure,
nurtured not on pious tracts but on science fiction and jazz
records. In their hands, however, militant middlebrowism
sometimes functions as a useful weapon in the fight against
a quiet, upper-class reign of terror based on a frozen high
style and a rigidified good taste.

The new writers are not above or beyond politics; yet
they seem in an elusive way to be *past it,* having come to
maturity after what the thirties had meant by politics had
lost most of its sense and significance. They are generally
pro-labor and opposed to anything that reminds them of
Fascism; but they are post-Marxist as they are post-
Freudian. In various political parties, they find fragments
of what seems to them a true view of society; in none do
they appear to find a sufficient embodiment of their own
aspirations. They vote Labor not unlike certain American
intellectuals, who, without great enthusiasm, support Adlai
Stevenson. The authors who most move them range in
politics from William Empson, whose sympathies with the
Communists have led him to swallow the most flagrant

tales of germ warfare in Korea, to George Orwell, whose vision of all that was worst in England and Russia blended into the anti-Utopia of *1984*.

If in politics they must be called post-Marxist, in religion they are *post*-post-Christian, pupils of teachers who themselves had lost all orthodox belief, unbelievers twice removed. The shadow of Wittgenstein falls over them and they tend to assume that metaphysics is meaningless. Yet they cannot avoid being shaped by the religious commitments of the class whom they represent in its final avatar; they are the last manifestation of English nonconformism, dissenters without God. Their most immediate ancestor is the Cambridge critic F. R. Leavis, harried veteran of a long war with "Bloomsbury"; and it is, in large part, his world-view that the new novelists adopt: areligious yet moralistic, nonpolitical yet aggressively class conscious, the faith of a British Last Puritan.

They are, indeed, secular Puritans, "distrustful of too much richness or too much fanaticism," and their protagonists, like all fictional projections of the Puritan mind, are typically on the run, a step or two ahead of fell temptation. The tempter is for them sometimes the homosexual (with alarming regularity, their characters brush off the clutching, pale hands of queers), sometimes intellectually pretentious upper-class women, offering sex as a bait in the trap of accommodation. Chiefly, however, it is some more abstract symbol of compromise which the hero flees: a raise, a promotion, a better job—finally, respectability itself. Typically enough, in our time of easy living, it is not failure and poverty against which the protagonist struggles but their opposites. In the book of the new young, nothing fails like success.

The hero of the new British novel is, then, the lonely individual narrowly evading respectability, or the harried, petty-bourgeois couple just escaping prosperity. Poverty and loneliness and exclusion are the touchstones of morality and merit—the Puritans' materialist measures of grace not refused but turned upside down. Rejection is offered as a way of life, though never *total* rejection which threatens to become religious or at least fanatic. The newer British fiction is plagued by knowing much better where to begin than where to end; its heroes flirt with self-destruction, suicide or utter declassing, but in the last chapters they tend to be bundled shamelessly into some sentimental compromise. Back goes the protagonist to the colliery in which his father worked, back to the old school or into the arms of a Good Woman.

One does not know exactly how to take these preemptory Happy Endings. Are they the outcome of utter confusion, or mere strategies to please the public, like the typical last scenes of movies? Certainly the new writers, though they woo failure in the name of their characters, are eager for success in their own right. They *want* to produce best sellers, and would consider it outmoded snobbishness to refuse to tickle the average reader in order to gain the approval of a sensitive few.

Yet plot is less important in revealing what the writers are after than are the attitudes of their protagonists: Jimmy Porter with his trumpet and sweet stall more important than the fable of *Look Back in Anger,* Lucky Jim and the "faces" with which he secretly mocks his fate more significant than what happens in the book called by his name. Whatever other characteristics the new hero possesses, whether he be a "card," a *schlemiel* or a self-torturer, he must possess two qualities: a fear of success and a talent for anger. As the fear is the substance of his politics, the anger is the substance of his self. These new heroes are irascible men above all, impossible husbands and lovers, impotent bullies gifted with a rough eloquence whose source is their rage at their own predicament and the state of the world. Such irascibility is at least a relief from the self-pity which has been too long the keynote of the novel; and it leads outward into action rather than inward into elaborate analyses of motive and sensibility, toward the picaresque rather than into stream of consciousness.

There have been impassioned arguments recently over whether these fictional figures are true to their own time—representative of the young as they are. Such debates seem most often to end in absurd, though heated, queries about why in hell Osborne's Jimmy Porter didn't get a job with a band if he were really all that talented; and they are, of course, essentially pointless from the start. It is a little like asking whether Hemingway's Jake Barnes really existed; whether, after all, there *was,* in fact, a Lost Generation.

What we are beholding is the creation of a *myth* of a generation, the response of a certain kind of just-short-of-thirty anti-intellectual intellectual to life in contemporary England. What such a writer renders is the way in which he enjoys being, or is forced to be (the two get mixed up), aware of himself, his consciousness of the drama of his existence. That drama is not history, it is an inner or imaginative drama that is felt rather than lived. Whether or not the Angry Young Men existed before the books which embody them, they exist now—for us as well as for themselves. It is their spokesman who is sent off to the Youth Congress in Moscow to register the "British view" for the British press, at the very moment that his right to represent anything is being challenged. And this is a joke that the younger writers can especially relish.

Indeed, they are very good at jokes in general; for though they look back in anger, they report in humor. The interior drama to which they bear witness, as well as the outer drama which it obliquely reflects, they regard finally not as tragic or pitiful, but as *funny*. Theirs is not, of course, the delicate, protective irony of an Isherwood, much less the superior and polished mockery of a Waugh or a Huxley. Amis, for instance, who is the funniest of them all, can sound like P. G. Wodehouse when he recounts the flight of his hero, dressed in female Welsh costume and pursued simultaneously by an angry husband and a drunk and amorous workman.

Most often the new writers plunge from satire to brutal farce, as deliberately vulgar as Wain's description of Edgar Banks (in *Living in the Present*) doing an imitation of himself vomiting in a phone booth and of a cop attempting to arrest him for committing that nuisance. Amis is the master of the pratfall, the minor indignity which forever bars his characters from seeming more than fools. Here is one of his husbands trying to strike a convincing attitude before a jealous and reproachful wife:

"No, we just met by chance. Honestly."
"I bet she was glad to see you like that."
"Like what?"
"You've got a bogey on your nose. Improves your looks no end."
I was near the mirror I used for shaving and which

hung above the washbasin. I peeped in and saw the bogey. It was large and vermiform and clung to the wing of my right nostril. I removed it feeling a little downcast. Even the dignity of Charles I on the scaffold, I reasoned, would have been deflated by the executioner telling him what Jean had just told me. . . .

At its furthest metaphysical reach, this becomes the grotesque gallows humor of Iris Murdoch's *Flight from the Enchanter*, a symbol of the Absurd in the full existentialist sense of the word. The new writers do, indeed, feel their lives as absurd, but usually with a small "a" rather than a capital. They have no vision of their plight as cosmically horrible or ridiculous, even as they have no vision of themselves as authors of cosmically significant works. If they write loosely strung, picaresque novels, "funny books," it is because this seems modest, proper to their diffidence. A poem by Philip Larkin (in the opinion of many, the best poet of the group) puts it quite candidly—so candidly, in fact, that it quite enraged one reviewer in *Encounter*, who found so bland a refusal to be outrageous the ultimate outrage.

TO THE DAUGHTER OF A FRIEND

> *May you be ordinary,*
> *Have, like other women,*
> *An average of talents:*
> *Not ugly, not good-looking,*
> *Nothing uncustomary*
> *To pull you off your balance,*
> *That, unworkable itself,*
> *Stops all the rest from working.*
> *In fact, may you be dull—*
> *If that is what a skilled,*
> *Vigilant, flexible,*
> *Unemphasized, enthralled*
> *Catching of happiness is called.*

Dedicated to such an ideal, it is no wonder that the poets of the Movement sound a good deal more like the English versifiers of the late eighteenth century than either William

Empson or Wallace Stevens, whom they like to speak of as their favorites. For similar reasons, the novelists turn rather to the consistently flat prose of Orwell than to more elegant examples for their models. "Amis," V. S. Pritchett has written in uncomprehending annoyance, "writes with his boots." This is true, as it is true that Wain is imprecise and clumsy in his polemics (his more graceful opponents leave him thrashing helplessly in their web of wit) and quite unsubtle in his fiction. Even Iris Murdoch, the most artistically ambitious of the lot, often is confused and blurred to the point of chaos. But this is, of course, exactly the point!

For too long the British novelist has had to submit to an imperious ideal of good writing which began as a liberation and has ended as a tyranny. The impulse of the new novel is back toward the popular ineptness of the Victorians: back through the drawing-room finish, the upper-class grace and wit, which give so odd a uniformity to English fiction from Firbank to Waugh, E. M. Forster to Isherwood, and Aldous Huxley to Henry Green. Once more we can see that it is a class war which is being waged in British literature; that we are witnessing an attempt to redeem fiction and poetry in theme, diction and decor from the demands of one social group in the interests of another. With the weapons of crudity and righteous anger and moral bluntness, the new writers are trying to deliver literature from the circles which captured it early in this century, and to restore it—to whom?

To a group not yet, it must be confessed, clearly defined even to itself—to the New Men in a New Society which proposes to itself the ideal of classlessness, to the real or imaginary Common Readers who are (or anyhow *should* be) emerging from the "Americanization" of British culture. The conflict over the new literature is sometimes spoken of in the correspondence columns as a debate between metropolitans and provincials, Londoners and outsiders; and it is true that many of the new writers live, or have lived, in places like Reading or Swansea or Sheffield, where they teach in "redbrick" universities. But it is hard to be provincial in the older sense in a world of mass communications and mass culture, where the former provinces threaten, indeed, to become the center. More properly, the new writers must be regarded not as provincials but as an "intellectual proletariat" of the Welfare State—perhaps even better as a kind of degraded petty bourgeoisie of the spirit.

Trained in the great universities themselves, though often as scholarship boys and after preparation in county or municipal schools, the members of the Movement find themselves compelled to teach literature, though they would like chiefly to make it. They are not "dons" in any traditional British sense, gentlemen by definition, living in semi-monastic retirement from the vulgar. They are plunged, armpit deep, into a society of largely misguided cultural aspiration and feebly camouflaged illiteracy, where their third-year students may never have heard of Homer and cannot without great pain make sense of a passage from Shakespeare.

The manners and codes of what they call contemptuously "Oxbridge" are irrelevant to their worlds, unreal; and yet these still hedge their lives about—in the form at least of shoddy emulation. Though the newer writers despise old-line philological criticism, having been trained by such "New Critics" as F. R. Leavis, they are urged to publish "scholarly" articles if they would hold their jobs and win promotions. Similarly, though they distrust the relaxed literary gossip of London and the amateur appreciation that passes for criticism in such circles, they find their own work unfavorably compared to that appreciation.

Most wounding of all, perhaps, though artistically most stimulating, is their sense of their own situation: their vision of themselves as the first self-conscious New Men of a dingy New World—not deposed aristocrats in the republic of letters, but minor cultural employees of a bureaucracy. The sordidness of their lives especially obsesses them, the ugliness of their habitual surroundings, which emerges not only in the backgrounds against which the buffoonery of their books is played out, but in their personal complaints and apologies. In 1953, John Wain begins by speaking of the "ugly, industrial city" in which he finds himself, then cries out in answer to those who have called him a "don," "I sit not in a gracious, panelled room—but in a tiny, slum-clearance bungalow."

Similarly, Kingsley Amis is quoted on the jacket of *Lucky Jim:* "I write in a small room facing the blank wall

of the house next door, between lectures in English literature at the University College of Swansea." From their
unspectacularly difficult position, the new writers judge
and portray their world in terms of a satire rooted in
bitterness and self-mockery. That bitterness and self-
mockery, as well as its seedy setting, we know in our
country, too. It is to be found among graduate students
and junior instructors in Bloomington or Evanston or
Madison or Chapel Hill—our own Readings and Swanseas,
where the young sit looking out of their windows at blank
walls.

Their critics sometimes accuse the "kitchen sink" school
of letters of indulging in sordidness for its own sake, of
exploiting the disgusting out of some obscure love of filth.
Yet it is no private nightmare but a real public world the
new writers have made their theme—a world more real
now than the lovelier world of the Sitwells and Russian
ballet, the dying world in which art is a final grace of
cultivated life and eccentricity its spice. The world of
Amis and Wain is the declassed, uniform world of mass
culture, where the country house and the common room
of Oxbridge enter only via the detective stories of Dorothy
Sayers: a world where graciousness has followed the last
servant out the door—or is about to. It is a world best
rendered by Kingsley Amis, who has made it impossible
for anyone in England to pretend any longer that it does
not exist:

> The baby, his upper lip hidden behind his lower
> one, was sitting on the pot, crying steadily; Eira was
> crouching naked with her face in Jean's lap . . . Jean,
> herself apparently wearing only a dressing gown, was
> vigorously towelling Eira's hair . . . Around them was
> a multitude of objects such as might, in a memory
> test, be shown to spectators for one minute and then
> withdrawn. Apart from clothes, adult and juvenile,
> male and female, ironed, newly washed and fit to be
> washed, there was a half-eaten browning apple, sev-
> eral broken biscuits, a plastic doll, the torso of a
> rubber doll, some children's books with pictures of
> clothed animals on the covers, a cup, a card of blue
> safety pins, an orange with one of my pencils stuck
> into it, a bottle of cod-liver oil, a pair of plastic

knickers . . . some nappies in varying states, the de-
faced cover of my *Astounding Science Fiction,* and
a lot of other things.

"Well, hullo," Jean said.

This, we must grant, is a world we inhabit, too—not any
of the exotic worlds of Evelyn Waugh or Nancy Mitford
Jones, but the depressing One World, with which all of
us must come to imaginative terms. It is the merciless
delineation of this long-familiar (to us) terrain which
is "new" to the British novel; and it is the acceptance of
such a world and of the limitation of passion and ambition
among those living in it—in short, the acceptance of the
declassing of experience—which makes such literature
new and disturbing in its own country. In Amis, Wain
et al., the "American novel" has arrived in England after
its more touted triumphs in France and Italy.

It has come not by deliberate invitation as in other parts
of Western Europe, but inevitably as the result of certain
changes in society, especially the shift in status of the
intellectual in general and of the writer in particular. The
embarrassment of the English reader at this unforeseen
and unsolicited event explains a little the almost hysterical
tone of his response to it. For us, the problem is considerably easier. No class allegiances or national pride stand
in the way of our recognizing a literature that makes an
attempt (whatever its crudity or occasional downright
philistinism) to possess imaginatively the classless, grim
world which has become our common home.

English Poetry Today
BY A. ALVAREZ

In 1932 the critic F. R. Leavis proclaimed that T. S. Eliot and Ezra Pound had between them brought about a significant reorientation of literature. Twenty years later he took most of it back again, blaming the anti-critical workings of the London literary circuit and the decay of an educated reading public. He may have been perfectly justified in crediting the metropolitan literateurs with setting up so many false gods. But the relative failure of talent is another matter entirely. So is the manner in which so much of the talent that has arrived has been misused. The London old-boy circuit may often be stupid, conceited, and parasitic, but I don't believe that it is a deliberate conspiracy against good work.

I once suggested (in *Stewards of Excellence*, 1958) that the experimental techniques of Eliot and the rest never really took on in England because they were an essentially American concern: attempts to forge a distinctively American language for poetry. Certainly, since Eliot removed himself into another, remote sphere of influence by proclaiming himself "Anglo-Catholic in religion, royalist in politics, and classicist in literature," the whole movement of English verse has been to correct the balance experimentation had so unpredictably disturbed. Sometime in the twenties Thomas Hardy remarked to Robert Graves that *"vers libre* could come to nothing in England. 'All we can do is to write on the old themes in the old styles, but try to do a little better than those who went before us.' " Since about 1930 the machinery of modern English poetry seems to have been controlled by a series of negative feed-backs designed to produce precisely the effect Hardy wanted.

The final justification of experimentalism lay, of course, beyond mere technique. The great moderns experimented not just to make it new formally, but to open poetry up to new areas of experience. The kind of insights which had already been substantiated by the novelists—by Melville, Dostoevsky, Lawrence, and even at times, by Hardy himself—seemed about due to appear in poetry. The negative feed-backs came into action to stop this happening.

The literary historians perhaps would see the process differently; and the English scene is peculiarly amenable to literary history: it is savage with gang-warfare which, at a distance, can be dignified as disagreements between schools of verse. So maybe a little potted, though rather partial, literary history would be in place.

The thirties poets reacted against those of the twenties by asserting that they had no time to be difficult or inward or experimental; the political situation was too urgent. W. H. Auden gave them the go-ahead because he combined the extraordinary technical skill in traditional forms with an extraordinary feel for the most contemporary of contemporary idiom. When he began, it must really have looked as though he were about to do something quite new in English. In a poem like "Sir, No Man's Enemy," for example, he used the new, difficult language of psychology with a concentration that was almost Shakespearian; or even in an unambitious piece like "Lurcher-loving collier, black as night" he managed triumphantly to re-create a traditional lyric—its ancestor is "Mistress mine, where art thou roaming"—in terms of the contemporary, unromantic, industrial scene. His trouble was that he was too skillful; he found both the art of verse and the art of success too easy. So he was able to channel his deep neurotic disturbances into light verse—much of it, admittedly, very fine—while his contemporary knowingness, his skill with references, with slang, with the time's immediate worries, went into the production of a kind of social, occasional verse, mostly traditional in form, but highly up-to-date in idiom. His example encouraged a whole swarm of poetasters who believed, apparently, that to be modern was merely a matter of sounding modern; it had precious little to do with originality. (I would exclude from this Louis MacNeice, whose social-political verse was mostly more effective and certainly more deeply felt than Auden's own.) By the end of the thirties experimental verse was out and traditional forms, in a chic contemporary guise, were back in. That was the first negative feedback.

The reaction to Auden took the form of anti-intellectualism. He was thought to be too clever and not sufficiently emotional for the extreme circumstances of the forties. The war brought with it a taste for high, if obscure, rhetoric. The log-rolling thirties were followed by the drum-rolling forties. The new master, of course, was Dylan Thomas. But Thomas was not only a fine rhetorician, he also, in his early poems, had something rather original to say. Admittedly, he was under constant pressure from the literary Public Relations Officers to continue at all costs less with his poetry than with his act as the blindly inspired poet; which meant that his rhetoric eventually ran on when the reasons for it had faltered. But the talent was there, however self-destructive it eventually became. His followers, however, used his work as an excuse to kiss *all* meaning good-by. All that mattered was that the verse should sound impressive. This was the second negative feed-back: a blockage against intelligence.

The third stage was yet another reaction: against wild, loose emotion. The name of the reaction was the Movement, and its anthology was Robert Conquest's *New Lines*. Of the nine poets to appear in this, six, at the time, were university teachers, two librarians, and one a civil servant. It was, in short, academic-administrative verse, polite, knowledgeable, efficient, polished and, in its quiet way, even intelligent. What it had to offer positively was more difficult to describe. Even the editor found he could define it only in negatives: "It submits to no great systems of theoretical constructs nor agglomerations of unconscious commands. It is free from both mystical and logical compulsions and—like the modern philosophy—is empirical in attitude to all that comes. . . . On the more technical side . . . we see the refusal to abandon a rational structure and comprehensible language. . . . It will be seen at once that these poets do not have as much in common as they would if they were a group of doctrine-saddled writers forming a definite school complete with program and rules. What they do have in common is, perhaps, at its lowest, little more than a negative determination to avoid bad principles."

Mr. Conquest is, I think, exaggerating when he says that his poets have nothing very much in common. For example:

> *Picture of lover or friend that is not either*
> *Like you or me who, to sustain our pose,*
> *Need wine and conversation, colour and light;*
> *In short, a past that no one now can share,*
> *No matter whose your future; calm and dry,*
> *In sex I do not dither more than either,*
> *Nor should I now swell to halloo the names*
> *Of feelings that no one needs to remember:*
> *The same few dismal properties, the same*
> *Oppressive air of justified unease*
> *Of our imaginations and our beds.*
> *It seems the poet made a bad mistake.*

Perhaps the logic seems a little tenuous? The shifts a little hard to follow? The content too fine-drawn? So they should. The piece is synthetic; it contains eight of the nine *New Lines* poets. I have omitted D. J. Enright since he rarely sticks to the metrical norms on which the rest insist. Otherwise I have not cheated in compiling the poem. I have taken the poets in the order in which they appear in the anthology, without using more than two lines from any one and without changing the punctuation except, in a minor way, between quotations. Yet though the poem may not be quite comprehensible, it is perfectly unified in tone. Wouldn't the impartial reader be hard put to know where one quotation ended and another began? Wouldn't he find a considerable similarity in the quality both of the language and of the experience? A kind of unity of flatness? The pieties of the Movement were as predictable as the politics of the thirties poets. They are summed up at the beginning of Philip Larkin's "Church-going": *"Hatless, I take off/My cycle-clips in awkward reverence."* This, in concentrated form, is the image of the post-war Welfare State Englishman: shabby and not concerned with his appearance; poor—he has a bike, not a car; gauche but full of agnostic piety; underfed, underpaid, overtaxed, hopeless, bored, wry. This is the third negative feed-back: an attempt to show that the poet is not a strange creature inspired; on the contrary, he is just like the man next door—in fact, he probably *is* the man next door.

Now, I am wholly in favor of restoring poetry to the realm of common sense. But there is always the delicate question of how common common sense should be. All three negative feed-backs work, in their different ways, to preserve the idea that life in England goes on much as it always has, give or take a few minor changes in the class system. The upper-middle-class, or Tory ideal—presented in its pure crystalline form by John Betjeman—may have given way to the predominantly lower-middle-class, or labor, ideal of the Movement and the Angries, but the concept of gentility still reigns supreme. And gentility is a belief that life is always more or less orderly, people always more or less polite, their emotions and habits more or less decent and more or less controlled; that God, in short, is more or less good.

. . . It is to the point that the two Englishmen who are most concerned to write in depth have spent the better part of their poetically formative twenties in America. I mean Ted Hughes and Thom Gunn. So they have been less open to pressures which would flatten both their intelligence and the sharp violence of their experience into a socially more acceptable middle style. If you compare, for instance, Larkin's "At Grass" with Hughes's "A Dream of Horses," the creative advantage of being three thousand miles away from the fog of English gentility becomes peculiarly clear. "At Grass" follows:

> The eye can hardly pick them out
> From the cold shade they shelter in,
> Till wind distresses tail and mane;
> Then one crops grass, and moves about
> —The other seeming to look on—
> And stands anonymous again.
>
> Yet fifteen years ago, perhaps
> Two dozen distances sufficed
> To fable them: faint afternoons
> Of Cups and Stakes and Handicaps,

Whereby their names were artificed
To inlay faded, classic Junes—

Silks at the start: against the sky
Numbers and parasols: outside,
Squadrons of empty cars, and heat,
And littered grass: then the long cry
Hanging unhushed till it subside
To stop-press columns on the street.

Do memories plague their ears like flies?
They shake their heads. Dusk brims the shadows.
Summer by summer, all stole away,
The starting-gates, the crowds and cries—
All but the unmolesting meadows.
Almanacked, their names live; they

Have slipped their names, and stand at ease
Or gallop for what must be joy,
And not a fieldglass sees them home,
Or curious stop-watch prophesies:
Only the groom, and the groom's boy,
With bridles in the evening come.

Larkin's poem, elegant, unpretentious and rather beautiful
in its mild way, is a nostalgic re-creation of the Platonic
(or *New Yorker*) idea of the English scene, part pastoral,
part sporting. His horses are social creatures of fashionable
race meetings and high style; emotionally, they belong
to the world of the ASPCA. It is a long way from Hughes's
"A Dream of Horses":

We were born grooms, in stable-straw we sleep still,
All our wealth horse-dung and the combings of horses,
And all we can talk about is what horses ail.

Out of the night that gulfed beyond the palace-gate
There shook hooves and hooves and hooves of horses:
Our horses battered their stalls; their eyes jerked white.

And we ran out, mice in our pockets and straw in our
*   hair,*
Into darkness that was avalanching to horses

And a quake of hooves. Our lantern's little orange flare

Made a round mask of our each sleep-dazed face,
Bodiless, or else bodied by horses
That whinnied and bit and cannoned the world from
    its place.

The tall palace was so white, the moon was so round,
Everything else this plunging of horses
To the rim of our eyes that strove for the shapes of
    the sound.

We crouched at our lantern, our bodies drank the din,
And we longed for a death trampled by such horses
As every grain of the earth had hooves and mane.

We must have fallen like drunkards into a dream
Of listening, lulled by the thunder of the horses.
We awoke stiff; broad day had come.

Out through the gate the unprinted desert stretched
To stone and scorpion; our stable-horses
Lay in their straw, in a hag-sweat, listless and wretched.

Now let us, tied, be quartered by those horses,
If but doomsday's flames be great horses,
The forever itself a circling of the hooves of horses.

The poem, by the standard of Hughes's best writing, is not all that good; it is less controlled than Larkin's and has a number of romantic, quasi-medieval trappings which verge on the pretentious. But it is unquestionably *about* something; it is a serious attempt to re-create and so clarify, unfalsified and in the strongest imaginative terms possible, a powerful complex of emotions and sensations. Unlike Larkin's, Hughes's horses have a violent, impending presence. But through the detail which brings them so threateningly to life, they reach back, as in a dream, into the depths of fear and sensation. Their brute world is part physical, part state of mind.

They have, of course, their literary antecedents: the strange, savage horses which terrorize Ursula Brangwen at the end of Lawrence's *The Rainbow*. But this is part of their wider significance. Dr. Leavis has come, apparently, to believe that Lawrence and Eliot represent the two warring and unreconcilable poles of modern literature. The best contemporary English verse, however, shows that their influences can be creatively reconciled. In the seriousness of what I have called the new depth poetry, the openness to experience, the psychological insight and integrity of D. H. Lawrence combine with the immense poetic skill and formal intelligence of T. S. Eliot. At its best, it is work which fulfills Coleridge's definition of the Imagination as the force which reconciles "a more than usual state of emotion with a more than usual order." If this is to be the new direction of verse, we might be in for an exceptionally fine creative period.

British Drama of the Fifties
BY JOHN RUSSELL TAYLOR

The British drama of 1956–62 is not so much a new wave as an explosion, with particles flying off in all directions and intense activity rather than coherent progression as its most evident feature. And it is not too unkind to say that the drama of the last five years is, in effect, all that matters in the drama of the last decade: certainly there is virtually nothing before *Look Back in Anger* (May 1956) which can begin to compare in vitality with what has come after.

Between the Festival of Britain and the advent of the English Stage Company at the Royal Court the British theatrical scene was bleak indeed. There was the hangover of the verse-drama revival, and so far as anyone supposed that Britain had anything at all comparable with the riches of new theatrical writing in other countries, it would have been the plays of T. S. Eliot and Christopher Fry. But Eliot's two plays subsequent to *The Cocktail Party*, *The Confidential Clerk* and *The Elder Statesman*, were widely spaced and met with only modified rapture, while Fry's reputation never quite lived up to the success of *The Lady's Not For Burning*; both, anyway, had been writing since before the war and could hardly be counted as exciting new talents, any more than Terence Rattigan, fluent arbiter of the commercial theatre. There *were* new dramatists, of course, but few and far between, and most of them very conventional: the only younger writers of any originality to get a hearing on the stage were John Whiting, who at least provoked violent disagreement with his Festival prize-winner *Saint's Day*, Denis Cannan, whose *Captain Carvallo* achieved a commercial as well as artistic success unequalled by any of his later plays, and Peter

Ustinov, the boy wonder of the war years, who had settled down by the early 1950's to being perpetually promising but never quite living up to expectations.

Even at this time, however unobtrusively, things were beginning to happen. The Third Programme of the B.B.C. offered a refuge for writers like Giles Cooper and Henry Reed whose talents were not easily adaptable to the commercial stage; Joan Littlewood had settled in East London with her own company, Theatre Workshop, which was working away quietly at building a production style and an audience, though good new drama was not yet its strong point; and the addition of commercial television to the B.B.C. service in 1955 meant that so many more spaces in the program had to be filled with drama and somewhere, somehow, the writers had to be found to do it. All of which might, or might not, be signs for the future. It was difficult to tell, just as there was no knowing whether a new company set up at the Royal Court in 1956 with the declared intention of being "a writers' theatre" would survive and succeed or whether it would prove just another well-meant financial disaster. Even when this new group, The English Stage Company, presented as their third production a play by an unknown writer called John Osborne, *Look Back in Anger,* the response was not immediate; the critics mostly seemed to feel that something new and exciting was afoot, even if they were not uncomplicatedly enthusiastic about the piece itself, but the public did not really begin to respond until some weeks later, after an act had been shown on television (the first instance, incidentally, of television in what was to become its habitual rôle of mediator between the advanced dramatist and his public).

Then, all of a sudden, the public started flocking to the Royal Court and the phrase "angry young man" was on every lip (aided by the currency of Colin Wilson's best seller *The Outsider*). A movement was under way. And, like the New Wave in the French cinema, it owed its momentum initially to basic commercial considerations: just as the enormous box-office success of *Et Dieu créa la Femme* planted the idea in producers' minds that there might be money in new film talent, so the vogue enjoyed by *Look Back in Anger* made people aware that there might be money in new dramatists and set the public and the pundits of the West End theatre alike off in search of a second Osborne.

What happened next is almost impossible to detail coherently without dropping into a list of names. Suffice it to say that if the "second Osborne" was expected to be another "angry young man," the expectation was rapidly disappointed, and if it was supposed that the next major commercial success would come from the English Stage Company that supposition was disappointed too. For, as we remarked at the beginning, what came after the first breakthrough of the new drama was not a wave or a tide but an explosion. Suddenly, all in the space of six years or so, dozens of new writers in all sorts of styles sprang up in all sorts of places, and set off briskly in all sorts of directions. At the Royal Court experiment continued unabated with the acquisition of two prize-winners from the *Observer* play competition of 1956, Ann Jellicoe and N. F. Simpson, and the encouragement of John Arden on the strength of a prize-winning radio play. None of these had much luck at the box-office, though one of Simpson's plays, *One Way Pendulum,* achieved a transfer to the West End, but new encouragement for the more commercially minded was not slow in coming from another unlikely source, Joan Littlewood's company at Stratford East, which brought forward in rapid succession Brendan Behan, Shelagh Delaney and the long-running Soho musical *Fings Ain't Wot They Used T'Be.* Meanwhile the impetus had transferred itself to the Provinces—to Coventry —where the Belgrade Theatre first staged Arnold Wesker's trilogy *Chicken Soup With Barley, Roots* and *I'm Talking About Jerusalem*; to Scarborough where Stephen Joseph's theatre-in-the-round discovered David Campton, author of such "comedies of menace" as *The Lunatic View* and *Four Minute Warning*, and brought a succession of new plays to a seaside audience who didn't care what name was attached to a play as long as it pleasantly occupied a wet afternoon. The West End theatre managers bestirred themselves and found a number of playwrights under forty, ranging from the safest and solidest, the Robert Bolts and Peter Shaffers, through the middle-of-the-road men like John Mortimer, to the most difficult and experimental, Harold Pinter and Henry Livings. And behind all this activity brooded the giant shape of television, taking writers from the theatre, introducing their work to a wider public than the theatre could ever provide and then giving them back with additions of its own: stage dramatists like Alun Owen who found their first major success on television, or occasionally by writers like Clive Exton who have chosen up to now to work entirely for the medium.

That is the scene as it stands at present. It is tempting, obviously, to start generalizing about "the new drama," but somehow the material resists such treatment. There are, of course, a couple of general points which can legitimately be made: all the writers concerned were born between the wars (N. F. Simpson, the oldest, in 1919, Shelagh Delaney, the youngest, in 1939); an unusual number of them in a largely literary theatre were actively involved in drama before they began writing (Osborne, Owen, Pinter, Exton and Livings were all actors, Ann Jellicoe ran an experimental theatre). . . . But that is about all, and even against the second point one might urge the numbers of writers recruited from outside the theatre: teachers (Simpson, Bolt), a lawyer (Mortimer), an architect (Arden) and others, like Arnold Wesker and Shelagh Delaney, who began writing directly for the theatre with no previous experience. And as for the styles they write in, though here and there affinities can be seen, no overall theory can be evolved to fit all, or even most, of the new dramatists neatly together into one coherent movement. At best one can indicate a few loosely defined headings under which two or three may be more or less arbitrarily grouped.

First of all, since it was first to catch the public's eye, there is the "angry" drama, the naturalistic drama of protest. This had proved in the long run the least durable phase; even its high priest, John Osborne, moved away from it after *Epitaph for George Dillon* and *Look Back in Anger,* leaving the field open to a handful of imitators, only one of whom, Willis Hall, won any success (with his war play *The Long and the Short and the Tall*). Instead, while Osborne in *The Entertainer* and *Luther* went haring off in pursuit of Brechtian "endistancement" and the frame of reference, social realism inclined in the hands of Arnold Wesker and Alun Owen to sorrow rather than to anger. Wesker's plays, particularly the Trilogy, make a number of worthwhile points clumsily; they are about the need of man to take a pride in his work, the struggle of the undereducated for self-expression and so on, but tend to obscure their messages in slipshod construction and to preach instead of exemplifying, so that we are all too palpably aware of the dramatist manipulating his puppets. Alun Owen, on the other hand, though nominally he might be regarded as a social realist and has taken the subjects for *Progress to the Park* and several of his television plays from working-class life in his native Liverpool, really uses his material for much more private ends than Wesker: much of his work is intensely subjective in form, and the characters, far from being puppets set up to explain the author's intention to the public, are aspects of his own nature in conflict, explaining, if they explain anything, the author to himself.

Most nearly akin, perhaps, to the social realists are the "academic realists," those who, however revolutionary their intention, start out with the ordinary materials of the old-fashioned middle-class drawing-room drama and the familiar idiom of the educated southern Englishman. These, anyway, are the materials Robert Bolt, Peter Shaffer and Clive Exton have begun with, though all of them seem to have found the conventions imposed unduly limiting, and consequently after their respective high-points of realistic contemporary drama (*The Tiger and the Horse, Five Finger Exercise, Where I Live*) each has been tempted away, to costume drama in the cases of Bolt and Shaffer (Bolt's biography of Sir Thomas More, *A Man for All Seasons,* Shaffer's play about the conquest of Peru, *The Royal Hunt of the Sun*) and in Exton's case to allegory (*Hold My Hand, Soldier*) and fantastic satire (*The Trial of Doctor Fancy*). Only John Mortimer, whose middle-class realism has always had a strong admixture of grotesque fantasy in the manner of Dickens or Gogol (*The Dock Brief, What Shall We Tell Caroline?*) remains faithful to this stable if rather over-rich combination, which in his latest play, *Two Stars for Comfort,* shows disturbing signs of becoming a conventional mold into which all materials can be poured with equal facility.

Between these in general realistically inclined dramatists and those who write in an evidently non-realistic style there is a small group whose work, influenced either directly by Brecht or indirectly by his leading English disciple Joan Littlewood, keeps a foot in both camps. This is so, for example, in the later plays of John Osborne, whose attempts to break out of the solidly realistic style of his early work have led him to experiment with realistic dialogue scenes interspersed with oblique comment (the music-hall songs in *The Entertainer*) or straight narration (in his television piece *A Subject of Scandal and Concern*) to keep the audience at a critical distance from the central matter of the drama. The result, for Osborne, has been a rather rough passage from critics and public and a number of awkward transitional works which may or may not prove to be paving the way for new complete achievements. In the case of Brendan Behan and Shelagh Delaney the influence (via Joan Littlewood) has been wielded to greater immediate effect, in that *The Quare Fellow* and *A Taste of Honey* were undoubtedly much the better textually for an unusual amount of directorial intervention and on the whole (with slight reservations in the latter) gained from the way they were staged. *The Hostage,* on the other hand, despite splendid moments, seemed to show the whole process running wild and in *The Lion in Love* Shelagh Delaney appeared, once away from the guidance of Theatre Workshop, to be feeling her way tentatively towards a loving and minute naturalism at odds with the fantasticated sub-Littlewood production the play was given. One has hardly the ground even to speculate on what line the future work of either writer will take.

Finally, and perhaps most interestingly, there are the writers whose work is evidently non-realistic in approach. Here comedy is usually uppermost, but otherwise the variety of styles is quite confusing. Whether one thinks of the highly intellectual farces of N. F. Simpson, with their rigidly methodical (and only sometimes funny) exploration of the mechanics of the "gag"; or the abrupt and violent plays of Ann Jellicoe, with their exaltation of action and their frequent reduction of dialogue to mere noise; or the philosophical North-Country farce of Henry Livings's *Stop It, Whoever You Are* and *Big Soft Nellie*; or the beautifully worked-out dramatic metaphors of David Campton's "committed" theatre; or the benignly macabre fantasy of David Perry's *Stuff and Nonsense,* there is no noticeable consistency except in the simple fact that whatever they are doing it is quite unlike anything in the British theatre before them. As to the two great figures in the reaction from realism, John Arden and Harold Pinter, they have taken the influences of, respectively, Brecht and Beckett and fashioned with them something completely personal and unpredictable. The intense tragi-comedy of *The Caretaker* or *A Night Out*, with their perfect control of form and their extraordinary feeling for the cadences of English speech, shows Pinter achieving paradoxically an hallucinatory super-realism in the very process of apparently abandoning realism altogether. And in *Live Like Pigs, Serjeant Musgrave's Dance* or *The Happy Haven* Arden's oblique methods, his sharp transitions from speech to song, from casual prose to highly formal verse, permit him to explore with relentless truth and no rigged "solutions" a number of vital questions in contemporary life—conflicting social standards, pacificism, old age. If naturalism flies out of the window in British drama today, it is becoming more and more likely that it does so only in order that a larger realism shall come in at the door.

Away From Lost Worlds
BY GEORGE WOODCOCK

There is a Lost World feeling about most of the minor English-speaking literatures. In remoteness, forms of expression that have passed away elsewhere still survive, or attitudes derived from England evolve in their own direction, as Georgian nature poetry has done—rather eloquently—in New Zealand. Anyone who has the courage to read what passed for Canadian literature in the early years of the present century, when Charles G. D. Roberts and Bliss Carman and Ralph Connor were still at the height of their reputations, may get the same feeling of antique forms blossoming nostalgically in isolation; even a twenties figure like E. J. Pratt, whom most Canadian critics now regard as the pioneer of a native poetry, can be convincingly presented as a phenomenon of the literary Galápagos, a latter-day didactic poet recording in a massively constructed adaptation of Victorian forms the epic stories that belong to a frontier society.

During the past quarter of a century, however, writing in Canada has passed beyond the Lost World phase. This is partly because of the recession into distance of the pioneer stage in Canadian social history; it is due also to the strains that arise in a society pulled by strong external influences and at the same time trying desperately to create and hold on to its own special identity. Culturally, as well as economically, Canada is largely dependent on the United States; what happens among writers in New York and San Francisco is likely to have some effect on what happens among writers in Toronto and Vancouver respectively, since cultural patterns in North America tend to run north and south like the mountains rather than east and west like the International Boundary.

Yet the link with Europe remains strong, and it has been somewhat reinforced during recent decades by the significant part which immigrants from Britain have assumed in the Canadian literary world. At the same time there has been a steady traffic on the part of Canadian writers to and from the literary metropolis; such novelists as Mordecai Richler, Norman Levine and Margaret Laurence are at present living in England but still writing out of their Canadian experience.

What English Canadian writers tend to seek in London, as their French-speaking compatriots do in Paris, is a concentration of writers—a complex and developed literary world—of the kind that does not exist in Canada. This absence of a native literary milieu (as distinct from the regional ambiance that originally shapes a writer's consciousness) is due partly to geographical reasons; Canada has no cultural metropolis, and writers group themselves loosely in places as far apart as Fredericton, Montreal, Toronto and Vancouver. But it is equally attributable to the vast inflow of British and American books and periodicals which has made difficult the emergence of either a really competitive publishing industry (ready to struggle over as well as encourage emerging writers) or a press of the kind that keeps writers in practice and in the public eye; there are literary quarterlies in Canada but no literary weeklies.

The lack of a true literary world, of either a Bohemia or an Establishment, has tended to force Canadian writers into institutional settings. An exceptionally high proportion of them are in some way linked with the Universities. This applies particularly to poets over thirty, and even some of the more successful Canadian novelists of the past twenty years have been unable or unwilling to break their academic ties; Hugh MacLennan, for example, still teaches at McGill. The result is that academic influences are exceptionally pervasive. A case in point is that of Northrop Frye, Principal of Victoria College, Toronto, authority on Blake, and dean of Canadian critics. Frye's myth-based criticism, carried on for many years in periodicals like the *University of Toronto Quarterly* and *Canadian Forum* and expounded week by week in his university lectures and seminars, has not merely set its mark deeply on Canadian critical writing in its early stages; it has also been largely responsible for the appearance of a whole school of mythopoeic poets, led by James Reaney, Jay Macpherson and Eli Mandel.

Where Canadian writers do not retreat into the colleges, they are likely to turn towards the Canadian Broadcasting Corporation and the Canada Council, both of which, though theoretically autonomous, are supported by government funds. The Canadian Broadcasting Corporation has consistently followed a policy of commissioning scripts from serious writers wherever possible, and has kept alive a series of high-caliber programs in which original plays, short stories and poems are regularly brought before a reasonably large public. Some of the best dramatic writing in Canada since the war has been for radio, including Earle Birney's *Trial of a City*, James Reaney's play *The Killdeer* and his opera *The Night-blooming Cereus*, and the many adept though rather didactic plays of Lister Sinclair. The Canada Council is the Canadian writer's substitute for the various private foundations which provide fellowships and other assistance to writers in the United States.

For all the good it has undoubtedly done, the Canada Council represents the final boxing in of Canadian literature by the structure of institutionalism. If we try to envisage an "average Canadian writer," we can see him living near a campus, teaching at least part time at university level, mingling too much for his own good with academics, doing as much writing as he can for the C.B.C., and always hoping for a Canada Council Fellowship that will take him away for a year in Menton or the Greek Islands. The mixture of the ingredients may vary, and it is true that some of the best writers working in Canada during the past few decades have managed to keep largely outside the pattern. Malcolm Lowry went unrecognized by the institutions until after his death in 1957, when the academics bought up his manuscripts and the C.B.C. began to broadcast programs about him. And such novelists as Morley Callaghan, Brian Moore, Mordecai Richler and Ethel Wilson have at least avoided too close connection with the universities, though all of them have been to some degree involved with the C.B.C. or the Canada Council, or both.

Yet the growing degree of institutionalism has not pre-

vented the two decades following the end of World War
II from being a period in which Canadian writing has acquired a variety, a sophistication, an ironic view of the
world it presents, and a critical view of its own productions which seem to mark it as a mature literature that
has grown out of colonial tutelage and is beginning to
interpret its own environment in an original way.

1945, the end of World War II, saw the major Canadian
writers of the period between the wars passing out of
existence or out of significant production. In 1944 Stephen
Leacock died and Frederick Philip Grove, that fumbling
giant among novelists, published his last important work,
The Master of the Mill; he was to die in 1948. The best
work of Morley Callaghan and E. J. Pratt was already in
the past. The writers who had appeared in the late twenties
and early thirties as the pioneers of a new, cosmopolitan
strain in poetry—A. J. M. Smith, F. R. Scott, A. M. Klein
and Dorothy Livesay—were becoming elder figures in
their turn, and during the war a group of poets who were
to dominate the decade immediately after the peace had
already begun to publish their work, either in volumes or
in periodicals; they included Earle Birney, Irving Layton,
Louis Dudek, Raymond Souster, Anne Wilkinson, P. K.
Page and Margaret Avison. Two impecunious magazines
played an extremely important part in introducing these
poets to the small literary public of 1945. *Contemporary
Verse*, edited by Alan Crawley from British Columbia,
had begun to appear in 1941 and was to cease publication
in 1951. *Northern Review*, edited by John Sutherland in
Montreal, emerged in 1945 from the amalgamation of
two wartime little magazines, *First Statement* and *Preview*; it continued to appear until Sutherland's death in
1956. These two magazines published almost every significant Canadian poet and prose writer who was at work
during the period when they were flourishing.

When we turn to the progress of particular literary
forms in Canada during the after-war years, it is evident
that the majority of Canadian novels published since 1945
can be classed as nothing better than "popular" in the
most inferior sense. Canadian publishers are still far too
partial to the lady writers who fabricate the kind of
colonial romance which Mazo de la Roche did very much
better a generation ago. There are still too many pseudo-

historical best sellers, and too many regional novels which
rely on shoddily homespun dialogue and a grossly sentimental vision of the pioneer past. A more justifiable popularity attaches to the works of the two writers who, in
terms of reputation at least, can be regarded as the leading Canadian novelists of the post-war era. These are
Hugh MacLennan and Morley Callaghan.

MacLennan is an academic and a classical scholar with
a sense of mission towards Canadian nationality. He is
preoccupied to the point of obsession with the fact of
living at a time and in a country where a sense of separate
identity as a nation is emerging; he is equally preoccupied
with the danger to the new nation which he expounded
in his novel *Two Solitudes*, the danger presented by the
division of Canadians into two mutually unassimilated
groups—the English-speaking and the French-speaking.
Every novel MacLennan has written is marred by the
didacticism which such preoccupations force upon him,
and by the distortion of both character and action when
they are bent to serve the prevailing argument. His best
novel up to the present, *Each Man's Son*, is the least
touched by MacLennan's nationalistic philosophy. It concerns a Cape Breton mining settlement shadowed by the
distortions of a puritanical attitude towards life, and in
its record of the downfall of a boxing professional brought
up in this environment, the fatalism which MacLennan
derives from his study of Greek drama serves well to
render the Calvinist view of existence. MacLennan writes
admirably on action (there is an extraordinary record of
a gigantic explosion at Halifax in his earliest novel, *Barom-
eter Rising*), but with a fatal embarrassment on anything
remotely erotic; his recent and most ambitious novel, *The
Watch that Ends the Night*, is ruined by the sentimental
implausibilities of the central sexual triangle between a
doctor who returns after having long been given up for
dead in the Nazi concentration camps, his former wife,
and the thin-blooded political commentator who has since
married her and who narrates the novel.

Morley Callaghan is justly regarded as a good short-
story writer, but a rather weak novelist, with a direct, lucid
prose that at times lapses into a colorless banality. Since
1945 he has published few stories and only three novels—
The Loved and the Lost, The Many-Colored Coat and

A Passion in Rome. The first two, which Callaghan kept down to the simplicity of a *récit*, are almost up to the standard of his pre-war work, direct in approach and spare in construction, though marred by a rather mawkish pseudo-compassion for the adult babes who wander in the dark wood of the modern city. *A Passion in Rome* is Callaghan's sole attempt at a complex, full-scale novel; it is a disastrous failure, structurally chaotic and written in a prose of appalling and gritty dullness. Callaghan's talent is lapidary in nature, not fitted for works on the grand pattern, and nothing he has produced since 1945 has equalled the best of his short stories of the 1930's.

The most vital Canadian fiction of the post-war period has in fact been written by people who for various regional or traditional reasons belong outside the main stream of ordinary Canadian life which writers like MacLennan and Callaghan seek to represent. There are, first, the immigrants. Probably the best novel to come out of Canada at any time has been Malcolm Lowry's *Under the Volcano*, completed when Lowry was living in the little shack on the foreshore near Vancouver which he inhabited during the fifteen years from 1939 to 1954. But *Under the Volcano* was conceived in Mexico and its first versions were written there. Much more truly Canadian were the short stories which Lowry wrote on the basis of his experience in British Columbia. Published after his death in the volume entitled *Hear Us O Lord from Heaven Thy Dwelling Place*, these stories showed clearly that Lowry had lived his way into his Canadian environment and could render its spirit as admirably and with as much fantastic originality as he rendered that of the Mexican plateau in *Under the Volcano*.

Brian Moore, in his own way, fits just as elusively into the pattern of Canadian writing as Malcolm Lowry. He is Belfast-born and, like Joyce, he has always carried his Ireland with him. The Irish lonely in their own land of his early novel, *Judith Hearne*, become the Irish lonely as aliens in *The Luck of Ginger Coffey*, a tragi-comic tale of the misadventures of an Irish bounder in Montreal, which is easily the best of many novels that have attempted to give expression to the predicament of the immigrant in Canada. Moore has now left Canada for the

United States, and his most recent novel, *An Answer from Limbo*, about Irish people lonely in New York, gives no hint of his Canadian experience and suggests that Moore still belongs to Ireland rather than to any of the lands where he may temporarily have settled.

Life abroad of a different kind from that which shapes the attitude of the immigrant has greatly influenced the work of one of the best of the recently published novelists of Canadian birth. Before she began writing, Margaret Laurence had lived for fairly long periods in Somaliland and West Africa, and out of her experiences in these lands she has written a number of fine short stories and a very evocative first novel about Africa, *This Side Jordan*. She has followed up with one of the very few good travel books written by a Canadian, *The Prophet's Camel Bell*.

One of the most interesting literary phenomena in post-war Canada has been the emergence of a body of excellent writers from a Jewish community that is minuscule in proportion to the whole English-speaking population of the country. These writers, who include poets as well as novelists, would object to being lumped together in a "Jewish school," since they are all strongly individualist in approach, but they write from a common background and they are all concerned in one way or another with the generation-by-generation progress by which a Jew in North America steps from his narrower traditional community into the wider community of the world; indeed, for many of them the Jewish youth at odds with his family or his neighbors is merely the aspect they know best of the general problem of the individual at odds with society in general. The best of the Canadian Jewish novelists are the poet A. M. Klein, who has written a single very moving allegorical novel of rather Zionist flavor, *The Second Scroll*, and Mordecai Richler. Richler is an iconoclastic novelist, nearer than any other Canadian writer to the British "angry young men," and very much concerned with the individual's self-liberation from his own as well as his world's hypocrisies. In such novels as *Son of a Smaller Hero* and *The Apprenticeship of Duddy Kravitz* he mounts a nihilistic attack on current moralities, using a prose that at best is brutally alive and direct and at worst as flat-footed as a policeman's walk. Other Jewish

novelists who rank high among Canadian writers are
Adele Wiseman (*The Sacrifice*), Jack Ludwig (*Confusions*) and Norman Levine, whose best book to date is
actually an autobiography-cum-travel book entitled *Canada
Made Me*.

Regional novels that rise above sentimental pseudo-
history or amiable rusticity are rare in Canada. Many
novelists have tried to encompass the life of the prairies,
but nothing in this field has been written during the last
twenty years to equal that admirable study of frustration
in an elevator town, Sinclair Ross's *As For Me and My
House*, which appeared in 1941. Ross's own later work
has not repeated this early triumph, and the best prairie
novel of the years since the last war, W. O. Mitchell's
Who Has Seen the Wind, is spoiled by the rather weak
comedy which breaks in constantly upon an otherwise
sensitive reconstruction of a child's developing recognition
of his environment and of the necessary presence of death.

Since the war Vancouver has tended to become a
western center of writing as important in its way as
Montreal and Toronto, with its own little magazines and
fleeting publishing ventures. Apart from Malcolm Lowry,
it is the home of at least one major Canadian novelist,
Ethel Wilson, who has woven the *données* of her environment into a series of highly sophisticated, ironical and
dry-humored *récits*. Ethel Wilson began to write short
stories in her forties; she did not start with novels until
her fifties, and she published her first novel, *Hetty Dorval,*
in 1947, at the age of 56. She is still writing, in her seven-
ties, with wry wisdom and an acute and careful sense of
style. Her best novels, *The Innocent Traveller, Swamp
Angel* and *Love and Salt Water*, are all set in the Vancouver region where she has lived since she came from
England in her childhood, but they are as universal in
their intent as a good nature poem.

A series of good one-shot novels remains to be mentioned to complete the fictional harvest of Canadian writing in the post-war years. Earle Birney's *Turvey*, the tale
of a Canadian Schweik in World War II, is a biting and
very amusing satire on what happens to a democracy when
it gets involved in the totalitarian operations of modern
war; Ernest Buckler's *The Mountain and the Valley* is a

good study of personal conflicts in rural Nova Scotia; Colin McDougall's *Execution* is an agonizing presentation of the conflict between human and military responsibilities among Canadian soldiers fighting in wartime Italy; Sheila Watson's *The Double Hook* is technically one of the most sophisticated of Canadian novels, revealing with complex allusiveness the hard underlying passions of life in a small British Columbian town.

Finally, one cannot leave fiction without mentioning the presence of a number of competent short-story writers who have kept writing despite the fact that there are very few magazines left in Canada which publish stories of any kind. Some of them, like Ethel Wilson, Mordecai Richler and Jack Ludwig, have already been mentioned as novelists; others, like Hugh Garner, Alice Munro and Henry Kreisel, are solely or mainly interesting for their stories. All of them are good writers with highly individual styles, but they get little encouragement, for the publishers are as reluctant as the popular magazines in Canada to handle short fiction. However, the Canadian Broadcasting Corporation still keeps up its policy of buying stories, and one of its executives, Robert Weaver, who is also editor of the influential *Tamarack Review*, has been assiduous in collecting anthologies of good Canadian short fiction—such as the recent Oxford collection of Canadian short stories —which give permanent form to at least some of the stories.

Canadian poetry has been rich in new trends and new poets since the last war, and here regional traditions and ways of speech, as well as the local influence of certain key figures, have all come into play. Montreal has been a strong center of Canadian poetry since the 1930's, and undoubtedly the English-speaking poets in that city are stimulated to a certain degree by the presence of a vital French Canadian verse tradition. F. R. Scott, A. M. Klein, Irving Layton and Louis Dudek, the principal figures in the Montreal movement during the 1930's, are now becoming its elder poets, while younger writers like Leonard Cohen and Harry Moscovich are moving into prominence. The Montrealers have always, in one direction, leaned towards a social realism that is linked with a politically radical tendency, while, in the other direction, tending towards metaphysical goals, varying from the Jewish mysticism of Klein to the Lawrencian vitalism of Irving Layton. Klein, the best of this group of poets, has published nothing since *The Rocking Chair* in 1948, and the center of the stage has been occupied for the last ten years by Irving Layton, a prolific and chaotic poet who has published almost a score of volumes and brochures of verse since his first book, *Here and Now,* came out in 1945. Layton's chief fault is an almost total absence of self-criticism; his best poems have always to be dug out from between thick layers of rhetorical rubbish. But when he succeeds in his exuberant game of hit-and-miss he can present as no other Canadian poet does a joy in the glory of life or a devastating contempt of life's enemies.

Generally speaking, the poets who are centered on Toronto have been less socially inclined, more metaphysical and more concerned with poetic craftsmanship than the Montreal group. These qualities were already evident in the work of the writers who carried over from the war period, such as Anne Wilkinson (*Counterpoint to Sleep*), Douglas le Pan (*The Net and the Sword*), and P. K. Page (*The Metal and the Flower*), but they have been developed more strongly by the mythopoeic group of poets, lately centering around the little magazine *Alphabet,* who arose under the influence of the critic Northrop Frye. The mythopoeic poets not only create mythological structures to illuminate the personal messages they wish to convey; they are also adept at a kind of wit which depends on the astonishing marriage of the ridiculous and the sublime, and at a rather recondite allusiveness. The best of them, Jay Macpherson (*The Boatman*), Eli Mandel (*Fuseli Poems*), and James Reaney, are among the most sophisticated and the finest poets writing today in Canada, though at times even their discrimination is dulled by a kind of intoxication with their own wit, so that their work is not of even quality. This applies particularly to James Reaney, who has experimented in many forms, and just as many moods, varying from the clotted Gothic melodrama of his early lyrics in *The Red Heart* to the allusive clowning of *A Suit of Nettles* and the strange mixtures of farce and pathos, inanity and depth, that emerge when he turns to play, opera and masque.

Among the other poets active in the post-war period in Canada it is hard to find such clearly marked groups as have existed in Montreal and Toronto. Even among the Toronto poets Margaret Avison stands apart in metaphysical isolation, one of the most self-critical Canadian poets as her single volume (*Winter Sun*) reveals, and one of the best. And, though there are a number of very distinguished British Columbian poets, it is hard to find a uniting thread. Earle Birney (*Ice Cod Bell or Stone*) writes a vigorous free verse, often satirical and richly allusive, while Roy Daniells (*The Chequered Shade*) is a fine sonneteer who handles spiritual subtleties with great wit and technical mastery. Wilfred Watson (*Friday's Child*) has a richness of image and vocabulary, but is still perhaps too much a follower of the English 1940's poets, while Phyllis Webb (*Even Your Right Eye*) writes with a honed-down intellectuality which is at times excessively chilling.

There remain two fields of writing in both of which the efforts of Canadians have until recently been rather rudimentary. One is drama, whose practitioners have been constantly frustrated by the virtual absence in Canada of a regular theatre that would handle original plays. As a result, only one stage playwright of real consequence has appeared in Canada since the war. He is Robertson Davies, a writer of somewhat heavily satirical novels and of stage farces characterized by a rather donnish skittishness. As I have already said, it is for the radio that most of the best dramatic writing in Canada has been done over the past twenty years, and unfortunately little of this has yet been published.

The appearance of criticism is the sign of a maturing and self-conscious literature, and it is significant that only in the past decade have Canadians turned with any seriousness or depth to the critical consideration of their own literature. Much that passes for criticism is still mere appreciation, for the Canadian literary world is small and has always over-rated the virtue of mutual kindliness. But the general situation has changed considerably since

1945, partly through the example of Northrop Frye as a theoretical critic, and partly through the appearance of a number of critics trained in the more rigorous standards of the English literary world, such as Paul West and George Woodcock. Together with such younger Canadian critics as Milton Wilson, F. W. Watt and Hugo McPherson, these writers have helped to create a more responsible view of literary criticism—an attitude crystallized largely by the appearance in 1959 of the first Canadian critical quarterly, *Canadian Literature.*

I cannot end this survey without mentioning the literary reviews and little magazines which, given the restricted nature of commercial publishing facilities, have played an important part in the pattern of Canadian writing. When *Northern Review* disappeared in 1956, there was no real literary magazine left in Canada, but later in the same year appeared the first issue of *Tamarack Review*, edited by a group of Toronto literati which included Robert Weaver, Anne Wilkinson and Kildare Dobbs (author of a fascinating semi-fictional autobiography called *Running to Paradise*). It was followed by other new literary magazines—Louis Dudek's *Delta* in Montreal (1957) and Jan de Bruyn's *Prism* in Vancouver (1959). All these magazines continue. But the most extraordinary development during the past two years has been the great crop of little magazines, printed, offset or merely mimeographed, which writers in their teens and early twenties have begun to publish all over Canada. Dozens of new poets and story writers are appearing in these new magazines of whose eventual achievement, even of whose promise, it is yet early to speak. In this undergrowth of little periodicals new trends are appearing; there is a tendency away from the mythological and the metaphorical towards a preoccupation with speech rhythms and rather direct statement, and there is also a tendency to turn more towards current movements in the United States than has been evident among Canadian poets in the past.

What is perhaps most significant, however, is the sudden spurt of vitality that is channeling hundreds of young people towards literature with a determination that makes them impatient of the limitations of ordinary publication. As they print and actively circulate their little magazines among steadily widening circles (one of the several mimeographed little magazines in Vancouver goes out to four hundred people), perhaps they are beginning to create that very literary world which Canadian writing has up to now lacked, and without which its best writers have often seemed so oddly unrooted.

Trends in the Contemporary French Novel
BY HENRI PEYRE

It is doubtless fortunate that the many prophecies ventured every year by literary critics are forgotten almost as soon as are the political and economic forecasts of historians and social scientists. The latter err most often on the side of excessive optimism and paint the material future of men in Western lands in glowing hues. The former prefer to be prophets of gloom. They nod their heads mournfully at the prospect of the death of tragedy, the moribund condition of poetry, the disappearance of the essay. The death of the novel was, until 1940 or so, one of their favorite topics. These conservatives, nostalgic for the solid, earnest fiction they had read in their youth, averted their horrified gaze from the "formless" novels which an anti-Victorian age offered them. They absorbed, lock, stock and barrel, the structure of frail generalizations handed over to them by Marxism. They glibly repeated that the rise of the novel had somehow and very mysteriously been bound up with the ascent of the bourgeoisie. They concluded that, as the bourgeoisie went on collapsing (has it ever been stronger than in its victorious answer to the many challenges thrown at it since 1917? has it ever been more fertile in literary and artistic talents who, emerging from its midst, whip it ferociously, because they know its capacity for endurance?), the novel would become the fixture of outworn creeds and of a bygone age.

The French novel almost perished three or four times in the last eighty years: first during symbolism and when Anatole France and Pierre Loti were taken to be its most skilled practitioners; then when some overconscientious workmen like Paul Bourget and Romain Rolland attempted to pour ideas and social preaching into it; then when autobiographical, thin novels on adolescents imprisoned in their solipsism followed perilously on the footsteps of André Gide, Julien Green, Jean Cocteau and others; again lately when philosophers turned into novelists, advocated commitment and lavishly disserted through their Kierke-gaardian characters on the human condition and on living existentially.

After every false death, however, a rebirth came. In the early nineteen fifties, the colorful flowering of the French novel of 1930–1950 (Bernanos, Céline, Giono, Malraux; then Camus, Sartre, Simone de Beauvoir) appeared to be withering into an autumnal decrepitude. The sturdy impulse once received from the new American fiction had ceased to spur French writers to emulation of transatlantic violence. Byzantine disquisitions on form in the novel and time in the novel, on symbolic structure and on the language of the novelist were paralyzing the fiction writers in a land where creators are perilously close to critics or where a critic lurks in the brain cells of every would-be imaginative talent. Joyce—following upon Mallarmé's meditations on *the* great work that was to supplant all other books and provide, through speculations on language and silence, the total orphic explanation of the world—was regarded as the grave digger of Western fiction.

The French, happily, are a fickle nation. Their usable past is so broad that they periodically decide to disregard most of it and to turn away from the impressive giants of yesterday to the defunct giants of an even earlier age, less likely to overshadow them. They treat these ancestors with insolent and refreshing familiarity. They redo Laclos, Rétif, Sade, Stendhal, and Benjamin Constant—with a difference. The novel, that phoenix among literary kinds, overprompt to return to dust, vigorously emerges from its heap of ashes. Critics and journalists hail "the new novel" of the new France. A Gaullist era in literature is ushered in, for which the grave sovereign is hardly more responsible than Queen Victoria was for Emily Brontë or Thackeray or Meredith. Publicity is promptly organized or encouraged. Foreign publishers order translations. English-speaking schoolboys will soon lay aside their favorite textbook, *L'Etranger*, and bid farewell to their nonvocal French hero, Meursault the involuntary murderer, for school editions of *La Jalousie* or *La Modification*. School girls will learn all about the French woman from *Le Repos du Guerrier* and *Aimez-vous Brahms*.

The new novelists of France are in truth a motley crowd, at least as varied as are the young and not-so-young men in anger in Britain or the crop of post-World War II American novelists ranging from Saul Bellow and Norman Mailer to William Styron and the author of *The Catcher in the Rye*. Being French, however, they had to formulate, hence to invent, a body of doctrinal views to clarify their own aims and to impress the philosophical reviewers. And, although they do not seem, like the Madrid writers, to be the habitués of a particular "tertulia" or to have yet selected their favorite café, they are labeled by the public as a school. Like all "schools," they would be more likely to agree on their grounds for disagreeing with their predecessors than on any common aims. The leftist Catholic *Esprit*, one of the most thoughtful monthlies in Europe at the present time and the freest from any constricting allegiance to any cause, devoted a substantial number, in July-August 1958, to the *"nouveau roman."* Ten of these younger novelists, ranging in age from twenty-five to fifty-five (Beckett) and fifty-seven (Nathalie Sarraute), were selected by the contributors to *Esprit* as the most significant: Samuel Beckett, Michel Butor, Jean Cayrol, Marguerite Duras, Jean Lagrolet, Robert Pinget, Alain Robbe-Grillet, Nathalie Sarraute, Claude Simon, Kateb Yacine. Another dozen might easily be added to that list: among the women, Françoise des Ligneris, Noelle Loriot, Christiane Rochefort and Françoise Mallet-Joris, already author of four novels though not yet thirty years old; among the men, if Roger Nimier, Roger Vailland, Romain Gary, Félicien Marceau, the revelation of the years immediately following World War II, are relegated to the antechamber of the Academy, the conspicuous names are those of André Gorz—lavishly praised by Sartre—Jacques Howlett, Bernard Pingaud, Bertrand Poirot-Delpech, Philippe Sollers and the author of a new epic novel of the persecuted Jewish race, Schwarz-Bart; lately, of Le Clézio.

It is naturally preposterous to attempt a generalization on the trends discernible in so many novelists which would fit all of them: individualism is not dead, even in a France which is supposed to show signs of Americanization and to accept austerity meekly if cheerlessly. Literary trends are ultimately imposed by the greatness of isolated individuals who happen to have broken through a previously blind alley and to have led many followers behind the trail they blazed. Proust and Malraux are now seen, in retrospect, as having expressed the trends, Proust of the 'twenties, Malraux of the 'thirties. Will any of the new novelists grow into an author of similar stature? The thing is by no means impossible. To our contemporary eyes, Michel Butor, perhaps Claude Simon and Claude Ollier, less probably Alain Robbe-Grillet and Nathalie Sarraute may develop into novelists of real greatness. But they write for their times and we, their immediate contemporaries, may naïvely state what we see in them as of today.

First the tradition of the *récit* is maintained by the younger writers: if they rebel against Flaubert and even more against Balzac, they revere Benjamin Constant and apparently Raymond Radiguet's classical restraint and naïve cynicism. Stendhal is the idol which knows no iconoclast. Communist writers, like Roger Vailland and Claude Roy, try to borrow his tone; Jean Giono labors to turn out adroit but almost embarrassing pastiches of *La Chartreuse de Parme;* rightist critics continue, long after Paul Bourget, Jacques Boulenger, and Maurice Bardèche, to be Stendhal's devotees. Such a cult makes the modern French novel too self-conscious and freezes its imaginative thrusts. Stendhal's irony and shy self-defense against his reader acted as a beneficent antidote against his romantic leanings: there is not much romantic exuberance to be tamed in our recent authors of *récits* and their sobriety often seems achieved with perilous ease. Of all masters of fiction, Stendhal may well be the most oppressive when his imitators steal only his outward mannerisms.

But sophisticated readers, who are repelled by the avalanche of wordy vitality which the American novel often rolls down upon them, turn with relief to several of the ingenious, tight-lipped and open-eyed short works of fiction in which the French excel. The best in the output of the last few years are: *L'Amour n'est qu'un plaisir* by Jean d'Ormesson; *Le Grand Dadais* (*Fool's Paradise* in the American translation published in 1959) by the new drama critic of *Le Monde*, Bertrand Poirot-Delpech; and *Moderato Cantabile* by Marguerite Duras. They are masterfully written, with that swift, racing, lucid pace of the eighteenth-century story tellers, rushing to their feminine conquests and eventually to the scaffold. *Le Grand Dadais* is a confessional tale in the first person, by a young man who appears to be a clumsy and innocent fool, but who in fact cherishes much cynical ambition behind his mask. He caused the death of another man, was indicted for murder, faced the judges with some insolence and was imprisoned for five years.

The age-old theme of a prisoner, to which the fate of Europe, turned into a huge prison camp during the war years, lent new and tragic significance, haunts several of the writers of today. Bernard Pingaud's *Le Prisonnier*, inspired by a painting by Georges de la Tour, gravely but coldly written, is another one of these indirect protests of man, "the innocent convict," against the prison of his condition.

Moderato Cantabile is a deftly wrought utilization of musical structure by an expert woman novelist. The words allude to the piano lessons taken, listlessly and rebelliously, by a child whom his mother fails to understand. His mother is strangely fascinated by a scene to which she is a witness: a man kills a young woman, for love, and kisses her dead body passionately. She identifies herself with the woman thus loved to the point of death and beyond it, while a factory worker whom she meets at a café appears to her, in spite of the class barrier between them, as he who might also have "killed the thing he loved." Nothing happens; an inner drama is merely hinted, with a superb economy of means.

Such self-control verges perilously on the sort of intellectual tyranny exercised by the novelist over his characters which has always been the weakness of French fiction. John Galsworthy, who used to admire that artistic discipline in Flaubert and Maupassant, contrasted it with the tendency of the English novel "to go to bed drunk." The American novel has, since Galsworthy's time, replaced the English one as the garrulous and torrential drunkard. The French have become weary of these characters who are led on a leash by their creator and never seem to waylay him where he had not premeditated to venture. Strict sparseness of language and cascades of little facts, in appearance insignificant, may also harm credibility and render the author's watchful presence obtrusive. It is easy to be amused by some of the most highly praised novels of the last five or ten years, but the intellect and our sense of delight in irony alone are concerned: our imagination and our feelings, after the brief intellectual or erotic titillation, remain cold.

Christiane Rochefort's *Le Repos du Guerrier,* translated as *Warrior's Rest,* sold generously, entertained widely and shocked no less violently, for it stands as far as can be from the *"roman de jeune fille"* which once was intended to preserve the virtue of the French woman up to the wedding-night revelation. A man, rescued from suicide by a girl of the French middle class, is selected by that young lady as the male who might have been a hero of the Kinsey report: he drinks as much as he makes love, and with the same zestful nonchalance. He beats his saviour lady with vigorous conviction; these scenes of correction of the female by the male must have won many feminine readers to that best seller, crowned with the Prix de la Nouvelle Vague. As some of them confessed in a subsequent questionnaire on women's aspirations, if the woman does not exactly wish to be beaten, she likes to be reassured that her male companion would at least be up to administering a few vigorous blows if he had to. In the end, after many a melancholy orgy, the woman brings her warrior to rest from whisky and probably from sex—through marriage. Then, naturally, they can be unhappy ever after in exemplary fashion. The tale is slight, though not devoid of social significance for those who wish to explore the strange forms assumed by feminine sexuality in our time; but it is told with winning naturalness.

The same could not be said of another best seller of our times, *Zazie dans le métro,* by Raymond Queneau. Like Wordsworth in his famous preface, the author, a student of language, and of Joyce, and an encyclopedist who seeks relief from his labors in prolonged flirtations with the comic muse, "brings his language near to the language of men." He waves the flag against the very notion of literature and rebels against the one convention which in the past remained sacrosanct to all revolutionaries: respect for language. But the characters are all wooden puppets, their manipulation of words is pedantic and heavy-handed and the teenager, Zazie, an insufferable and vulgar little girl, whose company would in real life prove even more tedious than Lolita's, seems to have been drawn by its ironical creator as a discouragement to the present strenuous efforts of the French at increasing their population. Many a discovery remains to be made in what Freud termed "the polymorphous perverseness" of childhood.

A more robust reaction against the traditional, brief, self-conscious, hyper-intelligent French *récit* appears in several attempts at rejuvenating the picaresque novel. Giono led the way after World War II, when his experience in a French prison cured him of preaching an idyllic life in harmony with nature and in sympathy with animals and drove him to galloping adventures across the plains and mountains of southern France and northern Italy. Louis Aragon, that underestimated Picasso of literature, a chameleon poet as Keats might have termed him and a plastic fictional talent, a master of metamorphoses yet never a posturing clown, delighted French readers in 1958 with *La Semaine Sainte*. The book is a dashing historical epic on the hundred days which preceded Napoleon's fall at Waterloo, colorful, tender, less rambling and less didactic than some picaresque novels which insist upon turning years of adventure into Goethean *"Lehrjahre,"* nostalgic for the warlike glamor of the Empire as only a Communist can be. Roger Nimier, who made a startling début *"à la hussarde"* into postwar fiction and should have become one of the masters of the new French picaresque, died before he fulfilled his promise. The analysis of love often waylays those impetuous young French conquerors into foolishly endeavoring to know women while they love them, and therefore into building up a structure of psychological labyrinthine staircases in order to pursue their baffling mistresses up and down every landing.

The most determined champion of the new picaresque has been, in the last fifteen years, Romain Gary. As early as 1946, that Russian-French diplomat, Gaullist airman, admirer of Malraux and of Stendhal, had challenged the existentialists by proclaiming: "The modern novel will be picaresque or it will not exist. Picaresque, in the sense of a fresco with a welter of adventures, of movement and of swarming characters. And of optimism, also." The author of *The Roots of Heaven* cannot help being a moralist and to hide many a message of gloom, yet of good will also, in the trunks and spacious legs of his elephants. But, with many a flaw in style and some off-handed contempt for structure, his work carried the reader along in its tempestuous sweep. The British tenants of the picaresque today, John Wain, Kingsley Amis, Angus Wilson, seem more bitter, more farcically satirical, more tightly and intellectually in rebellion against the conventions of social classes than their more generously Rabelaisian French counterparts.

The label of *"le nouveau roman"* has lately been appropriated by a particular group of novelists, far more earnest than the picaresque, the ironical and the salacious ones who maintain, in the midst of a world reveling in the absurd and proud of its sedulously cultivated anguish, the Frenchman's right to smile at what he cherishes most: women, sentiment, the illogic of life, and himself. Nathalie Sarraute and Alain Robbe-Grillet take us with pontifical gravity over the threshold of *"l'ère du soupçon."* They hold infinity, no longer in the palm of their hand, but within the crawling centipede which characters in *La Jalousie* crush repeatedly, in reality or in their nightmares, on a wall, or in the tropisms set in motion in some neurotic old lady by the imperfection of a lock applied upon an oaken door. The humor of Proust and of Sartre, the great masters of comedy, has been expelled from their Jansenist stories. So has any pampering to that vulgar expectation of naïve readers: "What is going to happen?" Their novel, like Joyce's, like Kafka's, like Gide's *Counterfeiters,* is, as it is now termed, an anti-novel. The most authentic predecessors of these doctrinaire new novelists are, even more directly, Sartre in *La Nausée* and Camus in *L'Etranger,* the two novels of the years 1935–45 that have exercised the most vivid fascination and have brought forth the most fecund progeny. But with the latest generation, absurdity is no longer encountered in the trappings of the middle class in their provincial Sunday best or in the luxuriance of a slimy root sprawling in the damp soil, in the alienation from society of an elementary hero speaking of himself as if he were *"l'étranger."* It lies in man's delusion that his existence could ever have been necessary or have mattered to objects surrounding him.

The characteristics of the "new fiction" may be defined

as follows; first, away with metaphysics. *Pourquoi des Philosophes?* is the title of one of the recent pamphlets by J. Revel, an acid and impatient iconoclast bent upon deflating the silvery bubbles blown by all the teachers of philosophy who, in the 'forties, had made French fiction their sole domain. André Gorz, whose volume, *Le Traitre*, is a masterful existential psychoanalysis of the author parading as fiction, is the only overt philosopher among the younger group. Speculations on man's fate and man's responsibilities in a world of derelict mortals condemned to be free appear to most others as mere escapism into cloudy speculations, away from the sway of hard, angular objects.

Then, down with psychology, which, as Paul Valéry hinted, ever saw and seized only the exterior of what is inward. Proust had certainly added a new density to our feeling for our inner life and made Flaubert and Zola, George Eliot and Hardy appear elementary; he had dissected love, jealousy, and the intermittences of the heart into what appeared to be their ultimate component molecules. But even Proustian analysis, once it had refined the perception of the readers fit to share it, became conventional; it resorted to ready-made formulas, to lavish botanical metaphors or to cascades of harmonious adjectives. Joyce's interior monologues, once revered as the paragons of subtlety, wear off their freshness and appear crude and tricky. The impact of American fiction, impatient of hairsplitting introspection and of the Frenchman's Valéryan obsession to see himself seeing himself (*"je me voyais me voir,"* as said La Jeune Parque), to watch himself eating, writing, feeling, has helped transform the French novel.

The leaders of the young movement also boast of their revolt against characters in the novel. Those characters in whom Balzac and his followers believed as if they were holy entities, became congealed into types: the lover, the jealous, the upstart, the inventor, the miser, the sadist, the self-sacrificing lady. But the era of suspicion forecast by Stendhal came with a hundred years' lag. Modern man's claim is to call everything in question: liberty, justice, equality, charity, saintliness, language and the fixity of characters. Beneath those artificial categories, Nathalie Sarraute discerns formless, nascent moves, slow repetitions

of our mental organs, elementary reactions of our flesh
or of our nerves which never reach the stage of half-
conscious elaboration in our brains. She wishes to be the
Columbus of those uncharted zoological tropisms. Proust
used to contend that his lenses were those of a telescope.
Mme. Sarraute prefers the microscope. She strikes at the
heart of the fictional phenomenon itself, by magnifying
those untold unformulable tropisms which make each of
us at times feel that, if only he could record them and
amplify them, he would grow into a novelist. There are,
few and far between, glimpses of freshness and poetry in
Le Planetarium, but also a perilous duel with tediousness,
a multiplication of minute nothings ("my son-in-law adores
grated carrots . . . new, tender carrots" repeats the ex-
asperatingly garrulous old lady) in *Le Planetarium* which
may strain the much vaunted resistance to boredom of
our age.

Alain Robbe-Grillet has been more explicit in his theoretical pronouncements and his novels are smoothly contrived, with at least the shell of a mystery-thriller plot, to
keep the reader breathless while he skips the geometric
passages. He wants to achieve nothing less than the final
break between man and the universe of things, to demystify the much abused adjective "human." Let man see
things "with no softness," detachedly, fully aware that
things never return to him his gaze, not any more than
God in His majesty. Let him cease boasting about the
tragedy of being forsaken by an indifferent world and
renounce the childishness of begging inanimate objects
for an echo of his own sorrows. Robbe-Grillet painstak-
ingly sizes up objects with compasses, T square and scale.
He describes longitudinal, rectangular, median lines in the
complexity of things, repressing all Balzacian temptation
to endow objects with a visionary existence of their own,
which would only be an egotistic delusion of our anthro-
pomorphism.

The tempo of fiction is also renovated: it is that of a
very slow camera, endlessly shooting at the same scene.
In *Les Gommes,* translated as *The Erasers,* as in *La
Jalousie,* there is no continuity of an irreversible passing
of time; there is no cumulative impact of a progressive
narrative. Holes of darkness are skillfully provided, into

which the reader may pursue one misleading track after another. Proust likewise induced us to put several fallacious interpretations on the behavior of Swann, Charlus, or Albertine, until all the masks were lifted and the truth flashed on the reader. In this new kind of cold geometric thriller, the reader remains baffled down to the end. We turn around in an eternal recurrence, living over again the same scene in anticipation, actuality and nightmarish memory. The novelist himself refrains from proposing his point of view; he wants to discover his laconic characters, exchanging few unconcerned words, at the same time as his reader does. He never analyzes them, never ponders over their psychology or moralizes on the significance of their deeds. Of the four novels published by Robbe-Grillet, *Le Voyeur* (translated as *The Voyeur*) is probably the most successful. *La Jalousie* is a trifle too tricky and *Dans le Labyrinthe* too puritanical in its fulfillment of Flaubert's dream: a novel made of and with nothing, a Mallarméean work of absence by an anti-poet.

The most authentic disciple of Robbe-Grillet is a novelist of great talent, Claude Ollier, whose *La Mise en Scène* received the newly founded Médicis prize late in 1958. He, too, is a seer, if not a visionary seer; like the painter Monet, he is an eye, but what an eye! Every particle of the desert sand, of the barren cliffs, of the hardy tufts of dry grass, every line along a track or shade of a teapot is patiently described. The hero, Lassalle (unlike Kafka and the characters in *La Jalousie,* he is endowed with more than a mere initial) travels across the North African desert to draw the road to a mining establishment. He is beset with suspicions of his guides, gradually discovers that his predecessor was murdered and the Arab women whom he had known a little too well have been brutally punished. The theme (it cannot be called a plot) is that of a mystery story laid in the desert. But all the talent, which is rich, is lavished on the inventory of objects. Man is relegated where he belongs: he is a being without communion with things, forbidden to play the cheap game of pathetic fallacy. *"Objets inanimés, avez-vous donc une âme?"* questioned naïve Lamartine. The answer is a sharp no: human beings themselves yearn only for geometric soullessness.

Claude Simon is also fascinated by objects, their shapes, weight and color. "To know is to possess," as he claims. His vocation was that of a botanist, and in *L'Herbe,* translated as *Grass,* a funereal symphony of characters who look back upon their whole lives "as they lie dying," he aimed at annihilating the story from the novel. "One does not see the story, not any more than one sees the grass growing," as he quotes from Boris Pasternak. *Le Vent* (translated as *The Wind* and courageously brought out by George Braziller) puzzled American reviewers—and understandably so. It is Faulknerian to the point of embarrassment. But the author showed that he could be at ease in a chaos and haunt us through repetitions. *L'Herbe* has more freshness and contrives striking effects of chiaroscuro in the midst of a gruesome dance of death. An old maid relives her life of devotion for creatures who did not deserve it; all is ripeness, or rather rottenness of the flesh shredded and devoured by death. There is more passion here than in *"l'école du regard,"* the school of the viewers, as the geometric land surveyors have been nicknamed; and an uncanny power over words: sentences of one hundred lines or more are child's play to that French Faulkner.

Michel Butor has been treated more generously by critics than Robbe-Grillet, Claude Ollier or Nathalie Sarraute, whom it is too easy to parody. He has not altogether renounced psychology, which reassures French academic reviewers. He, too, depicts objects minutely, but he does not dehumanize them with such fanatical relentlessness. He does not expel all symbolic connotations from his novels, and the stained-glass window of the old Bleston Cathedral, representing Abel's murder by Cain, stands for an original curse afflicting that rain-soaked city of Bleston, the forlorn Negro whom the protagonist encounters, the French man recapturing time and living it reversibly, with all its recurrences, during his dreary year in the British city of soot and fog. *L'Emploi du Temps* is, in our eyes, the richest, the most musically orchestrated and the most poetical novel of the last ten years. *La Modification,* published by Simon and Schuster as *A Change of Heart* and in London as *Second Thought* is something of a self-conscious *tour de force*. The long monologue of the traveler from Paris to Rome, observing, reminiscing, analyzing his feelings or watching them alter as he addresses himself as *"nous,"* miraculously eschews boredom. The Roman mistress, loved in association with the Eternal City, but in truth loved tepidly; the nagging wife in Paris, who wins in the end in the duel of which she is unaware, come to life with mysterious vividness. The technique is impeccable yet never obtrusive. Joyce and Faulkner are never altogether absent from these sprawling monologues and the thirty- or forty-line sentences, but their example has been assimilated and naturalized. "No great novel ever came from a superficial mind," wrote Henry James to R. L. Stevenson in the last decade of the nineteenth century. Butor's mind is rich, original and subtle. He is the most authentic novelist of his generation.

Too much has doubtless been made of the phrase "the New Novel in France," and publicity rushed in too fast and too arrogantly to cash in on the band of angels whom France, weary with existentialist mortalists and with eroticists, was awaiting to renovate fiction. There are many tricks in their manner, an arrogant and dogmatic self-consciousness in their doctrines, much tediousness in the practice of several of them. But this ascetic bath into purity and this "methodical experience," as Butor has called the modern novel, with lessons taken in all humility by writers from geometricians, engineers, and botanists is a salutary one. It is good that, periodically, literature in France should call everything in question, spurn the crushing weight of tradition and proceed to a systematic accumulation of new, if somewhat rough-hewn, materials. This era of suspicion is also an era of reconstruction and of faith in "a virgin and lively today."

Postscript, 1964: The new novel held its freshest appeal and was most hotly debated in France in the years 1958–60. American professors and critics were quick in lecturing about it, assigning *A Change of Heart* or *Jealousy* to their students as a required, and uplifting, reading, which replaced defunct Camus and Sartre, the latter no longer fashionable after his too great vogue in the early fifties. New York publishers arranged for translations of such esoteric books as *The Planetarium*, Butor's *Degrees* and *Mobile*, Simon's *The Road to Flanders* and *The Palace*. Scholarly journals rushed to print a number of grave essays in which academic detectives deciphered the pseudo riddles of who killed whom in *Le Voyeur*, did they sleep or did they not last year in Marienbad, how to disentangle the past from the present in Simon and Sollers' mushy and often gelatinous literary paste. The reception to the new French novel was cooler in Great Britain. In France, outside a relatively small band of readers hungry for innovations and in a hurry to hail the victory of "alittérature" over order and clarity, most critics and the general public remained unimpressed. The magazine *Esprit* wondered if it had been wise in getting the ball rolling. Traditional fiction, signed by Druon, Troyat or Zoë Oldenbourg, fared robustly with the purchasers of books. The task of renovating the novel may still be left to our descendants.

Discontent with the form of the novel is a venerable tradition with the French, who have always questioned that art form while practicing it zestfully. Predecessors of the worship of the object and of "le chosisme," foes of psychology and of the excessive share allotted to love in fictional stories could be found throughout the nineteenth century. An anthology of such indictments of the novel by novelists and of literature by its fervent but disquieted practitioners should some day be compiled. Mme. de Stael, in a 1795 piece entitled *Essay on Fictions*, advised novelists to devote their energies to the portrayal of passions other than love. Flaubert's *Correspondence* teems with lucidly prophetic remarks on the need to describe objects in the novel. Zola is a much greater critic than he is given credit for, one of the sharpest judges of Stendhal and Balzac in the second half of the century. Sainte-Beuve himself, often blind to the achievement of those who had proved their mastery in the art of fiction where he had ventured once and failed honorably, in a letter to Champfleury dated February 28, 1860, hailed the novel as "a vast trial field, open to all the forms of genius and to all manners. It is the future epic, the only one which modern customs will allow." But he added: "Let us not narrow it down. Let us not theorize about it; let us not organize it." And he advised novelists to write novels, but to beware of apologies or of expositions of their ideas on the novel.

The counsel is a hard one to follow for the self-conscious and hypercritical French. Between 1958 and 1964, the creative energy of the tenants of the new novel has flagged; few of their volumes have evinced signs of vigorous self-renewal. But they have lectured, printed essays on their theoretical views, answered interviewers on their intentions and their doctrine, attended learned conventions where they were being dissected by doctors of philosophy. Claude Simon, the most imaginative of the present-day novelists, is also the most distrustful of doctrines and manifestoes. Still, he was seduced into delivering a lecture at the Sorbonne on January 11, 1961, on "Significance, Novel and Chronology." He attacked Sartre's contention that an artist has to do with "significances." The world, to him, has no meaning. All is arbitrary; nothing is determined or ordained. Hence chronology is forsaken, as barely good enough for the novelists who construct their fiction with an eye on the dénouement and organize events in time accordingly. The recent novels by Claude Simon do not simply imitate reality. They render it present to the reader and they set it apart from the corroding influence of time.

Simon's *Road to Flanders* (1960) blends the French defeat of 1940, as lived by the protagonist haunted by the thought of suicide after the earlier suicide of an ancestor of his, experiences in a prisoners' camp with memories of his youth and fears of being jilted by his wife. All is senseless and absurd. Time revolves incessantly. Present participles rush upon each other. The sole order is the disorder in which sensations and memories succeed each other in the mind, carried along by "the incoherent, nonchalant, impersonal, destructive work of time," as the final sentence in the book describes it. *The Palace* (1963), in spite of its rich and sensuous style, smacks of trickery. The protagonist, staying in a palace hotel in Barcelona, recalls his stay in that same city during the Spanish Civil War, when he fought with the Spanish Republicans. None of the persons mentioned has a name, a past, or any definable character.

Michel Butor's reputation has hardly been enhanced by

what he has published since 1958; it must however be proclaimed that he has shunned treading in the same path where he had scored a remarkable technical success with *L'Emploi du Temps* (*Passing Time*), his most ambitious undertaking, and *La Modification* (*A Change of Heart*). His *Degrees,* however, had a harsh reception, while his next book, *Mobile,* not a novel but a collage of reminiscences of America, was an even worse failure. He continually experiments with several art forms and reflects on the technique of fiction. Of all the novelists under fifty, he is the acutest analyst of his own achievement and the ablest theorist. His *Répertoire* (1960) is replete with intelligent reflections on the novel in search of its nature and of its possibilities. Nathalie Sarraute, in connection with whose *Portrait of a Man Unknown* (1948) the "antinovel" had first been thus christened by Sartre and strikingly defined, has continued deserving the praise of her introducer to the French public: Sartre had lauded her for being able to "call the novel in question, to destroy it under our very eyes while appearing to erect it." Her collection of essays, *Era of Suspicion,* appeared in English in 1962 in New York and made more of an impact with the *literati* than her novels themselves. The latest of those, *Les Fruits d'or* (1963) is a virtuoso exercise: it has no action, no character, no core or focus. The episodes alluded to fleetingly, but never actually related, are trivial. With her tongue in her cheek, the novelist satirizes the reviewers who praise or blame a novel entitled *Les Fruits d'or,* each according to his own whims, prejudices, animosities, or to merely what he believes others expect from him or want to hear. She lays bare the faint, nascent tropisms in those critics of literature who, like many of us in life, lie to others and to themselves. But life has evaporated from such a novel, if novel it may be called. The reader finds it impossible to identify himself with characterless characters.

The most promising and the youngest of the innovators in recent fiction is Philippe Sollers. He has disowned his early, and very talented, attempt at a traditional love story, *A Curious Solitude.* His second novel, *Le Parc* (1961), is more bewildering, but emptied of action and characters. The narrator looks down, from his apartment, at a park, at the houses around it and the passers-by; he goes out for a brief while, takes up his observation post again. What he observes arouses in him memories of his childhood, of a woman he loved, a man killed in the war. Objects are meticulously described on page after page; the world is seen "tel quel," such as it is, or appears to be. *Tel Quel* is the title of a refined and beautifully written magazine which Sollers directed, in which appeared critical and poetical texts which he collected in *L'Intermédiaire* (1963): one of them is an elaborate and precious essay on Poussin's painting and another one, insolently preceded by an epigraph from St. Theresa of Avila, is a stilted but ironical piece on what is called "les lieux d'aisance" in dignified French. There lurks a claustration complex in many of those modern novels of aloneness.

Sollers is an avowed admirer of Robbe-Grillet, for of all those practitioners of the new novel, Alain Robbe-Grillet is indeed the most bellicose, the least encumbered with theories and intentions. His last attempts, since *In the Labyrinth* (1959) have not lain in the realm of fiction, but in that of the cinema. His sketches and stories, collected in the slim volume, *Instantanés,* had been written before 1959. *Last Year in Marienbad* and another "ciné-roman," *L'Immortelle* (whose scene is laid in a Moslem cemetery in Istanbul), are remarkably poetical evocations of an ambiguous world. Reality is sacrificed to that which is perceived and transformed by the mind which remembers or imagines. Any coherent order of the stable world outside is dissolved. Robbe-Grillet, an agricultural engineer by training, not to be outdone by Butor and Mme. Sarraute, his rivals, has emulated them in proposing his philosophy of the novel. His clearest statement appeared in English in *The New Statesman,* on February 17, 1961, as "The Case for the New Novel." There the novelist explained that man gropes in the modern novel as he has to grope in real life, "with the old conventions and principles crumbling under him." Against those critics who deplore that psychology, characters and plot are banished from the impoverished new novel, Robbe-Grillet argued that "man is there in every page, every line, every word. There are a great number of objects, minutely described, but they are always dominated by the eye that sees them, the thought that recalls them, the passion that distorts them. . . . In our books, it is a man who sees, feels, imagines, a man existing in space and time, embroiled in his passions, a man like you and me. And the novel can only offer *his* experience, limited and uncertain. It is a man, a man of today, who is his own narrator."

The New French Poetry
BY JEAN PARIS

For the past 150 years, every post-war period in France has marked the advent of a "new literature." Romanticism came out of Napoleon's campaigns as symbolism arose from the defeat of 1870, and the two main literary movements of our time, surrealism and existentialism, followed respectively the first and the second world wars. But while surrealism was essentially born from poets and painters, the existentialist school remained of a philosophical obedience, found its best success in essays, novels and theatre, and was almost fatal to poetry. This is why so many young poets today, in search of a new expression of life, are moving away from Sartre and his disciples, and looking to other writers who had formerly been eclipsed by their more flashy rivals. The real masters of this new generation are of a more discreet variety; their conception of language as personal incantation, together with the dignity of their poetry had, for many years, kept them from exercising much influence. I mention Victor Ségalen, O. V. de L. Milosz, Pierre Reverdy, Saint John Perse, Pierre-Jean Jouve, René Char, Aimé Césaire, etc.

In dealing with this new French poetry, it is almost impossible to present a complete, objective picture of it, as the most superficial look reveals such a diversity, ranging from the remnants of romanticism, symbolism, surrealism to the extravagances of lettrism, graphism, apoetry, and so on, that the genre seems at first a little confused. The poets I have chosen have not been selected as representing all major movements, but for their originality, for their genuine quality and their potential for the future. As different, as opposed as they may be amongst themselves, they share a common concern, they participate in a common dialectic, whose first phase is the destruction of the old lyricism and the second, the creation of a new one. It is from this dual requirement that the present-day poetry draws its contradictions and its ambiguities.

The first act of this drama was played by the historical event of this generation: the War. For the poets, this war absorbed their childhood, and conveyed to them the gravity and the darkness of negation. Thus Jean Laude:

> *Cities are deserted. Days are perverted. The ghost of a she-wolf grows along crumbling walls.*
> *No more hope, but lichen and dark fire where we dwell . . .*

Romain Weingarten:

> *I was haunted by alarm bells and I burnt and I ran away.*
> *Fire was raging in clothes, hands, hair. And as I ran, I howled. No one saw, no one heard.*

Jacques Dupin:

> *We grew up very fast, at random with wind and rain, thistles among the ruins, weeds between the tombs. In our orphan eyes, to awaken risk and gleam, a precocious gale arose. In vain they had us put on the Sunday harness, we wore black with such elegance that our nakedness shone through the darkest night. We did not cheat, but under our mourning weeds, our innocence saw . . . We grew up very fast, brothers! Our masters have learned nothing.*

Certainly the best examples of this period are Henri Pichette's *Apoèmes* and *Epiphanies*. Shattered sentences, broken rhythms, verbal bombardments, black, flaming howls of horror became the natural idiom of poetry. Under the twofold influence of Arthur Rimbaud and Antonin Artaud, the last great surrealist, Henri Pichette tried to raise his language to the level of the war itself, in a desperate attempt to endow poetry with the same violence, the same power of destruction. An upset of syntax, chopped machinegun style phrases, words poured out as a shower of bombs, monologues staggering between the outer apocalypse and man's inner terror, all these devices were tried successfully, as in this short passage from *Apoème 4* which reveals the soldier's panic during an attack:

> *Dreamers! camouflage yourselves! Glue hay to your teeth! Laughter is a mad weapon!* The transfigured gunners take a powder. Those are real bullets! The nightingale can't hear himself. *Fire!* The leaf, the tree, the forest tremble. *Fire! Fire!*

Fortunately some other poets chose a more discreet way to express the same terror. Poetry is less an art of description than transposition. For Jacques Charpier, war was not simply a frantic assault or a verbal alert, but the death of the word, the tumbling of man into nothingness.

> *I remember that eternal evening when all men on the earth embraced before the last idol that survived disaster.*
> *And united by the most beautiful language ever written, were silent.*

The last line of this short prose poem raised the most perplexing problem. How can poetry once destroyed be reborn? How can one believe in its powers, faced with the amplitude of its destruction? The war did not only annihilate millions of people; it has also put an end to all confidence in humanity. Poetry had then to question itself, to descend into its own chaos, its own night, in search of a new faith, of a new light. And naturally this long voyage into hell took on the character of an initiation, of a Quest.

Here we find three poets who form among themselves, despite obvious differences, a kind of spiritual family: Jean Laude, Roger Giroux and André du Bouchet. The first one, whose works proceed from a total despair, conceives the first exercise of poetry to be a constant awareness of its humiliation. Man is lost, he no longer has a grip on reality nor any means of expression:

> *At the level of the earth, words have no more depth. They thread their way like the base light under*

the doors. At the level of the earth, the dead.

Our reign is ending into a nightmare: in a wide-open space, time is swallowed, and oblivion spreads like the tide. The very situation of the poem is enunciated: a suffocation in the midst of an unintelligible universe.

> *The words sink in the sand. Surrounded by eggs, the numbers rot and the pendulum goes wild in the dead zone where the body of a new day takes form. Everything is a sign. On the ground strewn with bodies, clenched hands point in opposite directions, but I am the crossroad, the confluence where threats find their source.*

This agony is set in a twilight landscape *à la* Turner, a monotonous country, where *"in the north of hope,"* the dune is interrupted only by puddles and swamps. Yet it is within this *waste land* that we have to wander, and to wander is the beginning of an action. To walk in this desert implies a meaning, a direction, a possible reconquest of our native land. Perhaps this country is legible, perhaps there exists below its dismal waters *"a narrow pier, a channel of stones amongst the sands."* Laude's first book of poems bore a prophetic title in this respect: *Le Grand Passage.* Since then, the poet has adventured in search of this narrow gate. The symbol underlying his quest is the Zuydersee, this earth patiently conquered from the chaos, an image Goethe had already used to unify the mission of Faust. The legend of the Holy Grail provides also a background for a second voyage, a second book, *Les Saisons et la Mer* (The Seasons and the Sea) ending as a great departure towards the unknown, towards those horizons where a new earth will perhaps appear.

> *May an island emerge where our death soon fades. An island of reason where soon fades our fear.*

This final victory, or at least its prophecy, is obstinately refused by Roger Giroux. He also starts from silence but, contrary to Jean Laude, he denies every solution, every hope as illusory. For him, poetry must cling to its drama, which is to recover the *parole perdue*, the lost word, and since this paradise is never regained, poetry will only succeed in losing itself as well.

> *Every work is alien, every word is absent*
> *And the poem laughs and defies me to live*
> *This desire of a space where there would be no time.*
> *It's a gift of nothing to be able to name.*

One can see here the contradiction in which the new poetry becomes imprisoned. Giroux wrote a long poem entitled *Retrouver la Parole* (Regain the Word) to assert only that the poet has lost any ability to do so. Perhaps the only glory left to him is to persist at this impossible quest:

> *Nothing is ever said, but to say this nothing is the*
> *perpetual birth of the poet. And is he going to tear*
> *his face away? It is beyond that he must see, before*
> *this our space. . . .*

However, this condemnation of lyricism only applies to written poetry. But, far beyond the words, poetry can still be a way of life. Here, Roger Giroux rejoins several other poets for whom the poetic experience is to greet fully those mysterious moments that the mystic calls *visitations* and James Joyce "epiphanies." By a sudden incomprehensible act of grace, as Novalis already said, the least object, the most ordinary scenery becomes a symbol of divine presence. For Pierre Oster, for example, the world perpetually offers its wonders to man, wherein the secret will of God is revealed. The three books this very young and gifted poet has already published—*Le Champ de Mai* (The Field of May), *Solitude de la Lumière* (Loneliness of the Light), *Un Nom toujours nouveau* (A Name Forever New)— offer such moments of ecstasy and song to the glory of beauty.

> *A sensitive wood echoes the quiet heaven.*
> *I awake to sing the truth, as a chosen,*
> *To magnify my way!*
> *In my exile's eyes new landscapes are born*
> *The day blossoms, joined in wedlock to storms,*
> *A single leaf conjures in the heights of my soul*
> *The desperate echo of the wind's trump's howl,*
> *Summer! thy pure secret sighs: a new day dawns.*

Another young poet, Romain Weingarten, shares with Oster the privilege of these revelations, but gives them a more dramatic character, as this strange poem attests: *Troisième Vision de la Chambre* (Third Vision of the Room):

> *I would see, as far as eye could reach,*
> *The mothers' coffins still on the river*
> *And behind the great arch of white stone*
> *A clearness lighting up the chasm*
> *Where floated the last mists of the night.*
>
> *And as at the bedside of a dying woman*
> *Who could scarcely breathe any more*
> *I would wait for the word that might rend me apart*
> *But her lips remained silent beneath the stony weight*
> *And when she drew her last breath*
> *I felt her coming to me*
> *And handing me the keys*
> *Which for ever glittered in her palm.*

However, Roger Giroux remains separated from these two contemporaries by his awareness that these visions are, by nature, inexpressible. The world ignores us, sends us constantly back to our solitude, and even in our high moments of exaltation, we cannot break our prison of time, we cannot find the true word which would free us from our death.

> *A bird, when he goes*
> *On the sea as one breathes*
> *To bring remembrance of land to the end of this day*
> *Of light and love, a bird . . .*
> *How can one say that without undoing*
> *The work of the eyes, of the hands, of the face*
> *And without killing the bird and the language,*
> *How can one say that without shame?*

With André du Bouchet, the third part of this triptych, poetry reaches at last the extreme of negation. What Laude and Giroux had restricted to imagination is extended by this poet to existence itself. It is life, it is the very nature of human life which makes poetry impossible, or at least this poetry of joy and beauty that Pierre Oster and Romain Weingarten illustrate. Here we find, at the lowest of our misery, a quietly tragi-comic affirmation of our nothingness:

> *My share of earth is dry and covers me. It will soon be dark.*

André du Bouchet's relationship to poetry is much the same as Samuel Beckett's to the theatre. His imagery often recalls the desert landscape where the two bums of *Waiting for Godot* wander in a neutral yet hostile atmosphere, a blank world where one can only see signs or vague traces, without being able to understand their meaning. Thus,

> *Papers from all the fires in the white-washed day. A voice with thin needles. This earth on you like a hand, where the sky replaces the wall, the bare lime— at the foot of the stones.*

In almost every poem of André du Bouchet, the same shattered images reappear, as if their only value was derived from repetition. An existence reduced to a few gestures, a starvation in a depleted land, a poetry of famine which seems to grow thinner and whiter the more it develops . . . one could almost believe that the author depicts another planet, a strange and inhabitable world where everything has lost weight, meaning, color, life. *Volets* is a good example of this existential apoetry:

> *The woman going to the window, high in the house, at the level of the sun, draws the curtains, lowers the white blind, and the window vanishes. In native gold. Bird's eyeball.*
> *The restored manufacture of the room, at the iron age, downstairs, behind the albugo.*

that we can see in the three or four books André du Bouchet already published: *Air* (Air), *Sans Couvercle* (With no Lid), *Le Moteur blanc* (The White Motor), *Au deuxième étage* (At the Second Floor).

But, if poetry is an avowal of death, it is also and fundamentally a quest for a new life. The rare merit of

Yves Bonnefoy is to unite these two movements in the same profound drama. As a philosopher, Bonnefoy devoted much time to Hegel: he knows that every truth supposes its opposite. As a critic, he has written one of the best essays on Baudelaire, the first modern poet who mingled two contradictory notions in a single image (*Voici le soir charmant, ami du criminel . . . Here is the charming night, friend of the criminal . . .*). Combining these capacities, he developed an essentially dialectical poetry where hope and despair, darkness and light are presented as the two faces of the same mirror. While seeking life, this poetry has therefore to assume death, and then Bonnefoy's writings are basically founded on ambiguity. His first and most impressive book, *Du Mouvement et de l'Immobilité de Douve* (On the Movement and Immobility of Douve), joins in its own title these opposite realities and creates a language in which they constantly exchange their virtues.

As to the poetic entity that Bonnefoy called "Douve," he himself defined it as the relationship between consciousness and nothingness. From the outset, Douve seems to be provided with a twofold nature: she is referred to as death and, at the same time, as the awareness of our death, which is life. In a first section, written both in prose and verse, Bonnefoy describes the agony, death and burial of Douve; the rest of the book is an attempt to discover what may remain of her in the visible world. This pattern is highly symbolical, even mystical, as in Dante's *Inferno* and *Paradiso*, or Milton's *Paradise Lost* and *Paradise Regained*, or Proust's *Temps perdu* and *Temps retrouvé*, for poetry here confronts its own disappearance. In other words, death becomes the *vrai lieu*, the "real ground," of the poem, its vocation, its essence: Douve will be dismembered, she will return, like Ophelia, to her basic elements. But, at the same time, the ordeal will assert her nobility. A strange dignity will mark her departure *marching like suns in funeral spaces*. Dead in her flesh, she will be so alive in nature that the poet will hear her in the trees, in the wind. These two movements of death and resurrection form the central theme of Bonnefoy's poems, notably in *Vrai Nom* (Real Name):

The castle that you were I will name a desert
Night your voice, absence your face
And when you fall into the barren earth
I will name void the lightning that bore you.

Dying is a country that you loved. I come
But for ever along your sombre paths
I destroy your past, your shape, your memory
I am your enemy who will have no mercy.

I will name you war, and I will take
Upon you the liberties of war. And I'll have
In my hands your dark and empty face,
In my heart that country lighted by the storm.

Again we find the same dialectics in this splendid piece of verse:

The profound light in order to appear
Needs an earth trodden and crackling with night.
It is from a dark wood that the flame burst forth.
Even the word needs an inert substance,
A shore beyond all songs.

Thou must pass through death to live,
The purest presence is shed blood.

Thus, beginning under the star of nothingness, this poetry closes with an invocation. Life must be possible. Life must be found beyond despair and death. Certainly Yves Bonnefoy's second book, *Hier régnant désert* (Yesterday Reigning Desert), has not yet announced the outcome of the drama, but already, as if purified by its long journey into darkness, poetry has been revived, as in this beautiful prayer:

If this night is other than night
Arise, distant and blessed voice, awake
The gravest clay where the seed has slept . . .

Having lived through a quest similar to that of Laude and Bonnefoy, other poets are seeking in some manner to reconcile their art to the world. One possible approach is that of Claude Vigée who strongly emphasizes the theme of exile and retains in one of his last and very fine books, *L'Eté Indien* (Indian Summer), the same quality of ambiguity and beauty, each poem, like the dazzling moment of Indian Summer, embodying the splendor of the present and the threat of the future, the light of the sun and the cold of Winter. For Philippe Jacottet, a very great artist with an almost feminine delicacy, poetry is the unique means to transcribe the inexpressible in our world: a light touch of twilight, the soft glittering of certain hours, the furtive graces where dreams are woven. For Jacques Dupin, a poem is an alchemy of words, a meeting place of unusual images, where language might fulfill its highest powers. For Jacques Charpier, songster of his native Provence, poetry is enlarged little by little to the dimension of our earth and history, and like a mighty river flows into the whole cosmos, unto the stars.

Finally, there is a new element in French poetry which proved to be among the most important of the post-war period. I am referring to the French-speaking poets born in what one just recently stopped calling the "colonies." By Leopold Sédar Senghor from Mali, by Aimé Césaire from Martinique, our poetic language has been entirely renewed and deeply enriched. Formed by other civilizations, by traditions foreign to ours, these authors have injected a new vigor into our veins, with new rhythms and new images which have stimulated and miraculously rejuvenated our old blood. Despite the academic critics who fail to see in this poetry its kind of barbarian splendor, and blame it for its violence, its verbal audacity, its scorn of convention and its torrential character, I maintain that the use of the French language by these colored and colorful poets has been the most beneficial element our art has known since the war. At present, the two best representatives of this poetry are the Algerian Kateb Yacine and the Martiniquais Edouard Glissant. Their main theme is a deep concern for their people who suffered for so long and to whom one still barely concedes the right to exist. A superb example is to be found in a tragedy written by Yacine, the tragedy of the Algerian people struggling for its dignity: *Le Cadavre encerclé* (The Surrounded Corpse).

However, in closing, I would like to consider the extraordinary poem of Edouard Glissant, *Les Indes*. Author of several books of poetry: *Un Champ d'Iles* (A Field of Islands), *La Terre inquiète* (The Anxious Land), *Soleil de la Conscience* (Sun of Consciousness), *Le Sel noir* (The Black Salt), and winner of the 1959 Renaudot Literary Prize for his novel *La Lézarde* (*The Ripening*), Glissant depicts his native island of the Antilles as a place where history has incarnated its worst contradictions. Country of beauty and servitude, of opulence and misery, where men obsessed by their mother Africa *"stem the spirit of the river,"* toiling towards their past. *Les Indes* is an expression of both this ancestral spirit and the effort to rise above the atrocious memory of slavery.

> *They have nailed my people in their high ships. They have sold, rented, bartered flesh. The old for the little jobs, men for the sugar harvest, and women for the price of children. No more mystery, no more marvels. The Indies are a market of death . . . O desert of Language, mortuary grammar.*

This long poem, comprising a whole book, describes in six cantos the voyage of Christopher Columbus; the joyous departure, the anguish at sea, the discovery of the Windward Island, and so forth, up to its sinister consequences: the massacre of the Indians and the Negro slave trade. Here is a part of the *Chant II* narrating the throes of the long, long crossing.

> *Green goddesses, I hear you on this voyage, after the twenty-third night.*
> *More silent than the star, you have nailed those bearers of all stars, you.*
> *Arena of deaf sharks, the sea is the lists of the tournament. And two heroes rush in, and`their arms mow topmast and winds:*
> *From the land the Past lying in its warm night, And the Chaos! Courted dawn of all lands . . .*

But soon comes another voyage, and the poet relates the sufferings of his people aboard the slave ships:

> *One, taking advantage of the warder's inadvertence,*
> *turns his soul towards the sea and sinks. Another,*
> *whose body has no meadows, no river, no fire. One*
> *who dies in his dung, in the common fetidness. One*
> *who knows that his wife is chained up near by: he*
> *does not see her, but he hears her dying. And one*
> *who knows his wife is on another ship: he does not*
> *see her, but he hears her parting. And one with a*
> *broken rib, but they punish the sailor who does not*
> *spare the loot. And one they take to the deck once a*
> *week, so that his legs won't rot. One who can't walk,*
> *petrified in his death, but they make him dance on*
> *red-hot iron . . .*

Thus, from the sailing to this hell, the entire poem is intermingled with the movement of history, its unmerciful effects. In addition to the great beauty of his language, Edouard Glissant has renewed a literary genre which was scorned for too long: the epic poem. The events, related in chronicle form, are linked together in one gigantic fresco whose end describes the *commencement de l'unité* (the beginning of unity). For this voyage is not entirely negative; by reaching the East, by linking it to the West, Columbus' expedition achieved its mission: to circle the Earth and seal together all races in a common body: humanity. The ending of the poem decisively predicts the reconciliation of men on both sides of the Ocean, so that this nightmare may come to an end and this dark song to a fraternal light.

In this possible victory we cannot fail to see that of the word itself. What we find today in this French poetry is a seriousness, a gravity commensurate with the times we live in, and a greater honesty which will forbid our young artists from proclaiming their convictions too loudly. Having suffered not only the death of men, but the death of the most precious language, this new poetry is already indicating a path towards the future, towards a less chimerical, but more genuine and truer humanism. It can rightfully claim with Jacques Charpier that it will be *Le Paysage du Salut* (The Landscape of Salvation):

All night long heaven had been our king. The palm of the sun imprisoned the landscape. In the meadows of the city the girl fell asleep with her poisoned garments. I decided to live.

Another Tentative Start
BY JOSEPH P. BAUKE

"There is Goethe, and there are new starts," Hugo von Hofmannsthal once said, lamenting the fact that broken traditions have been the fate of German literature. But at the time of Hofmannsthal's death in 1929 no one could foresee that the most abrupt and complete break was yet to take place. A few years later, in the spring of 1933, the town-squares of Germany's major cities were lit by the blaze of burning books. In a ritual of barbaric solemnity, presided over in some places by professors of literature, the books of some twenty authors were consigned to the flames. In the years that followed the Nazi henchmen cleansed the libraries of the country and the minds of the people of all that was Jewish, Bolshevist, degenerate, or would otherwise hinder the total mobilization of the German race. Within months of the Nazi take-over the literary opposition ceased to exist, its spokesmen being either incarcerated or forbidden to write. Under the direction of a central agency, the *Reichsschrifttumskammer,* the Nordic renaissance held sway, and its atavistic glorification of blood and soil and martial prowess soon infected every printed page. Whatever was written and published to the applause of the Nazis, fiction and poetry as well as literary criticism, is now to us hopelessly provincial and without merit. To be sure, some respectable authors, such as Ernst Jünger, though hostile to the regime, continued to publish by withdrawing into an "inward emigration," as they called it, but their works were so far removed from the actualities of the day and so devoid of moral commitment that escapism would be a more proper term for this mental exile. They were able to wash their hands of the Nazis when the Third Reich went down, and they could often point to a record of personal integrity. Yet, having failed to be the conscience of the nation in its darkest era, they had forfeited any claim to moral authority and intellectual leadership. The new post-war generation of writers had to look elsewhere for guidance and inspiration.

With the fall of the Nazi regime, a way of life came to an end, and German history reached a zero point. Social patterns and political traditions were reshuffled along with millions of Germans who fled or were expelled from the eastern parts of the defunct *Reich*. Unbelief at the extent of Nazi atrocities, the difficulty of making a living in a ruined country with a stagnant economy, and a Wagnerian sense of final doom combined to produce the amnesia into which the Germans lapsed in the immediate post-war period. Armaggedon was over, and Germany had lost the battle. The apocalyptic despair of these years is admirably captured in Hermann Kasack's then widely discussed *The Town Beyond the River* (1947), a surrealistic novel about a modern necropolis where the dead pause on their way to metaphysical annihilation. As Oswald Spengler had done at the end of World War I, Kasack postulates that the Western World has liquidated itself and all its ideals; for "the material destruction merely confirms the bankruptcy of the mind." Germany at the end of her tether is the theme also of Thomas Mann's *Doktor Faustus* (1948), a much superior novel in which the nation's return to barbarism is brilliantly analyzed. The modern Faustus is condemned to hell again like his medieval prototype. Lessing and Goethe, in their versions of the legend, had saved the hero from damnation. Their message of *Humanität*, the ideal of Germany's greatest literary age, had lost its meaning in the chaotic post-war world when physical toughness was more important for survival than noble sentiments.

A note of faint hope was struck in the fiction of Elisabeth Langgässer, who because of her partly Jewish origins lived an agonized life in Hitler's Germany. Her symbolic novels, especially the daringly conceived *The Indelible Seal* (1947), are rooted in Catholic theology and evoke a Jansenist view of the depravity of human nature, which sees man redeemed in the end by divine grace alone. But the fortress of religious faith is of another age, and Langgässer impresses us more with her dazzling use of metaphor than her mystic belief in suffering as expiation. Next to her, Gertrud von Le Fort, Reinhold Schneider, and Werner Bergengruen must be mentioned as the chief representatives of the resurgence of Catholic writing. More conservative in form and subject matter than Langgässer, these authors remain popular with the older generation which finds in them the distant echoes of a well-ordered universe.

Traditional modes persisted, in the novel as well as in poetry, during the first years after the zero point. The stylistic revolutions of the early decades of the century, as radical as any in modern literature, were slow to influence the post-war writers, and the rich heritage of Georg Trakl, Else Lasker-Schüler, and Georg Heym in poetry, and of Franz Kafka, Robert Musil, and Alfred Döblin in prose, was integrated into literary life only from about 1950 on. The effect of these avant-garde writers on their contemporaries had been cut short by the Nazis, and they died as a generation without heirs. The young writers who had grown up under Hitler's dictatorship knew only what the Goebbels propaganda machinery had permitted them to know. Though their subject matter and their outlook on life were different, their style was that of the Nazi era. The bleak and tortured realism of the period right after the war stands in sharp contrast to the glorious decade that preceded the Nazis, and for a while it appeared as if the new freedom would not find the voices that could make use of it.

The first of the young writers to gain an audience was Wolfgang Borchert. His drama *The Man Outside* (1947) expressed the protest of the soldier who had fought Hitler's war to the end and then came home to find himself rejected by a fatherland that disavowed its past. Despite the rhetoric, the expressionistic gimmicks, and the self-pity, the play is a convincing document of the prevailing mood. The question of personal responsibility is not raised. The soldier is seen as the victim of evil leaders, an unworthy wife, and a god who has lost control over the universe. *The Man Outside,* though a deeply moving drama, illustrates the problematic character of nearly all German writing about the war. If it is patently impossible to describe Hitler's armies as bands of heroes, it is simply dishonest to skip over the moral issues altogether and to

depict the ordinary soldier as an individual suffering sense-
lessly in the Russian winter. The Germans were confronted
with the question of responsibility for the first time in Carl
Zuckmayer's *The Devil's General* (1946), a play about
a soldier fighting for a lost and corrupt cause. Zuckmayer,
famous since the twenties, is one of the few dramatists to
make a successful comeback, and the influence he continues to exert on young playwrights attests to the vitality
of his work. Akin to Zuckmayer's realism, but less explicit
in moral judgment, is Theodor Plivier's novel *Stalingrad*
(1946). The worst military disaster in German history is
faithfully reconstructed on the basis of interviews with survivors in Russian POW camps, and through the cool objectivity of the narrator, the book becomes a forceful
indictment of Hitlerism.

Zuckmayer and Plivier lived outside Germany after
1933, and their uncompromising attitude to the Nazis
comes as no surprise. But what of the young men who
fought the war on the German side? Borchert's emotional
outburst was caught up in the agony of the moment and
ends on a note of suicidal despair. He died on the day his
play was first performed, and his death, at the age of 27,
cast a luster on his work that its quality does not always
merit. Those who survived had to come to grips with their
experiences as soldiers and with post-war reality, and
the best of them succeeded admirably. The best, in this
connection, are not necessarily accomplished literary
craftsmen; their work springs from political conviction and
an outraged sense of justice. Hans Werner Richter, deeply
committed to *littérature engagée,* saw the zero point as the
great chance for a moral rejuvenation of the German
people. History, he argued, had proved the Germans
wrong, and therefore the trappings of the past must be
discarded to make room for new beginnings. To Richter,
it is truth, decency, and humane sobriety that one must
achieve. The subject and the intent alone are of consequence, not the form, and Richter despised as effete callig-
raphers those who continued to write "beautiful" prose
when truth was called for. His *The Vanquished* (1949)
and Heinrich Böll's *Where Art Thou, Adam?* (1951)
are examples of this quest for honesty and show the
psychological anguish of the individual soldier in the war.
The grand tradition of Prussian soldiering is found to have

been contaminated and perverted by the Nazis, and war itself is seen as the ultimate absurdity.

The prose of such good war novels is bare and sparse and has a reportorial flavor which implicitly condemns any kind of romanticism and pathos. These ex-soldiers aimed to be hard-hitting realists; and, convinced that a new faith in reality demanded a new style, they began to banish from their prose the artful conceits which the writers of the inward emigration so liberally employed. Proudly calling themselves *Kahlschläger,* no-nonsense lumberjacks, they cut down the forest of "poetic" verbiage and in their novels attempted to give the Germans exemplars of straightforward prose. Their task was not easy. The daily phlebotomy to which Goebbels and his minions had subjected the language had rendered it bloodless and hypocritical, and there were those, both in Germany and abroad, who wondered if the language of Hölderlin, Heine, and Nietzsche had not been polluted beyond redemption. Could words used at Dachau and Auschwitz ever again be the carriers of truth and sanity? A number of young men meeting as prisoners in the USA thought they could, and upon their return to Germany founded a journal *Der Ruf* (The Call) to popularize their vision of the new Germany. Their aims went beyond the reformation of language and literature. Aware that Germany had no vital democratic tradition, they advocated a complete overhaul of the country's social structure along leftist lines, vigorously opposed the restorative tendencies that grew ever stronger as the cold war intensified, and fought the influence of ex-Nazis now posing as pious democrats. Their program was too radical for many and their journal was eventually forbidden by the US military government. As a loose organization, "Group 47," with no statutes and no fixed dates for meetings, they continued to speak their mind on literary matters, but their influence on politics declined and now represents no more than a petulant protest. Group 47 has outlived its function as a reform movement, as Walter Jens, a leading member and the best of the younger critics, observed as early as 1953. Its annual literary prize, on the other hand, is one of Germany's most respected and is generally considered trend-setting. The historic achievement of the group is to have taught the new writers that the responsibility for language extends beyond esthetics—it is essentially a human commitment.

It is not without significance that a member of Group 47, Heinrich Böll, was the first new German voice to appeal to an international audience. He was almost immediately recognized as an atypical German author, one without a trace of romanticism and morbid introspection. In less than ten years his novels and short stories were translated into all major languages, including Russian, and Böll established himself as the spokesman of his generation. He succeeded better than any other writer in finding the language the German condition called for, a prose devoid of grandiloquence and fanciful artistry. More a disciple of Hemingway than of Thomas Mann, Böll started as a writer of short stories about everyday episodes in the lives of soldiers and ex-soldiers, who struggle vainly to maintain a modicum of human decency. They are not heroes in the traditional sense, and Böll does not even seem much concerned with their fate. War and the indolence of heart that makes it possible are the real heroes of his early work. Like Camus, whom he resembles in some respects, Böll is fundamentally a moralist, and a critique of society and its institutions runs through all his fiction. The hollow aspects of the German economic miracle have never been more mordantly satirized than in his story *Not Just at Christmas.* As the economic conditions improved, Böll was less inclined to write about the familial troubles of the lower middle class and forsook the tenements of the underlings to cast a critical eye at their betters. On the way up the social ladder, his style, quite fittingly, became more complicated, if less sure. With the slight proletarian smell of the cast went the supporting fabric from which Böll derived his strength as a narrator. In the ambitious novel *Billiards at Half-past Nine* (1959) Böll attempts to compress fifty years of German history and the lives of three generations of well-heeled burghers into the space of a few hours. A constant shifting of viewpoints and an awkward symbolism do not clarify the intricate web of the novel. Böll neatly divides his characters into those who partake of the Sacrament of the Lamb, and those who choose that of the Buffalo. Hitler is not once referred to by name—a dubious feat of artistic metamorphosis in a book about Germany in the first half of the century. Yet, under the garb of metaphor, the old Böll spirit of protest lives on. "Am I wrong," a German returning from exile inquires, "if I find the present Germans not less bad than those I left?" "You are probably not wrong," he is told. Böll's latest novel, *Views of a Clown* (1963), is set again in the milieu of his early work, without approaching its atmospheric density and critical cogency. It is mainly an attack on the social aspects of Catholicism.

In the years in which Böll rose to fame a large number of novels were published that dealt with the experiences of the immediate past, but most of these works remained emotional accounts of private sufferings and simplified large controversial issues to an alarming degree. Ernst von Salomon's *The Questionnaire* (1951) is a cynical auto-biography of a political opportunist in the years from the Weimar Republic to the end of the Hitler era. It is a major document of the mentality that made Hitler pos-sible. It gained notoriety because of the cheap mockery with which von Salomon lampoons the Allied de-Nazification program. While von Salomon makes no at-tempt at an apologia for the Germans, Bernt von Heiseler pleaded for them as innocent victims of *force majeure* in his long novel *The Reconciliation* (1953). Stefan Andres composed a massive trilogy about the origins and the functioning of a totalitarian system in *The Deluge* (1949 ff.). By relocating the phenomenon of the Third Reich in a fictional setting, Andres strove for an interpre-tation of Nazism from an objective point of view, *sine ira et studio.* The total result is an ambitious failure, for the supposedly detached view that analogous treatment was meant to provide taxed the imaginative powers of the author unduly. He was not able to maintain the stance of the impartial observer, nor could he hold the reader's interest. The inordinate length of the novel, a veritable deluge of words, illustrates the besetting temptation of German authors to inflate to a thousand pages a story that might well be told on half that number.

Most of the younger authors who have begun publishing since the end of the war write shorter novels and short stories. This preference is due less to the indigenous tradi-tion of the compact *novelle* than to the influence of Ameri-can, English, and French models that made their appear-ance in German translations as soon as the economic upswing gained momentum, from about 1950 on. Germany has always been the classic land of translations, perhaps because of its geographic position, and world literature, after all, is Goethe's concept. The enforced isolation of the thirties had created an artistic vacuum that was soon filled by enterprising publishers, and within a few years the contemporary literature of the Western world was available in German editions. About 600 American and 400 English authors are published annually in Western Germany alone, and the lively interest in foreign fiction shows no signs of abating. Under the impact of these imports from other cultures, the last vestiges of the provincialism cultivated by the Nazis have disappeared, and the literary climate of present-day Germany is not much different from that of other Western countries.

In addition to authors from abroad, the modern masters of German prose, suppressed as degenerate by the Nazis, were rediscovered. Of these past masters, Alfred Döblin and Hans Henny Jahnn were still alive and produced two of their most important works after the war. Döblin's *Hamlet, or The Long Night Comes to an End* (1957) is a vigorous novel about a young Englishman who returns home from World War II and identifies himself with Hamlet in his quest for the ultimate meaning of life. Despite religious suggestions, elaborate symbolism, and psychoanalytic overtones, *Hamlet* is an eminently readable novel, worthy of the company of the author's famed *Berlin-Alexanderplatz* (1930), a landmark in German fiction. Like Döblin, Hans Henny Jahnn was an expressionist, one of the rebels who spelled out the protest of German literature in our century. His early dramas, full of sodomy, pederasty, and necrophilism, are dark-minded visions of anarchic life that shocked Berlin audiences and haunted Bert Brecht for years. The savagery of his assault and the unorthodox erotic entanglements of his characters earned him the title of "Prophet of Lechery." His novel *Perrudja* (1929), despite its gigantic size, is a brilliant tour de force of expressionist writing, but his major work as a novelist is *River without Banks* (1949 ff.) a trilogy running to 2200 pages. *River without Banks* is the account an aging composer, Anias Horn, gives of his life, especially of his homosexual involvement with a young sailor who has murdered Horn's fiancée. Reminiscent of Thomas Mann in its preoccupation with the sources of artistic creativity, the novel attempts to assess the value of art in an absurd and brutal universe. Dionysian celebrations of life alternate with jeremiads on the relentless flow of time from which there is no escape, save perhaps in art. Following the patterns of archaic myths, the past and the present, the dead and the quick, are conjured up in a *danse macabre* that qualifies Jahnn as one of the supreme masters of the Gothic style. His view of life might well be summed up in the words of the heroine of his drama *Medea:* "You may kill me, if only you love me." His characters go down unappeased.

Jahnn, if anyone, is the most radical of the many German experimental writers in this century; thus, he has had little popular appeal. He has admirers among the younger authors, but his typically German fascination with general ideas and concepts, such as Life and Death, puts him outside the mainstream of post-war developments. The young novelists have grown more modest in their claims, if not their practices, and one notices a deliberate avoidance of the pose of the all-seeing, all-knowing author. The time-honored method of realism, with its attempt at objective description of situation and environment and its stress on psychological penetration of character, has been replaced by a variety of narrative forms designed to capture the ambiguity and tentativeness of human experience. The grotesque, the interior monologue, surrealistic and cinematographic devices, an odd angle of observation, or a combination of these modes, make reading modern German novels often a vexing and sometimes a tiresome affair. Moreover, the art of story-telling itself, plot construction, and a decent respect for the reader, are often disparaged as naïve and antiquated, and rejected in favor of a more cerebral approach better suited to convey the quality of multidimensional reality. As a consequence, the intellectual level of a novel may be extremely high, while its readability comes close to that of an abstruse treatise. A case in point is Uwe Johnson's *Speculations about Jacob* (1959), a sensitive novel about the relations of East and West Germany, and by implication, of East and West. It is a significant theme, and one of paramount importance to many Germans; but Johnson's ratiocinative distensions make Jacob's life and death appear vapid. Viewing the problems of Jacob, the man between East and West, as a philosopher rather than as a political writer, Johnson escapes the charge of creating propaganda for either side, at the risk of dissolving the issue in a bewildering array of possibilities. More mannered even than *Speculations about Jacob* is Johnson's second novel, *The Third Book about Achim* (1961). Its original title "description of a description" accurately summarizes the author's intention. The third book is the biography of an East German sports ace, to be written by a West German journalist at the request of an East German publisher. The account, however, is never finished, because the truth about Achim cannot be ascertained from the welter of conflicting opinions and rumors. Instead of a biography, we get the materials for one and the circumstances under which research for it was carried on. The box-in-a-box treatment extends to the characters, reducing them to pawns in an academic game. What keeps Johnson's novels from being refined into depictions of pure mental states is a sustained emphasis on objects. In the manner of the "new wave" French writers the meandering flow of conjecture and meditation is frequently interrupted by minute descriptions of everyday gadgets, bicycles, doorbells, and the nail in the wall. This device rivets the narrative to reality, and mirrors the labyrinthine confusion facing the protagonists. They are caught in the trap of life, much as their author is in that of his style.

Equally experimental as those of Johnson are the novels and stories of Arno Schmidt, who began by denouncing Goethe's prose as a viscous mush and proceeded to smash grammar and syntax of the German language. He is committed to the idea that modern life is an absurd succession of isolated facts and occurrences and that the individual is nothing but a conglomeration of habits and patterns. The disjointed elements of language are recombined arbitrarily to express this attitude in a series of loosely connected snapshots, usually in a utopian setting. If one shares his view of life, propounded by three of four wretched characters thrown together in a banal constellation, one might well enjoy the wit and the delightfully macabre humor that informs his work; however, the author's self-congratulations upon his feats of destruction put one on one's guard and call the seriousness of the assault into question. Most of Schmidt's hyper-intelligent fireworks burn up without illuminating anything (*Leviathan,* 1949; *Roses and Leek,* 1959; *Mare Crisium,* 1960).

Less talked about but more widely read are a number of novelists who have put to use the gains won by the experiments of others, without themselves being innovators. They are more concerned with social criticism than philosophical problems and have given some of the best accounts of present-day Germany. However, none of them is a straightforward realist, and their descriptions are often closer to satire and caricature than to the social realism preached and practiced in Communist East Germany, where literature has its definite place in the political economy. (By Western standards, most East German fiction is unreadable, and very little of it is ever published this side of the Iron Curtain.) Of West German novelists dealing with contemporary life, Wolfgang Koeppen, Gerd Gaiser, Alfred Andersch, and Heinz von Cramer are the most representative. Koeppen's *Pigeons in the Grass* (1951) presents a hectic panorama of US occupied Munich, the capital of the Nazi movement that has come to quick terms with democracy. A sinister and hell-bent cast of former Nazi bigwigs and their offspring populate Koeppen's second novel, *Death in Rome* (1954), which aroused much critical antagonism because of its uncompromising stand against some dangerous side effects of Germany's recovery. Gaiser's chief novel is *The Final Ball* (1958), an anatomy of a prosperous small town. Gaiser is a traditionalist who defends the values of a romanticized Germany in an age of technical progress and mass civilization.

The works of Andersch and von Cramer show a continuous wrestling with the immediate past. Andersch, a former Communist functionary, wrote a brilliant novel about freedom and commitment in a totalitarian society (*Zanzibar,* 1957), and analyzed, in *The Redhead* (1960), the motives of an upperclass woman who leaves West Germany and finds refuge among Italian proletarians. Technically imperfect, but morally compelling, is von Cramer's *A Figure of Art* (1958), the biography of an opportunistic writer who prostitutes his talents through forty years of German history. With this violent attack on certain features of the German national character, or at least of the German intellectual, von Cramer has recaptured for German prose some of the satirical fervor with which Heinrich Mann a generation before indicted his Wilhelminian contemporaries.

The most gifted novelist now writing is Günter Grass. His *The Tin Drum* (1959) hit its audience with the vehemence of a natural force and became a best seller in several languages. It is the picaresque autobiography of a lunatic dwarf who evokes the first thirty years of his life by beating a magic drum. Grotesque, blasphemous, and infinitely rich in narrative detail, the novel re-creates the atmosphere of the Third Reich in scenes and episodes of Dickensian vigor. By skillfully maintaining the stance of the infantile chronicler who knows neither guilt nor shame, Grass is able to view the years of the holocaust with an unflinching eye. *The Tin Drum* is free of the sentimentalities and the stilted allegorizing that mar too much of German fiction, and Grass even pulls off what, for obvious reasons, is impossibly difficult for most German writers— believable portraits of Jews. The Priapean gnome may carry a burden of symbolic meanings on his misshapen back; he is, above all, an imaginative creation that defies all academic theories about the imminent demise of the novel. What is lacking in the sprawling work is a sense of direction, intellectual or ethical, and the impression one carries away is that of absolute anarchy. Is it the anarchy that precedes a new order? Little Oscar, confined to bedlam, at least holds on to life.

Cat and Mouse (1961), Grass's second novel, is similar to the first in mood and setting and has the added virtue of brevity. With a few bold strokes, applied at the crazy angle that is his trademark, Grass takes us back to the Danzig of the war years, celebrating again a hero who retires to the citadel of his infancy. More overtly symbolic, *Cat and Mouse* is written with a showy elegance reminiscent of Thomas Mann's *Felix Krull*. Grass's new major novel, *Dog Years* (1963), deals with the final years of Hitler's power by tracing the fate of his missing dog. It is more episodic and structurally less cohesive than his other books, but just as provocative, and it corroborates on every page the fact that the author has a signature uniquely his own. The absurdities of war, mock philosophy, and a ferocious satire on the organizational genius of the Germans are fused into a compelling narrative. As a work of art, *Dog Years* lacks unity; as an account of war it is masterly. No one can tell what Grass's next book will be like, but there can be no doubt that there is more hope for German fiction in his violence and anarchy than in the chilly lucubrations of Uwe Johnson.

Like Grass, the Swiss Max Frisch has an international audience. In Europe, he is known primarily as a playwright; in England and the USA, as a novelist. An architect by profession, Frisch is a passionate individualist whose insistence on moral integrity and social commitment has existentialist overtones. His plays and novels are openly didactic in the manner of Brecht, except that Frisch has no ideological ties. On the contrary, he fights easy convictions and inflexible beliefs as enemies of human progress and professes no cause other than honesty and courage. Human dignity for him implies a willingness to discard all support from churches or any party doctrine, and presupposes a readiness to begin anew in the face of absurdity. Stiller, the hero of the novel *I'm Not Stiller* (1954), gives up his life in his home country, goes abroad, and finally returns under an alias. To his friends and the Swiss officials he is the man who departed, but he regards himself as a new man who has incorporated his past into his new existence. Quite properly, therefore, he may claim that he is not Stiller. *Homo Faber* (1957) treats the same problem of self-identification in inverted form by analyzing the attempt of its hero to assume the role of someone else.

Frisch's didacticism is even more outspoken in his plays. Indebted to Brecht for the technique of alienation, Frisch creates symbolic characters who move about on the stage like the dancers in a ballet and have as little individuality as the personages of a medieval morality play. The dangers of abstraction are not always avoided in these stylized plays that shun every illusion of reality and carefully avoid references to the contemporary scene. *Andorra* (1961), for example, a play about anti-semitism, does not take place in Andorra, or any similar locality, but is intended as a model that has no resemblance whatever to any existing country. The stylization of the play, together with its unabashed preaching, robs the lesson of much of its power. *Biedermann and the Arsonists* (1958) is a political allegory about the rise of Nazism and a general indictment of people who invite disaster through carelessness and then blame the catastrophe on fate. "Stupidity," the chorus sums up, "otherwise known as Destiny."

Friedrich Dürrenmatt, also a Swiss, is a prolific writer of dramas, detective novels, radio plays, and movie scripts. All his work centers on the questions of human guilt, justice, and punishment. A master of stagecraft, Dürrenmatt combines a variety of theatrical techniques in his macabre comedies that always end in tragedy or despair. The ethical impulse at the heart of his imagination gives his plays a moral force that sometimes rivals Brecht. Apocalyptic visions, a doomsday mood, gallows humor, and an unbridled *joie de vivre* form the atmospheric background for his quasi-metaphysical trials. In *The Visit* (1956), perhaps his best play, a rich old lady returns to the town of her youth, ready to buy the justice that was denied her as a young woman. In the course of her stay she exposes the hypocrisy and the greed of the town and provokes her former lover to the moral greatness of an expiatory death. *Romulus the Great* (1957), a play in Roman garb, is an effective attack on those who would save the West at the cost of betraying its ideals and accomplishments. It is also a hilarious evocation of a moribund civilization living out its empty days before the invaders arrive.

In Germany itself, no playwright has emerged as the leading contender for the vacancies left by Bertolt Brecht and Gerhart Hauptmann. Theatrical life flourishes in splendid new playhouses, equipped with the most modern stage apparatus, and many new plays have their premières every year. Yet few plays survive the season, and many sink into oblivion on opening night. There are imitations of Sartre, clever pieces in the manner of Ionesco and Adamov, and occasionally a realistic play in the vein of good US television shows. Leopold Ahlsen's *Philemon and Baucis* (1956) dramatizes the fate of an old Greek couple who, in the closing days of the war, are put to death for their acts of humanity. Though his *The Deputy* evokes a powerful and pertinent theatrical experience, Rolf Hochhuth's success comes more from his theme, that Pope Pius XII failed to condemn the extermination of the Jews, than his dramatic skill. In *The Beginning of the Age of India* (1955) the East German playwright Peter Hacks, a disciple of Brecht, introduces Columbus not only as the discoverer of a continent, but also as the herald of a new era in human history. Together with the progress of science, however, economic exploitation of the masses increases, and mankind is not any better off than before. Another promising East German dramatist, Heiner Müller, has developed Brecht's dialectics in directions independent of his master. The ideological control exerted by the government seriously interferes with his work, and his best play, *The Repatriation or Innovations in the Country* (1962) has never been performed. In East and West Germany, the ineffectualness of contemporary German drama is obvious. It may take some time before the German theatre again reaches its traditionally high level.

If the situation of the drama is depressing, lyric poetry enjoys a vogue that began right after the war and has not abated since. In poetry experiences found expression that proved overwhelming for the drama and frequently also for the novel. In comparison with other Western countries, the poetry published in the late forties is traditional in form and follows the mainstream of the German lyric, the confessional poem that dates back to Goethe. The anthologies of these post-war years, with their sonnets, careful rhymes, and traditional images, seem curiously dated now, despite their concern with the horrors of war. Old modes persisted until the fifties, when translations of foreign poets began to appear with increasing frequency. Authors as disparate as Dylan Thomas and T. S. Eliot were a revelation for the young poets, and soon a wave of experimental verse set in that also drew on the innovations of the native expressionists. Gottfried Benn, a lone survivor of the expressionist generation of Trakl, Lasker-Schüler, and Lichtenstein, became the rallying point of the young. It was not the pathos and the defiant gestures of the expressionists that attracted the new readers, but their linguistic experiments and their concern with form. Benn had been one of the first to use the language of medicine and the jargon of the newspapers for poetic effect. In his verse, Beauty and Art triumph as ultimate realities over man's insoluble dilemma between matter and mind.

Coupled with this praise of Art is a Nietzschean contempt for civilization and its taming effect on instinct. For a time, Benn flirted with the Nazis, only to discover that his cerebral barbarism had little to do with the uplifting spirit that the Third Reich expected of its artists. Nevertheless, his anti-humanism, his Spenglerian notions about Western Culture, and his hatred of democracy are constants in his work, and one may well wonder if the tradition of cultural despair has not been given a new lease on life in his fascinating verse. The significance of his artistic achievement, on the other hand, is beyond dispute.

Next to Benn, the nature poetry of Oskar Loerke and Wilhelm Lehmann must be mentioned as a source of inspiration for a whole group of younger poets. In their poetry, nature is minutely observed and interpreted in the framework of ancient myths. Past civilizations, Homeric heroes, Christian symbols, and contemporary experiences are described in an evocative language that strives to conjure up, through incantation, an eternal presence. The past is not seen as a model for the present, but as a substance of which we still partake. In the lines of such poets as Karl Krolow and Heinz Piontek the phenomena of nature are endowed with symbolic significance and become manifestations of hidden truths. The speculative, introspective quality of this verse, together with its often recondite allusions, renders it quite inaccessible to the uninitiated. Despite the exact descriptions, this poetry is essentially mystical and, at its best, as mysterious and tantalizing as inscriptions in undeciphered alphabets. It is historically significant that this kind of nature poetry should be written in a completely industrialized society. Far from being the naive nature worshippers of the Romantic era, these poets are as familiar with modern technology as they are with Jung's archetypes and Heidegger's nothingness. Their vision of nature is constantly threatened by *Angst*. In a bucolic setting of apparent tranquillity, Krolow suddenly discovers "the gap in the air, the emptiness that no one invented, / the accident that will dissolve the wall." The chill of outer space is as real as the consolations of nature.

Ingeborg Bachmann, Peter Huchel, and Paul Celan are the most prominent of contemporary poets. Bachmann, firmly rooted in the German tradition, combines a high intellectuality (she wrote a Ph.D. dissertation on Heidegger) with an apparently natural diction and thus achieves a realistic tone that does not have its equal in German poetry. Repercussions of cosmic catastrophes and private sorrows give her poems a haunting quality that is somewhere midway between the confessional mood of the romantics and the terseness of a text by Ludwig Wittgenstein. "The Unspeakable, softly spoken, walks the Land," we read in one of her best poems. Huchel's verse is less personal and not so intellectual, and shows a sense of commitment to society that is rarely found in lyric poetry. This is all the more remarkable since Huchel lives in East Germany where such candor is not always welcome.

Paul Celan, finally, is a Jew who was born in Rumania, lives in Paris, and writes in German. Surrealistic techniques, verbal paradoxes, and an absolute command of the poetic resources of language itself give his poems a highly personal quality that cannot be easily appreciated. His work is hermetic also in the sense that the reader in order to understand one poem, should be familiar with all of them. His best poem, however, needs no elaborate commentary and no philological exegesis. It is *The Death Fugue* (1952), a surrealist treatment of the mass murder in Hitler's concentration camps, a subject that would seem to defy language and strangle the imagination. In the form of a fugue, Celan combines isolated images in a recurring pattern, without regard for syntax and textual coherence, and creates a picture of universal death that is as horrifying as it is artistically perfect. It is surely the best German poem of post-war years.

BIBLIOGRAPHY

Bithell, Jethro. *Modern German Literature* (London, 1959).

Boeschenstein, D. "Trends and Symbols in Contemporary German Fiction," *University of Toronto Quarterly* (1956).

Exner, Richard. "German Poetry, 1950–1960: An Estimate," *Books Abroad,* 36 (1962).

Garten, H. F. *Modern German Drama* (New York, 1959).

Holthusen, H. E. "Crossing the Zero Point," *International Literary Annual* No. 3 (London, 1961).

—————. "German Lyric Poetry since 1945," *Poetry* (1956).

Klarmann, Adolf D. "Dürrenmatt and the Tragic Sense of Comedy," *Tulane Drama Review,* 4 (1960).

Lyon, James K. "The Poetry of Paul Celan," *Germanic Review* (January, 1964).

Plant, R. "The World of Heinrich Böll," *German Quarterly* (1960).

Waidson, H. M. *The Modern German Novel* (New York, 1959).

—————. "Dürrenmatt: The Comedy of Despair," *Nation,* 190 (1960).

Wellwarth, George E. "Dürrenmatt and Frisch: Two Views of Drama," *Tulane Drama Review* (Spring, 1962).

Wilson, Colin. "Dürrenmatt: Heir of the Existential Tradition," *London Magazine* (June, 1961).

Ziolkowski, Theodore. "Böll: Conscience and Craft," *Books Abroad,* 34 (1960).

—————. "Frisch: Moralist without a Moral," *Yale French Studies,* No. 29 (1962).

Italian Novels of the Fifties
BY SERGIO PACIFICI

It is always difficult for a critic of contemporary letters to attempt to draw an accurate assessment of a literary season just past. The risks incurred are many (they range from the possibility of errors of judgment to faulty evaluations of trends and currents), and the corresponding rewards are notoriously few. Moving in a virgin territory, without the aid of a historical perspective, the critic relies exclusively upon his personal taste and intuition to formulate a first, approximate synthesis of literary works produced within a recent period. These difficulties, under which all militant critics normally operate, are compounded in the present case by the relatively uniform character of the Italian literary landscape. In such a landscape there are no high peaks, scattered here and there, against which other works may be measured or with which they may be compared, if solely to pinpoint their uniqueness of meaning. In other words, while in the past the critic could confidently rely on Manzoni, Verga, D'Annunzio, and Pirandello as firm points of reference and as unanimously accepted landmarks, today, on the other hand, few would be ready to agree that even the most intelligent and prolific novelists (Moravia, Vittorini, Pratolini) possess the stature of a true *maestro,* whose work has traced new paths in the art of fiction, whose "presence" is constantly felt by other writers, and whose example is frequently emulated. To put the situation with a metaphor, we might compare present-day Italian fiction to a vast, ever-growing jungle, where it has become problematical to distinguish even the larger trees from the rest of the vegetation. It is precisely such a situation that makes a thorough discussion of the many interesting books that have appeared in Italy over the past decade rather futile. Their number, in fact, is so imposing that only by making a strict selection can one avoid the danger of turning these pages into an endless, monotonous catalogue of names, titles, and dates, whose only effect would be to demonstrate the fertility of the Italian imagination. The events, authors, and books mentioned in this essay will therefore be few: it is hoped, however, that they will give the reader at least a sense of the various phases undergone by recent Italian fiction and will persuade the reader that it is likely that the future historian of literature may regard the past decade as a productive as well as a critical phase of fiction writing in Italy.

Let us proceed through such uniform land by first mentioning some of the more important literary events of the past few years. The period under consideration begins with the death of Cesare Pavese who, in the summer of 1950, took his own life in a Turin hotel room. The sudden disappearance of a brilliant novelist who had rapidly emerged as one of the intellectual leaders of postwar Italy coincided with the rapid decline of prestige and influence of American fiction in Italy, already prophesied by Pavese himself some years before his death. From the early thirties through the better part of the forties, thanks to the brilliant translations and the perceptive critical comments of Pavese, Elio Vittorini, and a handful of Americanists, Italian readers had kept touch with a vigorous literature produced in a far-away land. For two decades the American example was assiduously studied, widely praised, and occasionally imitated, especially by those who had grown disillusioned with their own culture, or had grown weary over the years of the rhetoric and mediocrity of Fascist products. Reading the American authors became then equivalent to committing an act of defiance against the dictates of constituted authorities, and to an expression of faith in a literature that, however brutal and pessimistic, dared to believe in the idea that one of the basic functions of Art is to criticize both the nature and the order of our world. Finally, the great experience of reading the American writers was probably instrumental in producing a renewed awareness in Italy that it is the artist's duty to confront the reality of his history, his traditions, and his people with honesty and courage. Pavese's death, too, marked the beginning of a severe crisis that would gradually involve politicians and intellectuals alike, without regard to their ideological orientation. The dilemma (that has metamorphosed into an impasse) facing the generation born at the end of the First World War and matured during the Fascist years forms the subject of a compelling and complex recent novel by a former Communist, Fabrizio Onofri, published with the title *Roma 31 dicembre* (Rome, December 31). The book examines, with rare intensity, the tragedy of a society that finds itself periodically rejecting certain values to accept others necessitated by political changes. The climax of the novel is reached when the hero of the book (a successful playwright who symbolizes the disillusioned Italian intellectual) realizes that his gravest failure consists in his not having given to his daughter anything in which she can truly believe, that is to say, in his having been unable to set an example of moral and artistic integrity. The concern with such Hamletian questions is, however, the exception rather than the rule in present-day Italian fiction. The majority of Italian novelists have found their richest source of inspiration in the "real" situations of a country awakened, by the shock of defeat, to a pathetic social backwardness akin to the Middle Ages. Indeed, one of the distinguishing traits of postwar Italian writing has been an almost exaggerated eagerness to demonstrate to the world that the lesson of Fascism and of the humiliating tyranny it promulgated for over two decades has not failed to leave its indelible mark on the Italian sensibility. To deal with the reality of the new times has become, from the fall of Fascism onwards, a kind of solemn obligation every writer, big or small, has undertaken to discharge. The label ingeniously affixed to the new literature (and the new cinema) was that of "neorealism," a term that signified an almost violent *prise de position* (on the part of the younger writers in particular) with respect to those aspects of life many a novelist had, under Fascist pressure, conveniently or willingly ignored. The birth of a radically realistic literature was both a necessary and inevitable expression of a rejection of a certain literary heritage (that of the *Ronda,* too concerned with stylistic refinements, and of Hermeticism, incapable of reaching the general reader with its difficult modes of expression composed in ivory towers) as well as a condemnation of a style of life that had betrayed even the most modest expectations of dignity and freedom. Moreover, as the critic Carlo Bo once remarked, "it was necessary to react to recent past literature, to those that had been its qualities of meditation and decantation. It was necessary, in short, to oppose [real] life to our remembrance if it; action to meditation; and immediate and frequently careless writing to a calculated style, to artistic effort. In other words, [it was imperative] to contrapose a new image of creative writing to an old, partially tired and abused image that had dominated the period between the two [world] wars."

It was inevitable, therefore, that the themes of the new books should be the experience of the war and of the underground, the persecutions endured during Mussolini's dictatorship or in the Nazi jails, the chaos, the destruction and the desolation brought about by a war nobody had really wanted but which Italians had been compelled to fight. It is unlikely that such works as Carlo Levi's *Cristo si è fermato a Eboli* (*Christ Stopped at Eboli*, 1945), Giuseppe Berto's *Il cielo è rosso* (*The Sky Is Red*, 1947), Italo Calvino's *Il sentiero del nido dei ragni* (*The Path to the Nest of Spiders*, 1947), Oreste Del Buono's *La parte difficile* (The Difficult Role, 1947), Guglielmo Petroni's *Il mondo è una prigione* (The World Is A Prison, 1949), Carlo Cassola's *Fausto e Anna* (*Fausto and Anna*, 1952), Beppe Fenoglio's *I ventitrè giorni della città di Alba* (The Twenty-three Days of the City of Alba, 1952), and Natalia Ginzburg's *Tutti i nostri ieri* (*Dead Yesterdays*, 1952) will soon be forgotten. The polemical intention of these and other novels, short stories, and biographical essays was to review old postures so as to arrive at a just indictment of a way of life drenched with false promises, of problems left unsolved, of arrogant and empty claims. Even when depicting the vicissitudes of a nation defeated and ruined, most Italian writers expressed a measure of hope in the possibility that society would in the future work together toward a common goal of peace, justice, and work based upon brotherhood and human solidarity. The high esteem which contemporary Italian writing has been enjoying found a symbolic acknowledgment in the award, in 1959, of the Nobel Prize for Literature (the first to be given to an Italian in over twenty years) to the poet Salvatore

Quasimodo who had impregnated his work with an extraordinary amount of social content.

It is in the light of the apparently undiminished wave of success scored by neorealism that the recent publication of the first complete translation into Italian of James Joyce's *Ulysses* assumes special relevance, perhaps as an implicit indication of a growing restlessness with the unsatisfactory results of "engaged" fiction, and with what many regard as a definitely "monotonous" type of writing. The translation, admirably performed by an obscure teacher by the name of Giulio de Angelis, has at last made available a work that for the past decades had been frequently mentioned in literary discussions. It remains to be seen what effect, if any, it will have in encouraging the younger writers to seek fresh narrative techniques. The spate of effective books produced in Italy of late has dramatically underscored the extreme reticence novelists there display toward the business of rejuvenating the novel form. Overwhelmed by an unprecedented commercial success (it is no longer rare for a "good" novel to reach sales figures ranging from from fifty to one hundred and more thousand copies), they have begun to equate success with artistic excellence. Few Italian critics have boldly expressed radical opinions on this score. Renato Barilli, in a polemical essay published in *Il Verri* (No. 1, 1960) with the title "Cahier de doléance" has put his finger on what, by all standards, would seem to be one of the more negative aspects of Italian literary life:

[In Italy] there is no cultural room for swift, revolutionary movements; the texture of notions appears far swifter, unsuited to bending and to exceptions. And since it is true that a writer is partially conditioned by the milieu in which he finds himself acting, it follows that, being forced to act in Italy, he cannot experiment with techniques that are strikingly, impudently subversive, revolutionary, "avantgards."

Indeed, the only noteworthy innovation brought to the art of fiction in recent times has been the weaving of certain local dialects into the fabric of traditional narrative language, created by Manzoni [and realized in his *I Promessi sposi* (*The Betrothed*)] and handed down with considerable care from one generation to the next. Such an experiment [experiment may be its most suitable description, as it has not even remotely done to language what Verga was able to do in his *I Malavoglia* (*The House by the Medlar Tree*)] has been tried by many, but successfully brought off by two or three writers, chiefly Carlo Emilio Gadda [*Quer pasticciaccio brutto de via Merulana* (That Ugly Mess in Via Merulana)] and Pier Paolo Pasolini [*Ragazzi di vita, Una vita violenta* (Street Boys, A Violent Life)]. The majority of novelists, however, seldom question the validity of the traditional structures of fiction and are quite satisfied with holding their art up to reality, as a kind of lucid mirror where their readers may, willy nilly, recognize themselves or their problems. Perhaps at no other time than now has literature (and the cinema) reflected so faithfully the Italian reality. Perhaps the place of honor of neorealistic fiction is occupied by the so-called "southern school" which comprises such talented and diverse writers as Carlo Bernari, Domenico Rea, Michele Prisco, Mario Pomilio, Giuseppe Marotta, Fortunato Seminara, Luigi Incoronato, Saverio Strati as well as the late Corrado Alvaro, Vitaliano Brancati, and Francesco Jovine. Their novels usually focus on the poverty, hopelessness, and wretchedness of life in the *Mezzogiorno*, or on certain "flaws" typical of the southern temperament. Despite some notable exceptions, the bulk of fiction produced by southern writers has in the past been one-dimensional, betraying an excessive preoccupation with a photographic-documentary technique, too insistent on treating those aspects of life that may be called, *tout court*, folkloristic. The finest books about the South have not been works of fiction but essays and autobiographies, authored by Carlo Levi, Danilo Dolci, Giovanni Russo, Dante Troisi and others—all of whom have justly perceived that it is preferable to study the nature and origins of the present social structure in the South than to "narrate" a pathetic and deplorable facet of Italian reality. There are, to be sure, some writers whose work strives to achieve recognition of and insight into southern life: Leonardo Sciascia, for example, deserves to be singled out for his seriousness of purpose and depth of observation. His *Le parrocchie di Regalpetra* (The Parishes at Regalpetra) is a first-class report on the social, economic, and political deficiencies of life in the South; likewise his fiction [*Gli zii di Sicilia* (The Uncles from Sicily) and the recent *Il giorno della civetta* (*Mafia Vendetta*)] succeeds in presenting believable stories replete with an objective criticism of present conditions. His characters, to be sure, endure (and endure they must, true, repressed citizens that they are) their reality but manage to find in their experiences something that enlightens them, making them more aware of their condition and thus better able to cope with life, more prepared to ready themselves for a day of change that is sure to come.

The southern school (whose antecedents are Verga, Capuana, Deledda, and De Roberto) has not been the only group to take cognizance of special problems that are typical of certain regions: in recent years there has been a notable tendency to cover the spectrum of Italian society. As a consequence, fiction has succeeded in informing, if not always in illuminating, the world about such varied topics as the life of the Roman and southern sub-proletariat, of the Milanese industrial society (whose degradation and corruption has been dramatized in a facile manner by Uberto Paolo Quintavalle, whose *Tutti compromessi* [Everyone Is Involved] was 1961's *succès de scandale),* and even the life of the publishing world, whose foibles and ambitious "big projects" have been satirized in Luciano Bianciardi's novel *L'integrazione.* Another nucleus of novelists (Giovanni Testori, Luigi Daví, Giancarlo Buzzi, and Ottiero Ottieri, among them) have turned to dealing with those problems being confronted by their country during a period of increasingly faster industrialization. Although only certain parts of Italy (notably, the northern regions of Piedmont and Lombardy) are being exposed to such industrialization (and Americanization) of life, the review *Il Menabò* (edited by Elio Vittorini and Italo Calvino) deemed the question sufficiently vital to devote to it its fourth issue (1961) titled "Industry and Literature." A particularly good specimen of this tendency is Ottieri's *Donnarumma all'assalto (The Men at the Gate),* a remarkably sensitive novel that should be read in conjunction with Ottieri's essay "Industrial Notebook" (the feature piece of *Il Menabò* cited above). *Donnarumma all'assalto* is written in diary form by an industrial psychologist working in a model typewriter factory located in

the Mezzogiorno. The narrator-hero is in charge of screen-
ing employment applications and administering intelligence
and aptitude tests. From the very beginning of the tale,
the factory assumes the symbol of a terrestrial paradise
and, as Ottieri comments in his essay, "here one yearns
to work in a factory as much as to enter paradise. Here
the factory appears as a place of delights when compared
with the unemployment or the pseudo-jobs offered by the
region. Here the factory is dignity, honor, well-being. . ."
Thus, the protagonist is faced by a multitude of people,
of varying capacity and skills, waiting patiently at the
factory gates for the day when their patience will be re-
warded and they will be given a job that will no doubt put
an end to their precarious existence. Some (quite few) will
finally be called up to join the other workers: the majority
of the applicants, however, will never experience the profound happiness of knowing the meaning of assured and
continued earnings, working in pleasant surroundings. "The
world of the factory is a closed world. One does not easily
enter it or come out of it . . . The worker, the employee,
the manager, are silent. The writer, the movie director,
the sociologist are either outsiders and therefore do not
know [anything about it]; or, by chance, they enter it, and
then they say nothing more." Despite these obstacles,
Ottieri has been able to register, in his book, what Gianni
Scalia calls "the reality of working and the alienation from
it."

The canvas of Italian reality, in short, has seldom been
as vast as in the postwar period; seldom before has the
writer in Italy touched upon so many different aspects of
life in these difficult times. A few themes, however, remain too hot to handle for the cautious (and conformist)
novelist in Italy. The surface of such questions as the corruption in the government, or the dubious politics of the
Church, or the slovenliness of the bureaucratic machinery
of the state, or the abuses of the ruling class has barely
been scratched. I suppose this is what impelled the anonymous author of a survey published in the *Times Literary
Supplement* (October 13, 1961, "Italy after the Liberation:
Reality and Neorealism") to write:

This is the dilemma for the observer of the Italian
scene and fundamentally it is the weakness which

could close the era of neorealism. Sometimes it seems that a conspiracy of silence exists, or, better, a seeking refuge in rhetoric or in ideologies with the purpose of obscuring the fresco of Italian life as he senses it to be, and knows it to be from the few attempts at assessing things as they are.

Variety of content, diversity of inspiration, "hunger for reality," and conformity of points of view and of technique would appear to be the outstanding features of present-day Italian writing. A far more dangerous tendency (one that could pose grave consequences to creative writing) is represented by an increasing degree to which art has been turned into political tract. In a nation where many aspects of life have either been regulated, or modified, or shaped for and by political consideration, it is a telling sign of the times that the arts in general and literature in particular should be infused by an increasingly larger, and more overt, political message. How to make fiction politically and intellectually satisfying without degenerating art into propaganda is something all too seldom realized by the Italian genius. By the same token, in an era of intense ideological struggle it is becoming difficult to find many critics willing to evaluate a literary work dispassionately and serenely: witness the condemnation incurred by Giuseppe di Lampedusa's masterful novel, *Il gattopardo (The Leopard)*, rejected by leftist critics as being a reactionary novel that espoused conservative, or Fascist viewpoints. Writers themselves are not always strong enough to resist the trend: a pertinent example is provided by the noted novelist Alberto Moravia. The outspoken author of *Gli indifferenti (The Time of Indifference),* a self-declared anti-Communist who has espoused Marxism, has chosen to discuss Manzoni's *The Betrothed* from a vantage point that enabled him to speak "of Catholic realism, or better still of social realism, that is to say, of the art of propaganda as it is understood in modern times."

I have mentioned Moravia at this point because no general discussion of the state of Italian fiction can afford to ignore him. To speak of his literary output (which is considerable) signifies to take cognizance of a writer who, in the best and rare moments of creativity, has succeeded in synthesizing acutely and accurately certain malaises typical of our century. A glance at the books he has authored (few of which have fulfilled the expectation of his admirers) discloses an admirable continuity of inspiration and interest. He began his career in 1929 with a novel that dramatized "indifference" that soon became synonymous with absurdity. Through the following years, he proceeded by way of several stages aptly dubbed "mistaken ambitions," "disobedience," "conformism," "contempt," to give us a disconcerting tableau of the decay of the bourgeoisie. Recently, he has reached the extreme, but valid accusation that the cancerous disease corroding the fiber of a complacent, affluent, over-mechanized society is "la noia"—*tedium vitae*. Taking into account the numerous insights into modern life Moravia has given us over the past three decades (especially his illuminating studies of adolescent problems), it becomes necessary to stress that his recent books have not added much either to his reputation as a writer (which, judging by sales figures, is incredible, but judging from his critics is not always enviable), or to his artistic personality, more accurately defined in three of his works, *The Time of Indifference, Agostino,* and *La disubbidienza (Two Adolescents)*. The larger intention of Moravia, however, has been somewhat misjudged in the past: his last novel, *La noia (The Empty Canvas)*, has reaffirmed the fact that the novelist is less interested in criticizing his society than in analyzing an ever-increasing gap between man and his reality. Why modern man should feel estranged, or alienated from his environment, is a problem too complex to be adequately discussed in the present context. Suffice it to remark here that the predicament in which Moravia's heroes invariably find themselves is rooted in their incapacity to find something that may replace a long lost love for life, and an involvement with the human tragedy (or comedy), without which no reality can have any meaning.

For more than one reason, it is instructive to turn from Moravia to Elio Vittorini. If the former produces fiction with an almost exasperating regularity (to the point that some of his critics have urged him to write less and better than he has), the latter is, by contrast, almost too severe toward what he writes. Although I have been assured by his intimate friends that Vittorini's desk drawers are full of eminently readable material waiting to be published, he has in the past ten years brought out only two works: two novellas [titled respectively *Erica e suoi fratelli (Erica and Her Brother)* and *La Garibaldina (The Garibaldina)* and collected in a single volume, *The Dark and The Light* (1961)] and an anthology of his most important critical pronouncements and observations on the arts, politics, and culture of his three decades as a writer, *Diario in pubblico* (Public Diary). *Erica* was actually begun in 1936 but was left unfinished when its author became too distracted by political events to devote time to creative writing. Despite its stark realism, it anticipates the themes and stylistic manner of Vittorini's "second period" which begins with *Conversazione in Sicilia (In Sicily,* 1941). *The Garibaldina,* on the other hand, is the most balanced and felicitous postwar work of a writer whose interest is less in portraying an easy, "available" reality than in recapturing in a manner half allegorical and half surrealistic the moods of a world torn between opposing ideologies and finding itself in the midst of an unprecedented series of social upheavals. One of the fundamental differences between Moravia and Vittorini (it would be difficult to find two more opposing temperaments and personalities) is, *grosso modo,* the same as that between those who investigate, analyze, and interpret reality (frequently departing from certain conclusions reached *a priori*), and those who "invent" reality, that is to say those who allow the facts, characters, and happenings of their tales to find their moving spring, or their generating drive within and not without the work itself. Thus, while Vittorini's concerns are basically social and political (and not, as in Moravia's case, social and psychological), he allows the reader to discover by way of wonderfully poetic episodes the quality of the world we all live in. In his novels (but are they really novels rather than prose poems?) reality is accepted only to be subjected to a radical, necessary deformation where the possible *and* the impossible have an equal chance to exist, and where the milieu itself (a moving train, or a mythical land whose name of Sicily is really incidental) participates in the drama of a suffering humanity.

Moravia has busied himself with a careful reconstruction of the certain psychological problems of the middle class;

Vittorini has concentrated his energies in "singing" the individual's yearning to find dignity and harmony in a universe torn by hate. Vasco Pratolini, on the other hand, has directed his talent toward the completion of an ambitious trilogy, *Una storia italiana* (An Italian History), whose main purpose is to present, in fictionalized form, the progressive rise of consciousness of the proletariat as a social class fighting against the capitalist and to record the changing character of Italian society during the past six and a half decades. The first part of the trilogy, *Metello,* appeared in 1955. The novel tells of certain crucial events in the life of a Florentine stone mason and of his involvement with the rising labor unions. The excessive focusing on the hero's erotic-sentimental adventures, as well as an insufficiently penetrating and historically accurate depiction of the grave issues confronting Italian society during the first years of our century, gave rise to an intense polemical exchange of views between critics of various political leanings and resulted in an unfavorable reception and evaluation of the work. The second part of the trilogy, with the title *Lo scialo,* was brought out in 1960: but it, too, fared hardly better than *Metello.* In structure, *Lo scialo* (The Waste) is more episodic than any of his previous novels: through a series of self-contained vignettes, each centering on a select cast of characters, the author has painted an impressive gallery of unforgettable individuals, each of whom plays a particular role in a national drama that was to climax with the victory of Fascism. The decadence and corruption of Italian society (and not just the middle class) are amply documented and criticized: by doing so, Pratolini has dramatized the antecedents of the predicament in which Italy finds itself today, enjoying an unparalleled period of prosperity without having been able to solve some of her most basic and urgent issues. It is evident that the inordinate length of *Lo scialo,* and the convincing inclusion of the working class as co-responsible for the general decay of morals and values during the Fascist years have alienated several Marxist critics who had previously shown themselves sympathetic with the aims and views of the Florentine novelist.

The novels of Moravia and Pratolini exhibit a faithfulness to traditional modes of narrative in Italy. As someone remarked lately, they may well be taken as evidence of a desire to re-establish an orthodoxy that is equivalent to order so as to restore whatever unbalance may have been caused by current linguistic or structural experiments [the latest type of which is Raffaele La Capria's brilliantly executed novel *Ferito a morte (The Mortal Wound)*, winner of the 1961 Strega Prize, hedging by a single vote Fausta Cialente's *Ballata levantina (The Levantines)* and Giovanni Arpino's *Delitto d'onore (Crime of Honor)*, two competent but otherwise "conventional" realistic works]. One has to turn to a novelist like Italo Calvino for a type of fiction that is clearly out of the ordinary in that it does not propose the usual stereotyped representations of reality. Calvino's talent was already evident in his first book, *Il sentiero del nido dei ragni (The Path to the Nest of Spiders,* 1947) sponsored by his literary mentor, Cesare Pavese. After that novella, which narrates with an extraordinary lightness the adventures of a youngster named Pin and of a band of Partisans, Calvino espoused for a while the realistic approach and produced several tales, such as "La speculazione edilizia" ("The Building Speculation") and "La nuvola di smog" ("The Cloud of Smog"), which, interesting as they undoubtedly are as pieces of social criticism, have little of that inventiveness that happens to be Calvino's major resource as a narrator. The choice Calvino may be read in the short stories collected in an omnibus volume, *I racconti* (Short Stories), and *I nostri antenati* (Our Ancestors), consisting of three novellas previously published with the respective titles of *Il visconte dimezzato (The Cloven Viscount), Il barone rampante (The Baron in the Trees),* and *Il cavaliere inesistente (The Non-Existent Knight).* His models are the fabliaux of the Middle Ages and the eighteenth-century philosophical novel: but he has taken old models and made them his own by infusing them with an extraordinary degree of contemporary relevance. He has transformed his fiction into an elegant vehicle to dramatize, subtly and effectively, the foolishness and alienation of contemporary man. His views of our world are never abstractly presented: quite the contrary. Although his characters and situations are out of a "history" that could easily become absurd in the hands of a less skillful writer, they are transformed, through the magic of Calvino's sensibility, into delicate creations that succeed in existing on different levels, the first of which is always the literal.

As the foregoing remarks have tried to indicate, Italian fiction is today enjoying an enviable reputation. Its diversity, its closeness to reality (or at least, to a certain kind of reality), its courageous attempts to describe some of the manifold problems arising out of the conditions of the new times, have impressed the world. The shortcomings of contemporary fiction parallel strangely those characterizing the very fabric of Italian life: it is humorless, generally conventional and lamentably unconcerned with problems other than the basic ones. If there is an abundance of novelists who have given us incisive and convincing pictures of Italian life, there is only a handful of genuine writers who have succeeded in transcending their own time—the immediate present—and have given us compelling interpretations less of *how* things are, or of how times have changed, than of the precise meaning of such changes. Granted that the world of today is no longer the same as the world of yesterday, should not the novelist dedicate himself less to recording what is happening than to discovering in what way the evolutionary or revolutionary changes really matter, in what way they have affected *la condition humaine?* Elio Vittorini has correctly diagnosed such a literary situation with these words:

> It is certainly undeniable that literature, in comparison to the grandiose and terrible transformation that is taking place in reality around us and in each of our rapport with it, appears, on the whole, historically more backward not only than neo-Marxist sociology or certain innovating techniques . . . but also than artistic activities like painting or music which at least have left behind them their melodic dimension of old accomplices of "nature."

In conclusion, the fifties (and possibly even part of the sixties) stand a chance of being remembered as the era when the Italian novelist gained confidence in his *métier* and rid his writing of much of the rhetoric that had frequently plagued his literature and culture. Not much of what he produced, to be sure, was certain to survive the crucial test of time, but at least he could console himself with the fact that such is the fate of all writers in any historical period. Only the future events (the books yet to be written, the novelist yet to emerge) would tangibly demonstrate that the postwar experience had not been an excuse to "mark time," but that, rather, it had prepared the literary artist not only to mirror his time but to illuminate the tragedy as well as the joy of life in our time.

Something Old and Something New
BY SERGIO PACIFICI

> Chi parte non si volta
> non spera di tornare . . .
> —Alfonso Gatto

Why does contemporary Italian poetry continue to be little read abroad and all but ignored by even the best "informed" foreign critics? The question, puzzling as it may seem in light of the generous reception accorded to recent Italian fiction, should hardly evoke surprise. What Edward Sapir remarked (in his book *Language*) about the literary artist when he stated that "all his effects have been calculated or intuitively felt, with reference to the formal 'genius' of his own language; they cannot be carried over [into another language] without serious loss or modification" is especially relevant to the present discussion. Other reasons, too, are responsible for the relative "unpopularity" of Italian poetry. Indeed, the difficulties that make of poetry the least "exportable" of literary genres have been compounded, in the case of Italian poetry, with a charge of "academicism" that has most decisively hurt its cause abroad. Moreover, the Italian poet committed to improve an already solid and not too flexible tradition has shown a stubborn unwillingness to weave into his work the vast layers of socio-political meanings that account for a large share of the success enjoyed by other postwar cultural manifestations—notably the cinema of the so-called "neo-realistic" school.

Viewed from the present perspective, at once geographically remote and critically disinterested, the basic problem for the contemporary Italian writer appears to be twofold: how to simplify the language (making it less "aulic" than it has been) and how to introduce into poetry the burning problems of everyday reality. As for the dominant figures, they are still the elderly Giuseppe Ungaretti (b. 1888), Eugenio Montale (b. 1896) and the younger Salvatore Quasimodo (b. 1901). The other leading poet of this select group, Umberto Saba, passed away in 1957 at the age of seventy-three.

If statistics indicate that the last decade and a half has seen an imposing number of books of poetry published, a more serene assessment would soon reveal that relatively few "new" voices have been heard in this period. Perhaps no one deserves our attention more than Pier Paolo Pasolini, one of the youngest (b. 1922) and most mature poets to come to prominence after the last war. Pasolini, whose work is diversified enough to include philological and critical essays, anthologies of poetry in dialect and a novel partially written in Roman dialect (*Ragazzi di vita*, easily the most controversial book of 1955), achieved critical recognition in 1957 when his collection of poetry, *Le ceneri di Gramsci* (Gramsci's Ashes) was awarded the coveted Viareggio Prize. The numerous debts Pasolini owes to some of the great poets of Italian literature (Carducci, Pascoli and Saba, among others) in addition to his special usage of traditional forms and meters, are sufficiently indicative of the fact that the poet is trying to blend a new tradition with an older one, while simultaneously striving to lower "the language to the level of prose, that is, of the rational, the logical and the historical." Certainly the reference to Gramsci, the founder of the Communist Party in Italy, is more than a mere tribute, an acknowledgement of his non-political teachings or of his ever-growing stature in Italian culture. It was Gramsci who in the late twenties, writing from the jail where he was to die, urged the formation of a new culture that to become "popular" must reflect the aspirations of the people. It is particularly in this sense that Pasolini has already done much to narrow the gap that has always existed between life and literature in Italy. Whatever faults one may find in his poetry, it does represent, in its curious and often happy amalgamation of traditional and contemporary features, a passionate desire to further Man's understanding of reality in a more than merely technological sense. It is for this reason that while Pasolini has intellectually defined his position in the central section of the long poem entitled "Le ceneri di Gramsci"

Vivo nel non volere
del tramontato dopoguerra: amando
il mondo per odio—nella sua miseria
sprezzante e perso . . .

I live in the apathy
of the twilight of the post-war years: loving
a world I hate—in its wretchedness
contemptuous and lost . . .

his best composition is "Terra di lavoro" where he looks
at his southern companions in a third-class train compart-
ment, and relives with them all the bitter experiences that
make of the southern peasant the new "alienated" class.

While Pasolini is not the only poet who has succeeded in
finding a language more in keeping with the exigencies of
the postwar years, most poets active today still cling to
"hermeticism." They constitute a highly intelligent, serious
and articulate group that should receive more than my
necessarily brief mention. The consistently high caliber of
their work, the inventiveness and technical resources they
have displayed, make of them something more than
"minor" figures. Among them are Libero de Libero (b.
1906) and Sandro Penna (b. 1906), winners of the Viareggio Prize in 1950 and 1957 respectively. The oldest members of their group, they are widely read and highly
esteemed. Libero de Libero has produced a body of work
that, while it initially drew its inspiration from the Roman
countryside (he was born in Fondi, a village near Rome)
has become precious, academic and occasionally artificial.
Penna, on the other hand, is almost totally divorced from
the intellectual preoccupations of de Libero and eschews
the metaphysical themes of many of his contemporaries.
His poems are written in a simple style and are generally
autobiographical. As in the case of Saba, to whom he has
often been compared, his work does not show any substantial change: Penna writes today, as he has always, about
his simple joys and sorrows:

Sandro Penna è intriso di una strana
gioia di vivere anche nel dolore.

Sandro Penna is sodden with a strange
joy of living—even in sorrow.

His compositions have become progressively more "epigraphic" (in the modern sense of synthesis and lyrical illumination) to the point that they express the poem's total image in as few as three or four lines. They do captivate the reader, however, thanks to their graceful, almost feminine language, their haunting rhythm and the dreamlike manner in which people and things become blurred and magically transformed into sheer sensations.

Has the war, with its ensuing tragedy and wretchedness, changed in any important way the course of poetry in Italy, as it has in France? Though one finds it hard to make a strong case for a literature of the Resistance in Italy one should at least take cognizance of the few poets who did attempt to base their work on the war; among these are Franco Fortini and Alfonso Gatto (b. 1909). The former has devoted several of the lyrics of his *Foglio di via* (1946) to social polemics and has conjured up the horrors brought about by the war. He sees his native land as prison and prisoner at the same time:

> Ora m'accorgo d'amarti
> Italia, di salutarti
> Necessaria Prigione.

> Now I realize that I love you,
> Oh Italy, and greet you
> Necessary Prison.

and concludes by affirming that

> Ora non basta nemmeno morire
> per quel tuo vano nome antico

> Now it is no longer sufficient to die
> for that vain ancient name of yours.

where the emphasis is obviously on the adjective "vano," on the rapid disintegration of a myth no longer valid or useful.

Gatto, with a more colorful and vivacious imagination, has relived some of the most intensely dramatic and epic moments of the war, the days of the Liberation from the yoke in his *Il capo sulla neve* (The Head on the Snow), of which one of the most poignant poems is "Anniversario":

> Oh, l'Europa gelata nel suo cuore
> mai piú si scalderà: sola coi morti
> che l'amano in eterno, sarà bianca
> senza confini, unita dalla neve.

> Oh, Europe frozen in her heart
> will never warm up: alone with the dead
> who love her eternally, she will be white
> without boundaries, united by the snow.

Other poets have devoted part of their work to the war: Sergio Solmi (who shared with Gatto the St. Vincent Prize in 1948), Giorgio Caproni, Giorgio Bassani and Vittorio Sereni, probably the best of this group. His most significant work is *Diario d'Algeria* (1947) where he shed considerable light upon the plight of the Italian people and has eloquently spoken about the chaos and misery of Europe.

Leonardo Sinisgalli (b. 1908) has often been called the most versatile member of the "hermetic" group. He has written perceptive pages on architecture, the plastic arts, geometry, design, dance and optics. Himself a mechanical engineer, mathematician and student of metallurgy and electrical sciences, he began his diversified career in 1936 with a volume entitled *18 Poesie* (Eighteen Poems), later collected in *Vidi le Muse* (I Saw the Muses). As a poet he is quite difficult to define. Often accused of being too cerebral, too detached from reality, he has nevertheless written some very fine poems about his native Lucania, his family, and about the monotonous, hard life his parents and brothers lead in the country—and has thus turned his eye on the reality he previously neglected. His latest collection of poetry, *Tu sarai poeta* (Thou Shalt be Poet), reveals a more intimate fusion of the two tones, the epigraphic and elegiac, prevailing in his work; his best poems in this book reveal a new concern with life and death, and if the poet is still anxiously seeking to recapture all things past, he shows a new awareness of the present.

The last of the group of poets who, while not "major," have shown considerable maturity is Mario Luzi (b. 1914), winner of the Marzotto Prize in 1957 for his *Onore del vero*

(Honor of Truth). Learned and extremely perceptive, frequently obscure, Luzi has been more deeply influenced than his contemporaries by the sophisticated and often misunderstood tradition of European Symbolists. *Un Brindisi* (A Toast) and *Quaderno Gotico* (A Gothic Notebook) are still his most representative works. Perhaps not quite so allusive and metaphorical as some of his previous poetry they are, especially the latter, powerfully evocative. *Quaderno Gotico* dramatizes in a particularly sensitive manner the spiritual and carnal torment experienced by the poet, and thus justifies a recent critic who remarked that "to the immobile travail of the mind, the full and tumultuous travail of the heart has now been added."

BIBLIOGRAPHY

Bergin, T. G. "Italian Fiction Today," *Yale Review*, 39 (1950).

Cambon, Glauco. "Elio Vittorini: Between Poverty and Wealth," *Wisconsin Studies in Contemporary Literature*, 3 (1961).

Chase, Richard V. "Cesare Pavese and the American Novel," *Studi Americani*, No. 3 (1957).

Chiaromonte, Nicola. "Contemporary Italian Theatre," *The Literary Review*, 3 (1959).

—————. "Realism and Neorealism in Contemporary Italian Literature," *College English*, 14 (1953).

Croce, Elena. "Letter from Rome," *Hudson Review*, 12 (1959).

—————. "Notes on Italian Literature," *Hudson Review*, 16 (1963).

Della Terza, Dante. "Italian Fiction from Pavese to Pasolini, 1950–60," *Italian Quarterly*, No. 11 (1959).

—————. "Post-War Poetics and Poetry," *Italian Quarterly*, No. 16 (1960).

Fiedler, Leslie A. "The Rediscovery of Italian Literature: Chance, Chic and the Task of the Critic," *Italian Quarterly*, No. 9 (1959).

Lewis, R. W. B. "Elio Vittorini," *Italian Quarterly*, No. 15 (1960).

Norton, Peter M. "Pavese and the American Nightmare," *Modern Language Notes*, 77 (1961).

Pacifici, Sergio. *A Guide to Contemporary Italian Literature* (New York, 1962).

—————. "From Engagement to Alienation: A View of Contemporary Italian Literature," *Italica*, XL, 3 (1963).

Pandolfi, Vito. "Italian Theatre Since the War," *Tulane Drama Review*, 8 (Spring, 1964).

Tenenbaum, Louis. "Character Treatment in Pavese's Fiction," *Symposium*, 15 (1960).

Vittorini, Elio. "American Influences on Contemporary Italian Literature," *American Quarterly*, 1 (1949).

Williamson, Edward. "Contemporary Italian Poetry," *Poetry* (Dec., 1952, & Jan., 1953).

A Literature Appears
BY ANDREW FIELD

It is said that Vladimir Nabokov, when he was teaching at Cornell, would from time to time be sent listings of current Soviet publications from which he was asked to select those books he wished the library to purchase. These catalogs, so the story goes, were always sent back with the following legend written across the cover: "There is no Soviet literature." Nabokov's judgment, however waspish and whatever its political motivation, has a literary basis. It is a judgment with which, given certain reservations, the serious student of literature must concur—especially if we date "Soviet" (as opposed to "Russian") literature from 1928, when the authority of the Party over the artist was first actively asserted. One has only to compare the sometimes minor but always lively and original, occasionally even great (Babel, Olesha, Savich, Zamyatin) pre-1928 literature of Soviet Russia to what followed it to take the proper measure of the enormous difference.

There is, too, another view of Soviet literature, ultimately identical to Nabokov's, but having its own extra-literary circumstances. I am speaking of the disillusionment experienced by many of our leading critics in the 1930's when, beset with the problem of their own society, they turned hopefully to what they thought was the radically new conception of social organization and responsibility of Soviet Russia. "It was," wrote Lionel Trilling, "as if I had hoped that the literature of the Revolution would realize some simple inadequate notion of the 'classical' which I had picked up at college; and perhaps I was drawn to this notion of the classical because I was afraid of the literature of modern Europe, because I was scared of its terrible intensities, ironies, and ambiguities."

And so, forsaken by the best representatives of criticism, Russian and non-Russian, Soviet literature has been left to the devices of the political scientist and the journalist. One could hardly say that it has deserved any other sort of attention. But now, because of the "litero-political" efforts of writers like Ilya Ehrenburg and Evgeny Evtushenko (for which they deserve all gratitude *except* literary praise), the possibility of a literature of the *non*-litero-political variety has been gained. This incipient, supervening literature, which merits strictly literary judgment, requires an act of effort, a commutation of our set ways of thinking about Soviet literature.

The signs of cultural awakening in Russia are everywhere. One of the most significant occurrences on the Soviet literary scene has been the criticism from the liberal position, and on purely artistic grounds, of Evtushenko and poets similar to him. So far have things come.

There is now astonishingly diverse publishing activity not only in Moscow and Leningrad, but also in less noticed provincial areas such as Kaluga and Saratov. An essential aspect of the movement forward is a re-examination and re-evaluation of the literary past. Many previously forbidden poets have been published, including Nikolai Gumilyov, whose anti-Bolshevik activity and consequent execution in 1921 long placed him at the head of the list of proscribed poets in the Soviet Union. From the more recent past, the poems of Kseniya Nekrasova, the stories of Andrei Platonov, and the plays of Evgeny Shvarts—the only Soviet dramatist of major stature—have now been published. (These three outstanding artists, none of whom is now alive, had all experienced severe publication difficulties.) Still another encouraging sign is the fact that *émigré* poets and writers are now being recognized and brought back into the mainstream of Russian culture: Marina Tsvetaeva, the "poetess of the White Guard," the Nobel prize-winner Ivan Bunin, and the important Parisian *émigré* poet, Vladislav Khodasevich. A second, more complete edition of Boris Pasternak's poetry has been announced for 1964, and collections of the poetry of Nikolai Zabolotsky and Osip Mandelstam are "pending."

What all this means is simply that the uncomplicated way in which Soviet literature has long been presented to the West—rather like some sort of rudimentary Arthur

Murray dance pattern: two steps forward, one backward—is now inadequate to the reality. If we are reminded of how vicious are the forces of censorship which still plague the Soviet writer by the article of "Nikolai Gavrilov" (*New Leader*, Dec. 9, 1963), that is only cause for further astonishment at how much has, all the same, been accomplished.

The most productive genre in the Soviet literary renaissance is poetry, and, as at few times before in its history, Russian poetry means youth. Contemporary Soviet poetry ranges from the variations on ancient Russian themes by Viktor Sosnora to the (unpublished) "barracks poetry," highly surrealistic in form and often concerned with concentration-camp life, by young Soviet equivalents of our Beat poets. Andrei Voznesensky, the young poet best known in the West after Evtushenko, possesses genuine, original talent. Voznesensky is a virtuoso, and in that is precisely the delight and the limitation of his poetry, which mischievously darts and turns in unexpected ways. *The Triangular Pear*, a lengthy series of poems based on his trip to America (the title refers to New York subway lamps), allows this quality an added dimension in its zany juxtapositions of English and Russian. Thus Voznesensky places *Koka-kola* beside *kolokola* (the Russian word for bells). Anything can happen and does. His metaphors and images can be both bold (a rock-and-roll dancer becomes "a fish with an umbrella") and terse ("vehicular California"). The best single word to describe Voznesensky's poetry would be playful—

> *I'm a family.*
> *As in a spectrum, there're seven of me,*
> *Insufferable, like seven beasts,*
> *and the bluest has*
>   *a flute to blow.*
> *But just you wait.*
> *Come Spring I dream that I am eight.*

His very best poems, however, retain an essential boldness that transcends mere whimsy—

> *A ballad? About a fatal pill? A target?*
> *How dumb can you get!*

> *You've forgotten the Pushkin bullet!*
> *The winds whistling as in the holes of clarinets*
> *Through the pierced heads of our best poets.*

Some say that Voznesensky has been rated too highly, which may be true. But even when their images are incomprehensible to us, his poems seem finished, wrought objects. In his case at least, one feels no need to ask oneself the question that so many other young, avant-garde Russian poets bring to mind: What kind of poetry will he, could he write in twenty years? In the good sense of both terms, Voznesensky is a "modern" and a "traditional" poet.

Less noticed but, in my opinion, more accomplished than the avant-garde poets are the young poets of the "quiet school." One of the most outstanding among these artists is Evgeny Vinokurov. Vinokurov's poetic voice gives the appearance of being unintellectual (he himself says in one poem: "I believe in simple-mindedness"), but his "simplicity" is a conscious, studied manner, not unlike Robert Frost's. Here, for example, is a short poem, uncomplicated and yet perfect in its conveyance of felt life—

> *A man walked alone in the world,*
> *Lifted his collar, closed the flap,*
> *Lit a cigarette, bending over,*
> *Back to the wind,*
> > *at a corner.*
> *Went to the park. Greenish little pond.*
> *Freshly painted rowboats, all moored up.*
> *Whistling, snapped off a branch.*
> *For no reason, slapped it on his leg.*
> *He spat down from the wooden dock,*
> *Spat so lazily, not in anger.*
> *And nothing at all happened*
> > *except*
> *That he suddenly saw:*
> > *why life has passed me by.*

In one poem, Vinokurov describes how Picasso has taken the world apart, and then, tired from his labor but still full of gay malice, he visits a cafe where he sees a tear flowing down someone's cheek. "Take that apart! Just try!" concludes Vinokurov. The poem catches, I think, the attitude of most serious young Russian artists towards Western forms and techniques: after so many years in a suspended culture, they have a vast amount to reclaim from the Russian past before they can turn their attention to the West.

Another extremely talented young poet whose work is traditional in form and highly personal in content is Bella Akhmadulina. Akhmadulina's poetry is often compared to Anna Akhmatova's, though I find her poetry (at its best) has a much greater similarity to that of Edna St. Vincent Millay. The following poem has a stillness and a reserve which are belied by its emotive quality —

> It was all for a candle,
> A simple wax candle,
> That its ageless antiquity
> Would stand fresh in my memory.
>
> And your pen hastens
> On its florid navigations,
> Intelligent and thoughtful,
> While goodness floods the soul.
>
> You're thinking now of friends,
> Ever finer, in the olden way.
> You're a stearine stalactite
> Framed tenderly in my sight.
>
> And Pushkin looks on kindly,
> The candles are snuffed, night retreats,
> While the soft sound of our native speech
> Strokes the lips so coldly.

By virtue of her long poem *Ancestry* (the title and theme of the poem evidently derive from Pushkin's 1830 poem *My Ancestry*) published in the journal *Youth* (2, 1964) Akhmadulina is considered by some to have effectively challenged Voznesensky and Vinokurov for the title of Russia's leading younger poet.

Akhmadulina's affinity to Pushkin is also found in another contemporary poet, Naum Korzhavin. Korzhavin's verse is effervescent in character, yet far from being what we call "light verse." Korzhavin greatly admires precisely this quality in Pushkin (to whom several of his best poems are addressed), and he has succeeded in the difficult task of making himself master of Pushkin's light iamb. Korzhavin has published but one book of poetry, but I am quite at a loss to understand why he has not won wider recognition than he has—unless it is because people want even the very best poetry only by the pound. The work of still another poet, Boris Slutsky, is valued very highly, but, like Korzhavin, by far too limited a circle of readers. Finally, one can only list seven other young poets who seem to show real promise: Yury Levitansky, Vladimir Kornilov, David Samoilov, Bulat Okudzhava, Iosif Brodsky, and Vladimir Soloukhin. Nor must we overlook the contribution which is being made by such older poets as Andrei Dostal, Leonid Martynov, Veronika Tushnova, and, of course, Anna Akhmatova who is Russia's greatest living poet. Akhmatova's moving series of poems, "Requiem," is unquestionably one of the great poetic achievements of the decade. Thus there is now good reason to be optimistic about the future of Russian poetry.

Of the poets whom I have cited, seven are represented in an extraordinary literary collection, *Pages from Tarusa,* which was published in late 1961 at Tarusa, a writers' colony near Moscow. Its three-hundred-odd pages, fairly bristling with little known writers and poets, maintain a high literary quality. Although there is nothing overtly political in the collection, *Pages from Tarusa* was skillfully steered past normal publication procedures; because of that, when it appeared, it was quickly withdrawn from sale, but not before several thousand copies had been sold. The moving force behind *Pages from Tarusa* was the older writer Konstantin Paustovsky. Paustovsky makes no fuss but has probably done more, in his quiet way, to further the cause of artistic freedom in Russia, and to encourage young talent, than any other person. *Pages from Tarusa* gives an inclusive representation of both the strengths and the weaknesses of current Soviet writing; and it is revealing to compare this collection with yet another literary almanac, *Literary Moscow,* which played a significant role in the 1956 "thaw."

Russian prose, corroded and disfigured by the dead and pompous bureaucratic speech that has constituted the public voice for several decades, is far less advanced than poetry. The controversial novel by Vasily Aksyonov, *A Starry Ticket,* which appeared in 1961, illustrates both the desire of young writers to react against stilted language and the intrinsic weakness of most Soviet prose. Aksyonov's novel teems with slang, and that is refreshing, but over all, the novel is an embarrassingly poor imitation of *Catcher in the Rye*. Yet some very fine short stories show that Aksyonov is not without talent.

And in general, perhaps the clearest indication of the state of Soviet prose today is the marked success of the short story as against the novel. One of the very best of the Soviet short story writers, Aleksandr Solzhenitsyn, has written that long novels are ill-suited to a technological age. Because the novel is currently flourishing in the West, however, it seems more likely that the short story predominates in Russia because Russian fiction is just awakening from a long period of dormancy, and it is only natural that the first steps in serious fiction should be taken in a form of a more limited scope. On the whole, younger writers do not seem ready to "go the distance" in novels yet, or, as in the case of Aksyonov, one wishes that they had not.

Aleksandr Solzhenitsyn has to date published just five stories (new ones are promised), one of which, *One Day of Ivan Denisovich*, a description of a Stalinist concentration camp, brought him world-wide fame. The story has great literary merit, although it is not the "literary masterpiece" which it was proclaimed in many American journals as though the matter needed no explanation or justification. Ivan Denisovich is a Bruegel peasant plodding through a hellish Bosch landscape, and much of the force of the story comes from its determined restraint of feeling. The manner in which Solzhenitsyn refers to his protagonist by name and patronymic in the title is the first clue that, like Tolstoy's Ivan Ilich, Ivan Denisovich is to be at once something less and something more than an individual character. Solzhenitsyn's language is worthy of special note—its terseness and color call forth and magnify, rather than merely "tell" feeling. Another Solzhenitsyn story, *Matryona's House*, about a righteous old peasant woman "without whom, according to the proverb, no village can stand. Nor any city. Nor our whole land," is, in my opinion, the most impressive of Solzhenitsyn's stories from a purely artistic point of view.

Yury Kazakov has also attained a high degree of refinement in the short story. Kazakov has by now acquired a reputation as a rising star, but he also has many critics who claim that his style is too imitative of Turgenev, Chekhov, and Bunin. Such a charge is as unfair as it is true. Kazakov (by no means alone in this) turns deliberately to the pre-Revolutionary past to find models of style and language—but where else could a young writer turn? In Kazakov's best stories, the "imitation" is so perfect it can no longer be considered that at all. The prose is beautifully lucid and measured, and the fine and eloquent Russian one had thought the property of the past suddenly speaks again, sonorous and alive. Once again the "little man" has become a major theme, and once again stories are set in the country-side with scarcely a tractor or a quota in sight. A peasant couple, long out of love, set out for the city, and we seem to hear an echo of the plaintive cry from Chekhov's play: "To Moscow! To Moscow!" The wife knows she will die there and be buried with her family. She grieves and is consoled, alone. The husband dreams about how he will go to a cafe and be served there by a waitress. The poverty of his fantasy is grippingly effective. The only objection one can make about Kazakov's stories has to do with an occasional cloying excess of lyricism.

Another significant writer of the "Chekhovian" school is Natalya Tarasenkova who has published three collections of short stories. In the title story of one book, *Strange Dreams,* a wife and husband, Masha and Grigory, manage a small hotel which serves as a stopover for air travelers in a remote region. From boredom and neglect she turns in fantasy, but not in fact, to a handsome young man. The significance of her imagined act is shown vividly at the story's end as Masha prepares to wake her husband: "Grigory slept contentedly, his lips protruding foolishly as though he were about to whistle. Soon it would be necessary to wake him. And she felt pity towards her husband, pity and nothing more." Tarasenkova's talent, for all its modesty, is mature and imposing.

Vladimir Tendryakov has written a number of short novels which I consider the best long prose works to have appeared in the Soviet Union in recent years. *The Extraordinary* is a novella about a scandal in a provincial school that occurs when it is discovered that a teacher and one pupil are believers. The headmaster of the school, Makhotin, is both a member of the Party and a convinced atheist. In spite of this, he risks his own position in an effort to save the pupil from expulsion and the teacher from being fired. How very strange it is that a real, live "positive hero" should crop up in a story of great artistic merit after decades of drivel had convinced us that such a character cannot function in a work of art. In *The Extraordinary,* and in other works, Tendryakov promulgates a bold form of humanism that is supposed to restore to Communism the *moral* authority it once had for the Russians. One catches the same note in other writers of the younger generation—for example, in the reply by Naum Korzhavin to a literary questionnaire in a recent journal. "A man in a Communist society," he wrote, "must be, above all, spiritually rich."

Other prose writers worthy of note are Boris Balter, Bulat Okudzhava, Aleksandr Yashin, Vladimir Maksimov, and Ivan Stadniuk. Maksimov is the author of a fine novella, *A Man Survives,* about the rehabilitation of a renegade which is reminiscent in many ways of Warren Miller's *The Cool World;* Stadniuk's book, *People Aren't Angels* (which, by the way, deals in part with life in a concentration camp), stands out as conspicuously and uniquely successful among long Soviet novels. Besides these —and these names will be the ones most familiar to the Western reader—there is the grouping of writers which includes Abramov, Dudintsev, Ehrenburg, Tvardovsky, Viktor Nekrasov, Ovechkin, and Tarsis. Their primary virtue is not literary, and so judgment of them properly belongs in another essay.

One "political" writer, however, does command artistic respect. Abram Tertz is a stage name. The man is a ventriloquist by profession, only he is not playing for laughs or applause, but for keeps. From somewhere and someone in the Soviet Union a voice is talking to us, and if the tone is somewhat shaky at times—as all ventriloquial speech must be—its intent and character are not really open to question. In his essay, *On Socialist Realism,* Tertz called for a "phantasmagoric art." Then, in his *Fantastic Stories* (the title is borrowed from that of a collection of supernatural tales by E. T. A. Hoffmann), he set about to answer his own call. The six stories in this book (one of which, *The Trial Begins,* has been published as a separate book in English), in spite of the diversity of their themes, are unified by the passages they all share, which, while ostensibly direct statements from characters, are also asides from Tertz. He is the main attraction and, I think, very nearly the only one whom we accept as alive and important to us. This is not a fault, for Tertz can achieve superb artistic effects by sheer narrative manner.

Abnormal psychology, of which Tertz clearly has a deep understanding, figures prominently in all the stories. *You and I* is a brilliant and carefully executed examination of paranoia and internal sexual conflict. The protagonist of this story is a "double" personality who speaks now in one voice, now in another. The duality should be seen as an emblematic and not a clinical representation. The action begins in a dinner scene reminiscent of that in Dostoyevsky's *Notes from the Underground,* with the neat added suggestion of a political inquisition. The hero (one half of him, that is) has been invited to a 25th anniversary wedding party, but we are informed by him that the anniversary is bogus and, in fact, that the wife is really a man. The protagonist's revulsion at seeing his host, whom he hates, kiss this "man" is a clear Oedipal defense mechanism which is extended to include other women (in his eyes, the female guests are NKVD men in disguise). He does finally run away from the dinner party with a girl named Lida and has a brief affair with her which is presented in terms of a child's ravishment of his mother: "I stood before her on my knees. I well recalled one rule—a person is more accessible from below, and, if you are standing before him on your knees, you can at any moment seize him by the legs and throw him on his back." The struggle between the homo- and heterosexual elements of his personality continues to its logical end—suicide. One of the delights of Tertz's stories are the marvelous comic effects he achieves even while treating serious psychological and political themes, as, for example, in *The Graphomaniacs* where a writer sits in an editor's waiting room and dreams of performing "all the humiliating procedures" over the secretary, only to have that same secretary's "well-developed body, ripe for shame" block his path as he tries to get into the editor's office. These stories will be important *as literature* when (when?) the circumstances which caused their author to have to seek publication for them outside of Russia have become a chapter of history.

There remains only drama, the weakest of the Russian

literary arts today, and not much can be said in praise of it. The reason, of course, is not far to seek. In a controlled society, the staging of an original and good play, through the cooperative efforts of many people and for "public" display, is no easy matter. By comparison, the endeavors by which the writer works his way into print seem simple indeed. The result of this is that the talented writer in Russia is attracted least of all by drama. The three outstanding Soviet dramatists today, Volodin, Rozov, and Arbuzov, rise, at best, to the level of American television drama, a sad commendation. The most successful Russian dramatic productions are either foreign (Brecht, Gibson), classic (Gógol, Ostrovsky), or adaptations for the stage. In the last category, the experience of Vladimir Tendryakov's powerful novella, *The Miraculous,* is revealing: its dramatization played exactly one performance, after which it was temporarily suspended until it had been sufficiently "corrected." This state of affairs has, sad to say, had its effect upon all aspects of the Russian theatre, and the eighteenth century acting of the Moscow Art Theatre today could not possibly be farther removed from the principles of its founder, Stanislavsky.

Necessarily, my high-speed hopscotch through current Soviet literature omits and simplifies, but I trust that the profile at least is clear. Let me say clearly that Soviet literature is only beginning; it will not yet stand comparison with American. Still, it *is* a literature again, for the first time since the twenties; it can be taken seriously, and it repays reading.

BIBLIOGRAPHY

Blake, Patricia; and Hayward, Max, eds. *Dissonant Voices in Soviet Literature* (New York, 1962).

————, eds. "New Voices in Russian Writing," *Encounter* (April, 1963).

Field, Andrew. "Iosif Brodsky—Poet in Prison," *New Leader* (June 22, 1964).

————. "Rebel with a Cause," *New Leader* (Sept. 30, 1963).

————. "Socialist Surrealism," *New Leader* (May 13, 1963).

————. "A Soviet Eastern," *Partisan Review* (Summer, 1963).

————, ed. *Pages from Tarusa* (Boston, 1964).

Forgues, Pierre. "The Young Poets," *Survey* (Jan., 1963).

Gibian, George. "New Trends in the Novel," *Survey*, No. 36 (1960.)

Mathewson, Rufus. "The Obscene Tattoo," *Columbia University Forum* (Winter, 1961).

Monas, Sidney. "The Private Muse: Some Notes on Recent Soviet Literature," *Hudson Review*, 11 (1958).

Reeve, F. D. "The Autobiography of a World," *Hudson Review*, 16 (Winter, 1963-4).

————. "The House of the Living," *Kenyon Review* (Spring, 1963).

Viereck, Peter. "Alexander Solzhenitsyn," *Book Week* (July 5, 1964).

Whitney, Thomas, ed. *The New Writing in Russia* (Ann Arbor, 1964).

Spanish Literature Since the War
BY MANUEL DURAN

Spain has never been a gay country, except in the artificial description of its tourist posters. Yet it is hard to reflect upon the Spanish literature of the last twenty odd years without an acute feeling of nostalgia, as if for a lost Paradise. "A second Golden Age," Dámaso Alonso, a contemporary, has called Spanish pre-war poetry. In few other countries was the crisis brought about by the war so acute, the silence that followed it so stubborn, the feelings of isolation and despair among the new writers so overwhelming, as in Spain. We find more continuity in the literary trends of England and America, even of France— where Existentialism was being nurtured during the war and the German occupation—or in Russia. The Italian literary scene suffered a deep upheaval after the war, but it was a positive one, a release of energies. Only German literature remained temporarily depressed and has perhaps not regained yet the brilliance of the twenties.

It is necessary to begin an inventory of present Spanish literary resources by pointing out what Spain lost during the war and as a consequence of it. We must bear in mind, of course, that in Spain "the war" means the Spanish civil war, from 1936 to 1939; the post-war period, therefore, begins in Spain in 1939. Curiously enough, due to the disarray of writers and publishers, new trends were slow in developing: it may be said that Spanish post-war literature does not begin properly until 1944 or 1945, which would bring its starting dates in line with those of other countries. What Spanish writers lost during the war and after it can be summed up in a few words: an intellectual climate of openness, gaiety, self-confidence, optimism. Spain had been catching up with the rest of Europe without renouncing its uniqueness. Ever respected, sometimes acclaimed, writers were winning new, larger audiences. Schools were being built, universities reorganized; foreign books were read avidly. The "great leap forward" had been the work of the Generation of 1898, of men like Unamuno, Azorín, Valle-Inclán, Pío Baroja, most of them still alive and active before the war. This generation remained, and justly so, at the center of the Spanish literary scene. And a younger group, especially the generation of Lorca, Guillén, Aleixandre, Cernuda, and a half dozen more major poets, had come to reinforce the old-timers. For the first time in centuries all the genres were cultivated with success. The Romantic era, for instance, gave Spain interesting poetry, but no novels to speak of. The second half of the nineteenth century, good realistic novels, but no poetry worthy of that name. Now Spain had *both* novelists and poets, *both* essayists and playwriters (Lorca and Casona among the latter). Its literature could be compared to a well-tuned orchestra, with one titular conductor—the ever-popular philosopher-journalist José Ortega y Gasset, almost an intellectual dictator for certain avant-garde élites—and two guest conductors, the grand irascible old man, Miguel de Unamuno, and the imaginative, whimsical idol of the new generations, Ramón Gómez de la Serna.

Not all was perfect, of course, within the Spanish literary orchestra. Some sections were stronger than others. The new generations had produced a wealth of poetry but few good novelists. The theatre was just beginning to awaken. Yet the future was promising, the present happy enough. All this was lost in a few bitter, blood-drenched years.

The conflict itself produced very little literature of lasting value. Antonio Machado and Rafael Alberti wrote "populist" poetry for the trenches in which propaganda outweighed art. Pemán did the same thing for Franco's side. Only the war poems of a peasant-turned-poet, Miguel Hernández, may survive the test of time. If we compare Hernández's war poems, in their tense directness ("if I die, may I die / with my head unbowed"), with his slightly precious, neo-Baroque early poems, we detect a clue to the development of contemporary Spanish literature—the prewar styles were too subjective, too refined, too subtle to stand the test of conflict, war, collective emotions. They had to be discarded during the war and were to be replaced by simpler styles, more in keeping with the collective mood of war and the collective angers and frustrations of the post-war world. This applies not only to lyrical poetry, but also to the novel and drama.

Avant-garde estheticism and subjectivism simply would not do any more. New styles had to be found to fit the new moods, but the search was difficult, so difficult in fact that for the years following the war the main characteristic was, simply, silence. Many magazines had disappeared, many printing presses had been smashed by bombings, many publishers had closed shop. But the reasons for the silence were deeper than the mere material difficulties of the moment. Its roots were the inability to find an adequate voice, a fitting style, to express the overwhelming horror of the conflict. Many writers who stayed in Spain chose to remain silent, for silence was better than triviality. Others left Spain, and their books did not reach their homeland any more. (Yet in spite of Spain's prolonged indifference to such writers as Ramón Sender, Max Aub, Francisco Ayala and S. Serrano Poncela, they have won enormous prestige in the larger world of Hispanic letters.) Others yet were dead: Machado did not survive the long march into exile, Lorca had been murdered at the outset of the war, Unamuno had died, grief-stricken, a few months after the start of the hostilities. These key figures were not easily replaced. Exile had taken a heavy toll. Among the poets, for instance, the whole galaxy around Lorca and Guillén—Cernuda, Alberti, Prados, Altolaguirre, Guillén himself, Salinas—left Spain, and so did Juan Ramón Jiménez, the old Symbolist patriarch. Only Gerardo Diego and Vicente Aleixandre remained. Yet after 1944 new poets, for whom Unamuno and Machado were still vital, arose and found a way to express the collective anguish then gripping their country. Existentialism in contemporary Spanish poetry is not an imported movement, but rather a hard-won outpost conquered through suffering and the influence of some of the best poets of the old generation.

But before the way was clear for new developments an official attempt at channeling poetry through safe ways was made—and failed. Towards 1942 the silence of Spanish writers was beginning to worry the authorities. They tried to remedy it by subsidizing a number of literary magazines of which *Garcilaso* became the best-known. The poetry written and published in 1942 and 43 in the subsidized magazines appears today as a lifeless, bloodless attempt to withdraw into an ivory tower. The poems are on the whole very cold, formal, rigid and old-fashioned. No mention is made of the Spanish tragedy. Almost no introspection takes place. They remind us not so much of Garcilaso de la Vega, the great Renaissance Spanish poet who gave his name to the magazine, as of the Neoclassical poets of the eighteenth century—with their wealth of formal perfection, well-rounded musical lines, that yet failed to express deep emotion or to convey a sense of having been written in our century. Some of the poets that took part in this short-lived classical revival were, of course, much better than the movement they helped to launch: Dionisio Ridruejo, Leopoldo Panero, and especially Luis Felipe Vivanco went on to develop a more personal style. Yet it was a doomed trend, and its influence upon the new generations has been, on the whole, insignificant.

Towards 1944 the premises for a more personal and passionate approach to poetry were established in Spain by a series of complex circumstances. World War II was coming to an end. The Spanish government had backed the losing side, first with enthusiasm, then, as allied power grew, more and more coolly. Censorship became less rigid. Spain was aware once more of the existence of the outside world. Finally the year 1944 saw the publication of four significant books: Camilo José Cela's *El Nuevo Lazarillo (The New Rogue)*, a powerful, if rambling, neo-picaresque novel; Dámaso Alonso's *Sons of Wrath*, with some of the most dramatic, anguishing and desolate poems ever written in the Spanish language; Vicente Aleixandre's *Shadows of Paradise*, a major contribution to an already rich poetic career; and Carmen Laforet's first novel, *Nada* (a title which can be translated as "Nothing" or "Nothingness"), clumsy and sometimes contrived, but fresh and direct in its approach to the problems of an adolescent girl in post-war Barcelona. The impact of these four books, added to the vague news about Existentialism filtering into Spain from France, was enough to give a second wind to a literature some had judged dying or paralyzed.

The impact of these works can be partly explained by the fact that their authors, with the exception of Carmen Laforet, whose novel received the Nadal Prize, were already well-known to Spanish readers. Dámaso Alonso, for instance, was recognized as Spain's foremost critic. Aleixandre belonged to the Lorca-Guillén circle and was before the Civil War, along with Luis Cernuda, the great exponent of the Spanish version of Surrealism. Camilo José Cela's *The Family of Pascual Duarte,* a truculent first novel about an unlucky and lowly criminal who tells his life from the prison cell in which he awaits execution, had been acclaimed in 1942. The novel, which has been compared to Camus' *L'Etranger,* presents the same type of insensitive killer overwhelmed by circumstances who, in the course of the novel, explains himself and reaches a dispassionate acceptance both of himself and of his circumstances. Also, Cela's *Pascual Duarte* is actually the starting point of the new trends in Spanish prose. From 1944 on both the novel and poetry follow paths which, although closely related, are slightly divergent. If the archetype of Spanish post-war novels is to be found in Cela's *The Hive,* with its vast, grey, matter-of-fact hopelessness, its realistic description of social paralysis, the archetype for the new poetry could be Dámaso Alonso's *Sons of Wrath,* or perhaps one of the books by Blas de Otero, with their mixture of anguished metaphysics and human solidarity, of faith and despair. Cela's spiritual and literary forefather is Pío Baroja, the restless and forceful novelist of the generation of 1898; Blas de Otero's roots are to be found in the paradoxical poems by Miguel de Unamuno. We can thus say that today's Spanish literature elaborates themes inaugurated by the generation of 1898, with the important difference that a certain estheticism and admiration for some moments of Spain's glorious past, often present among the 1898 writers, are lacking today. This break with tradition, as well as Spain's present situation, go a long way towards explaining the exasperated, frantic quality of almost all contemporary Spanish literature.

On the whole the poets, as was to be expected, give us, in their appraisal of the individual and society, darker shadows and brighter highlights than the writers of prose. Miguel Hernández, dying of tuberculosis and sadness in a prison, still found the courage to write, "but there is a ray of sun in the struggle / that always conquers darkness in the end." Thus also Dámaso Alonso, after the initial outburst of *Sons of Wrath* ("Madrid is a city of a million and a half cadavers, according to the latest statistics"), after apocalyptic visions that remind us of Goya, Bosch and a horror film, finds in himself the courage and the faith to go on searching for God in his *Son of God* (1945). Vicente Aleixandre, a major poet by any standards, tempers his early cosmic despair—akin in some ways to that of Robinson Jeffers—with a serene, harmonious nostalgia: man is an exile on earth, his fall from some earlier, purer, Paradise is perhaps not irrevocable. Love is the forewarning, the glimpse of what death will achieve: a restitution of man to the unity of the world, the end of separateness, the destruction of limits and barriers.

Official censorship, intolerably rigid before 1944, still very strong until 1951, and present even today, has dealt more harshly with novelists than with poets. Since books of poetry are printed in limited editions in Spain, often in editions of no more than a thousand copies, and therefore do not reach large audiences, poetry is less feared, even if strongly critical of modern Spain, than fiction, which reaches a larger public and can be translated and published abroad. This explains, for instance, why time and again certain novelists, Cela and Juan Goytisolo especially, have been compelled to publish their novels in Buenos Aires or in Paris. Poetry, even the clearer, less esoteric poetry which is written today in Spain, is still obscure enough so that its meaning escapes the censor. Hence, the poets have greater freedom, which may explain, up to a point, their flashes of optimism. For their optimism is usually anchored in hope for the future, not in the description of the present—a hope which presupposes a deep social and political change in Spain.

As more and more poets became aware of their relative freedom, a significant change of direction took place in Spanish poetry. Towards 1944–1948 the dominant theme was what we might describe as "the struggle with the Maker." Dámaso Alonso's books describe a search for God by a man who does not yet believe fully, without reservations, without questioning or reproaching God. The same may be said about some of Carlos Bousoño's poignant, if somewhat colder, poems. Vicente Gaos' works, the early books by Blas de Otero, the posthumous poems of José Luis Hidalgo, *The Dead,* all move in the same direction—personal "existentialist" anguish, or the feeling of impend-

ing death, or the painful reflection about the decay and
suffering of a whole country, or a whole world, are used
as a springboard for an approach to metaphysical questioning of God, of the purpose of life, of the need for
suffering. This Dostoyevskian attitude is slowly replaced
around 1948–1950, and a new group of poets emerges:
Gabriel Celaya, Victoriano Crémer, Blas de Otero, Eugenio
de Nora. Most of them had published earlier, but their
poetry appears now substantially altered, more optimistic
and buoyant: "The poet," writes Gabriel Celaya, "must
turn his back on the half-educated petit-bourgeoisie, and
seek contact with certain neglected social strata that urgent-
ly invoke our conscience to call them to life." Thus is born
the poetry of social consciousness, of social struggle—in
other words, political and patriotic poetry. The poet is no
longer alone and naked before death, no longer does he
struggle until dawn with a Maker that does not deign to
make His designs, His terrible whims, clear to him. The
poet has found a mission. He sings of the humble and for
the humble. He sings of the beauty of manual work, of
the dignity of the poor, of the undying thirst for freedom,
of the strength of poetry itself: "I know that nothing is dead
while my song is still alive," writes José Hierro, one of the
best and most characteristic poets of the young generation.
And Blas de Otero: "I say live, live violently, die proudly,
make your challenge standing in the stirrups . . ."

The new poetic style is clear, transparent: "We must
speak clearly. Obscurity is a defect of style," claims Hierro.
The poet is not an exceptional being, but rather "one
of the crowd": "I, José Hierro, a man/ like many others
. . ." Simplicity, honesty, directness are the bywords of
the new poets. Their lines are often based on everyday
speech rhythms: The old-fashioned tricks of rhetoric
gone overboard, they talk to us as if in a private conversation. The struggle has shifted from God, to Society.
But since the enemy is not an overwhelming, eternal being,
but rather an old-fashioned social system, the individual
is no longer dwarfed and alone; and the poet is the voice
of the people, invulnerable, immortal: the future belongs
to the people and to the poet that sings of the people. The
present is black, yet not without hope for tomorrow.

The poet is a Seer, as the novelist is a mirror, recording
in its squalid nakedness the society in which he lives. Hence

the difference in attitude between poets and novelists. Not that all poets are alike: far from that. In an individualistic country like Spain, and in a field such as lyrical poetry, we could expect vast differences between the work of her different poets, even when they belong to the same school of social poetry. Dámaso Alonso has written that the modern poets are all traveling together in the same train, but no one knows where the train is going. Although it is becoming clearer where the train of socially conscious poetry is taking its passengers, their comments about the trip are not identical: a family air masks profound differences of temperament. José Hierro, for instance, is an intimist: he speaks to us in a subdued, restrained voice: we must occasionally make an effort in order to understand his message. Blas de Otero, on the other hand, is a stronger, more exuberant poet—he shouts incessantly, his explosions, invectives, screams of anger almost deafen us. Gabriel Celaya has a tone that is more even, more serene—the tone of a man who has made up his mind and is going to repeat his message, over and over, without fear of repetition—or of contradiction. Jaime Gil de Biedma, Carlos Barral, José Agustín Goytisolo are often more daring, sarcastic and ironical—sophisticated "fellow travelers" all going to the same place in a train that is adding new cars with each passing year.

According to the critic Alonso Zamora Vicente, *The Family of Pascual Duarte*, *The Hive*, and *La Catira (The Blonde Woman)*, a novel about rural Venezuela, are Cela's major novels to date. Of the three, *La Catira*, commissioned by the Venezuelan government during Cela's trip to South America in 1954, and published in 1955, taxes to the utmost the attention and the intelligence of the Spanish reader; rich in local color, in Venezuelan idioms, many of its pages cannot be understood without consulting constantly the glossary appended to the novel. It has not been translated into any language, to my knowledge, and no translation could do justice to the flavor of its well-built, if obscure, descriptions of violence and exuberance in the South American plains. It is a novel of the windswept American earth and the fanatic love it inspires in those who own it. As a foil to its epic overtones, Cela offers us a long series of quickly-sketched provincial characters, most of them ridiculous and pathetic. Because of these characters Venezuelans hate the novel and feel Cela betrayed them. Yet its heroine, a sort of Spanish-speaking Scarlett O'Hara, who uses men, sex, violence and power in order to keep her vast feudal holdings under her iron grip, is one of the most memorable female figures of Spanish literature.

Of lesser complexity and length, though not necessarily of less value, are Cela's "minor" novels: *Rest Home,* published in 1943, a slow meandering description of the thoughts of a group of patients in a sanatorium; *The New Rogue,* a poignant reconstruction in a modern setting of picaresque motifs, published in 1944; and *Mrs. Caldwell Talks to Her Son,* a hallucinating, nightmarish novel made up of a long "conversation" in which the heroine, a frustrated, anguished madwoman, talks to her sailor son, drowned long ago in the Aegean Sea.

But perhaps Cela's art comes to its climax in a third category of books which for lack of a name we might call "quasi-novels." In these Cela, who is fond of wandering on the lonely dusty roads leading to Spanish hamlets, talks to us about the people, the country, his own thoughts. They are much more than travelogues, for Cela's style makes use of one of the richest, most precise vocabularies ever employed by a modern Spanish writer in order to give us a subjective portrait of rural Spain. *A Trip to Alcarria* (1948), *From the Miño to the Bidasoa* (1952), *Jews, Moors, Christians* (1956), *First Trip to Andalusia* (1959) are inimitable descriptions of the real Spain, with its cruelty and tenderness, its dreams and its resignation. The over-all impression is more bitter than sweet. Cela is at his best when talking about the humble, the old, the blind, the shepherds, the dispossessed and marginal men, the children without a future; and yet we are made to feel they are the only ones who hold the key to the true riches of the country and know, subconsciously, all the secrets about Spain's inner self. How much deeper and more satisfying are these "quasi-novels" by Cela than the ambitious but slightly shallow novels about Spain's wealthy couples and their papier-maché "dolce vita," such as Juan Goytisolo's *Island of Women* and Juan García Hortelano's *Summer Storm!* If Cela is Spain's leading novelist, it is because of a rare combination of technique and intuition, experimentalism and love of the past. His subdued indignation wears the mask of a cold, sardonic humor. Some of his characters seem to have the grotesque unreality of deformed puppets, until we realize that these puppets love and suffer.

BIBLIOGRAPHY

Barea, Arturo. Introduction to C. J. Cela's *The Hive* (London, 1953).

Bosch, Rafael. "The New Nonconformist Spanish Poetry," *Odyssey*, 2 (1963).

Cohen, J. M. "Spanish Poetry since the Civil War," *Encounter* (Feb., 1959).

Feldman, David M. "Cela and *La familia de Pascual Duarte*," *Hispania*, 44 (1960).

Gullón, Ricardo. "The Modern Spanish Novel," *Texas Quarterly*, 4 (1960).

Ley, Charles David. *Spanish Poetry since 1939* (Washington, 1962).

MacMahon, Dorothy. "Changing Trends in the Spanish Novel," *Books Abroad* (Summer, 1960).

Palley, Julian. "Existentialist Trends in the Modern Spanish Novel," *Hispania*, 44 (1960).

St. Martin, Hardie. Introduction to Blas de Otero's *Twenty Poems,* (Madison, Minn., 1964).

de Torre, Guillermo. "Contemporary Spanish Poetry," *Texas Quarterly*, 4 (1960).

Yglesias, José. "Four Poets of Spain," *Massachusetts Review*, 3 (1962).

The Theatre of the Absurd
BY MARTIN ESSLIN

The plays of Samuel Beckett, Arthur Adamov, and Eugène Ionesco have been performed with astonishing success in France, Germany, Scandinavia, and the English-speaking countries. This reception is all the more puzzling when one considers that the audiences concerned were amused by and applauded these plays fully aware that they could not understand what they meant or what their authors were driving at.

At first sight these plays do, indeed, confront their public with a bewildering experience, a veritable barrage of wildly irrational, often nonsensical goings-on that seem to go counter to all accepted standards of stage convention. In these plays, some of which are labeled "anti-plays," neither the time nor the place of the action is ever clearly stated. (At the beginning of Ionesco's *The Bald Soprano* the clock strikes seventeen.) The characters hardly have any individuality and often even lack a name; moreover, halfway through the action they tend to change their nature completely. Pozzo and Lucky in Beckett's *Waiting for Godot*, for example, appear as master and slave at one moment only to return after a while with their respective positions mysteriously reversed. The laws of probability as well as those of physics are suspended when we meet young ladies with two or even three noses (Ionesco's *Jack or the Submission*), or a corpse that has been hidden in the next room that suddenly begins to grow to monstrous size until a giant foot crashes through the door onto the stage (Ionesco's *Amédée*). As a result, it is often unclear whether the action is meant to represent a dream world of nightmares or real happenings. Within the same scene the action may switch from the nightmarish poetry of high emotions to pure knock-about farce or cabaret, and above all, the dialogue tends to get out of hand so that at times the words seem to go counter to the actions of the characters on the stage, to degenerate into lists of words and phrases from a dictionary or traveler's conversation book, or to get bogged down in endless repetitions like a phonograph record stuck in one groove. Only in this kind of demented world can strangers meet and discover, after a long polite conversation and close cross-questioning, that, to their immense surprise, they must be man and wife as they are living on the same street, in the same house, apartment, room, and bed (Ionesco's *The Bald Soprano*). Only here can the whole life of a group of characters revolve around the passionate discussion of the aesthetics and economics of pinball machines (Adamov's *Ping-Pong*). Above all, everything that happens seems to be beyond rational motivation, happening at random or through the demented caprice of an unaccountable idiot fate. Yet, these wildly extravagant tragic farces and farcial tragedies, although they have suffered their share of protests and scandals, do arouse interest and are received with laughter and thoughtful respect. What is the explanation for this curious phenomenon?

The most obvious, but perhaps too facile answer that suggests itself is that these plays are prime examples of "pure theatre." They are living proof that the magic of the stage can persist even outside, and divorced from, any framework of conceptual rationality. They prove that exits and entrances, light and shadow, contrasts in costume, voice, gait and behavior, pratfalls and embraces, all the manifold mechanical interactions of human puppets in groupings that suggest tension, conflict, or the relaxation of tensions, can arouse laughter or gloom and conjure up an atmosphere of poetry even if devoid of logical motivation and unrelated to recognizable human characters, emotions, and objectives.

But this is only a partial explanation. While the element of "pure theatre" and abstract stagecraft is certainly at work in the plays concerned, they also have a much more substantial content and meaning. Not only *do* all these plays make sense, though perhaps not obvious or conventional sense, they also give expression to some of the basic issues and problems of our age, in a uniquely efficient and

meaningful manner, so that they meet some of the deepest
needs and unexpressed yearnings of their audience.

The three dramatists that have been grouped together
here would probably most energetically deny that they
form anything like a school or movement. Each of them,
in fact, has his own roots and sources, his own very personal approach to both form and subject matter. Yet they
also clearly have a good deal in common. This common
denominator that characterizes their works might well be
described as the element of *the absurd.* "Est absurde ce
qui n'a pas de but . . ." ("Absurd is that which has no
purpose, or goal, or objective"), the definition given by
Ionesco in a note on Kafka,[1] certainly applies to the plays
of Beckett and Ionesco as well as those of Arthur Adamov
up to his latest play, *Paolo Paoli,* when he returned to a
more traditional form of social drama.

Each of these writers, however, has his own special type
of absurdity: in Beckett it is melancholic, colored by a
feeling of futility born from the disillusionment of old age
and chronic hopelessness; Adamov's is more active, aggressive, earthy, and tinged with social and political overtones; while Ionesco's absurdity has its own fantastic
knock-about flavor of tragical clowning. But they all share
the same deep sense of human isolation and of the ir-
remediable character of the human condition.

As Arthur Adamov put it in describing how he came
to write his first play *La Parodie* (1947):

> I began to discover stage scenes in the most com-
> monplace everyday events. [One day I saw] a blind
> man begging; two girls went by without seeing him,
> singing: "I closed my eyes; it was marvelous!" This
> gave me the idea of showing on stage, as crudely and
> as visibly as possible, the loneliness of man, the ab-
> sence of communication among human beings.[2]

Looking back at his earliest effort (which he now regards
as unsuccessful) Adamov defines his basic idea in it, and
a number of subsequent plays, as the idea "that the
destinies of all human beings are of equal futility, that
the refusal to live (of the character called N.) and the
joyful acceptance of life (by the employee) both lead,
by the same path, to inevitable failure, total destruction."[3]

It is the same futility and pointlessness of human effort, the same impossibility of human communication which Ionesco expresses in ever new and ingenious variations. The two old people making conversation with the empty air and living in the expectation of an orator who is to pronounce profound truths about life, but turns out to be deaf and dumb (*The Chairs*), are as sardonically cruel a symbol of this fundamentally tragic view of human existence as Jack (*Jack or the Submission*), who stubbornly resists the concerted urgings of his entire family to subscribe to the most sacred principle of his clan—which, when his resistance finally yields to their entreaties, turns out to be the profound truth: "I love potatoes with bacon" ("J'adore les pommes de terre au lard").

The Theatre of the Absurd shows the world as an incomprehensible place. The spectators see the happenings on the stage entirely from the outside, without ever understanding the full meaning of these strange patterns of events, as newly arrived visitors might watch life in a country of which they have not yet mastered the language.[4] The confrontation of the audience with characters and happenings which they are not quite able to comprehend makes it impossible for them to share the aspirations and emotions depicted in the play. Brecht's famous "Verfremdungseffekt" (alienation effect), the inhibition of any identification between spectator and actor, which Brecht could never successfully achieve in his own highly rational theatre, really comes into its own in the Theatre of the Absurd. It is impossible to identify oneself with characters one does not understand or whose motives remain a closed book, and so the distance between the public and the happenings on the stage can be maintained. Emotional identification with the characters is replaced by a puzzled, critical attention. For while the happenings on the stage are absurd, they yet remain recognizable as somehow related to real life with *its* absurdity, so that eventually the spectators are brought face to face with the irrational side of their existence. Thus, the absurd and fantastic goings-on of the Theatre of the Absurd will, in the end, be found to reveal the irrationality of the human condition and the illusion of what we thought was its apparent logical structure.

If the dialogue in these plays consists of meaningless

clichés and the mechanical, circular repetition of stereotyped phrases—how many meaningless clichés and stereotyped phrases do we use in our day-to-day conversation?
If the characters change their personality halfway through
the action, how consistent and truly integrated are the
people we meet in our real life? And if people in these
plays appear as mere marionettes, helpless puppets without
any will of their own, passively at the mercy of blind fate
and meaningless circumstance, do we, in fact, in our
over-organized world, still possess any genuine initiative
or power to decide our own destiny? The spectators of the
Theatre of the Absurd are thus confronted with a grotesquely heightened picture of their own world: a world
without faith, meaning, and genuine freedom of will. In
this sense, the Theatre of the Absurd is the true theatre of
our time.

The theatre of most previous epochs reflected an accepted moral order, a world whose aims and objectives
were clearly present to the minds of all its public, whether
it was the audience of the medieval mystery plays with
their solidly accepted faith in the Christian world order or
the audience of the drama of Ibsen, Shaw, or Hauptmann
with their unquestioned belief in evolution and progress.
To such audiences, right and wrong were never in doubt,
nor did they question the then accepted goals of human
endeavor. Our own time, at least in the western world,
wholly lacks such a generally accepted and completely
integrated world picture. The decline of religious faith,
the destruction of the belief in automatic social and biological progress, the discovery of vast areas of irrational
and unconscious forces within the human psyche, the loss
of a sense of control over rational human development
in an age of totalitarianism and weapons of mass destruction, have all contributed to the erosion of the basis for
a dramatic convention in which the action proceeds within
a fixed and self-evident framework of generally accepted
values. Faced with the vacuum left by the destruction of
a universally accepted and unified set of beliefs, most serious playwrights have felt the need to fit their work into
the frame of values and objectives expressed in one of the
contemporary ideologies: Marxism, psychoanalysis, aesthet-
icism, or nature worship. But these, in the eyes of a writer
like Adamov, are nothing but superficial rationalizations

which try to hide the depth of man's predicament, his loneliness and his anxiety. Or, as Ionesco puts it:

> As far as I am concerned, I believe sincerely in the poverty of the poor, I deplore it; it is real; it can become a subject for the theatre; I also believe in the anxieties and serious troubles the rich may suffer from; but it is neither in the misery of the former nor in the melancholia of the latter, that I, for one, find my dramatic subject matter. Theatre is for me the outward projection onto the stage of an inner world; it is in my dreams, in my anxieties, in my obscure desires, in my internal contradictions that I, for one, reserve for myself the right of finding my dramatic subject matter. As I am not alone in the world, as each of us, in the depth of his being, is at the same time part and parcel of all others, my dreams, my desires, my anxieties, my obsessions do not belong to me alone. They form part of an ancestral heritage, a very ancient storehouse which is a portion of the common property of all mankind. It is this, which, transcending their outward diversity, reunites all human beings and constitutes our profound common patrimony, the universal language. . . .[5]

In other words, the commonly acceptable framework of beliefs and values of former epochs which has now been shattered is to be replaced by the community of dreams and desires of a collective unconscious. And, to quote Ionesco again:

> . . . the new dramatist is one . . . who tries to link up with what is most ancient: new language and subject matter in a dramatic structure which aims at being clearer, more stripped of non-essentials and more purely theatrical; the rejection of traditionalism to rediscover tradition; a synthesis of knowledge and invention, of the real and imaginary, of the particular and the universal, or as they say now, of the individual and the collective . . . By expressing my deepest obsessions, I express my deepest humanity. I become one with all others, spontaneously, over and above all the barriers of caste and different psy-

chologies. I express my solitude and become one with
all other solitudes. . . .⁶

What is the tradition with which the Theatre of the
Absurd—at first sight the most revolutionary and radically
new movement—is trying to link itself? It is in fact a very
ancient and a very rich tradition, nourished from many and
varied sources: the verbal exuberance and extravagant
inventions of Rabelais, the age-old clowning of the Roman
mimes and the Italian *Commedia dell'Arte,* the knock-
about humor of circus clowns like Grock; the wild, archetypal symbolism of English nonsense verse, the baroque
horror of Jacobean dramatists like Webster or Tourneur,
the harsh, incisive and often brutal tones of the German
drama of Grabbe, Büchner, Kleist, and Wedekind with its
delirious language and grotesque inventiveness; and the
Nordic paranoia of the dreams and persecution fantasies
of Strindberg.

All these streams, however, first came together and
crystallized in the more direct ancestors of the present
Theatre of the Absurd. Of these, undoubtedly the first and
foremost is Alfred Jarry (1873–1907), the creator of *Ubu
Roi,* the first play which clearly belongs in the category
of the Theatre of the Absurd. *Ubu Roi,* first performed
in Paris on December 10, 1896, is a Rabelaisian nonsense
drama about the fantastic adventures of a fat, cowardly,
and brutal figure, *le père* Ubu, who makes himself King
of Poland, fights a series of Falstaffian battles, and is finally
routed. As if to challenge all accepted codes of propriety
and thus to open a new era of irreverence, the play opens
with the defiant expletive, *"Merdre!"* which immediately
provoked a scandal. This, of course, was what Jarry had
intended. *Ubu,* in its rollicking Rabelaisian parody of a
Shakespearean history play, was meant to confront the
Parisian bourgeois with a monstrous portrait of his own
greed, selfishness, and philistinism: "As the curtain went
up I wanted to confront the public with a theatre in which,
as in the magic mirror . . . of the fairy tales . . . the vicious
man sees his reflection with bulls' horns and the body of a
dragon, the projections of his viciousness. . . ."⁷ But Ubu
is more than a mere monstrous exaggeration of the selfishness and crude sensuality of the French bourgeois. He is at
the same time the personification of the grossness of hu-

man nature, an enormous belly walking on two legs. That is why Jarry put him on the stage as a monstrous pot-bellied figure in a highly stylized costume and mask—a mythical, archetypal externalization of human instincts of the lowest kind. Thus, Ubu, the false king of Poland, pretended doctor of the pseudoscience of Pataphysics, clearly anticipates one of the main characteristics of the Theatre of the Absurd, its tendency to externalize and project outwards what is happening in the deeper recesses of the mind. Examples of this tendency are: the disembodied voices of "monitors" shouting commands at the hero of Adamov's *La Grande et la Petite Manoeuvre* which concretizes his neurotic compulsions; the mutilated trunks of the parents in Beckett's *Endgame* emerging from ashcans —the ashcans of the main character's subconscious to which he has banished his past and his conscience; or the proliferations of fungi that invade the married couple's apartment in Ionesco's *Amédée* and express the rottenness and decay of their relationship. All these psychological factors are not only projected outwards, they are also, as in Jarry's *Ubu Roi,* grotesquely magnified and exaggerated. This scornful rejection of all subtleties is a reaction against the supposed *finesse* of the psychology of the naturalistic theatre in which everything was to be inferred between the lines. The Theatre of the Absurd, from Jarry onwards, stands for explicitness as against implicit psychology, and in this resembles the highly explicit theatre of the Expressionists or the political theatre of Piscator or Brecht.

To be larger and more real than life was also the aim of Guillaume Apollinaire (1880–1918), the great poet who was one of the seminal forces in the rise of Cubism and who had close personal artistic links with Jarry. If Apollinaire labeled his play *Les Mamelles de Tirésias* a *"drame surréaliste,"* he did not intend that term, of which he was one of the earliest users, in the sense in which it later became famous. He wanted it to describe a play in which everything was *larger than life,* for he believed in an art which was to be "modern, simple, rapid, with the shortcuts and enlargements that are needed to shock the spectator."[8] In the prologue to *Les Mamelles de Tirésias,* a grotesque pamphlet purportedly advocating an immense rise in the French birthrate, Apollinaire makes the Director

of the Company of Actors who perform the play, define his
ideas:

> For the theatre should not be an imitation of reality
> It is right that the dramatist should use
> All the illusions at his disposal . . .
> It is right that he should let crowds speak, or inanimate
>   objects
> If he so pleases
> And that he no longer has to reckon
> With time and space
> His universe is the play
> Within which he is God the Creator
> Who disposes at will
> Of sounds gestures movements masses colors
> Not merely in order
> To photograph what is called a slice of life
> But to bring forth life itself and all its truth . . .

Accordingly, in *Les Mamelles de Tirésias* the whole
population of Zanzibar, where the scene is laid, is represented by a single actor; and the heroine, Thérèse, changes
herself into a man by letting her breasts float upwards like
a pair of toy balloons. Although *Les Mamelles de Tirésias*
was not a surrealist work in the strictest sense of the term,
it clearly foreshadowed the ideas of the movement led by
André Breton. Surrealism in that narrower, technical sense
found little expression in the theatre. But Antonin Artaud
(1896–1948), another major influence in the development of the Theatre of the Absurd, did at one time belong
to the Surrealist group, although his main activity in the
theatre took place after he had broken with Breton. Artaud
was one of the most unhappy men of genius of his age, an
artist consumed by the most intense passions; poet, actor,
director, designer, immensely fertile and original in his
inventions and ideas, yet always living on the borders of
sanity and never able to realize his ambitions, plans, and
projects.

Artaud, who had been an actor in Charles Dullin's company at the Atelier, began his venture into the realm of
experimental theatre in a series of productions characteristically sailing under the label *Théâtre Alfred Jarry* (1927–
29). But his theories of a new and revolutionary theatre

only crystallized after he had been deeply stirred by a performance of Balinese dancers at the Colonial Exhibition of 1931. He formulated his ideas in a series of impassioned manifestos later collected in the volume *The Theatre and Its Double* (1938), which continues to exercise an important influence on the contemporary French theatre. Artaud named the theatre of his dreams *Théâtre de la Cruauté,* a theatre of cruelty, which, he said, "means a theatre difficult and cruel above all for myself." "Everything that is really active is cruelty. It is around this idea of action carried to the extreme that the theatre must renew itself." Here too the idea of action larger and more real than life is the dominant theme. "Every performance will contain a physical and objective element that will be felt by all. Cries, Wails, Apparitions, Surprises, *Coups de Théâtre* of all kinds, the magical beauty of costumes inspired by the model of certain rituals. . . ." The language of the drama must also undergo a change: "It is not a matter of suppressing articulate speech but of giving to the words something like the importance they have in dreams." In Artaud's new theatre "not only the obverse side of man will appear but also the reverse side of the coin: the reality of imagination and of dreams will here be seen on an equal footing with everyday life."

Artaud's only attempt at putting these theories to the test on the stage took place on May 6, 1935 at the Folies-Wagram. Artaud had made his own adaptation ("after Shelley and Stendhal") of the story of the Cenci, that sombre Renaissance story of incest and patricide. It was in many ways a beautiful and memorable performance, but full of imperfections and a financial disaster which marked the beginning of Artaud's eventual descent into despair, insanity, and abject poverty. Jean-Louis Barrault had some small part in this venture and Roger Blin, the actor and director who later played an important part in bringing Adamov, Beckett, and Ionesco to the stage, appeared in the small role of one of the hired assassins.

Jean-Louis Barrault, one of the most creative figures in the theatre of our time, was in turn responsible for another venture which played an important part in the development of the Theatre of the Absurd. He staged André Gide's adaptation of Franz Kafka's novel, *The Trial,* in 1947 and played the part of the hero K. himself. Undoubtedly this performance which brought the dreamworld of Kafka to a triumphant unfolding on the stage and demonstrated the effectiveness of this particular brand of fantasy in practical theatrical terms exercised a profound influence on the practitioners of the new movement. For here, too, they saw the externalization of mental processes, the acting out of nightmarish dreams by schematized figures in a world of torment and absurdity.

The dream element in the Theatre of the Absurd can also be traced, in the case of Adamov, to Strindberg, acknowledged by him as his inspiration at the time when he began to think of writing for the theatre. This is the Strindberg of *The Ghost Sonata, The Dream Play* and of *To Damascus.* (Adamov is the author of an excellent brief monograph on Strindberg.)

But if Jarry, Artaud, Kafka, and Strindberg can be regarded as the decisive influences in the development of the Theatre of the Absurd, there is another giant of European literature that must not be omitted from the list—James Joyce, for whom Beckett at one time is supposed to have acted as helper and secretary. Not only is the Nighttown episode of *Ulysses* one of the earliest examples of the Theatre of the Absurd—with its exuberant mingling of the real and the nightmarish, its wild fantasies and externalizations of subconscious yearnings and fears—but Joyce's experimentation with language, his attempt to smash the limitations of conventional vocabulary and syntax has probably exercised an even more powerful impact on all the writers concerned.

It is in its attitude to language that the Theatre of the Absurd is most revolutionary. It deliberately attempts to renew the language of drama and to expose the barrenness of conventional stage dialogue. Ionesco once described how he came to write his first play. (Cf. his "The Tragedy of Language," *Tulane Drama Review,* Spring, 1960.) He had decided to take English lessons and began to study at the Berlitz school. When he read and repeated the sentences in his phrase book, those petrified corpses of once living speech, he was suddenly overcome by their tragic quality. From them he composed his first play, *The Bald Soprano.* The absurdity of its dialogue and its fantastic quality springs directly from its basic ordinariness. It exposes the emptiness of stereotyped language; "what is sometimes labeled the absurd," Ionesco says, "is only the denunciation of the ridiculous nature of a language which is empty of substance, made up of clichés and slogans. . . ."⁹ Such a language has atrophied; it has ceased to be the expression of anything alive or vital and has been degraded into a mere conventional token of human intercourse, a mask for genuine meaning and emotion. That is why so often in the Theatre of the Absurd the dialogue becomes divorced from the real happenings in the play and is even put into direct contradiction with the action. The Professor and the Pupil in Ionesco's *The Lesson* "seem" to be going through a repetition of conventional school book phrases, but behind this smoke screen of language the *real* action of the play pursues an entirely different course with the Professor, vampire-like, draining the vitality from the young girl up to the final moment when he plunges his knife into her body. In Beckett's *Waiting for Godot* Lucky's much vaunted philosophical wisdom is revealed to be a flood of completely meaningless gibberish that vaguely resembles the language of philosophical argument. And in Adamov's remarkable play, *Ping-Pong,* a good deal of the dramatic power lies in the contrapuntal contrast between the triviality of the theme—the improvement of pinball machines—and the almost religious fervor with which it is discussed. Here, in order to bring out the full meaning of the play, the actors have to act *against* the dialogue rather than with it, the fervor of the delivery must stand in a dialectical contrast to the pointlessness of the meaning of the lines. In the same way, the author implies that most of the fervent and passionate discussion of real life (of political controversy, to give but one example) also turns around empty and meaningless clichés. Or, as Ionesco says in an essay on Antonin Artaud:

> As our knowledge becomes increasingly divorced from real life, our culture no longer contains ourselves (or only contains an insignificant part of ourselves) and forms a "social" context in which we are not integrated. The problem thus becomes that of again reconciling our culture with our life by making our culture a living culture once more. But to achieve this end we shall first have to kill the "respect for that which is written" . . . it becomes necessary to break

up our language so that it may become possible to put it together again and to re-establish contact with the absolute, or as I should prefer to call it, with multiple reality.[10]

This quest for the multiple reality of the world which is real *because* it exists on many planes simultaneously and is more than a mere unidirectional abstraction is not only in itself a search for a re-established *poetical* reality (poetry in its essence expressing reality in its ambiguity and multidimensional depth); it is also in close accord with important movements of our age in what appear to be entirely different fields: psychology and philosophy. The dissolution, devaluation, and relativization of language is, after all, also the theme of much of present-day depth psychology, which has shown what in former times was regarded as a rational expression of logically arrived at conclusions to be the mere rationalization of subconscious emotional impulses. Not everything we say means what we intend it to mean. And likewise, in present-day Logical Positivism a large proportion of all statements is regarded as devoid of conceptual meaning and merely emotive. A philosopher like Ludwig Wittgenstein, in his later phases, even tried to break through what he regarded as the opacity, the misleading nature of language and grammar; for if all our thinking is in terms of language, and language obeys what after all are the arbitrary conventions of grammar, we must strive to penetrate to the real content of thought that is masked by grammatical rules and conventions. Here, too, then is a matter of getting behind the surface of linguistic clichés and of finding reality through the break-up of language.

In the Theatre of the Absurd, therefore, the real content of the play lies in the action. Language may be discarded altogether, as in Beckett's *Act Without Words* or in Ionesco's *The New Tenant,* in which the whole sense of the play is contained in the incessant arrival of more and more furniture so that the occupant of the room is, in the end, literally drowned in it. Here the movement of objects alone carries the dramatic action, the language has become purely incidental, less important than the contribution of the property department. In this, the Theatre of the Absurd also reveals its anti-literary character, its endeavor to link up with the pre-literary strata of stage history: the circus, the performances of itinerant jugglers and mountebanks, the music hall, fairground barkers, acrobats, and also the robust world of the silent film. Ionesco, in particular, clearly owes a great deal to Chaplin, Buster Keaton, the Keystone Cops, Laurel and Hardy, and the Marx Brothers. And it is surely significant that so much of successful popular entertainment in our age shows affinities with the subject matter and preoccupation of the avant-garde Theatre of the Absurd. A sophisticated, but nevertheless highly popular, film comedian like Jacques Tati uses dialogue merely as a barely comprehensible babble of noises, and also dwells on the loneliness of man in our age, the horror of overmechanization and overorganization gone mad. Danny Kaye excels in streams of gibberish closely akin to Lucky's oration in *Waiting for Godot*. The brilliant and greatly liked team of British radio (and occasionally television) comedians, the Goons, have a sense of the absurd that resembles Kafka's or Ionesco's and a team of grotesque singers like "Les Frères Jacques" seems more closely in line with the Theatre of the Absurd than with the conventional cabaret.

Yet the defiant rejection of language as the main vehicle of the dramatic action, the onslaught on conventional logic and unilinear conceptual thinking in the Theatre of the Absurd is by no means equivalent to a total rejection of all meaning. On the contrary, it constitutes an earnest endeavor to penetrate to deeper layers of meaning and to give a truer, because more complex, picture of reality in avoiding the simplification which results from leaving out all the undertones, overtones, and inherent absurdities and contradictions of any human situation. In the conventional drama every word means what it says, the situations are clear-cut, and at the end all conflicts are tidily resolved. But reality, as Ionesco points out in the passage we have quoted, is never like that; it is multiple, complex, many-dimensional and exists on a number of different levels at one and the same time. Language is far too straightforward an instrument to express all this by itself. Reality can only be conveyed by being *acted out* in all its complexity. Hence, it is the theatre, which is multidimensional and more than merely language or literature, which is the only instrument to express the bewildering complexity of the human condition. The human condition being what it is, with man small, helpless, insecure, and unable ever to fathom the world in all its hopelessness, death, and absurdity, the theatre has to confront him with the bitter truth that most human endeavor is irrational and senseless, that communication between human beings is well-nigh impossible, and that the world will forever remain an impenetrable mystery. At the same time, the recognition of all these bitter truths will have a liberating effect: if we realize the basic absurdity of most of our objectives we are freed from being obsessed with them and this release expresses itself in laughter.

Moreover, while the world is being shown as complex, harsh, and absurd and as difficult to interpret as reality itself, the audience is yet spurred on to attempt their own interpretation, to wonder what it is all about. In that sense they are being invited to school their critical faculties, to train themselves in adjusting to reality. As the world is being represented as highly complex and devoid of a clear-cut purpose or design, there will always be an infinite number of possible interpretations. As Apollinaire points out in his Preface to *Les Mamelles de Tirésias:* "None of the symbols in my play is very clear, but one is at liberty to see in it all the symbols one desires and to find in it a thousand senses—as in the Sybilline oracles." Thus, it may be that the pinball machines in Adamov's *Ping-Pong* and the ideology which is developed around them stand for the futility of political or religious ideologies that are pursued with equal fervor and equal futility in the final result. Others have interpreted the play as a parable on the greed and sordidness of the profit motive. Others again may give it quite different meanings. The mysterious transformation of human beings into rhinos in Ionesco's latest play, *Rhinoceros,* was felt by the audience of its world première at Düsseldorf (November 6, 1959) to depict the transformation of human beings into Nazis. It is known that Ionesco himself intended the play to express his feelings at the time when more and more of his friends in Rumania joined the Fascist Iron Guard and, in effect, left the ranks of thin-skinned humans to turn themselves into moral pachyderms. But to spectators less intimately aware of the moral climate of such a situation than the German audience, other interpretations might impose themselves: if the hero, Bérenger, is at the end left alone as the only human being in his native town, now entirely inhabited by rhinos, they might regard this as a poetic symbol of the gradual isolation of man growing old and imprisoned in the strait jacket of his own habits and memories. Does Godot, so fervently and vainly awaited by Vladimir and Estragon, stand for God? Or does he merely represent the ever elusive tomorrow, man's hope that one day something will happen that will render his existence meaningful? The force and poetic power of the play lie precisely in the impossibility of ever reaching a conclusive answer to this question.

Here we touch the essential point of difference between the conventional theatre and the Theatre of the Absurd. The former, based as it is on a known framework of accepted values and a rational view of life, always starts out by indicating a fixed objective towards which the action will be moving or by posing a definite problem to which it will supply an answer. Will Hamlet revenge the murder of his father? Will Iago succeed in destroying Othello? Will Nora leave her husband? In the conventional theatre the act always proceeds towards a definable end. The spectators do not know whether that end will be reached and how it will be reached. Hence, they are in suspense, eager to find out *what* will happen. In the Theatre of the Absurd, on the other hand, the action does not proceed in the manner of a logical syllogism. It does not go from A to B but travels from an unknown premise X towards an unknowable conclusion Y. The spectators, not knowing what their author is driving at, cannot be in suspense as to how or whether an expected objective is going to be reached. They are not, therefore, so much in suspense as to *what* is going to happen *next* (although the most unexpected and unpredictable things do happen) as they are in suspense about what the next event to take place will add to their understanding of *what is happening*. The action supplies an increasing number of contradictory and bewildering clues on a number of different levels, but the final question is never wholly answered. Thus, instead of being in suspense as to what will happen next, the spectators are, in the Theatre of the Absurd, put into suspense as to *what* the play *may mean*. This suspense continues even after the curtain has come down. Here again the Theatre of the Absurd fulfills Brecht's postulate of a critical, detached audience, who will have to sharpen their wits on the play and be stimulated by it to think for themselves, far more effectively than Brecht's own theatre. Not only are the members of the audience unable to identify with the characters, they are compelled to puzzle out the meaning of what they have seen. Each of them will probably find his own, personal meaning, which will differ from the solution found by most others. But he will have been forced to make a mental effort and to evaluate an experience he has undergone. In this sense, the Theatre of the Absurd is the most demanding, the most intellectual theatre. It may be riotously funny, wildly exaggerated and oversimplified, vulgar and garish, but it will always confront the spectator with a genuine intellectual problem, a philosophical paradox, which he will have to try to solve even if he knows that it is most probably insoluble.

In this respect, the Theatre of the Absurd links up with an older tradition which has almost completely disappeared from Western culture: the tradition of allegory and the symbolical representation of abstract concepts personified by characters whose costumes and accoutrements subtly suggested whether they represented Time, Chastity, Winter, Fortune, the World, etc. This is the tradition which stretches from the Italian *Trionfo* of the Renaissance to the English Masque, the elaborate allegorical constructions of the Spanish *Auto sacramental* down to Goethe's allegorical processions and masques written for the court of Weimar at the turn of the eighteenth century. Although the living riddles the characters represented in these entertainments were by no means difficult to solve, as everyone knew that a character with a scythe and an hourglass represented Time, and although the characters soon revealed their identity and explained their attributes, there was an element of intellectual challenge which stimulated the audience in the moments between the appearance of the riddle and its solution and which provided them with the pleasure of having solved a puzzle. And what is more, in the elaborate allegorical dramas like Calderón's *El Gran Teatro del Mundo* the subtle interplay of allegorical characters itself presented the audience with a great deal to think out for themselves. They had, as it were, to translate the abstractly presented action into terms of their everyday experience; they could ponder on the deeper meaning of such facts as death having taken the characters representing Riches or Poverty in a Dance of Death equally quickly and equally harshly, or that Mammon had deserted his master Everyman in the hour of death. The dramatic riddles of our time present no such clear-cut solutions. All they can show is that while the solutions have evaporated the riddle of our existence remains—complex, unfathomable, and paradoxical.

FOOTNOTES

1. Ionesco, "Dans les Armes de la Ville," *Cahiers de la Compagnie Madeleine Renaud-Jean-Louis Barrault*, No. 20 (October, 1957).
2. Adamov, "Note Préliminaire," *Theatre II* (Paris, 1955).
3. *Ibid*.
4. It may be significant that the three writers concerned, although they now all live in France and write in French, have all come to live there from outside and must have experienced a period of adjustment to the country and its language. Samuel Beckett (b. 1906) came from Ireland; Arthur Adamov (b. 1908) from Russia; and Eugene Ionesco (b. 1912) from Rumania.
5. Ionesco, "L'Impromptu de l'Alma," *Theatre II* (Paris, 1958).
6. Ionesco, "The Avant-Garde Theatre," *World Theatre*, VIII, No. 3 (Autumn, 1959).
7. Jarry, "Questions de Théâtre," in *Ubu Roi, Ubu Enchaîné*, and other Ubuesque writings. Ed. Rene Massat (Lausanne, 1948).
8. Apollinaire, *Les Mamelles de Tirésias*, Preface.
9. Ionesco, "The Avant-Garde Theatre."
10. Ionesco, "Ni un Dieu, ni un Demon," *Cahiers de la Compagnie Madeleine Renaud-Jean-Louis Barrault*, Nos. 22-23 (May, 1958). [Ionesco's essays, translated by Donald Watson, appeared as *Notes and Counter-Notes* (New York, 1964). Ed.]

Good-by to James Agee
BY ALFRED KAZIN

James Agee, who died in 1955, was a writer who gave all of himself, and often it was himself literally that he gave, to every medium that he worked in—poetry, fiction, reportage, criticism, movies, television. He was not only one of the most gifted writers in the United States, but such a natural as a writer that he found a creative opportunity in every place where drearier people pitied themselves for pot-boiling.

He was the only writer on *Time* who could reduce a managing editor to humility; the only critic who could ever conceivably write about movies for the *Nation* with love; the only documentary reporter for *Fortune* who could make a wholly original book (*Let Us Now Praise Famous Men*) out of an assignment to cover sharecroppers. He wrote two of the best and funniest movies of recent years, *The African Queen* and *The Bride Comes to Yellow Sky*. He wrote the commentary for that tender movie about a little Negro boy, *The Quiet One*. He did a series on Lincoln, for Omnibus, that has been called the most beautiful writing ever done for television; and John Huston thought that Agee was the best screen writer "we have."

In themselves, such distinctions can be meaningless, since not even the serious writers who work for movies or television always take them seriously. But Agee was a writer who actually did better in popular and journalistic media—where certain objective technical requirements gave him a chance to create something out of his immense tenderness and his high sense of comedy—than when he let himself go in purely speculative lyricism. He was a natural literary craftsman, not a literary intellectual,

222

and it was only *avant-garde* associations that ever misled him. His most beautiful poems—like the title poem of his first book, *Permit Me Voyage*—are those which are most traditional in form.

Like so many Southern writers (he came from Knoxville, Tennessee), he had such an immense capacity for feeling and such easy access to the rhetoric of English poetry that when not taken in hand by his medium, he could oppress the reader with merely beautiful words. His almost ecstatic feeling for music itself led him to seek unexpected dimensions in prose, and extraordinarily like Thoreau in this, he tried, in *Let Us Now Praise Famous Men,* to convey his feeling for the American land in highly charged rhythms that would stick close to the facts. Still, it is easy to overrate *Let Us Now Praise Famous Men,* for so many other books of the 1930's now seem unbelievable. Agee wrote of the sharecroppers with such love and rage that it is impossible to read the book without sharing his suffering. But despite its overpowering beauty of language and its immense personal nobility, the book is a turbulent preparation for a work of art that was not achieved.

Agee published in 1951 a short novel, *The Morning Watch,* and at his death he left a virtually complete manuscript which has now been published under Agee's own title, *A Death in the Family.* To anyone who knows how introspective and self-accusing Agee's less successful work could be, both these books show a disciplined control of his narrative material which, if anything, went too far. In both, Agee worked from his earliest memories in order to show the impact on a child of what was plainly a major factor in Agee's own life—the death of his father in the early twenties.

A Death in the Family is worked out with the most immense care and slowness, showing the effect of the father's death upon a family in Knoxville—on the mother, Mary; on the six-year-old Rufus and his sister Catherine; and on the circle of the mother's close relatives. There are several scenes in it that are really hair-raising—especially one where the family, sitting together, concertedly feel the spirit of the dead father coming into the room; and one where little Rufus, too young to realize the immensity of his loss, argues with the kids on the block that he now has a special distinction.

Yet what makes the book so significant is actually not the dramatic qualities of a novel, but a universe of feeling, of infinitely aching feeling, which is built up so thoroughly, with meticulous truth to the agony of bereavement, that we finally have the sense of a wholly tangible sorrow, a materialization of human grief. The book is remarkable as a literary performance because, although obviously written from within—almost as if in obedience to a hallucination—it tries entirely to describe it as an objective situation. The little boy is an unconscious participant in what will hit him only later; unlike his older self in *The Morning Watch*, here he is not old enough to be aware or "interesting."

The trouble with the book as a novel, however, is that although Agee wrote with an almost unbearable effort at objectivity, one feels from the writing that this effort was made to externalize a private grief, not because he thought of the characters in the book as outside himself. The personality of the dead father actually comes through better than any of the living, for he is the single fact outside them to which they all respond as one.

To speak of faults in a book by James Agee is to point up the absurdity of literary comparisons. Agee's book cannot be judged as another novel-of-the-week; it is an utterly individual and original book, and it is the work of a writer whose power with English words can make you gasp. A brother-in-law, looking at the dead man, feels that he is looking down "upon a horned, bruised anvil; and laid his hand flat against the cold, wheemed iron; and it was as if its forehead gave his hand the stunning shadow of every blow it had ever received." The sense of the father in this book, of both the place he filled in life and of the emptiness created by his death, is one of the most deeply worked out expressions of human feeling that I have ever read. And to think of Jim Agee, with his bad heart, writing with such fierce truth so soon before his own death is to marvel, all over again, how literally it is himself that a writer will give to his task.

Edward Albee
BY RICHARD KOSTELANETZ

Edward Albee is clearly the most promising and substantial of the several young American dramatists who have come forth in the last several years, for in a country where dramatists are notoriously unprolific and excellent plays relatively scarce, he has produced, above a few lesser pieces, two works, a short play and a full-length one, which are to my mind among the major achievements of the American stage. Moreover, though his development in the past has been uneven and he may be adversely swamped by the waves of his recent success, there are many good reasons to expect that Albee, now 36, will continue from time to time to write plays of high excellence. Though it is hard at first to define Albee's ultimate interests in a single sentence—his themes are as diverse as his subjects—one can trace the large lines of his style and sensibility as well as the import of each of his plays.

In his first and best one-act, *The Zoo Story* (1959), Albee tells a rather simple story which, largely because it remains so implicit, has often evaded audiences and critics. At base, Albee describes a failed homosexual pass. On the surface, though, the play remains innocent only to the innocent eye. Jerry, a young disheveled man, confronts Peter, a tweedily dressed, graying father in his middle forties, sitting on a bench in Central Park. Jerry solicits Peter's reluctant attention; and once he has a receptive audience, Jerry tells of his vain attempt to establish communication with his landlady's mangy dog. After this long monologue, Jerry starts to nudge Peter, provoking a fight. To make the battle more "evenly matched," Jerry gives Peter his knife which Peter holds out in front of him as a stiff-armed defense. Jerry impales himself on it—

quite deliberately, it seems—and once he feels death coming, he says, "Thank you, Peter, I mean that now," adding, "You have comforted me. Dear Peter."

Beneath this surface runs a homosexual undercurrent. Jerry never explicitly announces his desire to entice Peter, but Jerry's passions are implicit in nearly every speech he makes. Early in the play, Jerry addresses Peter as "boy" and then alleges that Peter can sire no more children. Jerry goes on to say that he lives next door to a "colored queen" and that he often tells strangers, "Keep your hands to yourself, buddy." Peter's usual reply is an indignant, "I must say I don't . . ."; and since throughout the play he is truly unaware of Jerry's real intention, his insensitivity becomes a major source of pathos and comedy.

Albee, like Tennessee Williams, knows how to transform a physical object into a dramatic symbol so that every time the object is mentioned we become more aware of its ulterior meaning. Here Albee has two major sets of symbols—dogs and cats, animals and vegetables. Dogs are surrogate-males, and cats become females. Thus, when Jerry says he wants companionship with a dog, he symbolically announces his homosexual designs. Secondly, an "animal" is a male who will not respond to a homosexual pass, while a "vegetable" is more acquiescent. Around the directions North and South, Albee weaves another stream of symbolic suggestions. Early in the play, Jerry makes sure he has been moving northward, but "not due north," through Central Park and then describes how he brought his mother's cadaver north; and just before he dies, he tells Peter, "I decided that I would walk north." In the north, of course, awaits death.

Once we recognize these symbols, much of the play's "mystery" dissolves into meaningful action. We can, for instance, easily grasp the significance of Jerry's attempt to befriend a dog and, in addition, appreciate it as one of the most moving speeches in contemporary theatre. When Jerry makes physical advances on Peter, first by tickling him until his voice becomes falsetto and then nudging him off the bench, Jerry says, "You're a vegetable! Go lie down on the ground." (Translation: You're a passive male so be a female with your back on the ground.) Again, Peter misses the point. In desperation, Jerry starts a fight with Peter, drawing his knife and giving it to Peter who holds it in front of him like an erected phallus.

Culminating the surrogate seduction, Jerry impales himself upon its blade with rhythms suggestive of an orgasm; and in his dying speech, Jerry confirms to Peter that because, "You've defended your honor, . . . you're not really a vegetable; you're an animal." In his desperate action, Jerry has solved his predicament—he finds both the sexual contact to assuage his desire and death to end it. On one level, then, Albee is writing about the predicament of the lonely homosexual who is never quite sure if the man he tries to pick up is "gay" and whose possible contacts are limited. On another level, he tells of one man's terrible isolation and his desperate need to break out of his shell. Either way, *The Zoo Story* is the most flawlessly wrought and tightly executed of all his plays and probably one of the great one-acts in American dramatic literature.

Soon after its success, Albee released two other one-act pieces, *The Death of Bessie Smith* (1959) and *The American Dream* (1960); and two short-short sketches, *The Sandbox* (1959) and *Fam and Yam* (1960). All but the last have stunning moments, scattered in a rather haphazard manner; but none has the impeccable coherence and emotional intensity of the first one-act. They all suffer from the same defect—in each Albee clumsily piles two dramatic actions into a single framework. *The Sandbox,* perhaps the best of the bad lot, opens with a satire on the ideal American family; but Albee, unable to continue, introduces a clumsy transition and ends with a somewhat mysterious and corny sketch about Grandma's death. In *Bessie Smith,* Albee tries to tell his two stories at once. The first, a tale of social injustice, remembers the historical travesty—because Bessie Smith, injured in an auto accident, was not admitted to a white hospital, she died. The second plot depicts the neuroses of Southern white folk. Only at rare moments do the two stories interact. *The American Dream* is a more disheartening failure, for here Albee becomes more ambitious, taking on the larger problem of the falseness of American ideals, only to sink into cheap comedy and contrived pathos. Too often in these early plays, Albee, letting his dramatic talents smother his good sense, creates a surface of theatrical brilliance on muddy foundations. *Fam and Yam,* even worse, has no defensible virtues, being merely a trivial joke about a young playwright's attempt to get an older successful dramatist to agree that dolts and money-makers control the American theatre. In his adaptation of Carson McCullers' brilliant novella, *The Ballad of the Sad Cafe*— also written early in his career but not produced until 1963 —Albee's failure stems from different causes. Here, it seems, nearly everything he added to the work had the texture of mush. Since the book has no dialogue, Albee wrote all the play's speeches; and since Albee, like most other northerners, has no sense of Southern language, they are embarrassingly inept. Moreover, because Albee's sensibility does not jibe with McCullers', the play lacks the coherence of the novel—whereas love is the dominant emotion of the book, hate becomes the central force in the play. In adapting McCullers' music, Albee sounds dissonant.

Some of Albee's early plays display his ability to create a sharp terror; other times, they contain moments of wit and comedy. In his full-length play, *Who's Afraid of Virginia Woolf* (1962), Albee succeeds in fusing terror and comedy into a single current and largely sustains this twofold tone for the entire play. For two of its three acts, *Virginia Woolf* is one of the most theatrically sharp, witty and moving plays ever written in America. The story's outlines are rather bare. George and Martha, a middle-aged professor at, satirically, New Carthage College and his slightly older wife, invite Nick and Honey, a handsome young biology instructor and his giggly, slim-hipped wife, home for drinks at 1:30 in the morning. For three hours —both on the stage and off—the four engage in drink, conversation and only a little action.

In the course of the play, as each character, his inhibitions slowly stripped by alcohol, comes to bare himself to the others, each reveals that the human appearance he presents to society is merely a façade for the hideous truth, the grisly wolf of the title. In the first act, a drunk Martha, whose father is the college's president, exposes a not-so drunk George by telling the guests that George married her in hopes of getting the presidency for himself; since then, despite the best of connections, he has always been a failure. George informs Nick, a newcomer to the school, that "musical beds" is the faculty sport and that, if you want to gain faculty support for your ambition, "The way to a man's heart is through his wife's belly." In the second act, the guests enter into the spirit of the evening, telling stories on each other, until we find out that the conceited and muscled Nick is too drunk to culminate his seduction of Martha (and, in Albee's cutting humor, is henceforth known as "the houseboy") and that the "son" that Martha continually mentions is merely a fantasy that she and George created to compensate for their inability to have children. In this stripping down is finally the major clue to the meaning of the play. Each of us creates illusions and masks to assuage psychological insecurities, to make us socially presentable—all to enable us to go on with life. Thus, what we as the audience should feel for Albee's four characters is not pity, which is a condescending emotion of sympathy for people who have problems that, by good fortune, do not plague us. Rather, for them we should feel the compassion that comes from an honest recognition that all of us experience a similar predicament, that the need to create a pleasant surface to mask our ugly selves is intrinsic in the human condition.

What sustains our interest, then, is first an awareness of personal complicity and, then, Albee's brilliant and masterful theatrical technique. His sense of timing is breathtakingly deft, particularly in the dialogues—a steady stream of sharp, punching speeches, full of memorable epithets, many of which have already entered the spoken language. His characters engage and challenge each other in credible terms, each one but Honey (defined by absence of clear definition) is a realized creation, and their neuroses are all terrifyingly real. Finally, at the play's heights, the theatre pulses with a nervous rhythm that is infectious.

Yet the play does not manage to escape a gaping flaw. The third act is the real problem, for what is supposed to sustain the audience's interest is the son supposedly about to return from college, and the crowning blow is the revelation that the kid is not. In contrast to the conciseness and speed with which Albee uncovers other hidden truths, he drags this one out to excessive lengths. The child's exorcism, it seems, was the root idea of the play, and all the others were variations on the theme. However, to most of us, many of these are more terrifying and damning than inventing a child.

All this suggests, nonetheless, that Albee's ultimate theme emerges, then, from a deeply felt sense of the universal tragedy of the human experience. A prime characteristic of his sensibility is his refusal to create heroes or anti-heroes, for essentially he deals in group predicaments. All his characters, no matter how different in outward appearance, suffer from similar failings. In *The Zoo Story,* Jerry is as much responsible for the failure of communication as Peter; and in *Virginia Woolf,* each character has some sort of sexual problem. Here, I think, is the key to understanding Albee's ultimate intentions. He wants to describe not the reality we see but the world he knows. At the center of his vision is human failure, an irrevocable picture of the inability of all of us to fulfill the images we cut out for ourselves, or even to satisfy our basic needs.

After several years of doldrums, extending from the peak achievements of Arthur Miller and Tennessee Williams in the early 1950's to 1959, American theatre has since undergone a minor renascence, once again overcoming the tradition of nearly total theatrical mediocrity that has always been our fate. Of all the figures who have become important in recent years, a group that includes Jack Gelber, Kenneth H. Brown, Arthur L. Kopit, Lorees Yerby, Kenneth Koch, Robert Hivnor, Jack Richardson, Lewis John Carlino, LeRoi Jones, James Purdy, and Murray Schisgal. As a playwright, Albee is unquestionably the most significant. Gelber and Brown, in conjunction with Judith Malina and Julian Beck, the founders and directors of The Living Theatre, have created manuscripts for two stunning theatrical experiences—respectively, *The Connection* (1959) and *The Brig* (1963). Gelber's play brilliantly uses the possibility of heroin addiction as an existential choice: if the world is absurd, if the aim of life for most Americans is irresponsible sensuality, then, the play seems to ask us, rather than take to drink or television watching, why not try heroin, which offers the euphoria we all desire quickly and directly. *The Brig,* in subject a portrait of the brutality in a Marine Corps prison, becomes in performance the most complete realization I know of the influential ideas of Antonin Artaud's *The Theatre and Its Double* (1938): that a true theatre poetry would exploit not language but the physical resources of the stage, emphasizing "gestures and postures, dance and music." Precisely because both these plays drew largely upon autobiographical materials and their artistic success depended so much upon the producing genius of The Living Theatre, neither Gelber nor Brown has yet really established himself as a sustaining and fertilely creative playwright. Both Kopit in his *Oh Dad, Poor Dad, Mamma's Hung You in the Closet and I'm Feelin' So Sad* (1959) and, with slightly less success, Miss Yerby in her one-act *Save Me a Place at Forest Lawn* (1963) and James Purdy in *Cracks* (1961) have created realized but minor works in the French absurd tradition of Ionesco and Beckett. Robert Hivnor and Kenneth Koch are older playwrights; and though each has created works of wild originality and exciting humor, respectively *Too Many Thumbs* (1947) and *George Washington Crossing the Delaware* (1959), neither has written a dramatic work whose realization measures up to their powers of mind and imagination. As for Richardson, LeRoi Jones, Carlino, and Schisgal, all are too derivative and unprofound to deserve the attention newspaper critics have given them. Thanks to the commercial vise that systematically chokes off nearly all living theatre in America from its natural audience, many of our most promising young playwrights have not received the attention or productions their work deserves: George Dennison, Maria Irene Fornes, Ely Stock, Robert Head, Bruce Woodford, and Rosalind Drexler. In short, playwrights are developing their talents, the American theatre is changing; and at the moment, in 1964, Albee is the young master.

In Defense of a Maltreated Best Seller
BY NORMAN PODHORETZ

Overpraising mediocre or merely passable or positively bad
novels is a regular habit with American reviewers—so
much so that anyone who takes literature seriously is forever finding himself in the tiresome position of having to
cry "fraud" at the latest masterpiece to be discovered by
the papers. The two most prominent examples in recent
years, of course, have been James Gould Cozzens' *By
Love Possessed* (whose reputation was utterly destroyed by
Dwight Macdonald's famous article in *Commentary*) and
Katherine Anne Porter's *Ship of Fools,* which is still
afloat on a sea of acclaim but is almost certain to be torpedoed before the year is out. Yet when a truly important
novel is either neglected (as was originally the case in this
country with William Golding's *Lord of the Flies*) or
gets a bad press (as, say, Norman Mailer's *The Deer Park*
did), the process of correction seems to require an uncon-
scionable length of time. The sooner the process begins,
however, the sooner it is bound to end, and I would therefore like to venture a step or two in the direction of literary
justice to a new novel that seems to me to have been
maltreated in an appalling way: James Baldwin's *Another
Country*.

In speaking of maltreatment, let me make it clear that
I do not mean to introduce a note of pathos into the discussion. Mr. Baldwin is certainly a victim of injustice at
the moment, but he is not a pathetic victim. For one thing,
his two earlier novels, *Go Tell It on the Mountain* and
Giovanni's Room, were both praised beyond their proper
deserts (especially the second), so that the general failure
to appreciate *Another Country* can be taken as an ironic
rectification of the balance. In addition to that, *Another*

Country has been on the best-seller lists since it came out at the end of June, so that Mr. Baldwin can at least read his bad reviews in comfort. Thirdly, far from being a perfect novel, *Another Country* is faulty to a degree that would wreck a work of lesser force and intensity and truthfulness, so that many of the charges that have been made against it are in themselves quite justified. Finally, the reviews were by no means uniformly hostile. Several pieces in scattered papers and magazines throughout the country—most notably Granville Hicks's moving and intelligent account in *The Saturday Review*—were enthusiastic, and many others, while finding fault with Baldwin's "lack of restraint," or his overly candid descriptions of sexual activity, or his use of dialogue, or his treatment of character, or his handling of plot, nevertheless acknowledged the novel's "power." All the reviewers, moreover (including those who detested the book), made sure to reserve enough space for an earnest tribute to Mr. Baldwin's talents, calling him one of our very best writers and voicing a pious confidence in his ability to do better in the future.

But in spite of all this, I will stand by the word "maltreatment." With few exceptions (*Newsweek* among them), the major reviewing media were very hard on *Another Country*. It was patronized by Paul Goodman in the *New York Times Book Review,* ridiculed by Stanley Edgar Hyman in *The New Leader,* worried over (with, it must be said, genuine distress) by Elizabeth Hardwick in *Harper's,* summarily dismissed by *Time's* anonymous critic, loftily pitied by Whitney Balliett in *The New Yorker* and indignantly attacked by Saul Maloff in *The Nation.*

Three of these reviewers—Goodman, Hardwick and Hyman—are first-rate critics, and I therefore find it hard to believe that their wrongheaded appraisals of *Another Country* can be ascribed to a simple lapse of literary judgment. How could anyone as sensitive and knowledgeable as Elizabeth Hardwick have been so led astray by Baldwin's occasional lapses into sentimentality in writing about love and sex as to call the book "conventional" and "uninspired"? How could a man of Stanley Edgar Hyman's sophistication have been so fooled by the large quantity of explicit erotic detail in *Another Country* as to accuse Baldwin of having cynically set out to fabricate a best seller? How could Paul Goodman, who most assuredly

234 James Baldwin

knows better, have taken the fact that all the characters
are cut off from the main world of the city as a sign that
this novel is a typical commercial product? My own guess
is that all these critics disliked the book, not because it
suffers from this or that literary failing, but because they
were repelled by the militancy and the cruelty of its vision
of life. Granville Hicks was right when he called the book
"an act of violence," and since it is the reader upon whom
this violence is being committed, perhaps one ought to
have expected that many reviewers would respond with
something less than gratitude.

Another Country is about a crucial year in the lives of a
group of people who inhabit a kind of underworld of in-
terracial and intersexual relations. Of the five main characters, two are Negroes—a once-famous jazz drummer,
Rufus Scott; and his younger sister, Ida, an aspiring singer
—and the other three are white—Rufus' closest friend, a
young, unpublished and unmarried writer (Vivaldo
Moore); a woman whose marriage is beginning to fail
(Cass Silenski); and a homosexual actor who comes
originally from the South (Eric Jones). Rufus—by far the
most impressive character Baldwin has ever created—has
a love affair with a pathetic white Southern girl named
Leona which ends for him in suicide and for her in insanity. After Rufus' death, his sister Ida falls in love with
Vivaldo, and while they are living together (less stormily
than Rufus and Leona had, but stormily enough), Ida is
unfaithful to him with a television producer who promises
to further her career; and he, though not a homosexual,
spends a night with Eric by whom, as Stanley Edgar
Hyman delicately put it, he permits himself to be "rectally
violated." By this time, we have already learned that
Rufus, although not a homosexual either, had also once
had an affair with Eric. As for Eric, he too crosses over
the line and enters into an affair with Cass, who is fed up
with the kind of man her husband has become since producing a successful but trivial novel.

Whites coupled with Negroes, heterosexual men coupled
with homosexuals, homosexuals coupled with women, none
of it involving casual lust or the suggestion of neurotic
perversity, and all of it accompanied by the most serious
emotions and resulting in the most intense attachments—
it is easy enough to see even from so crude a summary

that Baldwin's intention is to deny any moral significance whatever to the categories white and Negro, heterosexual and homosexual. He is saying that the terms white and Negro refer to two different conditions under which individuals live, but they are still individuals and their lives are still governed by the same fundamental laws of being. And he is saying, similarly, that the terms homosexuality and heterosexuality refer to two different conditions under which individuals pursue love, but they are still individuals and their pursuit of love is still governed by the same fundamental laws of being. Putting the two propositions together, he is saying, finally, that the only significant realities are individuals and love, and that anything which is permitted to interfere with the free operation of this fact is evil and should be done away with.

Now, one might suppose that there is nothing particularly startling in this view of the world; it is, after all, only a form of the standard liberal attitude toward life. And indeed, stated as I have just stated it, and held with the mild attachment by which most liberal and enlightened Americans hold it, is scarcely more shocking than the usual speech made at every convention of the National Society of Social Workers. But that is not the way James Baldwin holds it, and it is not the way he states it. He holds these attitudes with a puritanical ferocity, and he spells them out in such brutal and naked detail that one scarcely recognizes them any longer—and one is frightened by them, almost as though they implied a totally new, totally revolutionary conception of the universe. And in a sense, of course, they do. For by taking these liberal pieties literally and by translating them into simple English, he puts the voltage back into them and they burn to the touch. Do you believe, he demands of you, that racial prejudice is wrong, that all men are created equal, that individuals must be judged on their own merits? Then you must dare to surrender the objections you are still harboring in your soul against miscegenation. You must acknowledge that there is no reason why whites and Negroes should not sleep together and marry and produce children with as little interference as members of the same race now encounter. And that this is impossible you must recognize as a momentous fact about American life, signifying a moral sickness that may end by destroying our capacity for any kind of human contact whatever. Do you believe, he demands of you again, that love is the supreme value and that sex is the most natural expression of love? Then you must realize that the stifling of your own impulses toward a sexual articulation of the love you feel for members of your own sex is unnatural, signifying a warping of the instincts and of the body that may end by destroying your capacity for any sexual experience whatever.

Another Country, then, is informed by a remorseless insistence on a truth which, however partial we may finally judge it to be, is nevertheless compelling as a perspective on the way we live now. It is a cruel truth, and a demanding one, but it is not without an element of sweet spiritual generosity. For implicit in it is the idea that everyone carries his own burden, that every burden is ultimately as heavy as every other and that a man is either brave enough or strong enough to stand up straight under the weight on his back or he isn't; and if he isn't, he will pay the price and no one else has the right to judge him harshly; and if enough people are found to be lacking in enough bravery or enough strength, then there must be something wrong with the conditions they are being forced to endure and the values these conditions have bred.

Wherever Baldwin manages to remain true to this vision —as in the magnificent opening section about Rufus, the account of the relations between Vivaldo and Ida and scattered passages in every other part of the book—he is at his very best, achieving a unique blend of subtlety and forcefulness, anger and understanding. But there are situations and characters that tax Baldwin's power to sustain the burden of his moral attitude to the breaking point. Thus, he is merciless on Cass Silenski's husband Richard, who is a bad writer and a success, while remaining infinitely charitable toward Vivaldo, who is also a bad writer but a failure; he inclines toward sentimentality in most of the erotic passages involving either a white and a Negro, or a homosexual and a woman, whereas he is visibly skeptical of the validity of the more standard varieties of sex; he can trace every nuance in the relations of an unmarried couple, but in writing about marriage he falls into something very close to philistinism; and in general he judges his white characters (with the exception of the homosexual Eric) by more rigorous criteria than he is willing to apply to the Negroes in the book. All of which means that Baldwin, who speaks so passionately of the white man's need for the courage to know the Negro and the heterosexual's need to know the homosexual, is himself unable to summon up the courage to know and respect those who live in that other country usually designated as normal.

But in the end, the failures of *Another Country,* however serious, seem unimportant beside the many impressive things Baldwin has accomplished here. Within the context of his own development as a writer, I believe that *Another Country* will come to be seen as the book in which for the first time the superb intelligence of Baldwin the essayist became fully available to Baldwin the novelist, in which for the first time he attempted to speak his mind with complete candor and with a minimum of polite rhetorical elegance, and in which for the first time he dared to reveal himself as someone to be feared for how deeply he sees, how much he demands of the world and how powerfully he can hate. Is it perhaps this dangerous militancy that made so many reviewers dislike *Another Country?* The question is worth pondering.

John Barth: An Eccentric Genius
BY LESLIE A. FIEDLER

Nineteen-Sixty was a year in which two American eccentrics of great integrity and power produced ambitious
books which (once more!) have received neither the acclaim nor, I suspect, the kind of reading they deserve.
The first is Wright Morris, whose *Ceremony in Lone
Tree* was received generally with the stony respect it has
become customary to accord his work. His latest book
is the 13th he has published, and at this point the response
to him has become ritualized: the small sales, the impassioned pitches of a few critics, the baffled sense that
now, *now* he must surely be on the verge of popularity
(he has finally one book in paperback, *Love Among the
Cannibals*). Certainly, he has become the best known little-
known author in the civilized world—a "case" we would
all be loath to surrender; but even this indignity Wright
Morris will doubtless endure as he has endured all the
others visited on him in his exemplary career.

To be, like Morris, a really American writer these days
—doggedly provincial and incorruptibly lonely—requires
a special sort of obtuseness, with which Morris is lucky
enough to be blessed; and John Barth, who is my second
eccentric, shares this obtuseness. In his case, however, I
feel somehow that it is an obtuseness chosen rather than
given; for Barth is not only a younger man than Morris,
but is also, unlike Morris, an academic—with proper
degrees and a job in a university. All of which means,
it seems reasonable to assume, that Barth approaches
each of his inevitable publishing failures with an awareness of their inevitability; while Morris, one surmises,
launches each new book with an embittered but un-
broken hope. I see the first of these American types as a

character played by W. C. Fields and the second as one played by Buster Keaton: comics both of them, though reflecting on the one hand the absurdity of great expectations eternally frustrated, and on the other that of foregone defeat accepted with a kind of deadpan pleasure.

John Barth's *The Sot-Weed Factor*—the title is early American for a tobacco merchant—is his third novel, set like his first two in Maryland, or more precisely in the single county of Maryland which he knows best—his America. (Only such a European-oriented writer as Whitman at his worst believes that to portray America one must encompass its imaginary vastness, its blurred continental totality.) Barth works his corner of our land, reconstructs it with all the intensity of Morris re-imagining Nebraska, Hemingway Upper Michigan, Faulkner Northern Mississippi, or Whitman (in his less cosmic moments) Brooklyn; though Barth is surely aware that the territory he explores has less ready-made mythic import for other Americans than almost any region to which he might have been born. It does not represent the moral miasma we identify with the Deep South, nor the well-armed innocence of the East, nor the frigid isolation of New England, nor the niggling Know-Nothingism of the small-town Midwest, nor the urban horrors of the industrialized East.

Maryland, in fact, is not yet invented for our imaginations; and the invention of the place he knows is the continuing task Barth has set himself, the continuing interest that binds together his three books. His is not, of course, the interest of the pious antiquary or local colorist; what he discovers is scandal and terror and disreputable joy—which is to say, the human condition, the disconcerting sameness of human particularity. Yet John Barth is, on one level, a historical scholar; and his books, even when they deal with contemporary or nearly contemporary events (like *The Floating Opera* or *End of the Road*) give the odd effect of being worked up from documents, carefully consulted and irreverently interpreted. He finds in history not merely the truth, not really the truth at all—for each of his novels exploits the ambiguities of facts and motives —but absurdity. He is first of all a philosopher, and knows not only what Marx knew (that if history does, indeed, repeat itself, the second time is always comic) but also

what Heraclitus knew (that there is only a second time).
He is, in short, an existentialist comedian suffering history, not just because it happens to be *à la mode* to be
comic and existentialist, but because, born in Maryland
in his generation and reborn in graduate school, he can
scarcely afford to be anything else. He has, moreover,
talent enough to be what he has to be, against all the odds,
unfashionably.

Granted all this, it was predictable enough that Barth
would eventually try what looks like a full-scale historical
novel and is in fact a travesty of the form. And the probabilities were all along that when he attempted such a
book he would produce one not slim (like the *tour de
force* of Lampedusa's "The Leopard") but traditionally,
depressingly fat. This is in fact so.

The Sot-Weed Factor is a volume of over 800 pages,
dealing with the adventures of a rather unprepossessing
male virgin call Ebenezer Cooke, who in the declining
years of the 17th century came to America—equipped
with a doubtful patent as "Poet and Laureate of Maryland" which somehow involved him not only in the cultural life of his time but also in political and religious
struggles, Indian warfare and the miseries of love. That
the book is too long is obvious—*i.e.*, it is too long for
most reviewers to read through so that, though they are
respectful, they are also cautiously brief and non-committal. For 50 pages at a time it can even be boring or
confusing or both; but what are 50 pages in so immense
a text, and what do a little boredom and confusion matter
in the midst of so dazzling a demonstration of virtuosity,
ambition and sheer courage?

To have settled for less than 800 pages would have been
to accept timidly the unwritten edict that in our time only
bad books can be long, only the bestseller can risk dullness.
Why should the anti-historical novel not be equal as well
as opposite to the standard received historical romance in
fullest bloat? Why should it not also contain *everything*,
though everything hilariously transformed? Though Barth's
anti-history does not end as mere parody, it begins as such:
the reconstruction of a Good Old Time in which Sir Isaac
Newton, with buggery in his heart, pursues his students
across the quad; and the portrait of Lord Baltimore, a disguised master-spy, who is not even really the spy he claims

to be but a more devious counter-agent impersonating the impersonator.

Similarly, Barth's anti-novelistic form distorts the recognitions and reversals of popular literature, first in the direction of travesty and then of nightmare: Brother and sister recognize each other on the verge of rape; Indian and white man find they possess a common father when they confess a common genital inadequacy; the tomahawked and drowned corpses in one chapter revive in the next. Yet somehow the parody remains utterly serious, the farce and melodrama evoke terror and pity, and the flagrant mockery of a happy ending constricts the heart. And all the while one *laughs*, at a pitch somewhere between hysteria and sheer delight.

The book is a joke-book, an endless series of gags. But the biggest joke of all is that Barth seems finally to have written something closer to the "Great American Novel" than any other book of the last decades. In *The Sot-Weed Factor* he recapitulates (not by way of imitation but out of a sensitivity to the dark forces that have always compelled such concerns in our fiction) all the obsessive themes common to our classic novels: the comradeship of males, white and colored, always teetering perilously close to, but never quite falling over into, blatant homosexuality; sentimentalized brother-sister incest or quasi-incest; the anti-heroic dreams of evasion and innocence; the fear of the failed erection.

And the madness of the scene he calls up strikes us as a familiar madness, no recent surrealist import but that old disjunction of sense and order expected in American books, the homely insanity we scarcely notice in the work of Brockden Brown, Edgar Poe or John Neal. Indeed, in a way delightfully unforeseen, Barth's novel more closely resembles the horrendous farrago of John Neal's *Logan* (first published in 1822) than any more recent fiction, middlebrow or beat; though for the influence of *Werther* and Ossian, Barth has substituted that of Rabelais, Sterne, Sir Thomas Browne and the Marquis de Sade. No real American book, after all, can be born without some recognizable European ancestors.

The very styles of Barth's novel are based on Baroque and Mannerist models, and one of the charms of *The Sot-Weed Factor* is the insouciance with which it moves in and out of its counterfeits of 17th century diction. It is, however, no mere pastiche, but a piece of ingenious linguistic play, a joyous series of raids on half-forgotten resources of the language, largely obscene. If anyone has forgotten how many kennings there are in English for copulation, Barth's book will refresh his memory as it runs the gamut of unions, routine and recherché, between man and woman, man and man, man and beast. One important element of *The Sot-Weed Factor* is pornography, comic and serious; and in the book within a book (a secret diary of Captain John Smith which is discovered piece by piece throughout the action) Barth has succeeded in writing the kind of subversive erotic tale with historic trimmings which Mark Twain tried and failed at in *1601*. The point is that Barth—here parting company with his American predecessors—sees the world he renders primarily in terms of sex, and manages somehow to believe that even in America passion is central to the human enterprise.

He is, in the fullest and most satisfactory sense, a "dirty" writer; and this is one reason for his earlier books having dismayed critics, who want their sex programmatic (as in Lawrence, Miller, Durrell, Mailer, etc.), and the public, which wants it sniggering and sentimental (as in almost all bestsellers). Barth gives us sex straight, gay or vicious but never moralized, the literary equivalent of the painfully hand-copied erotica passed from cell to cell in the men's block of prisons; and since American literature has long lived in a jail labelled "For Men Only," he could not have found a more appropriate model.

The Sot-Weed Factor is, finally, not only a book about sex and society, but also one about art, a long commentary on the plight of the artist in the United States by a writer already initiated into contempt and misunderstanding, but preferring still irony to self-pity. After noticing in great detail the difficult relations of the poet with church, state and the opposite sex, the illusions of recognition and the reality of neglect, Barth entrusts his last word to a verse epigraph, presumably composed for his own gravestone by his anti-heroic poet, and, of course, left off by his heirs in the interests of piety:

Labour not for Earthly Glory:
Fame's *a fickly Slut and whory.*

From the Fancy's *chast Couch drive her:*
He's a Fool who'll strive to swive her!

And Barth adds, alluding wryly to the place he himself was born, that this warning must have got about, for the marches of Dorchester in Maryland "have spawned no other poet since Ebenezer Cooke, Gentleman, Poet and Laureate of the Province."

The Point Is Irrelevance
BY KENNETH REXROTH

Although Samuel Beckett has been around for a good many years, Roger Blin's production of *Waiting for Godot* —*En Attendant Godot*—at the Theatre Babylone, two years ago in Paris, catapulted him into an international reputation. Tennessee Williams is reported of the opinion that *Godot* is the greatest play since Pirandello's *Six Characters in Search of an Author*. Right off let me say that I agree with him. Furthermore, I think *Molloy* is the most significant—laying aside the question of greatness—novel published in any language since World War II.

Beckett is so significant, or so great, because he has said the final word to date in the long indictment of industrial and commercial civilization which began with Blake, Sade, Hölderlin, Baudelaire, and has continued to our day with Lawrence, Céline, Miller, and whose most forthright recent voices have been Artaud and Jean Genet.

Now this is not only the main stream of what the squares call Western European culture, by which they mean the culture of the capitalist era; it is really all the stream there is. Anything else, however gaudy in its day, has proved to be beneath the contempt of history. This is a singular phenomenon. There has been no other civilization in history whose culture bearers never had a good word to say for it. Beckett raises the issue of what is wrong with us with particular violence because his indictment is not only the most thorough-going but also the sanest. It is easy enough to write off Lautreamont, who seems to have literally believed that the vulva of the universe was going to gobble him up, or Artaud, who believed that bad little people inhabited his bowels. The cyclone fence around the mad house is certainly a great comfort. The trouble is, Beckett is on this side of the fence. He is not only an artist of consummate skill who has learned every lesson from everybody who had anything to teach at all —from Lord Dunsany to Marcel Proust and Gertrude Stein. (Compare the plot of *Godot* with that little theatre chestnut of Dunsany's, *The Glittering Gate*.) He also has a mind of singular toughness and stability—a mind like an eighteenth-century Englishman, as sly as Gibbon, as compassionate as Johnson, as bold as Wilkes, as Olympian as Fielding. I don't mean that he is "as good as" a mixture of all these people. I mean he is their moral contemporary. "Courage, sir," said Johnson to Boswell.

Beckett refuses to run off to Africa and die of gangrene, or write childish poems to prostitutes, or even see angels in a tree. When a prophet refuses to go crazy, he becomes a problem, crucifixion being as complicated as it is in humanitarian America. When *Godot* was put on in Miami, *Variety* and Walter Winchell, instantly recognizing themselves as two of the leading characters in the play, turned on it with a savagery remarkable even for them. Nevertheless, one of the most promising things about the reception of Beckett in America is the large amount of favorable notice he has received—not just in the quarterlies and *The Nation*, the *New Republic* and *Commonweal*, but in small-town book columns scattered over the country. The European reception of Beckett in the last couple of years, as you know if you keep up with things over there, has been dizzying. He has become an international public figure like Lollobrigida or Khrushchev.

Beckett's first published work was a six-page pamphlet, *Whoroscope* (Nancy Cunard, the Hours Press, Paris, 1930). This is a poem, like the poems we were all writing then—at least I was, and Louis Zukofsky, and Walter Lowenfels and a few other people—very disassociated and recombined, with two pages of notes. Its point is that although René Descartes separated spirit and matter and considered man an angel riding a bicycle, mortality caught up with him and the spirit betrayed him—the angel wore out the bicycle and the bicycle abraded the angel. This has remained one of Beckett's main themes—what is mortality for? And the point of view has never changed. That is, he has carefully pared away from what they call his universe of discourse everything except those questions which cannot be answered. He gives plenty of answers: Pozzo and Lucky in *Godot*—the sempiternal master and man— are, of course, an answer. And, of course, an irrelevant answer. They owe their existence, as does all the "matter" (in Aristotle's sense) of Beckett's art, to their irrelevance.

In 1931, he did for Chatto and Windus a seventy-two-page guide to Proust, a masterpiece of irascible insight worthy to rank with Jonson on Savage. It is one of the very best pieces of modern criticism and somebody should certainly resurrect and reprint it. It is difficult to resist quoting it extensively. In the concluding pages, he says,

> The quality of language is more important than any system of ethics or esthetics . . . form is the concretion of content, the revelation of a world. . . . He assimilates the human to the vegetal. . . . His men and women are victims of their volition—active with a grotesque, predetermined activity within the narrow limits of an impure world. . . . But shameless. . . . The . . . stasis is contemplative, a pure act of understanding, will-less, the "amabilis insania." . . . From this point of view, opera is less complete than vaudeville, which at least inaugurates the comedy of an exhaustive enumeration. . . . In one passage, he describes the recurrent mystical experience as a purely musical impression, non-extensive, entirely original, irreducible to any order of impression—sine materia . . . the invisible reality that damns the life of the body on earth as a pensum and reveals the meaning of the word defunctus.

The most cursory reading of five pages of *Molloy* or *Godot* will reveal the present significance of these words in the practice of Beckett himself.

Murphy (London 1938, Paris 1947) went unnoticed in the blizzard of "social" literature. It is the story of the quest for the person in terms of the quest for a valid asceticism. At the end Murphy has not found himself because he has not found what he can validly do without or safely do with. He may be on the brink of such a discovery, but mortality overtakes him. It is as though Arjuna had been poleaxed in his chariot while Krishna rambled sententiously on.

Watt was written in 1945 but published in Paris in 1953. "What" in Irish is pronounced "watt." It is a step forward in the best possible medium for Beckett's vision —the grim humor of *Iphigenia in Tauris, Lear,* Machiavelli's *Mandragola* and Jonson's *Volpone.* Its concern is the problem, who is who, and its corollary, what is what.

> Looking at a pot, for example, or thinking of a pot, at one of Mr. Knott's pots, of one of Mr. Knott's pots, it was in vain that Watt said, Pot, pot. Well, perhaps not quite in vain, but very nearly. For it was not a pot, the more he looked, the more he reflected, the more he felt sure of that, that it was not a pot at all. It resembled a pot, it was almost a pot, but it was not a pot of which one could say, Pot, pot, and be comforted.

I hope you noticed the sentence, "Well, perhaps not quite in vain, but very nearly." Because that is the gist of the matter and the plot of the novel, the point, so to speak. And it is the point of a good deal of Beckett.

Molloy is the story of two journalists, two keepers of personal, disorganized journals in the dark, light-years beyond the end of night. Molloy, a cripple, is left eventually on his belly in the gloom, clawing his way forward with his crutches. Possibly he is seeking his mother—at least at times that is the impression. Eventually he crawls to a room somewhere where "they"—the "they" of Edward Lear's limericks—bring him food and writing material and take away for their own purposes his narrative as he writes it week by week. It is a grim revery of empty progress through time and space, punctuated with doglike sex and paretic battle.

Moran, the subject of the second half of the novel, is a more recognizable literary figure—the hunter with all the characteristics of the hunted: Inspector Maigret with the personality of Gregor; the inspector in *Crime and Punishment* replaced by Smerdyakov from *Karamazov*. At the orders of a hidden boss whom Beckett, with a minimum of effort, invests with terrors of Fu Manchu, Moran hunts Molloy. In the process he loses his son and all the appur-

tenances of his personality, and becomes indistinguishable
from his quarry. At the end he possibly encounters and
kills Molloy without knowing it. On crutches himself, in
the night, in the rain, he discovers a voice, and writes in
turn his narrative.

Molloy is the drama, totally devoid of event, of relevant
event, of the seekers and the finders, of whom it has been
said: "Finders keepers, losers weepers."

In *Malone Meurt* (*Malone Dies*), Malone is another
lonely writer, locked in a room and fed like a beast. He
is trying to find his own existence by, as it were, describing
his anti-self, by describing a hero who will be progressively
differentiated from Malone, but he cannot do it. He cannot even keep track of the other's name, and he finally
comes to write a story that sounds like an exhausted Sade,
and which is, of course, the story of Malone. . . .

Where Now? Who Now?
BY MAURICE BLANCHOT

Who is doing the talking in Samuel Beckett's novels, who is this tireless "I" constantly repeating what seems to be always the same thing? What is he trying to say? What is the author looking for—who must be somewhere in the books? What are we looking for—who read them? Or is he merely going round in circles, obscurely revolving, carried along by the momentum of a wandering voice, lacking not so much sense as center, producing an utterance without proper beginning or end, yet greedy, exacting, a language that will never stop, that finds it intolerable to stop, for then would come the moment of the terrible discovery: when the talking stops, there is still talking; when the language pauses, it perseveres; there is no silence, for within that voice the silence eternally speaks.

An experiment without results, yet continuing with increasing purity from book to book by rejecting the very resources, meager as they are, that might permit it to continue.

It is this treadmill movement that strikes us first. This is not someone writing for beauty's sake (honorable though that pleasure may be), not someone driven by the noble compulsion many feel entitled to call inspiration (expressing what is new and important out of duty or desire to steal a march on the unknown). Well, why *is* he writing then? Because he is trying to escape the treadmill by convincing himself that he is still its master, that, at the moment he raises his voice, he might stop talking. But is he talking? What is this void that becomes the voice of the man disappearing into it? Where has he fallen? "Where now? Who now? When now?"

He is struggling—that is apparent; sometimes he struggles secretly, as if he were concealing something from us, and from himself too, cunningly at first, then with that deeper cunning which reveals its own hand. The first stratagem is to interpose between himself and language certain masks, certain faces: *Molloy* is a book in which characters still appear, where what is said attempts to assume the reassuring form of a story, and of course it is not a successful story, not only because of what it has to tell, which is infinitely wretched, but because it does not succeed in telling it, because it will not and cannot tell it. We are convinced that this wanderer who already lacks the means to wander (but at least he still has legs, though they function badly—he even has a bicycle), who eternally circles around a goal that is obscure, concealed, avowed, concealed again, a goal that has something to do with his dead mother who is still dying, something that cannot be grasped, something that, precisely because he has achieved it the moment the book begins ("I am in my mother's room. It's I who live there now."), obliges him to wander ceaselessly around it, in the empty strangeness of what is hidden and disinclined to be revealed—we are convinced that this vagabond is subject to a still deeper error and that his halting, jerky movements occur in a space which is the space of impersonal obsession, the obsession that eternally leads him on; but no matter how ragged our sense of him, Molloy nevertheless does not relinquish himself, remains a name, a site within bounds that guard against a more disturbing danger. There is certainly a troublesome principle of disintegration in the story of *Molloy*, a principle not confined to the instability of the wanderer, but further requiring that Molloy be mirrored, doubled, that he become *another*, the detective Moran, who pursues Molloy without ever catching him and who in that pursuit sets out (he too) on the path of endless error, a path such that anyone who takes it cannot remain himself, but slowly falls to pieces. Moran, without knowing it, becomes Molloy, that is, becomes an entirely different character, a metamorphosis which undermines the security of the narrative element and simultaneously introduces an allegorical sense, perhaps a disappointing one, for we do not feel it is adequate to the depths concealed here.

Malone Dies evidently goes further still: here the *vagabond* is nothing more than a *moribund*, and the space

accessible to him no longer offers the resources of a city
with its thousand streets, nor the open air with its horizon
of forests and sea which *Molloy* still conceded us; it is
nothing more than the room, the bed, the stick with which
the dying man pulls things toward him and pushes them
away, thereby enlarging the circle of his immobility, and
above all the pencil that further enlarges it into the infinite
space of words and stories. Malone, like Molloy, is a name
and a face, and also a series of narratives, but these narratives are not self-sufficient, are not told to win the
reader's belief; on the contrary, their artifice is immediately exposed—the stories are *invented*. Malone tells
himself: "This time I know where I am going . . . it is
a game, I am going to play . . . I think I shall be able
to tell myself four stories, each one on a different theme."
With what purpose? To fill the void into which Malone
feels he is falling; to silence that empty time (which will
become the infinite time of death), and the only way to
silence it is to say something at any cost, to tell a story.
Hence the narrative element is nothing more than a means
of public fraud and constitutes a grating compromise that
overbalances the book, a conflict of artifices that spoils
the experiment, for the stories remain stories to an excessive degree: their brilliance, their skillful irony, everything that gives them form and interest also detaches them
from Malone, the dying man, detaches them from the
time of his death in order to reinstate the customary
narrative time in which we do not believe and which, here,
means nothing to us, for we are expecting something much
more important.

It is true that in *The Unnamable* the stories are still
trying to survive: the moribund Malone had a bed, a room
—Mahood is only a human scrap kept in a jar festooned
with Chinese lanterns; and there is also Worm, the unborn, whose existence is nothing but the oppression of his
impotence to exist. Several other familiar faces pass,
phantoms without substance, empty images mechanically
revolving around an empty center occupied by a nameless
I. But now everything has changed, and the experiment,
resumed from book to book, achieves its real profundity.
There is no longer any question of characters under the
reassuring protection of a personal name, no longer any
question of a narrative, even in the formless present of an

interior monologue; what was narrative has become conflict, what assumed a face, even a face in fragments, is
now discountenanced. Who is doing the talking here? Who
is this *I* condemned to speak without respite, the being
who says: "I am obliged to speak. I shall never be silent.
Never." By a reassuring convention, we answer: it is Samuel Beckett. Thereby we seem to draw closer to what is of
concern in a situation that is not fictional, that refers to
the real torment of a real existence. The word experiment
is another name for what has actually been experienced—
and here too we try to recover the security of a name, to
situate the book's "content" at the stable level of a person,
at a personal level, where everything that happens happens with the guarantee of a consciousness, in a world
that spares us the worst degradation, that of losing the
power to say *I*. But *The Unnamable* is precisely an experiment conducted, an experience lived under the threat
of the impersonal, the approach of a neutral voice that is
raised of its own accord, that penetrates the man who
hears it, that is without intimacy, that excludes all intimacy, that cannot be made to stop, that is the incessant,
the interminable.

Who is doing the talking here then? We might try to say
it was the "author" if this name did not evoke capacity
and control, but in any case the man who writes is already
no longer Samuel Beckett but the necessity which has displaced him, dispossessed and disseized him, which has surrendered him to whatever is outside himself, which has
made him a nameless being, The Unnamable, a being
without being, who can neither live nor die, neither begin
nor leave off, the empty site in which an empty voice is
raised without effect, masked for better or worse by a
porous and agonizing *I*.

It is this metamorphosis that betrays its symptoms here,
and it is deep within its process that a verbal survival, an
obscure, tenacious relic persists in its immobile vagabond-
age, continues to struggle with a perseverance that does not
even signify a form of power, merely the curse of not being
able to stop talking.

Perhaps there is something admirable about a book
which deliberately deprives itself of all resources, which
accepts starting at the very point from which there can
be no continuation, yet which obstinately proceeds with-

out sophistry and without subterfuge for 179 pages, exhibiting the same jerky movement, the same tireless, stationary tread. But this is still the point of view of the *external* reader, contemplating what he regards as only a tour de force. There is nothing admirable in inescapable torment when you are its victim, nothing admirable in being condemned to a treadmill that not even death can free you from, for in order to get on that treadmill in the first place, you must already have abandoned life. Esthetic sentiments are not called for here. Perhaps we are not dealing with a book at all, but with something more than a book: perhaps we are approaching that movement from which all books derive, that point of origin where, doubtless, the work is lost, the point which always ruins the work, the point of perpetual unworkableness with which the work must maintain an increasingly *initial* relation or risk becoming nothing at all. One might say that The Unnamable is condemned to exhausting the infinite. "I have nothing to do, that is to say, nothing in particular. I have to speak, whatever that means. Having nothing to say, no words but the words of others, I have to speak. No one compels me to, there is no one, it's an accident, a fact. Nothing can ever exempt me from it, there is nothing, nothing to discover, nothing to recover, nothing that can lessen what remains to say, I have the ocean to drink, so there is the ocean then."

It is this approach to *origin* which makes the experience of the work still more dangerous, dangerous for the man who bears it, dangerous for the work itself. But it is also this approach which assures the experiment its authenticity, which alone makes of art an essential research, and it is by having rendered this approach evident in the nakedest, most abrupt manner that *The Unnamable* has more importance for literature than most "successful" works in its canon. Try listening to "this voice that speaks, knowing that it lies, indifferent to what it says, too old perhaps and too humiliated ever to be able to say at last the words that might make it stop." And try descending into that neutral region where the self surrenders in order to speak, henceforth subject to words, fallen into the absence of time where it must die an endless death: "... *the words are everywhere, inside me, outside me, well well, a minute ago I had no thickness, I hear them, no need to hear them, no need of a head, impossible to stop them, impossible to stop, I'm in words, made of words, others' words, what others, the place too, the air, the walls, the floor, the ceiling, all words, the whole world is here with me, I'm the air, the walls, the walled-in one, everything yields, opens, ebbs, flows, like flakes, I'm all these flakes, meeting, mingling, falling asunder, wherever I go I find me, leave me, go toward me, come from me, nothing ever but me, a particle of me, retrieved, lost, gone astray, I'm all these words, all these strangers, this dust of words, with no ground for their settling, no sky for their dispersing, coming together to say, fleeing one another to say, that I am they, all of them, those that merge, those that part, those that never meet, and nothing else, yes something else, that I'm quite different, a quite different thing, a wordless thing in an empty place, a hard shut dry cold black place where nothing stirs, nothing speaks, and that I listen, and that I seek, like a caged beast born of caged beasts born of caged beasts born of caged beasts . . ."*

—*Translated by* RICHARD HOWARD

Beckett and the Fiction of Mud

BY RAYMOND FEDERMAN

> comment c'était je cite avant
> Pim avec Pim après Pim
> comment c'est trois parties je
> le dis comme je l'entends
>
> *Comment c'est*

The novels of Samuel Beckett defy all classification. Their unorthodox form, their deceptive language, their lack of all elements of conventional fiction, their apparent incoherence, and above all their ambiguous suggestiveness lead to contradictory interpretations. However, on penetrating these works one discovers new concepts of fiction which reveal a most original view of man's existential dilemma. This vision was shaped progressively over a period of three decades during which Beckett exploited in a large number of works (poetry, drama, fiction) a complex and paradoxical method of creation. The ultimate result of these experiments produced the unusual work entitled *Comment c'est* (1961). To comprehend this novel, the unprepared reader—whether a critic or a dilettante—must rid himself of all preconceived notions he may have of the novel form. On first reading, *Comment c'est* appears as a confusing and incoherent mass of words which gains order and meaning only in the light of Beckett's self-generating previous fiction. From one novel to the next a deliberate process of disintegration reduces both form and content to a system whereby creation occurs simultaneously with destruction. In *Comment c'est,* Beckett reaches the outer limits of absurdity without ever falling into meaninglessness.

For what is this book which tells no story, has no plot,

has neither beginning nor end, and though divided into three distinct parts (before Pim, with Pim, after Pim) could go on with a fourth or a fifth or an infinite number of parts, as the anonymous narrator himself suggests? What is this novel which appears formless, which could be read from any page either forward or backward, which reveals the mechanism of its own creation, of its own difficult progress, while noting its aesthetic imperfection ("something wrong there")? Who is this naked being crawling a few meters at a time face down in the mud of some no-man's land toward his victim Pim in part one, establishing a strange and cruel relationship with Pim in part two, and then in turn becoming himself that victim in part three as he awaits his own tormentor, Bem or Bom, to reach him? Who are these creatures whose names change unexpectedly from Pim to Pem to Pam, from Krim to Krem to Kram, from Bim to Bem to Bom? Who is this weird creator-hero (tormentor-victim) who mumbles, out of a twisted mouth, a distorted language which hardly resembles human speech: "brief movements of the lower part of the face . . . quaqua"? What is this book which unravels and repeats the same sets of expressions for, in the French edition, 177 pages of punctuationless prose presented in a series of almost unrelated paragraphs (poetic stanzas?) of a most illogical syntax? Where is this unrealistic universe? Where, in man's experience, is this world of endless dimensions, of darkness and mud, where only a few incongruous objects are still recognizable: a can opener, a cord, a sack full of sardine and tuna fish cans?

To approach Beckett's universe through this novel can be disconcerting and frustrating. Readers of fiction are accustomed to find even in the most fantastic novels, if not a familiar landscape, at least identifiable characters and landmarks which show physical verisimilitude to man and to the real world. Even in Surrealist literature, through distorted images and verbal expressions the visions of the subconscious reflect external reality. The most daring works of science-fiction may posit unbelievable situations, yet despite their grotesque inventions and exaggerations the fantastic relates to the natural world. In other words, whether it pretends to imitate, reshape, evaluate, or interpret reality, or whether it intends to explain the world rationally and formulate ethical values, a work of fiction must rely on realistic norms. In that respect the novel must necessarily conform to a certain aesthetic order to avoid· dwindling into unintelligibility. The reader apprehends and accepts such fiction only within the frame of his own knowledge of language and of reality. Are we then to assume in reading Beckett's fiction that he consciously avoids all ethical statements, all affirmations of a rational and meaningful world? Beckett himself stated in a recent interview: "I am working with *impotence, ignorance.* I don't think impotence has been exploited in the past . . . My little exploration is that whole zone of being that has always been set aside by artists as something unuseable—as something by definition incompatible with art."

Thus by their very form and content the novels of Samuel Beckett question the validity of those criteria by which fiction is rendered believable and useful. While inventing stories and characters which annihilate their own shape and existence, Beckett offers a means of destroying, but also of purifying the traditional novel. His paradoxical creative method unmasks the counterfeit aspects of fictional realism. He confronts the reader with a bare illusion—the artistic lie through which writers transform reality into fiction. Beckett's novels progressively negate the substance of which they are made. Instead of creating a world which simulates reality, and offers social and psychological implications, Beckett presents situations that reject all concepts of truth. The reader is faced with an illusory existence situated in a fraudulent environment: the image of a man (creator-hero) sitting in a room, planted in a pot, crawling in the mud, or simply locked in his own mind, composing, inventing, with whatever words are still available to him, an absurd and totally false sub-reality.

If the grotesque landscape presented in *Comment c'est* bears little relationship to whatever knowledge one may have of real or fictional worlds, it is because this novel is not a projection of reality, but an experiment in willful artistic failure: the rejection of reality. It reveals in the course of its narration, on the level of pure consciousness, the chaos and agony of its creative movement. One can read this book as a satire of fiction—a masochistic expression of the futility of the creative act, or for that matter of all human actions. *Comment c'est* is a metaphorical world of abstractions and illusions which poses as fiction, just as conventional fiction pretends to pass for reality. If the book is successful, it is because it achieves what it set out to do: expose its own failure. In this novel, Beckett makes a conscious effort to avoid creating a finite and realistic world. He carries fictional form and setting into a third dimension as remote from traditional realism as poetry is from fiction. However, Beckett achieves this by parodying that which he is intent on destroying. Only through comic devices does he save himself from falling into cynicism. Each of his successive novels playfully mocks his preceding achievement, and in turn ridicules the whole of literature. *Comment c'est* is not only the story of a naked man who crawls in the mud and describes his progress, his association with a certain Pim, it is also a reflection on Beckett's own creative process.

The narration of *Comment c'est* may appear at first quite complex and unintelligible; but, it is, in fact, extremely simple both in form and content. It has been stripped of all the essential elements of fiction. It is literally made of *nothing:* an absurd and grotesque situation, an irrational and less than human character who barely preserves the basic attributes of man, a few common sentences repeated to the point of meaninglessness, and all of this in a language hardly coherent. Yet the novel progresses almost logically, and it is, as Hugh Kenner wrote, "built phrase by phrase into a beautifully and tightly wrought structure, a few dozen expressions permuted with deliberate redundancy accumulate meaning as they are emptied of it, and offer themselves as points of radiation in a strange web of utter illusion." This deceptive structure is based on nothing tangible. While the narrator-hero progresses painfully:

> push pull the leg slackens the arm folds all articulations play the head arrives at the level of the hand on the belly rest

> the other side left leg left arm push pull the head and the top of the trunk rise as much friction in less falls I crawl the amble ten meters fifteen meters stop

one realizes that the physical contortions of this strange creature have suddenly become verbal contortions. These no longer reflect the difficult progression of a naked body crawling in the mud, but that of a mind accumulating empty words. The reader is confronted with the agonizing growth of the novel. One page, one paragraph would have almost sufficed to describe the narrator's predicament. Beckett stretches the narration to the full length of a novel by merely relating the same events from three different perspectives: before Pim, with Pim, after Pim. The writer's, the creator's mind now appears naked before the reader as it struggles with an inadequate language to perform a futile creative act, while deliberately avoiding meaning and coherence. Failure and nothingness, the goals of this novel, become aesthetic experiences. The action of writing becomes a metaphor for the novel itself: the narrator-hero suffers the creation before the reader's eyes. As he proceeds toward his inevitable failure, he calculates what is left to be done, recognizes and acknowledges the errors of what has been written, and finally concludes with satisfaction: "good good end of the third part and last this is how it was end of the quotation after Pim how it is." What is presented then is a world in the process of disintegrating, in the process of *not* becoming.

The whole novel consists of utterances, of the narrator's recapitulations of his journey (his vain creative effort) toward Pim, of his suppositions and hopes as to how it will be with Pim, of his recollections as to how it was with Pim. Pim's obsessive presence in the narrator's mind governs the narration. Pim is the pivoting point around which every word, every thought, every calculation rotates. Yet to know who Pim is, whom he represents, or if he exists at all, is totally irrelevant, since, as the narrator suggests, it is possible that there "are a million" of Pims, Bems, Krems, or others, all of them interchangeable with "the 999 997 others whom from his position in the round he never has the occasion of encountering." Obviously, Pim and Co. merely serve as excuses for the novel's existence, for the novel to be written, uttered, or destroyed. This whole fiction lies in the realm of uncertainty. Admittedly, while composing his story, the narrator occasionally remembers a vague anterior existence which he situates somewhere above, "in life in the light." But these

realistic memories, presented as concrete images throughout the narration, seem incompatible with the narrator's
main stream of incoherent thoughts, and simply emphasize
the fraudulence of his fiction. The narrator's only concern
is for the novel to go on, regardless of its absurdity.
Therefore, he concentrates on Pim, on his quest for Pim,
on his relationship with Pim, and finally, in part three,
on his own predicament as he now replaces Pim and awaits
the coming of Bem or Bom, or of his alter ego, who
supposedly progresses slowly toward him in the mud.

By the end of part three, the novel has taken on a
circular shape. It has acquired such momentum in absurdity and irrationality that it could easily go on for an
infinite number of parts, simply repeating the same process, the same images, the same words and gestures, just
as the two tramps of *Waiting for Godot* could repeat their
useless comedy to infinity. Faced with this endless condition, in complete despair, the narrator suddenly affirms
that the whole story he told and experienced was a lie,
an illusion, that it is completely false, that none of it
really existed, that none of it was ever performed, spoken,
or written:

> if all this all this yes if all this is not how shall I say
> no answer if all this is not false yes

> all these calculations yes explanations yes the whole
> story from beginning to end yes completely false yes

> it happened otherwise yes entirely yes but how no
> answer how did it happen no answer what happened no
> answer WHAT HAPPENED howlings good

> something happened yes but none of that no bullshit
> from beginning to end yes this voice quaqua yes
> bullshit yes that a voice here yes mine yes when it
> stops panting yes

A novel such as *Comment c'est*, which discloses the
secret of its creation as it progresses, which exposes its
own shortcomings and imperfections, cannot be created
without some antecedent, at least from within the frame
of the author's previous works. To arrive at such complete disintegration of form and content, to achieve such

purity, such transparency and economy of language, to succeed in eliminating all necessary aspects of fiction, and yet preserve an apparent form of narrative, a pattern must precede such a creation. It must emerge from some concrete origin either in fiction or in reality. To grasp Beckett's vision in *Comment c'est*, to accept this novel without brushing it aside as a mere literary hoax, and experience fully the physical and mental deterioration of man as it occurs in Beckett's universe, it is essential to examine his previous achievements. From his 1934 collection of traditional short stories, *More Pricks Than Kicks*, to the English novels *Murphy* and *Watt*, to the unpublished short story *Premier amour* and jettisoned novel *Mercier et Camier*, to the *Nouvelles et Textes pour rien*, to the trilogy of *Molloy, Malone meurt, L'Innommable*, to the fragment entitled "From an Abandoned Work," and finally to the recent *Comment c'est*, not to mention the theater, Beckett has systematically removed from his fiction all the realistic features of what is commonly known as the novel. Therefore, to apprehend this process of reduction, which finds its ultimate expression in *Comment c'est*, one must investigate Beckett's universe chronologically. It is a world in constant motion, in a constant state of being reshaped while being destroyed.

Within this fiction, Beckett's derelicts endure their gratuitous predicament, and consciously invent a life for themselves, however trite, meaningless, absurd, comical, or fantastic it may be. They improvise their existence on the theme of self, with little concern for human norms. Their fictional progress corresponds to their own existence in progress, and becomes a dizzying performance which, like jazz improvisations, exploits its own imperfections as it discovers new zones of being. These creatures' shapes, thoughts, and actions are as unpredictable as the notes which jazz musicians emit from their instruments, and achieve coherence largely by virtue of that unpredictability. Beckett's fiction follows a culminating process which draws toward a single image, a single expression repeated stubbornly to a most irrational degree of infinity. It strives toward the creation of a unique and universal being caught in absurd immortality, and who cries out: ". . . I'll never know, in the silence you don't know, you must go on, I can't go on, I'll go on."

Existence On Stage
BY JACQUES GUICHARNAUD

Despite the success of Genêt, Adamov, and Ionesco, despite the recent interest in Jean Vauthier and Arrabal, Samuel Beckett is still considered the unquestionable originator of a new conception of theatre. Since the 1952–53 season, during which he was in danger of being eclipsed by more established names, critics and a great majority of the public have almost unanimously recognized the importance of his first play *En Attendant Godot*.

Today there is little point in defending Beckett's play. The play is "important," it is new, it lives, it represents a true insight into a way of feeling typical of our times, it goes even further and formulates a definition of man that transcends our times. It invents a new form of dramatic expression; in fact it would seem like the end result of a long search—through the bitterness of naturalistic plays, the mysticism of Catholic drama, the transcendency of poetic theatre—in the attempt to express man's fundamental drama. With *Godot* theatre avoids anecdote and established ideology without falling into abstraction.

Certain critics have described *Godot* as an "allegorical play," whereas *Godot* is in fact totally symbolic without being traditionally allegorical. Allegory consists of an analysis, an exteriorization, and a concrete representation of the elements of the analysis. And this is surely not the case in *Godot*. The elements of waiting (psychological, symbolic, or metaphysical) remain within the characters. They are not even individually thought out; they are continuously and synthetically experienced by the characters. In *Godot* there are no personifications of the abstract or the imaginary. Vladimir is not the personification of the soul or the thirst for God; Estragon is not the personification of material Hunger. Both characters are miserable. They wait and they suffer. They carry within themselves meanings which transcend the story they are living, but only because they are participating in a vaster meaning and a vaster story. Characters and objects (tree, hats, shoes, carrots, turnips) may have a symbolic value— just as Phèdre symbolizes love or Thésée's helmet and beard symbolize royalty-paternity. Although the subject of *Godot* is the waiting for what never comes, and although the play, from beginning to end, evokes that gaping emptiness within each of us which, according to the play, is our very condition, it does not contain the intermediary that is characteristic of allegory: the reduction to abstract elements.

The play also avoids the traps of expressionism and the dangers of the "play of ideas," as there is no question of abstract qualities or analyses of intelligence. Although Vladimir and Estragon sometimes "philosophize," they are in no way like those profound and lucid tramps occasionally found in theatre or films. *Godot* does not imply that wisdom comes from the mouths of tramps. What they say is not explicit and is immediately transposed into poetry. We witness an effort toward ideas, toward memories, toward a rough intellectualization of feelings or impressions—so that our interest is not in their reasoning, but in the effort they make to reason. The vague ideas they express are not there for themselves. They have a purely dramatic function; they are one of the poles toward which the characters desperately strain. There is neither debate nor confrontation, as in Giraudoux, Anouilh, or Sartre; there is merely the representation of the vacuum that separates the characters from what they want to attain.

The absence of any intellectual debate and the representation of a constant state of tension sets *Godot* radically apart from the "play of ideas" and recalls symbolist drama. The intellectual content is there but does not take a logical and discursive form of expression, unsuitable for treating a reality which in itself is experienced. The late nineteenth-century symbolist playwrights were concerned with reaffirming the reality of the Idea as against ideas, that is, the totality of an Essence grasped by intuition as against analytic categories. By the same token, Mood (*état d'âme*) was opposed to Discourse. Whereas Discourse gradually develops in time, advances through the moments of an action, Mood is immobilized in order to evoke an eternity. To the naturalistic discourse, to the sequence of events linked together by the relation of a cause and effect, in a time comparable to that of an office worker, a physicist, or even Darwin, symbolist drama opposed "moments, minutes that are eternal." By its almost Bergsonian intentions, it became "static drama"—a drama which does not move forward, in which nothing happens, similar to a "ball that seems inert" but is "charged with electricity." In extreme cases it has been reduced to the presentation of a painting on stage.

Rémy de Gourmont's description of symbolist drama would seem to anticipate *Godot:*

> Hidden in mist somewhere there is an island, and on that island there is a castle, and in that castle there is a great room lit by a little lamp. And in that room people are waiting. Waiting for what? They don't know! They're waiting for somebody to knock at their door, waiting for their lamp to go out, waiting for Fear and Death. They talk. Yes, they speak words that shatter the silence of the moment. And then they listen again, leaving their sentences unfinished, their gesture uncompleted. They are listening. They are waiting. Will she come perhaps, or won't she? Yes, she will come; she always comes. But it is late, and she will not come perhaps until the morrow. The people collected under that little lamp in that great room have, nevertheless, begun to smile; they still have hope. Then there is a knock—a *knock,* and that is all there is: And it is Life Complete, All of Life.

The play itself must flow; its time is that of the performance. But within the play time is neither that of the scientist nor that of the watch-wearing spectator; it is in the synthesis of the time of the anecdote that is played out and the time of "All of Life." Since waiting contains all of its dimensions at every moment, it is the same whether it lasts for one hour or for fifty years. Here the similarity is obvious. In each act of *Godot* there is an anecdote that takes place in the evening and continues for a few hours. The two evenings are consecutive, yet they are situated in different seasons and "one day we are born, one day we die, the same day, the same second." Moreover the inaction, characteristic of static drama, is closely related to that of *Godot*. Gestures or words—taking place in the flow of normal time—lose their inherent finality when considered in the light of eternity. They are all leveled off by the waiting, by the consciousness of a missing transcendency. Experiencing great love or eating a carrot are two "adventures" which dissolve in the same greyness, the same hollow.

A transcendency can color the world in two contrary ways. It can enrich it: two pieces of wood become the Cross; a red rag embodies the liberation of man. Or it can throw it into insignificance—which is exactly what happens in Rémy de Gourmont's description, as in *Godot*. The transcendency that strips the meaning or ordinary value from an action and substitutes no glorification on any other level can be found in another form in Shakespeare. The fury and sound of Macbeth's adventures dissolve into a final nothingness, and life becomes no more than a tumultuous story "told by an idiot." Didi's and Gogo's clownish tricks and screams, like Macbeth's machinations, would not be insignificant were they given for themselves, but their meanings are reduced to zero by the waiting for Godot. In *Macbeth* that zero is reached at the end of a long trajectory, a long evolution, whereas in *Godot* the zero is not revealed progressively; it is given in advance. Whence the play's apparent inaction, despite innumerable happenings; whence the fact that it marks time; whence the impeccable constancy with which the basic tension is maintained.

En Attendant Godot is a new form of static drama in which three levels are constantly interwoven: (1) the level of words and actions (poetry, clownish tricks, embryonic scenes); (2) that of the direct significance of those words and actions (love, misery, hunger, the role of the intellectual, the dialectic of master and slave, the dimness and confusion of memories, fear, bad faith, even a certain "miserabilism"); (3) that of the waiting which levels everything off. As raw material, Beckett used comedy and the drama of the bum, similar to Chaplin's art or to

Fellini's film *La Strada:* a farce about poverty or solitude, based on realistic observation, in which the spectator is asked to recognize an image of his own condition. Although *Godot* has a more universal and deeper meaning, Beckett used the same foundation, the same background of observation.

As the minutes pass by, Vladimir and Estragon produce an unpretentious mixture of "sound and fury"; they live, they eat, they suffer, they dance, they move about. Their activities are the stylization of a kind of tramp's slice of life. They make use of the objects they find; they eat the bones left by a rich picknicker; they are cold; they are beaten by the "others." On a psychological level, Vladimir and Estragon are much more coherent and individualized than Ionesco's "characterless" characters. They are characters in the traditional sense of the word. Each has a coherent and original personality, a body, a past. Yet they are often treated anonymously. They are called Vladimir and Estragon but only in the program: the young boy calls Vladimir "Monsieur Albert"; Estragon introduces himself as Adam (Catulle in the French version); between themselves they resort to childish nicknames, Gogo and Didi. According to Edith Kern, they are as anonymous as A and B in *Molloy*. Yet such anonymity would seem more comparable to that conferred on characters in farce or in Molièresque comedy through the use of conventional theatricalist names, than to the abstractions A and B or the numbered characters in certain expressionistic plays. Didi and Gogo are not interchangeable either between themselves or with the members of a collectivity. They are not far from the colorful, turbulent, diversified fauna that desperately peoples the works of the Irish.

In his radio play *All That Fall,* Beckett showed his gifts as an observer in the traditional style. The setting in *Godot* is less precise: an Irish landscape could hardly be evoked from that vague platform with one lonely tree. Nor are Gogo and Didi as localized as Mrs. Rooney, Mr. Tyler, Tommy, and Jerry of *All That Fall*. But Gogo and Didi are tramps. They have cut off all attachments to their places of origin; they come from different backgrounds; they met somewhere a long time ago. Indeed it seems as if each one's absolute uprootedness was part of his individual definition—an uprootedness accompanied by partial amnesia, and perhaps even explained by it.

Their partial amnesia is not gratuitous. It helps create the atmosphere of doubt, hesitation, the almost dreamlike haze that clouds the waiting for Godot. But on the level of characterization, the play presents a portrait of two tramps, separated from their pasts, rather vague about their memories, incapable of retracing their own lives or even understanding the ins and outs of their present situation. Yet the fact that they only dimly recall their pasts does not mean that they have none. They are suggested through passing illuminations of flashes. We know, for example, that their youths were more promising than their presents. "In the nineties," says Vladimir, "hand in hand from the top of the Eiffel Tower, among the first. We were respectable in those days. Now it's too late. They wouldn't even let us up." We also know that Estragon was a poet, that they harvested grapes together, that Estragon threw himself into the Durance and Vladimir fished him out—unconnected memories in a state of uncertainty which is in keeping with the characters' general psychological confusion.

The realism of Vladimir and Estragon is increased still more by their differences. The lines of one could not be spoken by the other. Vladimir thinks more; he is more cultured; his anguish is more intellectualized; he is more hesitant and more demanding in his choice of words. Estragon is more spontaneous and more lethargic; he is more childish; he sulks more; he is more eager for protection; he is more egotistical and more obstinate; he holds to his own vocabulary and refuses Vladimir's nuances. Vladimir is more restless, more active; Estragon, more inert. Vladimir has the responsibility; he is in charge of the carrots, radishes, and turnips which make up their meals. Estragon is more the victim; he is the one kicked by Lucky. It is Vladimir who tries to make conversation with Pozzo and who tries to seem "well-bred"; Estragon listens only because he is threatened or ordered to, otherwise he independently follows the flow of his own thoughts. Didi and Gogo clearly recall traditional couples in vaudeville. In fact their ancestors come directly from farce: the yokel and his sly partner, transformed in the modern world into the two soldiers of the nineties in French

military vaudeville, the comic teams in American movies,
Lennie and George in Steinbeck's *Of Mice and Men*.

On the level of anecdote, the difference between the two
characters creates a dramatic tension. Vladimir and Estragon are bound by a relationship that subsists on their
dissimilarities. Their dialogue is not only a kind of antiph-
onal chant of misery; it is also a theatrical dialogue in
which the two characters attract and repel, possess or
elude one another. Basically they need each other like an
old married couple. Vladimir needs someone to talk to,
a sound board for his verbal digressions, and tension is
created the moment Estragon refuses to "return the ball."
Estragon wants protection and in that respect he is the
feminine half. He actually demands protection, reproaches
Vladimir with singing in his absence, gets angry, leaves,
then is afraid and comes back—a kind of coquettish
friendship. This study of two tramps would be merely
grotesque or clinical were their friendship not profound.
It provokes emotion and recognition in that its basic
element, independent of needs or habits, is tenderness.
They talk about a common past, they help each other, they
kiss each other, and even when their actions are tinged
with farce they are steeped in compassion. Once again
we are reminded of Charlie Chaplin and the film *La Strada*,
although Beckett's works are infinitely less tearful.

Obviously the play's ultimate objective transcends the
anecdote and characterization. But despite its originality
as a whole, *Godot* is made up of traditional elements. In
the first production of the play in Paris, those elements
were stressed. The acting was similar to the inner realism
of the Stanislavsky method. As a result, the spectator's
participation was increased, the misery of the characters
made more striking, the tension between a life similar
to ours and an indifferent and forgetful universe made
more convincing and more poignant.

On another level, the spectator participates because that
slice of a tramp's life is charged with human suffering;
and even if he does not identify with the characters, he is
bound to be sensitive to the spectacle of misery in general.
For although *Godot's* "miserabilism"—similar to Chaplin's
—is one of the least important aspects of the play and
the virtues of the poor are not naïvely glorified, it is
constantly present.

In a broader sense Vladimir and Estragon symbolize man in general, and, on that level, the play presents a commentary on life and a definition of man. Edith Kern points out that Vladimir and Estragon are outside of society, that they are not what the existentialists would call *en situation*. Actually they are *en situation* in that they are beaten, they beg, etc. But they are detached from the machinery of society, in which they no longer have any function, and also from the historical situation, which the play ignores. Therefore they have the time to be men. They play at the kind of purity that the classics have bestowed upon certain tragic heroes.

The tramp then is the modern metaphor for universal man. The King in tragedy—risen above men, conducting his politics for himself, closed within his own glory, in direct contact with Fate and Values—represented man's condition in its pure state, without intermediaries and freed from bondage. When Voltaire and the Encyclopedists defined man by his function in and relation to the world of objects (manufacture, commerce), the Bourgeois became representative of humanity. He was Sedaine's citizen of the world. By comparison, the royal hero, who did not transform either economy or materials, would seem like an abstraction. Now that the bourgeois society has begun to doubt its own definitions, we have returned to the metaphor of man in the form of a detached character: the Proustian hero, for example, that bourgeois who does nothing. Leftist ideologies continue to define man by his relation to transformable materials but consider the bourgeois relation as abstract and take the proletariat as the symbol of humanity—a humanity *en situation*, defined both by its work and by the conquest of its freedom. But if one believes in the permanence of universal man it is difficult to accept the proletariat as a satisfying metaphor, for at this particular moment in history, the proletarian is no more than a "half-man" (Sartre). Beside him, we have the tramp—a symbol of humanity considered as residue, stripped of its functions and plans for transformations, and left face to face with itself. The tramp has become the image of our condition laid bare, with everything else a mere secondary quality or anecdote. He is an image of humanity reduced to zero, about to start again from nothing. Here there are possibilities for a new classicism:

A. J. Leventhal, for example, established a strict parallel between man according to Beckett and man according to Pascal.

The tramp represents man as such, as detached from society. He is in some ways the symbol of the inalienable part of every man, the irreducible element which transcends particularities and remains aloof from social, political, civic, or ideological brigades. He marks the renunciation of bourgeois participation in common values, as well as the idea of humanitarian *engagement* or commitment. Man now seems better defined by his solitude and his estrangement than by his participation.

All existence is solitary, and one of the signs of solitude is physical suffering. Where sympathy is possible in the case of moral suffering, physical pain seems to throw the individual into isolation. When Vladimir suffers, he is no more than a spectacle for Estragon. From the very beginning of the play, each tramp remains outside the other's pain:

> *Estragon:* Help me!
> *Vladimir:* It hurts?
> *Estragon:* Hurts! He wants to know if it hurts!
> *Vladimir:* . . . I'd like to hear what you'd say if you
> had what I have.
> *Estragon:* It hurts?
> *Vladimir:* Hurts! He wants to know if it hurts!

No one feels physical suffering *with* another. Here again a comparison can be made with man according to Pascal —the "Man without God," who cannot even use his suffering as a means to salvation. The idea of solitude as unbearable is Pascalian also. The friendship of the two tramps shows the incapacity of man to remain alone with himself. The drama of the human condition thus lies in the uncertainty of each man's relationship to others. The Sartrian analysis of the "others" gives the existentialist theatre its basic drama. The vision of man in *Godot* is similar to it: a perpetual series of rebounds, in which man is constantly thrown back into his solitude. At one extreme there is the idea of a kind of "togetherness" in common action, thanks to which emptiness and solitude seem to be filled:

> *Estragon:* We don't manage too badly, eh Didi, be-
> tween the two of us?
>
> . . . . . .
>
> We always find something, eh, Didi, to
> give us the impression we exist?

In contrast to Estragon's "we" is the other extreme: a total
absence of communication, even an absolute rejection of
the other as when Estragon, in a moment of brief but cruel
betrayal, closes his eyes and in the depths of solitude
calls to another, infinitely more powerful than Vladimir:

> *Estragon:* (*Stopping, brandishing his fists, at the top
> of his voice*). God have pity on me!
> *Vladimir:* (*Vexed*). And me?
> *Estragon:* On me! On me! Pity! On me!

Man's situation cannot be defined by his communion
with others, nor by an absolute absence of relations with
others, but by a fluctuation between the two extremes, by
élans toward communion that are perpetually broken off,
by a mobile synthesis between permanent solitude and the
effort made to come out of it. The fluctuation is characteristic of our activities and brands them as futile.
Vladimir and Estragon do not act; they try to act. They
invent games and then quickly tire of them. Their agitation
is a kind of Pascalian diversion practiced by characters
who know that they are only amusing themselves. What
Beckett's man has that Pascal's free-thinker lacks is lucidity, the consciousness of his own condition. Pascal's King
who hunts continues to hunt because he does not know
why he hunts. Vladimir and Estragon know that they act
in order to avoid thinking about their condition. They act
merely to fill up a vacuum, a fact of which the King was
unaware. The tragedy of their condition takes the form
of a circle: man's condition is unbearable, but the only
apparent means of escape are illusory.

Suicide was twice considered as a possible solution. In
the first act, presented as a sinister form of amusement
on the same plane as the others, it is attractive only
momentarily (for the sexual consequences of hanging)
and then rejected because it may separate the two tramps
should one of them fail to die. The idea is renounced

merely because it means complications. At the very end
of the play they come back to the same idea. But they still
do not commit suicide, this time because of a technical
accident: the cord breaks. Yet they never give up the idea
and the dialogue shows that suicide might be a solution
when, at the end, Estragon declares that he "can't go on
like this," suggests to Vladimir that they separate, and
Vladimir answers that they will hang themselves next day.
However there is no suicide, only two attempts. There
again, even in the case of suicide as a last possibility, the
true condition of man is not in the realization but in the
effort made. Since the attempt miscarried, it made suicide
an action like any other. Moreover it represents what is
most theatrical in any action—the moment when the
character tries to act and seems immobilized between two
modes of being: this time, the being he is and the non-
being he envisions. The drama is neither in the "to be"
nor in the "not to be," but in the "or" which links them
together. Thus another tension in *Godot* is that which
is established between the importance we ordinarily attach
to the "or" and the character's apathy in regard to it.
"Why don't we hang ourselves?" is a proposition that has
neither more nor less importance than: "We could do our
exercises." Although actions take on meaning when thought
of as actions-in-the-world, in *Godot,* just as in Camus'
l'Etranger, the character, thrown into solitude or estrangement, considers his own actions and the actions of others
equally meaningless.

Suicide is parodied in a way by the characters' inactivity
or desire for inactivity in the scene in Act II in which,
once they fall down, they remain lying down. That kind
of "Oblomovitis"—the lethargic irresponsibility of man
lying down—is made impossible by Pozzo's agitation. The
world of the others, who beat Estragon, also condemns
him to getting up and acting.

An intrusion into the monotonous flow of the tramps'
gestures and comments is provided by the entrance of
the couple Pozzo and Lucky. That type of intrusion, so
frequent in theatre, the arrival or passing through of an
apparently different kind of person, makes the spectator
wonder whether the intruder will succeed in transforming
the play's universe, or whether his difference will prove
to be no more than illusory. For the two tramps, Pozzo

and Lucky constitute a fantastic spectacle offered by the society of men from which they are excluded. By the same token, they are treated less realistically than the two heroes, for they are a sort of metaphor of what the tramps see in the society that is foreign to them.

Their nature and the nature of their relationship are immediately clear to the spectator. Pozzo, dressed like a country gentleman, carries a whip and holds, at the end of a rope, a pale and thin creature wearing a valet's vest and heavily burdened down. One is the master, the other the slave. They enter shortly after the following exchange of words:

> *Estragon:* (*His mouth full, vacuously*). We're not tied?
> *Vladimir:* I don't hear a word you're saying.
> *Estragon:* (*Chews, swallows*). I'm asking you if we're tied.
> *Vladimir:* Tied?
> *Estragon:* Ti-ed.
> *Vladimir:* How do you mean tied?
> *Estragon:* Down.
> *Vladimir:* But to whom? By whom?
> *Estragon:* To your man.
> *Vladimir:* To Godot? Tied to Godot? What an idea! No question of it. (*Pause*). For the moment.

Almost directly, Pozzo appears on stage holding the rope to which Lucky is *tied*. Is Lucky's rope similar to the bond that might possibly unite the tramps to Godot? Are they not in fact waiting for the opportunity to give themselves up to bondage? They are waiting to be taken over by Godot, they hope to be, but they never explain what they want of him. All that Vladimir and Estragon say is that they are waiting to be "saved." The idea of salvation without any concrete content is suddenly actualized by the rope that ties Lucky to Pozzo. If salvation consists in being possessed by Godot, the desire to meet Godot and the repulsion provoked by the rope would be the two poles of a fundamental hesitation, a movement back and forth comparable to that which attracts the two tramps to one another and then separates them. Here again is the tragic circle, similar to that in existentialist drama: the vacuum of freedom calls for something to fill it, for the nothingness is unbearable; but when the total commitment or possession is realized, the resulting state is just as agonizing. Man is caught between the vacuum of waiting for Godot and the bondage of a Lucky (Lucky: the lucky one who has found his Godot).

Neither possession nor bondage would seem to be solutions. The friendship between the two tramps and Pozzo's and Lucky's rope are only sketches or parodies of a true union—both desired and feared, yet never realized. They seem to imply that we never arrive at more than a pitiful or grotesque approximation of a union, just as, through action, we arrive at no more than the "impression we exist."

Our lives are farces of Life. The master-slave relationship and Pozzo's acts represent one aspect of the farce, the most ordinary and the least lucid. The rope is meant to reassure Pozzo, just as through his comments, Estragon reassures himself in stressing the friendship that ties him to Vladimir. But where Vladimir and Estragon make a pretense at acting, fighting, or playing, Pozzo takes his actions seriously and the least of his gestures becomes a whole spectacle, glorified by noble language. In exaggerating the simple processes of life—having Lucky serve him his lunch, sitting down again after having got up, describing the sky, lighting his pipe—Pozzo tries to drown his life in a general atmosphere of ceremony so as to cover up its insignificance. Either man waits for Godot, or he clutters up his life with all the outer signs of importance.

In the second act Pozzo is blind. For Edith Kern, Pozzo's blindness and Lucky's muteness are signs of the inevitable degradation of the master-slave couple. Actually Pozzo's blindness leads to a partial reversal of the relationship. He no longer drives Lucky, he follows him, and the rope has become shorter—a kind of parodic and concrete sketch of the master-slave dialectic. Besides, although the rope is shorter, Pozzo's blindness throws him into the shadows of his solitude. He thus grasps more accurately the horror of his condition, which has now become an amplification of Vladimir's and Estragon's. For even more than having doubts about time and his situation in space, Pozzo is in complete ignorance or total confusion.

Indeed it would seem that truth lies in the depths of the confusion. Pozzo's definition of life, implied by the play as a whole, is drawn from his darkness: "One day we were born, one day we shall die, the same day, the same second. . . ." Since the days are all alike, they merge into one indefinite day. There is no flow, only a state. Yet the words were spoken by a character who is in perpetual motion. Beckett plays with contrasts and creates a whole network of subtle tensions between the *state* and the *effort*. Pozzo, who passes by, clings to his state. The tramps, who remain, are always making an effort to get up and do something. When Estragon almost reaches a state (the death-like state of man lying down), it is Pozzo who, also fallen down, makes an effort to get up. That scene, in which Vladimir and Estragon call themselves "men" and Pozzo "all humanity," with all the characters who have fallen down, now trying to get up, now refusing, going from immobility to effort and vice versa, is the most developed metaphor of the human condition. It has an echo in *All That Fall*, when Mr. and Mrs. Rooney, he blind, she lamed by her obesity, try not to fall.

Pozzo tried to give his life a structure by his possession of Lucky and the visible sign of his possession, the rope. By the same token, Lucky is "saved" by that bond, by his function and his state of servitude. But servitude leads to a mechanization which crushes the individual. Lucky is reduced to basic reactions: he trembles, he cries, he kicks. He has a past: he had been a better dancer; he had been Pozzo's "thinker"; he had been, and still is his valet and his jester. Lucky is more than a servant in the ordinary sense of the word. He represents other servitudes, principally that of the intellectual and the artist. He thinks *for* Pozzo; he dances *for* Pozzo. Vladimir and Estragon think and play, or try to think and play, for themselves. Their efforts are perhaps ridiculous. But Lucky's are inhuman and abstract—at least they have become so in Pozzo's service. When independence (analogous with solitude) is opposed to service (analogous with union), the two situations result in grotesque failures. Moreover the complexity and incoherence of Lucky's long speech make it possible to see his situation at that moment as a farcical satire on the condition of professional intellectuals. Supported by a society for whom they are all valets, they "produce" thought, as they are asked to do, but exasperate their masters by their verbal delirium. The result of such deterioration is silence. In the second act Lucky has become mute.

Their new state introduces a usual notion of time. We are born and die the same day, but still the change indicates that we are born *before* we die (in *All That Fall* there is mention made of a little girl who dies because she has not been born). Pozzo and Lucky have changed from one act to the other, from one day to the next from winter to spring. The amount of time is undetermined but the direction of time is preserved. In the compressible but irreversible time that Vladimir and Estragon fill up in their monotonous way, the Pozzos and the Luckys "evolve":

Vladimir: How they've changed!
Estragon: Who?
Vladimir: Those two.
Estragon: That's the idea, let's make a little conversation.
Vladimir: Haven't they?
Estragon: What?
Vladimir: Changed.
Estragon: Very likely. They all change. Only we can't.

Where the two tramps are immobilized by their waiting for Godot, the couple Pozzo-Lucky, who are not waiting for anything, deteriorate in time. If they were meant to represent a society entirely concerned with itself, a kind of prophecy can be seen at that level. Desperately clinging to its present structure (the master-slave relationship) and its rites, amused by an abstract and anguished art (Lucky, who formerly danced the jig and the fandango, breaks out into a symbolic pantomime of "the net") and by means of an intellectual delirium that no longer has meaning, society will evolve into a world of blind Pozzos and mute Luckys—or toward the world of Hamm and Clov in *Fin de partie.*

The scenes including Pozzo and Lucky show the meeting of two living durations in different modes that merge: the perpetuation of waiting, a monotonous flow experienced by men who ask for happenings and change (*Estragon:* Nothing happens, nobody comes, nobody goes, it's awful!); and the transition, change, and deterioration experienced by men who cling to their state, although conscious of the speed of destruction and the unexpectedness of events (*Pozzo:* . . . night is charging and will burst upon us—pop! like that!). In contrast to social and historic man, who is in a hurry to be something or thinks he is, in the brief decrescendo that makes up the duration of a life or civilization, the play offers a portrait of man as withdrawn from history and society, left to his existence, and continuously yawning in the indefinite flow of monotonous time.

In both cases, the activities and effort are in vain and serve only to fill in time. What maintains and reinforces this particular meaning of the play, what keeps the spectator from attributing an inherent finality to any one activity are the constantly repeated references to Godot, who is awaited but never comes. Pozzo and Lucky come up to us like the person who stops and tells us the story of his life while we are impatiently awaiting a friend. The fact that we are waiting takes away all real finality from his words and relegates them to a negative universe marked by the absence of the friend we are awaiting. In the same situation, the drink we are having is not drunk for itself; it is drunk-while-waiting. And it is the *waiting* that permeates all of the tramps' gestures and comments and relegates their acts to a background of non-being such as Sartre analyzed in *l'Etre et le néant.*

And yet besides the agitation invented to pass the time, the moments of life marked by hunger, blows, fear, or physical suffering are real. They are experienced in horror. But even that reality is finally reduced to insignificance. It, also, becomes the negative background marked by the absence of Godot. The transcendency by which suffering is negated is itself no more than an absence. In the symbolist drama, the Idea—as mysterious, obscure, or chaotic as it may be—is reality. In *Godot* the real remains at the level of what is directly experienced, and Godot is systematically absent; his very existence is uncertain; he is the phantasm that is satisfying because it gives con-

tent to man's desire for a frame of reference. Man is
unable to accept insignificance, unable to understand that
his misery and his existence are themselves devoid of
meaning. Godot is that by which man both justifies and
confirms the insignificance of existence. He is the Hypothesis that explains a negative phenomenon. He is the
Yes dialectically necessary for life to be the No that it is.
The question is not to justify being, but to justify non-
being. The development in *En Attendant Godot* consists
in three movements: consciousness of insignificance; the
assertion of a meaning (Godot) in relation to which it
is possible to conceive of an absence of meaning; and the
strengthening of insignificance through a consciousness of
and the waiting for something that *has* meaning.

On the level of anecdote Godot is a character just like
the others. His absence makes him more blurred and
more uncertain, but enough details are given to form a
sketchy but concrete image. He has shepherds, agents, a
family, a bank account. He even has a beard. He is distant,
capricious, and powerful, like the Masters in Kafka's
world. Exactly who is he and whom does he represent?
Edith Kern suggests God plus the ending "ot" of Charlot,
the name given to Chaplin's Little Man by the French.
In fact the meaning of the play does not lie in explanations
of what Godot symbolizes. Whether he signifies God or
any other belief or illusion is of secondary importance. The
subject of the play and its drama is not the identity of
Godot but the waiting itself.

Therefore the play does not fall into any established
categories of religion or ideology, which in themselves
would suggest a definition of Godot. It represents a reversal of the Romantic attitude—that of Chateaubriand,
for example, for whom God came first and then the
vague à l'âme, a rather indefinite anguish and melancholy,
as a sign of our desire for God. Here the desire for Godot
to arrive comes first. Godot is the positive element created
to correspond to the feeling of emptiness and insignificance,
which alone is real and experienced.

The universe revealed by the play is one of insignificance. The drama that gives it tension is the conflict between insignificance and man's effort to have meaning
despite everything. The metaphor of waiting is the best
form of expression for that conflict, in which lies Beckett's

final definition of man. *En Attendant Godot* is not an allegory, an incompleted *Pilgrim's Progress*. It is a concrete and synthetic equivalent of our existence in the world and our consciousness of it.

En Attendant Godot is Beckett's most important work to date. His later works *Fin de partie,* the pantomime *Acte sans paroles,* the radio play *All That Fall,* and the mono-drama *Krapp's Last Tape* pick up certain of *Godot's* themes and express them in different metaphors, without ever quite reaching the plenitude and immediacy of his first play.

Yet all have one quality in common: their intense theatricalism. Besides the value of his vision of life, besides his drama, Beckett is acutely conscious of the essence of theatre itself. He writes for the Italian-type or picture-frame stage. His characters live within a stage frame; they must be seen from the same angle by the entire audience at the same moment. This is particularly notice-able when he tries to produce a "full-face" effect. In *Fin de partie* Hamm in his armchair must be seen from the front, just as Giacometti's figures, looming out of a space enclosed on three sides, are prisoners of their frames, or like one of Francis Bacon's horrifying apparitions. The play can only be performed in a box set, strictly limited by its frame. *Krapp's Last Tape* must also be played on the picture-frame stage if Krapp is to disappear into the background to drink in obscurity.

Using the traditional stage, Beckett is free to respect the convention of the fourth wall or break it at will. In *Godot,* by unexpectedly destroying the conventional illusions, he produces unoriginal but surprising effects. In the first act the audience is taken for a "bog" or is ironically considered as "inspiring prospects." The background itself suddenly stops being the space alongside a road and again becomes a stage set when Estragon, in a moment of panic (Act II, French version), rushes headlong "toward the backdrop, gets entangled in it, and falls." Certain lines are both a direct expression of the character's thoughts, and comments addressed to the spectator by the playwright:

Vladimir: This is becoming really insignificant.
Estragon: Not enough.

In *Fin de partie* the asides to the audience are more obvious. The play begins like a late nineteenth-century bourgeois comedy: the servant's pantomime of his domestic duties, followed by several remarks which explain the situation. Comments on the meaning of the play are more frequent. Clov's last declamatory speech, for example, is addressed directly to the audience.

Beckett's theatre goes even further and presents life as an imitation of theatre. The master in *Fin de partie* is called Hamm, implying a ham actor. Hamm tries to perform certain numbers, like Pozzo and Mr. Rooney. All of them feel they are giving a structure to their lives by choosing particular events and telling about them in an affected style with rhetorical effects, and conscious, not of reliving, but of replaying them. "How did you find me?" asks Pozzo after his description of nightfall. Hamm demands an audience and constantly interrupts to comment on his own style: "Nicely put, that . . . A bit feeble, that. . . ." And Mr. Rooney asks, after an interruption: "Where was I in my composition?" Such "composed" narratives are part of a system of rites by which Beckett's characters try to give form to life by fitting it into a framework of beautiful language or deliberately masking its horror. In *Krapp's Last Tape* the hero records the narrative of his life as it unfolds and listens to himself. Proust's hero set about saving his past by making it eternal through art; Beckett's heroes try to save their lives from insignificance through narrative. But for Beckett, literature is not salvation: Pozzo and, particularly, Hamm are conscious of the vanity of their attempts; Krapp's tape turns silently at the end of the act. Literature then is not necessarily salvation; it is an effort made to save oneself, perhaps as futile as any other. Yet Beckett himself makes the effort.

Presented as theatrical numbers, the "narratives" and, by extension, literature and theatre, are games. Conscious of the esthetic quality of their monologues, Pozzo, Hamm, Mr. Rooney, and Krapp (who found a tape recorder the best means for listening to himself) play and watch themselves play. By the same token, Vladimir and Estragon never succeed in taking their own actions seriously. They rapidly become aware of the fact that their actions are theatrical numbers and that they are actors and spectators at the same time. Life consists in pretending to live—like children pretend that they fly or are animals—and yet we have nothing more than our lives. Thus there is a correspondence between our lives in the world and the essence of theatre, in which, paradoxically, what is performed is both reality and a game, and requires both participation and detachment. Beckett's vision of life is made for the stage.

Life is no more than the comedy of life, no more than an attempt to play at living, no more than an embryonic farce. The often childish or capricious "games" that represent life on stage must necessarily be borrowed from genres in which failure, stumbling, and the resistance of objects make up the spectacle: circus and vaudeville sketches and their outgrowth, the motion picture farce. Among others, the hat number in *Godot* and Mrs. Rooney's difficulties with Mr. Slocum's car in *All That Fall* clearly establish the equivalence between daily life, made up of obstacles, repetitions, and failures, and the most elementary and grossest forms of theatrical comedy. Farce of that kind is grating, precisely because the equivalence is made so obvious and because our lives are directly concerned. The characters in Beckett's theatre are constantly caught between their own clumsiness and the resistance of objects, including their own bodies: shoes that are too narrow, hats too small, car doors too low, windows too high, prostate conditions, hemorrhages, itching. Moreover they forget necessary objects or misplace them, especially in *Fin de partie* and *Krapp's Last Tape*. Beckett's universe is one of perpetual irritation. Nothing in it works: a universe of imperfections in which things would seem to have been created, not for man, nor actually against him, but merely in order to exist in a state of passive resistance to his efforts. In *Acte sans paroles* Beckett is both more explicit and less convincing. Objects literally slip away from the character, and the remarkable atmosphere of concrete uneasiness that pervades his spoken plays is replaced by an abstract notion of frustration.

All the small obstacles of daily life cause man to make a series of efforts that represents, in a way, the more general attempt of giving a structure and meaning to life. The various attempts made are given a theatrical quality through techniques borrowed from the art of clowns and resulting in pure theatricalism. In *Godot* Beckett uses a twentieth-century myth—the one that best expresses man's attempt to live decently in a world of hostile objects and social groups: Charlie Chaplin's Tramp. In the second act of *Godot* the curtain rises on Estragon's boots placed "front center, heels together, toes splayed," and Lucky's bowler hat thrown somewhere in the background. Chaplin's cane is missing, as if the tramps, relatives of Chaplin's Little Man, had not managed to achieve his elegance.

Chaplin's Little Man is a modern myth and, apart from Hitler, the only modern myth sufficiently distant and individualized. Hollywood, the Party, the middle-class American and Frenchman, the Capitalist, are all institutions, collectivities, or abstractions raised to the level of myth. Chaplin's Little Man emerged directly as a myth, with his own individuality and his own past. His universality is guaranteed in part by his generality. He is known, recognized, and loved by about everyone. When Beckett suggests Charlie Chaplin, he is using a contemporary tradition in order to give a visible sign of the play's universality and also to show that the universal is in the present.

In *Godot* Beckett managed to multiply the Little Man's family. The character closest to the source is Vladimir, with his attempts at playing a certain worldly game: "Never neglect the little things in life," he says as he buttons his fly; or when he is asked his opinion on Lucky's dance: "There's something about it . . .," he says, "squirming like an esthete." On the other hand, Estragon's shoes most clearly recall the Little Man's classic attributes, and it is Estragon who kicks like him in order to have his revenge. All the characters wear bowler hats as a sign of their participation in the myth. For Chaplin's Tramp is the myth of man who, despite everything, *plays* at being a man.

Although Beckett's other dramatic works are not concerned with the myth, the idea of life as a game and man's attempt to play it remains a central theme. The myth is replaced by "explanations" that might be considered a weakness in Beckett's later works. In *Fin de partie* the theme is stressed in the title itself (*End Game*) and by passing remarks ("Me—to play," says Hamm). The attempt to play is opposed, as in *Godot*, to the desire for release through annihilation. The characters in *Fin de partie* waver between the two attitudes; Mrs. Rooney, in

All That Fall, wants to be transformed into a "big fat jelly" or disappear into her comfortable bed. The struggle between an attempt at playing and the wish for self-destruction is always accompanied by a consciousness of life's absurdity and brevity: "The same day . . . ," as Pozzo said; and Mrs. Rooney's: "Just one great squawk and then . . . peace. They would have slit her weasand in any case," after Mr. Slocum had squashed a hen with his car; and Hamm's: "Moments for nothing, now as always, time was never and time is over, reckoning closed and story ended," at the end of *Fin de partie. Krapp's Last Tape* ends in a kind of stupor and the tape recorder turns silently after Krapp's last words concerning the best years of his life: "I wouldn't want them back." Beckett's great feat is to make the spectator experience simultaneously the interminable series of minutes that make up his life, a game which never stops ending, in which he exists in a state of permanent tension, perpetually headed for defeat, and the somewhat objective consciousness of life's absurd brevity. "The end is in the beginning and yet you go on," says Hamm parodying T. S. Eliot. Life is a bad play, performed for nothing, yet it is the only one we have. Mrs. Rooney dreams of annihilation, but continues nonetheless to appreciate the landscape and makes every effort to walk without falling. Hamm and Clov call out for the end to come, but continue to play the hateful game of the man who can't sit down and the man who can't get up.

Beckett's characters are never alone in their efforts. They are bound two by two in differing forms of solidarity: Vladimir and Estragon, Pozzo and Lucky, Hamm and Clov, Nagg and Nell, Mr. and Mrs. Rooney, even Krapp and his recorded voice. The character of *Acte sans paroles* is in contact with a kind of invisible and superior being who plays with his desires just as Pozzo plays with Estragon when he is about to give him the chicken bones. Beckett's theatre is a theatre of couples. Each character rebounds against another. Each one acts now with, now against that other. The relationship with another seems necessary to the effort of playing at living, dialogue being one of the forms of the tension that is our existence. Tenderness, need, and hate are the psychological constituents of the bond, always treated with an irony in which sarcasm is mixed with emotion—emotion because the characters are bound by the recognition of a common misery; sarcasm because the bond remains unworkable and never transforms the misery, and because each one uses the other, pretending to communicate with him. When Nell and Nagg reminisce about a boat outing on Lake Como, they realize that, for different reasons, they had experienced the happy moments each alone, and their so-called common past had not saved them from final agony in separate garbage cans. The master-slave relationship is the most frequent and clearest sign of an absence of equality between people. Any relationship with others must needs be that of conqueror and conquered, executioner and victim, possessor and possessed—and theatre feeds on the contradictory efforts made by the characters to solidify the relationship or burst it wide open.

Although the themes and theatrical devices can be found over and again from play to play, and although Beckett's general vision of life and definition of man remain the same, each play is nonetheless situated in a different universe. *All That Fall* takes place in the peopled and known world of realism. Mrs. Rooney has gone out. She regrets it because of the dangers of the outside world, but persists in following the road to the station amidst people, animals, and flowers. The point of view is always Mrs. Rooney's, but the people she meets are treated with an objectivity à la Maupassant. *Godot's* universe is also that of the outside world, but its space is interpreted by the subjectivity of the characters, a kind of desert shot through with rare and unjustified happenings. In *Fin de partie* Beckett's characters no longer go out. They are voluntary prisoners of their own private dramas, just as the characters in *Huis Clos* refuse to leave their room in Hell when the door opens. The outside world, which continues to interest them, can only be seen through a telescope. It is an end-of-the-world landscape in which life has almost disappeared and the sea itself has become immobilized. "To hell with the universe," says Hamm, as he plunges back into the interminable quarrel that binds him to his servant, Clov. The indefinite space of *Godot* has been replaced by a closed room. The open image of waiting for salvation has been replaced by the closed image of waiting for annihilation. Finally, in *Krapp's Last Tape,* the room itself is a shadowy hole, in the center of which the character talks to himself, telling the story of his own life.

The silence of Krapp and his tape recorder is the last image to date of Beckett's man. Language has become powerless to express the dialogue of man with himself, and man remains suspended for an indefinite time between two states of consciousness: the interminable effort of living and the vanity of life. In Beckett's theatre, man is again put face to face with himself. After the successive demystifications represented by the works of post-war playwrights, Beckett has tried the supreme demystification. He attacks life itself. He does it without long speeches, without contradictory debates. He merely places existence on stage. His works cannot be called existentialist, although they can be explained through the use of existentialist categories. His is a *theatre of existence* which, in itself, is outside any one school of thought.

To exist, for Beckett, means to watch oneself trying to exist and, by the same token, to be either fully aware of the effort it takes or to attempt to blind oneself to it. The dogmatism of the Cartesian *cogito* is transformed into a skepticism tinged with Eastern philosophy: "I see myself trying to exist; therefore I exist." And as Pozzo says: "Sometimes I wonder if I'm not still asleep." In point of fact, the drama that makes up the substance of Beckett's theatre is the ironic duality of demystified man.

Beckett's characters silently struggle toward forms of being or structures that are suddenly disclosed by a gesture or in words. Lyricism, eloquence, invectives, and clichés are like fixatives which make existence intelligible and temporarily "save" it. The words hesitatingly move on from image to image toward the greatest possible precision or toward an enrichment or transformation of reality. Screams and swearing are often meant to "fix" a gesture or an impression. The poetry of the language is not in its profuse imagery but in its precision, in the music of intersecting voices, in the calculated alternation of pauses and transparent words. But the fixatives are ephemeral and the words fall back into silence, just as water subsides to form a new wave. The pulsation of effort, forever repeated and forever vain, gives Beckett's works their rhythm, their balance, their form. When all of life is a game, theatre, the game par excellence, has the last word.

Saul Bellow
BY LESLIE A. FIEDLER

With the publication of *Seize the Day,* Saul Bellow has become not merely a writer with whom it is possible to come to terms, but one with whom it is *necessary* to come to terms—perhaps of all our novelists the one we need most to understand, if we are to understand what the novel is doing at the present moment. Bellow has endured the almost ritual indignities of the beginning fictionist: his first novel a little over-admired and read by scarcely anyone; his second novel once more critically acclaimed, though without quite the thrill of discovery, and still almost ignored by the larger public; his third novel, thick, popular, reprinted in the paper-backs and somewhat resented by the first discoverers, who hate seeing what was exclusively theirs pass into the public domain; and now a fourth book: a collection of stories, most of which have appeared earlier, a play, and a new novella.

Suddenly, the novelist whom we have not ceased calling a "young writer" (it is a habit hard to break and the final indignity) is established and forty, a part of our lives and something for the really young to define themselves against. But it has become clear that he will continue to write, that he is not merely the author of a novel or two, but a *novelist;* and this in itself is a triumph, a rarity in recent American literary history and especially among the writers with whom we associate Bellow. We think of the whole line of Jewish-American novelists, so like him in origin and aspiration, of Daniel Fuchs and Henry Roth and Nathanael West, those poets and annalists of the thirties who did not survive their age, succumbing to death or Hollywood or a sheer exhaustion of spirit and subject. Or we think of Bellow's own contemporaries, the

Partisan Review group, urban Jews growing up under the threat of failure and terror, the depression and Spain and the hopelessly foreseen coming of war. We remember, perhaps, Isaac Rosenfeld or H. J. Kaplan or Oscar Tarcov or Delmore Schwartz or even Lionel Trilling, who had also to be twice-born, committed first to Stalinism and then to disenchantment, but who were capable of using imaginatively only the disenchantment. And remembering these, we recall beginnings not quite fulfilled, achievements which somehow betrayed initial promises. Certain short stories remain in our minds (flanked by all those essays, those explanations and rejoinders and demonstrations of wit): Kaplan's "The Mohammedans," Rosenfeld's "The Pyramids," Schwartz's "In Dreams Begin Responsibilities," Trilling's "The Other Margaret"; but where except in *The Dangling Man* and *The Victim* and *Augie March* do the themes and motifs of the group find full novelistic expression?

We must begin to see Bellow, then, as the inheritor of a long tradition of false starts and abject retreats and grey inconclusions. There is a sense in which he fulfills the often frustrated attempt to possess the American imagination and to enter the American cultural scene of a line of Jewish fictionists which goes back beyond the post-war generation through Ben Hecht and Ludwig Lewisohn to Abe Cahan. A hundred, a thousand one-shot novelists, ephemeral successes and baffled eccentrics stand behind him, defining a subject: the need of the Jew in America to make clear his relationship to that country in terms of belonging or protest—and a language: a speech enriched by the dialectic and joyful intellectual play of Jewish conversation.

Bellow's own story is, then, like the archetypal Jewish dream a success story; since, like the standard characters in the tales of my grandfather (socialist though he was!), the novelist, too, has "worked himself up in America." Bellow's success must not be understood, however, as exclusively his own; for he emerges at the moment when the Jews for the first time move into the center of American culture, and he must be seen in the larger context. The background is familiar enough: the gradual breaking up of the Anglo-Saxon domination of our imagination: the relentless urbanization which makes rural myths and

images no longer central to our experience; the exhaustion
as vital themes of the Midwest and of the movement
from the provinces to New York or Chicago or Paris;
the turning again from West to East, from our own heart-
land back to Europe; and the discovery in the Jews of a
people essentially urban, essentially Europe-oriented, a
ready-made image for what the American longs to or
fears he is being forced to become.

On all levels in the years since World War II, the
Jewish-American writer feels imposed on him the role
of being The American, of registering his experience for
his compatriots and for the world as The American
Experience. Not only his flirtation with Communism
and his disengagement, but his very sense of exclusion, his
most intimate awareness of loneliness and flight are demanded of him as public symbols. The Southerner and
the Jew, the homosexual out of the miasma of Mississippi
and the ex-radical out of the iron landscape of Chicago
and New York—these seem the exclusive alternatives,
contrasting yet somehow twinned symbols of America at
mid-century. *Partisan Review* becomes for Europe and
Life magazine the mouthpiece of intellectual America,
not despite but because of its tiny readership and its
specially determined contributors; and in Saul Bellow a
writer emerges capable of transforming its obsessions into
myths.

He must not, however, be seen only in this context. His
appearance as the first Jewish-American novelist to stand
at the center of American literature is flanked by a host
of matching successes on other levels of culture and sub-
culture. What Saul Bellow is for highbrow literature,
Salinger is for upper middlebrow, Irwin Shaw for middle
middlebrow and Herman Wouk for lower middlebrow.
Even on the lowbrow levels, where there has been no
such truce with antisemitism as prosperity has brought to
the middle classes, two young Jews in contriving Superman
have invented for the comicbooks a new version of the
Hero, the first purely urban incarnation of the most ancient
of mythic figures. The acceptance of Bellow as the leading
novelist of his generation must be paired off with the
appearance of Marjorie Morningstar on the front cover of
Time. On all levels, the Jew is in the process of being
mythicized into the representative American.

There is a temptation in all this to a kind of assimilation with the most insipid values of bourgeois life in the United States. It is to Bellow's credit that he has at once accepted the full challenge implicit in the identification of Jew with American, and yet has not succumbed to the temptation; that he has been willing to accept the burden of success without which he might have been cut off from the central subject of his time; and that he has accomplished this without essential compromise. In *Augie March,* which is the heart of his work (though technically not as successful as *The Victim* or *Seize the Day*), he has risked the final absurdity: the footloose Jewish boy, harried by urban machiavellians, the picaresque *schlimazl* out of Fuchs or Nathanael West, becomes Huck Finn; or, if you will, Huck is transformed into the footloose Jewish boy. It is hard to know which way of saying it gives a fuller sense of the absurdity and importance of the transaction. The point is, I think, that the identification saves both halves of the combination from sentimental falsification: Huck Finn, who has threatened for a long time to dissolve into the snubnosed little rascal, barefoot and overalled; and the Jewish *schlimazl,* who becomes only too easily the liberals' insufferable victim, say, Noah Ackerman in Irwin Shaw's *The Young Lions.*

The themes of Saul Bellow are not, after all, very different from those of the middlebrow Jewish novelists in step with whom he has "worked himself up"; but in treatment they become transformed. Like Wouk or Shaw, he, too, has written a War Novel: a book about the uncertainty of intellectual and Jew face to face with a commitment to regimentation and violence. But unlike Wouk and Shaw, Bellow has not merely taken the World War I novel of protest and adulterated it with popular front pieties. His intellectual is not shown up like Wouk's Keefer; his Jew does not prove himself as brave and brutal as his antisemitic buddies like Shaw's Ackerman or Wouk's Greenspan, whose presumable triumphs are in fact abject surrenders. The longing to relinquish the stereotyped protest of the twenties, no longer quite believed in, is present in Bellow's *Dangling Man,* but present as a *subject:* a temptation to be confronted, not a value to be celebrated.

Dangling Man is not an entirely successful book; it is a

little mannered, a little incoherent, obviously a first novel. But it is fresh beyond all expectation, unlike any American war book before or since; for Bellow has realized that for his generation the war itself is an anticlimax (too foreknown from a score of older novels to be really lived), that their real experience is the waiting, the dangling, the indecision before the draft. His book therefore ends, as it should, with its protagonist about to leave for camp and writing in his journal: "Hurray for regular hours! And for the supervision of the spirit! Long live regimentation!" In the purest of ironies, the slogans of accommodation are neither accepted nor rejected, but suspended.

Similarily, in *The Victim* Bellow takes up what is, perhaps, the theme *par excellence* of the liberaloid novel of the forties: antisemitism. In proletarian novels, though many were written by Jews, this was a subject only peripherally treated; for the Jew in the Communist movement, Judaism was the enemy, Zionism and the Jewish religion the proper butt of satire and dissent. But Hitler had made a difference, releasing a flood of pious protests against discrimination; from Arthur Miller's *Focus* to John Hersey's *The Wall*, via *Gentlemen's Agreement*, *The Professor's Umbrella*, etc., Jew and Gentile alike took up the subject over and over. In a time when the Worker had been replaced by the Little Man as a focus for undiscriminating sympathy, the Little Jew took his place beside the Little Negro, the Little Chinese, the Little Paraplegic as a favorite victim. Even what passed for War Novels were often merely anti-antisemitic fictions in disguise, the war itself being treated only as an occasion for testing a Noble Young Jew under the pressure of ignorant hostility.

In the typical middlebrow novel, it was seldom a real Jew who was exposed to persecution; rather some innocent gentile who by putting on glasses mysteriously came to look Jewish or some high-minded reporter only pretending to be a Jew. In part what is involved is the commercial necessity for finding a gimmick to redeem an otherwise overworked subject; but in part what is at stake is surely a confusion in the liberal, middlebrow mind about what a Jew is anyhow: a sneaking suspicion that Jew-baiting is real but Jews are imaginary, just as, to the same mind, witch-hunting is real but witches only fictions.

In Bellow's book about antisemitism, *The Victim,* once more the confusion becomes the subject. It is Asa Leventhal, not the author, who is uncertain of what it means to be a Jew, because he does not know yet what it is to be a man; and neither he nor his author will be content with the simple equation: the victim equals the Jew, the Jew the victim. In *The Victim,* Jew and antisemite are each other's prey as they are each other's beloved. At the moment when the Jew in general, when the author himself as well as his protagonist, have moved into situations of security, however tenuous, inflicting injury in their scramble to win that security, Bellow alone among our novelists has had the imagination and the sheer nerve to portray the Jew, the Little Jew, as victimizer as well as victim. Allbee may be mad, a pathological antisemite and a bum, but his charge that Leventhal's success was achieved somehow at his expense is not utter nonsense. It is the necessary antidote to the self-pity of the Jew, one part of a total ambiguous picture. In the slow, grey, low-keyed exposition of *The Victim,* Leventhal's violence and his patience, his desire to exculpate himself and his sense of guilt, his haunting by the antisemite he haunts, become for us truths, part of our awareness of our place as Jews in the American scene.

As *The Victim* is Bellow's most specifically Jewish book, *Augie March* (in this, as in all other respects, a reaction from the former) is his most generally American. Its milieu is Jewish American, its speech patterns somehow moulded by Yiddish, but its theme is the native theme of *Huckleberry Finn:* the rejection of power and commitment and success, the pursuit of a primal innocence. It is a strangely non-Jewish book in being concerned not with a man's rise but with his evasion of rising; and yet even in that respect it reminds us of *David Levinsky,* of the criticism of David implicit in the text and entrusted to the socialist characters. It is as if David had been granted a son, a grandson, to try again—to seek a more genuine Americanism of noncommital. Certainly, Bellow's character is granted a symbolic series of sexual successes to balance off the sexual failures of Cahan's protagonist. But the socialism of Cahan does not move his descendant; it has become in the meanwhile Soviet Communism, an alternative image of material success, and has failed; so that there is left to Augie only the denial of the values of capitalism without a corresponding allegiance, a desire to flee success from scene to scene, from girl to girl, from father to father—in favor of what? The most bitter of Happy Endings as well as the most negative, the truly American Happy Ending: no reunion with the family, no ultimately happy marriage, no return to the native place— only a limitless disponibility guarded like a treasure. It is, of course, the ending of *Huckleberry Finn,* an ending which must be played out as comedy to be tolerable at all; but unlike Twain, Bellow, though he has found the proper tone for his episodes, cannot recapture it for his close. *Augie,* which begins with such rightness, such conviction, does not know how to end; shriller and shriller, wilder and wilder, it finally whirls apart in a frenzy of fake euphoria and exclamatory prose.

Seize the Day is a pendant and resolution to *Augie March.* Also a study of success and failure, this time it treats them in contemporary terms rather than classic ones, reworking directly a standard middlebrow theme. Call it "The Death of a Salesman" and think of Arthur Miller. It is the price of failure in a world dedicated to success that Bellow is dealing with now; or more precisely, the self-consciousness of failure in a world where it is not only shameful but rare; or most exactly of all, the bitterness of success and failure become pawns in the deadly game between father and son. Bellow is not very successful when he attempts to deal with the sentimental and erotic relations that are the staples of the great European novels; his women tend to be nympholeptic projections, fantasies based on girls one never had; and his husbands and wives seem convincing only at the moment of parting. But he comes into his own when he turns to the emotional transactions of males inside the family: brother and brother, son and father—or father-hating son and machiavellian surrogate father. It is the muted rage of such relationships that is the emotional stuff of his best work; and in *Seize the Day,* it is the dialogues of Tommy and his old man, Tommy and the sharper Tamkin that move us, prepare us for Tommy's bleakest encounter: with himself and the prescience of his own death.

But how, we are left asking, has Bellow made tragedy of a theme that remains in the hands of Arthur Miller sentimentality and "good theatre"? It is just this magical transformation of the most travestied of middlebrow themes which is Bellow's greatest triumph. That transformation is in part the work of style, a function of language. Bellow is in no sense an experimental writer; the scraps of avant-garde technique which survive in *The Dangling Man* are purged away in *The Victim;* yet he has managed to resist the impulse to lifeless lucidity which elsewhere has taken over in a literature reacting to the linguistic experiments of the twenties. There is always the sense of a living voice in his prose, for his books are all dramatic; and though this sometimes means a deliberate muting of rhetoric for the sake of characterization, it just as often provides occasions for a release of full virtuosity. Muted or released, his language is never dull or merely expedient, but always moves under tension, toward or away from a kind of rich, crazy poetry, a juxtaposition of high and low style, elegance and slang, unlike anything else in English except *Moby Dick,* though at the same time not unrelated in range and variety to spoken Yiddish.

Since Bellow's style is based on a certain conversational ideal at once intellectual and informal, dialogue is for him necessarily a distillation of his strongest effects. Sometimes one feels his characters' speeches as the main events of the books in which they occur; certainly they have the impact of words exchanged among Jews, that is to say, the impact of actions, not merely overheard but *felt,* like kisses or blows. Implicit in the direction of his style is a desire to encompass a world larger, richer, more disorderly and untrammelled than that of any other writer of his generation; it is this which impels him toward the picaresque, the sprawling, episodic manner of *Augie March.* But there is a counter impulse in him toward the tight, rigidly organized, underplayed style of *The Victim:* and at his best, I think, as in *Seize the Day,* an ability to balance the two tendencies against each other: hysteria and catalepsy, the centrifugal and the centripetal in a sort of perilous rest.

But the triumphs of Bellow are not mere triumphs of style; sometimes indeed they must survive the collapse of that style into mannerism, mechanical self-parody. Beyond an ear, Bellow possesses a fortunate negative talent: a constitutional inability to dissolve his characters into their representative types, to compromise their individuality for the sake of a point. It is not merely that his protagonists refuse to blur into the generalized Little People, the Victims of sentimental liberalism; but that they are themselves portrayed as being conscious of their struggle against such debasement. That struggle is, indeed, the essence of their self-consciousness, their self-definition. Their invariable loneliness is felt by them and by us not only as a function of urban life and the atomization of culture, but as something *willed:* the condition and result of their search to know what they are.

More, perhaps, than any other recent novelist, Bellow is aware that the collapse of the proletarian novel, which marks the starting place of his own art, has meant more than the disappearance of a convention in the history of fiction. With the disappearance of the proletarian novel as a form there has taken place the gradual dissolution of the last widely shared definition of man: man as the product of society. If man seems at the moment extraordinarily lonely, it is not only because he finds it hard to communicate with his fellows, but because he has lost touch with any overarching definition of himself.

This Bellow realizes; as he realizes that it is precisely in such loneliness, once man learns not to endure but to *become* that loneliness, that man can rediscover his identity and his fellowship with others. We recognize the Bellow character because he is openly what we are in secret, because he is us without our customary defenses. Such a protagonist lives nowhere except in the City; he camps temporarily in boardinghouses or lonely hotels, sits by himself at the corner table of some seedy restaurant or climbs backbreaking stairways in search of another whose existence no one will admit. He is the man whose wife is off visiting her mother or has just left him; the man who returns to find his house in disorder or inhabited by a squalid derelict; the man who flees his room to follow the funeral of someone he never knew.

He is essential man, man stripped of success and belongness, even of failure; he is man disowned by his father, unrecognized by his son, man without woman, man face to face with himself, which means for Bellow face to face not with a fact but a question: "What am I?" To which the only answer is: "He who asks!" But such a man is at once the Jew in perpetual exile and Huck Finn in whom are blended with perfect irony the twin American beliefs that the answer to all questions is always over the next horizon and that there is no answer now or ever.

Postscript, 1962
BY JACK LUDWIG

Bellow's novella, *Seize the Day* (1956), which followed *Augie March,* shows the courage shown by, say, Joyce, in creating a hero like Leopold Bloom—a hero who is objectively unworthy.

Bellow's Tommy Wilhelm lives at the center of America's contradiction: on one hand we assume that *to be born is to be,* but our day-to-day existence follows the formula *to be is to succeed.* The American Way of Life says *all men are created equal, but only he who rings the bell gets the cigar.* Wilhelm, no bell ringer, is lamenting his denial by the world. America's standard is simple: anybody who can count can measure success. "How much is he worth?" has a double-entry bookkeeping rather than a metaphysical answer. By the money standard Wilhelm is a failure. Society's other standards rule against him: he is no longer a son (his successful old father turns him away), neither husband nor ex-husband (his wife Margaret refuses to make his leaving easy); he is no father, no businessman, no depositor, no spender. Cleaned out, he cries aloud for existential recognition because he is a "man" and "human," nothing more.

Wilhelm is Bellow's victim writ large, with just enough self-awareness to recognize his unheroic nature, his absurdity, his unimportance. Wilhelm's fate puts the question clearly: what does the world promise the untalented, the unsuccessful, the unlovable? Only as the gull of con-man Tamkin has Wilhelm made it. *I am a mark, therefore I am* answers no existential question.

Wilhelm sees himself as griffon-ridden, dragon-harried, vulture-torn, but, mock-Prometheus, he could not sup a starling: "I was the man beneath; Tamkin was on my back, and I thought I was on his. He made me carry him, too, besides Margaret. Like this they ride on me with hoofs and claws. Tear me to pieces, stamp on me and break my bones."

Bellow's legend makes Wilhelm cry, "Help!" in a bored world that hears it as "Wolf!" Wilhelm's last-mile walk ends with him crying in a commercial burial-parlor over the dead body of an unknown man in the company of stran- gers. The pathos of the objectively unworthy man is a high moment in Bellow's art.

Bellow's free-style *Augie March* language reappears in *Seize the Day* to objectify everything alive and vital and beautiful but missing from Wilhelm's life. The lyric vision of New York City accentuates Wilhelm's bleakness and his loneliness. Bellow has relentlessly brought a hero of the American middle-class world, who knows only how to measure with money, to the point at which there is no money to measure with. His "death of a salesman," un- like Arthur Miller's, blames no vague "somebody," and so does not shift the focus of pain and anguish off that sales- man, Wilhelm. Bellow, in a way, has gone beyond Joyce's Bloom with Wilhelm: added to Bloom's impotence and ineptness in a hostile world he has Wilhelm's untalented and unlovable nature. People think Bloom is "a bit of an artist"; Molly loves Bloom in her fashion; Bloom had a loving, if strange father, has had glowing moments with parents, wife, child, job, history—Wilhelm is nothing, has nothing, anticipates nothing. In his fate Bellow has written the meaning of money. Nihilism has a new definition: no money.

In an attempt to break with the givens of his earlier work, Bellow in 1959 left the Jewish, lower or middle middle-class level of his previous fiction and turned to the last shout of a dying American aristocracy. A former anthropology student, Bellow took his new hero, Hender- son, away from American sophistication and culture, to a concrete place, Africa, which, because of its weirdness to an American, becomes unreal, outside the press of space, time, and money. Africa allows for the confrontation of man as animal, as evolution, as spirit, rather than as function, statistic, category. Henderson is a recoil from Wilhelm: his question starts from the idea "What if one had plenty of money, and a place in society, and a wife, and children, and some role in history, some claim on tradition, some place in the given world—then what?" Will an affirmative check-mark in all man's questing categories add up to a significant answer—personally and generically—to the riddle of human existence?

Henderson the Rain King is Bellow's Karamazov novel: he tries to move his hero Henderson into situations which, like Dostoyevsky's, allow for endlessly intricate dialogues. Sporting the familiar Bellow motifs of gums and teeth and noses and knots in the chest, tightness in the throat, and assorted stress symptoms, Henderson still manages to leave his aristocratic home, his country's protections, to abandon his own fetishes; in darkest Africa, he confronts ultimate meaning in the flip of a log, a break in a dental bridge, the discovery of a dead body, the talk of a black King, the flight of a plane over water.

The escape clauses for Henderson are numerous: he's a bear, a boor, not his literary father's son. But Bellow in *Henderson the Rain King* attempts fiction which transcends definitions, and, so, escape clauses. One by one Henderson eliminates all the rationales and alibis of birth and upbringing, and talent, which would give him an out, let him "break up his lines to weep." Even his age— 55—he dismisses as a valid excuse for giving up the quest for change. He leaves America because society can't explain the things that happen to men and women, or offer any calming gift to still the voice in Henderson that cries out, "I want, I want." Henderson can attain much, sustain nothing. His feeling is intense, but evanescent: a flop with his children, he can feel love for a Persian child who will not be around to bug him in the morning. In Africa the emotional life is easy, because unreal. In Africa Henderson's flubbyknuckled blundering is as good a way to make it through the twenty-four-hour day as any other. But throughout his African sojourn Henderson looks for some clue, some carry-home message, some key to his personality or his physiology which will open him to undiscovered worlds.

Henderson the Rain King is a Bergsonian book, a saddened Nietzsche's book, in which Bellow's hero is trying to discover his meaning as evolution before re-entering the *Augie March* world of reality and history to define himself as individual. Bellow's forthcoming novel, *Herzog* (a section of which has already appeared) tries once more, as *Augie March* did, to merge man's double quest for a role in the present and in the history of the race. Herzog touches history by writing letters, real and imaginary, to the greats who "run things." In the name of himself and mankind he is entering a comic Metaphysical Complaint and a Mock-Lamentation against everyone in power and out who has trespassed on Herzog's and man's dignity. Herzog is Bellow's recognizable victim made comic, self-conscious, ironic, tranquilized. The victim as tensioneer has disappeared: his bill of particulars no longer serves to incriminate the universe.

Anthony Burgess
BY STANLEY EDGAR HYMAN

Anthony Burgess is one of the newest and most talented
of the younger British writers. Although he is forty-five,
he has devoted himself to writing only in the last few
years; with enormous productivity, he has published ten
novels since 1956; before that he was a composer, and a
civil servant in Malaya and Brunei. His first novel to be
published in this country, *The Right to an Answer,* appeared in 1961. It was followed the next year by *Devil
of a State,* and by *A Clockwork Orange* early in 1963. A
fourth novel, *The Wanting Seed,* is due out later in 1963.
Burgess seems to me the ablest satirist to appear since
Evelyn Waugh, and the word "satire" is inadequate to
his range.

The Right to an Answer is a terribly funny, terribly bitter smack at English life in a provincial city (apparently
the author's birthplace, Manchester). The principal activity
of the townspeople seems to be the weekend exchange of
wives, and their dispirited slogan is "Bit of fun" (pro-
phetically heard by Mr. Raj, a visiting Ceylonese, as
"bitter fun"). The book's ironic message is Love. It ends
quoting Raj's unfinished manuscript on race relations:
"Love seems inevitable, necessary, as normal and as easy
a process as respiration, but unfortunately . . ." the manuscript breaks off. Raj's love has just led him to kill two
people and blow his brains out. One thinks of *A Passage to
India,* several decades more sour.

Devil of a State is less bitter, more like early Waugh. Its
comic target is the uranium-rich East African state of
Dunia (obviously based on the oil-rich Borneo state of
Brunei). In what there is of a plot, the miserable protagonist, Frank Lydgate, a civil servant, struggles with the rival

claims of his wife and his native mistress, only to be snatched from both of them by his first wife, a formidable female spider of a woman. The humor derives mainly from incongruity: the staple food in Dunia is Chinese spaghetti; the headhunters upriver shrink a Belgian head with eyeglasses and put Brylcreem on its hair.

Neither book at all prepares one for the savagery of Burgess' next novel. *A Clockwork Orange* is a nightmarish fantasy of a future England where the hoodlums take over after dark. Its subject is the dubious redemption of one such hoodlum, Alex, told by himself. The society is a limp and listless socialism at some future time when men are on the moon: hardly anyone still reads, although streets are named Amis Avenue and Priestley Place; Jonny Zhivago, a "Russky" pop singer, is a juke-box hit, and the teenage language is three-quarters Russian; everybody "not a child nor with child nor ill" must work; criminals have to be rehabilitated because all the prison space will soon be needed for politicals; there is an opposition and elections, but they reëlect the Government.

A streak of grotesque surrealism runs all through Burgess' books. In *Right to an Answer,* at one melodramatic point, a corpse grunts and turns over in its coffin. In *Devil of a State,* a political meeting is held in a movie theatre while polecats walk the girders near the roof, sneer down at the audience, and dislodge bits of dried excrement on their heads. By *A Clockwork Orange* this has become truly infernal. As the hoodlums drive to their "surprise visit," they run over a big snarling toothy thing that screams and squelches, and as they drive back they run over "odd squealing things" all the way.

Alex has no interest in women except as objects of violence and rape (the term for the sex act in his vocabulary is characteristically mechanical, "the old in-out in-out"). No part of the female body is mentioned except the size of the breasts (it would also interest a Freudian to know that the hoodlums' drink is doped milk). Alex's only "aesthetic" interest is his passion for symphonic music. He lies naked on his bed, surrounded by his stereo speakers, listening to Mozart or Bach while he daydreams of grinding his boot into the faces of men, or raping ripped screaming girls, and at the music's climax he has an orgasm.

A running lecture on free will, first from the prison chaplain, then from the writer, strongly suggests that the book's intention is Christian. Deprived of his capacity for moral choice by science, Burgess appears to be saying, Alex is only a "clockwork orange," something mechanical that appears organic. Free to will, even if he wills to sin, Alex is capable of salvation, like Pinky in *Brighton Rock* (*Devil of a State,* incidentally, is dedicated to Greene). But perhaps this is to confine Burgess' ironies and ambiguities within simple orthodoxy. Alex always *was* a clockwork orange, a machine for mechanical violence far below the level of choice, and his dreary socialist England is a giant clockwork orange.

Perhaps the most fascinating thing about the book is its language. Alex thinks and talks in the "nadsat" (teenage) vocabulary of the future. A doctor in the book explains it. "Odd bits of old rhyming slang," he says. "A bit of gypsy talk, too. But most of the roots are Slav. Propaganda. Subliminal penetration." Nadsat is not quite so hard to decipher as Cretan Linear B, and Alex translates some of it. I found that I could not read the book without compiling a glossary.

At first the vocabulary seems incomprehensible: "you could peet it with vellocet or synthemesc or drencrom or one or two other veshches." Then the reader, even if he knows no Russian, discovers that some of the meaning is clear from context: "to tolchock some old veck in an alley and viddy him swim in his blood." Other words are intelligible after a second context: when Alex kicks a fallen enemy on the "gulliver" it might be any part of the body, but when a glass of beer is served with a gulliver, "gulliver" is "head." (Life is easier, of course, for those who know the Russian word *golova.*)

Burgess has not used Russian words mechanically, but with great ingenuity, as the transformation into "gulliver," with its Swiftian associations, suggests. Others are brilliantly anglicized: *khorosho* (good or well) as "horrorshow"; *liudi* (people) as "lewdies"; *militsia* (militia or police) as "millicents"; *odinock* (lonesome) as "oddy knocky."

Burgess uses some Russian words in an American slang extension, such as *nadsat* itself, the termination of the Russian numbers eleven to nineteen, which he breaks off independently on the analogy of our "teen." Thus *kopat*

(to dig with a shovel) is used as "dig" in the sense of enjoy or understand; *koshka* (cat) and *ptitsa* (bird) become
the hip "cat" and "chick"; *neezhny* (lower) turns into
"neezhnies" (underpants); *pooshka* (cannon) becomes the
term for a pistol; *rozha* (grimace) turns into "rozz," one
of the words for policeman; *samyi* (the most) becames
"sammy" (generous); *soomka* (bag) is the slang "ugly
woman"; *vareet* (to cook up) is also used in the slang
sense, for something preparing or transpiring.

The "gypsy talk," I would guess, includes Alex's phrase
"O my brothers," and "crark" (to yowl?), "cutter"
(money), "filly" (to fool with), and such. The rhyming
slang includes "luscious glory" for "hair" (rhyming with
"upper story"?) and "pretty polly" for "money" (rhyming
with "lolly" of current slang). Others are inevitable associations, such as "cancer" for "cigarette" and "charlie"
for "chaplain." Others are produced simply by schoolboy
transformations: "appy polly loggy" (apology), "baddi-
wad" (bad), "eggiweg" (egg), "skolliwoll" (school), and
so forth. Others are amputations: "guff" (guffaw), "pee
and em" (pop and mom), "sarky" (sarcastic), "sinny"
(cinema). Some appear to be portmanteau words: "chum-
ble" (chatter-mumble), "mounch" (mouth-munch),
"shive" (shiv-shave), "skriking" (striking-scratching).

There are slight inconsistencies, when Burgess (or
Alex) forgets his word and invents another or uses our
word, but on the whole he handles his Russianate vocabulary in a masterly fashion. It has a wonderful sound,
particularly in abuse, when "grahzny bratchny" sounds
infinitely better than "dirty bastard." Coming to literature
by way of music, Burgess has a superb ear, and he shows
an interest in the texture of language rare among current
novelists. (He confessed in a recent television interview
that he is obsessed by words.) As a most promising writer
of the 60s, Burgess has followed novels that remind us of
Forster and Waugh with an eloquent and shocking novel
that is quite unique.

After *A Clockwork Orange,* Burgess wrote *The Wanting
Seed,* which appeared in England in 1962 and will soon
be published in the United States. It is a look centuries
ahead to a future world almost as repulsive as Alex's.
Perpetual Peace has been established, and the main effort
of government is to hold down human reproduction. Con-

traceptive pills are universal, infanticide is condoned, homosexuality is officially encouraged, and giving birth more than once is a criminal act. We see this world as it affects the lives of Tristram Foxe, a schoolteacher, his wife Beatrice-Joanna, a natural *Urmutter,* and his brother Derek, Beatrice-Joanna's lover, who holds high office in the government by pretending to be homosexual. In this world of sterile rationalism, meat is unknown and teeth are atavistic, God has been replaced by "Mr. Livedog," a figure of fun ("God knows" becomes "Dognose"), and the brutal policemen are homosexuals who wear black lipstick to match their ties.

As a result of all the organized blasphemy against life, in Burgess' fable, crops and food animals are mysteriously stricken all over the world, and as rations get more and more meagre, order breaks down. The new phase is heralded by Beatrice-Joanna, who gives birth in a kind of manger to twin sons, perhaps separately fathered by the two men in her life.

But the new world of fertility is no better than the world of sterility that it supplants. Soon England is swept by cannibalism (the epicene flesh of policemen is particularly esteemed), there are public sex orgies to make the crops grow, and Christian worship returns, using consecrated human flesh in place of wine and wafer ("eucharistic ingestion" is the new slogan). The check on population this time is a return to old-fashioned warfare with rifles, in which armies of men fight armies of women; war is visibly "a massive sexual act."

At the end, Tristram, who as a representative man of both new orders has been in prison and the army, is reunited with his wife and her children, but nothing has changed fundamentally. The cycle, now in its Augustinian phase with the emphasis on human depravity, will soon enough swing back to its Pelagian phase, with the emphasis on human perfectibility.

The Wanting Seed shows Burgess' familiar preoccupation with language. His vocabulary rivals that of Wallace Stevens: a woman is "bathycolpous" (deep-bosomed), a male secretary is "flavicomous" (blond), a Chinese magnate is "mactated" (sacrificially killed), moustaches are "corniculate" (horned). The book is full of Joycean jokes: in a long sequence of paired names for the public fertility rites, one pair is "Tommy Eliot with Kitty Elphick," which is, of course, Old Possum with one of his Practical Cats; war poetry is read to the army on Saturday mornings, on order of Captain Auden-Isherwood.

On her way to the State Provision Store to buy her ration of vegetable dehydrate, synthelac, compressed cereal sheets, and "nuts" or nutrition units, Beatrice-Joanna stops to take a breath of the sea, and Burgess' beautiful sentence is an incantation of sea creatures: "Sand-hoppers, mermaids' purses, sea gooseberries, cuttle bones, wrasse, blenny and bullhead, tern, gannet and herring gull."

Like any satirist, Burgess extrapolates an exaggerated future to get at present tendencies he abhors. These include almost everything around. He does not like mindless violence, but he does not like mechanical reconditioning either; he detests sterile peace and fertile war about equally. Beneath Anthony Burgess' wild comedy there is a prophetic (sometimes cranky and shrill) voice warning and denouncing us, but beneath that, on the deepest level, there is love: for mankind, and for mankind's loveliest invention, the art of language.

Albert Camus
BY S. BEYNON JOHN

The English translation of Camus's *The Rebel* provoked a number of extravagant estimates of this talented French author and succeeded in distracting attention from what is, surely, his chief claim upon our interest: his power as an imaginative writer. So far as his philosophical forays are concerned, Camus is likely to remain something of an exotic in England. He typifies that marriage of intense intellectual abstraction and moral passion which excites across the Channel, whereas, in England, it more frequently exhausts. This English reaction is not simply the product of a bluff Philistinism, as some French critics affect to believe. It has its roots in our empirical tradition, our suspicion of those incandescent aphorisms, at once stylish and abstract, that dazzle the society of Parisian literary cafés where writers of imaginative fiction make their sudden raids into the territory of social and political theory. We turn, I fancy, with more ready sympathy to the play of the creative imagination in the medium of fiction, and here, Camus has most impressively configured for us a strange, haunting and significant world of his own.

As one might expect, the clues to any understanding of Camus lie, in the first instance, in the intellectual climate of his youth and young manhood and in his personal experiences during this period. Camus's own reaction to life was nourished and confirmed by the nihilism prevalent in much of French thought and literary sensibility between the last two wars. The elements which formed this climate of feeling were not novel. They had existed in the previous century, often provoking the usual reactions to nihilism, but in the twentieth century they reached a new degree of intensity which suggested to some of the sensitive and intelligent a new *kind* of experience. Repeated destructive wars, the accelerated growth of mass society, the generalized despair of mass unemployment, the unparalleled advances of technology, the doctrines and techniques of the totalitarian state—all represented what Peter Drucker describes as the "return of the demons." In a word, these forces tend to awaken in individual man the sense of his victimhood in the world. New scientific theories, too, seemed to challenge still further men's assumptions about the nature of experience. Among these we must count the delayed implications of Freud, and discoveries about the nature of the physical universe, especially those of Einstein. Two general conclusions were often drawn from the play of these factors. Firstly, they appeared to break up traditional values and beliefs about the nature of man and his place in the universe. Next, in the degree to which they menaced individuality or made it the prey of unconscious impulses (as with Freud), these forces seemed to impair the density of individual existence and to provoke the idea that man was adrift in an absurd universe. Such a climate of thought and feeling inspires, at least in part, the spirit of radical negation, *la hantise du néant* (the obsession with nothingness) that is to be found in the work of writers as various as Paul Valéry, André Malraux, and Albert Camus, and the temptation—evident in Malraux and Camus—to mistake intensity of sensation (a means of being confirmed in one's own existence) for the rhythm and warmth of life. It is as if, among the ruins of belief, subjective experience alone has validity, though it is often filled with an almost vertiginous sense of the suffering and estrangement of man.

The circumstances of Camus's own life in Algeria were such as to make this prevailing sensibility especially congenial. Born in 1913, in Mondovi, of a poor working-class family, he was reared by his widowed mother and knew a degree of privation. He entered the University of Algiers, maintaining himself by a variety of occupations, manual and clerical, but after completing the *licence* and a piece of post-graduate research on the relations between the thought of Saint Augustine and Plotinus, tuberculosis forced him to give up his hopes of a career in the University. During this period he underwent a number of important intellectual and literary influences, notably those of André Malraux and Dostoyevsky, whose work he met and, in a sense, lived in stage versions produced by an experimental theatre group to which he belonged. The nihilism and the spirit of revolt·evident in these writers were all the more influential in that they matched his personal vicissitudes. The other seminal experience of these early years was Camus's encounter with nature along the North African littoral. We find it expressed in two short collections of semi-autobiographical essays which provide a map, as it were, to his sensibility and his metaphysical preoccupations at this time. The more important of these, *Noces* (Nuptials) (1938), extends in range and power the travel sketches which had formed a part of his first collection, *L'Envers et l'endroit* (Betwixt and Between) (1937), raising them to the level of a sumptuous hymn to the world of physical beauty and the life of the senses. The four essays contained in *Noces* were composed between 1936 and 1937 and represent the notations of a metaphysical pagan in the face of changing landscapes. Each essay has its own distinctive resonance and mood but all are united in the persistent confrontation of the permanence of nature with what is sensual and mortal. Pervading all the muscular paganism and the insistence upon a "common resonance between man and the earth" is the horror and rejection of death. Man is revealed here as a web of sense, highly sensitive to the assault of sea, cloud and flower; obsessed with death, and caught up in a passionate revolt against the natural order of things in which he figures as a victim. In these essays, it is the décor that dominates, especially as Camus feels himself, at moments, to be just another element in the life of nature.

> Like a pebble made shiny by the tides, I was polished by the wind, worn down to the very soul. I was a bit of that force upon which I floated, then much of it, then all of it finally, merging the pulsings of my blood with the great sonorous beatings of that natural heart ever-present, everywhere. (*Noces*)

This identification of himself with nature leads Camus to treat wind, sun and sea almost like allegorical presences. Does not the very first page of *Noces* refer to the "gods that speak in the sun"? Here man is envisaged as the "locus of a polytheism," to borrow a phrase used by Aldous Huxley in describing the ideas of D. H. Lawrence, a writer with whom the early Camus has certain affinities. In this sense, *Noces* is directed away from the human world to a larger, non-human collectivity. The tendency of this polytheism is to personalize nature at the expense of man; it reflects the general and the non-human at the expense of the particular and the human.

What elements may be disengaged from these formative years? A pagan receptivity to nature complicated by a tragic apprehension of man's estrangement in the world; a rich sensuality married to the anguished anticipation of death; and, finally, a sense of man's victimhood coupled with the revolt against that order of the universe which permits it. From this point onwards, Camus's career offers a distinct shape.

First comes the period roughly contemporary with the Second World War (from 1938 until the middle of 1944), when his early tragic intimations are deepened and his sense of man's estrangement in the world raised to the power of obsession. During this phase, a marked congruity exists between Camus's philosophical themes and the situations and tonality of his imaginative fiction. Both reflect man's estrangement and the absurdity of human existence. The profound pessimism of Camus's work at this period may be thought of as the legacy of French military and moral collapse. At least, that collapse appears to sanction his earlier intuitions, since it is evidence of a world in which the arbitrary reigns supreme and men are crushed beneath the heedless pressure of history. On the other hand, the fact that Camus is engaged in the very positive activity of the French Resistance argues a commitment to life, an affirmation of the worth of living, which are at variance with the tone and themes of his literary production. It is the tension between these two attitudes that supplies the key to understanding *The Myth of Sisyphus* (1942), which both registers the force of the temptations of nihilism and attempts to find a way out of the nihilist impasse without flying into the arms of religion. *The Myth of Sisyphus* expresses, in terms of formal ideas, themes Camus had previously realized imaginatively in the first draft of *Caligula* (that of 1938, left substantially unchanged in the stage version of 1945), and in his novel,

The Stranger (early 1942); themes he will restate in dramatic idiom with *The Misunderstanding,* written in 1943 and first produced in 1944. The philosophical essay defines Camus's concept of the absurd as the encounter between man's innate need of order and purpose and the blank indifference of nature. A study that begins with suicide insists upon the recognition of the fundamental absurdity of life, urges the living out of this absurdity in a constant tension of revolt and, finally, arrives at an acceptance of life symbolized by the labor of Sisyphus. These ideas have their center of gravity in the experience of nullity and the absurd and it is this experience that animates Camus's imaginative writing.

The novel and the two plays of this period configure the sense of estrangement and create a tragically *elliptical* world through which the characters move as though in a trance. In *The Stranger,* as Sartre has brilliantly suggested, Camus deliberately suppressed all casual connections in the syntax and atomized the sense of temporal duration, by the constant use of the perfect tense, so as to stress the degree to which Meursault's world is arbitrary and absurd. The central dichotomy of the novel lies in the juxtaposition of two conflicting versions of the same set of events: Meursault's dry, laconic account of his Mother's burial, his liaison with Marie, and his eventual murder of a strange Arab, and, on the other side, the more sinister versions of these same events as seen through the eyes of the prosecution and its witnesses at Meursault's trial. This narrative technique adroitly conveys the sense of men's mutual incomprehension in the world. A number of grotesques (Salamano, with his mangy dog, and the eccentric lady absorbed in ticking off the radio programs are the most prominent) confirm the impression of absurdity. Meursault is not the villain of the piece. Villainy implies efficacy and responsibility, while he is just another *thing* in nature, obedient to the pulsations of the midday sun. *The Stranger,* far from being a transcription of the real world, is an allegory, a veritable myth of the absurd as incarnated in Meursault. Here, as in *Noces,* it is the inhuman and undifferentiated *collective* forces that dominate: sun and sea, presences of nature; the town of Algiers itself. The initiative, the particularity and the baffling complexity of men are absent.

Camus's mythopoeic faculty also finds expression in *The Misunderstanding,* where, by using for its plot a sensational news item discovered by Meursault on a scrap of newspaper hidden in his cell, he obviously intends to create a sort of contemporary myth about the nature of man's existence in the world. Camus combines the form of Grand Guignol and the substance of metaphysical anguish. This story—about a long-absent son who makes a fortune, returns home and is murdered by a mother and sister who fail to recognize him—is nothing but an extended metaphor on the human condition. This is the world without signs or sense, the absurd world in which man is never at home. Credibility, motivation—these criteria simply do not apply, since we are not in the human world but in that abstract zone of symbols where the puppets of the absurd twitch into counterfeit life.

Caligula confirms the impression of an abstract and over-intellectualized theatre. The same blank and inhuman world is crystallized about the career of this mad Roman emperor whose lunacy is transposed from the historical to the metaphysical level. His is that "encounter with nothingness" provoked by the death of his sister, Drusilla, with whom he has been enjoying an incestuous relationship. Death brings him up sharply against the central truth of existence: "Men die and they are not happy." Where Meursault and Martha register the fact of life's absurdity, Caligula attempts to outbid it. He demonstrates the bankruptcy of total revolt, the terrifying consequences of the lust for the absolute.

These three works reveal a deliberate transposition into fiction of the philosophy of the absurd. They are abstract and exemplary, the graphic expression of a myth. But, in his third period, from 1945 to 1951, Camus fails to realize imaginatively the transition from nihilism to a sort of "reverence for life" (to use Schweitzer's expression), which he successfully accomplishes at the level of the discursive intelligence, in his philosophical argument. Briefly, the ideas elaborated between these two dates, without marking a complete break with the desperate negativity of *The Myth of Sisyphus,* are distinguished by a more truly human accent and constitute, to a much greater degree than formerly, an affirmation of the value of human life. A significant shift in ideas takes place, beginning with the closing pages of *Letters to a German Friend,* passing through the many articles and lectures written between 1945 and 1948 in *Combat* and elsewhere, and culminating in the final words of *The Rebel.* Camus has moved away from the hectic metaphysical revolt and the moral scepticism evident in his early ideas so as to embrace, in the face of Nazi conquests, the moral conviction that "any mutilation of man is irretrievable." He has abandoned the notion of "total" revolt under the accumulated evidence he derives from his study of the anatomy of modern European revolutions. Man is fallible, political theories are relative, automatic progress is a mirage, and freedom is threatened in every generation. Man must resist the temptations of the absolute and return to the old Aristotelian concept of moderation. These conclusions are banal, but their timing makes them especially relevant and they bear the imprint of a lived experience.

These themes are transposed into the imaginative fiction of Camus's third period. Whereas his early heroes had been the victims of a sort of fatality of the absurd, the major figures of *The Plague* (1947), *State of Siege* (1948), and *The Just Assassins* (1949) revolt against the arbitrary. Unlike Caligula, though, they keep their revolt within human limits and, through it, manifest the fraternity of suffering by which men are united. Nevertheless, the imaginative world crystallized about this more human doctrine rarely conveys any convincing sense of life. Characters still lack human density, variety, and the element of surprise. Indeed, both *The Plague* and *State of Siege* are impressive in their total effect, but the individuals in them are reduced in scale and power by the force of great collective entities: the plague itself, the animated mass of the town, and the distant but disturbing presence of the sea. Consequently, neither Dr. Rieux nor Tarrou nor Father Paneloux quite comes alive for us. We perceive what they represent, but they do not seem to possess a life beyond the exigencies of this allegory in which an isolated and plague-stricken town symbolizes the human condition. Grand, however, that admirable comic creation, is above such criticism. He, and, to a minor degree, certain of the grotesques in *The Plague,* like the asthmatic Spaniard or the man who spits on cats, suggest something of the spontaneity of life. This is entirely absent from *State of Siege* where the deliberate adoption of the conventions of allegory intensifies the sense of abstraction. The conflict between death and suffering, that is, the power of evil, and the power of human love, construed in its largest sense and verging on the Christian concept of charity, is here articulated through a number of types and personifications. The Plague is incarnated in a sort of barrack-square martinet; Cadiz is the world, and a Chorus represents mankind. The action oscillates between the Plague and a young student, Diégo, who, along with his fiancée, Victoria, symbolizes Camus's attachment to purely human values. Both are insipid and lifeless, whereas a certain force is evident in the collectivities, the Plague, the Chorus and the sea that symbolizes liberty, which is not dispersed by Diégo's final victory, achieved through self-abnegation. Only at the level of political satire, in scenes of angry farce, does the play come to life.

The Just Assassins, it is true, is not dominated by these impersonal forces, but it is geared to abstract ideas. The debate over means and ends, which divides this group of Russian terrorists, imposes a rigid pattern on the characters involved. Hence, Ivan, the "delicate murderer," and Stépan, the case-hardened revolutionary for whom the end justifies all, draw life, less from their own personalities, which are "flat" and unexplored, than from the necessities of the dialectical counterpoint in which they are engaged. The debate between conscience and violence is remarkably well sustained, but an impassioned monotony continues to be the mark of Camus's characterization.

In the light of this brief interpretation, it may be possible to discern what factors inhibit the sense of life in Camus's fiction. They are, I suggest: the appeal of negation, the polytheistic experience of nature, and the force of abstraction.

Even when his thought passes beyond nihilism (and his whole intellectual development is an attempt to transcend its paralysing attraction), Camus retains the negative cast of mind that the encounter with nihilism had engendered. The act of faith, though not necessarily in a Divine Providence, required for a real acceptance of life and the possibility of human happiness is rarely made convincingly in Camus's imaginative work. His thought is centered on death, though certainly not as a "consummation devoutly to be wish'd," and this single-minded concentration inevitably affects the rendering of life in his pages. It falsifies life by equating it too readily with intensity of physical sensation. Camus's atheism is clearly an integral part of his experience of negation and it helps to drain his work of individuality and variety. I mean by this that Camus's use of myth is a response to the vacuum created by the "death of God" and the disintegration of traditional religious belief. Myth is a substitute for faith and the metaphors of religion, and myth, by its very nature, is anonymous and collective: it swallows up the individual life.

This tendency is intensified by the character of Camus's response to nature. He experiences nature so vividly that it comes alive, manifests itself in living presences which nullify man, and creates a feeling for allegory that permeates novels and plays alike. Allegory, like myth, is directed away from the life of particular men toward the general and the abstract. In a word, Camus has no difficulty in experiencing the reality of what is diffused and collective, but this very power impairs his feeling for the density of individual human existence.

Finally, Camus's philosophical intention is too obvious in all his imaginative writing. Situation and character often seem forced and contrived, as if the ratiocinative intelligence is, so to speak, too strong for the imaginative alloy in which it is working. In spite of this, Camus's novels and plays have an undeniable relevance and fascination for the contemporary reader. The vision of the world which he communicates may seem distorted, but it is a recognizable and significant distortion which illuminates man's predicament in the modern world. It was Camus's gift to recall us to an awareness of our human condition.

Solitary or Solidary?
BY NORMAN PODHORETZ

When Albert Camus won the Nobel Prize for literature
in 1957, the committee cited him for illuminating "the
problems of the human conscience in our times," but I
doubt whether even his most fervent admirers will find
much illumination in his new collection of stories, *Exile and
the Kingdom*. Camus has always been concerned with
experiences that belong not so much to individuals (love,
ambition, family) as to whole societies and even the
world at large (war, concentration camps, mass annihilation), and in this sense it is certainly true that he
has addressed himself to "the problems of the human
conscience in our times." But this preoccupation is precisely what accounts for the thinness of his fiction.
His books are parables rather than novels, anecdotes illustrating an idea, tales told not for their own sake but for
what they exemplify. Nor are there any characters in his
work.

Though the people he writes about have the usual ap-
purtenances of character—they are of such-and-such an
age, they look so, they live in this or that quarter of the
city—they are always types instead of individuals; they
are there because they stand for something in Camus's
conception of the world. In "The Stranger" (Camus's first
and best novel), this conception is stripped to essentials.

A young man with the most appallingly apathetic attitude toward everything and everyone suddenly, for no
compelling reason, shoots an Arab to death on a beach
in the glaring sunlight of a North African day; arrested,
he resists all the pressure put on him by the officials of
society to explain the senseless crime. They conclude that
he is a moral monster and condemn him to the guillotine.
While awaiting his execution, he is visited by a priest, who

tries to persuade him that there is an afterlife, and in the course of a violent argument (the only moment of passion he has ever known) he discovers that the source of his incorrigible apathy was an unexpressed conviction that death is the major fact of human existence—in the end, everything comes to the same. The rush of anger at the priest cleanses his soul of fear; now, on the brink of death, he feels ready to start life all over again, and he lays his heart open to "the benign indifference of the universe." On this note the book ends. But the final pages remain unclear even after several rereadings. Camus's intention is clear enough: he is asserting that life has value and meaning even when it appears most valueless and meaningless; he is trying to find a way to repudiate the implications of his own vision of the human predicament. Yet all he can do is to counter this vision with an abstract argument, and since he is a man of honesty and intellectual integrity, he will not permit himself a glib argument. The result is an obscure one—obscure not because it cannot be elucidated (it can) but because of its complicated philosophical trappings—that carries far less conviction than the strong nihilistic bias of the book as a whole. What remains after you have put "The Stranger" down—and this could be said, too, of his "The Plague" and "The Fall" —is a cry of despair and the memory of a writer doing his best to say no to the pronouncements of his own voice.

Three of the six stories in "Exile and the Kingdom" involve the same conflict between the nihilistic imagination that broods compulsively on death, executions, sickness, and doom, and the intellect seeking reasons to refute the evidence dredged up by the imagination. And these stories have the same peculiarity as the novels: they end in obscurity. In "The Adulterous Woman," Janine, a childless wife, accompanies her husband on a business trip from Algiers to a town in the desert. There she realizes that her life, like the desert itself, has all been an empty, barren waste. Staring at the desert from the parapet of a fort on the edge of the town, she sees an encampment of nomads, and "a knot tightened by the years, habit, and boredom" slowly begins loosening:

> Homeless, cut off from the world [the nomads] were
> a handful wandering over the vast territory she could

see, which however was but a paltry part of an even greater expanse whose dizzying course stopped only thousands of miles farther south, where the first river finally waters the forest. Since the beginning of time, on the dry earth of this limitless land scraped to the bone, a few men had been ceaselessly trudging, possessing nothing but serving no one, poverty-stricken but free lords of a strange kingdom. Janine did not know why this thought filled her with such a sweet, vast melancholy that it closed her eyes. She knew that this kingdom had been eternally promised her and yet that it would never be hers.

Seized with a fever in the middle of the night and suddenly terrified of the idea of death, she slips out of the hotel room she shares with her husband and rushes back to the parapet. There she submits to a sort of sexual union with the desert night. For a moment, it seems that this surrender to the indifferent universe, this acceptance of the paradoxical idea that all human beings are "poverty-stricken but free lords of a strange kingdom" which belongs to them and yet will never be theirs, this identification of herself with the very nature of the cosmos itself, is the answer to "the long anguish of living and dying," the "many years of mad, aimless fleeing from fear." Camus, indeed, tells us that "she seemed to recover her roots and the sap again rose in her body." But at the end of the story Janine is once more in her room, "weeping copiously" at the spectacle of her dull, fat husband staggering half asleep toward the washbasin to get a drink of mineral water. What is Camus saying here? That we are redeemed momentarily by the knowledge of our predicament? That there is no way out? A little bit of both, and yet it is significant that—just as in "The Stranger"—the dreadfulness of the predicament should be so much more vividly and forcefully presented than the possibility of redemption, a possibility Camus is able to suggest only in a piece of murky symbolism.

"The Renegade"—the best of the six stories in "Exile and the Kingdom"—provides an even clearer illustration of this difficulty. The narrator is a missionary whose fanatic religious zeal has led him to seek martyrdom by venturing

unprotected into a city built on a salt bed in the Sahara
and inhabited by a savage Bedouin tribe, which has apparently been allowed considerable sovereignty by the
French colonial authorities. The Bedouins subject him
to unthinkable cruelties (including the ripping out of his
tongue), but as a consequence he is converted to their
religion. Their idol, the Fetish, which must be worshipped
by barbarism, mercilessness, and hate, becomes his god;
their high priest, the Sorcerer, becomes his master. This
is to be the new order of things in the world; the Fetish
must triumph over "the whole of lousy Europe" and its
lying Christian ideals of love and charity. While the
narrator is in captivity, he learns that the French Army,
suddenly reversing its policy, has forced the Bedouins to
permit another Christian missionary to enter their city
with immunity, and he panics at the thought that they may
be defeated by this concession. He resolves to kill the
missionary, but the Bedouins, suspecting that he will
inform on them, set upon him once again and nearly tear
him to pieces. At the point of death, and welcoming it because it has been inflicted on him in the name of the
Fetish, he hears a voice say, "If you consent to die for hate
and power, who will forgive us?" He cannot tell whether
it is the voice of God, an old voice within himself, or the
voice of "that other fellow refusing to die, at my feet,
and repeating: 'Courage! courage! courage!' " For the
space of a paragraph, it appears that he has been recon-
verted; looking around him, he sees the signs of a recent
skirmish in which the Bedouins seem to have been defeated by French soldiers, and we get the impression that
the religion of cruelty and hate has been overcome by the
forces of Christian Europe. But Camus's final sentence ("A
handful of salt fills the mouth of the garrulous slave") puts
this impression in doubt; the garrulous slave, the name the
renegade had taken for himself after his conversion to the
religion of the Fetish, is silenced by a handful of salt—
and salt, we remember, is the very foundation of the
Bedouin city, symbolizing aridity and barbaric cruelty.
The obscurity of the ending (who *is* "that other fellow"
—the new missionary? the Sorcerer?) may derive from
Camus's own uncertainty; he himself doesn't know where
the mysterious voice came from and whether or not the
Fetish is triumphant. This ambiguity could be intentional

if the story is an allegory of the conflict between Eastern totalitarianism and Western civilization, the outcome of which is still uncertain. But I do not believe that "The Renegade" is so directly political, and even if it were, the obscurity would still be an aesthetic fault. Once again, Camus's creative power has gone into the construction of an image of doom and disaster, but he is unwilling to let his own impulses toward despair have the last word.

It is literally the last word that remains in doubt in the third story of this group, "The Artist at Work," a charming, if rather obvious, satiric fable about a painter who is swallowed up by the conditions around him. Camus portrays the artist as a holy innocent, a kind of saint, who obliges the demands made on him by the world at the tremendous cost of losing his ability to work. Gilbert Jonas (the name suggests the prophet Jonah) has always followed his star, trusting it to lead him safely forward, painting his pictures by its light. He becomes a great success, but he has to support his wife and three children in a tiny apartment on a small remittance from an art dealer. The baby squalls, the telephone rings, his disciples crowd in to watch him paint and to chat; he is busy with correspondence, petitions, interviews. It becomes more and more difficult for him to get anything done; even when he moves his studio from the parlor into the bedroom, the crowd follows after, sprawling over the conjugal bed. He begins drinking; the critics turn against him; his devoted wife is haggard and miserable. In a final act of desperation, he builds a platform just below the ceiling of one of his little rooms and closes it off from the world. Alone in his makeshift loft for days at a time, he starts painting so feverishly that he collapses from exhaustion. When a friend climbs up to the loft, he finds an empty canvas with a single word written in the middle, and he is unable to tell whether the word is "solitary" or "solidary"—whether the artist is properly an isolated creature following his private star or a man burdened with communal responsibilities. Here the uncertainty in Camus is turned against his own career; he seems to be mocking his perennial temptation to see himself as a saint and simultaneously expressing the bitterness of a writer who has been up to his neck in public affairs. And once more the way out is hidden in obscurity, for the "solitary" artist is a child and a fool and the "solidary" artist cannot work.

The remaining three stories in "Exile and the Kingdom," which offer solidarity as a hopeful possibility, have none of the uncertainty that troubles the three dealing with the human being in his "solitary" condition, the lone person confronting the universe directly and nakedly. And yet these "solidary" pieces are less interesting. The point of "The Growing Stone" is, very simply, that a sharing of the burdens of the oppressed can be the way to salvation. A French engineer, D'Arrast, comes to a town in the Brazilian jungle to build a bridge, and there he meets a native, a former ship's cook, who has vowed to carry a hundred-pound stone on his head in a ceremonial procession to the church. The cook collapses under the weight of the stone, whereupon D'Arrast picks it up and carries it on his own head, not into the church (i.e., this is not a Christian act) but back to the miserable hovel where the cook lives. "And there, straightening up until he was suddenly enormous, drinking in with desperate gulps the familiar smell of poverty and ashes, he felt rising within him a surge of obscure and panting joy that he was powerless to name." "The Silent Men," making a similar point from the opposite direction, is about a paternalistic shop owner who has held out against his striking employees and tries to resume friendly relations with them after they return to work. Disaster overtakes his family, but his men, in their anger at his behavior during the strike, cannot bring themselves to offer sympathy and consolation. In "The Guest," the weakest of the stories, Camus is apparently criticizing a simple-minded notion of solidarity common on the French Left—that one must always side with the criminal against the police.

The difficulty in Camus's "solitary" stories is of a piece with the difficulty in his essays in the earlier "The Myth of Sisyphus," in which he begins by defining the human predicament as "absurd"—we are all exiles in an indifferent universe—and then tries to answer the question Why should a man not commit suicide? The answer he finds, if it can be called an answer, is unsatisfying, for the problem as he states it is insoluble. Life in the large may be absurd, but no individual life can be summed up in a single concept, and it is individuals who commit or do not commit suicide, not abstract figments of life. Most philosophers who engage in such speculations go on assuming—as David Hume did when he left his study—that the sun will rise every morning, though they know that this assumption is not strictly warranted in logic. Camus, as it were, always carries his study with him. To a novelist, the fact that a man enjoys swimming may be as big a fact about him as that he lives in a period which has seen horrible catastrophes and mass annihilation or that the principle of absurdity governs his stay on earth. But for Camus, even in his novels and stories, the character of the times and the nature of the universe are always encroaching upon the reality of merely personal experience and threatening to obliterate it altogether. He is a Hume who spends all his time worrying about whether the sun will rise tomorrow, a Dr. Johnson who kicks the stone and continues to regard the metaphysical proposition that matter is an idea in the mind of God more real than the pain in his foot.

How easy it is to be smug about this, to ascribe Camus's way of looking at the world to the decline of French power in the postwar period, or to his special political tribulations, or to a French atheist's battle with the Church. All these factors are present; there is something parochially French and not at all universal in his work. Yet what we want to say of Camus is not any of these things. For he is one of those writers who by sheer force of character make clever critical discriminations seem beside the point. He is marvelously endowed with nobility and courage and honesty, and we watch his career less in hope of seeing him produce a great novel (though he may yet do that) than for the spectacle it offers of a man grappling more and more bravely with his impulses toward a fruitless nihilism.

The Protean World of Lawrence Durrell

BY JOHN UNTERECKER

When Lawrence Durrell is finally put in his place—say a
hundred years from now—two "facts" will undoubtedly
glare at the assessing critic: the fact of Durrell's variety
and the fact—underlying variety—of his unvarying themes.
For Durrell may be both the most protean modern writer
and at the same time the most predictable. Though what
he has to say seems essentially unchanging, his exploration of the ways in which ideas can be set down has been
limited so far only by the limitations time imposes on any
man: Durrell hasn't lived long enough to try out *every*
form.

I stress his variety, for I strongly suspect that Durrell,
consciously or unconsciously, must at some time or other
have toyed with the idea of being literature's Leonardo—
the master of each literary form. Even if one hits only
the high spots, it is easy to see that his range is extraordinarily wide. He has so far written thrillers (*White
Eagles over Serbia*); intricate poems (the sonnet of sonnets, "A Soliloquy of Hamlet," for instance) and bawdy
ballads (Dylan Thomas' favorite being "A Ballad of the
Good Lord Nelson"); a trilogy of "travel books" which,
of course, more accurately should be described as island
portraits (*Prospero's Cell, Reflections on a Marine Venus,*
and *Bitter Lemons*); several plays; the "solipsistic," raw
fictional account of pre-war London, *The Black Book;*
comic interludes about life in the diplomatic corps (*Esprit
de Corps* and *Stiff Upper Lip*); *The Dark Labyrinth*, a
novel which Durrell accurately described to Henry Miller
as "an extended morality, but written artlessly in the style
of the detective story"; literary criticism (*A Key to Modern British Poetry*) and—by far his most popular work—

the extraordinarily-complex, expanding study of the emotional education both of a hero and of his friends, *The Alexandria Quartet.* He has also in his time turned out public-relations copy, newspaper columns, and—presumably unavailable to the public—a whole series of confidential reports, the bulky stuffing of diplomats' bags and home-office files. He has published some of his letters to Henry Miller, and a smaller group of letters (to Alfred Perlès) about Henry Miller. He has acted as translator (Emmanuel Royidis' novel *Pope Joan*), anthologist, and magazine editor.

But though his forms may be as infinitely varied as Cleopatra, Durrell himself, like Antony, takes on the proportions of a "marble constancy." For in all the broad range of his work, themes, motifs, even images connect and interconnect until the body of his output—for all of its surface variety—fuses together into something that begins to feel like an organic whole. To demonstrate that, however, would take a small volume. What can comfortably be accomplished in an essay is a brief analysis of the ways these obsessive materials show up in a single work. Because it has been read by more people than any other of his works, I shall settle on *The Alexandria Quartet.*

When two paragraphs back I tried to compress the *Alexandria Quartet* into a phrase by describing it as "the extraordinarily-complex, expanding study of the emotional education both of a hero and of his friends," I was not so much attempting to define the novel as to insist on some of its most basic elements.

Its complexity is, I suppose, obvious; and, as Durrell makes clear in his headnote, it is deliberate. The work is laid out in a kind of up-to-date geometry, the first three sections constructing for us a three-dimensional "solid" Alexandria, while the fourth, adding the dimension of time, allows us to experience between the covers of a single work what T. S. Eliot might call an objective correlative for the space-time continuum—or more accurately, for the self-consciously perceived space-time continuum.

Durrell is careful to keep this structure constantly before his readers; and, though he is sometimes heavy-handed in his treatment of it (perhaps mirrors and masks obtrude so much as to be conspicuous), he is also at times extremely subtle, extremely delicate. But it may be that in order to enjoy later subtleties, we need the heavy-handedness, the obtuseness, of such early remarks as those of Justine on the nature of fictional reality. Less than a dozen pages into the first book and barely introduced as a character, she spells out for the reader what he must not miss. She sits in front of a dressmaker's "multiple mirrors" and speculates on the art of the novel: " 'Look! five different pictures of the same subject. Now if I wrote I would try for a multi-dimensional effect in character, a sort of prism-sightedness. Why should not people show more than one profile at a time?' " This is, of course, clearly a case of author forcing dogma into the mouth of one of his characters. But it is, nevertheless, explicit statement of this sort which we must have if later we are to be able to accept Durrell's characters' expansion of it. We must, for example, have in the back of our mind this passage of Justine's if we are later to be able to see it qualified from a slightly different point of view, as, for example, by Justine herself in the last book. There, mirrored images transform themselves into fictions. She is again speaking to Darley: "We are after all totally ignorant of one another, presenting selected fictions to each other! I suppose we all observe each other with the same immense ignorance." For none of the pictures in any of the mirrors presents truth—though all present reality of a kind. Truth, finally, as Darley realizes, exists only in relationship: "I . . . saw that lover and loved, observer and observed, throw down a field about each other. . . . Then they infer the properties of their love, judging it from this narrow field with its huge margins of unknown. . . . I had only been attesting, in all I had written, to the power of an image which I had created involuntarily by the *mere act of seeing* Justine. There was no question of true or false. Nymph? Goddess? Vampire? Yes, she was all of these and none of them. She was, like every woman, everything that the mind of a man . . . wished to imagine. She was there forever, and she had never existed! Under all these masks there was only another woman, every woman, like a lay figure in a dressmaker's shop, waiting for the poet to clothe her, breathe life into her."

Reality becomes for Durrell something very much like a masked ball—but the masks are nothing less than our own numerous false faces and those false faces we project onto the faces of all men and women around us. The difficult trick for the novelist is to discover a way of revealing the different realities each of his major characters observes—and, as well, as many as possible of the "selected fictions" those major characters to disguise the poverty of their irresolute and private selves.

Durrell's solution is a little like Gide's in *The Counterfeiters:* a storyteller finds variant accounts of what ought to be a single story. In *The Alexandria Quartet*, Darley's initial version of a set of events is corrected by Arnauti's *Moeurs* and by the diaries of both Justine and Nessim; these versions are in turn corrected by Balthazar's interlinear; that interlinear is corrected by the objective history of events in *Mountolive* and by a number of sets of letters, most significant of which are those between Leila and Mountolive, Pursewarden and Mountolive, and Pursewarden and Liza. Finally, time itself offers a shifted perspective; and in *Clea,* the one novel which moves forward in time, each of the central characters is allowed the opportunity to re-examine and re-evaluate his past and the pasts of the group of wounded survivors from the first three books.

For just as *Justine* is a book of mirrors, *Balthazar* a book of masks, and *Mountolive* a book of intrigues—the first two offering private false faces and the third offering the public false face of political action—*Clea* must properly be seen, I think, as a book of wounds, damaging but in a way life-giving wounds which strike through all of the false faces to the quick body beneath and which can be healed only by the tenderness of human affection. There are of course wounds—as there are mirrors, masks, and intrigues—through all four books; in one way or another, hardly a character in the *Quartet* escapes disfigurement or death (think of the crowds of blind or half-blind figures alone: from one-eyed Hamid, through one-eyed Scobie, one-eyed Capodistria, and one-eyed Nessim, to totally blind Liza and the whole host of minor figures—blind servants, sheiks, and priests—who fumble through the novel). But in *Clea,* some at least of the wounded are not only cured but actually transformed—given a new and fuller life—thanks to apparent disaster. The virtuous Semira, complete with the new nose designed for her by Clea and fashioned for her by Amaril, dances triumphant-

ly before the affectionate assembled Alexandrians; and
Clea herself—cured by Amaril of her troublesome vir-
ginity—is freed, tenderly, to cure not just anyone but the
bankrupt and broken doctor, Balthazar, who must finally
wound her and—aiding Darley—bring her with rough
tenderness back to life. Even Scobie, battered to death in
his Dolly Varden, is tenderly ("How much the city misses
him") elevated to sainthood and then, thanks to Nim-
rod's delicate, ironic hint, saluted by his murderers, "the
boys of H.M.S. *Milton*," with a fine display of naval fireworks.

For it is, in the long run, only tenderness which illuminates for an instant the solipsistic darkness, the lonely,
terrible darkness onto which the more perceptive of Durrell's major characters see projected the crucial figures of
a private "heraldic universe." It is no accident, therefore,
that in the last book, just after Darley realizes both his
limitations as an artist and at the same time the nature
of that universe he must attempt to represent ("It was life
itself that was a fiction—we were all saying it in our different ways, each understanding it according to his nature
and gift") that fictive Clea, "all tenderness," drops for a
moment the mask of her reserve to step out of her fictional
world and in a transparent interval, bring Darley back to
a world of action. And it is here too, in the last book, that
the reader, if he has been attentive, will recall that passage
from *Balthazar* in which Pursewarden has set down for
Clea the plan for his own "last volume": "I feel I want
to sound a note of . . . affirmation—though not in the
specific terms of a philosophy or religion. It should have
the curvature of an embrace, the wordlessness of a lover's
code. It should convey some feeling that the world we
live in is founded in something too simple to be over-
described as cosmic law—but as easy to grasp as, say, an
act of tenderness, simple tenderness in the primal relation
between animal and plant, rain and soil, seed and trees,
man and God."

If tenderness—an "utterly merciless" tenderness rescued
from sentimentality by the distancing power of irony—is
the principal lesson in the "emotional education" which
the central characters experience, they learn their lesson
most frequently from painters and from writers, also
wounded—and some of them healed—in their efforts to

transmit their vision of human process.

The book, in fact, is overrun with artists of one kind or another. For in addition to the professional writers and painters—Arnauti, Pursewarden, Darley, Keats, and Clea—there is a battallion of casual diarists and Sunday painters, most conspicuous among them Nessim, Mountolive, and Justine. And behind all the fictional characters are the flesh and blood writers and painters of the flesh and blood world. For not only does Durrell allow Pursewarden to give a quick two-page survey of English literature, he also has the ingenuity to set him corresponding with D. H. Lawrence! Some of the characters in the novel have also known Cavafy, the poet of the city. And Sir Louis, Mountolive's senior in Moscow, is permitted, after his retirement to Italy, both to meet Claudel and to pass on to Mountolive one of Claudel's diplomatic stories! Like the living landscape, living and recently-deceased "real" writers ground the book in reality and feed their truths to the fictional artists and writers who live only in the novel.

And the writers in the novel feed on each other.

By offering us this collection of writers, Durrell has left himself open to the sort of criticism reviewers are fond of making: the problem, some have argued, is not that Durrell identifies with one of the writers in his book—Darley, of course, who is equipped both with Durrell's initials and with his ideas—but with several of the writers and painters. This, they feel, is confusing. And, to an extent, they are correct. Pursewarden, for example, seems, in some ways, the real author-identification figure. He is by far the most intelligent person in the book; and he is even made the author of a novel famous for an asterisk which refers to a blank page! He seems, therefore, just right as "author" of *Justine*; but, alas, he's killed off half-way through the series, and Darley survives until the last page, where, putting pen to paper, he writes, "Once upon a time."

But I think we need not be misled by Pursewarden's inventive asterisk, and I think we need not be troubled by the whole problem of author-identification. (An author is, I suppose, never one of his characters, but rather the sum of them; and so far as Pursewarden is concerned, if a model need be found for his ideas, that model is as likely to resemble Henry Miller as it is to resemble

Lawrence Durrell.) Within the novel, Pursewarden seems
to me to be less author-spokesman than teacher of Darley.
Like Clea, another teacher, he shows Darley not just how
to see but what to see; and he suggests one method—the
ironist's—of capturing those figures of the "heraldic universe" who, like Capodistria's homunculi, scramble—
desperate for love—out of their life-sustaining fluids into
the thin air of the artist's "real" world.

For love, as Pursewarden explains in his long, ironic,
"imaginary" dialogue with Darley, is finally what makes—
the only thing which makes—the world go round. And
the great book—when it is written—"will be characterized," he goes on to say, "by a *total lack of codpiece.*" It
will strip us, if not to the bone, to the flesh which drives
those bones and it will present, without editorializing, the
enormous variety of love: "I mean the *whole bloody
range*—from the little greenstick fractures of the human
heart right up to its higher spiritual connivance with the
. . . well, the absolute ways of nature, if you like." Such
a book, Pursewarden argues, might allow us to "rediscover
in sex the key to a metaphysical search which is our
raison d'être here below."

And though the *Quartet* is not quite the book Pursewarden visualizes—perhaps Miller's two trilogies come
close to it—it is a book which does explore in the right
way the right territory. For its range is very wide: from
rape to homosexual passion, from child prostitution to
narcissistic masturbation, from the unrequited love of
Narouz for Clea to the tender exchanges of Clea and
Darley, from the random skirt-chasing of Pombal to the
intricate incestuous relationships of Liza and Pursewarden
and the suppressed, but just as real, incestuous quad-
rangle set up by Leila and Nessim, Mountolive and his
mother. Durrell's project is, if you want, mere presentation, not judgment. But it is presentation designed to show
something significant about the structure of the human
heart.

So ambitious a project, though it may eventually reduce, as Pursewarden suggests, to boy meets girl, involves,
before it reduces to that level, each boy and each girl in
a complex design of affection; to turn again to the physicist's metaphor, it involves each figure of the novel in a
"field" of emotional entanglement. This field, radiating

out from him, in intricate ways distorts the "fields" set up around each of the other characters. No figure, therefore, is uncomplicated. Justine, for example, is caught in a tangle of loves—wife of Nessim, former wife of Arnauti, mistress of Darley and Pursewarden, lover of Clea; she is as well obsessed by her childhood experience of Capodistria's rape and by her passionate desire to recover her child. Yet she experiences sexual passion only when it can be coupled with political intrigue! Virginal Clea is in some ways more complex still; for, involved in the affair with Justine, she is loved by Narouz, loves Amaril, is freed by him to love Darley, and is loved by Keats. Melissa, given so little personality as to seem at times merely an object, is nevertheless involved in her own tangle of love; for, mistress to Cohen and to Darley, she sells herself for one night to Pursewarden and bears a child by Nessim. Yet each of these lovers—pair them up as we will—sees not even the false face his beloved presents to him! He sees only something he projects onto that false face: "If you can't do the trick with the one you've got," Pursewarden tells Justine, "why—shut your eyes and imagine the one you can't get. Who knows? It's perfectly legal and secret. It's the marriage of true minds!"

But if, in Durrell's world, *everything* admits impediment to the marriage of true minds, Durrell does suggest in his imagery of interacting fields of personality, a world not strictly private, a world which, though misunderstood by each person in it, can be understood by an outsider in terms of the interaction of those persons. And if, sometimes, the machinery creaks—Clea reading lips through a telescope, say; or, in the last book, Scobie being imitated by three different characters—the machinery does finally present to us a believable landscape, a believable landscape on which believable characters, mired in time, struggle—not only with each other but as well with themselves—toward a tender acceptance of things as they are.

The Rebirth of the Artist
BY ELLIN HOROWITZ

Welcome O Life! I go to encounter for the millionth time the reality of experience and to forge in the smithy of my soul the uncreated conscience of my race.

James Joyce, *A Portrait of the Artist as a Young Man*

Invisible Man is another kind of portrait of the artist, the making of an exile. Ralph Ellison's book, like Joyce's, takes its hero through a series of initiatory episodes from which he emerges a new man, an individual with the god-like power to create. The pattern is generally that of a quest for identity, the birth of the individual out of the chaos of man's manifold potential. In both stories the narrator's art will arise from the conflicts of his hero's quest.

Ralph Ellison has specifically employed the pattern of man's mythic descent into the pit, or womb, and his emergence with the power to prophesy—the ancient initiation of the great going down into the darkness of symbolic death and the resulting resurrection. *Invisible Man* is cyclical in form and resembles the ritual cycle it re-enacts. The narrator begins his story in an underground hole. The underground, as in Dostoyevsky, is identified with the subsconscious, the world outside of time and reason. His hole however is warm and fantastically lit, neither dark, damp nor cold as a grave.

And remember, a bear retires to his hole for the winter and lives until spring; then he comes strolling out like the Easter chick breaking from its shell. I say all this to assure you that it is incorrect to assume that, because I'm invisible and live in a hole, I am dead. I am neither dead nor in a state of suspended animation. Call me Jack-the-Bear, for I am in a state of hibernation.

The artist tells us that his hero is an invisible man; he is unnamed and invisible because people refuse to see him. This book is a search for his identity, denied both by society and himself.

At the onset the hero is seen as a kind of seasonal god whose underground death will cause new life to rise from the earth. The pattern is a variation on the descent of the initiate: he must go down into the pit and face the mystery in order to be reborn. The narrator functions as a Jonah in the womb of the whale, and his prophecy, his book, will be born out of the pit.

The greatest obstacle in the Negro's search for identity arises out of the incompatibility of individual values with a community whose thinking is preindividual, for the Negro is aware that he is seen only in terms of his category. He exists as a specimen of an ostracized group and to wander from the behavior pattern laid down for that group is to disrupt the community's pattern of thinking. Because every American is, in some sense, an outsider, the Negro is a prototype experiencing the national problem of alienation and isolation. As the outsider and stranger, the insulted and injured, he externalizes the darkest part of all our souls. Ellison's conflict belongs to all of us. Even beyond the failure of man to recognize the identity of those about him is the failure of man to exert himself, to become himself, and to run the risk of humanity. Thus we contribute to our own invisibility.

In his article on Richard Wright in the *Antioch Review* (Summer, 1945), Ellison discusses the various strategies with which the Negro confronts his American destiny. He may choose invisibility and accept the role created for him by the white world, resolving his resulting conflicts in the hope and catharsis of Negro religion. In repressing the hatred for Jim Crow and striving for a middle way of respectability, he consciously or unconsciously becomes the accomplice of the white man in oppressing his brothers. Thus invisibility, as it appears in Ellison's hero, becomes, like Hamlet's madness, both plight and device. The alternative is to reject the stereotype and become the criminal, the revolutionary carrying on a constant psychological, often physical, battle against the white world. Ellison's own hero must make this choice between invisibility and Lucifer's "non serviam."

A profitable method of dealing with *Invisible Man* is to see the action as a series of initiations in which the hero passes through several stages and groups of identification. The changes of identity are accompanied by somewhat formal rituals resembling the primitive's rites of passage. The primitive recognizes that man changes his identity as he passes from one stage or group to another and accompanies this transition by rituals that are essentially symbolic representations of birth, purification and regeneration in nature.

Ellison's narrative is a series of such initiatory experiences set within a cyclical framework of the mystic initiation of the artist. The rites of passage take the hero through several stages in which he acts out his various and conflicting sub-personalities. When he has won his freedom he is reborn as the artist, the only actor in our society whose "end" is a search beneath the label for what is individual.

The narrator begins his story in the pit and in a flashback takes his hero through the experience that led up to his descent. Finally, in the epilogue, there is a union between the innocent hero and the artist who has achieved wisdom; the central duality lies in that juxtaposition between the two I's. The element of confession in the first person narration of *Invisible Man* suggests its function as a cathartic. The artist tells us his story from the pit so that he may rise at the end.

The hero begins his career in a Southern town as a docile innocent who dreams of becoming educated and pleasing the white community. The narrative is the story of his expulsion from this Eden of illusion.

The first uneasy note in the hero's youthful paradise is the recurring voice of his grandfather who on his deathbed told the boy that he had been a spy all his life. "I want you to overcome 'em with yesses, undermine 'em with grins, agree 'em to death and destruction, let 'em swaller you 'till they vomit or bust wide open." Though the

meekest of men he had spoken of his meekness as something dangerous. This is essentially the ancient Chinese
strategy of absorbing the conqueror in order to keep one's
own identity. When things go well for the hero he feels
guilty, as though he were unconsciously obeying his grandfather's advice. For conduct defined as treachery he is
praised by the most "lily-white" men of the town (i.e.,
"that's pretty white of you"). Throughout the hero is
fearful of upsetting white domination, and the meaning
of his grandfather's sphinx-like riddle becomes a key
problem ("The old man's words were like a curse").

The smoker scene is the crucial initiatory experience of
the hero's boyhood. His art will be born out of blood,
chaos, and humiliation—the conditions under which he
gives his first speech on The Virtue of Humility. At the
height of a battle-royal he sees the prostitute who taunts
him as a bird girl, and, as in Joyce, this is the moment
the hero's art is born. He will suffer anything in order to
give his speech. Ironically, the only prophecy born out of
the dark bloody arena is a speech on humility, and the
reward, a scholarship, is the key to the world of Negro
yes-sayers and repressed respectability. It is the first item in
the prize briefcase the hero will always carry. He is told:
"Keep developing as you are and someday it will be
filled with important papers that will help you shape the
destiny of your people." The irony is pointed at the articles
he will later carry in the briefcase, which is equated
throughout with the hero's unconscious; he will continue
collecting things in it, the things he wishes to put away,
the symbols of his disillusionment. It becomes a record
of his being and his "badge of office" like the Shamen's
magic bag.

At the second stage the hero is seen at college aspiring
to be an educator and identifying with the college president Bledsoe (long suffering bled-so). Bledsoe is one of
various types of Negroes pictured here as tempters; others
are a Booker T. Washington Negro, the Uncle Tom educator, the kind who "keeps his place," the semi-mythic
Founder, and blind Barbee who says "see ahead." Bledsoe
himself is the seemingly unctuous servant who is in truth
deadly aggressive. Despite power, prestige, white friends,
and Cadillacs he somehow arranges his pants so they will
sag at the knees and his feet shuffle to suggest a past on

a chain gang. Like the hero's grandfather he says, I seem obsequious but really rule them all. For power he will say yes and aid white men in subjugating his people. The hero's grandfather, however, made no claim to rule. He simply allowed himself to be swallowed so that the white man would choke.

The fall from the college paradise occurs when the hero inadvertently shows a Northern trustee do-gooder the seamier side of Negro life outside the Utopian college grounds. The seamy side appears in the countryside's most notorious Negro, a kind of monster described by progressive Negroes with disgust as "field niggerism." The scene itself is a monstrous parody of Southern genre writing about Negroes, highlighted by an Erskine Caldwell account of the Negro's incestuous relations with his daughter. Not so strangely, minorities seem to be traditionally characterized as oversexed and immoral, and here the image of the Negro as an uncivilized instinctive animal and "big black rapist" is clearly the transference of the forbidden on to the scapegoat people. The trustee, Norton (perhaps a nasty pun on Charles Eliot Norton, as the other Northerner is called Emerson), listens with a voyeur's perverse fascination because he has had just these desires towards his own daughter, and he concludes by paying the old Negro for doing it for him.

For this crime, the acceptance of reality and an unconscious revolt against yesing the white man, the hero is expelled from grace and must leave the sanctuary of school. "Here with the quiet greenness I possessed the only identity I had ever known and I was losing it."

The great exodus following the expulsion is a transition from the South to Harlem. Travel itself suggests a symbolic change of identity but in these first days in the North he continues to pattern himself on the old college ideal. Despite the escape by geography he remains invisible in Harlem's black against black. Dreaming of a great future he remembers always to deodorize so "they" won't think "all of us smell bad," and to be on time, "not any c.p. (colored people) time." He rejects pork chops and grits for bacon and eggs, but hearing an ashman's song begins to "go back to things I had long ago shut out of my mind."

The letter of introduction which was to bring him suc-

cess proves to be the letter his grandfather showed
him in a dream—the letter that says, in essence, "keep
this nigger boy running." Kenneth Burke speaks of this
advice as a Belerophontic letter, the message the character
carries that contains his fate. Now the innocent first sees
himself as deceived and betrayed. This is exactly what will
happen to him; they all keep this "nigger" running. Everyone, white and black, seems in a conspiracy to keep him on
the inexorable journey towards a self.

The following factory scene is a wild vision of the
position of the Negro in a black-white world. Seeing the
building at a distance "was like watching some vast patriotic ceremony." Flags flutter around a great white sign
bearing the company slogan: "Keep America pure with
Liberty Paints," The factory's chief patriotic contribution
is their color "optic white," related to the dominant theme
of sight and blindness, visibility and invisibility, white and
black. The hero's job is to make white paint by putting a
drop of seemingly magic solution into a can of black
liquid, but he cannot seem to make it white enough and
when it is white he sees only grey (recalling the white
campus and the dim Negro cabins nearby).

Again the Negro appears as the victim, the result of
the conscious or unconscious torture of one man to
another. The hero remains unseen to those about him who
see only what they need or want to see. To the unions he
is a company fink, while to Lucius Brockway he is an
educated Negro who doesn't know his place and probably
belongs to the union. Each uses him for his own ends.
Lucius, the old Negro who tends the furnace, says he is
the one who really makes the paint white; "I dips my
finger in and sweets it." This black finger and the black
liquid are needed to make the paint white. It is the Negro
who keeps America pure by acting as the scapegoat for
all sins (a deliberately grim joke for purity is identified
with whiteness).

Lucius Brockway is the Negro who maintains his invisibility, going underground (he works in the basement),
and worshipping the boss and white supremacy. He created
the company slogan: "If it's optic white it's the right
white," reminiscent of the folk song's refrain, "If you're
white you're right, but if you're black, get back, get back,
get back."

The hero's first act of revolt is his unconscious inability to make white paint, for implicit in his failure is the overthrow of Lucius Brockway, one of the dominant authority images. The act of rebellion culminates in a furnace explosion with its images of the inferno, and a loss of consciousness which functions as the ritualistic-death of the initiate.

The scene that follows in the factory hospital is clearly a strange vision of birth with suggestions of lobotomy and castration. The hero lies in a womb-like box as figures in white perform a macabre operation intending to turn him into a "vegetable." During the mock shock therapy he appears as a ludicrous dancing minstrel darky, the harmless silly fellow the white world would like to believe in to allay their fears. Recovering consciousness he feels his limbs amputated; he is like a child, without a past, helpless, and lost in a "vast whiteness." The "delivery" is complete with the literal cutting of an umbilical cord. The old personality is dead and the initiate has a new identity born out of the machine. Because he has lost his past he is considered cured but when questioned about Buckeye the Rabbit he remembers playing this part as a child and is brought back through reversion to the folk tradition of which he is an unacknowledged part: "I could no more escape than I could think of my own identity. Perhaps, I thought, the two things are involved with each other. When I discover who I am I'll be free."

Man is never a constant unified being. Always in a state of transition, he is not one but many multiple sub-identities. Thus duality is essential in the notion of rebirth. The hero, caught in the conflict between old and new, is described in terms of a disassociated personality: "I had the feeling that I had . . . used words and expressed attitudes not my own, that I was in the grip of some alien personality lodged deep within me." The schizophrenic behavior of the tribal shamen is thought to indicate possession by the gods and Ellison's hero displays some of the symptoms of the mad prophet. Later, before his first speech for the Brotherhood he describes his ambivalence:

This was a new phase, I realized, a new beginning, and I would have to take that part of myself that looked on with remote eyes and keep it always at the distance of the campus . . . Perhaps that part of me that observed listlessly but saw all, was still the urging part, the dissenting voice—the traitor self that always threatened internal discord.

Throughout the narrative the hero stands between submission and rebellion like a tragic hero torn between two conflicting necessities. In order to achieve the new life of the ritual, the god, in Freud's terms the father, must be slain. The guilty answering voice demands submission, for parricide is the greatest of man's crimes. The hero's traitor voice is the voice of the rebellious son. A dream in the prologue re-creates the Freudian myth of the primal horde in racial terms. Here a Negro woman poisons her white master-husband to save him from a more brutal sacrifice by their white-hating sons. She tells the hero that she loved her husband but she loved freedom more. While she cries her sons laugh and the hero observes: "I too have become acquainted with ambivalence."

The alternate strategies offered the Negro, to submit or to rebel, reflect the traditional ambivalence of the son. The notion of the great white father and the simple Negro children who must be protected by the parental taboos of white supremacy would suggest that the entire racial division can be seen in terms of the relationship between father and son. The white man's advice to the Negro to "keep his place" is the father's advice and the threat in both cases is sexual. In *Invisible Man* the authoritarian figures consistently play the role of subjugating the hero, punishing him for the crime of asserting his identity, seen as the son's rebellion. The displaced guilt running throughout the narrative can be traced to the desire to overthrow the father and is certainly linked with the dominant castration imagery. Throughout, the hero identifies with authority figures, torn between submission and rebellion, feeling like a criminal but not knowing why he is guilty.

Each of the hero's crimes is essentially the Oedipal crime. At the smoker the town's leading white men watch as a naked prostitute taunts the Negro boys who are alternately threatened if they look and threatened if they don't. The hero submits to the humiliation of watching the woman he cannot have but unconsciously says "equality" instead of "responsibility" in his speech. Bledsoe expels the hero from college because his unconscious defiance threatens Bledsoe's position. He must leave school, the alma-mater, and the protection of the father Bledsoe, his only source of identity. He is willing to do anything to stay, obey Bledsoe and worship the god-like Founder, but another expulsion from Eden occurs because the son would not keep his place. The price of freedom is wrath and banishment.

The hero's inability to make white paint and his physical attack on Lucius Brockway are his crimes at the factory. Here again he is feared as a threat to an older man's position and must be punished by castration in the rebirth fantasy. Brockway too had advised the boy to "keep his place." Again in the Brotherhood his crime is the assertion of his individuality, ostensibly called opportunism, that would threaten the communal group. In reality he is expelled by Brother Jack because he has gained too much power and is a rival for his position. When the hero sleeps with a Party leader's wife she is described as a surrogate for Brother Jack's mistress. Here he plays the expected role of "big black rapist" to a masochistic white woman. In effect he is acting out the ultimate crime in terms of both family and racial taboos. The result is the riot and the final destruction.

Such rebellion is punishable by castration. The authoritarian figures in white in the factory hospital are the castrators while in the concluding dream sequence we actually see Bledsoe, Norton, and Emerson castrating the hero because he will not return to their domination. In both cases castration is equated with the dispelling of illusions. When Bledsoe first smashed his dreams and called him "nigger," it was as shattering as if "I learned the man whom I called father was actually of no relation to me."

It should be made clear that the father-god figures in the narrative are not always white men although white seems to function generally as the image rebelled against. Actually almost every major character in the novel is a variation on this theme. The college Founder, described as part Horatio Alger, part Christ, is called a "cold father symbol" and the narrator derives great pleasure from seeing pigeons soil his statue. Norton is "a god, a force," a "messiah" and a "great white father." Later Brother

Jack is called a "great white father" who, for all his seeming liberalism, should really be called "Marse Jack" as he is the field boss in a white supremacy state. He watches his underlings "like a bemused father listening to the performance of his adoring children," and is later compared, in a quite Freudian sense, with a bulldog the hero feared as a child. Finally, at the conclusion, Ras appears as an angry black god wreaking destruction.

After the factory explosion the hero begins a new life mothered by Mary. Not so curiously his family, like Christ's, is fatherless. Mary is a reminder of his past, stable and comforting, but she demands some notable achievement that will benefit the race. As Mary's son he must seek his appointed role. Now he can accept his true identity symbolized in the acceptance of Negro food. He eats yams boldly on the street; "They're my birthmark . . . I yam what I am." This realization, in turn, enables him to deliver the eviction speech (in echo of Antony's address to the Romans) that wins him a position in the Brotherhood.

Even as he is drawn into the Party he suspects that they only wished to use him for something. A drunken member wants him to sing because "all colored people sing" and they wonder if he shouldn't be a little blacker for their purposes. They see him as The Negro, and he, in turn, is unable to see them. He enters the Party only on the assurance that he can become as great as the Founder, and still deluded, strives towards his old identification even at the price of submission.

With the entrance into the Brotherhood comes another transformation. The change in group identification is symbolized by a new set of clothes, a new name, and a new family. (With the concept of maternity conferring rebirth all initiates become brothers.) Despite his new family and role the hero cannot rid himself of a broken bank, the grinning comic Negro image he carries in his briefcase. Brother Jack too speaks of the sacrifice of the old self for new life: "You have not completely shed that old agrarian self, but it's dead and you will throw it off and emerge with something new."

The first speech for the Brotherhood is delivered in an arena reminiscent of the earlier smoker scene. The hero feels curiously unsure of his identity, fearing he will forget his new name, or be recognized. It is a feeling of schizoid disassociation; the hero is seen as the possessed prophet whose magic lies in his speeches and his power to convert. The entire narrative, in fact, is later described as his "raving."

He speaks on blindness and this theme becomes related to the notion of invisibility and the imagery of black and white. In the arena he is blinded by a spot light (white) and looking at the audience sees only a black pit. He says: "They've dispossessed us each of one eye since the day we were born. So now we can see only in straight 'white' lines." The preacher Barbee was blind and Brother Jack has only one eye. The hero tells his audience that under the Brotherhood's leadership the one-eyed men will join and the blind will lead the blind, but the hero himself cannot see and he is invisible to his audience. He speaks of becoming "more human . . . with your eyes upon me I have found my true family . . . I am a citizen of the country of your vision." But he exists only in the vision of the audience and coming off the platform, blinded by the light, "I stumbled as if in a game of blindman's bluff." The next time, he decides, he will wear dark glasses. Later, when he affirms his invisibility, dark glasses become his disguise.

The hero does not begin to understand the meaning of his speech but he is reminded of a teacher who told him that we create our race by creating ourselves. He remembers Joyce's *Portrait of the Artist as a Young Man* and thinks, "Stephen's problem, like ours, was not actually one of creating the uncreated conscience of his race, but of creating the uncreated features of his face; our task is that of making ourselves individuals."

The hero's crime in the eyes of the Brotherhood is that of asserting his individuality over the unity of the organization; it is called his striving for personal power. The disillusionment culminates in the betrayal and sacrifice of Tod Clifton. Clifton had turned against the Brotherhood, reverting to the darky notion of the Negro by selling dancing minstrel dolls, mocking self-images like the hero's bank. The doll itself is a hoax; it dances because of a thread tied to its back that is invisible because it is black.

The hero on his own initiative sees this as the time to play up the murdered Clifton as a sacrificial victim to the cause. With the committee's resentment of his tactics comes the realization that the Party does not care for his cause and will exploit the Negro for power. Even they do not see beyond their own ends. Brother Jack has a glass eye which he says he got in discipline to the Party; the price of discipline is blindness.

In the concluding chapters the hero stands between the opposing forces of the Brotherhood and Ras the Exhorter, the Negro nationalist leader; both sides see him as a traitor. To escape his only recourse is the ultimate invisibility and his initial move in this last transformation is the disguise of dark glasses in which he can neither see nor be seen. Speaking to a friend he had the feeling "that the old man before me was not Brother Macao at all, but someone else disguised to confuse me." The glasses here function as the blindness of Oedipus.

In the large hat and uniform of a zoot suiter, he no longer has any identity. "It was as though by dressing and walking a certain way, I had enlisted in a fraternity in which I was recognized at a glance—not by features, but by clothes, uniform, by gait."

The key to the novel then is not actually invisibility. In the new disguise "I'd be seen in a snowstorm but they'd think I was someone else." He can be seen but not in his own identity because he is constantly changing. The metaphysical center of the novel is Rinehart for whom the hero is mistaken. Rinehart is a chameleon: confidence man, runner, gambler, briber, lover and Reverend. Could he himself be both rind and hart? The hero seizes upon this possibility of invisibility through multiple personality. He had never seen the notorious Rinehart who is not invisible but many things, the charlatan-Reverend who advertises, "Let there be light," and "Behold the seen unseen." Perhaps only this man of many possibilities is at home in a world without boundaries where no one is anyone. Freedom, he discovers, is not only the recognition of necessity, it is the recognition of possibility. "I was and yet I was invisible, that was the fundamental contradiction. I was and yet I was unseen . . . I sensed another frightening world of possibilities. For now I could agree with Brother Jack without agreeing." Now he understands how to follow his grandfather's advice. This "choke 'em

with yesses" strategy is metaphorically the going underground.

The action concludes with a vast apocalyptic image of
the end of the world and the destruction of an angry god.
The riot grows out of the Party's sacrifice of Harlem and
the death of Tod Clifton avenged by Ras in the costume
of an Abyssinian chieftain. The hero, caught between the
opposing forces, runs through streets flooded with water
(anticipating a new creation) as he tries to return to the
mother Mary. His glasses are broken and he still carries
his briefcase.

The running ceases only when he is driven into the
pit—a coal cellar, for a Negro in a coal cellar is invisible.
This is the dark womb which will be the source of new
life just as the black coal cellar is the source of heat and
light. To light his way out of the pit he must literally and
symbolically burn the contents of his briefcase—the
threatening letter written by Brother Jack, his Brotherhood
name and identity, the scholarship, the letter that kept
him running, Mary's bank and the dancing doll, Brother
Tarp's chain gang link which he received instead of his
grandfather's watch as a son's legacy, the Party pamphlets,
and Rinehart's promise to "Behold the seen unseen."

In his dream, Norton, Bledsoe, and Emerson return to
demand his submission and castrate him for this final
rebellion. The castration acts as the ultimate dispelling of
illusions whereby the hero gains the right to see. Like
the Fisher King his impotence seems a prerequisite for
his life-giving role. Here, as in ancient ritual, the powers
of reproduction are sacrificed and scattered on the water
for ever-renewing life.

The hero can no longer return to Mary (because he is
castrated), or to his old life (because he has no illusions).
In the meantime he will remain underground. "The end
was in the beginning."

"I am an invisible man and it placed me in a pit." In
an epilogue the narrator reviews his experience.

Now I know men are different and that all life is
divided and that only in division is there true health.
Hence again I have stayed in my hole, because up
above there's an increasing passion to make men
conform to a pattern. Just as in my nightmare, Jack

and the boys are waiting with their knives, looking for the slightest excuse to . . . well, to "ball the Jack," and I do not refer to the old dance step . . .

Apparently castration is necessary for conformity because it is the punishment for rebellion. Diversity becomes the narrator's creed and he warns that there will be no tyrant states if man keeps his many "parts" (in the two-fold sense). "Why if they follow this conformity business they'll end up by forcing me, an invisible man, to become white, which is not a color but a lack of one." The hero himself loves light because he is invisible; "Light confirms my reality, gives birth to my form."

The hibernation is over. I must shake off the old skin and come up for breath. There's a stench in the air which, from this distance underground, might be the smell either of death or of spring—I hope of spring. But don't let me trick you, there *is* a death in the smell of spring and in the smell of thee as in the smell of me. And if nothing more, invisibility has taught my nose to classify the stenches of death.

A brief discussion of a few of Ellison's sources might clarify his novel. *Invisible Man* is the result of a union between the Negro folk culture (blues, jazz, folk tales, the Bible, etc.) and the modern Western art of such men as Joyce and Eliot. Like Eliot among many others, Ellison is concerned with the use of pagan ritual as an objective correlative for his experience, and he has been influenced by Joyce in the use of the initiatory experience as related to the sense of the artist as an exile. The hero, like Stephen Daedalus, is the rejected, isolated figure on the border of human activity who must pass through several stages and survive various tests before winning the freedom to create. He is the modern hero seen in Conrad, Hemingway and Lawrence; the alienated passive hero in a de-personalized world who must become an exile in order to search for the "reality of experience." Like the Faulkner and Hemingway hero he is something of a lonely figure on the shady side of the law; the man with a mystic wound who cannot hunt with the pack. The resemblance to Joyce includes the almost paranoic sense of deception and betrayal as well as such consciously borrowed symbols as the bird girl.

Images of birds and flight are extremely important in Ellison's work and are more fully developed in his short story published in 1944, *Flying Home*. Flight is equated with Daedalus, the mythic figure of the artist whose craftsmanship is potentially the source of his freedom. The augury of the birds in *A Portrait of the Artist* is re-created at several points in *Invisible Man*, notably after the hero has given his successful eviction speech.

For the concept of the underground there is a wealth of background in folk literature and several possible modern sources in the guilty fear-ridden creatures of Kafka's *The Burrow* and Dostoyevsky's *Notes from the Underground*. A more direct source would probably be Richard Wright's story, *The Man Who Lived Underground*. Here the hero is specifically an invisible Negro driven into a sewer, where he erects a fantastic world and emerges as the mad prophet of the ritual who speaks with wisdom, although no one will listen to him.

The spirit of the novel is that of the blues, which Ellison has elsewhere defined as the impulse to keep painful details alive, to rub the sore and to transcend it, not by philosophy but by "squeezing from it a near tragic, near comic lyricism." The narrative opens with the ceaseless question of the blues: "What did I do to be so black and blue?" The hero wants to listen to Louis Armstrong play it while he eats a dish of vanilla, his favorite ice cream. "I like Louis because he .has made poetry out of being invisible." Ellison's book too is a search for the meaning and experience of being black and blue. It possesses the spirit of the blues in that it tells of the agony of life, and of the possibility of conquering it through sheer toughness of spirit, but like the blues it falls short of tragedy by offering no scapegoat other than the self. *Invisible Man* rubs the sore and probes the festering. It is a blues expression of pain and does not presume an answer. At the conclusion he is enabled to face his experience: "They were me, they defined me, and blind men no matter how powerful they became, even if they conquered the world, could take that, or change a single taunt, laugh, cry, scar, ache, rage, or pain of it."

The half-tragic, half-comic quality of the blues is reflected in the tone of emotional ambivalence in the novel. Through his hero's varied roles the author has acted out the opposing strategies offered the Negro, of being "for" society or "against" it. The new vision born out of the hero's conflict seems to be an attitude of comic ambivalence that allows him to embrace the complexity. Within the paradox of acceptance-rejection the world becomes one of infinite possibility. Thus the hero is neither white nor black but invisible in a world which is neither good nor evil but good-and-evil. "So it is that now I denounce and defend, or feel prepared to defend. I condemn and affirm, say no and say yes, say yes and say no." Ellison's hero is not reborn in traditional triumph. He will emerge with a realistic acceptance of the limitations of society (". . . for all life seen from the hole of invisibility is absurd"), and his own role (". . . and humanity is won by continuing to play in face of certain defeat").

The curious note in this almost neat equation is the stronger emphasis given the sense of limitation and doubt. The narrator's view often appears to have less of the positive quality of union than the tentative quality of hedging. Ellison seems strangely divided about his theme and the sense of hesitancy and confusion in the epilogue would seem to deny the affirmation to be gained by a descent into darkness. The hero has not come very far beyond his initial understanding of invisibility, a fine but limited notion. He has become a prophet but does not have much to prophesy. While the author need not offer us glory and salvation, the structure of the narrative does suggest a rebirth in proportion to the intensity and conviction of the fearsome descent. Ellison's hero, it seems, will emerge simply because he has no real choice and the epilogue, his prophecy, is certainly the least effective piece of writing in the novel. We feel that the author searches for something positive but seems undercut by doubt; significantly, almost all of the writing in the epilogue is qualified or framed as questions. The conclusion is haunted by a curious sense of fear that would deny affirmation and one cannot help but associate this with the castration fear which undercuts all the hero's attempts at rebellion.

Ellison has made poetry out of being invisible by putting it down in black and white, and the hero's failure to find affirmation in his darkness is recompensed by the

savage and enlightened vision of that darkness. Ralph
Ellison has written an extremely important novel, one
that goes far beyond social protest though it is a protest
and could scarcely help but be. Ellison neither rises above
nor renounces his identity as a Negro, but uses it as the
key to an understanding of the meaning and experience of
alienation and isolation. His conflict belongs to all of us.
It is externalized in the very real division of our society
into white and black; white does not see black and this
is all our fates. Having descended into such darkness
Ellison has gained the right, the insight and the responsibility to prophecy. The narrator concludes: "Who
knows but that, on the lower frequencies, I speak for you?"

Jean Genet
BY RICHARD KOSTELANETZ,
WITH JONATHAN COTT

The great modern writers have, in general, progressed from a concern in their early works with the real world, a concern which usually involved a protest against its harshness and deceit, to an emphasis upon the essence of man outside of history—a development exemplified in literary careers as diverse as those of Thomas Mann, T. S. Eliot, Samuel Beckett and James Joyce; and in this respect, Jean Genet's writings strikingly contrast with the dominant modern pattern. Whereas most contemporaries "mature" from cynicism into a lofty acceptance of or disinterest in man's ills, Genet develops from the subjective, almost polymorphously perverse, dream world of his first work *Our Lady of the Flowers*, best characterized by lines from Lewis Carroll's *The Hunting of the Snark*—"I engage with the Snark / Every night after dark / In a dreamy, delirious fight."—to an engagement with the realities of the present in his later plays. Of all the major modern writers, perhaps only Bertolt Brecht, whose work has likewise evolved from lyric to epic dimensions, also fits into this counter-pattern. Though Genet's writings clearly move in this direction, he never thoroughly suppresses one facet of his imagination beneath another. The fantasy elements of the recent plays echo aspects of the early novels and, conversely, the early novels sound protest notes that become dominant in the plays. Throughout his career, then, Genet balances the demands of fantasy and reality so that all his works become, in different degrees, both protest and vision.

For these reasons, one should view each of Genet's works from the particular perspective it demands. Rather than bringing outside issues such as Cartesian philosophy or the metaphysics of rebellion to bear upon *Our Lady of the Flowers*—a work that cannot carry the burden—it is more illuminating to see it as a certain kind of literary work, a novel of pure imagination. In the past, this kind of interior fiction survived only as an undercurrent of the classic novel, which attempted primarily to depict reality; and only in recent times has it, like so many other anti-traditions, entered the mainstream of literature.

"Reality" and "imagination," the two prime components of all prose fiction, confront each other in different measures. At the far extreme from *Our Lady* are totally naturalistic novels, a tradition running from Emile Zola to James Farrell in which human imagination is a negligible force. Next to them on the spectrum are novels in which imagination encounters reality and, to use Shaw's phrase, the "adjustment of moral and social scales" takes place—novels like *The Charterhouse of Parma,* Thomas Mann's *Buddenbrooks* and, more recently, J. F. Powers' *Morte D'Urban*. In another kind of work, reality is colored and instructed by imagination, until the tension between them becomes the novel's central issue—one thinks immediately of *Don Quixote* and Goethe's *Werther* and, in this century, of E. M. Forster's *The Longest Journey* and Saul Bellow's *Henderson the Rain King*. At the other extreme of the spectrum is the fictional creation in which God-like imagination makes little compromise with reality, except perhaps at a distant symbolic remove—the kind of literature we associate at its best with Lewis Carroll, Emily Dickinson and Franz Kafka. What characterizes their work is the writer's completely original sensibility, which is the cultivated and self-perpetuated vision of the closed artistic world of the "singular boy"—a phrase also taken from Lewis Carroll, this time his *Sylvie and Bruno:* "Then I's very glad I *is* a singular boy! It would be horrid to be two or three boys. P'raps they wouldn't play with me!" Jean Genet's *Our Lady of the Flowers* is among the best realized and most successful examples of this kind of literature.

In all his novels, Genet creates a series of "landscapes," externalizing worlds out of his psychic system. Thus, Sartre writes that *Our Lady* "is the height of aloofness," for it, more than any other of Genet's works, is the most "closed." To say that Genet's self-isolation is the prime reason for the novel's beauty is false in human terms; rather, self-isolation defines the limits Genet willingly imposes on himself to enable him to write such a book.

> A gesture that went beyond the room, entered into the night, where it continued on to the stars, among the Bears, and even farther; then, like the snake that bites its tail, it returned to the shadow of the room, and into the child who drowned in it.

In this extraordinary statement, Genet compresses into a sentence the movement and gestures of the entire novel. Genet's masturbatory and homosexual fantasies originate in his mind's prison, and all Genet's characters are his fantasy projections of the pin-ups on his wall—"(They) will fall from the wall onto my pages, like dead leaves, to fertilize my tale." Even on this level, they are astonishing creations—Clement Village, the "real" Negro convict who serves as a model for Seck Gorgui, plays with toy soldiers in Genet's cell and cries in despair when "the foreman brought the soldier that was one too many." Transformed through Genet's imagination, he is a dream character very much like Lewis Carroll's Red Queen and Mad Hatter and Kafka's Red Indian, his K's, and his Milena— that "real" lover whose personality, one gradually realizes, Kafka creates as if she were a character in his novel and the mirror of his emotions—all of them exist on the level of projection. Genet differs from these predecessors in the freedom of his imagination, for he is able to absorb characters into himself and transform them into others at his mere pleasure, announcing by an act of will that metamorphosis is as much a part of his aesthetic ground rules as his far-fetched metaphors and inconceivable oxymorons.

All the characters exist in an intangible area—floating uncircumscribed just above the ground, but usually unable to fly away. Of Darling, Divine's lover, Genet writes: "A Greek, he entered the house of death walking on air." Of Divine: "Now she is asleep in the lace, and their married bodies are afloat." Or in the magnificent passage describing Divine's funeral procession, Genet writes:

> In the rain, this black cortege, bespangled with multi-

colored faces and blended with the scent of flowers
and rouge, followed the hearse. The flat round um-
brellas, undulating above the ambulating procession,
held it suspended between heaven and earth. The
passersby did not even see it, for it was so light that
it was already floating ten yards from the ground. . . .

Genet's fantasies bathe in elegant and sensuous imaginary
waters, for his works successfully illustrate his own pro-
nouncement that, "The role of the artist is to impart value
to words." White enameled lilies, gilded candelabra, sugared
almonds, snow-white petticoats, wax orange blossoms,
white tulle, sky-blue denim—all are imagined and continue
to extend Genet's daydreams into an infinite and beautiful
heaven, and he is continually able to infuse his descriptions
with some of the lushest metaphors in modern writing.
Everything Genet touches, particularly experiences most
of us find distasteful, becomes transfigured and purified
through his vision. When a character wants to move his
bowels, he says: "My two bouquets of violets" or "I've
got a cigar at the tip of my lips." And when Darling
picks his nose, Genet writes: "From his nostrils he plucks
acacia and violet petals." Through his magical use of
words, Genet establishes and regulates "a whole internal
astronomy." In this respect, his aesthetic sense merges with
his psychological needs: "I need merely evoke (a warm,
gilded luxury)," Genet writes, "from time to time in its
snug details for the vexations of my poor life as prisoner
to disappear, for me to console myself, console myself
with the idea that such luxury exists." Moreover, through
the sheer power of his literary imagination, especially his
rhetoric and imagery, Genet obliterates in the sensitive
reader any moral response to what he describes. Poetry,
Genet once told an interviewer, consists "in transforming,
by means of language, reputedly base matter into what
[is] regarded as noble matter. If my books arouse readers
sexually, they're badly written, because the poetic emotion
should be so strong that no reader is moved sexually."
Then, by accepting Genet's private mythology of deities and
devils, the reader empathizes with his sense of the beauty,
and sometimes the sacredness, of homosexuality and
thievery.
    Yet it is wrong to think that Genet has any intention

to reform. Rather, he, deprived by his imprisonment of
the capacity to act, imagines acting only through his
imagination and thereby denies the possibility of action
itself. Likewise, Genet suffers from the tragic predicament
of recognizing that his dreams escape from him. For once
the characters of the novel—embodiments of Genet's desires—attain their own life, they destroy themselves:

> Darling, Divine, and Our Lady flee from me at top
> speed, taking with them the consolation of their
> existence, which has its being only in me, for they
> are not content with fleeing; they do away with
> themselves, dilute themselves in the appalling in-
> substantiality of my dreams, or rather of my sleep,
> and become my sleep; they melt into the very stuff
> of my sleep and compose it. I call for help in silence:
> I make signals with the two arms of my soul, which
> are softer than algae. . . .

But precisely in the comfort of sleep and the excitement
of dreams lies Genet's salvation, for, he tells us, "The
importance of any event in our life lies only in the
resonance it sets up within us, only in the degree to
which it makes us move toward asceticism." With Genet,
there is always, on one hand, the sense of Emily Dickinson's "Say, sea,/Take me"—Genet's cry of "Hold me
back! Fasten me!"—but also, on the other, of her knowledge that ". . . thyself may be/Thine enemy; / Captivity
is consciousness,/So's/liberty"—for Genet's prison cell,
like Emily Dickinson's Amherst cottage or Kafka's room
in Prague, is "sweet": there one can feel the "joy" and
"ecstasy" which all three writers experience alone.

Spider, snake and guitar images proliferate in the novel.
Describing Culafroy as a type of child, Genet writes:
"[These kind of children's] slightest gesture proves to
them that a crystal mirror, which their fist sometimes
bespangles with a silvery spider, encages the universe of
houses, lamps, cradles, and baptisms, the universe of
humans." And talking of young Culafroy's relationship
with his girl friend Solange, Genet interjects the unidenti-
fied quotation: "You are your own fate, you have woven
your own spell." Here Genet has gotten out of himself
far enough to reveal—in the imagery of a spider's web—

the truth of his psychology and to portray that subtle and difficult scene in which Solange, jealous, discovers that Divine-Culafroy loves Alberto: "She had difficulty finding enough saliva to ask: 'You like him?' and her swallowing was painful, as if she were swallowing a package of pins." Through Alberto, Genet becomes initiated into both snakes and homosexual love, and a guitar is Genet's apt symbol for a naked male backside.

Genet employs more conventional patterns of symbolism usually to invert them. Many of his figures of speech are references to God and the Church usually, through elegant blasphemy, to express his sense of the negative state of grace. However, the purity and intensity of his vision, while specifically denying God and Christian grace (the ciborium proves to be hollow), offers him the possibility of salvation. By an act of imaginative will, he can make "the toilet of the slate house" his heaven on earth:

It was my refuge [as a child]. Life, which I saw far off and blurred through its darkness and smell—an odor that filled me with compassion, in which the scent of elders and the loamy earth was dominant, for the outhouse was at the far end of the garden, near the hedge—life, as it reached me, was singularly sweet, caressing, light, or rather lighted, delivered from heaviness. I am speaking of the life which was things outside the toilet, whatever in the world was not my little retreat with its worm-eaten boards. It seemed to me as if it were somewhat in the manner of floating, painted dreams, whereas I in my hole, like a larva, went on with a restful nocturnal existence, and at times I had the feeling I was sinking slowly, as into sleep or a lake or a maternal breast or even a state of incest, to the spiritual center of the earth.

Immediately after writing this, Genet states that, "If I were sick, and were cured by a miracle, I would not survive it. Miracles are unclean; the peace I used to seek in the outhouse, the one I am going to seek in the memory of it, is a reassuring and soothing peace." Again, Genet affirms that he finds his own salvation in a state of immanence.

As a closed literary work, *Our Lady of the Flowers*

does not, of course, break out of itself as do, say, *Don Quixote* and *The Brothers Karamazov*. Genet concludes by describing a pimp drawing the outline of his penis on a letter. Genet must return to this position—he ends and begins alone with his genitals. But on the way he created a work whose intensity is nearly overbearing, whose internal universe is a sustained and coherent whole, whose original style befits its materials, and into the novel form itself he infused a freedom and possibility for which future novelists will be indebted. In all, *Our Lady of the Flowers* is one of the most remarkable prose works of our time.

In his later prose, Genet slowly opened himself to the world outside, moving first into the semi-fantasy of his second prison narrative, *Miracle de la rose* (1946, yet untranslated) in which history and dream are not quite fused; the untranslated *Pompes funebres* (1947); and the semi-autobiographical and very confused *Querelle de Brest* (1947, also untranslated), the story of a young man's quest for identity; and several poems of little consequence; until in *The Thief's Journal* (1948), his second major prose work, Genet seems to confront the reality of his own experience.

In many ways, *The Thief's Journal* is distinctly inferior to *Our Lady*. The falling off is immediately evident in the language, for absent from *The Journal* is the intensity and originality of style that marked the earlier book. Rather, the images tend to be disappointingly flat, and the metaphors conspicuously few and obvious. However, the overall incoherence of the book—its fragmented narrative, its shifts in tone, and its changing attitudes—is probably a deliberate approximation of the incoherence of the experience he describes.

Nonetheless, the incoherence of one aspect, the character of the novel's "reality," works against Genet's achievement, for instead of being necessary, or intrinsic to Genet's purposes, it needlessly muddles his intentions. He gives us autobiographical "facts," tells us of his adventures as a beggar, thief and prostitute in all the countries of continental Europe, lists his contacts and lovers in the major cities of his travels, remembers how his youthful love for Stilitano urged him to crime; and most of the time we believe that Genet is relating a kind of colored reportage, very much (perhaps too much) like Ferdinand-Louis Céline's travels through America, *Journey to the End of Night*. But at times he undercuts this by allowing fantasy elements to enter his world, such as the dream-juxtapositions typical of *Our Lady*. The opening page contains the bald, italicized assertion: *"There is a close relationship between flowers and convicts. The fragility and delicacy of the former are of the same nature as the brutal insensitivity of the latter."* This sort of highly imaginative metaphor would be appropriate in *Our Lady*, but in *The Journal* it appears incongruous and faked. The aspiration to realism is also undercut by the book's final passage where Genet says that he has just passed "through the region of myself which I have called Spain." That is to say, the "Spain" of the book exists totally in Genet's imagination. Precisely because these two dimensions, dream and reality, remain so needlessly confused, the reader is never quite sure how to comprehend Genet's book.

Through the series of journal notes and short narratives, Genet weaves several themes that permeate his entire work. He became a writer, he remembers, to satisfy his desire for a purely subjective beauty that he could infuse into his actions and perceptions. "The beauty of a moral act," he writes, "depends upon the beauty of its expression." In Genet's particular experience, to judge from *Our Lady*, this means that the beauty of the form of an act, or the beauty of Genet's way of seeing it, can cross out any moral dimension it may have previously had. If Genet can deftly pick the pocket of a handsome sleeping Negro and softly feel his crotch too, then he has successfully committed two beautiful acts. The proof of their loveliness is that they are worth remembering and setting down in his journal. In Genet's radical reformulation of values, the prime fount of aesthetic pleasure is, of course, homosexual relations—not because of their Platonic purity but because Genet, always the subjective egoist, finds them the most pleasurable experiences in his life. The appearance or suggestion of homosexual energy, it follows, can render an ugly person beautiful. In his description of the ideal lover, the one-armed Stilitano, Genet writes, "All his brilliance, all his power, had their source between his legs. His tool, and that which completes it, the whole

apparatus, was so beautiful that the only thing I can call
it is a generative organ."

In tracing the causes that prompted him to a life of
crime and homosexuality, Genet argues that since he was
orphaned from birth, assigned to live in public institutions,
and rejected by the normal world, he, in turn, rejected
those who did not care for him. In this intense negation,
he began to admire all those whom society hated; from
this stems his fondness for murderers and criminals. At
times, Genet suggests that all the rejected men of the
world, from criminals to orphans to Negroes to homosexuals, are united in their revolt against society, acting as
an Hegelian antithesis to normalcy, very much like Marx's
proletariat. Though Jean-Paul Sartre in his book on Genet
finds a wealth of significance in this implication, it remains in the end a lesser, more tentative idea in the Genet
canon.

In this book, Genet's ideas are more significant than
the style, for he was turning away from the world of pure
imagination of *Our Lady* to a literature that attempts to
influence the spectator. "This is my last book," he pledges
in *The Thief's Journal,* and at that time Genet had already
begun to write in a more communicative genre, the drama.
"A performance that does not act upon my soul is vain,"
he writes in a preface to *The Maids,* and in his subsequent
work he pursues this more external path.

Despite the sustained high intensity of the pitch of
conflict, the many sharp passages and stunning gestures,
and the presence of certain compelling themes, *Deathwatch* (1947–9) is a curiously incoherent play. The dramatic high points do not seem to relate to each other, and
the conflicts fail to jell into unifying themes. For his
materials, Genet remains within the prison world of *The
Thief's Journal,* but in the play he has extracted himself
from the situation. Three Prisoners await their fate—
Green Eyes, aged 22, who is anticipating his conviction
for murder and his possible execution; Maurice, aged 17,
who in his inability to accept imprisonment nervously
taunts his cell-mates; and Lefranc, aged 23, who kills
Maurice to prove himself the equal of Green Eyes—also
capable of gratuitous murder. As in *Our Lady,* Genet is
obsessed with homosexual power—the prisoners are all
handsome and sensual, Lefranc strangles Maurice with

the motions of a rape, Maurice's hero-worship of Green Eyes has homosexual overtones, and Snowball, the Negro prisoner who is called the "King" of the cellblock, is described, like Divine, as floating above the earth.

Though the play contains elements from the earlier works, Genet's prime purpose here is testing the possibilities of the stage. In performance, non-verbal effects assume a certain importance, as though Genet were moving towards the kind of total theatre outlined in Antonin Artaud's influential polemic, *The Theatre and Its Double* (1938). Artaud, we remember, called for a theatre in which gesture and posture, dance and sound would create "violent physical images" that could dominate the play's language. In *Deathwatch*, language, rather than action, remains the major mode of expression, but the clanking of Green Eyes' chains, the gestures that culminate in the strangling of Maurice; and Green Eyes' mad dance in a vain attempt to escape the oppressive consciousness of impending death all contribute towards creating a violent, tense stage.

Since the action focuses upon Green Eyes, one assumes that Genet wants to illustrate a prisoner's desperate predicament in the face of death. Though the other prisoners admire him for the enormity of his crime, he cannot respond to their worship; for imprisoned doubly and finally in the cell of himself and unable to control his fate, Green Eyes can only shout in protest, "It [fate] fell on my shoulders and clung to me." But fate seems an inadequate way of explaining Green Eyes' and Lefranc's actions; and even if we accept this as the play's prime theme, many of the conflicts, as well as the lines, seem superfluous. So rather than understand Genet's *Deathwatch*, the audience remains excited and, regrettably, confused.

Genet's second play, *The Maids* (also 1947), is likewise at bottom a flawed play, for here Genet seems to deal with two distinct themes, neither of which quite relates to the other. The first, which critics such as Martin Esslin and Sartre have chosen to emphasize, is the exposure of the human being who, possessing in himself no essence, achieves a sense of identity and pride only by playing the role of another. The play opens with an elegant lady being dressed by "Claire," her maid; but when the telephone rings and this make-believe world is terminated, as sleep by an alarm-clock, "Claire," we discover, is really the maid Solange, while "the lady" is really Claire, the elder of the two maids. Likewise, the lady whom they tend is a kept woman who imitates passion and devotion to earn the support of her Monsieur. Since Genet in his stage directions suggested that the three women should be played by male actors, we as audience then witness *X* imitating a distinctly different *Y* playing a more different *Z*. To Esslin Genet's "game of mirrors . . . is a device to uncover the fundamental absurdity of being, its nothingness." But is the message of *The Maids* really that universal? Elsewhere, Genet has created integral beings of unequivocably defined character; so what he is really defining here is the contrary, the inauthentic character whose essence is so hollow he can assume any identity society or his dreams force upon him. In this direction, Genet may even be saying something about the character of the actor—for whom he has in prose expressed severe contempt—but this interpretation should not be pushed too far.

The play also succeeds on another thematic level; for particularly if women are cast in the roles, as is usually the case, the maids become rather sympathetic figures. After all, they, like criminals and Negroes, are the outcasts of a society that offers little to satisfy their needs; so in lieu of any other excitements, they relish making themselves important by pretending to hold higher places in the ladder of existence. Their response to feelings of insignificance is a perfectly normal one, practiced by children who dress up in their parents' clothes as well as adults. In fact, Genet himself wrote in *Our Lady,* "We occupy our minds with giving ourselves splendid roles through luxurious lives." In this interpretation, interest focuses upon the demonic attachment the maids express towards each other and towards their mistress—like all of Genet's emotions a seething fusion of equally intense love and hate—and, later, we sympathize with the maids' vain attempt to cover up their mistake which caused the arrest of their mistress's patron. Rather than face her punishment, Claire dresses in her mistress's clothes; and drinking the poisoned tea she prepared for her mistress, she dies in a role of importance. Precisely because the play sustains itself on both levels, neither of which meshes

with the other, *The Maids,* like *Deathwatch,* finally remains unfocused and unchallenging.

In *The Balcony* (1956), Genet expands upon one of the
two themes of *The Maids;* but with *The Balcony* he has
matured so considerably as a dramatist that it is the first
play that is full-length, coherent and truly rebellious. His
theme, dramatized relentlessly in every scene, is that reality
and illusion are indistinguishable, or rather that illusion
is the only reality we know. From this follows a secondary
theme: good and evil are also too amorphous to be clearly
discerned, for man, both in his own life and in his perception of the world, is destined to succumb to the comforting illusion that gives him what he wants to believe, not
the reality he is unwilling to face.

The Grand Balcony is a palace of illusion occupied by
prostitutes willing to enact a client's fantasies. A gas man
who pretends he is a bishop needs a servile penitent,
another piteous creature becomes a General who accepts
a costumed girl as his faithful horse, while a third becomes a Judge with a thief whom his executioner can
whip. By wearing cothurni, high platform shoes, and a
costume with padded shoulders each creates an illusion of
power to compensate for his own insignificance. This
suggests that Genet sees power as a stronger motivating
force than sex (i.e., the ego as more demanding than the
libido).

The Balcony is Genet's metaphor for the world; the
playing of roles defines his sense of the human condition.
Irma, the boss of The Balcony, calls her patrons "visitors"
rather than "clients," deceiving herself into thinking she
offers a more distingushed service. The Police Chief, discovering that none of Irma's clients want to imitate him,
oppressively aware of his own impotence, dreams that
his splendid mausoleum will be topped by an enormous
phallus. When the Envoy describes the mausoleum's inner
room as a place "where mirrors will reflect to infinity—I
say to infinity!—the image of the dead man," he pulls out
from all role-playing the final underpinning: death reduces us all to an inescapable insignificance, for zero
reflected to infinity is still zero.

Rather than merely condemning the vanity of role-
playing, Genet shows us that disguise is inevitable. Outside The Balcony is fomenting a political rebellion whose

prime tenet is "despising make-believe . . . and complacency." (Too many directors, it should be noted, unwisely omit this and other scenes.) Although they know that to deal in illusion is to corrupt the cause, the rebels resort to illusion-making to achieve their aims—Chantel, an ex-Balcony girl, is transformed into a Joan of Arc–like–heroine-figurehead, while in a later scene the leaders discuss at length how best to exhibit themselves to the press photographers. When the revolution succeeds, the small men who impersonated the Bishop, the Judge, and the General assume these roles in reality, but each, feeling embarrassed by the power and responsibility of genuine authority, wishes to return to the "absolute dignity" of merely pretending the role. In this sequence, Genet, by numerous historical allusions from before Joan of Arc to the present, dramatizes a critique of political reality which while partly true—the public sees more posed illusions than real men—does not finally tell us much about political existence. Another deficiency stems from Genet's continued inability to differentiate his characters sufficiently.

In *The Balcony,* Genet makes several ultimate statements about existence, and these are more pertinent. Because society forces upon us roles that it wants us to play—so that the world knows how to understand us—and, it follows, because man is able to gain significance (as well as immortality) for himself only by aspiring to an Identity, man is forever fated to repudiate any essence he may have had. The Envoy, Genet's truth-telling character, says the rebels cannot win because "What they want is that each individual be both himself and a shining specimen of himself." In the end, Genet says that man, caught between essence and dream, finds "reality" a chaos of illusions. Because the world deceives us at every turn, moral judgments are impossible—the Bishop says, "Here (in The Grand Balcony) there's no possibility of doing evil." Though the Judge pretends to make judgments, he cannot distinguish good from evil. In the brilliant final scene, Irma, who with the revolution's success had become the Queen, returns to her existence as "Irma" and then, in a second shift, to the relaxed personality of the actress playing Irma (though, of course, this is a theatrical role too), to address the audience, "You must now go home, where everything—you can be quite sure—will be even falser than here. . . . You'll leave by the right, through the alley." In these perfect moments, all the tensions of the play are held in suspension, for Genet does not let his audience forget that it is *our* world of illusions he describes. The theatre itself and the production of the play become the epitome of Genet's image of, respectively, the universe and its events.

Though Genet's next play, *The Blacks* (1958), is filled with enough inversions and subtleties to confuse many a sophisticated spectator and critic, its central action is quite clear. It depicts the Negro's fantasy of the ascendancy of the black race to ultimate world power and the extermination of the whites as punishment for milleniums of exploitation. On one level, several Negroes overthrow the Queen, her valet, a colonial governor, and a missionary who once lorded over them; but since Genet instructs that these "white" roles are to be played by white-masked Negro actors and adds a dosage of improbable events, he implies that all this takes place in the world of dream. For these reasons, the central conflict of the play is not between the characters themselves but between the play and the audience—the former to be composed, at Genet's demand, entirely of Negro actors and the latter of whites. If the audience should be entirely Negro, then, Genet suggests, they should either import a white spectator or don white masks.

Genet intends to tell his white audience that the antagonism between white and black, both as people and as colors symbolizing opposing values, has grown so strong through history that as the black man rises to power, he will have as little tolerance of white as the white man, in the past, has had of black. A Negro character, Village, rapes and kills a white woman solely out of hatred for the color white, as though he wanted to exterminate not a single person but an entire race and even the notion that whiteness stands for purity. In contrast, Diouf, the male Negro who preaches the possibility of love and racial reconciliation between the races, is condemned as a traitor; and since he is too impotent to resist, his fellows dress him in the clothes and mask of a little white girl. Likewise, just after the white exploiters are overthrown, the missionary reverts to a cow-like primitive existence and a Negro woman, ironically named "Snow," expels the deposed

Queen to a Hell that is "Pale, White, Infernal." Like the revolutionaries in *The Balcony,* the Negroes assume, by inversion, their predecessors' illusion that equates color with human value. At times, the black-white conflict assumes larger dimensions as though Genet were suggesting that any long-standing antagonism between the entrenched and the outcast, whether they be bourgeois and criminal (one black character says, "We are like guilty criminals"), client and prostitute, and audience and actor—in short, between the "white" world and those it has condemned to blackness—can be resolved not by compromise but only by an apocalypse in which the underdog will expell his master from the earth. Beyond that, Genet believes that so long as there are differences between people, inequities of authority or good fortune, human society is fated to be forever rent with hate. Despite the gushing power of his own fierce anger, Genet controls *The Blacks* as a fantasy, never letting us forget that he depicts a dream of revolution. At the start, the figures on the stage are introduced as actors; and at the end, Village and Virtue (aptly, a Negro prostitute) affirm their love to a background minuet from *Don Giovanni* in a scene too sentimental to be anything but a dream.

More than in his previous work, Genet here, in a symbolic sense, engages the realities of the external world; and though his commentary is a bit too narrow to pass for political wisdom, the play itself represents Genet's first real attempt to come to terms with history. Likewise, he intends to move us in the present (though in what direction is unclear); for, in repudiating naturalistic or even absurd theatre, which presents a scene as a self-contained whole, Genet creates a play that, if it is to succeed, must "speak" directly to its spectators, cutting into the sinews of their existence by telling them that they have every reason to fear their future. Also in *The Blacks,* Genet demonstrates his increasing maturity as a playwright, for he has moved away from conventional narrative drama to a theatre composed, like absurd plays, of a series of rituals along a single theme. At the same time, Genet for the first time creates a gallery of full characters who, with their distinct personalities, transcend the mirror images of the earlier book. In all, despite some unnecessary obtuseness, this is Genet's most successfully realized play—the images

are as coherent and compelling as is the whole. Of all his
plays, it evokes, if we are white, the strongest disturbance
in our souls.

Genet's most recent play, *The Screens* (1961), exhibits
in its published version (unlike the earlier plays, it has
not yet been performed in America) a distinct falling off
from the realized excellence of *The Blacks.* His subject
is again a basically political one, the Algerian revolution;
but instead of focusing the action, Genet creates a work
of sprawling diffuseness that seems to push in many directions, to suggest a multitude of themes without coalescing
around any definite purpose. At times, Genet, revealing
Brecht's influence, seems to be working towards a new
conception of a theatre with epic overtones. The play
has nearly a hundred characters, many of them interchangeable; and instead of scenery Genet uses a plethora
of screens, some of which depict or symbolize certain
backgrounds, others contain suggestive drawings put on,
often by actors, for the occasion. For instance, while two
Frenchmen talk, several Arabs draw flames on the background screens and blow on them to signify the impending
cataclysm. A brilliant director could possibly employ these
effects for a profit, but in manuscript they seem to clutter
needlessly an already jumbled and confused stage. (Genet,
to discourage further the possibility of performance, pre-
scribes an open-air theatre.) Moreover, the play's language
is conspicuously weak and colorless—the scatology, in
particular, is uninspired and grating—as though Genet
had forced himself to repress his natural lyricism. Finally,
the play is permeated with heavy doses of preposterousness
—a woman finds a pair of hanging trousers more attractive
than her husband and in another scene a glove suspended
in mid-air intones the voice of its owner. These cute
effects, serving no discernible purpose, distract from the
final impact.

Just as it is difficult to see importance in all the technique, critics find it hard, to judge from the variety of
published interpretations, to unweave the most important
strands from the uneven and multiple plot. Their confusion is excusable, for *The Screens* really is a puzzling
play. The interpretation offered here admittedly neglects
many aspects presented in the manuscript. Its main character, Said, is a degenerate and impoverished Algerian,

opportunistic and totally corrupt. In becoming an active fighter for the rebel cause, Said progressively comes to resemble his French enemies, assuming their arrogance, their shameless filth and their unconcern for individual life. Instead of repudiating terror and poverty, he merely continues all the evils of French rule, perpetuating an Algeria in which, as one character puts it, "There are no more judges, there are only thieves, murderers, fire-brands. . . ." In rising to military eminence, Said loses contact with his followers; and too arrogant to escape his fate, he is shot to death by five Algerian soldiers. As in *The Balcony,* Genet creates a symbolic microcosm to comment critically on all revolutions in history, and again Genet tells us that they are caused by the *ressentiment* of the underdog, that the underdog desires primarily to imitate his master, that its leaders are devoured by its children, and thus that the revolution in the end achieves nothing but needless violence and loss of life. Genet also suggests that Said is the prototypical devil of modern times and that, repeating another theme from *The Blacks* —as long as there is social difference, there will continue to be revolutions. Thus, in his sense of the tragedy of all social change, Genet unequivocally rejects Sartre's strong belief in the necessity and inevitable success of all rebellions; for Genet in his refusal to say that the Algerians embody all virtue and the French all vice, contends that, despite all man's hopes and actions, life is cyclical, rather than linear, and basically immoral. "As long as there are soldiers," one character says, "there'll be whores." In the final scenes in the world of the dead, Genet clearly adds to these themes the dimension that death makes all in-significant; for in the end, the actions of one man, whether for evil or good, ultimately causes no distinct change in life on earth and counts for naught in heaven. Although Genet in *The Screens* seems once again to want to make large statements about human existence—that life is doomed to be anomic, tragic, filthy and immoral and the world affords neither love nor refuge from its terrors—he is unable to cast his vision in an appropriate theatrical technique. The failure of *The Screens* does not signify the end of Genet's career; for its inadequacies stem, it seems, more from a creative restlessness that has yet to resolve itself than a dissipation of talent or concern.

Because Genet's development as a writer proceeded outside what generally pass for literary circles, his work does not easily fit into the cubbyholes of literary tradition. In his early prose, he synthesized the sustained negativism of the wildly imaginative, violently rebellious, *poet maudit* tradition of French writing running from the Marquis de Sade through Baudelaire and Céline as well as the pregnant fantasy of writers as diverse as Lewis Carroll, Sade and Emily Dickinson. As a playwright, he developed parallel to the absurd movement in France, obliquely confirming their view of the world while not employing their distinctive absurd techniques. In this respect, as well as others, Genet's work has been needlessly confused. Though Martin Esslin in his early essay on "The Theatre of the Absurd," in *The Tulane Drama Review* did not mention Genet, Esslin mistakenly included him in the book of the same title, offering, to double the fault, very misleading interpretations of the individual plays. Even by Esslin's definitions, Genet is not an absurdist. In absurd theatre, the playwright uses absurd events, as in Ionesco's *The Chairs* where a hired lecturer addresses a non-existent audience in an indecipherable tongue, to convey his sense that life is fundamentally nonsensical and meaningless—absurd. The events in Genet's plays are too riddled with meaning to be absurd; for Genet, as we noted, has a more tragic conception of existence. His characters are not haunted by metaphysical impotence; rather their efforts, no matter how strong, are doomed to failure; and whereas Ionesco's language is characterized by disembodied cliché, Genet's has a black eloquence and a knack for imaginative metaphors. For Ionesco and Beckett the central fact of modern life is unbelief, for Genet it is filth and terror. In some respects, Genet's theatre is more Brechtian than absurd—at times Genet, like Brecht, appears to believe that theatre should stimulate feeling as well as articulate it—but not even that term tells us much about Genet's plays.

Genet's ideas may be too idiosyncratic and limited to influence most of us greatly, and his work exhibits certain glaring aesthetic weaknesses which are the inevitable undersides of his distinctive strengths. Nonetheless, his prose and plays are valuable to us, first, for enlarging our conception of what is possible stylistically in literature, secondly, for permitting us to see through his vision aspects of life we are all too ready to dismiss as filthy and non-existent and, third, for creating an elegant and powerful theatre of unforgettable images and challenging themes.

William Golding

BY FRANK KERMODE

The critical reception of Mr. Golding's fourth novel, *Free Fall* (1959) was on the whole hostile; that of its predecessor (*Pincher Martin,* 1956) uncomprehending. Not since his first, *Lord of the Flies* (1954) has he enjoyed general acclaim; yet the opinion that he is the most important practising novelist in English has, over this period of five or six years, become almost commonplace. One reason for this apparent paradox is that Golding's books do not (if only because each is extremely original in construction) yield themselves at one reading: *The Inheritors* (1955) and *Pincher Martin* have been better understood with the passing of time, and the same will be true of *Free Fall*. This suggests that Golding is a difficult writer; and it would not be strange if this were true. We have become accustomed, for intelligible historical reasons, to the idea that significant works of art are necessarily obscure.

It is, however, true only in a limited sense. We may note at once that despite the roar of baffled critics Mr. Golding's intentions are always simple. Of *Pincher Martin* he says "I fell over backwards in making that novel explicit. I said to myself, 'Now here is going to be a novel, it's going to be a blow on behalf of the ordinary universe, which I think on the whole likely to be the right one, and I'm going to write it so vividly and accurately and with such an exact programme that nobody can possibly mistake exactly what I mean.' "[1] But he goes on to admit that his handling of the story was "unspecific"; he did not actually *tell* the reader that Martin drowns on page 2; the evidence that he did so is oblique, and is completed only by the last sentence of the book. Golding is unlike many modern writers in his willingness to state the "programme" of his book (and also in denying the reader much liberty of interpretation); but he does not pretend that what seems to him simple must be so explicitly and directly set down that the reader will not have to work. In short, his simplicity is a quality best understood as intellectual economy. His theme takes the simplest available way to full embodiment. But embodiment is not explanation; and all that can be guaranteed the reader is that there is no *unnecessary* difficulty, nothing to make the business of explaining and understanding more difficult than, in the nature of the case, it has to be.

The best course for sympathetic critics is to be a shade more explicit, to do what the novelist himself perhaps cannot do without injury to the books, which grow according to imaginative laws, and cannot be adjusted to the extravagant needs of readers. If critics have any reason for existence, this is it; to give assurances of value, and to provide, somehow—perhaps anyhow—the means by which readers may be put in possession of the valuable book.

It is worth notice that Golding is to a marked degree isolated from intellectual fashion: "I think that my novels have very little genesis outside myself. That to a large extent I've cut myself off from contemporary literary life, and gained in one sense by it, though I may have lost in another." He is more interested in Greek than in modern literature. Thus there are in his books preoccupations one would not expect in a highbow modern novelist—that Ballantyne was wrong about the behaviour of English boys on a desert island, or H. G. Wells about the virtue of Neanderthal men, are not opinions many would care to dispute, but few would find in them points of departure for passionate and involved fictions. In the same way Mr. Golding, though he is in some degree an allegorical writer, is entirely free of Kafka's influence, which makes him very unlike Rex Warner, with whom he is sometimes implausibly compared. His technical equipment is as sophisticated as Conrad's; yet like Conrad he begins each new book as if it were his first, as if the germination of the new theme entailed the creation of its own incomparable form. (There are, however, some habitual devices—the sudden shift of viewpoint at the end of the first three novels, for instance.) Perhaps the resemblance to Conrad could be developed: an isolated indeed exiled sensibility, a preoccupation with guilt, desperate technical resource. Sometimes this last power re-invests what others have done before, old devices labelled in text-books: stream of consciousness, changing point of view, time-shifts. There was a time according to the author himself, when he wrote novels intended to meet the requirements of the public, as far as he could guess them; but these novels failed, were never even published. Then, with *Lord of the Flies,* he saw that it was himself he had to satisfy; he planned it in very great detail, and wrote it as if tracing over words already on the page. How, in pleasing his own isolated taste, and doing it in these essentially unmodish and rather private ways, has he come to represent to so many the best in modern English writing?

The answer to this is necessarily involved, though the situation is in itself simple enough. One thinks of Mr. Golding's world: he sees it swinging through its space, its wet or rocky surfaces lifting under the pull of the moon; its inhabitants, locked on to it by gravity, walking upright, containing floating brains, peristaltic entrails, secreting seed at the base of the spine, somehow free and somehow guilty. Golding once called himself "a propagandist for Neanderthal man"; his way of looking at the world has something of the candour of Lascaux. In *The Inheritors* Neanderthal man is superseded by *homo sapiens,* who has a better brain, and weapons; but it is the innocence of the doomed predecessor that we see enacted, for, until the last pages, we see the activities of the new man, intelligent and so capable of evil, through the bewildered eyes of the old. And Golding, though he admits that we belong with the new man, supposes that we could not recapture that innocence, that natural awe for Oa, the mother-goddess, had not something of it survived in us.

I am groping for an answer to the question, how such a writer can strike us as profoundly attuned to contemporary sensibility? It seems to be that in his own way, and short-circuiting a great deal of fashionable and sophisticated mythologizing, Golding gives remarkably full expression to a profound modern need, the need for reassurance in terms of the primitive; the longing to know somehow of a possible humanity that lived equably in the whole world; the need for myths of total and satisfactory explanation. Our developed consciousness, our accumulated

knowledge are marks of guilt; the fragmentary nature of
our experience is the theme of our artists. To discover
again the undifferentiated-myth, is to return to Eden or to
Neanderthal man—or indeed to the primary germ-cell
the splitting of which is the beginning of guilt: that is to
find innocence and wisdom.

Golding has been called a writer of "fables"; "what I
would regard as a tremendous compliment to myself," he
says, "would be if someone would substitute the word
'myth' for 'fable' . . . I do feel fable as being an invented
thing on the surface whereas myth is something which
comes out from the roots of things in the ancient sense
of being the key to existence, the whole meaning of life,
and experience as a whole." And he accepts the description, "myths of total explanation" for his works. The genesis
of these myths is naturally obscure. They do not much
resemble the myths of Joyce or those of Mr. Eliot or Mr.
David Jones; yet they are related to the same Symbolist
aspirations towards prelogical primitive images which
animate all these authors. The differences are attributable
to Mr. Golding's relative isolation from any mainstream
of speculation. To put it too simply: he sees a world
enormously altered by new knowledge. He understands
the strong reaction against this new knowledge which is
characteristic of modern art, an art in love with the primitive; also the patterns of human behaviour are now very
generally explained by reference to psychic residua or
infantile guilt. It is a world you can blame "science" for if
you like, a world in which the myth of progress has failed;
but the rival myth of necessary evil and universal guilt
has come back without bringing God with it. He looks at
this world understanding what it contains, as the painters
at Lascaux understood theirs. He thinks of the books of
his childhood—*Coral Island,* Wells's *Outline of History*—
and observes that they are wrong about the world, because they thought cannibals more wicked than white men
and Neanderthal man less worthy than his conqueror.
These books have, in his own figure, rotted to compost in
his mind; and in that compost the new myth puts down
roots. When it grows it explains the ancient situation to
which our anxieties recall us: loss of innocence, the
guilt and ignominy of consciousness, the need for pardon.
Mr. Golding owns that he is a religious man. He believes

that some people are saints: in *Lord of the Flies* Simon is a saint, and this is why, he says, literary people have found Simon incomprehensible; "but he *is* comprehensible to the illiterate person . . . The illiterate person believes in saints and sanctity." (This is not the first time a modern artist has found his allies among the illiterate—Yeats and Eliot have made similar declarations.) Golding believes in human guilt and human sense of paradise lost; he also believes in divine mercy.

The evidence for holiness lies scattered among the fragments of our world, and those fragments are represented in Golding's books; they form part of the whole. But this whole is a world of imagination, where everything is related, everything counts and truth is accessible; the world of myth. For Golding's own term is the right one; out of the single small seed grows this instrument "for controlling . . . ordering . . . giving a shape and significance to the immense paradox of futility and anarchy which is contemporary history." These are Mr. Eliot's words on Joyce's myth; but they will serve for Golding. Art, says Cassirer, requires a step back into mythical thinking; perhaps this has always been so since mythical thinking became obsolete, but never has the step back been more consciously taken than in our times. And in the contrast between our consciousness of this, and the momentary forgetfulness of our Darwinian grandfathers, Golding found the theme of his first novel.

Lord of the Flies has "a pretty big connection" with Ballantyne. In *The Coral Island* Ralph, Jack and Peterkin are cast away on a desert island, where they live active, civilized, and civilizing lives. Practical difficulties are easily surmounted; they light fires with bowstrings and spyglasses, hunt pigs for food, and kill them with much ease and a total absence of guilt—indeed of bloodshed. They are all Britons—a term they use to compliment each other—all brave, obedient and honourable. There is much useful information conveyed concerning tropical islands, including fieldworkers' reporting of the conduct of cannibals: but anthropology is something nasty that clears up on the arrival of a missionary, and Jack himself prevents an act of cannibalism by telling the flatnoses not to be such blockheads and presenting them with six newly slaughtered pigs. The parallel between the island and the Earthly Paradise causes a trace of literary sophistication: "Meat and drink on the same tree! My dear boys, we're set up for life; it must be the ancient paradise— hurrah! . . . We afterwards found, however, that these lovely islands were very unlike Paradise in many things." But these "things" are non-Christian natives and, later, pirates; the boys themselves are cleanly (cold baths recommended) and godly—regenerate, empire-building boys, who know by instinct how to turn paradise into a British protectorate.

The Coral Island (1858) could be used as a document in the history of ideas; it belongs inseparably to the period when boys were sent out of Arnoldian schools certified free of Original Sin. Golding takes Ralph, Jack and Peterkin (altering this name to Simon, "called Peter") and studies them against an altered moral landscape. He is a schoolmaster, and knows boys well enough to make their collapse into savagery plausible, to see *them* as the cannibals; the authority of the grown-ups is all there is to prevent savagery. If you dropped these boys into an Earthly Paradise "they would not behave like God-fearing English gentlemen" but "as like as not . . . find savages who were kindly and uncomplicated. . . The devil would rise out of the intellectual complications of the three white men." Golding leaves the noble savages out of *Lord of the Flies* but this remark is worth quoting because it states the intellectual position in its basic simplicity. It is the civilized who are corrupt, out of phase with natural rhythm. Their guilt is the price of evolutionary success; and our awareness of this fact can be understood by duplicating Ballantyne's situation, borrowing his island, and letting his theme develop in this new and more substantial context. Once more every prospect pleases; but the vileness proceeds, not from cannibals, but from the boys, though Man is not so much vile as "heroic and sick." Unlike Ballantyne's boys, these are dirty and inefficient; they have some notion of order, symbolized by the beautiful conch which heralds formal meetings; but when uncongenial effort is required to maintain it, order disappears. The shelters are inadequate, the signal fire goes out at the very moment when Jack first succeeds in killing a pig. Intelligence fades; irrational taboos and blood-rituals make hopeless the task of the practical but partial intellect of Piggy; his glasses, the firemakers, are smashed and stolen, and in the end he himself is broken to pieces as he holds the conch. When civilized conditioning fades—how tedious Piggy's appeal to what adults might do or think!—the children are capable of neither savage nor civil gentleness. Always a little nearer to raw humanity than adults, they slip into a condition of animality depraved by mind, into the cruelty of hunters with their devil-liturgies and torture: they make an unnecessary, evil fortress, they steal, they abandon all operations aimed at restoring them to civility. Evil is the natural product of their consciousness. First the smallest boys create a beastie, a snake—"as if it wasn't a good island." Then a beast is created in good earnest, and defined in a wonderful narrative sequence. The emblem of this evil society is the head of a dead pig, fixed, as a sacrifice, on the end of a stick and animated by flies and by the imagination of the *voyant,* Simon.

Simon is Golding's first "saint, and a most important figure." He is "for the illiterate a proof of the existence of God" because the illiterate (to whom we are tacitly but unmistakably expected to attribute a correct insight here) will say, "Well, a person like this cannot exist without a good God." For Simon "voluntarily embraces the beast . . . and tries to get rid of him." What he understands—and this is wisdom Golding treats with awe—is that evil is "only us." He climbs up to where the dead fire is dominated by the beast, a dead airman in a parachute, discovers what this terrible thing really is, and rushes off with the good news to the beach, where the maddened boys at their beast-slaying ritual mistake Simon himself for the beast and kill him. As Piggy, the dull practical intelligence, is reduced to blindness and futility, so Simon, the visionary, is murdered before he can communicate his comfortable knowledge. Finally, the whole Paradise is destroyed under the puzzled eyes of an adult observer. Boys will be boys.

The difference of this world from Ballantyne's simpler construction from similar materials is not merely a matter of incomparability of the two talents at work; our minds have, in general, darker needs and obscurer comforts. It would be absurd to suppose that the change has impoverished us; but it has seemed to divide our world into "two cultures"—the followers of Jack and the admirers of

Simon, those who build fortresses and those who want to name the beast.

Lord of the Flies was "worked out carefully in every possible way," and its author holds that the "programme" of the book *is* its meaning. He rejects Lawrence's doctrine, "Never trust the artist, trust the tale" and its consequence, "the proper function of the critic is to save the tale from the artist." He is wrong, I think; in so far as the book differs from its programme there is, as a matter of common sense, material over which the writer has no absolute authority. This means not only that there are possible readings which he cannot veto, but even that some of his own views on the book may be in a sense wrong. The interpretation of the dead parachutist is an example. This began in the "programme" as straight allegory; Golding says that this dead man "is" History. "All that we can give our children" in their trouble is this monstrous dead adult, who's "dead, but won't lie down"; an ugly emblem of war and decay that broods over the paradise and provides the only objective equivalent for the beast the boys imagine. Now this limited allegory (I may even have expanded it in the telling) seems to me not to have got out of the "programme" into the book; what does get in is more valuable because more like myth—capable, that is, of more various interpretation than the rigidity of Golding's scheme allows. And in writing of this kind all depends upon the author's mythopoeic power to transcend the "programme." Golding has this poetic power, and nowhere is it more impressively used than in his second book, *The Inheritors*.

Prefixed to *The Inheritors* is a passage from Wells's *Outline of History,* and this serves the same purpose as Ballantyne's novel in the genesis of the earlier book; it sets off an antithetical argument. "Wells's *Outline* played a great part in my life because my father was a rationalist, and the *Outline* was something he took neat. It is the rationalist gospel *in excelsis*. . . . By and by it seemed to me not to be large enough . . . too neat and too slick. And when I re-read it as an adult I came across his picture of Neanderthal man, our immediate predecessors, as being these gross, brutal creatures who were possibly the basis of the mythological bad man . . . I thought to myself that this is just absurd . . ." The difference between Golding and the Wells of the *Outline* is simple; to Wells the success of the high-foreheaded, weapon-bearing, carnivorous *homo sapiens* was progress, but to Golding it was the defeat of innocence, the sin of Adam in terms of a new kind of history.

Golding's real power, the true nature of his mythopeic obsession, became evident only with the publication of this second book. This root-idea is, as I have suggested, a variant of the Fall, transplanted from theology. Golding is fascinated by the evidence—in the nature of the case ubiquitous—that human consciousness is a biological asset purchased at a price; the price is the knowledge of evil. This evil emanates from the human mind, a product of its action upon the environment. *The Inheritors* is about the accumulation of guilt that necessarily attended the historical success of *homo sapiens;* the intellectual superiority of Man over his simian victims is precisely measured by the cruelty and guilt which dominate his life and are relatively absent from his predecessor's. The creatures to be exterminated are almost innocent, as near it as we can imagine; they practise no deceit, have an obscure sense of life as a mystery, understand wickedness as killing, but their lives are controlled by the seasons, by inhibiting fears of water, above all by a physiological equipment excellent in its way but prohibiting intellect. They know the world with senses like an animal's; they depend much upon involuntary reflexes—keen scent, night vision, acuteness of ear; they are not men at all, and that is why they are innocent. Only after prolonged observations of the new men can Lok associate sex with cruelty, derange his senses with alcohol, offer violence to a friend, or even think of one thing or process as "like" another. Not to know evil is, in a sense, to know nothing. The new men sail away, successful and guilty, leaving Lok with the doll-goddess which is his only image of the intelligent and creative mind. Clutching this toy, he who had known useful fear is now the prey of useless terror as well as of his animal enemies; they, the real creators, plan a bloody and intelligent future.

Technically *The Inheritors* attempts a little less than *Pincher Martin,* but has fewer flaws. The natural setting, of obvious importance, needed to be wonderfully done and is. Above all, the feat of recording observations of the

activities of *homo sapiens* made with the sensory equipment of Lok is of astonishing virtuosity. We are constantly
reminded of the involuntary powers that sustain him;
his ears speak to him even if he will not listen, small areas
of skin react with useful knowledge, the nose marvellously
distinguishes and identifies. We can always see, too, that
the extinction of this animal is *necessary,* as in the passage
where he observes a new man aiming at him with a bow
and can no more conceive of what the man is doing than he
can impute enmity to so similar a being or explain his tall
face—his senses simply report a series of inexplicable
events. In the heart of the book there is a remarkable
passage of some fifty pages in which Lok and the female
Fa observe the communal activities of the new people
from a vantage-point in a tree. This is carried out with a
fierce imaginative power that is not in the least inconsistent
with a very minute attention to the complicated effect to be
communicated. What we have to be shown is that although we are experiencing these events innocently, by
way of the passive, vegetarian, inhuman senses of Lok,
we *belong* down below in the clearing, corrupt and intelligent. And at the end we abruptly leave Lok; suddenly,
with a loss of sympathy, observe him with our normal
sight, joining the new men, our own sort. With these anxious and responsible technicians we sail away, with only
a last glimpse of superseded innocence stumbling about on
the shore of a dead world. *The Inheritors* does not, like
Lord of the Flies, qualify as a spanking good tale, and
with its publication Golding met for the first time that
uncomprehending reception with which he is now so
familiar. The book was written, presumably at white-heat,
in a few weeks. It has not been surpassed.

Pincher Martin is, however, a bigger book. It is another
imaginative "forcing" of the same seminal idea, but more
densely written, with much interweaving of image and
reference—more like a poem, in fact, for undoubtedly this
kind of novel "aspires" to the condition of poetry. It takes
more reading than the others; it lacks the adventitious
accessibility of *Lord of the Flies* and is less recognizably
a story than *The Inheritors.* For all that, its wisp of narrative is handled with great skill, and after all the full import
of the book depends upon a most ingenious narrative device. The talent remains clearly that which produced the

earlier books, and some of the procedures, particularly those involving the extraction of significance from symbolic objects, are easy to recognize. And there is a continuity of theme. But it is, all the same, a book demanding unremitting attention.

Golding has himself provided "a mental lifeline" to readers who find the book difficult; it appeared in *Radio Times* and it might be useful to copy part of what he said.

Christopher Hadley Martin had no belief in anything but the importance of his own life, no God. Because he was created in the image of God he had a freedom of choice which he used to centre the world on himself. He did not believe in purgatory and therefore when he died it was not presented to him in overtly theological terms. The greed for life which had been the mainspring of his nature forced him to refuse the selfless act of dying. He continued to exist separately in a world composed of his own murderous nature. His drowned body lies rolling in the Atlantic but the ravenous ego invents a rock for him to endure on. It is the memory of an aching tooth. Ostensibly and rationally he is a survivor from a torpedoed destroyer: but deep down he knows the truth. He is not fighting for bodily survival but for his continuing identity in face of what will smash it and sweep it away—the black lightning, the compassion of God. For Christopher, the Christ-bearer, has become Pincher Martin who is little but greed. Just to be Pincher is purgatory; to be Pincher for eternity is hell.

The man is called Martin so that his worldly name may be Pincher (a naval nickname for all Martins) and nobody calls him "Christopher" until God does so at the end, out of the black lightning, as the resisting Martin shrinks to a mere pair of claws. Again the myth is worked out in fanatical detail; Martin calls his rock "Rockall" not only because that is a real rock, but because he remembers a poor joke turning on a word which is a bad rhyme for Rockall, and which is an obscene word for "nothing." The geology and animal life of the rock he invents out of memories of childhood holidays. He is horribly aware of the self-deceit, the Promethean posing, the shrinking

identity; he will do anything rather than accept the loss
of himself, even in exchange for the mercy of God.

Martin is "fallen man—fallen more than most"; a type
of depravity. His human consciousness is an evolutionary
specialization, like a pig's snout, used to ensure handsome
survival. He is hideously greedy, hence the recurrent
metaphors from eating. "He takes the best part (Martin
had been an actor), the best seat, the most money, the best
notice, the best woman. He was born with his mouth and
his flies open and both hands out to grab. He's a cosmic
case of the bugger who gets his penny and someone else's
bun." But this efficiency only makes his suffering more
characteristic; he declares for madness rather than extinction, intellect rather than love, and makes his own
most appropriate purgatory. Martin's boast is that he
controls and imposes his will on the world: "I can outwit
you; you are a machine." He is relieved to discover that
the cause of apparently "evil" manifestations lies entirely
within himself; that his fear of the gull which makes him
think of lizards originates in something he's read; that
he can cure the world by curing his own disorder. There
is a crucial and astonishing episode in which, with all the
gestures of heroism, he undertakes to expel the poison
from within him. He has eaten disgusting food, and it has
made his mind sick as well as his body. "I am in servitude
to a coiled tube the length of a cricket pitch. All the
terrors of hell can come down to nothing more than a
stoppage. Why drag in good and evil when the serpent lies
coiled in my own body?" His intelligent solution is a self-
inflicted enema.

But although it is true that the evil proceeds from within
him, it will not be dispersed by intelligence. That only
preserves him alive for torture, and he creates his hell with
the same effort that he puts forth to preserve his identity.
Of the plenitude with which this and all the related paradoxes inherent in the theme are developed I have room
to say virtually nothing. But one of them requires notice,
since I argue for the totality of the imaginative act. Martin's acts are willed, but also necessary; and this is beautifully translated into narrative at the point where, as officer
of the watch, he gives a helm-order a moment before the
torpedo strikes. The order was freely willed and murderous; it was also necessary and proper in the circumstance.

All that happened was "because of what I did," but it could not have been otherwise. Only the best in fiction has invention of this order.

This is not quite the whole story. It would seem, as a hypothesis stemming from the situation described, that another heaven might be possible, a God to whom some other question than "If I ate them, who gave me a mouth?" might be addressed. Golding's Nathaniel, whose natural goodness Martin recognizes and resents, is there to say that only in the abandonment of the beloved self is there any way to this. Nathaniel is the second in what may be a band of Golding's elect, those who see and know. But Nathaniel is anything but a respectable saint; his religion has a seedy quality and it contributes to Martin's agony as well as shadowing it with some ecstatic alternative. It isn't a pill of doctrine but another part of the imaginative structure.

Pincher Martin is a wonderful achievement, the book of a drowned man soaked and battered by an actual sea, making substantial rock out of nightmare; it is as if one's own hands grew soft and swollen in the idiot water and bruised on the dripping stone. It is a horrible book too; because the man is shrunk so mercilessly into his minimal disgusting humanity, the fattest maggot of all; and because Golding's knowledge of human egotism and cruelty is horrible. What makes all this bearable and Golding a major novelist is the total technical control: nightmare, hysteria, every kind of beastliness and depravity are given the virtue of form. There is no distinguishing here between a compassion that might be called religious and the skill of an artist; they are the same thing. There are those who find Golding sadistic; it is a judgment that calls in question their ability to read any book whatsoever, because it betrays an insensitivity to the moral quality of form. Yeats spoke of an intellectual construct which enabled him to "hold in a single thought reality and justice"; *Pincher Martin* is such a thought.

Of *Free Fall*, Golding's fourth and perhaps his most ambitious book, I must say that although I do not feel that I have yet got to know it well I have no expectation that it can ever possess my mind as the others have done. It should be remembered that Golding asks a lot of his critics —this is a matter, I think, of emphasis, of his not saying

"The first page and the last page are crucial." He does not say so because it seems to him self-evident.[2] It is not in such reticences that Mr. Golding fails (if he does fail); for in everything related to the shape of this myth his skill is all that it was in *Pincher Martin*. Technically *Free Fall* (which depends upon a system of "time-shifts" devised to expose the religious significance of a man's experience) is at least accomplished as any of the others. It is a mark of Golding's integrity that in every book he employs technical devices of remarkable ingenuity but never indulges his skill; it is never a hair's-breadth in excess of what the moral occasion demands. One's coolness towards the book has other causes.

The myth of *Free Fall* is, basically, that of all Golding's books: the Fall of Man, the expulsion from Paradise, erected wit and infected will. It is a myth which has accumulated an enormous and various theology, which does not matter until the novelist turns theologian himself. Golding's hero is examining his life (made typical life by many allegorical devices) with a view to discovering a pattern, some connection between his two worlds of experience, one deterministic, the world of empirical observation, the other a world in which the burning bush is not consumed, a world of horror and glory, heaven and hell. Sammy's conclusion (which is not the conclusion of the novel) is that "there is no bridge." In his brooding over different episodes in his life, Sammy Mountjoy is necessarily theologizing; in other words, there is within the book continuous comment—admittedly not directly vouched for by the author—on the myth. I do not think that this works; there is an unwonted hollowness in these passages, the shabbiness of a do-it-yourself theology; and the book at moments lies open to the Coleridgean charge of mental bombast—"thoughts and images too great for the subject" —the subject being not the Fall but a *commentary* upon it. In Golding's earlier books—and this is unique in modern fiction—guilt, unconscious innocence, the taste of isolation, good and evil, are made actual, like vomit in the mouth. It is this actuality that is lacking in *Free Fall;* its absence takes the nature out of Golding's prose, it takes the plasticity out of the narrative. The crucial episode, a nightmare experience in a prison-cell, calls for, and is not provided with, the savage compassion which went into the writing of *Pincher Martin.* Yet it is in a way wonderfully composed, passionate and cunning; there is no question of a failure of power or of nerve, only—to be bold—of a flaw in the original conception.

This flaw is one to which Mr. Golding's gifts render him peculiarly liable. Myths of total explanation are religious; comment upon them is theology. *Free Fall,* like *Paradise Lost,* is about *everything;* the author knows this, devises his narrative and even names his characters accordingly. Samuel Mountjoy at first misunderstands his vocation (like Samuel in the Bible) and is as a child in his slum an inhabitant of Paradise (Mountjoy). As he writes, he lives on Paradise Hill, "thirty seconds from the shop and the local." A central event of his life is the recognition of the beauty of a girl called Beatrice; later, by a positive act of will, he rejects the possibility of living by this vision, and subjects her to his lust. The two worlds between which his life is suspended (in a condition of "free fall" as understood in science fiction) are represented by a religious schoolmistress and a science master called Nick. The child does not have to choose; in childhood the two worlds interlock. He chooses, as a young man, to desecrate Beatrice. The other world he finds again in a prison-camp, where he is subjected by a German officer named Halde[3] to an interrogation modelled on that of Christ in the desert. Will he reject the "world"? Is he a son of God? He does not know enough to betray his comrades, and Halde sends him to a cell which he peoples with his own egotistical terrors; at the height of his agony he bursts out (or is let out) of the cell, forgiven. He walks into the world of vision: "The power of gravity, dimension and space, the movement of the earth and sun and unseen stars, these made what might be called music and I heard it." Beatrice has been reduced (and this passage is as fine as anything in Golding) to an incontinent idiot in an asylum; but Sammy still finds himself called to Paradise. He cannot reconcile the two worlds but the novelist, on the last page, builds a kind of bridge between them.

That it is mythologically substantial, this bridge, I do not doubt; but I do not understand it. The novel is about delivery from the body of this death; not only about the Fall but also about regeneration. This account of it is too scanty to be fair even to my imperfect understanding of the book, but it may be enough to help me make my point: that it is not the religious but the theological element that limits the imaginative scope, and brings into the writing a kind of dry heat, a brittleness, absent before. I ought to say that Messrs. Gregor and Kinkead-Weekes, in the intelligent article I have already quoted, find the theology satisfactory, and indeed orthodox. But Mr. Golding is not orthodox. He has done what writers in the Romantic tradition have done before—as Mallarmé discovered Nirvana without knowing Buddhism, or as Yeats dwelt, though heretically, on the Annunciation, he has found in experience and embodied in his own myths the truths that inform all others. But to provide accounts of mystical experience is one thing—admittedly a difficult thing, if only because of the qualitive differences between St. John of the Cross and a mescalin addict; to invent a mystical theology is another. The first is work for a genius, the second for a church. Not to see this is the flaw of all the Romantic and Symbolist writers who lapsed into the pseudo-theologies of occultism.

A final word on "simplicity." Golding's novels are simple in so far as they deal in the primordial patterns of human experience and in so far as they have skeletons of parable. On these simple bones the flesh of narrative can take extremely complex forms. This makes for difficulty, but of the most acceptable kind, the difficulty that attends the expression of what is profoundly simple. For all that I have said against *Free Fall* it is this kind of book, like the others a work of genius by a writer from whom we can hope for much more, since he is in superbly full possession of his great powers.

Postscript, 1964: William Golding's *Lord of the Flies* has sold over a million copies in the American paperback edition alone. It has, by all accounts, succeeded *The Catcher in the Rye* as the *livre de chevet* of educated American youth. I doubt if anybody is really qualified to say why this should be so; books make their way inexplicably. This one was published in 1954, and certainly it was noticed; E. M. Forster commended it and "everybody" talked about it, but with a sense that it was caviar rather than chowder—a book to tempt an intellectual into believing he had discovered a classic at its birth, but hardly a best seller. In the years that followed Golding did much to confirm this belief, but very little toward making himself a popular novelist. *The Inheritors* is a technically uncompromising, fiercely odd, even old-fashioned book about the overthrow of Neanderthal man, wonderfully distinguished but inconceivable as a big seller; *Pincher Martin* is as difficult as it is masterly; and *Free Fall* is complex, original, and in many ways reader-repellent. Golding's fifth and latest novel, *The Spire,* coming five years after *Free Fall,* is unsurprising in one way at least: it is firenew, magnificently written in what, despite its novelty, we can identify as a style bearing the impress of Golding's peculiar presence; but difficult, inviting only slow and submissive readers. . . .

The Spire tells the story of Jocelin, Dean of some cathedral, and his efforts to realize a vision and a vow by building on to his church a 400-foot spire. That is all. And we see the entire action not so much through the eyes as over the shoulder of Jocelin; such facts as where the money came from, and what other interested parties think about the crazy dean, we gather by using the corners of our eyes. It is sometimes, for Golding's other books, both easy and useful to know his point of departure; nobody is the worse for understanding how *Lord of the Flies* is related to Ballantyne's *The Coral Island,* or for taking note of the epigraph of *The Inheritors,* which is from H. G. Wells's *Outline of History* and congratulates *homo sapiens* on his successful campaign against the Neanderthals. Here we are not told of any similar starting point; but Mr. Golding must have got up the subject of how to build a spire, and the one he has in mind is Salisbury. He makes the spire 400 feet high—Salisbury is a little over that— and the highest in England as Jocelin wants it to be. It is surmounted by a capstone and a cross, as Salisbury spire is. It is octagonal, with a skin of diminishing thickness, and has no orthodox foundation, like Salisbury, of which it has been said that the dangers and difficulties of adding the spire were enough to frighten any man in his senses from trying it. Iron bands strengthen the structure. The four columns over which the spire was raised settled or bent in Salisbury, as in the book, and the spire at once slipped out of its true perpendicular, as here. In short, this is basically the spire at Salisbury. There was even a twelfth-century bishop called Jocelin. Despite some topographical mystification, the scene is consistent with this, and especially the Hanging Stones, which must be Stonehenge. And although it is no business of ours, Mr. Golding lives near Salisbury. I don't know exactly where he got the facts about the mason's craft, however, and I should like to.

In outline the story tells how the making good of the vision entails endlessly disagreeable and unforseeable discoveries. It seemed simple enough; yet it has sordid material causes, unsuspected sexual motives; and it can be realized only in the teeth of technical obstacles which a sane man would regard as prohibitive. The cathedral being a bible in stone, the spire will be the Apocalypse; but it is also a human body and the spire its erect phallus. It all depends upon how your attention is focused. As Dean Jocelin himself observes, "the mind touches all things with law, yet deceives itself as easily as a child." The opening paragraph shows us Jocelin laughing, shaking his head so that a glory consumes and exalts Abraham, Isaac, and God; his ways of looking, the moods of his mind, make and unmake vision and sacrifice. At this point Jocelin controls a manageable glory. But there is the question of the foundations, the palpitating human substratum that must maintain this glorious erection. And to its splendor the church is sacrificed, defiled by pagan workmen. Obscenely superstitious, they work as if taking part in some pagan rite. When they pry up the slabs at the crossways, it is clear that there are no foundations.

Against the will of the other principal Persons, against the skilled advice of the master builder, Jocelin forces the business on; whatever the foundations of the spire— whether you take them to be mud, or the corrupt money of his aunt—he will have his four hundred feet and his cross with its Holy Nail, a diagram of prayer. Rain water in the excavations finds the corpses and makes the church foul; the master builder seduces the wife of a church servant; the spire seems founded on human filth, the earth "a huddle of noseless men grinning upward." The workmen fool about with the model spire obscenely between their legs; but the vision persists, even in the crossways, above the pit itself: "Here, where the pit stinks, I received what I received." The four slender pillars are not divine

but human lovers, founded precariously on filth; they
sing in agony under the growing weight. The church
servant disappears, and Jocelin finds pagan mistletoe in the
crossways—a typical Golding narrative device, to issue in
a revelation as horrible as the recognition of Beatrice in
the madhouse of *Free Fall.* Jocelin fares forward: "the
folly isn't mine. It's God's Folly . . . Out of some deep
place comes the command to do what makes no sense at all
—to build a ship on dry land; to sit among the dunghills;
to marry a whore."

Whereas Jocelin thinks of each new foot of the building
as a godsent challenge to his strength personally to uphold
the structure, the master builder has material problems;
he devises a steel band to hold the outward thrust of the
spire. Each is clear about the cost, in life and lust and
increase of foulness, of this "unruly member." The mason's
mistress dies for it—a violent death in childbirth, Golding's
recurrent figure for violence and creation. "This have I
done for my true love," thinks Jocelin with terrible but
perhaps only apparent inconsequence. The workmen desert
for pagan midsummer fire festivals, and Jocelin's own
unruly member is tormented by the memory of the dead
woman. Reporting to the Visitor from Rome, he presents
himself—filthy, crazy—as "Dean of the cathedral church
of Our Lady," the church he has desecrated, deprived of
services, made the scene of deadly lust. His spire is
finished, the Nail driven in; it is at once half-destroyed
in a storm. And yet, though built imperfectly, in folly and
anguish, it is (he thinks in hubris) a spire of prayer. Then
the angel strikes him. He has brought ruin and loathing on
himself and on the master builder and the church; he can
see only the hopeless conflict between the kind of love he
thought he had, and the kind that really made the vision,
so that the red hair of the dead woman hangs between him
and heaven, preventing prayer. On his deathbed he finds a
formula for this: "a tangle of hair, blazing among the
stars; and the great club of his spire lifted towards it . . .
that's the explanation if I had time . . . Berenice." The
antinomies of love are reconciled there; Jocelin's final
gesture of assent is not to the priests around his deathbed,
but to the beautiful maimed spire.

So much of the story one can tell without giving anything important away; such is the nature of Golding's

power. It derives from patterns assumed by the language of the book from certain figures I haven't even mentioned: a tent, a net, a tree, as well as the mistletoe berry. Like *Lord of the Flies* it could be called a fable; but it is not a diagram. We are not to think of a prayer-spire and a phallus-spire, of Christian and pagan, devotion and lust, vision and graft. All these antinomies swirl together in the tormented mind of Jocelin, and in ours. We are even allowed to see how a deaf-mute carver understands Jocelin, and how the sacrist, a jealous, embittered, even venal man, is properly shocked by the pagan outrages on the holy vessels in his care; but Golding eschews the deliberate double vision which constitutes the plot of his first three books. Scholarly enquirers will have to look hard for a scenario here. Or, indeed, for a simple issue. Jocelin's dying thought is this: "There is no innocent work. God only knows where God may be." But that is not quite the point; nor is the suicide failure of the master builder (who, having gained weight by drinking, miscalculates at last the breaking strain of a rafter). Whether the vision was innocent or not, the technique sound or not, the spire is still there at the end, damaged but beautiful.

Briefly then, this is a book about vision and its cost. It has to do with the motives of art and prayer, the phallus turned spire; with the deceit, as painful to man as to God, involved in structures which are human but have to be divine, such as churches and spires. But because the whole work is a dance of figurative language such an account of it can only be misleading. It requires to be read with unremitting attention, and, first time perhaps, very little pleasure. It is second-period Golding; the voice is authoritative but under strain. The style might have been devised by some severe recluse for translating the Old Testament; it is entirely modern, without the slightest trace of godwottery, yet it is almost unnaturally free of any hint of slang—a modern colloquial English but spoken only by one man.

Trying to characterize the dry hot urgency of this prose, I found myself unexpectedly thinking of a musician: of Vaughan Williams in the mood of *Job*. The parallel has some use, I feel. The ballet for which this music was written was based on the Blake engravings—the Old Testament in an extremely heterodox interpretation. The music is in the full voice of Vaughan Williams's already slightly archaic but fully idiomatic, mere English, pentatonic manner; it goes directly to the large statement about good and evil: Satan falling, Elihu beautiful, the sons of the morning at their sarabande. Vaughan Williams had some of the sensitive bluffness, much of the true privacy, of Golding; and he was another late starter who continually experimented but stayed out of touch with the contemporary avant-garde. There is a squareness, a clumsiness; but in some works—in *Job* especially, and in the later music which remembers *Job*—we hear the clear strange tones of the visionary whose idiom we can learn (a saxophone for the comforters) and who speaks as directly as may be of good and evil.

Golding writes rather like that. Look at this passage, chosen quite at random:

> The evening turned green over the rim of the cup. Then the rim went black and shadows filled it silently so that before he was well aware of it, night had fallen and the faint stars come out. He saw a fire on the rim and guessed it was a haystack burning; but as he moved round the rim of the cone, he saw more and more fires round the rim of the world. Then a terrible dread fell on him, for he knew these were the fires of Midsummer Night, lighted by the devil-worshippers out on the hills. Over there, in the valley of the Hanging Stones, a vast fire shuddered brightly. All at once he cried out, not in terror but in grief. For he remembered his crew of good men, and he knew why they had knocked off work and where they were gone.

The "cone" is the unfinished spire; we note how unashamedly the sentence passes from its rim to the easy grandeur of "the rim of the world." We might regret "terrible dread," and yet it is somehow purged by the absolute plainness of reference elsewhere, by "knocked off work," for instance. The last sentence might seem altogether too artless were it not that on this very page the whole strange plot is undergoing a subtle change of movement, modulating into violence.

It is a prose for violence. All Golding's books are violent; as I say, his basic figure for terror, violence, and bloody creation is childbirth. As such it is used in this book, and it breaks out of the language into the plot. This is part of a private vision; and one might hazardously conjecture that this novel, like some of its predecessors, is as much about Golding writing a novel as about anything else. But one need not believe that to agree that it is deeply personal. It gives one some idea of the nature of this writer's gift that he has written a book about an expressly phallic symbol to which Freudian glosses seem entirely irrelevant. It is remote from the mainstream, potent, severe, even forbidding. And in its way it is, quite simply, a marvel.

FOOTNOTES

1. This, and several other remarks attributed to Mr. Golding in this article, are derived from a transcript of a B. B. C. discussion programme.
2. There is a perceptive study of the opening and conclusion of *Free Fall* in an article by Ian Gregor and M. Kinkead-Weekes called "Mr. Golding and his Critics" (*Twentieth Century*, February, 1960).
3. It has been pointed out that *Halde* means "slope," and that this name is also allegorical, since Halde is the agent by which Sammy moves into the gravitational field of his spiritual work. Mr. Golding tells me he did not think of this. It is allegorist's luck.

A Deadly Serious Lunacy
BY SHIMON WINCELBERG

As the theater lately has discovered, or rediscovered, when the artist deals with human experience at those levels which are almost literally worse than death, the resources of naturalism prove pitifully inadequate. The alternative, requiring not only a high order of poetic vision but also a willingness to shock, to challenge, to spit in your audience's eye, is what goes currently under the label of the Absurd. This encompasses farce, gibberish, surrealism and even that sub-branch of show-business called "sick humor" —all with good, honorable roots reaching back to Aristophanes, Homer, Cervantes, Swift and just about every other writer, painter or poet who ever had the audacity to attempt works of art out of the meaningless deaths, tortures and degradations some men undergo at the instance of others.

At the moment, of course, Absurdity as a literary or theatrical device is not only respectable but fashionable. And while fashion creates the hazard of attracting opportunists, it also makes it possible for the occasional work of genuine originality and power to find a far wider audience than someone like Nathanael West did in his time.

Joseph Heller's novel, *Catch-22*, lives up almost completely to its ecstatic notices. It is a sprawling, hilarious, irresponsible, compassionate, cynical, surrealistic, farcical, lacerating and enormously readable account of what happened (though it couldn't have, really; not quite *that* way) to some American flyers on a small island in the Mediterranean during the Italian campaign of World War II. Despite its determination to be as unreliable as possible about that particular war and why it might have been fought, it manages to reduce such fine, naturalistic war novels as those of Norman Mailer, James Jones or Irwin Shaw to mere talented journalism, and their portrayal of the bumbling or malevolent high brass into a positive whitewash.

Having served *my* time both on the other side of the globe and as close to the ground as I could get, I don't know whether the term "Catch-22" is an authentic piece of Air Corps folklore or the author's own happy invention. But, as the central symbol of his characters' predicament, it serves his purpose with devastating precision.

Catch-22 is the principle which keeps the half-crazed and exhausted bomber crews of the unspeakable Colonel Cathcart's squadron flying a quota of missions outrageously raised each time they are about to reach it. One of its definitions goes, "they have a right to do anything we can't stop them from doing." "They" are Heller's preposterous (perhaps just a shade too preposterous) colonels and generals, a gallery of childish, senile, vain, malicious, frightened incompetents playing a paper-helmet war for the gratification of their corkscrew egos and titanic insecurities, for some nebulous form of social or commercial advancement, little exercises in one-upmanship between rival brass, or simply to get themselves written up in the *Saturday Evening Post*.

There is almost no plot to speak of, at least until the very end, by which time practically everyone you care about, with the exception of the hero, is dead or missing. There is only a string of sometimes overlapping, sometimes disconnected, events, some as outrageously lunatic as an early Marx Brothers film, some as realistic and sickening as anything ever written about the strange things war can do to the fragile bodies and minds of a lot of once-healthy young animals in uniform.

The book's "hero" is Captain Yossarian, engaging, stubborn, lecherous, saintly, and excruciatingly sane as he flails back at the system symbolized by Catch-22. Sample dialogue between Yossarian and his friend Doc Daneeka, the crabbed, self-pitying, powerless medical officer:

"Is Orr crazy?"

"He sure is."

"Can you ground him?"

"I sure can. But first he has to ask me to. That's part of the rule."

"Then why doesn't he ask you to?"

"Because he's crazy. . . . He has to be crazy to keep flying combat missions after all the close calls he's had. But first he has to ask me."

"And then you can ground him?"

"No. Then I can't ground him."

"You mean there's a catch?"

"Sure there's a catch. Catch-22. Anybody who wants to get out of combat duty isn't really crazy."

At times, however, Heller's brilliant and original comic vision, as well as his splendid rage at the homicidal and suicidal stupidity with which wars may be fought at the headquarters level, is somewhat weakened by his evident delight in his own cleverness. Not that the jokes, by and large, aren't both fresh and funny—especially the grisly ones. But it soon becomes apparent that most of his characters can be summed up in terms of a joke, which might make them easy for a reviewer to describe, but greatly limits their ability to grow, develop, or expose themselves to revelation.

There is Colonel Cathcart, the one who keeps raising the number of missions, and before a particularly nasty one exhorts his men to be sure and make tight bomb patterns in order to produce "a good clean aerial photograph he won't be ashamed to send through channels." All the disclaimers in the world will not convince me that this man is fictitious.

Another far from atypical character, I suspect, is the sweet and crushingly ineffectual chaplain, who "used to think it was immoral to be unhappy." It is his ambitious but lazy assistant who is responsible for that moving and time-saving form letter to the next-of-kin, which reads:

"Dear Mrs., Mr., Miss, or Mr. and Mrs. ——————: Words cannot express the deep personal grief I experienced when your husband, son, father or brother was killed, wounded or reported missing in action."

There is also Doc Daneeka, bitterly resentful of the impending collapse of the German armies because it means he will be sent to the Pacific. And the "licensed psychiatrist" who accuses Yossarian of being immature, "with a morbid aversion to dying" and "deep-seated survival anxieties." And the luckless flyers forced to abandon their plane in the waters off Marseilles, who find that their Mae

Wests wouldn't inflate because their mess-officer, the remarkable Milo Minderbinder, had stolen the carbon-dioxide capsules to make ice cream sodas for the officers' mess. Nor will I find it easy to forget "ex-Pfc." Wintergreen, the elusive mail clerk, who is "probably the most influential man in the whole theater of operations."

For the last 30-40 pages Heller seems abruptly to have been persuaded that even a novel as original as his would be better for some sort of a plot, preferably in chronological order. So he hastily furnishes one, involving his startled hero in one of those soul-searching conflicts between conscience and self-interest which used to be so popular on live TV. It is very well done and all but, in contrast to the rest of the book's splendid contempt for such niceties, I find it a little on the square side.

That, however, is a minor quibble against a novel which, on almost every page, offers such felicities as: "There are now fifty or sixty countries fighting in this war. Surely so many countries can't *all* be worth dying for."

The Inner and the Outer Reality

BY RICHARD SCHECHNER

Ionesco is the closest thing we have to an abstract expressionist in the theatre. His plays are plainly autobiographical and confessional. "I try to project on stage an inner drama (incomprehensible even to myself) telling myself, nevertheless, that since the microcosm is the image of the macrocosm, it may happen that this torn up, disarticulated inner world is in some way the mirror or the symbol of universal contradictions." He discovers the astonishing in the banal, the unreal in the real, the new in the old, the fresh in the stale, and the archetype in the stereotype. His work is romantic and subjective, mirroring his own anguish and inner struggles and translating them into symbols and patterns that have been empathetically embraced by audiences throughout the world. But this empathy should not confuse us. Ionesco's vision is private —as private as de Kooning's or Pollock's—and our warm response to it is not due to the fact that Ionesco has been watching us carefully; the truth is rather that our obsessions resemble his: the artist precedes his work into existence. Like Kafka's, Ionesco's most personal insights are public coin, at least for this moment in history.

But what is the exact relationship between the microcosm and the macrocosm, the inner and outer worlds, and what exactly are the universal contradictions? In the most simple terms the outer world is the setting and the inner world the action of Ionesco's plays. The heroes—Jack, Amédée, Choubert, Bérenger—are forced to undergo an action within a setting, and these two are never in harmony with each other. This is the most striking contradiction in Ionesco's work, one which is theatrical and visual as well as dramatic and literary. The roots of his comedy (the angry humor of tragedy, as Peter Selz says) are set firmly in this dialectic. The corpse is growing in Amédée's *apartment;* the Pupil is murdered in the Professor's *study.* Both the corpse and the murder are bold externalizations of the inner reality—visualizations of the underlying anguish inherent in the human condition as Ionesco sees it. But the apartment and the study are there also; the banal setting silently affirms the existence of the external reality. The greater the gap between the action and the setting the more violent and comic the effect. Ionesco's comedy, we must not forget, is very primitive, springing from the chthonic, sado-masochistic sources of laughter itself. The hilarity of the first scene of *Jack,* for example, is an expression of the tension wrought from the triple disparity between the setting (bourgeois domesticity), the tone of voice (sentimental family love), and the action (sado-masochistic cruelty).

> *Mother Jack.* It was I, my son, who gave you your first spankings, not your father, standing here, who could have done it better than I, for he is stronger, no, it was I, for I loved you too much . . . Oh, ungrateful son, you do not even remember how I held you on my knees and pulled out your cute little baby teeth, and tore off your toenails so as to make you bawl like an adorable little calf.

This unresolved triple dialectic of setting, tone, and action persists even in the more "rational" Bérenger plays. The Killer is loose in the Radiant City, the rhinoceroses plague a small, provincial town in southern France, Bérenger takes a stroll in mid-air while the English town-folk chatter with their children. It is this coexistence of banal setting and outrageous action that makes us feel that Ionesco's world is our own. We live in an age where nuclear annihilation is a fine casual topic during a coffee break. Ionesco's settings are always "real" and, as in Kafka, each detail of the nightmare is "realistically" documented. The form—the virtual shape—of reality is left untouched, as are the tiniest details; it is in the middle ground—the vast range between minutiae and pattern—that Ionesco dislocates and disarticulates. It is the inclusion of phrases like "pulled out" and "tore off" in Mother

Jack's speech that is disturbing—giving us a glimpse of what underlies her "love"—eliciting laughter and anguish at the same time.

Ionesco uses this same device in his treatment of language where, for the most part, he leaves the word and sentence intact, while tampering with the choice and order of words within a sentence. A character in *The Bald Soprano* can say "I'd rather lay an egg than steal a cow" (*"J'aime mieux pondre un oeuf que voler un boeuf"*), and it will almost slip by our ears before we realize that it is complete nonsense. It looks and sounds like a sentence; its rhyme scheme disguises it as a proverb; it has all the grammatical necessities of a sentence. But it lacks the *intention* of a sentence. In plays like *The Lesson* or *The Maid to Marry* this same device is amplified. Instead of tampering with the sentence, Ionesco vitiates entire sentences, thereby destroying the intention of paragraphs or even larger units.

> *Professor.* That which distinguishes the neo-Spanish languages and their idioms from other linguistic groups, such as the group of languages called Austrian and neo-Austrian or Hapsburgian, as well as the Esperanto, Helvetian, Monacan, Swiss, Andorran, Basque, and jai alai groups, and also the groups of diplomatic and technical languages—that which distinguishes them, I repeat, is their striking resemblance which makes it so hard to distinguish them from each other. I'm speaking of the neo-Spanish languages which one is able to distinguish from each other, however, only thanks to their distinctive characteristics, absolutely indisputable proofs of their extraordinary resemblance, which renders indisputable their common origin, and which, at the same time, differentiates them profoundly—through the continuation of the distinctive traits which I've just cited.

This speech sounds erudite and yet it is hard to understand and murderous to memorize (ask any actor who has played the role). It is impossible to *grasp* the Professor's idea; the speech as a whole is elusive and vaporous. The trick is simple. While preserving all the grammatical rules and using a scholarly vocabulary and tone, the speech pivots around a central contradiction: "That which distinguishes them, I repeat, is their striking resemblance which makes it so hard to distinguish them from each other." The Professor—and through him, language—is but another example of the universal contradictions; and the dialectic created between his scholarly, heavy tone and the weightlessness of what he says—its pivotal nonsense—is analogous to Mother Jack's opening speeches or the situation in which Amédée finds himself. Naturally I am citing only several examples of what saturates each play. Wherever we look in Ionesco's work—language, setting, characterization, action—we discover the same pattern of coexistent opposites; each dialectical pair adds texture to the whole scheme; we are thrown back and forth between irresolvable opposites, and we are trapped in this world of unresolved contradictions much in the same way as we are trapped among Genet's infinitely faceted characters.

To carry this point still further, the very ordinary appearances of Ionesco's heroes are contradicted by the nature of their acts. The timid Professor murders his pupil; Jack, the "poetic" and rebellious son, can hardly speak an intelligible sentence; hermetic Amédée floats away into the wide sky; irresponsible Bérenger defies the herd. It is as if, at last, the inner life of these characters forced its way to the surface, thrusting through the crust of banality. At this moment of "realization" (and the actor would do well to remember this), their very appearance changes and they look like what they are. The Professor stands taller, his voice deepens and he becomes more authoritative; Jack goes down on all fours, mumbling the single word "cat"; weak and immobile Amédée lugs the corpse outside; Choubert is reduced to a tortured infant; Bérenger accepts the skin of a man. After this "realization" only the setting remains to remind us of the outer reality.

What Ionesco gives us is an intricate pattern of contradictions, one transcending the next; but whatever dialectical pair is dominant at the moment, the unbearable tension between opposites remains constant—there is at least one contradiction between the inner and the outer reality operating at all times in each of his plays. It is this dialectical tension which replaces plot. At each moment we are gripped by the dialectic, while at the same time the play moves forward rhythmically, thrusting itself onward in a

series of ever intensifying and tightening circular patterns
or figures until a climactic, paroxysmal instant is achieved.
Then the knot relaxes, the spasm is over, silence wins, and
the curtain falls. But we must learn to watch his plays
(particularly his work before the Bérenger plays) as the
Greeks, we are told, watched dance. We must pay attention not only to the moment, the beat, but also to the
completed figure—the trajectory traced by the rhythm.
It is a difficult task, perhaps too difficult for our theatre
and its audience, but we are asked to grasp the play as a
completed form, as an action which is over, as an action
in repose. If we will do this the contradictions will become
more obvious and they will each fall into their own pattern,
tracing their own musical line through the play.

> *The Bald Soprano* as well as *The Lesson:* . . . ab-
> stract theatre, nonpersonality theatre . . . Thus to
> make the characters not characters. All intrigue, all
> particular action is stripped of interest. It is merely
> accessory. Everything is channelled into a dramatic
> tension . . . One must liberate the dramatic tension
> without the help of any real plot or particular goal.
> Everything will point to the revelation of something
> monstrous—it must be because theatre is, finally, the
> revelation of the monstrous, or of states of mon-
> strosity, without characters or with the monstrous
> characters that we find within ourselves. To come to
> that exaltation or those revelations without the justifica-
> tion of motivation . . . Progression of a passion with-
> out object . . . Abstract theatre. Pure dream . . .
> Under a burlesque text, a dramatic motion. Under a
> dramatic text, a burlesque motion.

This selection from Ionesco's working notes (April, 1951)
is an accurate statement of both his intention and achievement in his early work. It means simply that his plays are
incremental without being culminant; the final moments
may be more intense but they are not more important in
terms of the completed figure than the early moments. In
The Lesson, for example, the final "scalp dance" between
the Professor and Pupil would be pointlessly shocking if
it were not for the several analogous dances between them
which precede the rape-murder. The little game they play

over taking seats, the more formal game of addition, the arguments they have over subtraction, the impasse they reach with multiplication, all cut the same pattern as the final dance. The earlier moments do not "prepare" us for the ultimate dance; they are early symphonic motifs which will finally be consummated and musically resolved in the rape-murder. The tension and contradictions so blatant at the end are subtly present at the beginning; there is no "development," but there is orchestration: variations on a theme, amplification, and then modal resolution.

To return now once again to Ionesco's characters. The gap between the inner and outer reality—that gap which informs Ionesco's entire technique—lays bare the alienation of his heroes from themselves and from the world. The Ionesco hero can neither reach and understand himself nor grasp the things of the world. Yet these things—his apartment, his wife, his coffee cups, his tables and chairs—are *his;* they are his only connection to the flow of life, to the abundance of life, and as the hero becomes conscious of his separation from these things he tries ever more desperately to unite himself to what is his. The Smiths and the Martins argue vehemently with each other over nonsense—then they rush across the stage looking for something—their own identities; The New Tenant tries to find peace and security amid his household furnishings; Madeleine, in *Victims of Duty,* fills the stage with numberless coffee cups while her husband Choubert is being tortured by the Detective. But each attempt at locating the self within things fails, and the characters can only try harder the next time. This next attempt is paced at an increased tempo, and the next still more rapidly, and so on, until the play reaches its climactic moment of realization and frustration. As Ionesco's heroes try to relate to the world around them they lose contact not only with that world, but also with themselves. Their very existence—or more exactly, the felt conviction that they exist—is threatened, and even the simple processes of life become dangerous. They substitute speed for substance, activity for act. The climax of this increasingly rapid acceleration which forms the penultimate moment in so many of Ionesco's plays reflects the utter inability of his heroes to resolve the living dialectic between the emptiness they *are* and the fullness which the world presents teasingly to them. In the ecstatic paroxysm both the inner and the outer realities break apart, the multi-colored dome of their lives shatters, revealing the dark radiance and silence of nothingness. At this point only the memory of pure whirling motion remains—activity without substance, activity without reality—and the rest is fragmentary, chaotic, useless.

This alienation can best be understood if we adopt a term from existential psychoanalysis—ontological insecurity. According to R. D. Laing, who has explored this notion with brilliance and clarity, the ontologically insecure person experiences the world in totally different terms than does "the individual whose sense of self is securely established in its health and validity. Relatedness to other persons will be seen to have a radically different significance and function . . . In the individual whose being is secure in this primary existential sense, relatedness with others is potentially gratifying; whereas the ontologically insecure person is preoccupied with preserving rather than gratifying himself; the ordinary circumstances of living threaten his low threshold of security." We have only to remember the Professor at the beginning of *The Lesson* or Amédée's encounter with the Postman to understand how well Laing's description fits Ionesco's characters. The ontologically insecure person "may lack the experience of his own temporal continuity. He may not possess an overriding sense of personal consistency or cohesiveness. He may feel more insubstantial than substantial, and unable to assume that the stuff he is made of is genuine, good, and valuable. And he may feel his self as partially divorced from his body." Ionesco puts the same experience in only slightly different words. "We are astounded to discover that we exist in this world that appears illusory, fictitious—where human behavior reveals its absurdity, and all history its absolute uselessness; all reality, all language seems to become disjointed, to fall apart, to empty itself of meaning so that, since all is devoid of importance, what else can one do but laugh at it?" Needless to say, this laughter expresses anguish, not joy.

During the early years of his public career as a playwright (1950–1953), Ionesco felt most uneasy in the world. "I have never succeeded in becoming completely used to existence, neither to that of the world, nor to that of others, nor above all to my own." The world itself seemed threatening, and it was in turn threatened. "Words are only noise stripped of all meaning. These houses, the sky, are only facades of nothingness; people seem to move automatically, without any reason; everything seems to evaporate, everything is threatened, including myself, by an imminent, silent sinking into I know not what abyss." The Ionesco hero, like Laing's patient, "feels that like a vacuum he is empty, but this emptiness is him." The nothingness which Ionesco's characters *are* may, at any time, annihilate the world of things by annihilating the consciousness which conceives this world. The noisy plays, the full stages, always stand on the brink of silence and emptiness. Remember that fine theatrical moment in *The Chairs* immediately after the suicide of the old couple when we realize that we have been fooled, that these chairs are not full, but utterly empty. Writing to Sylvain Dhomme, the first director of *The Chairs,* Ionesco made his intent clear. "The theme of the play is nothingness." At the moment of annihilation—the paroxysm, the climax, the point at which the intolerable tension between the inner and the outer reality can no longer be borne—the string snaps, both the inside and the outside disappear, and everything hurtles down the "black hole," so vividly named by the Old Woman in *The Chairs*. (Note how at the end of *The Future is in Eggs* the stage collapses and the characters "all unwittingly gently sink and disappear without interrupting their actions." Note also Ionesco's original plan for the end of *The Bald Soprano.* "In the first version the stage remained empty until the spectators began to rise from their seats. Then the director of the company came on stage with a machine gun and killed everyone.") The world is neither permanent nor substantial; the most routine processes are not to be depended on. The question debated with such vigor in *The Bald Soprano* is a real and indicative one: Is there someone at the door when the bell rings?

Her Early Novels
BY WALTER ALLEN

One of the best first novels of our time was Doris Lessing's *The Grass Is Singing* (1950). The story of a town girl married to a farmer in Africa, and of her behavior towards her Negro servants—behavior reflecting her own inner uncertainty and in the end with fatal consequences to herself—it satisfies both as a novel and as a parable on the nature of relations between black and white in Africa. It heralds one of Doris Lessing's two main themes, the relationship between the races in Africa. The other is the problem of being a woman in what is largely a man's world. Both themes come together in her work in progress, *Children of Violence* (the overall title), of which so far *Martha Quest* (1952), *A Proper Marriage* (1954) and *A Ripple from the Storm* (1958) have appeared. The sequence traces the life of Martha Quest from her childhood and adolescence on a farm in what seems to be Rhodesia to the break-up of her marriage in the country's capital during the war and her involvement in left-wing political activities at the time. In these books Doris Lessing does for a young woman something very similar to what Arnold Bennett in *Clayhanger* and D. H. Lawrence in *Sons and Lovers* did for a young man, but the closer parallel is probably with George Eliot. In the passionate seriousness of her response to life, Martha Quest is in the direct line of descent from Maggie Tulliver, and Doris Lessing shows her kinship to George Eliot both in her technique here and in her sober, unsentimental scrutiny of behavior, motives and morals. As the work goes on, there is a deepening irony, so that one sees Martha with as it were a double vision, as she sees herself and as she is seen from the outside by a mature observer.

How the work will continue it is difficult to say. In *A Ripple from the Storm* Martha Quest seems no longer the channel through which the action flows. She has become smaller, overshadowed by the events described, lost in the minute political detail of the book, which relates the breakdown during the war of a raw provincial society, in which the color problem can still be seen in terms of crude white and black, under the impact of invasion from the outside, by Jewish refugees from Nazis and by class- and politically-conscious airmen of the Royal Air Force. What had begun as a full-length portrait of a young woman has become a study of a society in a process of disintegration. . . .

Free Women
BY ROBERT TAUBMAN

The first inset in *The Golden Notebook* is a narrative
called "Free Women," which gives us Anna and Molly in a
London flat in 1957, and a provisional definition: they lead
"what is known as free lives, that is, lives like men." This
discontinuous narrative frames four huge sections devoted
to Anna's notebooks of the 1950's: the black dealing with
the African experience out of which she has written her
only novel; the red for politics—the decline and fall of
the communist myth; blue a record of relations with men,
and of dreams and sessions with her analyst; yellow in
which she "makes up stories," mostly drafts of a novel in
which "Ella" re-enacts a large part of Anna's experience. In
all this, what it means to be a "free woman" is thoroughly
worked over. Not only the question of "lives like men"—
an illusion, for if Anna enters a sexual relationship as freely
as a man, she nevertheless ends it in humiliating dependence—but also the freedom of choice that paralyses her as
a writer, the freedom allowed by the irresponsible state of
the world, and the ironical freedom of a woman haunted
by the idea of integrity who is condemned to act at random to find out what her actions mean.

Structure and scene are both more complex than this
suggests, and it may be unfair even to pick out freedom as
the key idea. But the scenes are pretty familiar ones, and
the book's striking quality is not that it is difficult in a
profound or original way, but rather the reverse—the conviction it carries of being a close transcription of actual
experience, in which most of the expected preoccupations
of a writer in the mid-20th century naturally find their
place. Its unusual structure is less a matter of subtle organization than of simple, rather haphazard naturalism:

Anna's journals seem to lie half in and half out of the novel, as if the bulk of them had existed before it—a section of them has indeed been reconstructed for the theatre as *Play with a Tiger.* The multiple views of Anna which they provide make excellent material for argument—there is no doubt she is going to be talked about, like one of Ibsen's or Shaw's "new women" when they first appeared; but it will be out of the sort of curiosity aroused by a real person and not for any interest established in her as a character in a novel. If there is anything new here, then it is an advance in naturalism; but in the sort of naturalism, abetted by the way Anna's life is compartmented in her separate journals, that tends to devalue its object. Sex is an obvious example, since it occupies much of Anna's attention, and is treated as a natural experience with a freedom impossible only a year ago: and welcome as this is, one effect is that it never gets off the level of a natural experience, which is not the same as a fully human one.

This sort of limitation comes to mind partly because the opening scene between Anna and Molly so strongly provokes comparison with the opening chapter of *Women in Love,* and looking back over this record of other women in love 50 years later inevitably suggests how little comparable it achieves. It would be wrong to regard this book as a creative experiment on the same terms: it is not a creation but a document, as the insistent consciousness of Anna is there to remind us all along. Simply as a record of how it is to be free and responsible, a woman in relation to men and to other women, and to struggle to come to terms with one's self about these things and about writing and politics, it seems to me unique in its truthfulness and range. Its interest will certainly be felt; it is the sort of book that determines the way people think about themselves. May it, for one thing, soon displace the Simone de Beauvoir paperbacks in the hands of all those who want what she is supposed to provide—a sort of intelligent woman's guide to the intelligent woman. Doris Lessing says far more of genuine interest, is less self-conscious and much less boring.

From the Kingdom of Necessity
BY RANDALL JARRELL

Many of the reviews of *Lord Weary's Castle* have been conscious that it is an event of the order of Auden's first book; I know no poetry since Auden's that is better than Robert Lowell's. Everybody who reads poetry will read it sooner or later. I hope that I can help readers by pointing out its distinguishing features, by tracing its development, and by analyzing the themes that unify it.

Underneath all these poems "there is one story and one story only": when this essential theme or subject is understood, the unity of attitudes and judgments underlying the variety of the poems becomes startlingly explicit. The poems understand the world as a sort of conflict of opposites. In this struggle one opposite is that cake of custom in which all of us lie imbedded like lungfish—the stasis or inertia of the complacent self, the satisfied persistence in evil that is damnation. In this realm of necessity the poems place everything that is closed, turned inward, incestuous, that blinds or binds: the Old Law, imperialism, militarism, capitalism, Calvinism, Authority, the Father, the rich who will "do everything for the poor except get off their backs." But struggling within this like leaven, falling to it like light, is everything that is free or open, that grows or is willing to change: here is the generosity or willingness or openness that is itself salvation; here is "accessibility to experience"; this is the realm of freedom, of the Grace that has replaced the Law, of the perfect liberator whom the poet calls Christ.

Consequently the poems can have two possible movements or organizations: they can move from what is closed to what is open, or from what is open to what is closed. The second of these organizations—which corresponds to an "unhappy ending"—is less common, though there are many good examples of it: "The Exile's Return," with its menacing *Voi ch'entrate* that transforms the exile's old home into a place where even hope must be abandoned; that extraordinary treatment of the "Oedipus complex," "Between the Porch and the Altar," with its four parts each ending in constriction and frustration, its hero who cannot get free of his mother, her punishments, and her world even by dying, but who sees both life and death in terms of her, and thinks at the end that, sword in hand, the Lord "watches me for Mother, and will turn/The bier and baby-carriage where I burn."

But normally the poems move into liberation—even death is seen as liberation, a widening into darkness: that old closed system, Grandfather Arthur Winslow, dying of cancer in his adjusted bed, at the last is the child Arthur whom the swanboats once rode through the Public Garden, whom now "the ghost of risen Jesus walks the waves to run/Upon a trumpeting black swan/Beyond Charles River to the Acheron/Where the wide waters and their voyager are one." (Compare the endings of "The Drunken Fisherman" and "Dea Roma.") "The Death of the Sheriff" moves from closure—the "ordered darkness" of the homicidal sheriff, the "loved sightless smother" of the incestuous lovers, the "unsearchable quicksilver heart/Where spiders stare their eyes out at their own/Spitting and knotted likeness"—up into the open sky, to those "light wanderers" the planets, to the "thirsty Dipper on the arc of night." Just so the cold, blundering, iron confusion of "Christmas Eve Under Hooker's Statue" ends in flowers, the wild fields, a Christ "once again turned wanderer and child." In "Rebellion" the son seals "an everlasting pact/With Dives to *contract*/The world that *spreads* in pain'; but at last he rebels against his father and his father's New England commercial theocracy, and "the world *spread*/When the clubbed flint-lock broke my father's brain." The italicized words ought to demonstrate how explicitly, at times, these poems formulate the world in the exact terms that I have used.

"Where the Rainbow Ends" describes in apocalyptic terms the wintry, Calvinist, capitalist—Lowell has Weber's attitude about the connection of capitalism and Calvinism—dead end of God's covenant with man, a frozen Boston where even the cold-blooded serpents "whistle at the cold."

(Lowell often uses cold as a plain and physically correct symbol for what is constricted, static, turned in upon itself.) There "the scythers, Time and Death,/Helmed locusts, move upon the tree of breath," of the spirit of man; a bridge curves over Charles River like an ironic parody of the rainbow's covenant; both "the wild ingrafted olive and its root/Are withered" (these are Paul's terms for the Judaism of the Old Law and the Gentile Christianity grafted upon it); "every dove [the Holy Ghost, the bringer of the olive leaf to the Ark] is sold" for a commercialized, legalized sacrifice. The whole system seems an abstract, rationalized "graph of Revelations," of the last accusation and judgment brought against man now that "the Chapel's sharp-shinned eagle shifts its hold/On serpent-Time, the rainbow's epitaph." This last line means exactly what the last line in "The Quaker Graveyard"—"The Lord survives the rainbow of his will"—means; both are inexpressibly menacing, since they show the covenant as something that binds only us, as something abrogated merely by the passage of time, as a closed system opening not into liberation but into infinite and overwhelming possibility; they have something of the terror, but none of the pity, of Blake's "Time is the mercy of Eternity."

The worshiper climbs to the altar of the terrible I AM like a victim, to breathe the rarefied and intolerable aether of his union with the divinity of the Apocalypse; he despairs even of the wings that beat against his cheek: "What can the dove of Jesus give/You now but wisdom, exile?" When the poem has reached this point of the most extreme closure, when the infinite grace that atones and liberates is seen as no more than the bitter and useless wisdom of the exile, it opens with a rush of acceptant joy into: "Stand and live,/The dove has brought an olive branch to eat." The dove of Jesus brings to the worshiper the olive branch that shows him that the flood has receded, opening the whole earth for him; the olive branch of peace and reconciliation; the olive branch that he is "to eat" as a symbol of the eaten flesh and blood of Christ, of atonement, identification, and liberation. Both the old covenant and the new still hold, nothing has changed: here as they were and will be, are life and salvation.

Lowell seems a strange opposite of the usual Catholic convert, who distrusts freedom as much as he needs bondage, and who see the world as a liberal chaos which can be ordered and redeemed only by that rigid and final Authority to which men submit without question. Lowell reminds one more of those heretical enthusiasts, often disciplined and occasionally sanctified or excommunicated, who are more at home in the Church Triumphant than in the church of this world, which is one more state; a phrase like Lowell's "St. Peter, the distorted key" is likely to be appreciated outside the church and overlooked inside it, *ad maiorem gloriam* of Catholic poetry. In Lowell's poems the Son is pure liberation from the incestuous, complacent, inveterate evil of established society, of which the Law is a part—although the Father, Jehovah, has retained both the violence necessary to break up this inertia and a good deal of the menacing sternness of Authority as such. (It is interesting to compare the figure of the Uncle in early Auden, who sanctifies rebellion by his authority; the authority of Lowell's Christ is sanctified by his rebellion or liberation.)

Anyone who compares Lowell's earlier and later poems will see this movement from constriction to liberation as his work's ruling principle of growth. The grim, violent, sordid constriction of his earliest poems—most of them omitted from this book—seems to be temperamental, the Old Adam which the poet grew from and partially transcends; and a good deal of what was excessive in the wonderful rhetorical machine of a poem like "The Quaker Graveyard at Nantucket," which catches and twists to pieces the helplessly enjoying reader, is gone from his latest poems, or else dramatically justified and no longer excessive. "The Quaker Graveyard" is a baroque work, like *Paradise Lost;* but the coiling violence of the rhetoric, the harshly stubborn intensity that accompanies its verbs and verbals, the clustering stresses learned from accentual verse, come from a man contracting every muscle, grinding his teeth together till his shut eyes ache. Lowell's later work has moved in the direction of the poem's quiet contrast-section, Walsingham; the denunciatory prophetic tone has disappeared, along with the early satiric effects that were one of the poet's weaknesses. The later poems depend less on rhetorical description than on dramatic speech; their wholes have escaped from the hypnotic bondage of the details. Often the elaborate rhetorical stanzas have changed into a novel sort of dramatic or narrative couplet, run-on but with heavily stressed rhymes. A girl's nightmare, in the late "Katherine's Dream," is far more open, classical, and speech-like than the poet's own descriptive meditation in an earlier work like "Christmas at Black Rock." It is important to understand this development; the reviews I have read have not realized that it exists.

Lowell has a completely unscientific, but thoroughly historical mind. (It is literary and traditional as well: he uses the past so effectively because he thinks so much as it did.) Lowell's present contains the past—especially Rome, the late Middle Ages, and New Englind—as an operative skeleton just under the skin. This is rare among contemporary poets, who look at the past as Blücher looked at London: "What a city to sack!" (Actually he said, "What a mix-up!" But this fits, too.) War, Trade, and Jehovah march side by side through these centuries: it is the fundamental likeness of the past and present, and not their disparity, which is brought out. "Cold/Snaps the bronze toes and fingers of the Christ/My father fetched from Florence, and the dead/Chatters to nothing in the thankless ground/His father screwed from Charlie Stark and sold/To the selectmen." This is the history of New England's nineteenth century in a sentence. Lowell's period pieces, which range from Propertius to Jonathan Edwards, are notable partly for their details—which are sometimes as magically and professionally illusionary as those of "I, Claudius"—but mainly for the empathy, the historical identification, that underlie the details. These period pieces are intimately related to Lowell's adaptations of poems from other languages; both are valuable as ways of getting a varied, extensive, and alien experience into his work. Dismissing these adaptations as "translations" is like dismissing "To Celia" or "Cathay," and betrays an odd dislike or ignorance of an important and traditional procedure of poets.

Lowell is an extremely professional poet, and the degree of intensity of his poems is equaled by their degree of organization. Inside its elaborate stanzas the poem is put together like a mosaic: the shifts of movement, the varied pauses, the alternation in the length of sentences, the counterpoint between lines and sentences, are the outer form of a subject matter that has been given a dramatic, dialectical internal organization; and it is hard to exaggerate the strength and life, the constant richness and surprise of metaphor and sound and motion, of the language itself. The organization of Lowell's poems resembles that of traditional English poetry—especially when compared to that type of semi-imagist modern organization in which the things of the poem seem to marshal themselves like Dryden's atoms—but often this is complicated by stream-of-consciousness, dream, or dramatic-monologue types of structure. This makes the poems more difficult, but it is worth the price—a great many of the most valuable dramatic effects cannot be attained inside a more logical or abstract organization. Lowell's poetry is a unique fusion of modernist and traditional poetry, and there exist conjoined in it certain effects that one would hitherto have thought mutually exclusive; however, it is essentially a post- or anti-modernist poetry, and as such is certain to be influential.

Lowell is wonderfully good at discovering powerful, homely, grotesque, but exactly appropriate particulars for his poems. "Actuality is something brute," said Peirce. "There is no reason in it. I instance putting your shoulder against a door and trying to force it open against an unseen, silent, and unknown resistance." The things in Lowell's poems have, necessarily, been wrenched into formal shape, organized under terrific pressure, but they keep to an extraordinary degree their stubborn, unmoved toughness, their senseless originality and contingency: no poet is more notable for what, I have read, Duns Scotus calls *haeccitas*—the contrary, persisting, and singular thinginess of every being in the world; but this detailed factuality is particularly effective because it sets off, or is set off by, the elevation and rhetorical sweep characteristic of much of the best poetry of the past. Lowell is obviously a haptic rather than a visual type: a poem like "Colloquy in Black Rock" has some of the most extraordinary kinesthetic effects in English, perfect duplications of what is being described. It is impossible not to notice the weight and power of his lines—most others look a little threadbare or transparent beside them. Because of passages like

In the great ash-pit of Jehoshaphat

The bones cry for the blood of the white whale,
The fat flukes arch and whack about its ears,
The death-lance churns into the sanctuary, tears
The gun-blue swingle, heaving like a flail,
And hacks the coiling life out . . .

the smooth, calm, and flowing ease of some passages, the flat ease of the ordinary speech of others, have more than their usual effectiveness: the dead mistress of Propertius, a black nail dangling from a finger, Lethe oozing from her nether lip, in the end can murmur to the "apple-sweetened Anio":

. . . Anio, you will please
Me if you whisper upon sliding knees:
"Propertius, Cynthia is here:
She shakes her blossoms when my waters clear."

The poems' wit is often the wit of things: the "poised relations sipping sherry/And tracking up the carpet," the "postgirl sounding her French horn" over the snows of Maine, the "stern Colonial magistrates and wards/of Charles the Second." The "corn-fed mouse/Reined in his bestial passions"; the "red-flanneled madmen looked through bars." One laughs out in church.

Lowell, at his best and latest, is a dramatic poet: he presents people, actions, speeches, things as they feel and look to people; the poet's generalizations are usually implied, and the poem's explicit generalizations are there primarily because they are dramatically necessary—it is not usually the poet who means them. He does not present themes or generalizations but a world—and the differences and similarities between it and the ordinary one bring home to us themes, generalizations, and the poet himself. There is never any exploitation of the "personality" of the poet; the *I* who stands meditating by Hooker's statue or the Quaker graveyard is closer to the different *I's* of the dramatic monologues than to the man who wrote them. It is partly because of this that atheists are vexed by his Catholic views, and Catholics by his heretical ones, so much less than they normally would be.

But there are other reasons. The poet's rather odd and imaginative Catholicism is thoroughly suitable to his mind, which is so traditional and dramatic that no images from the sciences, next to none from philosophy, occur in his poems. Such a Catholicism is thoroughly suited to literature, since it *is* essentially literary, anthropomorphic, emotional. It is an advantage to the poet to have a frame of reference, terms of generalization, which are themselves human, emotional, and effective as literature. "Bodily Changes in Fear, Rage, and Hunger" may let the poet know more about the anger of Achilles, but it is hard for him to have to talk about adrenalin and the thalamus; and when the arrows of Apollo are transformed into "a lack of adequate sanitary facilities," everything is lost but understanding. (This helps explain the dependence of contemporary poetry on particulars, emotions, things—its generalizations, where they are most effective, are fantastic, though often traditionally so.) Naturally the terms of scientific explanation cannot have these poetic and emotional effects, since it is precisely by the exclusion of such effects that science has developed. Lowell's Catholicism represents effective realities of human behavior and desire, regardless of whether it is true, false, or absurd; and, as everyone must realize, it is possible to tell part of the truth about the world in terms that are false, limited, and fantastic—else how should we have told it? There is admittedly no "correct" or "scientific" view of a great many things that a poet writes about—values, emotions, and so forth—and he has to deal with them in dramatic and particular terms, if he has foregone the advantage of pre-scientific ideologies like Christianity or Marxism. (Of course it seems to me an advantage that he almost necessarily foregoes; I remember writing about contemporary religious poems, "It is hard to enjoy the ambergris for thinking of all those suffering whales," and most people will feel this when they encounter a passage in Lowell telling them how Bernadette's miraculous vision of Our Lady "puts out reason's eyes." It does indeed.)

It is unusually difficult to say which are the best poems in *Lord Weary's Castle:* at least a dozen are realized past changing, triumphs that vary only in scope and intensity—a number of others are poems that almost any living poet would be pleased to have written. But certainly some of the most wonderful things in the book are "Where the Rainbow Ends," "Between the Porch and the Altar,"

"The Quaker Graveyard in Nantucket," "Colloquy in Black Rock," "The Death of the Sheriff" (especially the first of the two poems that compose it), and "At the Indian-Killer's Grave." Close to these are "The Exile's Return," "The Ghost," "Charles the Fifth and the Peasant," "Death from Cancer," "Mr. Edwards and the Spider," "Christmas Eve under Hooker's Statue," "Mary Winslow"—and I cannot leave unmentioned poems like "After the Surprising Conversions," "The Drunken Fisherman," "The Blind Leading the Blind," "The Shako," "France," and "New Year's Day." I do not list a number of small or partial successes that will delight anyone who loves poetry.

When I reviewed Lowell's first book I finished by saying, "Some of the best poems of the next years ought to be · written by him." The appearance of *Lord Weary's Castle* makes me feel less like Adams or Leverrier than like a rainmaker who predicts rain, and gets a flood which drowns everyone in the county. A few of these poems, I believe, will be read as long as men remember English.

Robert Lowell's New Book
BY JOHN HOLLANDER

Robert Lowell is probably the most distinguished American poet of his generation, and under any circumstances, the appearance of his first book in eight years would have to be a considerable event. For those readers who have not followed the periodical publication of a good many of the poems in *Life Studies* during the past few years, the event may be a rather surprising one as well. An abrupt change in subject and style appears at first glance to have taken place. The opening section of the book follows recognizable cadences (as at the end of *Beyond the Alps:* "Now Paris, our black classic, breaking up / like killer kings on an Etruscan cup") and casts itself in familiar forms (dramatic monologues, for example, of Marie de' Medici and of *A Mad Negro Soldier Confined at Munich*) that are as characteristic of Mr. Lowell's previous work as is their excellence. But the remainder of the book (with the possible exception of two poems to Ford Madox Ford and George Santayana) will seem to represent an extremely sharp turning off an undeniably ascending straight path. This new course is made all the more startling, as well as all the more apparently divergent, perhaps, by reason of the currency, at the time of the book's publication, of a somewhat militant esthetic position equating strict prosody with a kind of literary repression—a poetic Reichian character armor, so to speak, and demanding a more "natural" national mode of poetic expression. For what seems most prominently to govern this new direction in Mr. Lowell's work is the association of a new autobiographical subject matter and a poetic form that has loosened almost unrecognizably in logic and meter.

I say "*seems* most prominently to govern" because I

think that the continuities between these poems and the earlier ones are stronger, after all, than the divergences. The book's thematic structure is dominated by a pivotal, thirty-five page prose fragment of reminiscences, themselves somewhat fragmentary in nature, of the poet's family and of his native city. This prose section, entitled "91 Revere Street," glosses, and is in turn glossed by, the eleven poems that make up the first group of the section of the book called, after the title of the whole, "Life Studies." The final poems in this first group and those of the second concern the poet's recent life, rather than his childhood. The diction of all these poems varies considerably. In *Sailing Home from Rapallo*, for example, we find a vocabulary and a measure as hitherto well-known in Mr. Lowell's poetry as these:

> The graveyard's soil was changing to stone—
> so many of its deaths had been midwinter.
> Dour and dark against the blinding snowdrifts,
> its black brook and fir trunks were as smooth as masts.
> A fence of spear-hafts
> black-bordered its mostly Colonial grave-slates.

Despite the almost startling relaxation of the poet's accustomed iambic rhythm, the voice is utterly familiar here. On the other hand, something rather new appears when the tension of a whole, bare, almost prosaic passage of report will be packed into what is more image than figure, more glimpse, even, than image:

> All night the crib creaks;
> home from the healthy country to the sick city,
> my daughter in fever
> flounders in her chicken-colored sleeping bag.

These are the opening lines of *During Fever*. Again, at the end of what is almost the diary-entry and the easy ironies of the first paragraph of *Memories of West Street and Lepke*, we get much the same thing:

> I have a nine-months' daughter,
> young enough to be my granddaughter.
> Like the sun she rises in her flame-flamingo infants' wear.

The remainder of the poem, with its memories of the violence of imprisonment, is thus introduced with an image of passionate disruption of a kind that is ubiquitous in much of the poet's work (see the beginning of *Man and Wife*, for example: "Tamed by *Miltown,* we lie on Mother's bed; / the rising sun in war paint dyes us red").

Then, too, there are passages of some length that seem to function as isolated fragments of intensely felt and even more intensely remembered experience, existing prior to, and underlying, the rather witty and polished paragraphs of *91 Revere Street,* with their predominantly scenic organization. The autobiographical poems of *Life Studies* are constructed around the glimpse, the remembered object, rather than, in a more novelistic way, around the scene, the event or the confrontation. In them a mere inventory often takes on a menacing air, a promise of either psychic violence or unimaginably deep comfort, even before some final, clinching image will strike the tone, finally committing the poem's attitude. Some lines from further on in *During Fever* exemplify this:

> Mother your master-bedroom
> looked away from the ocean.
> You had a window-seat,
> an electric blanket,
> a silver hot water bottle
> monogrammed like a hip-flask,
> Italian china fruity
> with bunches and berries
> and proper *putti*.
> Gold, yellow and green,
> the nuptial bed
> was as big as a bathroom.

From what I have quoted so far, it will be obvious that the poet has left behind him several of the schemes that typified the poems of *Lord Weary's Castle* by which he is best known. Tight stanza forms, melodramatically invoked Christian imagery, an almost rhetorical allusiveness now and then, all served to illuminate a Hell set not in contemporary Boston, but in a mythically powerful metamorphosis of that city into a half-actual, half-historical apparition—a metaphysical Boston yoking the felt present and the known past by violence together. But there has also existed another strain in Mr. Lowell's poetry that appears in several poems in *Lord Weary's Castle* and may be traced through the shorter poems in *The Mills of the Kavanaughs* (such as *Her Dead Brother, David and Bathsheba in the Public Garden* and, most particularly, *Thanksgiving's Over*, one of his finest poems altogether). It is this line that may be said to have reached fruition in the recent poems; its course may be followed from the section called "The Attic" from *The First Sunday in Lent,* or the opening of *Mary Winslow* ("Her Irish maids could never spoon out mush / Or orange juice enough") and other poems in the earlier book. The speaker is in most of these cases the protagonist of a dramatic monologue, as, for example, in *Between the Porch and the Altar:*

> It must have been a Friday. I could hear
> The top-floor typist's thunder and the beer
> That you had brought in cases hurt my head;
> I'd sent the pillows flying from my bed,
> I hugged my knees together and I gasped.

But the genre is the same even where the "I" of the poem seems to be more the poet himself, as in *The Death of the Sheriff:*

> The popping pine-cones flash
> Like shore-bait on his face in oils. My bile
> Rises, and beads of perspiration swell
> To flies and splash the *Parmachenie Belle*
> That I am scraping with my uncle's file.

It is true that, in both of these cases, it is the rigor of the rhymed pentameters and their unique energy that we associate with Mr. Lowell's work of this period. The attentive rigor of stanzas and often of couplets is generally absent from the newer poems. But this is not to say by any means that metrical control and power have been abandoned here. A characteristic quality of Mr. Lowell's pentameter lines has always been one of lumped tension, of a half-awkward clotting-up of the otherwise strict alternation of weak and strong syllables with consonantal clusters that seem always on the verge of dominating the rhythm. The grotesque opening lines of the poem to Ford Madox Ford in the present book seem almost self-parody in their overuse of this phenomenon: "The lobbed ball plops, then dribbles to the cup . . . / (a birdie, Fordie)." This sort of texture is used far more successfully, however, when the commanding pentameter movement is no longer there to "save" it. The conclusion of *Waking in the Blue* starts off with just such a jerky, fretful music:

> . . . Cock of the walk,
> I strut in my turtle-necked French sailor's jersey
> before the metal shaving mirrors,
> and see the shaky future grow familiar
> in the pinched, indigenous faces
> of these thoroughbred mental cases,
> twice my age and half my weight.
> We are all old-timers,
> each of us holds a locked razor.

The control exercised by the syntactical line-breaks, by the occasional half and full rhymes, and by the pulsations of metrical tension between more strictly and more loosely related lines is very much like, *mutatis mutandis,* the kind of control exercised by the tighter prosody of the earlier poems. It is merely that the material is less violent and less likely itself to get out of hand, seeming to require less in the way of restraining devices, metrical, metaphorical or mythical. Often when writing of his baby daughter, Mr. Lowell moves into an apocalyptic mode through the use of a glimpse of color, as in the passages quoted earlier, or in *Home After Three Months Away:*

> Though I am forty-one,
> not forty now, the time I put away
> was child's-play. After thirteen weeks
> my child still dabs her cheeks
> to start me shaving. When
> we dress her in her sky-blue corduroy,
> she changes to a boy,
> and floats my shaving brush
> and washcloth in the flush. . . .
> Dearest, I cannot loiter here
> in lather like a polar bear.

Only after the shock of "sky-blue" has expended itself, does the poem move into the wry mode. Here as elsewhere in *Life Studies,* however, the imagery unites not the actual and the imagined, but rather the worlds of child and adult, the realms of the variously remembered, near and distant. The over-arching cosmos that contains all of these, seeing them simultaneously, is the world of these poems. In considering the interior of that world, I remember Delmore Schwartz's line: "How all things flash! how all things flare!" But the light on the objects and people in these poems is generated with less heat than is that of the refining fire of the previous books. In *Where the Rainbow Ends,* Mr. Lowell concluded *Lord Weary's Castle* by asking almost of his own poetic imagination

> . . . What can the dove of Jesus give
> You now but wisdom, exile? Stand and live,
> The dove has brought an olive branch to eat.

The question remained for some time exactly what sort of wisdom it was toward which the poet was to move in his subsequent work. In the title poem of *The Mills of the Kavanaughs* he made what was perhaps a last, not completely successful attempt to criticize in a state of near-prophetic terror a world that he had himself created; his theme was still "History" (as he rang a surprisingly fundamental change on T. S. Eliot's line) "is now and New England." In the present book, the olive branch symbolic of both peace and of sustenance after the deluge appears only in the facts of life and the things of this world, in the bountiful harvest of the "Fallings from us," the "vanishings" into whose nature the Imagination must needs direct its most unrelenting researches. *Life Studies* is withal a much less spectacular book than its two predecessors, but it is unbelievably moving.

The Masterpiece of the Forties
BY WALTER ALLEN

Malcolm Lowry's *Under the Volcano* (1947) is, it seems to me, the finest and profoundest work of fiction written by an Englishman during the decade. Lowry, who died in 1957 at the age of forty-eight, published a first novel, *Ultramarine*, in 1930 while still an undergraduate; very much an experimental novel, it recounted the experiences of a very young middle-class Englishman as a deckhand on a cargo ship. It was, one assumes, based on immediate experience, experience later to find its way into *Under the Volcano*. Lowry spent most of his life in Mexico, the scene of *Under the Volcano*, the United States and British Columbia, and as a novelist could probably be regarded as no less American than English. Certainly if one were looking for affinities in contemporary fiction one would find him closest to Faulkner.

This is because of their common heritage: both are the sons of Conrad and of Joyce and learned, better perhaps than any others, the real lessons to be gotten from Joyce. Apart from the first chapter, which is set a year ahead and has the function almost of a chorus to the action, *Under the Volcano* is concerned with the events of a single day, the Day of the Dead, November, 1938, the last day in the life of Geoffrey Firmin, British Consul in the town of Quauhnahuac in Mexico, a town lying beneath the two volcanos of Popocatepetl and Ixtaccihuatl. The point is made more than once in the novel that the ancients placed Tartarus under Etna: *Under the Volcano* is a novel about hell.

Firmin is a compulsive drunk. He is a man who is in the deepest sense alienated, knows himself alienated and, clear-sighted in the imprisonment of his sloth, is yet unable to make the necessary gestures, speak the necessary words, that would heal the breach between himself and the world. The theme of the novel is the necessity of love and the appalling difficulty of love; and during the Consul's last day on earth we watch him in his drunken progress of flight from those who love him and would save him—his wife, an ex-Hollywood film star who has divorced him but returned to him that day, and his half-brother Hugh, an anti-Fascist journalist haunted by the Spanish Civil War—a progress of evasive action from bar to bar, made almost against his will, until it ends with his murder by Fascist thugs who throw his body into the ravine—one of the novel's most powerful symbols—that splits the landscape. One says the flight is almost against his will. He is more in love with damnation than with being saved; he can think the words of love but is unable to say them aloud. In a sense, the climax of the book, in that it represents the point of no return, is the argument he has with Hugh on the value or otherwise of political action. The Consul is a man who in every conceivable way has abdicated. To his wife's pleadings, to all the demands made on him to save himself, he might have said, with Eliot's Gerontion:

> I have lost my passion: why should I need to keep it
> Since what is kept must be adulterated?

It is Lowry's great achievement that he has made the Consul a genuinely tragic figure who never loses our respect and our admiration. There are many echoes of Marlowe in the novel: the Consul's friend Laruelle, a French film director, is planning a Faust film; and we think of the Consul as Marlowe thought of Faustus: "Cut is the branch that might have grown full straight." And though the novel is a vision of hell, given the most precise and vivid actuality in terms of the Mexican scene, and certainly, one feels the most thorough-going rendering of dipsomania that has ever been written, there are still glimpses of heaven, of the possibility of a good life. Heaven, though not for the Consul, is even attainable, and, while the novel abounds in symbols of hell, it also has its symbols of release, of freedom, of which the freeing of the birds is the most obvious, and of the possibility of natural happiness, as in the beautiful description of Yvonne's and Hugh's morning ride around the environs of Quauhnahuac, with the foals trotting beside the mares they are riding and, going before them, the dog hunting snakes.

Then there are the wider implications. It is not by chance that, when the book opens with Laruelle's contemplation of his dead friend, the war in Europe has already begun and that during the main action Chamberlain has returned only a few weeks before from Munich and the war in Spain is dragging to its end. The novel is set firmly in the context of its time, and the wider relevance is established even to the point of being rammed home when Hugh, who has been trying to cure his brother's alcoholism, bursts out: "Good God, if our civilization were to sober up for a couple of days it'd die of remorse on the third. . . ."

Though its indebtedness in a general sense both to *Ulysses* and to *The Waste Land* is obvious, *Under the Volcano* stands uniquely by itself as a great tragic novel, a masterpiece of organization and of elaborate symbolism that is never forced or strained but right, springing largely as it does out of the scenes in which the action takes place. The harmony between the characters and the phenomena of the external universe through which they move is complete; and so are the correspondences between them. In this respect, Joyce in *Ulysses* did no better.

The Fiction of Norman Mailer
BY HARRIS DIENSTFREY

Andrea: Unhappy is the land that breeds no hero.
Galileo: Unhappy is the land that needs a hero.

Brecht: *Galileo*

Norman Mailer began his career as a more or less ordinary, if very talented, social realist. He took the measure of his characters' lives from the economic and political structure of the society about them; men were and could be no more than this structure let them be. But as Mailer has developed, he has shed this framework of determinism, and the nature of his concerns has changed entirely. He has become a novelist bent upon exploring the ways a man can use his will and experience to break the accepted limits of feeling and behavior, and by so doing make both himself and his society more alive. Mailer is now one of the few contemporary novelists of any country whose work is passionately in search of a hero.

The change has been piecemeal. Mailer maintains his ideas with an extraordinary, almost quivering earnestness, and one has the sense that for him the development he has undergone has been something like the sloughing off of an old skin and the making of a new one. There is no doubt that from the literary viewpoint of neat and fully articulated structures, several of his novels have suffered. Both *Barbary Shore* and, to a lesser degree, *The Deer Park*, move in directions that Mailer seems not to have intended. But it goes without saying that a novel can have more vital sources of strength than a tidy structure.

Mailer's first novel, *The Naked and the Dead* (no doubt the best-known American novel to come out of World War II), is a book he would have written in one form or another even if the war had never occurred. Its characters, their strengths and weaknesses, and the possibility for their change have all been determined, as though writ in stone, by the American life out of which they emerged. They funnel into one end of the island campaign that forms the immediate subject of the book and come out the other merely more of what they were at the start. In this sense, that its ultimate locus is America, one might even say that *The Naked and the Dead* is not a war novel at all.

The action of the book is structured around the campaign of a division task force to capture a small South Pacific island. There is a remarkable ease to *The Naked and the Dead*, as if its author were completely confident he was describing the marrow of reality. The writing is always direct and concrete, and objects and sensations are recorded with spare metronomic precision. Mailer staffs the book's action with a full array of personnel, from privates to a commanding general, and builds the novel out of details that lock together like links in a chain. Episodes and scenes follow one another with a sure sense of proportion. "I doubt if ever again," Mailer once observed, "I will have a book which is so easy to write."

The most impressive achievement of *The Naked and the Dead* is its brilliantly meticulous, almost monumental re-creation of the exhaustions and terrors of war. In this regard, it has no peers. (James Jones' recent novel, *The Thin Red Line,* often favorably compared to Mailer's book, is actually a creation of quite a different order, a black lyric poem about the fantastic and insane incongruities of war.) Except for the few men to whom it provides a feeling of violent release, the war in *The Naked and the Dead* is totally without glory, an endless stitch in the side whose degrees of physical misery—fatigue, exhaustion, stupor— Mailer renders with almost exquisite subtlety. It is a war with no chance of heroism and no heroes—only men who suffer more or less.

But there are really two wars in *The Naked and the Dead,* the one being fought on a Pacific island and, by implication, the one that rages in America—the class war that has shaped the book's characters. Like John Dos Passos' *U.S.A.,* on which in so many respects it is patterned, *The Naked and the Dead* is a novel of social protest. Its characters occupy points all along the American social spectrum, and Mailer supplies their backgrounds in short biographical cameos that constitute a bravura display of his ability to handle the varied patterns of American life. (For the Negro whom the Army kept segregated until after the war, Mailer substitutes a Mexican-American born and raised in Texas.) To the last man, these people are without happiness or personal satisfaction or decent hope of self-fulfillment: "a bunch of dispossessed. . . . from the raucous stricken bosom of America." The country has worn them away, thwarted and blunted them, and destroyed their capacity to imagine a better life. The Pacific war in which *The Naked and the Dead* plunges them only exchanges a physical misery for the emotional and spiritual misery they have experienced all their lives.

Four characters dominate the book: General Cummings and his aide, Lieutenant Hearn, the novel's moral consciousness; and a pair of enlisted (lower-class) counterparts, Sergeant Croft ("who hated weakness and loved practically nothing") and Pfc. Valsen ("He'd do no man harm if he could help it, and he'd take no crap"). Amid the dense factuality with which he records the entire campaign, Mailer molds the actions of these four men into a shrill allegory that presumably foretells America's coming descent into fascism. "You can consider the Army," Cummings tells Hearn, "as a preview of the future." The allegory is quite unconvincing. Mailer does nothing to make one believe that it symbolizes historical inevitabilities. Yet this graft onto the novel provides a neat example of how he originally viewed the relation between men and their society.

Cummings is an American fascist; he confidently foresees the time when the country's democratic structure will topple and the restoration of order will depend on a dictator of sufficient ruthlessness and intelligence, a man such as himself. Hearn, both repelled by Cummings' vision and yet drawn by the force of his certainty, is a younger man who has spent his adult life trying unsuccessfully to find some way to realize his nebulous democratic hopes. Intellectually a socialist, emotionally an anarchist, he cannot give himself to either very confidently. At the outbreak of the war he voluntarily enlists as an officer. By the time he comes to end his vacillation—he decides to give up

his commission and take on the rank (and the related
political and social commitments) of an enlisted man—it
is too late. Through a combination of separate stratagems
by Cummings and Croft, he is shot by a Japanese soldier
and killed instantly. The story is much the same with his
lower-class counterpart, Valsen. Like Hearn, he is uncertain, politically isolated, and without a sustaining vision.
When at last he forces himself to make a stand against
Croft, he finds he no longer has the necessary strength
and courage. As *The Naked and the Dead* would have it,
the bleak American heritage of capitalism has inevitably
exhausted him.

In *The Naked and the Dead,* the world is a machine,
rigid and inexorable, and America a country doomed by
unalterable conditions.

Barbary Shore, published in 1951, was to take Mailer
from his view of an ordered world to a view of chaos.
Studded with wild starts and abrupt stops, the novel reads
as if Mailer intended one sort of book (a didactic, third
force summary of present world conditions from the viewpoint of American radicalism) but kept finding himself
writing another (a fevered vision about the emotional circuits moving below the face of history). The book is taut
with ideas barely articulated. Quite unlike *The Naked
and the Dead, Barbary Shore* gives the impression of having been wrenched out of the imagination by an enormous
effort of will.

As in the second novels of several important writers
who found their initial subject in war (John Horne Burns'
Lucifer with a Book, Vance Bourjaily's *The Hound of
Earth*), the physical setting has violently contracted. In a
claustrophobic Brooklyn rooming house, during a steamy
hot summer, six Americans, spanning three generations,
act out "the phenomena of the world today." The weird
double vision of the book develops when the characters,
as though by a will of their own, suddenly behave in ways
quite unrelated to the political considerations that brought
them into being.

The novel's central character, and its oldest, is McLeod,
a one-time revolutionary Communist who betrayed most
of his hopes and ideals (and many of his friends) in the
"bureaucracy" of the revolution. He eventually fled to the

State Department, then fled it also, taking with him an undefined "little object." Whatever it is, it is the only small hope left to man. And guilt-ridden McLeod, reduced to writing analytic, Trotskyite pamphlets that condemn both "state" and "monopoly" capitalism, has it.

The book—in a quite literal sense—puts McLeod on trial. Through tireless interrogations ostensibly concerned with the whereabouts of the "little object," *Barbary Shore* examines whether the man can still claim a touch of honor and true insight into the forces controlling the world after the worst about him has been told. Three people sit in judgment. Between the ages of twenty-five and thirty, they are in effect his political offspring.

Of the three, the figure who represents what *Barbary Shore* takes to be the most common contemporary political type is Hollingsworth, a secret agent for the State Department. Like McLeod, Hollingsworth is a "bureaucrat." He is in the rooming house to discover whether or not McLeod has the "little object" and to this end he institutes the interrogations. Unlike the older man (whom he rather likes), Hollingsworth represents the type of bureaucrat—*Barbary Shore* sees them managing the world—who has no hope or ideal beyond himself. "A good-time Charley, that's myself," Hollingsworth declares, "and that's why I'm smarter than the lot of you." Alternating between whiny self-pity and brutal sadism, he is driven not by ideological considerations but by a vast indiscriminate resentment. The only judgment Hollingsworth is capable of rendering upon McLeod is an utterly personal, psychological one, neither moral nor political, but full of rage and frustration. "You're an old man," he cries after listening to a long visionary speech, "and you indulge yourself. . . . Babble, babble, babble about how sweet it used to be. Only you make it the future."

The other two characters who attend the interrogations represent for *Barbary Shore* the state of contemporary radicalism. Like McLeod, they are powerless, and one, Lannie, is near madness. She lost her reason when the man she calls her father lost his life, an axe in his head. The novel presents Lannie, for an unclear reason, as the quintessential victim. Helplessly caught in a downward spiral of violent self-abasement, she burns with hatred for McLeod and his first masters, and obsessively aids Hollingsworth in his interrogations. "If you are to be destroyed, you must love your destroyer, for who else is there to love when that's the world?" Lannie's brother radical is Lovett, the book's narrator. Lovett suffers from amnesia. "Probably I was in the war," he begins his story. But he finds a kinship of spirit in McLeod that helps draws him out of his isolation. Through this relationship and the pain of his confrontations with Lannie, he convulsively feels his way back to the great socialist passion that once informed his life. At the end, his action provides the novel's ultimate judgment on McLeod. In a gesture of intense psychic effort, he accepts from the older man the "little object" and the burden of his own past along with it. While the police come in the front door, he flees through a back window, taking the unknown object with him.

For the remaining two characters of *Barbary Shore,* the outcome of the interrogations could not be less important. Both Guinevere, the landlady, and Monina, her four-year-old daughter, are ruled—like Hollingsworth—by impulses and emotions rising from some realm of being where only the self exists. And like him, they are meant to represent the condition of most men today. Each of these three figures is an extraordinary creation.

Within the scheme of *Barbary Shore,* Guinevere signifies nothing less than the masses. A large fleshy woman, she sometimes glows with vibrant sensuality, sometimes appears like the worst drab of a housewife. "A jewel," Lovett describes her. "But set in brass." She is at the beck and call of almost everyone. It turns out that she is McLeod's secret wife, though she no longer knows why she married him. She sleeps with Lannie, and with Hollingsworth, and refuses only Lovett—the radical outside history.

Monina, the daughter of Guinevere and McLeod, is in many ways the most remarkable figure of the book. She is obviously a token of the generation to come, a child of the mass media as Mailer sees them. Hardly able to speak, she nonetheless is a consummate narcissist, brilliantly aware of the most delicate sexual nuance. Like a celluloid vamp, she can counterfeit the full ceremony of seduction with appalling intensity—and then burst into hysterical tears. She lives in fantasy and emerges into the real world only to be shocked into fright.

It is in Monina's behavior that one can see most clearly

the throbbing underside of *Barbary Shore*. In one episode,
murder under its surface, the young child, "like a missile
whose fuse was her mouth," inexplicably sinks her teeth
into Hollingsworth's hand and clings to it fiercely.

> Unguarded, a moan escaped from his mouth, his
> eyes opened in fright. What nightmares were resur-
> rected? He sat helpless upon the chair, . . . a convict
> in the deathroom, his body violated in the spasms of
> the current.
> "I'm innocent," he screamed.
> And with the cry, Monina released him, ran weep-
> ing out the door and wailing down the stairs.

The rest of the episode—its pinched metaphoric prose is
characteristic—registers the obsessive force of the tortured
psychic world that keeps erupting into the tight political
framework of the book.

> Doubled with pain, Hollingsworth grunted, his paw
> held out before him to reveal in bleeding outline the
> opposed small scimitars of Monina's teeth. He writhed
> back and forth upon the chair, and then tentatively
> his unmarked hand fumbled through his hair. There
> was no spot shaven, no electrode upon his skull. . . .
> As his anguish receded, he sat back, arms dangling,
> his face pale, sweat upon his brow. "Ohhhhh," he
> shuddered. Then he drew upright in his chair, his
> mouth deadly. "When I see that kid again," he said,
> "I'll cut her fucking heart out."

In trying to give fictional form to what he considered "the
phenomena of the world today," Mailer was pitched headlong outside his ideological scheme into a tangle of emotion
entirely more vivid—the terror, fantasy, and violence that
surround the three characters meant to represent the most
typical kinds of contemporary consciousness. Hollingsworth, Guinevere, and Monina stalk through the novel
like quivering animals, ready to fly or strike, kill or cry,
bursting with fear and venom and at the same time longing
for love and peace. They do not really know what they
want or how to get it, and the only guides they any longer
recognize are the visions of their fabulous and sinister

fantasies. "Suppose I was to ask you to go away with me now," Guinevere hungrily questions Hollingsworth. "Would you go?"

"Go where?"
"Anywhere. To the ends of the earth. To Barbary —I like the sound of that."

Barbary Shore is like a tale told by a man whose senses know he is teetering on the edge of a sheer drop but whose mind protects itself by worrying when the next forty-day deluge is likely to begin. As if to nail down his wildly careening story, Mailer gives McLeod a long wind-up speech during the last of Hollingsworth's interrogations. Intended as an abstract summary of the novel's meaning, it discusses the twin colossi bestriding the world, "state capitalism" and "monopoly capitalism," and how each is kept in working order by comparable groups of increasingly totalitarian bureaucrats (bound to rebel, McLeod prophecies, in an attempt to regain the personalities they have lost serving the machines of government), and how the two systems inevitably must war because of inner economic contradictions. Out of the resulting destruction, McLeod concludes hopefully, the Phoenix of socialism will rise. This is the speech that Hollingsworth angrily denounces as so much "babble, babble, babble."

For Mailer, *Barbary Shore* seems to have been an unconscious working out of the limitations of his political beliefs and the limitations of political theorizing in general. After this, his work takes a decisive turn. The difference is not that he revokes the Marxism informing his first novels. Mailer never seems to revoke much of anything, usually managing to incorporate old ideas, re-shuffled, into new perspectives. He still believes that capitalism ("state" or "monopoly") is inherently inequitable and that the fruit of living within capitalism is frustration and outrage. The difference is that he concerns himself with areas of experience which political ideas can no longer adequately explain, and indeed become less and less adequate with each new step his fiction takes.

The change in perspective begins with "The Man Who Studied Yoga," the translucent short novel that originally was to serve as the prologue to Mailer's eight-volume conception of *The Deer Park*. The eight volumes reduced themselves to one, but "The Man Who Studied Yoga" still stands as a prologue to the fiction that has followed.

In style and tone, the short novel is as different from *Barbary Shore* as that book was different from *The Naked and the Dead*, and in a general way "Yoga" is a return to the mode of the first work. With much the same directness and exactitude, though with a new edge of humor and personal involvement—the entire story has something of the texture of a candid documentary movie—Mailer examines a Sunday in the life of Sam Slovoda, a forty year old continuity writer for comic books. He is married and modestly affluent. The unnamed narrator provides a thumbnail sketch of his character. "He is better than most. He would prefer to see a more equitable world, he scorns prejudice and privilege, he tries to hurt no one, he wishes to be liked. I will go even further. He has one serious virtue—he is not fond of himself, he wishes he were better."

As always, Sunday for Sam is a yeasty compost of boredom, irritation like an itching sore, enervation, self-disgust, unaccomplishment. It starts with the promise of a gesture toward reality—he has planned to do some work on the novel he has been preparing to write for years— but he cannot focus enough energy for the task. It ends with he and his wife watching a pornographic movie with two other couples. Like him, they are also "progressives" —"It's all economic," one of the women is prone to say. After they leave, Sam and his wife run the movie through again and make love on the couch before it. Their sex is enjoyable for her but not for him, though he is warmed by the fact of her pleasure. Yet before he can find sleep, he suddenly recalls his novel, for which he cannot even devise a hero, and he lies in a sweat caused by the waste of the day, of all his days, of all that he had hoped once to do but never will. "What a dreary compromise," the narrator closes with mute anger and sadness, "is life!"

A simple way to suggest the distance between the concerns of *The Naked and the Dead* and those of "The Man Who Studied Yoga" is to recall that Hearn and Valsen want to change the system, Sam merely wants to change himself. Hearn and Valsen fail because of "objective" conditions: the system has the power. Sam fails too, but no

similar explanation suggests itself. Something in his spirit
has gone dead, and he does not know what or why. It is
in this regard that "The Man Who Studied Yoga" is a
prologue to fiction that follows it. The story presents the
essence of that poisoned state of being and society whose
dissection, and the search for whose remedy, now forms
the center of Mailer's work (fiction and magazine journalism alike).

The subject of *The Deer Park*, published in 1955, like
that of "The Man Who Studied Yoga," is the suffocation
of spirit. Set in a Hollywood resort, Desert D'Or (the
literal and associative meanings of whose name are both
relevant) the novel first of all is a graphic report—in a
flexible, muscular style studded with metaphor—on the look
and sound of the Hollywood milieu. There is an almost
anthropological passion to this element of the book, as if
Hollingsworth's cry of "babble, babble, babble" had burned
Mailer's own ear; as if it had been to him, and not to the
young narrator of *The Deer Park*, Sergius O'Shaugnessy,
that the mystic-cum-hipster, Marion Faye, had remarked:
"You don't know how anything works." Since *Barbary
Shore*, Mailer seems deliberately to have set himself the
task of confronting and understanding as many different
constellations of America's vast social landscape as he can.
Certainly his journalism for *Esquire*, much of it reprinted
in his most recent collection, *The Presidential Papers*, fits
such a program. And it is in this light that the background
of *The Deer Park* should be understood.

But Desert D'Or is not just a piece of America, it is also
a metaphor for it, just as the rooming house of *Barbary
Shore* was, and if some of the same claustrophobia remains
—it may now be a permanent aspect of Mailer's work,
an inevitable by-product of the psychic underworld he has
taken as part of his subject—the nature of the metaphor
has changed entirely. From an image of depression barrenness and economic inequity, Mailer has moved to an
image of golden sun and money, and to a place which is
the source of the mass fantasies that have as their product
someone like Monina. Indeed, it comes as no surprise to
find Monina herself in Desert D'Or, her child's guise thrown
off and revealed in her true aspect: Lulu Meyers, Holly-

wood star, whose Bimmler rating looks to be slipping out
of the top twenty.

The heart of *The Deer Park* concerns the parallel experiences of Sergius O'Shaugnessy, its royally named narrator just discharged from the Air Force (he had been a First
Lieutenant and a small hero in Korea), and Charles
Francis Eitel, a blacklisted film director in whom Sergius,
for a while, finds a spiritual mentor. "I felt that he was a
man like me, only many times smoother and he knew
more." Both are at turning points in their careers. Sergius
must make some decision about his future. He comes to
Desert D'Or with a lucky $14,000 poker windfall looking
for a good time and to give himself a brief moratorium on
decision-making. Eitel is there trying to write an original
script for a film (which he intends to produce himself)
that "can justify so much bad work."

In Sergius, Mailer has created a brilliant portrait of a
young man balanced on the edge of his culture, both
fascinated and repelled by it, and in need of a guide (that
they are so rare in this day is part of Mailer's theme)
to help him sort out the pressures working on him and
find the confidence to make his own decision. At times
in *The Deer Park,* Sergius becomes fuzzy or schematic,
particularly at its end, after he has decided to leave
Desert D'Or to begin the arduous task of trying to become
a writer; and there are times when he fades away, merely
a passive reporter of events whose impact on him is lost
below the details. But during those sequences when he
emerges into the book and frames its events, the shape
of his character and the essence of his predicament is
unmistakable. No other figure in contemporary American
literature embodies with such clarity the complex of contradictory forces that mark the young and rebellious. Sergius is emotionally throttled, yet he burns with unused
emotion; he is exhausted, yet filled with a sense of giant
possibility. He hungers rapaciously for all the sweets of his
culture—its prizes and power—yet he bursts with a desire
to tear the entire culture down, to root out each and
every one of its sweets as corrosive rot. At the base of
his bewilderment and confusion is the fact that he does
not know what is at stake, that he has no sense of what
he might ultimately lose or gain by saying yes or no to
any of the conflicting impulses moving in him.

It is the figure of Eitel who provides the answer. If Sergius is a blunt hammer, Eitel is a stiletto, and Mailer renders his trembling passage in Desert D'Or with great subtlety. Eitel had come to Hollywood during the depression, had made several low-budget films of raw force, and had then become a commercial director, producing no better work than that of an intelligent craftsman. His refusal to be a co-operative witness before a congressional investigating committee—not for political reasons but for his own sense of dignity—has given him the chance to try and be what he once seemed to have the power to become. But he finds he cannot. The script he aches to write remains locked in his imagination. He has lost the strength to pry it out during the years he cheated his talent and spirit in the service of a world of masquerade.

For *The Deer Park,* the masquerade is not simply Hollywood but a style of life, most blatantly symbolized for Mailer in the work of Hollywood, that pervades the root and being of American society. Everyone in *The Deer Park* is its victim. The characters form a kind of chain of reflecting mirrors, each providing a different angle of vision to the disorder that affects them all. At one end is Marion Faye (almost an alter ego of Sergius and at times too schematically developed), so fierce in his loathing for the false world he sees that he will allow no one, least of all himself, the smallest salve of a lie or an emotional impurity. At the other end is "Uncle" Herman Teppis, king of the masquerade, the head of Supreme Pictures, as fierce as Faye in his loathing of the world he helped make, with the difference that he will allow no one in it the least piece of honesty. Somewhere in the middle is Elena, the "near-beauty" who has a long affair with Eitel while he struggles to write his script, and who fights no less passionately than he to let herself break free. (It should be said that Mailer is one of the few American novelists to concern himself directly and convincingly with the experiences and feelings of women. The character of Elena is one of his major achievements.) In the remarkable letter she writes Eitel after he breaks off their affair—a letter at once arrogant, sullen, abusive, eloquent, and anguished —she suddenly explains: "In a way you could eat up the whole world if you wanted to, if only you didn't fall for all the talk that the middle-class squares give you."

The America that *The Deer Park* portrays is a world lost in masquerade and lie, its inhabitants so caught up in a continuous swirl of fantasy that they no longer have any sure sense of themselves or any sure knowledge of where the fantasy ends, or what is underneath it. Even if, like Eitel, they finally come to realize how badly they are cheating themselves, like him, they rarely have the strength to change. The whole weight of the culture is against it. "For do we not gamble to the heart of the mystery," Sergius tells Eitel in the goodbyes the two men bid each other in the imagination of Sergius' mind, "against all the power of good manners, good morals, the fear of germs, and the sense of sin. Not to mention the prisons of pain, the wading pools of pleasure, and the public and professional voices of our sentimental land." In *The Deer Park's* America, most men are like Sam Slovoda, trapped in self-estrangement and loss of spirit.

But as in *Barbary Shore, The Deer Park* contains a theme that develops somewhat outside of Mailer's control. How does one break the process of self-estrangement? How does a man become better than his world? If socialism is the answer to economic and political exploitation, what is the answer to a spiritual exploitation in which the individual himself becomes his own worst exploiter? Like a loose string not quite in place, this theme turns up at the edges of *The Deer Park,* fretful and nagging. It shows itself in Marion Faye's search for an absolutely pure emotion, in Eitel's suggestion that he draws great psychic energy from sex with Elena, in his "theory" about "the buried nature" and "the snob" hidden and at war in each man. ("If people were lucky and if they were brave," he explains to Sergius, "sometimes they would find a mate with the same buried nature and that could make them happy and strong.") At the very end of *The Deer Park* the impulse behind these musings breaks loose, and all in a rush one feels, produces those strange last lines, opaque, yet oddly affirmative, that bring the book to a close and that more than anything else seem to be the opening to another work.

There are hours when I would have the arrogance to reply to the Lord Himself, and so I ask, "Would

You agree that sex is where philosophy begins?"

But God, who is the oldest of the philosophers, answers in His weary cryptic way, "Rather think of
Sex as Time, and Time as the connection of new
circuits."

Then for a moment in that cold Irish soul of mine,
a glimmer of the joy of the flesh came toward me,
rare as the eye of the rarest tear of compassion, and
we laughed together after all, because to have heard
that sex was time and time the connection of new
circuits was a part of the poor odd dialogues which
give hope to us noble humans for more than one
night.

Whatever these lines mean, their general intent is clear:
they are a gnomic prescription for the modern hero, for
the man who would make "new circuits" and so gain
more life, and destroy the habitual lifeless connections that
would destroy him.

It is this concern—the making of "new circuits"—that
has now moved to the center of Mailer's fiction. In the
few sections that have appeared of the thousand page
novel he has predicted it will take him ten years to write,
and in the novel that he wrote against monthly deadlines
for *Esquire* magazine (*An American Dream*), the drive
that motivates the protagonist is always the desire to grow
and become more alive. In the logic with which Mailer
views the world, not to grow is to die. There is no space
here to examine this work in detail. But four points should
be made. First, an assertion: that the work displays a
richer sensitivity to the most disturbing states of contemporary consciousness than is shown by any other novelist
of Mailer's generation. Second, a matter of style: that the
Mailer who began his career with a prose style that found
a model in the spareness of Hemingway and Dos Passos
now has developed a style that in its own way calls to mind
the rhetorical virtuosity of Faulkner. Third, a matter of
perspective: that the Mailer who began with a political
ideology learned in his youth now is developing a body
of ideas that would seem to have as its grandiose ambition a calculus of the modern psyche. And finally, a

matter of morality: that the most disturbing aspect of
Mailer's recent fiction is its implicit argument that to be
more alive in these times is rarely to be more virtuous and
almost always to be more violent.

The Magic and the Dread
BY ALFRED KAZIN

The stories of Bernard Malamud are a striking example of the opportunities—and hazards—that are faced these days by "minority" writers who have rejected special pleading in favor of modern art. Writers like Ralph Ellison and James Baldwin are no longer tempted to sing the chain-gang blues once favored by Negro writers in this country; originals like Saul Bellow, Daniel Fuchs, and Bernard Malamud are not likely to retrace the kind of sentimental or aggressive pathos that has afflicted so many recorders of Jewish experience in this country, from Fannie Hurst to Michael Gold—a style that has found its last haven in the Hollywood of Irwin Shaw and other nostalgic readers of *PM*.

The newer writers (who seem "new" not because they are young but because it has taken them so long to climb out of the depression and war and to discover themselves as individuals) have turned their backs on what James Baldwin has jeeringly called "everybody's protest novel" —Uncle Tom, the Negro or the Jewish Christ dead of American capitalism, the saintly victim. But agile and really gifted as these new writers are, they have been just as unwilling or unable as Jewish and Negro writers always have been to let their experience alone, to describe it as something that may be valued for its own sake. It is here that one sees the peculiar nemesis of writers who feel that they can fit themselves to American life only by trying to give universal meaning to each piece of their experience.

The patron saint of these writers is always Dostoyevsky —the supreme example of the novelist whose characters must always search for meaning, who cannot for a moment allow life to exist without scrutinizing intervention. But where Dostoevsky had equal ability to embody the emptiness and sloth of nineteenth-century Russia, these new American writers itch with symbolism. They have been exposed so continually to modern literature and modern art that they find it hard to find their way back to what Herbert Gold has called the lesson of Balzac's "stupidity." Although these writers have produced a peculiarly penetrating kind of fiction, haunting as well as haunted, there is a certain overeagerness in them all to stand and deliver, to be freed of certain painful experiences through the ritualistic catharsis of modern symbolism. The Jewish or Negro writer, far from being mired in his personal pathos as of yore, is now so aware that his experience is "universal" that he tends to escape out of his particular experience itself, to end up in the great American sky of abstractions.

Of all these new writers, Bernard Malamud seems to me the most unnecessarily tempted by symbolism. For he is the most compassionate, the most concerned and involved of them all, and whenever I turn back to the best scenes in his fine novel, *The Assistant*, or to the little masterpiece about a rabbinical student in search of a wife who went to a marriage broker (the title story of this collection), I get something of the same deep satisfaction that I do from the great realistic masters of Yiddish literature.

Malamud's world has its own haunting archetypes: the desperate and sickly storekeeper, the refugee who turns up in Rome or New York to accuse his fellow Jews of heartlessness, the lonely student with ovoid eyes in staring search of love, the American intellectual abroad who finds it impossible to escape his Jewish past. The scene is always the down-at-heels grocery, the winter street, the irreversible hardness of the modern city. Malamud has caught as one the guttural toughness of big-city speech and the classic bitterness of Jewish dialogue. The remarkable story "Take Pity" contains the typical situation of all his work—a great love condemned to ineffectuality. A man who has committed suicide so that he can leave all his property to a widow who always refused to accept him during his lifetime sits in the other world telling a "census-taker" (his name is Davidov) how the woman's husband

died. "Broke in him something. . . ." "Broke what?" "Broke
what breaks. He was talking to me how bitter was his
life, and he touched me on my sleeve to say something
else, but the next minute his face got small and he fell
down dead, the wife screaming, the little girls crying that
it made in my heart pain. I am myself a sick man and
when I saw him laying on the floor, I said to myself,
'Rosen, say goodbye, this guy is finished.' So I said it."

This is the talk of people who are not merely on edge
but who really live on the edge. Their tense expressiveness
is one of the cultural symbols of the Jews, in art as in
religion; just as the great Rabbi Hillel could be challenged to give the whole meaning of the Law while standing on one foot, so there is a Doomsday terseness to
Jewish speech—as if the book of life were about to close
shut with a bang. Malamud has caught this quality with
an intimacy of understanding that is utterly remarkable.
But in their terseness, his characters fundamentally express
despair rather than any spiritual refusal of the great world.
His world is all too much an inner world—one in which
the city streets, the houses, the stores, seem, along with
the people who broodingly stand about like skeletons, some
with flesh, always just about to fold up, to disappear into
the sky. People talk to each other disbelievingly, as if
each felt that the other was about to disappear, as if the
world under their feet were itself unreal. People flit in and
out of each other's lives like bad dreams.

It is a curious, almost uncanny transformation of the
old Jewish mysticism, where earth is so close to heaven
—or to hell—that the supernatural and the trivial jostle
each other. From the historic standpoint of Jewish theology, of the seemingly incredible Jewish experience itself,
everything is entirely real. Life is always strange and God
always moves in unpredictable ways. In Malamud's stories
everything real becomes unreal; we are under the sign not
of theology but of surrealism. Sometimes this is unbearably effective; but when the symbols become too explicit,
as in "The Lady of the Lake" or "Angel Levine," Malamud's own tone is undecided between the mysterious and
the silly. In "The Mourners," an old man, suffering for
the guilt of having deserted his family years back, is about
to be evicted; the landlord is driven half mad trying to
get the dirty old man out of the tenement. The old man

begins mourning for him, the landlord, as dead—he is
spiritually dead—and the landlord, staring in unbelief, is
engulfed in the sudden upsurge of his own shame and
becomes a mourner too. The symbolism here is not only
explicit, it is positively allegorical. And indeed, Malamud
explains, in his Hawthornesque touches, why Hawthorne
and symbolist novelists like Kafka so often read alike.

But Malamud is at his best in those stories which depend
not on surprise but on the moment of ungovernable human feeling. In "The Loan," an old friend turns up in a
baker's shop to ask for a loan—to pay for a headstone
for his wife's grave. The baker's wife, his *second* wife,
steadfastly refuses to countenance the loan, and at the end
of the story the two friends, each bereft in his own way,
"pressed mouths together and parted forever." In the title
story, Malamud's usual attempt to escape "realism" is brilliantly, triumphantly justified. It is the marriage broker's
own daughter whom the rabbinical student falls in love
with, from a photograph, and at the end of the story the
ambiguities of life and death are so close that one has
the sense of being caught in a dream. Life is never very
solid for these Jews, these people "who live on air"; they
are always on the verge of saying good-by and departing
for the other world.

II

The otherworldly feeling in the great Jewish writers of
the past was supported by a conviction that earth and
heaven are connected. Malamud captures the strangeness
of Jewish experience brilliantly, but he relies on compassion, not on the covenant. He is so concerned with the
dread, the flimsiness of the human material in our age,
that he has to outwit his own possible sentimentality. This,
as I see it, is why he so often turns to symbolic endings,
goes through his material so quickly. The result is that
while this book seems to me masterful and indescribably
haunting, it is surprising to note, when one closes it, how
many of the people fade indistinguishably into each other.
What remains in the reader's mind is not a world, *the*
world, but the spectral Jew in his beggarly clothes—always
ready to take flight.

It is an extraordinary fact that although the great Yiddish writers in Czarist Russia could not call the country their own, they gave the earth of Russia, the old village, a solid reality, as if it were all the world they had left to cherish, like the Jewish graveyard that is lovingly kept up even when the houses decay. Malamud, the closest in wit and depth of feeling to the great Yiddish writers, nevertheless falls into the same abstractness that is the bane of so many new writers in America. Unlike those who are abstract because they have only their cleverness to write from, Malamud is abstract out of despair: despair of the world itself, which can no longer be represented.

In this one sees the curious danger of the American writer who has been influenced by Kakfa, Joyce, Eliot, *et al.* Life in America changes so quickly, and people are so quick to change into each other, that the everlasting thinness and abstractness of American writing, which comes from our lack of "society," of a solid core of leaders, manners, tradition, is likely to be intensified by our new writers, who have a society but don't believe in it enough to describe it—to deal with it not merely as it is but as something that *is*.

One of the things we now long for in contemporary literature is escape from the tyranny of symbolic "meaning." We want to return to life not as a figure in the carpet but as life in its beautiful and inexpressible materiality—life as the gift that it actually is rather than as the "material" that we try to remake.

Malamud provokes these reflections because he is so gifted. There seems to me no writer of his background who comes so close to the bone of human feeling, who makes one feel so keenly the enigmatic quality of life, for the body of this world—for that which cannot be explained because it is too precious to turn into symbols.

A New Life for a Good Man
BY STANLEY EDGAR HYMAN

Bernard Malamud's *A New Life* is the first new novel of consistent excellence that I have found since beginning this column, a lovely oasis after an interminable crawl through the hot sands. It is the story of S. Levin, a 30-year-old failure, who leaves New York to be an English instructor at Cascadia College on the West Coast. The novel covers one year of rich experience, and at its end we see Levin, fired and disgraced, setting off for San Francisco with his booty: a second-hand Hudson, the wife of the chairman of his department, her two adopted children, and Levin's own child inside her.

A New Life, as a fable of redemption or rebirth, is accurately titled. "One always hopes that a new place will inspire change—in one's life," Levin says tentatively when he arrives in Cascadia. Later, "he felt like a man entering a new life and entered." At the height of his affair with Pauline Gilley, she says, "Oh, my darling, we must do something with our lives." When he despairs of her, he thinks of her as "the small town lady who talked of a new life but had been consistently afraid of it." Finally determined, she tells Levin: "I want a better life. I want it with you."

The action of the novel is Levin's development into a kind of saint. To the outward eye, he is a typical *schlemiel*: He steps into cow pies, teaches with his fly open, makes the ruinous remark every time. But in truth he is a holy *schlemiel*, God's innocent, a Fool in Christ. Levin attains to sanctity (and I think that this represents a considerable advance for Malamud) not through denying and mortifying the flesh, like the anchorite Frank Alpine in *The Assistant,*

442

but through indulging the flesh, and his adultery is a holy adultery.

It begins in lust, and after his first adventure with Pauline in the forest, Levin thinks vulgarly: "his first married woman, sex uncomplicated in a bed of leaves, short hours, good pay." The affair progresses, and Levin suddenly realizes: "The truth is I love Pauline Gilley." It then goes beyond love, or beyond what Levin understands as love, to the sacrificial acceptance of responsibility. Feeling his love gone, he nevertheless accepts the burden of Pauline and her children. "Why take that load on yourself?" Pauline's husband Gerald challenges, itemizing the disadvantages, and Levin answers, in the true voice of a Malamud saint: "Because I can, you son of a bitch." It is a classic progress from *eros,* fleshly love, to *agape,* the spiritual love of one of God's creatures for another.

Malamud's vision of life in the novel redeems its ugliness and nastiness with humor, and redeems the humor with charity. Cascadia College is a dreadful place, narrow and mean, but it is also a terribly funny place where "there are no geniuses around to make you uncomfortable," fly-casting is taught for credit, and a textbook containing Hemingway's story "Ten Indians" is banned on the pretext that it might offend, "as degrading the American Indians." Gerald Gilley is a repulsive careerist, a golf-mad professor who is compiling a picture-book of American literature, but he is a comic masterpiece of a careerist, and Levin's ultimate understanding is that he too is a suffering fellow human, and he feels compassion for him.

Where the sex scenes in Malamud's earlier books were always interrupted at their climax, constituting a prolonged tease of the reader, or else were consummated under the aegis of death, producing an unlovely *liebestod* effect, here (although traces of the old bad habits remain) sex is funny, earthy and sometimes beautiful. Before becoming involved with Pauline, Levin has had: an encounter with a waitress in a barn, ruined at the dramatic moment when a disappointed rival steals their clothes; a wrestle with an unmarried colleague on the floor of his office, broken off by Levin out of an obscure compassion; and a gay weekend with Nadalee, a student, resulting in her efforts to get her class grade raised from a C to a B.

His involvement with Pauline is hardly more glamorous:

he is disturbed by her flat chest; at one point in the affair he has excruciating muscle spasms in bed with her; at another point she is temporarily frigid, and he thinks bitterly, "Now we have truly come to adultery." At the novel's end, in one of the most wonderfully embarrassing scenes in modern fiction, Gerald warns Levin of Pauline's constipation and menstrual irregularities. Funny, awful, it nevertheless is love, and beauty, and value.

Levin's past, when it is finally confessed to Pauline, seems unnecessarily melodramatic: his father a thief, "Harry the Goniff"; his mother insane and a suicide; himself a gutter alcoholic. Levin's future, as we can picture it at the end of the novel, is less extreme: Pauline will develop breasts in pregnancy; Levin, with a new identity, will again have a first name; their life together will be responsible, hard-working and devoted. If this is not joy, the top-gallant delight Father Mapple's sermon promises the righteous in *Moby Dick,* it is a happy ending nevertheless, and perhaps as much as our shabby modern world can promise anyone.

Malamud's technical mastery is impressive. His apparently episodic novel is tightly woven, mostly by means of foreshadowing. When the chairman of the department warns Levin against dating students or prowling among faculty wives, the weekend with Nadalee and the affair with Pauline are implicit in his warning, as though created by it ("Nay, I had not known sin, but by the law," says St. Paul, "for I had not known lust, except the law had said, Thou shalt not covet"). When Levin arrives in Cascadia, the Gilleys take him to their house for dinner, and Pauline spills the tuna fish casserole in his lap; when he has changed into a fresh pair of pants, the little boy wets on them. It is an uproarious scene, and announces Levin as the book's *schlemiel,* but it is also the annunciation of his future role as husband and father, victim and protector, of the woman and child who pour their love in his lap.

Some of *A New Life* is scandalously funny. C. D. Fabrikant, the department's scholar, is rarely seen except on horseback, and gallops off by way of punctuating his remarks. Levin first meets the dean carrying a bag of grapefruit, and, as in an old silent movie, while they talk they scramble for the grapefruit after the dean has walked into a telephone pole, then scramble again when Levin walks into a tree. Like that of Malamud's best stories in *The Magic Barrel,* the humor is wild and surrealistic. The cold bare trip back to town with the waitress cursing Levin is nightmarish comedy.

At the height of his emotional disturbance, Levin walks into a bar, orders "Love," and when the bartender goes in search of the bottle, madly flees. When Levin goes to confront the wronged husband in his hotel room, Gerald greets him earnestly with: "Pardon the small room." In the terrible period when Levin has bravely given up Pauline, and is tormented by erotic dreams, Malamud writes:

"Amid such pleasures Mrs. Beaty's white cat fell in love with him, laying a broken-feathered bird at his door, fat headless robin. He asked the landlady to keep the cat out of the house but pussy in love was faithful, finding more ways in than he could block off, depositing another bloody-breasted bird. 'Eat my heart,' he cried and kicked the beast down the stairs. Ascending on three legs she delivered a mangled rat, then went into heat, her raucous cries sounding through the house."

Malamud's expressionist device, which he shares with several of the best writers of our time, is writing dreams, fantasies and even similes as though they were literal realities. When he reads a theme of Nadalee's about swimming naked, "Though Levin's legs cramped after a too hasty immersion in cold water, he jumped in after her and spent most of the night swimming with Nadalee."

Malamud's work has some of the bitter comedy of Yiddish literature, some of the preoccupation with sin and redemption of Russian literature. It particularly resembles the work of that remarkable Soviet-Jewish writer, Isaac Babel, who combines both traditions, and combines them *within* the current of modern European literature. *A New Life,* in its progress from affair to bondage, may remind readers of *A Farewell to Arms,* but Malamud faces up to problems that Hemingway kills Catherine to evade. It has some of the grubby comedy of the British Angries, the compassion of Salinger, the moral earnestness of George P. Elliott. Yet this novel, like Malamud's work generally, remains unique, in its totality unlike the work of anyone else.

Certainly there are flaws. *A New Life* is too slow getting
started, and the book is half over before its action really
begins. There are infelicities of style and syntax, although
fewer than in the earlier books, and occasional weaknesses
of diction, as when Malamud gets fancy and writes "dew"
for "tears." Some of the plot, in which Levin becomes a
candidate for chairman of the department and meets espionage with counter-espionage, is absurd, although Malamud saves himself at the worst point by writing a human
and moving confrontation scene between Levin and the
woman colleague who has just gone through his files.

In progressing from *The Natural* to *The Assistant* to
A New Life, Malamud has achieved a new mature acceptance. Pauline is the Iris of *The Natural,* no longer
scorned; Levin rakes leaves with the frenzy of Frank Alpine, but he has an insight into his nature and destiny
that Frank never achieves. In a sense, Malamud has moved
from the story of Samson, punished for the misuse of his
powers, to Job, suffering because chosen to suffer, to Jesus,
suffering voluntarily to redeem. If Malamud continues to
be able to find modern plots to embody his powerful
redemptive themes, I know no limit to what he can accomplish.

Alberto Moravia: Eros and Existence
BY R. W. B. LEWIS

"So as to have a new life": was what she wanted
to answer; but she had not the courage. That remote reason of hers, now that she saw nothing was
changed except her surrendered body, appeared to
her ridiculous and unworthy.

MORAVIA, *The Time of Indifference*

THE SEXUAL ASPECT

Alberto Moravia is the most precocious and among the
most gifted and prolific of the novelists now referred to
by younger Italians as the second generation. Italian intellectuals in their twenties have taken to calling themselves the third generation (a periodical bearing that name
was even founded to promote the notion[1]); and they are
now lumping together, as their elders if not betters, all
those novelists whose art was formed out of the experience
of the Fascist era: Silone, Moravia, Elio Vittorini, Cesare
Pavese, Vitaliano Brancati, Carlo Levi, Mario Soldati, and
a number of others. Moravia belongs properly with this
group and is probably its leading practitioner of the craft
of fiction. But beyond that, he is perhaps the most emphatic annalist anywhere of one widely featured explanation of life.

The explanation seems to have come to him, all rounded
and complete, at the moment he first became aware of
his own literary talent, and this was a very early moment indeed. He has complained with apparent seriousness
that he was able to write nothing from his ninth to his
seventeenth years; but his first and perhaps best novel,

The Time of Indifference, was written before he was eighteen (though not published until 1928, when he reached his majority), and his first story—"Tired Courtesan"—came out in the Italian journal *Novecento* in 1927, when he was twenty years old. "Tired Courtesan" was published in French, in line with the magazine's policy of supporting a pan-European culture by offering its wares in any of the major languages. A good deal of Moravia was announced in the subject and tone of the title itself, and in the sophisticated trickery of the French translation. The substance of the tale—a murky assignation during an illicit affair that both parties, for diverse financial reasons, are anxious to terminate—introduced much of what has ever since been Moravia's controlling image of experience.

It is an image of the world in its sexual aspect: or at least of that part of the world that, according to Moravia, is touched and accounted for by the sexual aspect. To say merely that Moravia's fiction is erotic is a truism that can stifle rather than enlarge our sense of his achievement: like saying, with a final simplicity, that Dante's poetry is religious. For Moravia's fiction provides a major treatment of a minor but honorable and suggestive view of things: the sexual view, the view of human relations and of everything that arises in or impinges upon human relations as beginning and ending in the sexual encounter. Everything other than sex is, in the stories of Moravia, an extension of sex; or perhaps better, everything other than sex is sooner or later converted into it. Moravia, in fact, is a minor master of the strategy of conversion in literature: that is, of *artistic* conversion, of the transformation of one set of values into another. The typical Moravian narrative shows us, not the precise and detailed moment of the sexual encounter (in this respect, there is less "sex" in Moravia than in a good many other modern writers; much of the time the "sex" remains hidden, like the divinity in certain religious poems), but the full amount of life that culminates in the sexual encounter or is an observable deflection from it. And the purpose behind Moravia's strategy is strikingly similar to that of the other novelists we are considering. If Moravia's encounters are sexual rather than political, as in Silone, or religious, as in Greene, the aim is identical—to recover a more faithful image of man at a time when that image has been singularly deformed and betrayed. Measured against that purpose. Moravia's achievement is impressive but partial.

"The use of man as a means and not as an end," Moravia has insisted, "is the root of all evil." An ancient and recently urgent European tradition echoes in the remark; and in the case of Moravia, the urgency arose from the Fascist habit of reversing the formula. It was chiefly because fascism was the enemy of man that it was also the enemy of art. Moravia had to discover, as Silone rapidly discovered, that human reality in art was heresy in the Fascist view. *The Time of Indifference* was a notable public success, but its combination of clinical honesty and lyrical sadness went so against the official vulgar heartiness sponsored by the Italian government that an order was issued forbidding the mention of the author's name in any newspaper or magazine. His next novel, *Mistaken Ambitions* (1935), consequently went unreviewed, and Moravia was forced, like Silone, to adopt a pen name, "Pseudo," for articles, and the mild evasion of "Alberto Moravia" for stories (the author's real name is Alberto Pincherle-Moravia). Moravia traveled a good deal during the thirties—to Mexico, China and the United States.[2] In the same period he abandoned realism for more indirect and furtive pictures of the contemporary scene. Several of his literary colleagues were driven by the political climate of the day into the same area of the fantastic and the hermetic, and not always to their disadvantage;[3] but Moravia's surrealistic and satirical writings in the thirties (*L'Epidemia,* for example) do not, in my opinion, show him at his best.

Moravia's sufferings under Mussolini were not abnormal, nor was his early life unduly adventurous; what was abnormal was Moravia's creative sensitivity. He was born in Rome in 1907, and much of his childhood was colored by a painful bone disease that required a prolonged stay in a sanitarium and the use first of crutches and later of a cane. He still walks with discomfort; but his illness was to serve him by recompense, and in a manner not uncommon in the history of literature, both as stimulus and as sheer material for his fiction: *Sick Boy's Winter* (1930) was a brilliant early fruit of the days at the Istituto Codavilla in Cortina. His worst experience during the war came toward the end of it, when he tried to flee southward from Rome to Allied-occupied Naples, in 1943, and got stuck en route. He spent nine months of hideous boredom, hiding out with his wife and some shepherds in a kind of covered pigsty, silent, inactive, watching the endless rain descend (as he has said) "like a liquid wall and always the same." This episode, too, was to be fruitful. Out of the discomfort and the boredom, Moravia, fourteen years later, fashioned one of his solidest novels: *Two Women,* a meticulous account of the winter he still vividly remembered.

He had written *The Fancy Dress Party,* a curious short novel, in 1941, and the eloquent *Agostino* three years later; but his uninterruptedly fertile period began with the arrival of spring and the Allied armies in 1944. *The Woman of Rome* followed in 1947; *Luca* (another short novel, coupled with *Agostino* as *Two Adolescents* in English) in 1948; *Conjugal Love* in 1949, *The Conformist* in 1950, and *A Ghost at Noon* in 1954. It is in these works (along with *Two Women*) that Moravia's image of human nature and human experience—though present, as I have said, from the beginning—assumed its full and unmistakably Moravian shape.

THE STRATEGY OF CONVERSION

Perhaps the element most often vitalized by the sexual impulse, in Moravia's treatment of it, is money—the element closest indeed to sex in the center of Moravia's vision of human affairs. Moravia's characters are relentlessly grasping; but they or their observers intermittently realize that it is not the acquisitive but the sexual instinct that grasps after satisfaction. One of *Racconti Romani,*[4] for example, shows us a real-estate agent with designs upon a beautiful and aristocratic young widow, some of whose property he has been asked to sell. His hopes fade as he discovers that the woman derives her sexual gratification not from men but from money—from the very fantasy of making money, from demanding many times more money for the property than she can possibly expect to get. The lines cross skillfully: the widow's interviews with prospective buyers are forms of flirtation aimed at increasing the price in the pursuit of an essentially nonfinancial pleasure. The agent gives up. "I had been the agent in a business affair, but now she had made me become the agent in a sordid love affair. Before I knew what I was doing, I burst out, 'Princess, I am a broker, not a pimp'; and red in the face, I hurried away."

The child Agostino (in the novella bearing his name), reveals only his innocence when he wonders—gazing at a country villa turned into a brothel—"what the relation was between money, which usually served to acquire well-defined objects of measurable quantity, and caresses, nudity, female flesh." A connection is readily intuited by the initiated. Adriana, the woman of Rome, remembers her surprising willingness to accept money the first time it is offered her—and by a man she dislikes, at a moment she believes herself "engaged" (in the fine free Italian meaning of the word) to someone else:

> The feeling I experienced at the moment bewildered me . . . a feeling of complicity and sensual conspiracy such as none of his caresses in the restaurant bedroom had been able to arouse in me. It was a feeling of inevitable subjection. . . . I knew, of course, that I ought to refuse the money; but at the same time I wanted to accept it. And not so much from greed, as from the new kind of pleasure which his offering had afforded me.

The young woman who narrates "The English Officer" (1946) recalls, like Adriana, the "spontaneity" and "attitude of surrender" with which she took the first money offered her for going to bed with an Allied soldier.

Moravia's repertoire is not a large one; in fact, he has insisted that it must not be. "I never trust a writer who can say too many things," he has told a *New Yorker* interviewer. "By that I mean a writer who has too many tunes to play. One good tune is enough. Good writers are monotonous, like good composers. Their truth is self-repeating. They keep rewriting the same book. That is to say, they keep trying to perfect their expression of the one problem they were born to understand."[5]

The political dimension of life yields not much less easily than does the economic. Fascism and underground anti-Fascist activities enter *The Woman of Rome* as a shadowy other world; they are made to seem an unreal intrusion—

via the insubstantial character of Mino—into the reality
of the heroine's sexual history. In an essay on communism
and the West (1954), Moravia alluded resentfully to the
recent "politicization" (his word) of life; and he has attempted, in his own writings, to reverse that tendency.
"Moravia distrusts politics," his friend and colleague Paolo
Milano has said about him; "and he has a qualified indifference towards history—individual men interest him,
not crowded events."[6] Moravia's distrust leads, in his fiction, to the conversion, or attempted conversion, of the
political into the sexual: an effort which compares interestingly to that of Ignazio Silone, who has sought to transform the political into the charitable, out of an even more
radical distrust of the former.

Moravia's attempt is projected with entertaining directness in "Bitter Honeymoon" (1951), in which a young
couple, starting on their honeymoon, run into one of the
bride's political colleagues, a fellow worker in "the Party."
The husband, Giacomo, is (he says) not interested in politics, though he is vitally interested in consummating the
marriage after a failure to do so the night before. The
Communist intruder, Livio, argues that everything has its
political implications: "How could it be otherwise? Politics
is everything." Simona, the wife, wobbles between the two
men in a state of uncertain potentiality; she had failed
to report her marriage to the Party, but she had also
resisted her husband's advances. Listening to the two comrades talking together, Giacomo suspects gloomily that
"comrade" may represent a more intimate relation than
"lover." But love conquers all, or nearly so; at least, the
human element seems vindicated; and the story ends with
the first instant of consummation. In *The Conformist*, an
admirably ambitious but on the whole unsuccessful novel,
Moravia attempts nothing less than a philosophical demonstration in narrative of the sexual origins of political
commitment—the Fascist temperament as rooted in a
youthful homosexual trauma. And in his *Portrait of
Machiavelli* (1950), Moravia intimates that the peculiar
quality of Machiavelli's political passion was the consequence of sexual frustration, or the consequence at least
of an utter moral exhaustion that Moravia perceives in
Machiavelli's cold comedy of seduction, *Mandragola,* and

which he defines by means of a close comparison with
the Marquis de Sade.

Friendship, to judge from Moravia's fiction, is determined and measured by a man's sexual conduct toward
his friend's wife or mistress: several rather amiable items
from the *Racconti Romani* underline this criterion. Family relations are shaped in the same manner. The theme
of *Agostino* is examined in the context of the predominantly, almost overtly sexual relation between a young
mother and her child. An awareness of that relation is
the beginning of Agostino's transition to manhood, of the
decline of his innocence and the toughening of his heart:
when, secretly watching his mother undress, he says to
himself—with an attitude that "seemed to him almost
scientific but which in fact owed its false objectivity to
the cruelty of sentiment which inspired it"—"She is a
woman . . . nothing but a woman." In *The Time of
Indifference*, the relations between mother and daughter,
mother and son, and sister and brother are elaborately
defined by the sexual aspect: as incarnate in the businessman, Leo, who moves in the novel from an affair with
the mother to an affair with the daughter, while the brother
looks on, alternating between a dreary effort to feel morally indignant over his family's behavior and the thought
that he might turn his sister's quasi-incestuous degradation to his own account by borrowing money from her
new lover. *"L'Architetto"* (1935) is a lighter and less
contorted variation on this same singular design. And when
Moravia wrote his first original play (he had already
dramatized his short novel *The Fancy Dress Party*), he
was drawn quite naturally to the tale of Beatrice Cenci
and her repulsive father—"since," as he has remarked,
"the relations between father and daughter . . . lend themselves to a psychological interpretation very close to the
modern sensibility, and have indeed an almost existentialist
flavor."

These illustrations are typical. These are the inhabitants
and these the characteristic involvements in the somewhat
lopsided Moravian universe. It is to be noted that there
is no historical or religious or mythological dimension to
this universe, either pure or converted; this is one of the
many ways in which Moravia should be differentiated from
D. H. Lawrence, who may also be said to have described

the world in its sexual aspect, but with a sense of incipient force and with a rich and tender carelessness altogether distinct from the meticulously ordered proceedings of Alberto Moravia. Nothing, for example, could be more alien to Moravia than Lawrence's own achievement of deep-flowing artistic conversion in *The Man Who Died,* in which the crucified but not wholly dead Christ is restored to life by the sexual devotion of a priestess of Isis. The religious impulse is thus converted into the erotic impulse in a manner that converts near death into a *vita nuova.* Moravia's view of the mythic as well of life in general and of family relations was plainly indicated in the comment introducing his second novel, *Mistaken Ambitions,* in 1935. "In *The Time of Indifference,*" he wrote, "the author tried to create tragedy based on traditional motives —those, so to say, which grow out of the tensions and disequilibria of a badly tangled family situation: those for example of Aeschylus in the *Oresteia,* or of Shakespeare in *Hamlet.*"[7] It should be added, in fairness, that Moravia has recently satirized his earlier attitude by including, in *A Ghost at Noon,* a preposterous interpretation of the *Odyssey* as a bleak story of sexual incompatibility—a view of that spacious poem that Moravia's hero-narrator is permitted violently to reject.

But the literary allusions are none the less significant: for perhaps the major tactic within Moravia's broad strategy of conversion—of transforming a familiar moral note into an essentially sexual note—is to invoke the literary echo, in a partly joking and partly jaundiced manner. He is quoted as relating the scene in *The Time of Indifference* in which Leo and Carla embrace behind the curtains, their guilty pleasure heightened by peeking out at the betrayed but unsuspecting mother, to the famous "curtain scene" in *Hamlet;* and it may be, as Daniel Aaron has suggested,[8] that the seduction of Leda by the barber in *Conjugal Love* wryly re-enacts, and willfully debases, the more ancient seduction of Leda by the god as swan. In *The Time of Indifference* again, there is a manifest echo—within the context of an affair gone stale before it has started—of one of the best-known and most poignant soliloquies in Italian literature. It is the classic *addio monti* passage in chapter eight of Manzoni's *I Promessi Sposi,* the farewell of chaste Lucia to her homeland and her lover: "Farewell mountains springing from the waters and rising to the sky . . . farewell house that was still not hers. . . ." This turns up in *The Time of Indifference,* echoed by Carla's soliloquy as she hastens through the inevitable rain toward her mother's lover: "Farewell streets, farewell deserted quarters," and so on. The transformation implicit in the echo depends crucially upon the purity, the firm moral character of the original.

THE TRAGICOMEDY OF EXISTENCE

All of this brings us to a central quality, or combination of qualities, in Moravia's fiction, a recognition of which must modify our first impression of frankness and realism. I mean its literary and especially its theatrical quality, and its pervasive semicomic mood.

Moravia's work is to some extent impressively realistic, and it has an exceptional vividness of presentation. His words at their best provide instantaneous openings on to the actions they describe; persons and things are observed with a camera-eye exactness, tinged all the while with an elusive wistfulness; but the style rarely *rises,* for there seems to be nothing, as it were, for the style to rise to— the here-and-now, sharply delineated and sadly contemplated, is everything. But his scenes stay fixed in our minds, and our recollection is that we have seen them, not read them; we recall people and places, not words and pages. This is to say, precisely, that his writing is theatrical— and theatrical, it should be insisted, rather than dramatic. Italians for twenty years have been speaking of "the Rome of Moravia"—a crowded, hurried, modernized, and mechanized Rome, full of brief cases and cocktails and very different from the Rome of somewhat older Italian literature; for example, the poetic, heroic, archeological Rome of D'Annunzio.[9] It is true that Moravia has accomplished one of the great feats of the artist in narrative; he has created a world, and he calls it Rome. But Giuseppe Borgese was probably right when, reviewing *The Time of Indifference* in 1929, he contended against the claim for Moravia of sociological accuracy in his portrait of Rome: "There is not much Rome here . . . the scene is made up of lights and draperies, as in certain contemporary *mises en scénes.*"

When Moravia won the Marzotto award for fiction in 1954, he was introduced, aptly enough, as "the last Goldonian in Italy." The reference was to the eighteenth century Venetian playwright, author of several scores of comedies of intrigue and manners. Moravia works assiduously in the whole tradition of Italian culture; Boccaccio, Machiavelli, Ariosto, Manzoni, and many others are very notably reflected in his writing, and he is, in fact, one of the most incorrigibly *literary* novelists of his generation; but he is perhaps closest to Goldoni, and reading Moravia's stories we come upon many signs of his affection. The rhythmic comings and goings, the startling confrontations, the heated dinner conversations, the mistaken identities, the cross-purposes, the deceits, the peepings, the gifts or billets-doux received and mislaid and inopportunely discovered: these are what move the plot in a narrative by Moravia, and they are the devices of conventional farce.

Above all, the device of the accidental witness to the intimate or even the shameful act. The use of it is endless: Agostino, lurking outside the window of a country brothel, peering in at a prostitute and her customer; Marcello, in *The Conformist,* returned unexpectedly to his Paris apartment, hiding in the dark to watch a Lesbian make overtures to his wife; the protagonist of *Conjugal Love* happening, during an evening stroll, upon an adulterous interchange between his wife and the local barber—and a host of other such occasions. One sign of the interesting development represented by Moravia's novel, *A Ghost at Noon,* is—along with the implicit satire it contains of Moravia's own earlier attitude to myth, as mentioned above—the way the hidden-witness motif is turned back on itself. The husband in *A Ghost at Noon* finds himself on one occasion seated next to his wife, badly rattled by her obdurate attitude toward him and furtively watching the fall of her *négligé.* "Suddenly . . . I told myself that this was what I had come to at last: to look at my wife's nakedness in hiding, with the pleasure of forbidden things, like a boy who peeps through a crack in the cabin of a beach resort." That reflection, typical of *A Ghost at Noon,* suggests a deepened moral estimate of the erotic theatricality with which Moravia has for long busied himself. But for much of his earlier work, the device of the secret observer was a valid necessity. It is, to be sure, a classic motif of pornographic literature as well as of farce; but in Moravia, it is primarily a piece of theatrical mechanics, not lingered over for its own sake but essential to the progress of the action. It is the turning point or even the climax. For the very core of Moravia's fiction *is* theatrical. He begins not on a clearly felt literal level, nor even on the so-called symbolic level; he begins on a theatrical level, with the dramatis personae poised toward each other in postures of skilled artifice; and the moral content follows from there. His fiction, that is, moves under the compulsive effort of both author and character to squeeze genuine sentiment out of traditional stage business.

Now genuine sentiment, in these stories, is the first dependable mark of being alive. In fact, given the human condition reflected by Moravia, it is precisely a sentiment *about* being alive; the Moravian character suffers from the need attributed by Moravia to Machiavelli—the need "to feel himself alive."[10] What is gradually revealed to us as Moravia's pervasive theme, a theme even more pervasive than sex and in fact served by the erotic theme, is nothing else than the sensation of existence. This is the end to which Moravia's fiction may be seen to be pressing; and it is to this that the sexual encounter regularly and treacherously seems to promise the clue.[11] As a consequence of his theme, Moravia's stories are more ridden by anxiety than the Goldonian comedies they draw upon; the stake is so much more important. Goldoni's work, too, had its measure of realism, along with a certain hardness of tone; Goldoni lacked the warm romantic humor, say, of Goldsmith or the rational gaiety of Beaumarchais. But his comedies were firm in outline and unstrained in manner; they centered on the complicated steps of the intrigue in question, and intrigue could provide Goldoni with a set pattern of action in which he might take a detached, if sometimes uncharitable, delight. But despite the morbid amusement they may contain, Moravia's tragicomedies of intrigue are (like *Mandragola*) darker and more desperate; for Moravia focuses not upon the intrigue but—through the intrigue—upon the encounter the intrigue was to bring about, and upon the reward the encounter was to assure; and comedy dissipates in panic as the outcome of the adventure seems ever more dubious.

Or perhaps we should say that only the laughter dissipates: the comic mood, however discolored, remains. Traditional comedy, from the Greek stage onward, has defined a particular rhythm of experience that concludes with the unmasking of impostors and the celebration of marriage. Impostors are for the most part unmasked in the fiction of Moravia, but anything like a marriage is just what dismally fails to take place. That is why his stories may more properly be called tragicomedies; and why, in this respect, they are like many of the narratives of Henry James (a writer with whom Moravia might not otherwise be easily associated)—in particular, like *The Ambassadors,* where the imposthume represented by the adultery of Chad Newsome and Mme. de Vionnet is exposed, but where the potential marriage between Strether and Miss Gostrey is fastidiously renounced. The tone of that novel is explicitly stated at the moment of renunciation: "She sighed it at last all tragically, all comically away." With a shift in pronoun, the sentence could conclude Moravia's *Conjugal Love.*

James was congenitally interested in the question of living. Moravia has been obsessed with a more radical mystery—the mystery of existence itself, the fundamental enigma that, I venture to say, has been the chief concern of Moravia's literary generation, both in Italy and elsewhere: as this book will, I trust, sufficiently testify. What the concern amounts to in Moravia's case may best be suggested by tracing through his stories the process by which he arrived at it; as the sexual intention gradually invades the whole of observable life only to pause before the threshold of the source of life itself. I have rehearsed the "sexualization" of money, politics, friendship, and family relations; to these may be added the moral virtues —courage, honor, good will, kindness, truthfulness, self-respect, all of them tested and given their meaning in sexual terms. And even beyond those, the trivial rituals of the daily round: dressing and undressing, shaving, bathing, eating and drinking, the trip to the seashore, the afternoon walk, the leisurely times in the neighborhood cafe. The same inclination energizes them all, the same atmosphere surrounds them. But here and there we detect a deepening of penetration to the more elementary conditions of human survival. Health and sickness, for example:

we can cite the rapidly sketched *"Infermiera" (Racconti Romani)*, in which the gardener of a Roman villa fails in the courtship of his patron's nurse because the latter was more attracted by sickness than by health. Her taste was "to make love with sick people; but I, unhappily, was healthy, and so there was absolutely no hope for me." Better than that, and one of Moravia's finest novellas, is *Sick Boy's Winter*, the whole of which takes place in a sanitarium, with the narrative prose fairly breathing the sterilized air of its corridors. Here, the progress of the young hero's convalescence is entirely implicated in the development and expression of his sexual pride; he seduces a wan little English girl, a fellow patient, and both he and his mute pitiful victim suffer nearly fatal relapses. In *Luca*, adolescent sexuality leads through a grave illness to the longing for death, and then onward to partial recovery and the meager promise of a new life.

Dealing as he does so persistently with the sexual element, Moravia could scarcely help sounding the note already familiar in modern literature: the ambiguous relation between sex and death; and he has not failed to offer his own erotic variation on the grand pattern of death and rebirth—for instance, the combination of murder, suicide, and impending childbirth that turgidly concludes *The Woman of Rome*. But life and death are stripped by Moravia to their innermost essence. They are very simply existence and nonexistence. They are the plus and minus of radical vitality, as affected by sexual action. In the fiction of Moravia, we have a recurring picture of Eros moving between being and nonbeing. It is this that distinguishes the fiction once and for all from pornography; for the incessant peepings and pryings in Moravia's stories are, beyond pornography and even beyond farce, symptoms of an insatiable desire to catch a glimpse of the secret reality of human beings—their primary existence, what is hidden or misrepresented by public morality, conventions and clothing. They are symptoms, in short, of a hectic and self-conscious and yet ambiguous romanticism; they are symptomatic, too, of an author whose characters, as inveterate spies, are surrogates for their creator, whose work may be called the most thoroughgoing job of private espionage in modern fiction. But again, a distinction must be pressed; for as to Moravia's anatomical concern, his repeated and detailed descriptions of the naked body, what this suggests, as more than one critic has asserted, is not a salacious interest in nudity but an aptitude for still-life painting. The Italian phrase for still-life, more telling than ours, is *natura morta;* and it is exactly Moravia's ambition and that of his principal characters to transform *natura morta* into *natura viva.*

The ambition offers a peculiar challenge to Moravia's artistic talent, for existence, as it seems to be conceived in the Moravian ethic, is anything but a dramatic subject. The ethic itself contains few seeds of the dramatic; it is personal and nonphilosophical in its nature; it is a feeling, rather than a theory; a mood and a tone, rather than a discourse. We could perhaps say that it is a fragment of existentialism that evaporates at the critical moments; for while Moravia's characters, like those in certain of the writings of Sartre and Camus, reach for wholeness and identity *through* action (through cautiously staged sexual action, in the case of Moravia), they almost always fail.[12] Carla, the heroine of *The Time of Indifference,* enters the affair with Leo out of muddled desire for a "new life": a phrase that, in typical Moravian fashion, sings ironically in Italian with its flattened reminder of Dante's *Vita Nuova,* an account of spiritual rebirth through ennobling love. And Carla fails so abysmally that she cannot answer her brother Michele when he asks her why she had behaved so. Life, as she had anticipated it, was too scanty a thing to have striven for. " 'So as to have a new life': was what she wanted to answer; but she had not the courage. That remote reason of hers, now that she saw nothing was changed except her surrendered body, appeared to her ridiculous and unworthy." Michele and his sister are the first in Moravia's long catalogue of failures: mostly masculine failures, be it noted in passing, for Moravia's women are occasionally endowed with a sort of hulking secret, just as they are given personal names (Leda, Adriana, etc.) more consistently than are the men. Moravia's heroes are apt to be small, indistinct, ill-favored, and hesitant; and there is a portion of verisimilitude here that I will not labor, both in the portrayal of Italian women and men and in the exposure everywhere on the chosen scene of the sexual preoccupation. But what the men do acquire is the consolation of a rueful humor, a

still faintly comic reflection of *This is the way things are;*
how foolish, ultimately, is the human posture and the
human destiny. For the price of failure is to be condemned to a second-class existence, a form of nonexistence, something that is to be suffered rather than enacted.
Moravia's stories are therefore, and by design, pathetic
rather than dramatic; pathos is the middle and the end
of his characteristic narrative.

In *Luca,* a little sum of existence is actually retrieved:
enough to give this excellent short novel a rarely positive
and almost (but not quite) a hopeful quality. Luca, an
adolescent of good family, undergoes a nervous breakdown and is brought back from the edge of nonexistence
by a robust woman who nurses him, bathes him, and finally makes love to him; but his recovery is isolated and
private, almost metaphysical; it relates him to existing
things qua existing, but in no sense does it relate him to
humanity. The suggestion of a Camus or a Silone, that
the answer to the sense of nonexistence is companionship
and compassion, has yet to appear in the pages of
Moravia. Hence the dispirited, prematurely exhausted
quality that so often pervades these pages: the absence,
that is, of creative tension. Such tension as his fiction
does manage to generate is elaborately exemplified in *The
Woman of Rome,* in the contrast between the natural,
inframoral bias toward life of Adriana, the Roman prostitute, and the bias toward death of her succession of lovers.

Adriana has a simple capacity for existence; and it is
that capacity—rather than any rage to live—that is challenged, bruised, and seduced, but never destroyed in the
course of her recorded experiences. For along with a talent
for existence, Adriana has a distinct taste for the deathly.
Her lovers are death symbols, symbols of anti-existence,
recognizable variations on deadliness: and the drama they
engage her in is an antic, sensual, and highly traditional
danse macabre. The men in her life cavort ominously before her, beckoning and grinning: Astarita, the police
administrator, who looks like a death's-head and who
speaks of himself as a "garbage-can for rubbish" and
curses the day he was born; Sonzogno, the murderer, in
whose embrace Adriana "felt a pleasure made sinister and
atrocious by fear [so that] I could not restrain a long wail-
ing cry in the dark, as if the final clasp had been the clasp

of death, not of love, and my cry was life departing from me"; Mino, the hapless revolutionist, who is faithless to his calling and who tells Adriana in bed that he has "died —just died. Died forever." For her part, on her side of the bed, Adriana acknowledges the deeply seductive appeal of nothingness in a meditation of singularly erotic detail:

> I began to think about the sea again and was over-
> come by the longing to drown myself. I imagined it
> would only be a moment's suffering, and then my life-
> less body would float from wave to wave beneath
> the sun for ages. The gulls would peck my eyes, the
> sun would burn my breast and belly, the fish would
> gnaw my back. At last I would sink to the bottom,
> would be dragged head downwards towards some icy
> blue current that would carry me along the seabed
> for months and years among submarine rocks, fish
> and seaweed, and floods of limpid salt water would
> wash my forehead, my breast and my belly, my legs,
> slowly wearing away my flesh, smoothing and refin-
> ing me continually. And at last some wave would cast
> me up on some shore, nothing but a handful of
> fragile, white bones . . . and perhaps someone without
> noticing it would walk on my bones and crush them
> to white powder. With these sad, voluptuous thoughts,
> I fell asleep.

But Adriana survives the self-annihilating impulse of her lovers; and while Mino commits suicide and Astarita and Sonzogno deliberately get themselves killed, Adriana's tribute is the only pregnancy I can recall in Moravia's fiction.

THE SUPREMACY OF SADNESS

The Woman of Rome is, on balance, a distinguished piece of fiction; but it is distinguished, I suggest, in the terms proposed above, as an image of Eros moving be- tween being and nonbeing. To speak of its affinities with French realism, as some readers have done, or to identify it as an Italian *Moll Flanders,* is to miss its real quality by extracting the subject matter from the texture. The

tone of Daniel Defoe and the world it informs (hard, dry,
virile, and epiphenomenal) have almost nothing in common
with the lyrical reflectiveness, the muffled nostalgia, that
modify the happenings in *The Woman of Rome,* or any
other work by Alberto Moravia. That tone is most effectively rendered, perhaps, in *Conjugal Love;* over which
we may briefly linger by way of conclusion, since it seems
to me his most elegantly wrought romance of existence.

Conjugal Love has a kind of subdued perfection; and
it illustrates memorably Moravia's personal sense of the
poignant foolishness of human aspiration and illusion. It
tends, too, to confirm the suspicion aroused by *Agostino*
and *Luca* that Moravia is usually happier with the short
novel (and the short story) than with the novel proper;
his resources and his themes appear to lack the variety
and the inward momentum that novels require. *Conjugal
Love* seems aware of these limitations, and never seeks
to extend itself. The husband's narration gives the impression of some tidy person leafing through his private scrap-
book. For what happens in the book—more important
than its plot, which is a reshuffle of Moravia's theatrical
stock in trade—is the creation through the arts of narrative of a feeling or a mood: the sense of existence as
suffering.

The story introduces us to a married couple of independent means, enjoying the graceful leisure of a Tuscan
villa. The wife, Leda, is a fastidious and affectionate person, marked however by an observably ambivalent attitude
—a combination of attraction and disgust—toward the
sordid and ugly in human experience. The husband is
marked by the sort of taste, intelligence, and fussy kindness
—all genuine, but when taken together, pathetically inadequate—that characterized Lambert Strether, whose
unlucky fate it was also, in James's *The Ambassadors,* to
stumble upon an adultery that his very kindness and taste
had prevented him from guessing at. Like Strether, the
husband is a man of mild literary pretensions; and when
we meet him, he is settling down to the composition of a
story—a small work of art that will be called, of course,
Conjugal Love. Creative power and sexual power are established in the familiar but always fertile tension of
similarity and hostility: the husband's brief fit of artistic
energy demands from him a marital abstinence, as his

entire fund of potency is given over to his writing. We
are not left in doubt over the outcome, for the tone from
the beginning has reduced drama to pathos; and we forsee,
without the need for bracing, the evening when the husband will discover at once his wife's infidelity and his own
irrevocable failure as a novelist. But the moral of the book
—and perhaps it is the moral of Moravia's fiction in
general—has been reached several chapters earlier.

The husband has been puzzled by some elusive quality
in Antonio, the barber who comes to shave him daily and
who will eventually cuckold him—dragging from his wife
the full physical expression of her fascinated revulsion. The
barber's secret, the husband learns, is simply that his de-
mure and courteous exterior masks an indefatigable Don
Juan, an erotomaniac. But the husband goes on to realize
that the discovery answers nothing; and his meditation at
this point is almost a personal apologia of the author.

> The mystery I had noticed when I knew nothing
> about him survived even now when I thought I knew
> everything. That mystery had been pushed backwards
> into a less accessible zone, that was all. It was a
> little, I began to think, like the mystery of all things,
> the big and the small: you can explain everything
> except their existence.

The perception of the enigma of existence beneath the
puzzle of devouring sexuality shapes the husband's final
attitude and hence the feeling diffused through the book.
The disasters, such as they are, do not spring from vicious
or chronically self-willed deceitfulness. They are due to
an impersonal fraudulence in the nature of things, the way
things ineluctably are; and so the book closes on a note
of simple acceptance—not with anger or bitterness, but
with rue for remembrance and sadness for all the im-
aginable future. The husband confides at the end his acceptance of a second class existence, a shrunken assignment to perpetual mediocrity; he will become "a much
more modest man."

Sadness is thus the supreme emotion in the Moravian
universe. It is the one emotion that transcends indifference
—as indifference itself is an achieved condition that transcends the vulgar credulity, the unexamined faith in human

debasement, of the Antonios and the Leos. Indifference is the final response to the world in its sexual aspect; but sadness is what a man feels when he has "pushed [the mystery] backwards into a less accessible zone"; it is the only sentiment remaining to those who have arrived at the condition realized at a stroke by Moravia in the first of his novels, *The Time of Indifference*. This is why, as some Italian critics have complained, there is not much "story" to Moravia's career: his themes, his characters, his devices, his moral range were all exemplified by the time he was twenty. His story is the story of an endeavor to move beyond indifference, and for reasons of art as well as morality. Sadness is as far as he has been able to get. For what Moravia is unable to portray—because in all honesty he is unable to detect it—is a moral world more real and resilient than the condensed and decaying world in which his characters glumly move: a more remote machinery, even if it turns out to be infernal machinery, at work behind the stage machinery so prominent in the middle distance.

The absence of such a counterworld means the absence, too, of any sharply defined vision of evil; for the betrayals Moravia describes are not flanked by the persuasive imagery of innocence and conscience. There is consequently only a slight and shadowy moral tension, little actual resistance and no tragedy. At most, the minds of his characters are fleetingly troubled, not by a sense of sin, but by a sense of having forgotten something that might once have been a sense of sin. "The fault was Carla's as well," muses Michele, ". . . and his mother's too. The fault was everyone's; impossible to discover its source, the original cause of it." And behind that, a sense, fainter than perfume in an empty room, of a lost paradise: "a paradise of reality and truth," as Michele vaguely tells himself; "a paradise where everything—gestures, words, feelings— would have a direct connection with the reality in which they had originated."

The memory of this paradise appears as an occasional mirage in the stories of Moravia, something to serve as the basis for resentment but not strong enough to promote rebellion. The representative hero of Moravia, like modern man himself in Camus's definition, feels himself a stranger "in a universe suddenly emptied of illusion and light,"

an exile fatally deprived "of the memories of a lost home
country or the hope of a promised land." In the world
of Albert Camus, revolt has gradually emerged as man's
only dignifying act; but Moravia's is a world in which
revolt is improbable. It lies dormant, a painless hell, un-
disturbed by the expectancy of a fresh revelation, a larger
conversion: the conversion, perhaps, of existence into life.
The contents of that world are fairly indicated in the
very language of Moravia's titles (especially in the original), with their invariable allusion to indifference, contempt, sickness, weariness, poor judgment, equivocation,
deceit, crime, smallness, ugliness, conformity, bitterness,
unhappiness, or solitude. The word "hope" or anything like
it has never appeared except once, and then in the title
of an essay rather than a narrative: *"La Speranza."* But
La Speranza is not an affirmation of hope, it is a skeptical
analysis of its phenomenon, and an analysis that—by defining hope as the illusory impulse that spurs men on in
the endless pursuit of the impossible—permits Moravia to
identify *The Castle* of Franz Kafka as the very type of
hope-filled book.

FOOTNOTES

1. *La Terza Generazione*, initiated in Rome in 1953, and dedicated
to "solutions," other than political, of the cultural crisis of our
time. The magazine was discontinued in 1957.
2. I should acknowledge here a sensible review of Moravia's
career by Aldo Paladini, in the Milanese periodical *Settimo Giorno*,
December 2, 1954.
3. The very form and the peculiarly haunting music of Elio
Vittorini's brilliant *Conversazione in Sicilia* (1937) were a necessary
and happy response to the Fascist challenge.
4. A collection of sixty-odd "short short stories" or anecdotes,
published originally in newspapers and dealing with the comic or
seedy side of the city of Rome. They have not all been translated
into English. The one referred to here is *"Il Mediatore."* [Since
this was written, some have been published as *Roman Tales*. Ed.]
5. Interview in the *New Yorker*, May 7, 1955.
6. In a review of Moravia's collection of articles, *Un Mese in
URSS; L'Espresso* (Roman weekly), April 13, 1958. Milano continues: "For the massive facts of history . . . Moravia has the same
dark respect that the phenomena of nature excite in others. This is
one of the forms of Moravia's pessimism, on which his vigor as a
novelist depends, as well as his analytic acumen and his anti-

rhetoric." The book under review, incidentally, is the only collection of Moravia's journalistic writings yet published.

7. For this and for several other references, I am indebted to *Introduzione a Moravia* by Euralio de Michelis (Florence, 1954).

8. *Hudson Review,* Summer, 1951.

9. Paladini, *loc. cit.*

10. *Sentirsi vivo. Vivo* is only partly rendered by "alive"; it contains the note also of making one's presence felt, of being recognized and acknowledged.

11. After reading this chapter, which was published as a separate essay in *Modern Writing No. 3* (1956), Moravia addressed a letter to me, in English. I have permission to quote the following (dated April 13, 1957): "It is quite true that sex has been for me the key to open many doors. The fact is that I started to write in 1925 . . . and in that time there were very few or no values at all which, after the terrible crisis of the so-called twenties, resisted a close examination. Everything in this faraway time seemed tottering, inconsistent, contradictory and false. There were only a few things which seemed to me solid and true and these things were connected with nature and with the less objectionable and analysable and ineffable sides of the human soul. Among these things no doubt was sex, which is something primordial and absolute. I have said the word: absolute. Looking for the absolute, it was impossible to find it then in the upper spiritual world but only in the depths of the unconscious and of the lowest and most obscure instincts of man."

12. In the letter addressed to me by Moravia, and already quoted in part, he adds the following: "Ten years before Sartre's *Nausée,* I wrote *The Time of Indifference* which was an existentialist novel avant-la-lettre. From existence to being it is very difficult to pass; there is a big gap between the two. I tried hard to fill the gap, to cross the line between existence and being. Maybe I didn't succeed."

The present chapter is clear, I hope, in its conviction that the failure to cross the line in Moravia's novels is a failure of the characters and not of the author; that Moravia is dramatizing a failure, but not himself failing. In this respect, he may be compared with Chekov. The failure of will and nerve in Chekov's plays is a quality of his dramatis personae, and not of himself; hence Chekov may aptly and ironically call *The Cherry Orchard* "a comedy," as I would call most of the stories by Moravia.

The Novels of Iris Murdoch
BY FRANCIS HOPE

Miss Murdoch's new novel *A Severed Head,* is very strange indeed; both in itself and as coming from her. Like Mr. Angus Wilson in *The Middle Age of Mrs Eliot,* she seems almost to have made a deliberate effort to pare away the characteristics by which she was becoming best known. Possibly both writers were afraid of the distortions inseparable from a widely accepted public image. More probably, they genuinely wanted to extend their own range, to avoid the mere repeated practice of a technique already mastered. In Mr Wilson's latest book, the morality was there undisguised, quite free of all the satirical observation and deliberate "unpleasantness" which had previously decorated—or for many people obscured—the basic didactic structure; not surprisingly, many of his readers mourned for the plumage and forgot the living bird. In the same way, those who have been delighted by the grace of Miss Murdoch's writing, by its complexity and depth of imagination, by its extraordinary mixture of the real and the fantastic, will probably be surprised and may perhaps be disappointed. Even the blurb-writers will have to find some new clichés to describe her; the ones in the last sentence are already out of date.

It is primarily, I think, a question of form. *Under the Net* was in a sense a refusal to write a novel at all (as all picaresque novels are); the life shown in it is too fragmentary to be forced into the conventional novelist's pattern of turning-points and crises, problems and solutions, significant incidents and revelatory experiences; there is only a series of contingent adventures, with ownership of a dog and the vague promise of some future creative writing for the hero at the (arbitrarily chosen) end. As Jake makes Hugo say in his account of their conversations: "All theorizing is flight. We must be ruled by the situation itself and this is unutterably particular." In speaking at all, we are condemned to some kind of over-simplifying falsehood; in the same way, Miss Murdoch is cheating a little by using a novel to make the point that points should not be made by novels; as Hugo says, only actions can be entirely truthful. But a refusal to generalize is at least an approach to truth.

In *The Flight from the Enchanter,* Miss Murdoch seemed to have come to terms with the novel far enough to permit herself a more elaborate plot, and to choose an impersonal narrative form which allows her to generalize about her characters (Rainborough, for instance) in a series of epigrammatic asides which Hugo could hardly have sanctioned. Again, the point seems to be partly that no satisfactory points can be made; but, as the scholar Peter Saward says of his labours over an indecipherable script, "one reads the signs as best one can, and one may be totally misled. But it's never certain that the evidence will turn up that makes everything plain. It was worth trying." The epigraph applies perhaps equally well to Annette's attempts to "educate herself in the school of life" or to Rosa's to escape the consequences of her own and her brother's actions in her pursuit of Mischa Fox to Italy. Miss Murdoch's characters seem in this book to move more obviously along lines she has laid down for them: one real and one attempted suicide, a convenient death in the last pages, the mechanism of intrigue which finished Rainborough's career—all these are controlled if not contrived events. On the other hand, they are still only a beginning. For the most part, one is still left with the impression that Miss Murdoch is recording rather than creating a world which defies explanation, full of loose ends and disturbing ambiguities (the Polish brothers, Mischa Fox's fish, the destruction of Rainborough's garden wall), which may be symbolic or not, which are magic, but only, as Mischa says about his netsuke, "in the way in which magic can be part of ordinary life."

When *The Sandcastle* appeared, many people welcomed it as a sign that Miss Murdoch's writing had become more "realistic." It would be truer to say that it had become more conventional. The world of *The Sandcastle* is not necessarily more everyday than that of the earlier novels— the gypsy-like man who appears announcing disaster is quite as fantastic as anything in them—but it is more neatly

and recognizably an artifact. It is the coherence as well as
the plausibility of the plot that reassured critics that Miss
Murdoch had, as it were, settled down to her trade. Rain
Carter's car falling into the stream not only demonstrates
the cogent mechanical reality of the external world (like
any of Miss Murdoch's engineering set-pieces); it also symbolizes the irreparable emotional disaster that has fallen on
Mor. After the point of balance is reached, there is no
turning back. The situation is *not* merely particular, even
though its connection with other situations may be hidden.
"Our actions are like ships which we may watch set out to
sea, and not know when or with what cargo they will
return to port." *(The Bell.)*

I have stolen this last point, which I failed to recognize
for myself, from a more intelligent friend; but it would be
difficult to miss the unity of theme which *The Sandcastle*
possesses. It revolves around a central and eminently general issue: the issue of freedom. Mor, like most human
beings, cannot escape the fact that he is free. When he
realizes that he can walk into Demoyte's house and speak
to Rain at night, "the pain of knowing that it was possible
was for a moment extreme." And when Rain leaves the
dinner at which Nan (herself in many ways the least free,
and yet the most powerful, of the characters) has attempted to reclaim her husband, "although Mor struggled
in his seat he could not bring himself to get up. A lifetime
of conformity was too much for him." He is like the cock
in the experiment, whose beak is pressed against a chalk
line on the floor, and who cannot lift his head until the
line is rubbed off; he is imprisoned in his own refusal to be
free.

But the novel is also concerned with the problem of
deception. Mor deceives his wife, but cannot be entirely
truthful even in doing so; he conceals his political ambitions from Rain, and through this gap the laws of consistency can reach him, and take a terrible revenge. The
same problem recurs in *The Bell*. The bell itself is called
Gabriel (the archangel of the Annuciation) and is inscribed
Ego Vox Sum Amoris. In the monastic legend, this is
exactly what it is; its miraculous flight into the lake reveals
the fact that one of the nuns had a lover. But even in
twentieth-century fact, that voice cannot be silenced: Catherine's love for Michael, Michael's for Nick or for Toby,
break through their profession of religious vocation as

irresistibly as Dora is forced to ring the bell which she and Toby have dragged out of the lake. Dora herself cannot eventually conceal the fact that she is free to leave Paul, and must use that freedom. In the long run, self-deception is not so much immoral as impossible.

This is partly, of course, a technical device for maintaining suspense; where the characters deceive each other, the process of discovery can be used to hold the reader's interest. The more basic moral issue of *The Bell* is that of fundamentalist or interpretive ethics, as reflected in James's and Michael's sermons. It raises the infinitely difficult question of how far one can be guided by rules as opposed to experience, how far it can be good to renounce the world without knowing it, how far one must know one's own limits before setting oneself any moral objectives at all. "Those who hope, by retiring from the world, to earn a holiday from human frailty, in themselves and others, are usually disappointed." *The Bell* is an account of such disappointments. It is in every way an astonishing book, and one of its most impressive features is the extreme ease with which so tightly disciplined a conception is carried out. Even the style is supremely confident. *The Sandcastle* was often stiltedly written, in a form of Revived Mandarin ("In his own household Evvy was able to proceed unchecked, especially as he had refused to draw the considerable entertainment allowance which Demoyte had established as part of the Headmaster's emoluments") which perhaps reflects a certain stiffness in Miss Murdoch's new approach to the novel. But *The Bell* contains whole pages of analysis written with marvelous aphoristic clarity, and its narration never falters for lack of a word or a phrase. Structurally, it is equally imposing, and equally carefully worked over. It is a very long way from a world too random to be forced into any moral or artistic order.

In the light (if it is a light) of this, what can one make of *A Severed Head?* Obviously, Miss Murdoch has become more formal still—perhaps following as large a change of course as was marked by the publication of *The Sandcastle*. In her two previous novels the figures move to some extent in a pattern; in *A Severed Head* they go through an elaborate minuet worthy of Mr. Henry Green, in which six partners try out every possible heterosexual combination except one (Honor Klein and Alexander). Indeed the novel contains, in a sense, nothing but form. With the exception of

Honor Klein cutting up napkins with a Japanese sword, and the entry of the removal men on to a scene between Martin and Antonia, there is neither the strangeness nor the juxtaposition of minor incident that Miss Murdoch's admirers have come to expect; the characters' backgrounds and occupations seem merely designed, as in the most crudely romantic novel, to give them the money and the leisure to pursue an intricate scheme of personal relations; and their personalities vanish in the mist of their own involvements. As Martin says, his love for Honor is an inexplicable phenomenon which has nothing to do with personality; as she says, it has nothing to do with happiness either. It has no conceivable connection with Rain Carter's love for Mor, or Jake's for Anna Quentin; and it makes total nonsense of the pretensions to rationality of Palmer and Antonia, who insist that everything must be discussed and can be settled. In a sense, Miss Murdoch has come full circle: she is again arguing against too much seeking for explanations, although she has now chosen a highly sophisticated rather than a loose-knit form for her argument. In another sense, she has started on a new track which may lead further. The imperfections of *The Sandcastle* were a small and (if the suggestions of this article are true) a necessary price to pay for the smooth perfection of *The Bell;* the sequel to *A Severed Head* may be equally remarkable.

Postscript, 1964: Sustaining her productivity, Miss Murdoch wrote a pair of novels in the following two years, *An Unofficial Rose* (1962) and *The Unicorn* (1963). The first presents a comic collection of inadequate, immature people, each rendered through his own perception of things. In the second, Miss Murdoch finds even another novelistic form to carry her pet themes: the horror story. The novel describes an innocent young woman becoming aware of two truths: that the world offers evil at every turn and that it defies neat explanations; and, in contrast, a priggish middle-aged man's escape from this recognition. Within this small range, *The Unicorn* is efficiently realized; but more, it provides further evidence of Miss Murdoch's versatile talent and her enormous, but still unfulfilled, promise for truly superior fiction.

—Richard Kostelanetz

VLADIMIR NABOKOV

The Defenseless Luzhin
BY ANDREW FIELD

An unusually malevolent reviewer of Nabokov's *Pale Fire* —he is one of the few authors who regularly raise mediocre critics to true fury—asserted that Nabokov came to this country from Europe "with forty pounds of intellectual luggage, to which he has since added nothing." In fact, of course, Nabokov came to the United States by ship, and he brought with him not forty pounds but many intellectual steamer trunks. Nor is Nabokov difficult only because of his Russian background: Western critics now strain under his "Russianness" just as *émigré* Russian critics in the thirties had to contend with his "Westernness." That is precisely the problem: to read Nabokov requires a fine knowledge of almost all (Spanish is not absolutely essential) European literatures, including our own. We are able to understand him only to the degree that we are able to approach him culturally and intellectually. Not many do.

To take but one example, perhaps the most frequently encountered cliché about Nabokov is that of the unique position within his work of *Pnin*, the novella about an eccentric Russian professor in America. If only, according to the anti-Nabokov, pro-*Pnin* critics, Nabokov would write more delightfully charming and human books like *that* one instead of. . . Alas, *Pnin*, appearances to the contrary, is also a dark Nabokovian fiction in which the reader, through laughter, is drawn into the circle of those who mock and torment Pnin. Pnin is another of Nabokov's heroes who, through eccentricity or abnormality, hover fitfully on the brink of society and sanity. A bit of literary history is helpful here: The "real" Pnin was a minor Russian poet of the late eighteenth century, the bastard son of Prince Repnin (truncated names for illegitimate children were quite common at that time). Even the name, then, is both intrinsically funny and cruel. The poet Pnin was an outcast from society because his father would not grant him legal recognition, just as the fictional Pnin is a curiosity within society whom no one will "recognize" as a human being. The eighteenth-century Pnin's best known work is "The Wail of Innocence" which concerns the fact of his illegitimacy, and Nabokov's Pnin, of course, in his frequent moments of great stress never cries, he always "wails." Again, there is in Nabokov—let us not forget his credentials as a natural scientist—as little or as much as the reader is capable of perceiving.

The Luzhin Defense, a short novel written in Russian by the young Nabokov in France during the summer of 1929, has as its protagonist a grand chess master named Luzhin. Luzhin is a Pnin-figure (his fiancée at one point calls him "absent-minded like an old professor") in whom comedy has been made the handmaiden of tragedy. He is a former Wunderkind who has, however, never mastered those little gestures whose sum is society. As a strategist, he sees only the more significant gestures or patterns through which the real course of life is played out. And in *Speak, Memory* it is interesting to note how Nabokov uses an impersonal chess analogy when speaking of his own childhood and the death of his father: "But no shadow was cast by that future event upon the bright stairs of our St. Petersburg house, and the large, cool hand resting on my head did not quaver, and several lines of play in a difficult chess composition were not blended yet on the board." These patterns have a fascination which is quite independent of the people (or rather, figures) who participate in them. Nabokov has always had a marked predilection for the view from above, and there is his own description of the "subliminal co-ordinates" by which a novel is "plotted."

Luzhin's helplessness before life's manners occasions an endless succession of comic scenes in which he either misunderstands or understands too precisely. When asked a polite question: "How long have you played chess?", he at first says nothing and then, suddenly, replies: "Eighteen years, three months and four days." If his courtship *à rebours* in which he succeeds by making all the wrong moves is a literary Chapliniad (in a hilarious mockery of the stereotype, his future fiancée runs after him to return the filthy handkerchief he has dropped), the scene in which the dazed Luzhin becomes involved with a group of tipsy Berliners is pure Keystone comedy. But the comedy is the beginning of Luzhin's madness (the title of the French translation of the novel is *La course de fou*), and by the time Luzhin's chess promoter, a ubiquitous knave who has his counterparts in other novels, tries to involve him in the making of an actual movie, Luzhin understands chess so well that life itself becomes the abstraction to him and he can scarcely resolve the problem of how to leave a room. The character of Luzhin is based in part on that of the chess master Rubinstein and of another, lesser known master (Nabokov once worked as the chess editor of an *émigré* newspaper), but, as in the instance of Pnin who is also made up of recognizable bits (of eccentric Russian professors in America), the entire fictional structure cannot be adequately perceived in terms of its elemental, real "pieces."

In the pitiful and charming chess master Nabokov plots in extreme the unpierceable isolation of the individual. Luzhin was taught how to play by his father's lover, and the melodies and combinations of chess serve as a surrogate for life which is "not entirely comprehensible" to him. His choice is an anti-Platonic one in which the illusion, chess, is consciously chosen over the reality, life (as if in confirmation of the cave allegory, shadows of people and objects in the novel do in fact give rise to chess combinations in Luzhin's mind), and it would not be too much to suggest that all of Nabokov's novels are, in essence, ironic, anti-Platonic propositions.

When life intrudes upon and destroys his control of chess, Luzhin is put on the defensive and ends in flight from both sun and shadow. The expression of his tenuous stance between the two realities is his acrophobia: Luzhin is terrified of heights, the third dimension which takes him beyond the chessboard. His mental illness is brilliantly anticipated in scenes on balconies and staircases. In the final scene Luzhin barricades himself in a room and hurls himself downward, imagining in that moment that eternity is a chessboard towards which he is falling. "The door was broken down. 'Aleksandr Ivanovich, Aleksandr Ivanovich!'

screamed several voices. But there was no Aleksandr Ivanovich." In one sense there never was an Aleksandr Ivanovich, for these last lines are the first time that the reader learns Luzhin's given name. In Nabokov's fiction the function (or in this case, absence) of a character's name is to point past itself to that "clear madness"—the phrase *(yasnoe bezum'e)* which in various forms possesses each of his heroes.

The Luzhin Defense is Nabokov's finest short novel as well as his first work of real significance. It is important beyond this because it may be seen as a cornerstone to all of Nabokov's writing wherein many important melodies and combinations of his art are first made apparent.

The Perilous Magic of Nymphets
BY JOHN HOLLANDER

In the bizarre mixture of vintage 1830 sham editorial note and parody *Saturday Review* piece that serves as an introduction to this remarkable book, we are earnestly informed that "As a case history, 'Lolita' will become no doubt a classic in psychiatric circles." There is no doubt that it will not. The shades of Stavrogin, Lewis Carroll, Tiberius, Popeye, or worse hinted at in the foreword, the pornographic promises implicit in its publication by a Parisian erotica house, seem only ghosts to be dispelled almost in the very first chapter. Even to state that the book is *about* a cultivated European emigré in love with a twelve-year-old girl is misleading: modern readers cannot help but refer such a theme to the wrong novelistic conventions. There is no clinical, sociological, or mythic seriousness about *Lolita,* but it flames with a tremendous perversity of an unexpected kind. Readers of Mr. Nabokov's earlier work will be more prepared than most to relate such a theme to a style weird enough to support it in a new way. They may understand what it means to say that this book often suggests a terrifyingly semi-serious parody of *Manon Lescaut* by James Thurber. Nearly everything about *Lolita* is parodic, save for the primary love story, which ridicules only itself.

The story is told by one Humbert Humbert, presumably writing from a psychopathic ward, and, later, from jail. He comes, he informs us, from a mélange of European stock, and was raised on the Riviera, where his father ran a hotel. There, at the age of twelve, "in a princedom by the sea," he met his first and archetypal love, Annabel Leigh. Their brief affair having terminated in her untimely death, Humbert crystallizes around her image an ideal type of girl, between the ages of nine and fourteen, whose sexual power is to forever hold him prisoner. "Nymphets," he calls such creatures:

> Between those age limits are all girl children nymphets? Of course, not. Otherwise, we who are in the know, we lone voyagers, we nympholepts, would have long gone insane. Neither are good looks any criterion; and vulgarity, or at least what a given community terms so, does not necessarily impair certain mysterious characteristics, the fey grace, the elusive, shifty, soul-shattering, insidious charm that separates the nymphet from such coevals of hers as are incomparably more dependent on the spatial world of synchronous phenomena than on that intangible island of entranced time where Lolita plays with her likes.

"Lolita" is an American nymphet, one Dolores Haze, whose affair with Humbert occupies the bulk of the book. After some rather telescoped description of a scholarly career, Humbert tells of his unfortunate early marriage with the chronologically mature but otherwise infantile Valeria. She resolves his misery by running off with a Tsarist taxidriver in Paris, ending up, before her death, in typically Nabokovian fashion ("the couple had somehow got over to California and had been used there, for an excellent salary, in a year-long experiment conducted by a distinguished American ethnologist. The experiment dealt with human and racial reactions to a diet of bananas and dates in a constant position on all fours"). Finally landing him in America, chance leads Humbert to a small New England town and the role of roomer in the house of the widowed Charlotte Haze, whose bobby-sox daughter, Lolita, strikes up in him irresistible reverberations of the lost Annabel. Humbert marries Mrs. Haze solely in order to murder her and gain legal guardianship of the child. It is through no action of his own that he finds himself a widower again, driving to Lolita's summer camp to remove his daughter, take her home, and possess her.

On their first night together, Lolita turns out to be completely corrupt. From then on, their affair consists of a frenzied car-and-motel tour of the whole country, finally culminating in the loss of Lolita to Clare Quilty, a playwright, and the murder of that hated rival in one of the funniest and most grotesque scenes in the book.

Throughout all this, Mr. Nabokov's attention is fixed on the sentimental treatment of the love affair itself, and the satiric portrayal of the American *kitsch* through which the lovers peregrinate. It is Humbert's own amazingly flexible rhetoric, primarily, which permits of rapid switches back and forth from: "and feeling as I did her warm weight on my lap (so that, in a sense, I was always with Lolita as a mother is with child)" to: "We had breakfast in the township of Soda, pop. 1001." Much of the book's comic genius lies in the style, which alternates elements of Turgenev and mock Proust, rigorous Constant-like *analyse de l'amour* and parody and pastiche. There are moments of surrealoid super-clarity, but unlike true surrealism, these glimpses never stake all on the effect of the moment, abandoning any further dramatic utility. They seem to spring from the kind of Dickensian eye which lets Esther Summerson in *Bleak House* notice, before any more concrete signs of familial disorder, the fact that one of Mrs. Jellyby's curtains is secured with a fork. But the most pervasive single device of style is the verbal diddle. Humbert fiddles with his own name ("Hamburg," "Humbug," "Homburg," etc.) and indeed, with everything else. "Guilty of killing Quilty," he mutters toward the beginning of the narrative, "Oh my Lolita, I have only words to play with." Usually the games are even more Joycean, especially in a long section in which are described the recondite *noms de guerre* with which his pursuing rival, the more to pique him, fills out motel registers. One thinks of Thurber's mad fixation on the linguistic games with which he avoids social confrontations. But in *Lolita*, the word-play leads back to the love-play always; it is a little like an extended trope on the pathetic fallacy, in which verbal hocus-pocus makes the obsessive object light up, in intellectual neon, everywhere.

The problem of what to make of *Lolita* has led certain of the book's admirers to beg off its sexual and literary outlandishness by remarking that the whole thing is *really* Mr. Nabokov's love affair with America. Certainly Dolores herself, with her outrageous jargon and tastes, is part of what Auden has called the "heterogeneous dreck" of the American landscape through which she and her doting lover move. But there is something more here, surely, some better way for the reader to escape (if he must) the too-serious acceptance of the suburb of heterosexuality in which Humbert dwells. His particular Lecherville has, as far as I know, no well-known clinically respectable name of long standing (Old Can't-tell-the-players-without-a-score-card Krafft-Ebing has to resort to "violation of persons under the age of fourteen" for his map). This is important, I feel. Humbert himself tells us: "I am not concerned with so-called 'sex' at all. Anyone can imagine these elements of animality. A greater endeavor lures me on: to fix once and for all the perilous magic of nymphets." Indeed, the "sex" in this book is all subject to tender exegesis (after one rare moment of melodramatic tenderness from Lolita: "It may interest physiologists to learn, at this point, that I have the ability—a most singular case, I presume—of shedding torrents of tears throughout the other tempest"). The not-quite-teen-age girl herself, of course, providing her learned lover with duties involving the procurement of sundaes and movie magazines, is the only plausible modern *femme fatale.* She is elusive, perverse, and, above all, *transient* (each nymphet has but a few years of affinitive power). Indeed, there *is* a term for the moral condition that is the subject of this book, but it comes from the lexicon of purely literary pathology. "Nympholepsy," the frenzy of attachment to an unattainable object, was a common word for a commonly cultivated romantic state. I rather think that Mr. Nabokov's strategy was to literalize the word's metaphor, and to write of a class of real nymphets who could produce in their palely loitering admirers the rhetorical action whose fruit is romantic writing. Swinburne and Poe provide the names of the two lost loves, and the lost child and the Lady of Pain unite, for Mr. Nabokov himself, in one "fair, nasty nymph." *Lolita,* if it is anything *"really,"* is the record of Mr. Nabokov's love affair with the romantic novel, a today-unattainable literary object as short-lived of beauty as it is long of memory. It is also, not to change the subject for a minute, just about the funniest book I remember having read.

Nabokov's Obtuse Fool

BY RICHARD KOSTELANETZ

O wad some Pow'r the giftie gie us
To see oursels as ithers see us!
It wad frae mony a blunder free us,
    An' foolish notion!
What airs in dress an' gait wad lea'e us,
    An' ev'n devotion!

Robert Burns

In *Pale Fire* (1962), Vladimir Nabokov presents in Charles Kinbote the latest version of that figure who haunts much of his fiction, perhaps as an ominous possibility of Nabokov's own existence—the writing man as fool. Kinbote's predecessors include John Ray Jr., Ph. D. who insists in the foreword of *Lolita* (1955) that the book "should make all of us—parents, social workers, educators—apply ourselves with still greater vigilance. . . ," Humbert Humbert who composes his memoirs of *Lolita* from "a psychopathic ward," the narrator of *The Real Life of Sebastian Knight* (1941) who mistakenly thinks his deceased half-brother was an important novelist; but Kinbote is easily the richest of these creations. Though he may lack the mythic resonance that made "nymphet" part of the currency of American culture and *Lolita* a best seller, Kinbote is the prime reason why *Pale Fire* is both Nabokov's best work and one of the most hysterically funny novels in contemporary literature.

Developing an idea faintly presented in *The Gift* (1937), that literary criticism itself could be the novel's subject and determine its form, *Pale Fire* has an unprecedented novelistic structure of three unbalanced parts: a 999-line poem entitled "Pale Fire" by the American author John Shade

(who considers himself second only to Robert Frost), a
foreword to it by Kinbote, an admirer of Shade, who for
a semester was guest professor of Zemblan, his native
tongue, at Wordsmith College, New Wye, Appalachia,
U.S.A. The third section, following the poem, is Kinbote's
commentary on it. The poem itself is a rather innocuous
piece about nothing in particular, written in a fairly orthodox form, which echoes at various times Alexander Pope,
T. S. Eliot, Robert Frost, and Wordsworth's lines about the
growth of the poet's mind. It occasionally becomes interesting, as in Shade's description of his sensitive daughter's
suicide or his (rather, Nabokov's) parodies:

> Time means succession, and succession, change:
> Hence timelessness is bound to disarrange
> Schedules of sentiment.

The third section, Kinbote's line-by-line commentary on
the poem, is the comic center, for his remarks are a masterful example of what in graduate schools is glumly called
"over-reading," in the outside world "egomania," and in
literature brilliant comic irony.

Most of the humor in *Pale Fire* comes from the ironic
relation between what Kinbote sees and what the reader
perceives is actually happening; and Nabokov, like the
Marx Brothers, knows how to multiply our laughter by
repeating the same joke in a different form. In his earlier
novels, in contrast, the comedy stems from his ability to
crack a joke, particularly to execute a cuttingly satirical
description such as, in *Pnin* (1957), the campus' "murals
displaying recognizable members of the faculty in the act
of passing on the torch of knowledge from Aristotle,
Shakespeare, and Pasteur to a lot of monstrously built
farm boys and farm girls." In *Pale Fire*, however, the
satirical blade is swallowed, so to speak, by an ironic
narrator who unintentionally wields it against himself, for
his blabberings continually *reveal* more than they explicitly
tell. Kinbote's characteristic fault is missing the point, and
being doubly gifted he can persuade himself that his failures
are really virtues. In one of the funniest passages in the
book, he remembers with his usual pomposity, his early
days at Wordsmith:

> "On one of my first mornings there, . . . I noticed
> that Mr. and Mrs. Shade . . . were having trouble

with their old Packard in the slippery driveway where it emitted whines of agony but could not extricate one tortured rear wheel out of a concave inferno of ice. . . . Thinking to offer my neighbors a ride to campus in my powerful machine, I hurried out toward them, . . . and I was about to cross the lane where I lost my footing and sat down on the surprisingly hard snow. My fall acted as a chemical reagent on the Shades' sedan, which forthwith budged and almost ran over me as it swung into the lane. . . ."

Kinbote's madness transcends mere egotism—it is unadulterated egomania; for, able at all times to exaggerate his own importance, he insists upon understanding Shade's poem "Pale Fire" as a symbolic re-creation of all the Zemblan history that Kinbote unloaded on Shade's reluctant ears. Therefore, in his interpretation, Shade's trivia actually tells of Kinbote's life, perhaps fantasied, as King Charles Xavier II, the deposed monarch of Zembla. (Unlike Frederick C. Crews who in *The Pooh Perplex* parodies the clichés of the *methods* of literary criticism, Nabokov, wisely I think, blames the abuses of criticism upon the practitioner's lack of good sense.) Kinbote's obsessive egotism is fused to a thorough insensitivity to the written word. "How to locate in blackness, with a gasp, / Terra the Fair, an orbicle of yasp," a line whose archaic vocabulary masks an inappropriate image, he finds "the loveliest couplet in this canto"; either "Housman's *The Shropshire Lad* [sic] or Tennyson's *In Memoriam*" are the "highest achievement of English poetry in a hundred years"; and his quotations from Shakespeare, retranslated back from the Zemblan, make one wince.

From his failure to question himself and his perception of things follows a chronic inability to recognize reality, for when he finds after a party in "my coat pocket a brutal anonymous note saying: 'You have hal. . . . .s real bad, chum,' " he interprets that half-spelt word as "meaning evidently 'hallucinations,' although a malevolent critic might infer from the insufficient number of dashes that little Mr. Anon . . . could hardly spell." Exemplifying both sides of the coin of priggishness, Kinbote is both boastful and hypocritical, for along with his platitudinous religious devoutness and his condemnations of extra- and pre-marital sexual relations goes a compelling and rather indiscriminate admiration for young men. (At their first meeting, his former wife, he innocently tell us, was dressed as a boy.)

All this means that, to Nabokov, Kinbote's greatest crime is a thorough lack of self-consciousness. Doomed to be a fool and not to recognize it, Kinbote can report that the first time he read Shade's *Pale Fire* he could see no reference to Zembla. Likewise, he fails to recognize that when someone calls him "The Great Beaver" it is derogatory, that his capacity to rationalize all failures and criticism is immense, that he regularly commits all sorts of misspellings and greater intellectual errors (which can be interpreted as an undercurrent of ironic commentary), that he has a natural inclination for overblown and inappropriate similes and metaphors and needlessly multisyllabic adjectives and adverbs, and that in his superficially correct index to Shade's poem several names, usually those of young attractive males, do not exist in the text. He continually commits the faults he decries in others and brags he lacks in himself. "I have no desire," he writes early in his commentary, "to twist and batter an ambiguous *apparatus criticus* into the monstrous semblance of a novel," and nothing, but nothing, could convince him he has.

What is remarkable about *Pale Fire,* then, is Nabokov's ability to realize successfully a three-fold effect—to sustain at once the sheer comedy of Kinbote's stupidity, secondly to create consistently and subtly the writings of a deeply mad, but superficially sane, intellectual mind, and thirdly the inescapable terror of Kinbote's isolation and constant failure. At times, one feels that Nabokov is too harsh on Kinbote, giving him more deficiencies than one character can bear; but Nabokov also knows, I believe, that Kinbote is in superficial respects much too like himself—an offbeat, exiled writer of aristocratic background and haughty character, teaching his native language at a rural American college (Nabokov for many years lectured at Cornell), who once wrote a prodigious commentary on a beloved poem, Pushkin's *Eugene Onegin*—not to sympathize with his predicament.

By using Kinbote as a counter example to, say, Timofy Pnin of his earlier novel and perhaps himself, Nabokov, despite his insistent proclamation that his work lacks ethical dimensions, has a moral point to make. What separates

Pnin and the narrator of the supposedly autobiographical *Speak, Memory* (1949)—Nabokov's closest approximations of "heroes"—from Kinbote, the prototypical fool, is that both of the former characters possess a strong self-consciousness, which expresses itself in a capacity for self-irony; for this reason, while Pnin's madness and incompetence are charming and sympathetic, Kinbote's is largely repulsive.

Too many intellectuals feel inclined to dismiss *Pale Fire* as a thoroughly evil and tasteless book, for Nabokov, like Dostoyevsky, depicts the perils of a way of life that is, like that of most intellectuals, proudly eccentric, apparently self-reliant, individualistic, and analytical; and Nabokov disturbs us by tying all these admirable qualities to a few fatal flaws. However, once we recognize that a major theme of all Nabokov's writing is that self-awareness is the prime mark of the mature human being, we can define Kinbote not as a true intellectual, but an incomplete one. At this point Nabokov is vulnerable to another criticism more apt than anti-intellectualism. Precisely because its thematic resonance is so narrow, *Pale Fire*, one of his two best novels, remains in many ways faintly trivial. Whereas John Barth in *The Sot-Weed Factor*, and Eugène Ionesco, for examples, can lift a similar feeling about the joke of knowledge and life into a serious vision of the absurdity of existence, in *Pale Fire*, in contrast, nearly every line of action culminates in just a guffaw so that, one feels in the end, Nabokov, despite his extraordinary inventiveness and comic sense, in lacking a true seriousness about human life, lets his work fall short of what we recognize as major fiction.

About Zhivago and His Poems
BY FRANK O'HARA

We are used to the old saw that poets cannot write great novels or indeed any novels. The adherents of this cliché, hoping to perpetuate a mystery-distinction between two kinds of writing, are cheered on by the novelists who hate "poetic" novels and the poets who hate "prosaic" poems. Virginia Woolf gets hers from one quarter and William Carlos Williams gets his from the other. The argument is usually bolstered by phrases like "Joyce *turned to* prose," which would have been an amusing scene, but never occurred. For what poetry gave to Joyce, as to Pasternak, is what painting gave to Proust: the belief that high art has a communicability far superior in scope and strength to any other form of human endeavor. The Nobel Prize committee was correct in making the award include Pasternak's poetry as well as the novel. To admirers of his poetry *Doctor Zhivago* is the epic expression of many of the themes first found in individual lyrics and short stories; the present epic form is the poet's response to the demand of his time for its proper expression.

With one prose masterpiece behind him, *Safe Conduct* (1931), Pasternak insists in *Doctor Zhivago* on identifying poetry with truth to the supreme extent: in no other work of modern literature do we wait for the final revelation of meaning to occur in the hero's posthumous book of poems. The political ramifications of the novel's publication have thrust the poet (author *and* hero) into dramatic relief for a vast international public and established the efficacy of the poet's stance in realms far beyond personal lyricism. The clamor over *Doctor Zhivago* has been denounced by various literary figures as damaging to Pasternak personally, but let there be no mistake about this clamor: it comes not from anything Pasternak has said in the press, nor from the phrasing of the Nobel Prize citation, nor from Western or Soviet political commentaries on the novel's content, it comes from the nature of the work itself. Of the critics only Edmund Wilson has seen this quality in its proper perspective. Pasternak has written a revolutionary and prophetic work which judges contemporary society outside as well as within the Iron Curtain. And if Pasternak is saying that the 1917 Revolution failed, he must feel that the West never even made an attempt. Far from being a traitorous work, *Doctor Zhivago* is a poem on the nobility of the Soviet failure to reconstruct society *in human terms,* and it is not without hope. The two disillusioning heroes of *Safe Conduct,* Scriabin and Mayakovsky, give way to the triumphant hero of *Doctor Zhivago.*

It is plain that this hero must be an artist; to Pasternak the artist is the last repository of individual conscience, and in his terms conscience is individual perception of life. This is not at all a counter-revolutionary attitude based on an intellectual-aristocratic system. It has not to do with a predilection for "culture." The lesson comes from life. Zhivago himself becomes a doctor, but he finds that his usefulness to society is everywhere stymied, that his social efficacy is incomplete and does not contribute to his understanding of his own predicament. To be a twentieth-century hero Zhivago must leave for subsequent generations a living testament. It does not suffice that he "live in the hearts of his countrymen" by remembered deeds alone. It is a question of articulation: the epic events of *Doctor Zhivago* demand from their participants articulate perception or mute surrender. Pasternak's epic is not the glorification of the plight of the individual, but of the accomplishment of the individual in the face of almost insuperable sufferings which are personal and emotionally real, never melodramatic and official. And it is the poet's duty to accomplish this articulation.

Everywhere in the work of Pasternak published in English, we saw this meaning growing. It is a world very like that of Joyce's characters as we meet them in *Dubliners* and *The Portrait of the Artist as a Young Man* and find them later older, clearer, changed, in *Ulysses* and *Finnegans Wake.* Obviously the young Larisa Feodorovna bears this kind of resemblance to the adolescent Zhenia

Luvers of the early story (mistakenly printed as two distinct stories under separate titles by New Directions); several scenes in *Aerial Ways* anticipate events in the novel, and indeed Pasternak draws attention to this aspect of his writing in the opening passages of *A Tale* (called *The Last Summer* in English). It is the writer of the *Letters to Tula* who bears the strongest resemblance to Zhivago himself: "Everything that happens happens from the nature of the place. This is an event on the *territory of conscience,* it occurs on her own ore-bearing regions. There will be no 'poet.'" In this passage Pasternak reveals early (1918) his belief that the poet must first be a person, that his writings make him a poet, not his acting the role. I cannot agree with Elsa Triolet when she recently attacked Pasternak for having betrayed Mayakovsky in writing *Doctor Zhivago.* On the contrary, the principles which were later to seduce Mayakovsky had been exposed in *Letters to Tula* already: ". . . I swear to you that the faith of my heart is greater than ever it was, the time will come—no, let me tell you about that later. Tear me to pieces, tear me to pieces, night, burn to ashes, burn, burn brilliantly, luminously, the forgotten, the angry, the fiery word 'Conscience'! Burn maddening, petrol-bearing tongue of the flame . . .

"This way of regarding life has come into being and now there is no place on earth where a man can warm his soul with the fire of shame: shame is everywhere watered down and cannot burn. Falsehood and dissipation. Thus for thirty years all who are singular live and drench their shame, old and young, and already it has spread through the whole world, among the unknown . . .

"The poet, henceforward inscribing this word, until it is purged with fire, in inverted commas, the 'poet' observes himself in the unseemly behavior of actors, in the disgraceful spectacle which accuses his comrades and his generation. Perhaps he is only playing with the idea. No. They confirm him in the belief that his identity is in no way chimerical . . ."

This passage is like a rehearsal of the talks Zhivago has with his uncle when they discuss principles. That it also bears on Pasternak's relationship with Mayakovsky is witnessed by the following passage from *Safe Conduct:* "But a whole conception of life lay concealed under the Romantic manner which I was to deny myself from henceforth. This was the conception of life as the life of the poet. It had come down to us from the Romantics, principally the Germans.

"This conception had influenced Blok but only during a short period. It was incapable of satisfying him in the form in which it came naturally to him. He could either heighten it or abandon it altogether. He abandoned the conception. Mayakovsky and Esenin heightened it.

"In the poet who imagines himself the measure of life and pays for this with his life, the Romantic conception manifests itself brilliantly and irrefutably in his symbolism, that is in everything which touches upon Orphism and Christianity imaginatively. In this sense something inscrutable was incarnate both in the life of Mayakovsky and in the fate of Esenin, which defies all epithets, demanding self-destruction and passing into myth.

"But outside the legend, the Romantic scheme is false. The poet who is its foundation, is inconceivable without the nonpoets who must bring him into relief, because this poet is not a living personality absorbed in the study of moral knowledge, but a visual-biographical 'emblem,' demanding a background to make his contours visible. In contradistinction to the Passion plays which needed a Heaven if they were to be heard, this drama needs the evil of mediocrity in order to be seen, just as Romanticism always needs philistinism and with the disappearance of the petty bourgeoisie loses half its poetical content."

What then, after rejecting the concept of the Romantic "pose" in relation to his own life and art, does Pasternak's position become? He had already moved towards this decision in the poems written previous to 1917 and in a later volume he chooses the title from a poem, *My Sister, Life.* This expresses very clearly his position: the poet and life herself walk hand in hand. Life is not a landscape before which the poet postures, but the very condition of his inspiration in a deeply personal way: "My sister, life, is in flood today . . ." This is not the nineteenth-century Romantic identification, but a recognition. In the later work Zhivago says to the dying Anna Ivanovna: ". . . But all the time, life, one, immense, identical throughout its innumerable combinations and transformations, fills the universe and is continually reborn. You are anxious about whether you will rise from the dead or not, but you rose from the dead when you were born and you didn't notice it . . .

"So what will happen to your consciousness? *Your* consciousness, yours, not anyone else's. Well, what are you? There's the point. Let's try to find out. What is it about you that you have always known as yourself? What are you conscious of in yourself? Your kidneys? Your liver? Your blood vessels? No. However far back you go in your memory, it is always in some external, active manifestation of yourself that you come across your identity—in the work of your hands, in your family, in other people. And now listen carefully. You in others—this is your soul. This is what you are. This is what your consciousness has breathed and lived on and enjoyed throughout your life— your soul, your immortality, your life in others. And what now? You have always been in others and you will remain in others. And what does it matter to you if later on that is called your memory? This will be you—the you that enters the future and becomes a part of it . . ."

There is every reason to believe that Pasternak's recognition of self was accompanied by great pain. He adored Mayakovsky at the time and indeed was forced to this decision of self by Mayakovsky's presence in that time, ". . . because poetry as I understand it flows through history and in collaboration with real life." Mayakovsky made a fatal error and became a tragic hero. Like Strelnikov in the novel, he succumbed to a belief in the self-created rhetoric of his own dynamic function in society. That society needed him and benefited from this rhetoric is obvious. But both he and the character in *Doctor Zhivago* ended in suicide when their usefulness in this function came to an end, and while their response to social demand seems shortsighted to Pasternak, he also condemned society for the temptation:

> *The great Soviet gives to the highest passions*
> *In these brave days each one its rightful place,*
> *Yet vainly leaves one vacant for the poet.*
> *When that's not empty, look for danger's face.*

The chair of poetry must remain empty, for poetry does not collaborate with society, but with life. Soviet society is not alone in seducing the poet to deliver temporary half-truths which will shortly be cast aside for the excitement of a new celebration of nonlife. The danger is that life does not allow any substitute for love.

It is not surprising then that this sense of poetry and its intimate connection with his relationship to life is one of the strongest elements in Zhivago's nature. It makes of Zhivago one of the most original heroes in Western literature, a man who cannot be interpreted by nineteenth-century standards, which I suspect Lionel Abel attempts to do when he says, writing in *Dissent*, ". . . how can he not have understood that in yielding to the impulse to write of his beloved immediately after his loss of her, he was taking a practical attitude toward his grief, trying to get something out of it, literature, maybe even glory?" What Mr. Abel misses finding here is the grief-expression of the romantic hero, which had been eschewed by Pasternak himself in an early poem which fits oddly well into the present scene of loss:

> . . . *O miraculous obit, beckon, beckon! You may*
> *Well be astonished. For—look—you are free.*
>
> *I do not hold you. Go, yes, go elsewhere,*
> *Do good.* Werther *cannot be written again,*
> *And in our time death's odor is in the air;*
> *To open a window is to open a vein.*

Far from shallow or opportunistic in his grief (being left alone in the Urals with the wolves closing in would hardly raise hopes for literary fame), Zhivago weeps, drinks vodka, scribbles poems and notes, is subject to hallucinations, and begins the decline which will end in his death. But at this crucial period of his life in which he unexpectedly suffers the ultimate loss, that of Larisa Feodorovna, the period in which he had hoped to accomplish his poetic testament, his creativity does not desert him. We must remember that the events of the post-revolution period have robbed him of the time to think, the time to write. He saves his sanity by crowding the writing and the speculations of a lifetime into these days of isolation, coming to conclusions about certain events, and thus approaching once again, after this interval of grief, his "sister, life": ". . . Mourning for Lara, he also mourned that distant summer in Me-

liuzeievo when the revolution had been a god come down
to earth from heaven, the god of the summer when everyone had gone crazy in his own way, and when everyone's
life had existed in its own right, and not as an illustration
for a thesis in support of the rightness of a superior policy.

"As he scribbled his odds and ends, he made a note
affirming his belief that art always serves beauty, and beauty
is delight in form, and form is the key to organic life,
since no living thing can exist without it, so that every
work of art, including tragedy, expresses the joy of existence. And his own ideas and notes also brought him joy,
a tragic joy, a joy full of tears that exhausted him and
made his head ache."

He decides to forego the virtual suicide of his retreat in
the snowy wilderness, in the abandoned house which has
offered him, for the first time since he was a student, the
solitude for his poetry, and to return to Moscow. The
inverted commas have been purged from the word poet.
And unlike Chekhov's *Three Sisters* he does reach Moscow. And there he has a tangible reality even after his
death, as recognized by his two childhood friends as they
read at dusk the posthumous poems which Zhivago's mysteriously angelic half-brother Evgraf has collected: ". . .And
Moscow, right below them and stretching into the distance,
the author's native city, in which he had spent half his
life—Moscow now struck them not as the stage of the
events connected with him but as the main protagonist
of a long story, the end of which they had reached that
evening, book in hand.

"Although victory had not brought the relief and freedom that were expected at the end of the war, nevertheless
the portents of freedom filled the air throughout the post-
war period, and they alone defined its historical significance.

"To the two old friends, as they sat by the window, it
seemed that this freedom of the soul was already there, as
if that very evening the future had tangibly moved into the
streets below them, that they themselves had entered it
and were now part of it . . .

"And the book they held seemed to confirm and encourage this feeling."

This is Zhivago's triumph over the terrible vicissitudes of
love and circumstance which we have witnessed, the "ac-

tive manifestation" of himself—his soul, his immortality, his life in others.

Though the greatness of scale in *Doctor Zhivago* bears a resemblance to Tolstoy's achievement, this is not a massively documented and described war-novel like those we have had from American, French and Russian neo-Tolstoyans, where the scheme is that of nineteenth-century prototypes swamped by the events of their time. On the contrary, one of the great beauties of Pasternak's technique is that of portraying events through the consciousness of principal and minor characters. In this he resembles Joyce and Proust; often we hear of an event from a character *after* it has changed him, so that we apprehend both the event and its consequences simultaneously. The intimacy which this technique lends to the epic structure, particularly when the character is relatively unknown to us, and the discretion with which it is handled, remind one of two other works of perfect scale, Lermontov's *A Hero of Our Time* and Flaubert's *A Sentimental Education.*

Nowhere in the novel is this method more rewarding than in the presentation of the hero, and here it is varied beyond what I have described. Of Yurii Andreievich Zhivago we know a great deal as we progress through the novel. We not only know his feelings and his response to and attempted evaluation of events, but also his longings. We even know what he considers the most important elements in his life and how he intends to evaluate them in his work. But here Pasternak's devastating distrust of the plane of action in human affairs becomes clearest and makes its strongest point. In the post-epilogue book of poems we find that Zhivago has not written the poems he wanted to, nor the poems we expected (except for the one on St. George); in the course of creating the poems he has become not the mirror of the life we know, but the instrument of its perceptions, hitherto veiled. This is the major expression of a meaning which Pasternak has implied often in the novel proper. The human individual is the subject of historical events, not vice-versa; he is the repository of life's force. And while he may suffer, may be rendered helpless, may be killed, if he has the perceptiveness to realize this he knows that events require his participation to occur. In this context we find another revolutionary reinterpretation of the human condition: Strelnikov, the "active" Red Army Commissar, is rendered passive by his blind espousal of principles whose needful occasion has passed; Zhivago, passively withdrawn from action which his conscience cannot sanction, finds the art for which an occasion will continue to exist. This qualitative distinction between two kinds of significance is as foreign to our own society as it is to that of the U.S.S.R.

The poems with which the novel culminates, as we read them in English, are truly Zhivago's own, not Pasternak's. They deliver us a total image of the hero's life which is incremented by details of that life from the prose section. While we recognize the occasions of many, we find their expression different from what we, or Zhivago, expected. As an indication of how different they are from Pasternak's own poems, we need only compare two poems on a similar theme, Pasternak's lyric "If only when I made my début" and Zhivago's *Hamlet*. In the one, Pasternak deals with one of his central themes which is mentioned above in relation to Mayakovsky. The poem is full of the tragedy of human involvement, but in a pure, nonsymbolic manner: it is the role taking over the actor, of course, but it is also the word consuming the poet, the drama of the meaning, which the poet has found through the act of creating this meaning, transporting him to an area of realization beyond his power, where he has been joined to the *mortal* presence of life:

> *A line that feeling sternly dictates*
> *Sends on the stage a slave, and, faith,*
> *It is good-bye to art forever*
> *Then, then things smack of soil and Fate.*

How different is Zhivago's poem on this theme. Not only does he assume a "masque," that of Hamlet, but before we are through the second stanza he has made the symbolic connection of Hamlet with the Hebraic-Christian myth of father-and-son positive by reference to Christ in the Garden of Olives. The poem ends on a reference to Zhivago's own physical circumstance, a personal note that has saved many a Symbolist poem:

> *I stand alone. All else is swamped in Pharisaism.*
> *To live life to the end is not a childish task.*

Because of the novel, we cannot resist the idea that this poem was written in the snowy forests of Varykino after Lara's departure, where Zhivago endures his agonizing "vigil" and decides to forego suicide and to return to Moscow.

The Christian poems are extraordinary achievements as poems, and also reveal how complicated the structure of the novel is. In reading them we realize for the first time how enormously influential on Zhivago was the interpretation of Christ's significance by a minor character who was speaking to Lara and overheard by him from the next room. It becomes clear that Zhivago's Christianity is no hieratic discipline, but a recognition of social change: ". . . you have a girl—an everyday figure who would have gone unnoticed in the ancient world—quietly, secretly bringing forth a child . . .

"Something in the world had changed. Rome was at an end. The reign of numbers was at an end. The duty, imposed by armed force, to live unanimously as a people, as a whole nation, was abolished. . . . Individual life became the life story of God . . ." For those who have interpreted *Doctor Zhivago* with some smugness as a return to Christianity as the Western World knows it, it should be pointed out that this historical interpretation bears roughly the same analogy to Protestantism and Catholicism as they are practiced that Marxism does to Capitalism. It is not only based on historical distinctions, but "faith" is further set aside by the distinctions made in the poems between human life and nature, and the ambiguities of this relationship as they affect the Christ legend. When the fig tree is consumed to ashes in *Miracle*, Zhivago writes:

> *If at that point but a moment of free choice had*
>   *been granted*
> *To the leaves, the branches, to the trunk and roots*
> *The laws of nature might have contrived to*
>   *intervene.*

And in *Holy Week* our dependency on nature becomes the rival of God:

> *And when the midnight comes*
> *All creatures and all flesh will fall silent*

> *On hearing spring put forth its rumor*
> *That just as soon as there is better weather*
> *Death itself can be overcome*
> *Through the power of the Resurrection.*

It is not difficult to ascertain that for Pasternak the interdependency of man and nature is far from theological. It is in these clarifications of feelings and thoughts, in these poems, that Zhivago becomes a true hero. Here we find his inner response to his wife's moving letter from exile which also contains his reasons for not joining her outside Russia (*Dawn*), in other poems his ambivalences and his social nobility. In the most revealing of all, the love poems to Lara (including the superb *Autumn, Parting, Encounter* and *Magdalene*), we find the intensity which had so moved her and which Zhivago himself reveals nowhere else except in the secrecy of their own intimate hours. Her greatness in responding to this love becomes even more moving in retrospect than it was when one first read her thoughts at his bier, one of the greatest scenes in literature: ". . . Oh, what a love it was, utterly free, unique, like nothing else on earth! Their thoughts were like other people's songs.

"They loved each other, not driven by necessity, by the 'blaze of passion' often falsely ascribed to love. They loved each other because everything around them willed it, the trees and the clouds and the sky over their heads and the earth under their feet. Perhaps their surrounding world, the strangers they met in the street, the wide expanses they saw on their walks, the rooms in which they lived or met, took more delight in their love than they themselves did."

And the posthumous response to her love is on as grand a scale:

> *You are the blessing in a stride toward perdition,*
> *When living sickens more than sickness does itself;*
> *The root of beauty is audacity,*
> *And that is what draws us to each other.*

It is this inevitability which makes *Doctor Zhivago* great, as if we, not Pasternak, had willed it. And if love lives at all in the cheap tempestuousness of our time, I think it can only be in the unrelenting honesty with which we face animate nature and inanimate things and the cruelty of our kind, and perceive and articulate and, like Zhivago, choose love above all else.

JAMES PURDY

The Damaged Cosmos
BY JONATHAN COTT

The terrible, destructive private self each one of us possesses, reflected in the suppressed violence of contemporary social life, is a central subject in the works of James Purdy. He has explored this inner realm in his two extraordinary collections of short stories, *Color of Darkness* and *Children Is All*; a novelette, *63: Dream Palace;* and two novels, *Malcolm* and *The Nephew*. Purdy shows us the "Nightwood" Djuna Barnes had to explain; he reveals the loneliness Marguerite Duras has attempted to elucidate, but without the latter's cloying self-conscious approach. He never intrudes as he makes us see the desperation with which we live; and the objectivity of his observation finally extends to the furthest limits of grief.

What makes Purdy's stories so vital is the hard esthetic veneer in which he freezes the violent emotions his stories contain. If these emotions were loosened into a "free" form, they would release and dissipate the stories' power. Because his style is so rigid and matter-of-fact, the reader, in Purdy's characteristic device, is shocked as an apparently meaningless event in a character's life reveals a tragic and irreversible truth. A mother forces her son to burn photographs of his dead father; a young man shocks his mother by growing a beard; a little boy misplaces his tooth and thus cannot make a special and terrible wish; a woman complains about her husband's last name; a wife asks her crippled husband for a raven. These are occurrences in which Purdy reveals essential truths.

Despite this hard "veneer," Purdy is still capable of exploring innumerable and subtle gradations of character motive; and his unswerving eye for the small gestures of daily existence beautifully penetrates those most private recesses of feeling that few contemporary authors have been able to disclose. In *The Nephew,* for example, we read of Alma Mason and her brother Boyd who live in Rainbow Center—an *echt*-distillation of rural America—and who suffer from their slowly acquired knowledge that their nephew Cliff, "missing in action" in Korea, will never return:

"I know you think Cliff's not coming back," Alma said, and her voice broke.

He had not seen Alma cry for too many years to remember. He did not know whether she could. However, at this moment for the first time in recent memory, he saw her come very close to breaking.

"I hope against hope is all," Boyd finally said in a subdued reverent voice.

"If it's the best you can do!" Alma's voice was hard and clear again.

She rose and went upstairs without her usual dispassionate *goodnight.*

Sometimes, after they had done battle together, as they had tonight, he would hear her later furiously breaking wind in her bedroom, and since she was such a proper fastidious person, he wondered whether she went to her bedroom at such times for the reason that she knew she was going to break wind, or whether she broke wind as an aftermath of their disputes together.

The narrative progression of this gentle story of a love —missed but ultimately redeemed through the quiet comforting of aged brother and sister—is, on the surface, as slow and unexultant as Rainbow Center itself. But like all of Purdy's literature, *The Nephew* is dramatic in the sense that Joyce meant when, in the person of Stephen Daedalus, he wrote: "The dramatic form is reached when the vitality which has flowed and eddied round each person fills every person with such vital force that he or she assumes a proper and intangible esthetic life." And it is the characters in *The Nephew* who manifest this "form" so perfectly: the "old monarch" Mrs. Barrington, Professor Mannheim, Minnie Clyde Hawke—and Mrs. Laird watching TV:

At that moment shots rang out from the TV screen, a horse whinnied, cries of other men were raised, and a pane of glass, perforated by bullets, fell to the mud of a frontier town.

"Kill all those good-for-nothing rotters!" Mrs. Laird's voice rose above the machine's crescendo. "Shoot to kill or you'll regret it later." . . .

"It'd be a better world, you can believe me, if they killed more of the no-good rotters that are running this world today. You can quote me on that, too, girls. I was never afraid of a fight." . . .

More gunfire rocked the TV set as Federal troops marched on the frontier town to rescue those imperilled by the outlaws.

"Shoot to kill!" Mrs. Laird's voice was supreme now even among the gunshots.

Then as the noise of bullets was dying down, they could hear the old woman cry softly:

"Faye, come in here and watch. They are raising the American flag. Old Glory. Doesn't it make your heart beat faster to see our flag, Faye? Come in here, dear, and salute the flag with me, and get your mind out of the gutter reading those books and papers. Do you hear me, Faye? Come in here with your mother and salute the flag."

A moment later they could hear her intoning as a Sousa march was played.

Writing about Purdy, one is too often tempted to over-quote, as Edith Sitwell and David Daiches did in their introductions to Purdy's work. But it is a sin easy to condone. Mrs. Laird's TV speech or Purdy's description of Fenton's deathwatch over his brother Claire in *63: Dream Palace* are testaments to this writer's powers to disclose the core of emotional truth.

In the autumn of 1963, a poorly realized dramatic adaptation of several Purdy stories appeared off-Broadway under the title of his first book *Color of Darkness;* and Purdy has in fact written two plays—*Children Is All* and *Cracks*—both of which appear in the most recent of his published volumes. Ironically enough, they seem less successful that his more dramatic "non-dramatic" works. But this is not to deny the special beauty of *Children Is All* —a play about the return after fifteen years in jail of a middle-aged woman's son who, as the play concludes, dies in her arms, unrecognized. It communicates—after a perhaps too-slow development—both the pain and the strange joy of unresolved longing, transfigured into an acceptance of human estrangement. As the mother Edna says in her last speech:

> . . . I feel so at ease with this perfect stranger who came in like from nowhere. For the first time in my life, Leona, I feel so close to my own son . . . I feel like I did today when Reverend Stover came, like I'm soaring, soaring!

Cracks—an allegory of life-and-death and the redemptive power of "Creation"—fails because the transcendence over pain—"I felt the zephyrs of death blowing from the cracks in my surroundings"—is arrived at too unconvincingly. Unlike *The Nephew*, which arrives at its redemption through the gradually worked-out, changing psychological motions of Alma and Boyd, *Cracks* imposes its redemption willfully, as if from the outside. One has only to read Purdy's *Sermon*—tough in its insistence on the continual reality of despair—to realize that grace must, in the main body of Purdy's work, come somehow violently.

But if the allegory of *Cracks* leaves us unsatisfied, we must finally focus on Purdy's best work so far, *Malcolm*— an allegory in the fullest sense and one of the most extraordinary literary creations of our time. Purdy has subtitled *Malcolm* "A Comic Novel," and the author's style —seemingly as hard and disinterested as the stars—manifests a comic sensibility that, even with the lightest of echoes from Ronald Firbank and Nathanael West, remains *sui generis*. What must be emphasized, however, is that Purdy's comic sensibility operates most significantly as a means to the allegorical end. For *Malcolm* is an allegory of *growing up*. The physical setting of the novel is the "city," but there is no sense of place or community transmitted. The novel does away with the physical plant not in order to evade "what is there," but in order to invent an allegorical structure which, like Chrétien's fright-

eningly modern-sounding *Perceval,* concerns itself with
the "quest for identity" and the difficulty the sensitive
boy has in making a home for himself. Malcolm is a
young Everyman who must live without the possibility of
salvation; and the novel's putative vitiosity is only a world
of a confused and amorphous understanding of the self.

The first sentence of *Malcolm* suggests the elusive,
dream-like quality of the story:

> In front of one of the most palatial hotels in the
> world, a very young man was accustomed to sit on a
> bench which, when the light fell in a certain way,
> shone like gold.

Malcom has lost his father and, completely lost, he sits
on the bench all day, not feeling, he says, that he "exists."
One day he meets an astrologer named Mr. Cox who gives
him addresses to visit. In this way, Malcolm becomes acquainted with a number of characters. Estel Blanc, an
Abyssinian mortician, is the symbol of death. " 'I do wish
you wouldn't be so final,' Malcolm said, but too low for
Estel to hear him." Nothing mitigates Malcolm's fate; and
we endure it only because of the book's comic style. To
Kermit, a midget artist friend, Malcolm cries: "But you're
so small. . . . You *must* be a midget!" The scene develops
its humor as the characters posture and take the ludicrous
situation seriously.

Kermit's wife Laureen tends fifteen cats, runs away
with a wrestler, and finally marries Girard Girard, a tycoon
who wants Malcolm to be his son. And Girard's first
wife, Madame Girard, simply "wants" Malcolm. She is one
of Purdy's most fantastic creations—a woman of great
disdain and frustration, whose motto is: "Texture is all,
substance nothing."

Finally Malcolm, recognized as a "contemporary,"
meets Melba, "America's Number One Chanteuse," who
sings:

> When you said goodbye, dark daddy,
> Did you know I had not yet said hello?

Malcolm marries Melba, but one day he wakes up, and his
hair, "except for where the blood had dyed it a startling

crimson, was now snow white." A few days later Malcolm dies from "sexual hyperaesthesia."

Even in the midst of the most degenerate scenes, Purdy can reveal Melba—nymphomaniac, conscienceless—in a moment of weakness and allow her to touch us:

> "Malcolm insists a dog bit him," Melba said, and she looked at her drink, which she had carried with her to the car.
>
> The physician, excusing her near forgetfulness, then hastily wrote out a prescription which he handed to her.
>
> Melba still waited on, her glass in hand, why she never understood later, until the doctor got into his broken-down car and drove off. She even waved to him from the drive with her glass.

And throughout the novel, characters and events assume deeper meaning: a chauffeur inquiring of Malcolm his "Destination"; the famous "bench" which Malcolm must leave; a dog bite Malcolm imagines receiving; or that seemingly vague, delicate song Cora Naldi sings:

> And is it so that you were there?
> And is it so you were?
> And is it so that while you were
> Cherries were your ware?
> Pale cherries were your ware?

Most of all, Purdy communicates his characters' aloneness. "I am always alone in victory," says Madame Girard. Or as jazz pianist George Leeds yawns:

> "You see, Malcolm I just stick to the piano. And the rest of the world and the people, too, even nice people like you, well, I just kind of tend to let them go, if you don't mind me saying so."

Cats—the most uninvolved of animals—appear frequently. And the mood of lonesomeness is conveyed in that most beautiful of passages describing Malcolm, "hopelessly alone in Eloisa Brace's apartment:

> Everywhere in the house, no matter at what hour, one felt that it was afternoon, late afternoon breaking into twilight, with a coolness, too, like perpetual autumn, an autumn that will not pass into winter owing to some damage perhaps to the machinery of the cosmos. It will go on being autumn, go on being cool, but slowly, slowly everything will begin to fall piece by piece, the walls will slip down ever so little, the strange pictures will warp, the mythological animals will move their eyes slightly for the last time as they fade into indistinction, the strings of the bass will loosen and fall, the piano keys wrinkle and disappear into the wood of the instrument, and the beautiful alto sax shrivel into foil.

"You can't go on yourself!" Girard Girard tells Malcolm. But Malcolm cannot be saved. " 'Take me with you,' " he says to Girard Girard, "with strength, though his voice cracked a little because it was changing." Malcolm has, as he says, "nothing to go back to." But he gets "involved" with Melba and dies after living his "short long life."

Malcolm is a kind of Christ. (There are references to this throughout the novel. Malcolm might, in fact, be interpreted as a kind of saint.) He is an innocent, a child, who makes his "quest," becomes "initiated," and, in Cox' words, "gives himself up to things." But he is treated as a "thing" as well. He remains passive and people use him. As with Rimbaud's "I" in *The Drunken Boat,* things *happen to* Malcolm. No one truly concerns himself with him —except Girard Girard who, nevertheless, does not return to "take" Malcolm away. In this true novel of growing up, Malcolm, unlike Paul Morel or Stephen Daedalus, never experiences a sudden recognition of what life was, and is, and might be. Precisely because there is no final realization of duty, calling, and truth, Malcolm can be seen as a symbolical contemporary figure; in his life the purposeless nature of the modern world is disclosed. *Malcolm* is a novel of disintegration, of a damaged cosmos:

"I have lost everything!" the boy said, and then his violence disintegrated into a sudden calm and even sweetness.

This thought, so simply stated, is the most terrifying truth there is.

The Goddess and the Schlemihl
BY STANLEY EDGAR HYMAN

A new sort of American novel seems to be emerging in the '60s. I am led to that conclusion by the appearance of a first novel, *V.*, by Thomas Pynchon. It strikingly resembles another recent first novel, Joseph Heller's *Catch-22*, and it has a number of things in common with other first novels of the decade, including two excellent ones that I reviewed recently, Walker Percy's *The Moviegoer* and Bruce Jay Friedman's *Stern*. *V.* is raw and formless in comparison with those two, but it is powerful, ambitious, full of gusto, and overflowing with rich comic invention. Pynchon is a writer of enormous talent and potential, and before making some observations about the new sort of fiction that I think he represents, I will discuss some features of his remarkable novel.

V. is almost impossible to synopsize, or even to describe. It has an interwoven double plot. In one action, an ex-Navy Italian-Jewish drifter named Benny Profane pursues the good life with little success; in the other, a friend of his named Herbert Stencil dredges up the history of a fabulous adventuress and secret agent named "V." (Stencil discovers, or invents, everything about her except the important fact which the reader eventually figures out, that she was Stencil's mother.) The relationship between these two plots is a subtle and complex one. The international hi-jinks of the chapters involving V., with their grand amours and exotic wickedness, oddly serve to make the random lechery and low carousing of Profane's world seem not sordid but human and sympathetic. At the same time, V., as a Platonic myth of the passions, enlarges the significance of the contemporary action.

Pynchon takes advantage of his international melodrama

for all sorts of fine mean parody. Sometimes he writes like E. Phillips Oppenheim or the Baroness Orczy; at other times like Lawrence Durrell or the French New Wave. The international incidents are deliberately preposterous, from the first armed assassin disabled by a kick from a well-shod boot, to the last double agent going numb at the threat of exposure and fiendish retribution.

Pynchon is even more wildly imaginative, high-spirited and funny in the Profane episodes. A Brazilian salad man at a *borscht* resort acquires a machine gun, camouflages it with watercress and endive, and sits through meals pretending to strafe the guests, dreaming that they are Arabs and that he is an Israeli soldier. "Yibble, yibble, yibble," he says, pointing at one well-fed Jew after another, "got you dead center, Abdul Sayid. Yibble, yibble, Muslim pig." A Jesuit priest, Father Fairing, convinced that the rats are about to take over New York City, moves down to the sewers to convert the rats to Roman Catholicism, and by blessing and exorcising all the sewer water between Lexington and the East River and between 79th and 86th, creates Fairing's Parish.

At other times Pynchon seems principally interested in harrowing the reader. A nose-lifting operation is described in detail for five pages, a young ballerina is horribly impaled during a performance, and one chapter is devoted to the sadistic atrocities against natives committed by the Germans in German South-West Africa in 1904 and later. Only the last of these has any relevance that I can see. It soon becomes clear that Pynchon is indirectly commenting on the Nazi crimes against the Jews, one of the things that has created Profane's numbed world.

· The least successful feature of *V.* is Pynchon's whimsy. As in musical comedy, his characters sometimes interrupt their conversation to break into duets. The characters' names, like those of *Catch-22,* are juvenile: Dewey Gland, Baby Face Falange, and such. New York is usually referred to as "Nueva York." The comical behavior of drunken sailors gets to be a bore after a while. When Pynchon's invention flags he flogs it, and the reader may be reminded of *Mad.*

The garish fantasy of V. dominates the book. We see her first as a 19-year-old Yorkshire girl named Victoria Wren, deflowered by a British agent in Cairo during the

Fashoda crisis in 1898; then in Florence in 1899, seducing
Stencil's father on a couch in the British consulate; after
that nameless in Paris in 1913, a Lesbian fetishist in love
with a young ballerina she dresses as a boy; then as Veronica Manganese in Malta in 1919, by which time she has
a star sapphire sewn into her navel and a glass eye with a
clock for a pupil; then as Vera Meroving of Munich in
German South-West Africa in 1922, punctuating a garden
conversation by braining a goldfish; finally disguised as a
nameless priest on Malta in 1939, dying in an air raid
when some children find her unconscious and despoil her,
killing her in their efforts to dig out her star sapphire.

These are only the few of V.'s impersonations that we
see. Stencil reports that she spent a year disguised as an
old fisherman in Mallorca, that she was a partisan in Asia,
that she crashed a stolen airplane in Spain. Beyond that V.
is some great female principle, embodied even in the rat
Veronica, who was either Father Fairing's saintly nun-to-be
or his mistress, "depending which story you listened to."
She is the goddess Venus and the planet Venus, the Virgin,
the town of Valetta in Malta, the imaginary land of Vheissu
with its iridescent spider monkeys and Volcanoes. She
is Vesuvius, Venezuela, the Violet of a vulgar mnemonic;
ultimately she is the V of spread thighs and the mons
veneris.

None of the real characters in the book can quite come
up to this fertility goddess. Profane is a self-identified
schlemihl who works at such jobs as hunting alligators in
the New York sewers or being night watchman in a labor-
atory that mutilates plastic human dummies. Women throw
themselves at him, but something always goes wrong. If he
is not interrupted by a comic intruder he is repelled by the
girl's eagerness and changes his mind. Profane finally
manages an affair with Rachel Owlglass, a Bennington
alumna who loves him and wants to transform him.
There are several beautiful and moving love scenes between them, written with power and honesty. Profane
turns out to be incapable of accepting the responsibility
that Rachel represents, and when last seen he is on Malta,
with a new girl, looking for sewer work.

Surrounding Benny and Rachel are a group of young
eccentrics who call themselves the Whole Sick Crew.
Slab devotes his life to painting a series of Cheese Danish

canvases; Esther Harvitz is the mistress of her plastic surgeon; Roony Winsome tapes street fights; his wife Mafia plays Musical Blankets with male roomers named Charisma and Fu; and so on. Just outside the Crew are two sympathetic characters: Paola Maijstral, a Maltese who disguises herself as a Negro whore named Ruby; and McClintic Sphere, a Negro jazz musician and parody of Ornette Coleman, who plays a hand-carved ivory alto saxophone. In a wider circle are two truly grotesque figures: Shale Schoenmaker, Esther's nose surgeon and lover, who cannot control his impulse to remodel the rest of her; and Dudley Eigenvalue, a "psychodontist" who diagnoses his patients' emotional difficulties as "malocclusion," "deciduous dentition," or "heterodont configuration."

Along with *Catch-22* and other recent first novels, *V.* represents a deliberate return to old-fashioned literary conventions. It has the long chapter headings of older comic fiction ("In which Rachel gets her yo-yo back, Roony sings a song, and Stencil calls on Bloody Chiclitz"), the comic capitals of George Ade ("a ghetto for Drunken Sailors nobody knew what to Do With"), and an omniscient narrator who explains things to the reader. Where the British Angry Young Men derive from the tradition of Fielding, Smollett and the picaresque novel, *Catch-22*, *V.* and the others derive principally from Sterne's *Tristram Shandy*, Twain, and the conventions of digressive oral narrative. What has been lost is the innocence. If Pynchon has been influenced by Sterne, he has also been visibly influenced by our bitter symbolists of the '30s, Nathanael West and Djuna Barnes.

These new novelists also delight in impure forms. The doomed love between Profane and Rachel is the material of tragedy, and Pynchon handles it with great purity of feeling, but jostling their scenes in the book are wild comedy, outlandish melodrama, and bloated caricature. The hero of the modern novel has been unheroic for a long time—one has only to think of Swann and Leopold Bloom —but rarely so unheroic as these protagonists. Benny Profane is as soft and fat as Friedman's Stern, as cowardly as Heller's Yossarian, as addicted to "yo-yoing" (traveling aimlessly back and forth on subways and ferries) as Percy's Jack Bolling is to escapist moviegoing. Hemingway's Lieutenant Henry in *A Farewell to Arms* made a separate

peace and deserted the war after he had fought bravely;
Benny Profane, who never fought in any war, has made
a separate peace in every human struggle, even the one
against mice (pro-mouse, Benny springs traps).

These heroes are in neurotic withdrawal and thermonuclear shock. They suffer from meagerness of aim, asking
only to be physically gratified and otherwise left alone.
Pynchon wants more of life than Benny does, and his
message is delivered as a series of slogans by the book's
sympathetic characters. "Love with your mouth shut,"
McClintic tells us, "keep cool, but care." (How treacherously that last appears to resemble Krishna's message to
Arjuna in the *Bhagavad Gita:* Do your duty without attachment.) "You have to con each other a little," Rachel
tells Profane, trying to prevent a quarrel.

What Pynchon and his fellows are really offering us
are the slogans of revisionist psychoanalysis: kindness, consideration, mutuality, unselfish love. But outside and beyond this world of moderate adjustment is V., who wants
more of life than Pynchon does. She wants passion, danger,
total immersion in the destructive element, rebirth in the
artifice of eternity. It is a sign of Thomas Pynchon's intelligence and imagination that he knows that too.

Robbe-Grillet Today
BY ROLAND BARTHES

> Don't give them any name. . . They could
> have had so many other adventures . . ."
> —*Last Year at Marienbad*

The realistic intention of our literature is singular. Is
reality, then, so lost that in order to recover it we must
on each occasion mobilize an institution, a tradition, a
market, a technique, a talent or even a genius? It seems,
as a matter of fact, that the exercise of a certain *distance*
(and consequently of a certain *function*) is necessary to
the modern writer: he must believe (by what necessity?)
that there is on the one hand *the real*, and on the other
language; that one is antecedent to the other, and that
the task of the latter is somehow to run after the former
until it catches up with it. What is the reason for this
analogic vocation of our literature? The answer probably
lies in a certain arrangement of the models themselves:
the real that is "available" to the writer can doubtless
be multiple: now psychological, now theological, social,
political, historical, or even imaginary, each in its turn
replacing the other; these realities nonetheless have a
common characteristic which explains the constancy of
their projection: they are all and entirely imbued with
meaning: a passion, a fault, a conflict, a dream inevitably refer back to a certain transcendence—soul, divinity, society or supernature, so that all our realistic literature is not only analogical but *significative* as well.

Among all these psychological and social realities the
object itself had no original place; for a long time, literature was concerned only with a world of inter-human
relations (if a harp is mentioned in *Les Liasons Danger-
euses,* it is because it serves to conceal a love-letter); and
when things, tools, spectacles or substances began to
appear with some abundance in our novels, it was as
esthetic elements or human indications in order to refer

more effectively to a certain mood (romantic landscape) or to a specific social misery (realistic detail). As we know, Alain Robbe-Grillet's work deals with this problem of the literary object; do *things* induce meanings, or on the contrary are they "mat"? Can and should the writer describe an object without referring it to some human transcendence? Significative or meaningless, what is the function of objects in a fictional narrative? How does the way in which they are described modify the story's meaning? The character's consistency? The very relation to the idea of literature? Now that Robbe-Grillet's *oeuvre* has developed, now that the cinema has given it a second wind and a second public, we can put these questions to it in a new way. Depending on our answer, we shall quickly realize that we are faced, with the help of Robbe-Grillet, with *two* Robbe-Grillets: on the one hand the Robbe-Grillet of immediate things, destroyer of meanings, chiefly described by his first critics; and on the other, the Robbe-Grillet of mediate things, creator of meanings, analyzed by Bruce Morrissette in his study *Les Romans de Robbe-Grillet* (Paris, 1963).

The first Robbe-Grillet (I am not concerned here with a temporal antecedence, but merely with an order of classification), the first Robbe-Grillet decides that things mean nothing, not even the absurd (he rightly adds), for it is obvious that the absence of meaning can very well be a meaning. But since these same things are buried under a heap of various meanings by which men, through their sensibilities, poems and various uses, have imbued the name of each object, the novelist's task is in a way cathartic: he purifies things of the unwarranted meanings which men ceaselessly deposit upon them. How? Evidently by description. Thus Robbe-Grillet produces certain descriptions of objects sufficiently geometrical to discourage any induction toward a poetic meaning; and sufficiently detailed to interrupt the fascination of the narrative; but by doing so he encounters realism; like the realists, he copies, or at least seems to copy, a model; in formal terms, we might say that he proceeds as if his novel were merely the event which occurs to fulfill an antecedent structure: it matters little whether or not this structure is *true*, and whether Robbe-Grillet's realism is subjective or objective; for what defines realism is not the origin of the model but its external relation to the language accompanying it. On the one hand, the realism of this first Robbe-Grillet remains classical because it is based on a relation of analogy (the slice of tomato Robbe-Grillet describes resembles a real slice of tomato); and on the other, it is new because this analogy does not refer to any transcendence, but claims to survive enclosed within itself, content when it has necessarily and sufficiently designated the too-famous *dasein* (being-there) of the thing (this slice of tomato is described in such a way that it is supposed to provoke neither desire nor disgust, and to signify neither season, nor site, nor even sustenance).

It is apparent that description can neither exhaust the tissue of the novel nor satisfy the interest traditionally expected of it: there are many *genres* besides description in Robbe-Grillet's novels. But it is also apparent that a small number of descriptions that are both analogical and non-significative, according to the place the author gives them and the variations he introduces into them, is enough to modify the general meaning of the novel altogether. Every novel is an intelligible organism of an infinite sensibility; the least point of opacity, the least (mute) resistance to the desire which animates and carries along all reading, constitutes an *astonishment* that is transferred to the whole of the work. Robbe-Grillet's famous objects have, then, no anthological value; they truly involve the anecdote itself and the characters it collects in a kind of silence of signification. This is why the notion one might have of a "chosiste" (or thing-dedicated) Robbe-Grillet can only be unitary and, so to speak, totalitarian: there is a fatal reversion from the non-significance of things to the non-significance of situations and of men. It is in fact quite possible to read all of Robbe-Grillet's work (at least up to *In the Labyrinth*) in a "mat" way; one need merely remain on the surface of the text, it being understood that a *superficial* reading is no longer to be condemned in the name of the old values of inwardness. It is even the indubitable merit of this first Robbe-Grillet (even if he is a fictional one) to demystify the so-called natural qualities of the literature of introspection (the *profound* being by rights preferable to the *superficial*) to the advantage of a *dasein* of the text (which we must be sure not

to confuse with the *dasein* of the thing itself), and in a
way to refuse the reader the pleasure of a world that is
"rich," "profound," "secret"—in short, significative. It is
evident that according to Robbe-Grillet No. 1, the neurotic or pathological state of his characters (one oedipal,
another sadistic and a third obsessive) has in no way the
traditional value of a *content*, of which the elements of
the novel would be the more or less mediate symbols
available to the decoding of the reader (or of the critic):
this state is only the purely formal term of a function.
Robbe-Grillet, then, seems to manipulate a certain content
because there is no literature without a sign, and no sign
without that which it signifies; but his whole art consists
precisely in *deceiving* meaning at the very moment it suggests it. To name this content, to invoke madness, sadism
or even jealousy is thus to exceed what we might call the
novel's highest level of perception, the one on which it is
perfectly and immediately intelligible, just as when we
look very closely at a photographic reproduction we doubtless penetrate its typographical secret, but we also no
longer understand anything about the object it represents.
It follows that this *deception* of meaning, if authentic,
would in no way be gratuitous: to provoke meaning in
order to arrest it is merely to prolong an experiment
which has its modern origin in the surrealist movement
and which engages the very being of literature, that is,
finally, the anthropological function it possesses within the
entirety of historical society. Such is the image of Robbe-
Grillet No. 1 which might be formed from certain theoretical texts and novels, to which we must add, in general,
the commentaries of the first period.

From these same texts and these same novels (but not,
of course, from these same commentaries) we may just
as well form the image of a Robbe-Grillet No. 2, no
longer a "chosiste" but a "humanist," since the objects,
without turning back into symbols in the usual sense of
the term, do recover a mediating function in the direction
of "something else." Of this second image, Bruce Morrissette has made himself, in the course of the study mentioned above, the detailed constructor. His method is both
descriptive and comparative: on one hand, he patiently

recounts the novels of Robbe-Grillet, which permits him
to reconstitute the often very complex arrangement of
episodes, that is, in short, the structure of the work, which
no one has hitherto dealt with; and on the other hand, a
wide learning permits him to relate these episodes (scenes
or descriptions of objects) to models, archetypes, sources,
echoes, and thus to re-establish the cultural continuity
which unites an *oeuvre* reputed to be "mat" to a whole
literary and consequently human context. Morrissette's
method produces, in effect, an "integrated" image of
Robbe-Grillet, or better still, an image reconciled with the
traditional goals of the novel; it doubtless reduces the
work's revolutionary share, but on the other hand it establishes the excellent reasons the public may have for
finding itself at home with Robbe-Grillet (and the critical
success of *In the Labyrinth* in France, the worldwide public career of *Marienbad* seem to bear that public out).
This Robbe-Grillet No. 2 does not say, like Chénier: "Out
of new thoughts, let us make old verses." He says, on
the contrary: out of old thoughts, let us make new novels.

What does this reconciliation concern? First of all, of
course, those famous "objects" previously regarded as neutral and non-significative. Morrissette acknowledges the
originality of the Robbe-Grilletist vision of things, but he
does not believe that in this universe the object is cut off
from all reference and that it radically ceases to be a
sign; he has no difficulty discovering, in Robbe-Grillet's
collections, several objects which if not obsessional, are at
least sufficiently repeated to induce a meaning (for what
is repeated is supposed to signify). The eraser (in *Les
Gommes*, published in America as *Erasers*), the little cord
(in *The Voyeur*), the centipede (in *Jealousy*)—these objects, repeated, varied throughout the novel, all refer to a
criminal or sexual act, and beyond this act to an inwardness. Morrissette nonetheless refuses to regard them as
symbols; in a more reserved (but perhaps somewhat
specious) manner, he prefers to define them as simple props
for sensations, emotions, memories; thus the object becomes a contrapuntal element of the work; it belongs to
the story with the same prerogatives as a periptery, and it
is certainly one of Morrissette's great contributions to
Robbe-Grillet criticism to have been able to rediscover a

narrative in each of these novels; thanks to his scrupulous and detailed summaries, it is clear that the Robbe-Grillet novel is a "story" and that this story has a meaning: Oedipal, sadistic, obsessional, or even simply literary, if *In the Labyrinth,* as he believes, is the story of a creation; doubtless this "story" is not composed in a traditional way, and Morrissette, concerned with the modernism of the technique, skillfully illuminates the variations and complexities of the narrative "point of view," the distortions Robbe-Grillet imposes on chronology and his rejection of psychological analysis (but not of psychology). It remains no less true that, provided once again with a story, a (pathological) psychology and a substance which if not symbolic is at least referential, the Robbe-Grillet novel is no longer the "flat" diagram his early critics described; it is an object in the round, and full of secrets; now the critic must begin considering what there is behind this object and around it: he takes to deciphering, becomes hermeneutic: he seeks "keys" (and in general finds them). This is what Morrissette has done for Robbe-Grillet's novels: the courage of such a critic is apparent, who dares straight off and in the case of a writer not only contemporary but still quite young, to use a method of decipherment we have taken a half century to apply to authors like Nerval and Rimbaud.

Between the two Robbe-Grillets, "chosiste" the Robbe-Grillet No. 1 and the "humanist" Robbe-Grillet No. 2, between that of the early criticism and that of Bruce Morrissette, must we choose? Robbe-Grillet himself will not help us here; like every author, and despite his theoretical declarations, he is, about his own work, constitutively ambiguous: further, it is obvious that his work is changing, which is its privilege. And it is actually this ambiguity which counts, which concerns us, which bears the historical meaning of a work that at first glance seems to refuse history. What is this meaning? The opposite of a meaning—that is, a *question.* What do things *mean,* what does the world *mean*? All literature is this question, but we must immediately add, for this is what constitutes its speciality: *it is this question minus its answer.* No literature in the world has ever answered the question it asked,

and it is this very suspension that has always constituted
it as literature: it is that very fragile language which men
possess between the violence of the question and the silence
of the answer: both religious and critical at the moment
during which it questions, it is both irreligious and conservative at the same moment during which it does not
answer: a question itself, it is the question which the centuries ask within it, it is not the answer. What god, Valéry
once said, would dare take as his motto: "I deceive"?
Literature would be such a god; perhaps it will one day
be possible to describe all of literature as the art of deception. The history of literature will then no longer be the
history of the contradictory answers afforded by writers
to the question of meaning, but the history, on the contrary, of the question itself.

For it is apparent that literature cannot directly raise
the question which constitutes it: it has not been able, will
never be able, to extend its interpellation to all discourse,
without passing through the stages of certain techniques;
and if the history of literature is ultimately the history of
these techniques, it is not because literature is only technique (as some tried to say in the days of art for art's
sake), but because technique is the only power capable of
suspending the meaning of the world and of keeping open
the imperative question addressed to it; for it is not *answering* which is difficult, it is questioning, it is speaking
interrogatively and answering in silence. From this point
of view, Robbe-Grillet's "technique" was, at a certain
point, radical: when the author believed it was possible to
"kill" meaning directly, so that the work revealed only
the fundamental astonishment which constitutes it (for to
write is not to affirm, it is to be astonished). The originality
of the attempt derived, then, from the fact that the question was not disguised by any false answer, though without
of course being formulated in terms of a question; Robbe-
Grillet's (theoretical) error was merely to believe that there
was a *dasein* of things antecedent and external to language,
which it was literature's responsibility, he thought, to recover in a last impulse of realism. As a matter of fact,
anthropologically, things signify immediately, in every case
and with good reason; and it is precisely because signification is their "natural" condition, so to speak, that by

simply stripping them of their meaning literature can affirm itself as an admirable artifice: if "nature" is significative, a certain task of "culture" can be to make it "designify." Whence, quite logically these "mat" descriptions of objects, these anecdotes narrated "on the surface," these characters without confidence—all of which produce, at least according to a certain reading, the style, or one might say the choice, of Robbe-Grillet.

Yet these empty forms irresistibly call for a content, and we gradually observe, in the criticism, in the author's own work, certain temptations to sentiment, certain returns of archetypes, certain fragments of symbols—in short everything that belongs to the realm of the adjective— creeping into the proud *dasein* of things. In this sense, there is an evolution of Robbe-Grillet's work, which is paradoxically accomplished by the author, the critics and the public all at once: we are all part of Robbe-Grillet, insofar as we all set about replenishing the meaning of things as soon as we open the work in front of us. Considered in its development and in its future (which we cannot assign to it), Robbe-Grillet's work then becomes the *ordeal of meaning* suffered by a certain society, and the history of this work will be in its way the history of that society. Already meaning is returning: driven out of the famous slice of tomato in *Erasers* (but doubtless already present in the eraser itself, as Bruce Morrissette demonstrates), it fills *Marienbad*, its gardens, its mirrored paneling, its feather cloaks. Yet though it is no longer non-existent, meaning here is still variously conjectural: everyone has explained *Marienbad*, but each explanation was a meaning immediately contested by the next: meaning is no longer deceived, henceforth it remains suspended. And if each novel by Robbe-Grillet contains "en abyme" its own symbol, doubtless the final allegory of this work is the statue of Charles III and his wife which the lovers of *Marienbad* ask each other about: a splendid symbol, moreover, not only because the statue itself induces various uncertain and nonetheless named meanings (you and me, classical gods, Helen and Agamemnon, etc.), but further because the prince and his wife are pointing in a certain way at an uncertain object (situated in the fable? in the garden? in the hall?):

this, they are saying. But what is *this?* All of literature is perhaps in this slight anaphora which both calls our attention and keeps silent.

—*Translated by* Richard Howard

Two Dream Poets
BY JONATHAN COTT

Westward, hit a low note, for a roarer lost
across the Sound but north from Bremerton,
hit a way down note.
And never cadenza again of flowers, or cost.
Him who could really do that cleared his throat
and staggered on.

The bluebells, pool-shallows, saluted his over-needs,
while the clouds growled, heh-heh, & snapped & crashed.

No stunt he'll ever unflinch once more will fail
(O lucky fellow, eh Bones?)—drifted off upstairs,
downstairs, somewheres.
No more daily, trying to hit the head on the nail:
thirstless: without a think in his head:
back from wherever, with it said.

Hit a long high note, for a lover found
needing a lower into friendlier ground
to bug among worms no more
around um jungles where ah blurt "What for?"
Weeds, too, he favoured as most men don't favour men.
The Garden Master's gone.

John Berryman's "A Strut for Roethke" was written after
the death of the fifty-five year old American poet in the
summer of 1963. It is the song of one extraordinary
dream poet to another; and it explodes with what at first
reading seems to be "the muck and welter, the dark, the
dreck" that Roethke ascribed to his own works of art.
Both are writers of poems that are in some sense dream-

work—"psychic shorthand" as Roethke called it—writers whose exacerbated sensibilities project to us two unique and startling perceptions of the world. Both are painfully conscious of the world in inverse proportion as, in Roethke's words, they "wake to sleep and take their waking slow." To Roethke and Berryman, dreams are not "toys." They are the confrontation and working-out of the poet's psychic and spiritual identities in relation to the moral and political decline of the West in Berryman's *Dream Song*s and, in Roethke's poems, to the world of the "minimal"—a world in which even the dirt breathes "a small breath," a world in which external and internal realities exist on the same psychic terrain and eventually become identical.

Roethke searches below the external surface of his self in order to arrive at the inner soul; the "delineation of the ideal" becomes apparent through the poet's scrutiny. With *The Far Field*—a collection of Roethke's last poems —and the earlier collected verse, *Words for the Wind*, we have Roethke's full testament of this search. As he wrote in "Open House":

> My secrets cry aloud.
> I have no need for tongue.
> My heart keeps open house,
> My doors are widely swung.
> An epic of the eyes
> My love, with no disguise.
>
> My truths are all foreknown,
> This anguish self-revealed.
> I'm naked to the bone,
> With nakedness my shield.
> Myself is what I wear.
> I keep the spirit spare.

The poet consistently presents himself to us, naked and rampaging his Self. "A man's a beast prowling in his own house," he writes in the later poem, "The Pure Fury." And only in an induced dream-state can the poet arrive at what in "Otto" he calls his "lost world." To reach this world, Roethke must make a poetic journey from "exhaustion to exhaustion" (a phrase he takes from Yeats) during which he dives down in his dream state through all layers of his psyche. Redintegration often occurs in the greenhouse, Roethke's lost world, his self-styled "symbol for the whole of life, a womb, a heaven-on-earth" ("Open Letter," in *Mid-Century American Poets,* edited by John Ciardi). For Roethke, as for Emil Nolde, Father is the Great Gardener. After having "returned" to his "heaven-on-earth" in "The Lost Son," the poet cries out: 'Ordnung! Ordnung! Papa is coming."

It is almost embarrassing for a critic to interpret Roethke's work in terms of Freud and Jung. Roethke's series of fourteen child-like, dream-like monologues in *Praise to the End* succeeds so beautifully in communicating "the spring and rush of the child—and Gammer Gurton's concision" ("Open Letter") and in revealing secondary-elaboration of subconscious roots of thought and feeling that one would rather think that psychologists obtained their perceptions of dreams and childhood fantasies from Roethke. Conceptions such as "Dreams as a Form of Ideation" and "Nightmares as Objectifications of Organic Sensations," etc., seem foolish when applied to Roethke's work. To say that the line "I have left the body of the whale, but the mouth of the night is still wide" ("The Longing") has "Freudian overtones" is quite idiotic. The rock-bed reality and radically "regressive" images of Roethke's poems are so striking and essential that Freud is superfluous. Roethke's work is the discovery of himself; and his poems need no symbolic correlatives to explain them.

The manifest dream content in Roethke's poems consists of objects existing in the world of the "minimal." This is a world of sweet-peas, weeds, stones, meadow mice, little girls. But as we can see from almost any quotation from Roethke's poems, the poetic materials spring up from the greenhouse where the poet spent much of his childhood, from the soil of the garden, from the marsh. "Weeds, too, he favoured as most men don't favour men," Berryman wrote about him. And although in "The Abyss" Roethke writes that "too much reality can be a dazzle," he wants only to tell of his intense love for the objects and events of the natural world. In "Night Journey" he writes how on a cross-country train he "stays up half the night/To see the land I love."

Roethke employs images of the world of the "minimal" in all his love poems (hardly equalled for their passion in our time) or meditations or songs: "Love, love, a lily's my care"; "I remember the neckcurls, limp and damp as tendrils." But this world also includes "A kingdom of stinks and sighs,/Fetor of cockroaches, dead fish, petroleum,/Worse than castoreum of mink or weasels,/Saliva dripping from warm microphones,/Agony of crucifixion on barstools" ("The Longing"). For Roethke's world is his mind; his mind, the world: "A ghost comes out of the unconscious mind/To grope my sill: It moans to be reborn!" And it is reborn. Roethke's poems are the means by which he connects the everyday world with his unconscious ghost. We see, for example, how a creature of the world and the creature of the poet's mind in "Night Crow" become one—because they are one:

> When I saw that clumsy crow
> Flap from a wasted tree,
> A shape in the mind rose up:
> Over the gulfs of dream
> Flew a tremendous bird
> Further and further away
> Into a moonless black,
> Deep in the brain, far back.

Ghosts are made real, animals made human; for in Roethke's dream-world there is little distinction between the two. The Bat—a Christian Morgenstern character-creature—"loops in crazy figures half the night." Yet "his fingers make a hat about his head"; and Roethke finally reveals "him" wholly and terribly:

> But when he brushes up against a screen,
> We are afraid of what our eyes have seen:
>
> For something is amiss or out of place
> When mice with wings can wear a human face.

Plants, too, are seen animistically. In "Orchids," the flowers have "soft luminescent fingers . . . loose ghostly mouths." In one of Roethke's last great poems, "The Geranium," the poet's relationship with a flower is as human as his love for Jane in his often-anthologized "Elegy for Jane." "The Geranium" resembles the poem in its beautifully cadenced lines and tone of loneliness and grief:

> When I put her out, once by the garbage pail,
> She looked so limp and bedraggled,
> So foolish and trusting, like a sick poodle,
> Or a wizened aster in late September,
> I brought her back in again
> For a new routine—
> Vitamins, water, and whatever
> Sustenance seemed sensible
> At the time: she'd lived
> So long on gin, bobbie pins, half-smoked cigars,
>   dead beer,
> Her shrivelled petals falling
> On the faded carpet, the stale
> Steak grease stuck to her fuzzy leaves.
> (Dried-out, she creaked like a tulip.)
>
> The things she endured!—
> The dumb dames shrieking half the night
> Or the two of us, alone, both seedy,
> Me breathing booze at her,
> She leaning out of her pot toward the window.
>
> Near the end, she seemed almost to hear me—
> And that was scary—
> So when that snuffling cretin of a maid
> Threw her, pot and all, into the trash-can,
> I said nothing.
>
> But I sacked the presumptuous hag the next week,
> I was that lonely.

In Roethke's poems, the ideal is delineated only by the identity the poet makes between his psyche and the world. Both are the same—as in the womb or in dreams—and this is the world of Roethke's poetry. The fact that Roethke is one of the great craftsmen—his use of slant and oblique rhymes is wonderfully subtle (lives/ leaves; stone/moon; all/temporal); the villanelle form in "The Waking" and his ballad and song forms of "The

Saginaw Song," "A Wheeze for Wystan," and "My Papa's Waltz" are extraordinary—almost escapes mention. For Roethke writes of such extremes of emotions that one wishes to judge his poems on their power and his imagination alone. As in a perfect dream, we break through to the beauty of "The Moment"—the moment in which events, things, persons, and feelings are transfigured to become All:

> We passed the ice of pain,
> And came to a dark ravine,
> And there we sang with the sea;
> The wide, the bleak abyss
> Shifted with our slow kiss.
>
> Space struggled with time;
> The gong of midnight struck
> The naked absolute.
> Sound, silence sang as one.
>
> All flowed: without, within;
> Body met body, we
> Created what's to be.
>
> What else to say?—
>   We end in joy.

* * *

Turning it over, considering, like a madman
Henry put forth a book.
No harm resulted from this.
Neither the menstruating   stars (nor man) was
moved at once.
Bare dogs drew closer for a second look

and performed their friendly operations there.
Refreshed, the bark rejoiced.
Seasons went and came.
Leaves fell, but only a few.
Something remarkable about this
unshedding bulky bole-proud blue-green moist

thing made by savage & thoughtful
surviving Henry
began to strike the passers from despair,

so that sore on their shoulders old men hoisted
six-foot sons and polished women called
small girls to dream awhile toward the flashing &
    bursting tree!

The book "put forth" is John Berryman's *77 Dream Songs,* one of the great achievements of American poetry. Curiously enough, the *Dream Songs* perfectly exemplify the suggestions Roethke addressed to himself in his "Open Letter" on how a poet can derive his important powers. The poet, Roethke, writes:

> must be able to telescope image and symbol, if neces-
> sary, without relying on the obvious connectives: to
> speak in a kind of psychic shorthand when his pro-
> tagonist is under great stress. He must be able to
> shift his rhythms rapidly, the "tension." He works
> intuitively, and the final form of his poem must be
> imaginatively right . . . . obscurity should break open
> suddenly for the serious reader who can hear the
> language: the "meaning" itself should come as dramat-
> ic revelation, an excitement.

Berryman, in a note of introduction to his early poems of 1940, wrote of the "strain," the "torsion" of his poetry. In retrospect, we see how the poet's now-famous twisting, elliptical style emerges in the fourth and fifth sections of Berryman's first volume, *The Dispossessed* (e.g., "Rising wind rucks from the sill/The slack brocade beside   the old throne he dreams on."—"The Long Home"). *Homage to Mistress Bradstreet,* published in 1956 and unfortunately little read, is a poem of fifty-seven eight line stanzas of shifting end rhymes in which the phrasal cadence of the speaking voice conflicts violently with the iambic line. Berryman's latinate diction, wrenched accents, and occasional sprung rhythms combine to produce the haunting study of the torn and deracinated early American poetess. In monologues and interspersed conversations with the poet himself, the poet's heartbreakingly exposed love for and understanding of Anne Bradstreet is revealed:

> Outside the New World winters in grand dark
> white air lashing high thro' the virgin stands
> foxes down foxholes sigh,

surely the English heart quails, stunned.
I doubt if Simon than this blast, that sea,
spares from his rigour for your poetry
more. We are on each other's hands
who care. Both of our worlds unhanded us. Lie
  stark. . . .

(Stanza 2)

Veiled my eyes, attending. How can it be I?
Moist, with parted lips, I listen, wicked.
I shake in the morning & retch.
Brood I do on myself naked.
A fading world I dust, with fingers new.
—I have earned the right to be alone with you.
—What right can that be?
Convulsing, if you love, enough, like a sweet lie.

(Stanza 27)

It is in the *Dream Songs*, however, that Berryman finds
the perfect vehicle for his style and vision. The eight line
stanza becomes six-lined. The "roiling & babbling &
braining"—to use Berryman's phrase—is spoken and sung
by Henry, the dreamer of the *Dream Songs*. He talks
about and converses with himself, but also with Mr. Bones,
perhaps of minstrel show derivation, who is somewhat an
alter ego: "Easy, easy, Mr. Bones. I is on your side,"
says Henry. As Roethke wrote:

> The revelation of the identity of the speaker may
> itself be a part of the drama; or, in some instances,
> in a dream sequence, his identity may merge with
> someone else's, or be deliberately blurred. The strug-
> gle for spiritual identity is, of course, one of the
> perpetual recurrences. . . . *Disassociation often pre-
> cedes a new state of clarity*" ("Open Letter," emphasis
> added).

For there is a marvelous clarity to these songs. They
abound, of course, in the condensation and displacement
of dream-work. But loneliness and despair have rarely been
expressed with such quietness and restraint as in the song
titled "Snow Line":

It was wet & white & swift and where I am
we don't know. It was dark and then
it isn't.
I wish the barker would come. There seems to be
  to eat
nothing. I am unusually tired.
I'm alone too.

If only the strange one with so few legs would come,
I'd say my prayers out of my mouth, as usual.
Where are his notes I loved?
There may be horribles; it's hard to tell.
The barker nips me but somehow I feel
he too is on my side.

I'm too alone. I see no end. If we could all
run, even that would be better. I am hungry.
The sun is not hot.
It's not a good position I am in.
If I had to do the whole thing over again
I wouldn't.

Beyond performing in complete darkness "operations of
great delicacy/on myself" for the sake only of his Self,
Berryman approaches our life today with the moral stature
and compassion of Sam Johnson and Gibbon. He goes
naked to show our "moral nudity." In many respects he
has an eighteenth-century mind although his speaking voice
is the singing brawl of the declamatory sot (Pope's "sot
as hero"). It is through these drunken lurchings of syntax,
however, that the extirpation of our respect for ourselves
and others is witnessed and proclaimed. I have heard
Berryman read his *Dream Songs* in public—intoxicated,
slurring, emphasizing words so wilfully as to destroy the
"line"—yet the majesty of his vision finally broke through
like his "flashing and bursting tree." Nothing less than the
decline and fall of the contemporary West is revealed in
Berryman's "non-tipsyish" drunken songs.

Sometimes Berryman rages against the "teen set":

"Scads of good eats" dere own t'ree cars, the 'teens
(until of them shall be asked one thing, they romp
  or doze)
have got it made;

no prob. was ever set them, their poor ol' jerks
of parents loved them, with deep-freeze, & snacks
would keep a Hindu family-group alive.

Well, so they're liars & gluttons & cowards: so what?
. . . It's the Land of Plenty, maybe about to sigh.
Why shouldn't they terrify
with hegemony Dad (stupido Dad) and "teach"? . . .

One waits for the Houyhnhnms to set the "teens" to "hard work."

Or Berryman will see the chaos and lunacies of the Eisenhower years in fragments of Henry's dreaming mind. In another song Henry alias Henry Hankovitch—doing his "short Zen pray"; déraciné?—plays with his girl friend Phoebe "both happy as cockroaches/in the world kitchen woofed, with all away." But the "political" comment is not far off:

The international flame, like despair, rose
or like the foolish Paks or Sudanese

Henry Hankovitch, con guitar,
did a praying mantis pray
who even more obviously than the increasingly
   fanatical Americans
cannot govern themselves. Swedes don't exist,
Scandinavians in general do not exist,
take it from there.

Berryman writes in one song about fall-out shelters and in another of the final destruction after which: "Bars will be closed./No girl will again/conceive above your throes." The world is crumbling because, unlike Henry whose self is fragmented but aware of its own and others' fragmentation, we "hardly know [our] selving":

All virtues enter into this world:')
A Buddhist doused in the street, serenely burned.
The Secretary of State for War,
winking it over, screwed a redhaired whore.
Monsignor Capovilla mourned. What a week.

Berryman realizes that our "squeamish comfy ruin-prone proud national mind" is the small cause from which extend the greater evils. But the cocktail parties go on—parties like the one in which "Henry's pelt was put on sundry walls." (One is reminded of Roethke's "The flying fabric stitched on bone."):

> Golden, whilst your frozen daiquiris
> whir at midnight, gleams on you his fur
> & silky & black.
> Mission accomplished, pal.
> My molten yellow & moonless bag,
> drained, hangs at rest.
>
> Collect in the cold depths barracuda. Ay,
> in Sealdah Station some possessionless
> children survive to die.
> The Chinese communes hum. Two daiquiris
> withdrew into the corner of the gorgeous room
> and one told the other a lie.

And finally we have Berryman's songs of grief for those like Roethke and Robert Frost who are "in friendlier ground"; for their virtues and feelings were so "unusual," patent and open-to-wounding in the face of the everyday evils. About Frost, Berryman writes:

> His malice was a pimple down his good
> big face, with its sly eyes. I must be sorry
> Mr. Frost has left:
> I like it so less I don't understood—
> he couldn't hear or see well—all we sift—
> but this is a *bad* story.

Berryman faces ruin and frustration with high comedy and low comedy and sorrow; with "ancient signs, infamous characters, new rhythms." How can we help but be moved by the courage of:

> The high ones die, die. They die. You look up
>   and who's there?
> —Easy, easy Mr. Bones. I is on your side.
> I smell your grief.

> —I sent my grief away. I cannot care
> forever. With them all again & again I died
> and cried and I have to live.

And even when we read this, we know John Berryman's
fortitude and artistic power will endure the clawing de-
generations of these years:

> these fierce & airy occupations, and love,
> raved away so many of Henry's years
> it is a wonder that, with in each hand
> one of his own mad books and all,
> ancient fires for eyes, his head full
> & his heart full, he's making ready to move on.

A Novelist of Great Promise
BY STANLEY EDGAR HYMAN

Television has destroyed boxing in our time, perhaps permanently by killing the neighborhood clubs at which young fighters learn their craft. As a result boys are brought up into the big time too soon, and acclaim and fortune are won by the semi-skilled who then naturally continue to be semi-skilled. Consequently, we will probably never again see fighters with the artistry of Archie Moore or Ray Robinson.

In the literary arenas the same thing is done by gushy reviewing. Philip Roth is a case in point. In 1959, at the age of 26, he published his first book, *Goodbye, Columbus*, consisting of the title novella and five short stories. It was greeted with a cascade of adulation, of which some remarks quoted on the back of the paperback reprint are a fair sample. "One catches lampoonings of our swollen and unreal American prosperity that are as observant and charming as Fitzgerald's," Alfred Kazin wrote in the *Reporter*. "At twenty-six he is skillful, witty, and energetic and performs like a virtuoso," Saul Bellow wrote in *Commentary*. "What many writers spend a lifetime searching for—a unique voice, a secure rhythm, a distinctive subject —seem to have come to Philip Roth totally and immediately," Irving Howe wrote in the *New Republic*.

The next year, *Goodbye, Columbus* won the National Book Award as "the most distinguished work of fiction published in 1959." Roth was promptly awarded a Guggenheim fellowship as well as a grant from the National Institute of Arts and Letters with a citation saying in part: "*Goodbye, Columbus* marks the coming of age of a brilliant, penetrating, and undiscourageable young man of letters." Undiscourageable? Who had tried?

The merits of *Goodbye, Columbus* and its author are immediately evident. The novella shows a sardonic wit, and the sharp eye of a born writer. The Patimkin way of life, with its white hair "the color of Lincoln convertibles" and its 23 bottles of Jack Daniels each with a little booklet tied around its neck, decorating the unused bar, has been rendered for all time. There are other sure touches: the cherry pits under Neil's bare feet in the TV room; the Ohio State sentimental record of the title. The long mono-logue by Patimkin's unsuccessful half-brother Leo at the wedding is a masterpiece: funny, moving, perfect.

But the faults of *Goodbye, Columbus* are as readily visible. The novella has no values to oppose to Patimkin values other than a small Negro boy who admires Gauguin's Tahiti, which seems a considerable overmatch. Some images are bad, like Brenda treading water "so easily she seemed to have turned the chlorine to marble beneath her"; the language is sometimes as inadequate as: "I failed to deflate the pout from my mouth." Most important, the novella shows Roth's architectonic weakness. Many of the incidents do not advance the action; the end is merely a running-down.

The stories show the same balance of strength and weak-ness. "Defender of the Faith" is the only one of them that seems wholly successful to me. "Eli, the Fanatic" reaches one high point of power and beauty, when Tzuref replies to all the smooth talk about the 20th century with: "For me the Fifty-eighth," but the rest of the story is rambling and diffuse. "The Conversion of the Jews," with its pat moral, "You should never hit anybody about God," is ultimately hokum, as "You Can't Tell a Man by the Song He Sings" is immediately hokum. "Epstein" is an inflated joke.

The minor result of the shower of praise and coin that Roth received was to make him arrogant. In a speech, "Writing American Fiction," at a 1960 symposium, he knocked off his elders and betters: Malamud displays "a spurning of our world," Salinger tells us "to be charming on the way to the loony bin," and so on. The major, and really unfortunate result has been to convince Roth that he has nothing further to learn. Three years later, *Letting Go* appears with the same merits and the same faults as *Goodbye, Columbus.*

Let us get the faults out of the way first. Since the novel is six times as long as the novella, it shows Roth's architectural weakness six times as strongly. It never in fact becomes a novel, with a unified dramatic action, but falls apart into two narratives which have only a pat complementarity: the failure of Gabe Wallach in the world of personal relations, specifically with the divorcée Martha Reganhart, despite every advantage; and the limited success of Paul and Libby Herz in the same world, despite every handicap. For the rest, it is a series of comic set pieces and vignettes: dirty diapers and high thought among the instructors at Midwest universities; Swedish modern and espresso in Jewish apartments in Brooklyn; the Kodachrome European trips of Central Park West dentists.

The prose is still quite lame in spots. Characters experience "relief—though by no means total relief" and children eat "manipulating their food like Muzak's violinists their instruments." There are letters that no one would ever have written, and long pedestrian explanations of past events by the author. In the style of college humor magazines, Roth will interrupt a scene to remark: "It's the little questions from women about tappets that finally push men over the edge." At the same time, there is a balancing pomposity; the book has no fewer than *three epigraphs*—by Simone Weil, Wallace Stevens, and Thomas Mann—any one of which would do for a dissertation on Covenant Theology.

A two-page history of the marital sex life of the Herzes has a clinical leadenness that would sink the most buoyant novel. Beyond that there is cocktail-party Freud. A pathetic event finally ends the liaison between Gabe and Martha. Martha's older child, Cynthia, pushes her younger brother, Mark, off the top of a double-decker bunk, which results in Mark's death. Roth spends laborious pages showing us why—it was penis-envy! Finally, Gabe's weakness is Hegelian essence: "He is better, he believes, than anything he has done in life has shown him to be." Not being the sum of his actions, Gabe is not really anything in the book.

The virtues of *Letting Go*—of Roth, really—are equally impressive. He has the finest eye for the details of American life since Sinclair Lewis. When Margie Howells of Kenosha moves in with Gabe as an experiment in

Bold Free Union, she comes with Breck shampoo, an Olivetti, an electric frying pan, a steam iron, and a copy of the *Oxford Book of Seventeenth-Century Verse*. The Spiglianos (he is the chairman of Gabe's department) have 11 budgetary tins in their kitchen, one labelled: "John: Tobacco, scholarly journals, foot powder."

Roth's ear is just as remarkable as his eye. When Blair Stott, a Negro on pot, talks hip, it is the best hip, and a delight. When Gabe and Martha quarrel over money, every word rings true, and the reader can feel a sick headache coming on. No manner of speech seems to be beyond Roth's powers. An elderly Midwest woman says to Gabe: "You talk to the top professors and you see if they're not Masons." Paul recalls necking with a girl in high school, sitting in her living room while her father called out from the bedroom: "Doris, is that you, dolly? Is somebody with you? Tell him thank you, dolly, and tell him it's the next day already, your father has to get up and go to work soon, tell him thank you and good night, dolly."

If Gabe is a thin Hegelian essence, Martha is a gorgeous rich *Existenz*. She *is* the total of what she does. "A woman at least realizes there are certain rotten things she's got to do in life and does them," Martha explains to Gabe. "Men want to be heroes." She is bawdy and vulgar, honest and decent, funny and heartbreaking. Gabe's effort, as he finally recognizes when he loses her, had been to turn her into a sniveling Libby. Martha's vitality dominates the book, and if Gabe's final "letting go" of the world is at all poignant, it is poignant chiefly in that he had a chance to keep Martha and failed it.

The best of *Letting Go* comes from the marvelous quality of Roth's imagination. A fellow-dentist with whom Gabe's father goes ice-skating is characterized in a phrase; he only makes "little figure eights, and all the time, smiling." The failure of Paul's father in the frozen foods business is one magnificent sentence: "One day, creditors calling at every door, he got into the cab of a truckful of his frozen rhubarb and took a ride out to Long Island to think; the refrigeration failed just beyond Mineola, and by the time he got home his life was a zero, a ruined man." At her low point, Libby, who has converted from Roman Catholicism to Judaism on marrying Paul, tries to

Philip Roth

commit suicide; when that fails she decides to make potato pancakes, "to bring a little religion into her house."

Two episodes of almost indescribable complexity, at once awful and uproarious, are the clearest sign of Roth's great promise. One is Libby's abortion, which becomes entangled with the effort of an elderly neighbor, Levy, to steal a job-lot of jockey briefs from another elderly neighbor, Korngold; it culminates in a horrifying and splendid scene when they both invade the Herz bedroom just after Libby comes home from the operation. The other is Gabe's mad effort to persuade a scoundrel named Harry Bigoness to sign a legal document that will enable the Herzes to keep their adopted baby. Eventually Gabe steals the baby in the night and drives it to Gary, Indiana, to confront Bigoness.

Roth may be the Lewis of Suburbia, but he is potentially much more. His "Writing American Fiction" speech rejects all the easy affirmations of America, and concludes on Ralph Ellison's sombre final image of the Invisible Man waiting underground. Roth really does know how hard life is. *Letting Go* concludes with Gabe, who has tried to do good without attachment, as Lord Krishna recommends in the *Gita*, left with little good achieved and no attachments either. I think that after he has seasoned longer, after another book or two, if he is prepared to learn from his mistakes, Philip Roth will be a fine novelist. Providing, that is, that all the matchmakers and promoters leave him alone.

Saints, Pilgrims and Artists
BY DONALD BARR

Breaking, sick with revulsion, a combat soldier reads a
letter from his little sister, overcomes despair and falls
asleep. A boy of sixteen, flunking out of prep school, runs
gently amuck in Manhattan, talks to his little sister and
ends in a sanitarium. A staff sergeant on occupation duty
in Germany, just released from a neuropsychiatric ward,
is shaking in black isolation in his billet, finds a letter
from a little English girl who has befriended him and falls
into a quiet sleep. A pretty college girl lunching with her
date on a football weekend suddenly loses control, and
after a sweating attempt to explain a religious book she
has read, faints and lies ejaculating silently, "Lord Jesus
Christ, have mercy on me," over and over.

Those who regard stories as symptoms will find a whole
syndrome in the works of Jerome David Salinger. He is
preoccupied with collapses of nerve, with the cracking
laugh of the outraged, with terrifying feelings of loneliness
and alienation. He seems to correspond peculiarly to the
psychological aura of our moment of history. And since
he appears chiefly in a slick magazine written for the
urban upper and would-be-upper middle classes, it seems
easy to find in his tormented souls the insulted psyche of
the "other-directed man" of Professor Riesman's *The
Lonely Crowd*. A recent article in the *Nation* was hopefully titled, "J. D. Salinger: Mirror of Crisis."

But this is wrong. First, Salinger, though he served an
apprenticeship in the *Saturday Evening Post* and writes
for *The New Yorker*, is an artist and art is not for
diagnosis—not until we are through with it as art. Once
we have made it a source of data, we cannot treat it as
a source of wisdom. Second, Salinger does *not* write about

the Lonely Crowd, the man made in the image of
B.B.D.O., the Great American Oral Type, the consumer of
love and Rauwolfia. He writes about saints, pilgrims and
artists.

Salinger's first published work was a sketch in *Story* of
a girl trying too hard at a party, done in the slice-of-life
fashion, its very point lying in its seeming pointlessness.
It is witty and concentrated, but it was followed by stories
of army life in *Collier's* which are coy, maladroit, patriotic
lies. The stories which appeared while Salinger himself was
in training are different. Only thinly falsified, they show
his special emphasis, the disclosure of character—not public character in its social relations or in questions of right
conduct, but private character. The personality is always
at grips with a problem which is almost too strong for it.
The problem is always love. (By always, I mean, of
course, usually. By love, I mean the willing exposure of
the soul to pain, not the appetite.) They also show an ear
trained to everyday speech and thought, preparing for the
great bravura of *The Catcher in the Rye*. Few novels have
been written throughout in so strongly marked an idiom,
for that is essentially a short-story device. Yet through
seventy-five-thousand words it does not pall; and for two
reasons.

First, there is no insinuated laughter *at* Holden Caulfield's idiom, though it is very funny. This sort of narration
is almost never intended to get an effect of ultimate dignity.
Ring Lardner mixes parody with very little pathos. "Is
this a human being?" we say. "Well, well, it takes all
kinds." Nelson Algren, while he wishes us to feel the bitter
pathos of freakishness, must also invite us to feel guiltily
superior to it. "Is *this* a human being?" we say. "It is the
tragic price of the System that supports me." But of Holden
Caulfield we say, *"This* is a human being." He is troubled,
lost, but in the image of God.

Second, Salinger has an ear not only for idiosyncrasies
of diction and syntax, but for mental processes. Holden
Caulfield's phrase is "and all"—"She looked so damn *nice,*
the way she kept going around and around in her blue
coat and all"—as if each experience wore a halo. His
fallacy is *ab uno disce omnes;* he abstracts and generalizes
wildly, and his closing words are, "It's funny. Don't ever
tell anybody anything. If you do, you start missing every-

body." Each experience fills the whole universe for a moment.

Let us put down some statements about Holden Caulfield. His terrible word of condemnation is "phony." He is kept celibate by compassion. ("I thought of her going in a store and buying [the dress] and nobody in the store knowing she was a prostitute and all. . . . It made me feel sad as hell—I don't know why exactly.") Even his anger is a twisted compassion. (To the pimp who beats him up he cries, "You're a stupid chiseling moron, and in about two years you'll be one of those scraggy guys that come up to you on the street and ask for a dime for coffee. You'll have snot all over your dirty, filthy overcoat, and you'll be . . .") He feels the injustices done others as done to himself. What he wants to be is "the catcher in the rye," the only big person in a field of playing children, with the job of catching them, keeping them from falling off "some crazy cliff." He wakes up a schoolmate to ask, "What's the routine on joining a monastery?"

Holden Caulfield is not a finished saint, but the Beatitudes apply to him better than Professor Riesman's valuable book does.

Some graduate-student girl in flats and a grown-out Napoleon cut, schlepping her *Finnegans Wake,* loose-leaf notebook with colored tabs and *Reporter* magazine around Columbia, could do a good master's essay on the sources of the *New Yorker* tradition in the short story. She would have chapters, of course, on Chekhov and Maupassant (ordinariness, and the unresolved cadence at the end); Joyce (the story turning on an "epiphany," a moment of awareness when some incident brings the inner meaning of experiences into clarity), with a well-hedged comparison to Zen Buddhism (enlightenment coming from sudden flashes of perception rather than from thought); Henry James (compassion, sensitivity and taste making their possessors terribly vulnerable to the world); Somerset Maugham and Aldous Huxley (neutrality toward passion, and the punishment of the characters' hubris or pride by the author's observation); and the immediate founders like Benchley, Dorothy Parker, Thurber, E. B. White, Perelman (variously: unmuscular agnosticism, fullback-hating, hatred of whimsy, laughing in a relieved way at one's lack of power, the use of pregnant trivialities, admiring people who have faith as if they were gamblers who had won and measuring oneself ruefully against the literature of competence and strength that flourished in the boyhood of the world before World War I).

It is during this last chapter that our girl would begin to have trouble with Salinger, for even when he wrote his classically *New Yorker* stories, he did not conform wholly to a certain sickish ethos which runs in the magazine's tradition, and which happens to be what Holden Caulfield's teacher describes as the "terrible, terrible fall" that awaits the merely sensitive, "where at the age of thirty, you sit in some bar hating everybody who comes in looking as if he might have played football in college."

Our graduate student could state the difference in terms of poems. For the magazine's ethos, she will, of course, turn to her well-loved *Collected Poems of T. S. Eliot*, to the overheard voices of the Waste Land, and to Prufrock, with his social obligations, his hospital metaphor to describe the world he lives in and his mermaid metaphor to describe the world he cannot live in, his "No! I am not Prince Hamlet, nor was meant to be." For Salinger's ethos, I would suggest the poem by Shaemas O'Sheel that begins: "They went forth to battle but they always fell," especially the lines from "It was a secret music that they heard," down to

Ah, they by some strange troubling doubt were stirred,
And died for hearing what no foeman heard.

I have been moving by heavy hints and preparations to a theological conclusion. In Salinger's early stories, a growing sense of a man's estrangement from his world and his kind, of his being marooned on the island of himself, is attributed to the war. Babe Gladwaller feels that those who have not shared his experience cannot really understand his mind. In the second phase, the Veteran gives place to the Lover: Holden Caulfield loves; Seymour Glass loves; the husband of the wanton girl loves; Sergeant X loves. Some love a single object, and it is inaccessible through coldness or coarseness or circumstance. Others love the whole world, and it is busy. A few are content in their lonely benevolence; but most suffer from the feeling that they have failed at loving.

Sergeant X in his German billet finds a book left by a Nazi woman who has been interned. She has written in it: "Dear God, life is hell." He writes a quotation from Dostoyevsky underneath: "Fathers and teachers, I ponder 'What is hell?' I maintain that it is the suffering of being unable to love."

Most of Salinger's work, therefore, is about those who think they were in hell, a place where the soul suffers according to its qualities, and without escape.

Ordinarily, we all are interested in hell. Ten people have read and enjoyed the *Inferno* for every one who has read the *Purgatorio* or the *Paradiso*. It is fun; like looking at real estate, it gives us a sense of our own possibilities. But Salinger's hell is different. It is hell for the good, who can feel pain, who really love or hope to love. On the gate of this hell we do not read the words "*Lasciate ogni speranza, voi ch'entrate.*" Hope is not abandoned here— hope is the implement of torture, hope deferred. We identify ourselves both with the victims and the devils. And it is not strange real estate. It is home.

To the Christian hell is in the afterlife; to the atheist it is in this life; but to both hell is eternal, because it lasts as long as the soul does. But to the Mahayana Buddhist, for example, hell is not eternal. He does not admit the three laws of thought, that whatever is, is; that no thing both is and is not; and that a thing is or is not. In his Nirvana, the soul both is and is not; it exists egolessly. It has given up living and dying. What the body is doing meanwhile, I am not sure. Nirvana may be an oblivious afterlife, or a state of miraculous unconcern in the midst of this world. In any case, this—and not surprisingly, when we recall the stories in which sleep is the end of suffering —is the exit of hell which Salinger now sought.

In January, 1953, after a year and a half of literary fame and literary silence, Salinger published in *The New Yorker* a story called "Teddy," which began his latest phase. It reads *methodically,* as if the impulse had first been to write something that was not a story. It has dialogue of a kind then new to his work but now his standard: no longer seducing our belief and lighting up characters with things we had heard but not listened to, but expounding an ordered set of ideas as plainly as can be done without actually destroying the characters into whose mouths they are put. The ideas are mostly Zen. The direct, mystical glimpsing of God behind the identities of this world is the way. An unsentimental and unpossessive love is the practical result. But the God—one feels this—is not our God, only divinity in the abstract. The love—one could not prove it—is no longer our love, only benignity.

In the stories Salinger has published since then, "Franny," "Raise High the Roof Beam, Carpenters," and "Zooey"—poignant, beautifully managed philosophic dialogues, really—the doctrine is developed sometimes in the language of Christian mysticism (after Meister Eckhart) and sometimes as a rather highflying syncretism.

This mysticism aims not at a rejection of the world, a flight from life, but an affirmative feeling for life that transforms it to the terms of its essential godhead, and gives peace. It is the triumph of Salinger's third phase that he elevates almost into a bodhisattva, a Buddhist saint, the young man Seymour Glass, who nine years before had been given to us as a critically wounded soul.

What is definite in doctrine and what is definite in fiction are virtually opposite. Salinger's prose has not improved as he carries his answers to these many decimal places. No longer are the trivialities pregnant; they are delivered by Caesarian. When Buddy Glass overhears a lady say, ". . . and the next morning, mind you, they took a pint of pus out of that lovely young body of hers," the incident is worked up into a regular symbol. His characterizations are less telling. The Veteran became the Lover; now the Lover has become the Perfectionist.

Salinger's kind of mystic is a spiritual perfectionist, and the members of the Glass family who carry on his recent, immensely long dialogues are artist-perfectionists as well. Their standards are their author's, just as their learning is their author's. It is not a humble attitude. For no one was ever ashamed to admit that he was a perfectionist. As a self-accusation, it has everything; it diagnoses one's neurotic ailments, wraps one in a small but fetching mantle of mystery, implies great refinement and intense suffering, and even threatens one's audience a bit. For we all can love a little, but none of us is perfect.

Yet Salinger remains one of the most powerful talents now practicing the short story. For the many who are involved in an effort like his, his struggles are more meaningful than other men's successes.

Manifesto For a New New French Novel
BY ANNE KOSTELANETZ

Not since Henry James have the acumen of the critic and the psychological sensitivity of the accomplished novelist been so well fused as in Nathalie Sarraute. This is particularly evident in her essays, collected as *The Age of Suspicion* (originally published in 1956 as *L'Ère du Soupçon*), which reveal her awareness of the novel both as an artistic craft and as a means of communicating "psychological reality." Here she traces the development of the psychological novel from Dostoyevsky to the present, defines her own original approach to the form and describes the fictional techniques necessary to realize this new kind of fiction. Thus these essays serve two functions: they provide a lucid analysis of the nature and practice of the psychological novel since Dostoyevsky and they also, like Henry James' *Prefaces,* contain the most illuminating critical discussions we have of Mme. Sarraute's own novels.

In her longest essay, "From Dostoyevsky to Kafka," Mme. Sarraute defines the tradition of the psychological novel to which she belongs. Her few discerning comments on Dostoyevsky, Kafka, Proust, Joyce and Camus incisively pinpoint their characteristic concerns and techniques and also indicate the direction in which her own fiction has moved.

For Dostoyevsky, writes Mme. Sarraute in "From Dostoyevsky to Kafka," the primal human motivation is the "desire for contact." This overwhelming need drives all his characters to expose their most private selves in grotesque and distorted acts of hatred and love, of pride and humility. Hypersensitive to others' opinions and feelings towards them, Dostoyevsky's characters are forced to see themselves as others see them, thus becoming disembodied "states of consciousness" which register every submerged reaction in their audience. Consequently, as Mme. Sarraute points out, these characters let their personalities become mere masks which they change at will to win the love of others. This single insight illuminates many of those confusing Dostoyevsky dialogues in which one character postures before another. For instance, the grotesque charade in which Karamazov consciously transforms himself before Father Zossima's eyes from a penitent sinner to a buffoon to a sneering atheist is all an attempt to establish a true contact with the Father, whether of hatred, respect or affection.

In all of Dostoyevsky's books but one, his characters do achieve some sort of ultimate contact with another human being. But, Mme. Sarraute notes, that one example of unalleviated despair paved the way for the entire work of Kafka and all the "existential novelists" who followed him. She is referring, of course, to that scene in *Notes from Underground* in which the underground man capers ludicrously before his dinner companions in a desperate effort to win their friendship or respect while Zherkov, the stupid officer, "examines him in silence as though he were some curious insect." Here Dostoyevsky describes a total separation in which one human being is reduced to an insignificant, squirming bug. Mme. Sarraute's analysis of this scene does much (perhaps even more than Sartre's philosophical tomes) to clarify the origin of existential "angst."

Historically, Kafka's tales grew out of this single image of unalleviated despair. His characters try desperately to establish contact with the external world of society; but Kafka's concept of "contact" is both less ambitious and more unachievable than Dostoyevsky's. Because Kafka's characters desire only to present a *respectable* exterior to the world, they systematically discard their personalities (his last protagonist is only a 'K.,' his own initial) and reduce themselves to mere objects in order to make it easier for others to define and accept them. But this willful destruction of identity leads inevitably to a world of absolute inhumanity, or, in Mme. Sarraute's moving phrase, of "un ne-pas-comprendre définitif et total."

In tracing Kafka's thought from its inception to this end beyond which no one can go, Mme. Sarraute has also defined the contemporary literary sensibility. She sensitively portrays her contemporaries' total disillusion with the psychological possibilities of the novel which so interested writers a generation ago. Not only had Kafka shown that man could not hope to understand himself or the world, but psychoanalysis had demonstrated the superficiality of all fictional techniques (including Proust's careful dissections of dialogue and Joyce's interior monologue) in even approaching the complex depths of human motivation. The single motivations of the great literary "types"—Balzac's avaricious Grandet, Thackeray's ambitious Becky, Stendhal's "hero manqué" Sorel—seemed incredibly naive.

In this "age of suspicion" when neither novelist nor reader could believe in the traditional claim of fiction to represent "reality," novelists, aware of their own ignorance, were forced to limit their fictional world. The result was the movement commonly called the "new French novel" which she more accurately pinpoints as the "behaviorist novel." These writers insisted first, that psychological motivation can be comprehended only by the psychoanalyst and secondly, that the "reality" known by the ordinary reader and writer is nothing more than the surfaces which our senses register. Their position was strengthened by the ability of the cinema and the "American novel" (by which the French mean Steinbeck, Dos Passos, Hemingway) to present a convincing reality with "objective" vision alone. She records the joyful relief with which her avant-garde contemporaries threw up the traditional obsession with psychological motivation and returned to the novel of clear outline, detailed description, elegant style and classical form. She outlines with precision the aims and techniques of the behaviorist novel from its inception to Robbe-Grillet's *Jalousie.*

And with perfect justice, Mme. Sarraute destroys their earlier position, tearing down the idol of the behaviorists, the book which "proved" their ideas, Camus' *L'Étranger.* With a wry smile, Mme. Sarraute points at what the behaviorists refused to see when they hailed Meursault as the "homo absurdus" whose inner emotions are identical with those observed from the outside—namely, that Meursault is a man of great psychological profundity. She points to Meursault's taste, his awareness of others (especially his understanding of the curious love-hate relationship between Salamano and his dog), his frequent psychological insights, as well as his self-indulgent ennui and consciously refined egotism. Thus she shows that since Meursault deliberately acts from psychological motivations and inherent prejudices, Camus was not supporting the behaviorists, but rather challenging them.

Since, she concludes, after Kafka and Camus a further development of the "homo absurdus" theme was impossible, Mme. Sarraute devotes the next three essays, "The Age of Suspicion," "Conversation and Subconversation," and "What Birds See," to a polemical outline of a new area of fictional psychology. Despite the smack of the personal manifesto in these essays, they do illuminate Mme. Sarraute's fictional intentions and are therefore indispensable to an accurate understanding of her novels. She explicates in detail the area of psychology with which she is concerned: the subterranean feelings and thoughts on the outermost fringe of consciousness which give truth and significance to our surface lives. She defines this area as that

immense profusion of sensations, images, sentiments, memories, impulses, little larval actions that no inner language can convey, that jostle one another on the threshold of consciousness, gather together in compact groups and loom up all of a sudden, then immediately fall apart, combine otherwise and reappear in new forms; while unwinding inside us, like the ribbon that comes clattering from a telescriptor slot, is an uninterrupted flow of words.

To present this "uninterrupted flow of words," she has developed a new form of dialogue, one which discards all conventions of indentation, colon and quotation mark, as well as the cumbersome "he said" of the nineteenth-century novel and the even more awkward dialogue repetitions or stilted introductions of Claude Simon. Instead, she uses only the sparsest punctuation: dashes or line spaces to indicate change in speaker or interruption of thought and three dots to record transitions from the spoken to the unspoken thoughts of the speaker or an amplification of the previous thought. She never allows a third person or an omniscient narrator to interrupt or analyze the dialogue—her conversations flow smoothly and quickly, carefully paced by her supple style.

This new form of dialogue, which she did not perfect until *The Planetarium* (1959), is described in "What Birds See" as:

> A technique that might succeed in plunging the reader into the stream of these subterranean dramas of which Proust only had time to obtain a rapid aerial view, and concerning which he observed and reproduced nothing but the broad motionless lines. This technique would give the reader the illusion of repeating these actions himself, in a more clearly aware, more orderly, distinct and forceful manner than he can do in life, without losing that element of indetermination, of opacity and mystery that one's own actions always have for the one who lives them.

How satisfactorily Mme. Sarraute transformed this critical, analytical ideal into fictional reality only a reading of her most recent novels can demonstrate. Her four novels both illustrate her critical dicta and reflect the increasing subtlety and sureness of her understanding of this new area of psychological fiction.

In her earliest novel, *Tropismes* (1939; reissued, 1957), Mme. Sarraute probes the psychic lives of those *nouveaux bourgeoise* women who have moved from the country to a Paris apartment. Since she confines herself to a single social class, she can treat the psychology of all these women as one mind and show how the innermost thoughts of each reflect the notions of all. Flickering from one mind to another, she grasps those "tropismes" (a biological term meaning the response, usually an orientation, of a plant or animal to the influence of external stimuli) which characterize these women's response to their daily routines. Although Mme. Sarraute's fictional concern wavers between lyrical description and psychological probing, although she has not yet discovered the means or the material to construct an effective fictional vision, she has already defined the direction in which her work will move—the definition of psychological depths beneath the objective surface of situation and character.

Her next novel, *Portrait of a Man Unknown* (1947),

continues to test the hard surfaces of appearance for signs of underlying realities. The narrator, an anonymous "I," tries desperately to penetrate the motivations and characters of the alternately rough and charming father and his "hypersensitive" daughter who live in his apartment-house. Despite repeated encounters and surreptitious spyings, the narrator is unable to crack their external masks —what he thinks are moments of insight are actually nothing more than imaginative projections. Ironically, it is the narrator's own acute sensibilities, as they play over these two figures, which suggest that kind of perceptive introspection which becomes the mark of her best fiction.

Martereau (1953) is a crude attempt to define that area of psychology her later novel grasps so surely. The narrator poses his own affectionate responses to Martereau against his uncle's suspicions and his aunt's concern (perhaps adulterous) in an attempt to define the essence of this man. He succeeds only in destroying his own relationship with Martereau without ever discovering the truth of the man's character. But already we find Mme. Sarraute capturing the unspoken nuance of social encounters, for it is the barely hinted suggestions, the delicate plots and counter-plots, the constant awareness of the listener's reaction to one's statements, and the eternal anxiousness to please and satisfy which make up the real matter of this novel. Here, however, it is her sluggish words—heavy, static, defined—which keep the novel from moving forward. Only in the most recent novel are these words metamorphosed into movements which generate the form of the novel from their own energy.

The "characters" in *The Planetarium* are only named consciousnesses, each speaking in the first person, each rotating in his own orbit until a sudden collision throws him into contact with another and stirs his submerged thoughts and feelings into rapid turmoil. Nathalie Sarraute skillfully expands these isolated collisions in time and in relevance until the universal conflict of rebellious youth and parental authority is constructed. The basic pattern of collision is the archetype of initiation into or rejection from a defined social group. The "groups" presented vary from the writers' clique commanded by Germaine Lemaire, which the young critic Alain hopes to enter, to the familial communion which their parents wish to re-establish with Alain and Gisèle after their marriage, to the "special place" in Alain's heart which his Aunt Berthe must maintain even if it means sacrificing her apartment, to the perfect marriage which Alain and Gisèle are incapable of achieving.

It is not these social situations which make up the novel's texture, however, but the sensations aroused within the characters when they collide. Their spoken words flow smoothly, but beneath are hidden depths of half-grasped, often inarticulate, desires and fears. Mme. Sarraute suggests these barely conscious movements with a slight nuance, a fleeting metaphor, an undeveloped suggestion and, very rarely, an image as developed as the surrealist description of natives stalking their victims in the jungle which evokes the sensation of terror with which Berthe awaits the loss of her apartment.

The listener in these dialogues, like all of us in everyday life, is wholly unaware of these submerged movements in the speaker. The listener interprets, reads in, but never grasps—Nathalie Sarraute illustrates this in the encounter between Berthe and her brother Pierre. At this point only, the dialogue is repeated, first from Berthe's point of view and then from Pierre's. The total disparity between the two dialogues—the same words are spoken, but the underlying purposes, feelings and interpretations are totally different—emphasizes the layers of the human mind unseen by the objective observer. Each mind encloses the empty forms which the external world gives it—the unfilled words, the crude actions, the placed objects—in a filled world of nuance and emotion. Each mind generates an atmospheric coloring which plays upon and transforms the external world so uniquely that it becomes incomprehensible to another mind.

Nathalie Sarraute's style, which is her subject (insofar as the rhythms of a mind's feelings are the rhythms of words), creates that sense of the infinite possibilities and actual limitations of human existence which we receive from Henry James' heavy noun clauses, but with a lightness perfectly suited to the subtlety and swiftness of the hidden motions of consciousness with which she deals. Series of adjectives and nouns over which the eye moves quickly, interspersed with "that's" which give the illusion of having captured the thought exactly, and frequent interruptions, either in speaker, in point of view or in the object of the mind's concern, break up the lengthy dialogues; while the carefully controlled rhythm and pace of the flow of words sustain the continuity of thought. This monologue, in which Berthe prepares to ask Pierre to save her apartment from Alain's grasping hands, reveals Mme. Sarraute's gift for introspection:

> They mistake for diffidence, for excessive sensitiveness, that terribly embarrassed, uneasy, retiring manner he has at times, as at this moment, that toneless, slightly hoarse voice—in their eyes, it's part of his charm, people believe in him so easily—but she knows him too well: it's a feeling of annoyance, almost of rage, that he has, and which gives him that look, that voice, it's sly, shameful resentment, against anyone who takes the liberty of interfering with his comfort, of disturbing his timid, cramped bachelor's peace . . . marriage, paternity changed nothing, he was like that already, at the age of ten. . . .

And the ensuing dialogue between Alain and his idol, Germaine Lemaire, when she visits the apartment they have stolen from Berthe is the essence of Nathalie Sarraute's style:

> Delighted, emboldened, self-confident, he nods, pointing towards the little dark oak bench in the corner by the window: "And that, that corner under the window, do you like that?" She looks, she's considering it, and he feels anxious, the solid ground on which he was standing, starts to move . . . she hesitates . . . What does she see? what can she be thinking? . . . He waits. Finally, she makes up her mind: "Now there, really, I don't know. It seems to me that a good comfortable easy chair in front of that window, that view . . ." He stumbles, he's reeling, he hangs on . . . "Ah . . . Whereas we, that is, I . . . thought it was so pretty . . . it's an old church bench . . .—Yes, I see that . . . But I'm not so sure . . ." Something is swaying, trembling over there, too, in the slender, silent figure that is busying itself about the tea-table, something in it too has begun to totter,

from one instant to the other, something may collapse . . . he perceives, coming from there, directed
at him alone, in a mute language, their own language,
an appeal, more than an appeal, an objurgation not
to betray, not to cast under the heel of the outsider,
in a moment of weakness, in a moment of despicable
cowardliness, under the heel of the insolent, unman-
nerly intruder, their secret treasures which together
both of them, they have chosen reverently, fervently,
contemplatively . . . "Gisèle, listen . . . she must not
desert him, she must join with him . . . this bench is
very pretty, but perhaps here, in front of the window . . . it's true, a big armchair . . ."

With *The Planetarium*, Nathalie Sarraute achieved that
new kind of psychological novel which her critical essays
describe, a novel which captures those movements which
cannot be seen directly and clearly by the conscious mind,
those movements which form and disintegrate with utmost
rapidity "on the extreme edge of consciousness." She has
internalized character, plot and description and has discarded from her form all the antiquated conventions of
the traditional novel which impede the flow of these movements beneath and around the levels of spoken dialogue.
She has subtly evoked complex and varied personalities
and diverse social situations with which we can identify
(perhaps more easily than with James' limited "drawing-
room" situations). She has articulated the very real sensations which we all feel whenever we are intensely involved
in an uncertain situation, the numerous and complex
movements that give meaning to our actions and our
words. She has taken from Dostoyevsky his sensitivity
to the complicated and contradictory feelings which are
never revealed in conventional dialogue and developed
a new instrument—nothing more nor less than her style—
to present them to the reader. But her style so deftly
captures the dimly perceived pattern of our innermost
lives that we, too, echo the final communion between
Alain and Germaine. . . "I think we're all of us, really,
a bit like that."

Postscript, 1964: It was perhaps inevitable that Nathalie
Sarraute, being both a critic and a novelist, should write

a novel about literary critics. One suspects, however, that *The Golden Fruits* (1963), a satire on contemporary French literary critics, is, like Simone de Beauvoir's *Mandarins*, a *roman à clef* written more to attack her peers than to advance the art of fiction. This extra-literary dimension of *The Golden Fruits* also explains the confusing but deliberate anonymity of the "characters," all critics. Since they are living persons, their names, sexes, occupations and appearances are rigidly suppressed—we get only a series of conflicting judgments about the latest novel, M. Brehier's *The Golden Fruits*. The accomplished style of this novel only partially overcomes the total lack of characterization—we find the same deft use of language, the carefully fixed images and the subtle conversations and sub-conversations that *The Planetarium* achieved. This style, however, is obviously inappropriate for satirical purposes. Satire demands language which can score its hits directly and concisely—something which Mme Sarraute's complex, sensitive sentences just cannot do.

Nonetheless, Mme. Sarraute's precise depiction of the opinions, social relations and taste of this French literary circle is often telling, more often very funny. The novel is "about," of course, a novel. M. Brehier's *The Golden Fruits* is the latest discovery of the "Maitre" (surely Robbe-Grillet) of this particular literary circle and is acclaimed by all as "su-perb." No one dares disagree, for fear that the most intangible of things, his "taste," will be denied. In their efforts to vindicate their rave reviews of this mediocre novel, the "critics" indulge in delightful parodies of literary jargon:

> "This book, I believe, establishes in literature a privileged language which succeeds in investing a correspondence that is its own structure. It is a very new and very perfect appropriation of rhythmic signs that transcend by their very tension the inessential in all semantics. . . .
>
> "Yes. Undoubtedly. We have here a take-off that abolishes the invisible by blending it with the ambiguity of what is signified."
>
> —We agree absolutely. Thus an a-temporal dimension is dissolved here in the becoming of a the-

matic. Because of this fact, this work, down to its most structured strata, is a poem.

—I would go even farther. In my opinion, it is by apprehending the inexpressed simultaneously, in different modes, that this book avoids the petrification of what is structured. In this way, it deploys—and how magnificently!—gratifying, literally, our every exigence.

Indeed, it is not until the "Country Boy" arrives that their conviction in the magnificence of this new novel is shaken. He insists that *The Golden Fruits* is a pastiche of platitudes. Although he is temporarily vanquished by the inevitable last shot of the cornered critic—

They would say: Now listen, is it possible you don't see that that banal, platitudinous side you speak of, is precisely what Brehier was after, he did it on purpose.—

his sacrilege has made the Master vulnerable. First Jacques writes a "discarded fragment" of *The Golden Fruits* which the Master insists is the finest thing Brehier has done. Then, forced by an unbeliever to defend his extravagant review, the Master condescends, saying "Every page is perfect," only to find no page worth reading aloud. The unmasking both of Brehier and his critics culminates in their crude anecdotes about his personal vulgarity, his cheap clothes, his addiction to pop songsters, comic books and boorish boasting. Within two weeks, Brehier's book is never mentioned—and the "critics" are hailing the next work of genius.

Mme. Sarraute's deft parodies of literary jargon and "fashion" plus an occasional psychological insight into the mentality of the connoisseur make this an interesting novel for "litterateurs." However, as far as her career as a novelist and critic is concerned, this book is a distinct setback. One can only hope that Mme Sarraute has paid off her literary debts and will now explore even further the new fictional area she has discovered.

Sartre
BY WILLIAM BARRETT

We may as well begin with Sartre in a moment of heroism. Much in his writings is distinctly unheroic in nature, but the note of heroism does sound, and here it is in *The Republic of Silence*, where Sartre is describing the life of the French Resistance from 1940 to 1945:

> We were never more free than during the German occupation. We had lost all our rights, beginning with the right to talk. Every day we were insulted to our faces and had to take it in silence. Under one pretext or another, as workers, Jews, or political prisoners, we were deported *en masse*. Everywhere, on billboards, in the newspapers, on the screen, we encountered the revolting and insipid picture of ourselves that our suppressors wanted us to accept. And because of all this we were free. Because the Nazi venom seeped into our thoughts, every accurate thought was a conquest. Because an all-powerful police tried to force us to hold our tongues, every word took on the value of a declaration of principles. Because we were hunted down, every one of our gestures had the weight of a solemn commitment. . . .
>
> Exile, captivity, and especially death (which we usually shrink from facing at all in happier days) became for us the habitual objects of our concern. We learned that they were neither inevitable accidents, nor even constant and inevitable dangers, but they must be considered as our lot itself, our destiny, the profound source of our reality as men. At every instant we lived up to the full sense of this commonplace little phrase: "Man is mortal!" And the choice

that each of us made of his life was an authentic
choice because it was made face to face with death,
because it could always have been expressed in these
terms: "Rather death than . . . " And here I am not
speaking of the elite among us who were real Resist-
ants, but of all Frenchmen who, at every hour of
the night and day throughout four years, answered
No.

And a few years later (1947), in his *What is Literature?*
he draws another philosophic conclusion from this experience:

> We have been taught to take Evil seriously. It is
> neither our fault nor our merit if we lived in a time
> when torture was a daily fact. Chateaubriand, Ora-
> dour, the Rue des Saussaies, Dachau, and Auschwitz
> have all demonstrated to us that Evil is not an ap-
> pearance, that knowing its cause does not dispel it,
> that it is not opposed to Good as a confused idea is
> to a clear one, that it is not the effect of passions
> which might be cured, of a fear which might be
> overcome, of a passing aberration which might be
> excused, of an ignorance which might be enlightened,
> that it can in no way be diverted, brought back, re-
> duced, and incorporated into idealistic humanism,
> like that shade of which Leibnitz has written that
> it is necessary for the glare of daylight. . . .
> Perhaps a day will come when a happy age, look-
> ing back at the past, will see in this suffering and shame
> one of the paths which led to peace. But we are not
> on the side of history already made. We were, as I
> have said, *situated* in such a way that every lived min-
> ute seemed to us like something irreducible. There-
> fore, in spite of ourselves, we came to this conclusion,
> which will seem shocking to lofty souls: Evil cannot
> be redeemed.

It is necessary to emphasize passages like these for
American readers who wish to understand Sartre, because
Americans have not yet comprehended what the French
have lived through: that we have at last arrived at "the
age of assassins" which the poet Rimbaud predicted. Sartre

came to maturity during the 1930's. The atmosphere of Leftist politics was over everything, and Sartre has never ceased politically to be on the Left. But over France also was the stale and tired atmosphere of a world already doomed to defeat: The Popular Front government of Léon Blum drifted, nerveless and flaccid, incapable of meeting the crisis of the times; the French bourgeoisie hung on, entrenched and petty, unable even to conceive the possibility of any great action. *"Les salauds"* became a potent term for Sartre in those days—the *salauds,* the stinkers, the stuffy and self-righteous people congealed in the insincerity of their virtues and vices. This atmosphere of decay breathes through Sartre's first novel, *Nausea,* and it is no accident that the quotation on the flyleaf is from Céline, the poet of the abyss, of the nihilism and disgust of that period. The nausea in Sartre's book is the nausea of existence itself; and to those who are ready to use this as an excuse for tossing out the whole of Sartrian philosophy, we may point out that it is better to encounter one's existence in disgust than never to encounter it at all—as the *salaud* in his academic or bourgeois or party-leader strait jacket never does. The Resistance came to Sartre and his generation as a release from disgust into heroism. It was a call to action, an action that brought men to the very limits of their being, and in hearing this call man himself was not found wanting. He could even rediscover his own irreducible liberty in saying No to the overpowering might of the occupying forces.

The essential freedom, the ultimate and final freedom that cannot be taken from a man, is to say No. This is the basic premise in Sartre's view of human freedom: freedom is in its very essence negative, though this negativity is also creative. At a certain moment, perhaps, the drug or the pain inflicted by the torturer may make the victim lose consciousness, and he will confess. But so long as he retains the lucidity of consciousness, however tiny the area of action possible for him, he can still say in his own mind: No. Consciousness and freedom are thus given together. Only if consciousness is blotted out can man be deprived of this residual freedom. Where all the avenues of action are blocked for a man, this freedom may seem a tiny and unimportant thing; but it is in fact total and absolute, and

Sartre is right to insist upon it as such, for it affords man his final dignity, that of being man.

The experience of this freedom is not so new in philosophy as it might seem. It is this kind of freedom, in fact, that accompanied Descartes throughout the course of his famous Systematic Doubt, in which he proposed to say *No* to every belief, no matter how plausible, so long as he saw a possibility of doubting it. For the young and brilliant Sartre, teaching philosophy before the Second World War, Descartes was a special hero—a hero of thought if not of the life of action. The experience of the Resistance gave the figure of Descartes even greater importance for Sartre, since in the Resistance Cartesianism could be incarnated in the life of action. As Descartes proposed to say No to that imaginary demon who might seduce him into assenting to a proposition that was not altogether clear and indubitable, though everything in society and nature around him also urged him to assent, so the Resistant could say No to the might of the Occupation.

Sartre is a Cartesian who has read Proust and Heidegger, and whose psychological explorations of man go far beyond those of the seventeenth-century philosopher; more important still, he is a Cartesian who has experienced war and terror in the modern world and who is therefore situated historically in an altogether different relation to the world. But a Cartesian he is, nonetheless, as perhaps no Frenchman—or no French thinker—can help being when the chips are really down. Descartes and the French Resistance—Descartes *in* the French Resistance—these are the simple keys to the whole of Sartre's apparently complicated and involved philosophy.

To see this clearly we need only go back to Descartes at a certain moment in his Systematic Doubt. He proposes to reject all beliefs so long as they can in any way be doubted, to *resist* all temptations to say Yes until his understanding is convinced according to its own light; so he rejects belief in the existence of an external world, of minds other than his own, of his own body, of his memories and sensations. What he cannot doubt is his own consciousness, for to doubt is to be conscious, and therefore by doubting its existence he would affirm it. In the dark void in which Descartes hovered there shone only the light of his own mind. But before this certitude shone for him (and even after it, before he passed on to other truths), he was a nothingness, a negativity, existing outside of nature and history, for he had temporarily abolished all belief in a world of bodies and memories. Thus man cannot be interpreted, Sartre says, as a solid substantial thing existing amid the plenitude of things that make up a world; he is beyond nature because in his negative capability he transcends it. Man's freedom is to say No, and this means that he is the being by whom nothingness comes into being. He is able to suspend all of nature and history in doubt, to bracket it against the backdrop of nothingness before which the Cartesian doubter hovers. Sartre here merely draws conclusions from what is existentially implicit in the Cartesian doubt.

Descartes, of course, was a good Christian and a Catholic, and as a practical matter he had no intention of imperiling his immortal soul by placing his religious faith in doubt while he was performing his intellectual gyrations in the void. As a canny and sagacious Frenchman, he proposed to abide by the customs of his time and place (which included the practice of religion). Hence, when he launched himself into the Doubt, he made certain of securing his lines of communication behind him; he took no chances when he made the descent into the painful night of the void. The next step after the certitude of the *Cogito*, the "I think," thus turns out to be a proof of the existence of God; and with God as guarantee the whole world of nature, the multitude of things with their fixed nature or essences that the mind may now know, is re-established around Descartes. Sartre, however, is the Cartesian doubter at a different place and time: God is dead, and no longer guarantees to this passionate and principled atheist that vast structure of essences, the world, to which his freedom must give assent. As a modern man, Sartre remains in that anguish of nothingness in which Descartes floated before the miraculous light of God shone to lead him out of it. For Sartre there is no unalterable structure of essences or values given prior to man's own existence. That existence has meaning, finally, only as the liberty to say No, and by saying No to create a world. If we remove God from the picture, the liberty which reveals itself in the Cartesian doubt is total and absolute; but thereby also the more anguished, and this anguish is the irreducible destiny and dignity of man. Here Cartesianism has become more heroic—and more demoniacal.

Thus Sartre ends by allotting to man the kind of freedom that Descartes has ascribed only to God. It is, he says, the freedom Descartes secretly would have given to man had he not been limited by the theological convictions of his time and place. Descartes' God derives from the absolutely free God of Duns Scotus rather than from the God of St. Thomas Aquinas, who is bound by the laws of logic. This Cartesian God, says Sartre, is the freest God that man ever invented. He is not subordinate to a realm of essences: rather, He creates essences and causes them to be what they are. Hence such a God transcends the laws of logic and mathematics. As His existence precedes all essences, so man's existence precedes *his* essence; he exists, and out of the free project which his existence can be he makes himself what he is. When God dies, man takes the place of God. Such had been the prophecy of Dostoyevsky and Nietzsche, and Sartre on this point is their heir. The difference, however, is that Dostoyevsky and Nietzsche were frenzied prophets, whereas Sartre advances his view with all the lucidity of Cartesian reason and advances it, moreover, as a basis for humanitarian and democratic social action. To put man in the place of God may seem, to traditionalists, an unspeakable piece of diabolism; but in Sartre's case it is done by a thinker who, to judge from his writings, is a man of overwhelming good will and generosity.

1. BEING-FOR-ITSELF AND BEING-IN-ITSELF

Sartre's philosophy is based on a dualism which, if not Cartesian to the letter, is certainly Cartesian in spirit. Being, says Sartre, is divided into two fundamental kinds: (1) *Being-in-itself* and (2) *Being-for-itself*. *Being-in-itself* (Sartre's *en-soi*) is the self-contained being of a thing. A stone is a stone; it is what it is; and in being just what it is, no more and no less, the being of the thing always coincides with itself. *Being-for-itself* (*pour-soi*) is coextensive with the realm of consciousness, and the nature of consciousness is that it is perpetually beyond itself. Our thought goes beyond itself, toward tomorrow or yesterday, and toward the outer edges of the world. Human existence is thus a perpetual self-transcendence: in existing we are always beyond ourselves. Consequently we never possess our being as we possess a thing. Our existence from moment to moment is a perpetual flying beyond ourselves, or else a perpetual falling behind our own possibilities; in any case, our being never exactly coincides with itself. It could do so only if we sank into the self-contained form of the being of a thing, and this would be possible only if we ceased to be conscious.

This notion of the For-itself may seem obscure, but we encounter it on the most ordinary occasions. I have been to a party; I come away, and with a momentary pang of sadness I say, "I am not myself." It is necessary to take this proposition quite literally as something that only man can say of himself, because only man can say it *to* himself. I have the feeling of coming to myself after having lost or mislaid my being momentarily in a social encounter that estranged me from myself. This is the first and immediate level on which the term yields its meaning. But the next and deeper level of meaning occurs when the feeling of sadness leads me to think in a spirit of self-reproach that I am not myself in a still more fundamental sense: I have not realized so many of the plans or projects that make up my being; I am not myself because I do not measure up to myself. Beneath this level too there is still another and deeper meaning, rooted in the very nature of my being: I am not myself, and I can never be myself, because my being stretching out beyond itself at any given moment exceeds itself. I am always simultaneously more and less than I am.

Herein lies the fundamental uneasiness, or anxiety, of the human condition, for Sartre. Because we are perpetually flitting beyond ourselves, or falling behind our possibilities, we seek to ground our existence, to make it more secure. In seeking for security we seek to give our existence the self-contained being of a thing. The For-itself struggles to become the In-itself, to attain the rocklike and unshakable solidity of a thing. But this it can never do so long as it is conscious and alive. Man is doomed to the radical insecurity and contingency of his being; for without it he would not be man but merely a thing and would not have the human capacity for transcendence of his given situation.

There is a curious dialectical interplay here: that which constitutes man's power and glory, that which lies at the very heart of his power to be lord over things, namely his capacity to transcend himself and his immediate situation, is at one and the same time that which causes the fragility, the wavering and flight, the anguish of our human lot.

With enormous ingenuity and virtuosity Sartre interweaves these two notions—Being-in-itself and Being-for-itself—to elucidate the complexities of human psychology. The principal work in which he does this is *L'être et le néant (Being and Nothingness),* a great, uneven, brilliant and verbose tome which he worked on during the resistance and which appeared in 1944. Sartre's debt to Heidegger is great, but his own originality is unquestionable. He is one of the most brilliant minds alive—sometimes we feel too brilliant, for the greatest mind needs a little saving streak of earth-bound stupidity somewhere, so the feet can be planted mulishly on the soil of some unshakable fact. Sartre has learned all the dialectical tricks of Hegel, and he can trot them out as he chooses with a virtuosity that is at times excessive. It is a use of Hegel's means toward an existential rather than an idealistic end, of course, for Sartre can never go the way of Hegel: he believes, in opposition to the idealist, that Evil is real and cannot be redeemed, that the negative can never be sublimated in the pure positive being of the Absolute. Dachau and Belsen have taught him that. Where Sartre goes beyond Heidegger is in giving a more detailed elaboration of the negative side of human existence. For Heidegger the essentially temporal being of man is pervaded by the negatives of the *not*-yet and *no*-longer; but Sartre does much more with this, nosing out all the sordid and seedy strands of nothingness that haunt our human condition like a bad breath or body odor. Never in the thought of the West has the Self been so pervaded by negation. One would have to go to the East, to the Buddhist philosopher Nagarjuna (*circa* 200 A.D.), with his doctrine of *Anatman,* the insubstantiality of the Self, to meet as awesome a list of negations as Sartre draws up. The Self, indeed, is in Sartre's treatment, as in Buddhism, a bubble, and a bubble has nothing at its center.

But neither in Buddhism nor in Sartre is the Self riddled with negations to the end that we should, humanly speaking, collapse into the negative, into a purely passive nihil-

ism. In Buddhism the recognition of the nothingness of ourselves is intended to lead into a striving for holiness and
compassion—the recognition that in the end there is nothing that sustains us should lead us to love one another, as
survivors on a life raft, at the moment they grasp that the
ocean is shoreless and that no rescue ship is coming, can
only have compassion on one another. For Sartre, on the
other hand, the nothingness of the Self is the basis for the
will to action: the bubble is empty and will collapse, and
so what is left us but the energy and passion to spin that
bubble out? Man's existence is absurd in the midst of a
cosmos that knows him not; the only meaning he can give
himself is through the free project that he launches out of
his own nothingness. Sartre turns from nothingness not to
compassion or holiness, but to human freedom as realized
in revolutionary activity. In this final appeal to the will to
action there is a secret kinship with Nietzsche; and nothing
justifies more fully Heidegger's contention that Nietzsche is
the secret master of Western metaphysics in its final stage
than the way in which Sartre's thinking comes around in
the end to join Nietzsche's.

However great his initial dependence upon Heidegger,
Sartre's philosophy moves finally in an altogether opposite
direction. He misses the very root of all of Heidegger's
thinking, which is Being itself. There is, in Sartre, Being-
for-itself and Being-in-itself but there is no Being. How can
the For-itself and In-itself meet unless both stand out in
the open space of Being? We have here, in Sartre, the
world cleft once again into the Cartesian dualism of subject and object, the world of consciousness and the world
of things. Sartre has advanced as the fundamental thesis
of his Existentialism the proposition that existence precedes
essence. This thesis is true for Heidegger as well, in the
historical, social, and biographical sense that man comes
into existence and makes himself to be what he is. But for
Heidegger another proposition is even more basic than this:
namely, Being precedes existence. For without the open
clearing of Being into which man can transcend himself, he
could not ex-sist, i.e., stand out beyond himself. Man can
make himself be what he is only because all his projects
are revealed to him as taking place within the open field
or region of Being. This is why Heidegger has declared,
"I am not an Existentialist"—because the Existentialists of

the Sartrian school do not grasp this priority of Being, and so their thinking remains, like that of Descartes, locked up in the human subject.

To be sure, Sartre has gone a considerable step beyond Descartes by making the essence of human consciousness to be transcendence: that is, to be conscious is, immediately and as such, to point beyond that isolated act of consciousness and therefore to be beyond or above it. Descartes, at the extreme point of his thought, had envisaged consciousness as absolutely enclosed in itself, with the world of external objects shut out, and all the past and future suspended. But this step forward by Sartre is not so considerable if the transcending subject has nowhere to transcend himself: if there is not an open field or region of Being in which the fateful dualism of subject and object ceases to be. Modern philosophy from Descartes onward has asked itself the question: How can the subject really know the object? By the time of Kant (and despite all the advances in physical knowledge since Descartes) the human mind felt itself so estranged from nature that Kant's answer was that the subject can never know the object-in-itself. And from there it is but a short step to Nietzsche, who declares that knowledge of the object-in-itself is unnecessary—all we need is to be able to master it, and hence the Will to Power becomes primary. (In Sartre what becomes primary is rather the will to action.)

Now, Heidegger's reversal of this development in modern philosophy is radical and goes to the root of the matter; and I do not think Sartre has seen this aspect of Heidegger's thought. For what Heidegger proposes is a more basic question than that of Descartes and Kant: namely, how is it possible for the subject to *be?* and for the object to *be?* And his answer is: Because both stand out in the truth, or un-hiddenness, of Being. This notion of the truth of Being is absent from the philosophy of Sartre; indeed, nowhere in his vast *Being and Nothingness* does he deal with the problem of truth in a radical and existential way: so far as he understands truth at all, he takes it in the ordinary intellectualistic sense that has been traditional with non-existential philosophers. In the end (as well as at his very beginning) Sartre turns out thus to be a Cartesian rationalist—one, to be sure, whose material is impassioned and existential, but for all that not any the less a Cartesian in his ultimate dualism between the For-itself and the In-itself. And the curious irony about this is that Sartre, whose name the general public has come to take as synonymous with Existentialism, is the one existential philosopher who does not deal with the prime question that has been the central passion of nearly all the Existentialists—the question, namely, of a truth for man that is more than a truth of the intellect.

It is altogether consistent therefore that Sartre should advertise his brand of Existentialism to the public as a new humanism. Like every humanism, it teaches that the proper study of mankind is man, or, as Marx put it, that the root of mankind is man. But, again like every humanism, it leaves unasked the question: What is the root of man? In this search for roots for man—a search that has, as we have seen, absorbed thinkers and caused the malaise of poets for the last hundred and fifty years—Sartre does not participate. He leaves man rootless. This may be because Sartre himself is the quintessence of the urban intellectual —perhaps the most brilliant urban intellectual of our time, but still with the inevitable alienation of this type. He seems to breathe the air of the modern city, of its cafés, faubourgs, and streets, as if there were no other home for man.

2. LITERATURE AS A MODE OF ACTION

Such too is the impression with which his more strictly literary works leave us. It is a paradox that although the Existentialists have often been accused of really being literary men or poets rather than philosophers (in the strict academic sense), Sartre, the only Existentialist who has fulfilled himself as a literary man, pouring out novels, plays, and literary essays, and who indeed earns his living now as a professional writer, is in his philosophy the most intellectualistic of all the Existentialists. The fact is that despite Sartre's enormous strictly literary output, men like Kierkegaard and Nietzsche had more of the artist in them. They were poets, and not only is there nothing of the poet in Sartre, but he even shows little real feeling for poetry when he talks about it. His conception of literature is a thoroughly intellectual one: in his *What is Literature?* (1947), a long and brilliant essay in critical theory, he develops the fundamental view that literature is a mode of action, an act of the writer's freedom that seeks to appeal to the freedom of other individuals and eventually to the total free collective of mankind. Stripped of its metaphysical language, his theory leads him to espouse a kind of social realism in literature. Thus the greatest living writer, he tells us, is John Dos Passos. Such a judgment is rather shocking as evidence of Sartre's literary taste—or lack of it. But the philosopher is really responding to the *idea* of Dos Passos' fiction, not to the novels as works of art. Dos Passos is, for Sartre, the perfect example of what he believes a writer should do and what he himself tries to do in his own later fiction: that is, grapple with the problems of man in his time and milieu. Sartre's novels are a technically dazzling, streamlined variety of social realism. It is always to the idea, and particularly the idea as it leads to social action, that Sartre responds. Hence he cannot do justice, either in his critical theory or in his actual practice of literary criticism, to poetry, which is precisely that form of human expression in which the poet—and the reader who would enter the poet's world—must let Being be, to use Heidegger's phrase, and not attempt to coerce it by the will to action or the will to intellectualization. The absence of the poet in Sartre, as a literary man, is thus another evidence of what, on the philosophical level, leads to a deficiency in his theory of Being.

Sartre is a writer of very powerful gifts, nevertheless, who succeeds in his effects whenever the idea itself is able to generate artistic passion and life. His first novel, *Nausea* (1938), may well be his best book for the very reason that in it the intellectual and the creative artist come closest to being joined. Much as ideas and the elaboration of ideas figure in the book, the author has not shirked the novelist's tasks, and the remarkable thing is the life with which the ideas are invested, which forms the intimate texture of the hero's experience and sensibility. The mood of this life is disgust, which can as well as any other mood become the occasion of discovery, a radical plunge into one's own existence. It is authentically human, this disgust, and turns out to be novelistically exciting, though it has nothing like the grand scope and implications of Céline's disgust. Sartre's treatment is more self-conscious and more subtle, philosophically, but also more static; his disgust is not embodied, as Céline's is, in the desperate picaresque of common life and the anonymous depths of street characters. *Nausea* is not so much a full novel as an extraordinary fragment of one. In his later fiction Sartre has turned away from the narrow and intense form of the early book to a broader panorama, and not always with entirely happy results.

These later novels—originally a trilogy, *Les Chemins de la Liberté (The Roads to Liberty)* and now a tetralogy—may go on being issued as endlessly as the *roman fleuve* of Jules Romains, if Sartre's volcanic activity as a writer continues. One does wish that Sartre would pause for a while and regroup his forces. The man really writes too much. Perhaps if literature becomes a mode of action one gets so caught up in it that one cannot stop the action. These later novels of his contain remarkable things—great scenes and passages—and their theme is the central Sartrian one of the search for liberty, or rather for the realization in life of that liberty that we always and essentially are, sometimes even in spite of ourselves. Yet they are so uneven in achievement, one regrets to see Sartre's great talents wandering and thinning out like spilt milk.

Of his plays too, it may be said that his two earlier and shorter ones—*Les Mouches (The Flies)* and *Huis Clos (No Exit)*—are his best. They are at any rate the things to recommend to the reader who wishes to get the concrete drift of Sartre's philosophy but has no stomach for the elaborate dialectic of *Being and Nothingness*.

The Flies, first produced while the Resistance was still going on, is in form something of a set piece, since it deals with the myth of Orestes and the Furies; but it is charged throughout with a passion and eloquence born of Sartre's own personal convictions. Orestes is the spokesman for the Sartrian view of liberty. The solution of the play is not at all like that in Aeschylus, for here there are no supernatural agencies that can deliver Orestes from his guilt. He has to take that guilt upon himself, and he does so at the end of the play in a superbly defiant speech before the cosmic Gestapo chief Jupiter; he accepts his guilt, he exclaims, knowing that to do so is absurd because he is a man and therefore free. In discharging his freedom man also wills to accept the responsibility of it, thus becoming heavy with his own guilt. Conscience, Heidegger has said, is the will to be guilty—that is, to accept the guilt that we know will be ours whatever course of action we take.

No Exit, the most sensational of Sartre's dramatic successes, displays perhaps to their best advantage his real talents as a writer: the intense driving energy of the play, the passion of the ideas expressed, we can recognize as authentically his. The three characters of *No Exit* are planted in Hell; they are being punished, rather in the manner of Dante, by being given exactly the fruit of their evil itself. Having practiced "bad faith" in life—which, in Sartre's terms, is the surrendering of one's human liberty in order to possess, or try to possess, one's being as a *thing*—the three characters now have what they had sought to surrender themselves to. Having died, they cannot change anything in their past lives, which are exactly what they are, no more and no less, just like the static being of things. These three persons have no being other than that each has in the eyes of the others; they exist in each other's gaze, in fact. But this is exactly what they longed for in life—to lose their own subjective being by identifying themselves with what they were in the eyes of other people. It is a torment that people do in fact choose on earth; the bourgeois *salaud* and the anti-Semite, Sartre says, have chosen as themselves their public stance or role, and thus really exist not as free beings for themselves but as beings in the eyes of others.

Despite the excitement and intensity of *No Exit* as theater, the distinctly intellectual nature of Sartre's gifts once again reveals itself. The three characters are thinly blocked out, hardly more than single intense curves of action, illustrating the three evils of cowardice, Lesbianism, infanticide. Beyond a certain point they hold no surprises for us, they are without contingency—and this from an author who denies the existence of "character" as a fixed thing. The same is true here as we observed earlier of *Nausea:* Sartre succeeds most surely where the fusion of intellectual with creative writer is most intimate and passionate. But this is always achieved by the writer's drawing secret drafts on the philosopher's credit. As a writer Sartre is always the impassioned rhetorician of the idea; and the rhetorician, no matter how great and how eloquent his rhetoric, never has the full being of the artist. If Sartre were really a poet and an artist, we would have from him a different philosophy, as we shall see from turning back now to that philosophy.

3. AN EXISTENTIAL PSYCHOLOGY

One would expect that Being-in-itself, as the realm of self-identical objects, would be invested by Sartre with imagery suggesting stiffness and rigidity. Quite the contrary: this vast realm is associated for him with images of softness, stickiness, viscosity, corpulence, flabbiness. There is too much of it, and it is heavy, like a fat lady in the circus. In the famous episode in *Nausea* where the hero, Roquentin, discovers existence in the experience of disgust, he is looking at a chestnut tree in a provincial park: the roots are tangled and excessive; the tree itself is *de trop*, too much, excessive. Since it has no ultimate reason for existing, Being-in-itself is absurd: its existence is a kind of superfetation. Its softness has the quality of the feminine. Behind all Sartre's intellectual dialectic we perceive that the In-itself is for him the archetype of nature: excessive, fruitful, blooming nature—the woman, the female.

The For-itself, by contrast, is for Sartre the masculine aspect of human psychology: it is that in virtue of which man chooses himself in his radical liberty, makes projects, and thereby gives his life what strictly human meaning it has.

It is necessary to call attention to these feminine and masculine images that circulate in the background of Sartre's more formal concepts because in *Being and Nothingness* and certain other writings he has attempted to sketch a new and radical type of psychology. He calls it "existential psychoanalysis," and it has already caught on somewhat in Europe; a group of psychiatrists there has espoused it, and even in this country it has its professional adherents. This new type of psychoanalysis, Sartre says, will replace or at least supplement the older forms. The essence of man, according to the French thinker, lies not in the

Oedipus complex (as Freud held) nor in the inferiority complex (as Adler maintained); it lies rather in the radical liberty of man's existence by which he chooses himself and so makes himself what he is. Man is not to be seen as the passive plaything of unconscious forces, which determine what he is to be. In fact, Sartre denies the existence of an unconscious mind altogether; wherever the mind manifests itself, he holds, it is conscious. A human personality or human life is not to be understood in terms of some hypothetical unconscious at work behind the scenes and pulling all the wires that manipulate the puppet of consciousness. A man *is* his life, says Sartre; which means that he is nothing more nor less than the totality of acts that make up that life. And to understand truly a man's life we have simply to grasp the structure, at once single and complex, that binds together all those overt acts—this structure being, in fact, just the unique and irreplaceable project that *is* that individual's life.

Sartre has given his theory a remarkably concrete application in a biographical study, *Baudelaire*, published here in 1950. We cannot, according to Sartre, understand Baudelaire's life—his poetry, his ideas, his quarrels—by relating all these things to his sexuality; on the contrary, the sexuality must be seen to take its place in the whole life, and indeed to take its form and direction from the total project that is that life. The choice of himself that made Baudelaire's life what it was occurred, says Sartre, when he was sent off to school as a boy and thus for the first time was separated from his mother: alienated and intimidated by his schoolfellows, he withdrew into himself, and there the choice of himself as solitary and different began. Sartre shows how this choice radiates, like the ripple from a stone, through the whole life that followed: the cultivation of the poet's mind as a mirror of his solitude; his withdrawal from the fatness and lubricity of nature in visions of a completely inorganic world, a city of metals without a single tree, etc., etc. Sartre assembles a great number of details and correlates them well, so that we are left with a powerful and unified image of Baudelaire's life. But how convincing is his picture as rendering the total truth about Baudelaire? And how convincing is this new psychoanalysis he has here put to the test?

In the first place, the choice of himself that Baudelaire is supposed to have made at around the age of twelve hardly appears to have been a conscious and resolute project, elected then and there for a whole lifetime. If it was *not* conscious, then Sartre would be forced to admit the existence of an unconscious; for if Baudelaire's life was a single project—that is, a choice of himself as the being he was to be—reflected in all the myriad details of his life, the way in which it was to be reflected was unknown to him at twelve, and therefore the project itself, as a totality, was in good part unconscious. If a human life is a concrete liberty radiating outward into all the details of our actions, some people may indeed know what their project is, what their life means, but at any one time a vast portion of this project as manifested in all our actions must be hidden from us. Sartre does not admit this, but if he did he would be compelled to take refuge in the notion of an unconscious project. In any case, the unconscious has to be reintroduced as soon as we seek to apply existential psychoanalysis concretely.

The merits of Sartre's theory as psychology we leave to the psychologists to determine; what concerns us here is the philosophic thought that lies at the root of the psychology. And once again the root is Cartesianism: the identification of mind with consciousness, with the *Cogito*, is a Cartesian identification. When Descartes said "I think, therefore I am," the statement—apart from its merely functional usage as marking a certain stage in his reasoning— was, humanly speaking, the statement of a man who identifies his own reality with his thought. The unconscious is something alien and opposite: Consciousness is a realm of clear and distinct ideas, but the world of the unconscious is the fat, formless, fructifying domain of the In-itself of nature. This latter world can be forgotten and finally denied to exist. A Cartesian subjectivity (which is what Sartre's is) *cannot* admit the existence of the unconscious because the unconscious is the Other in oneself; and the glance of the Other, in Sartre, is always like the stare of Medusa, fearful and petrifying.

This relation to the Other is one of the most sensational and best-known aspects of Sartre's psychology. To the other person, who looks at me from the outside, I seem an object, a thing; my subjectivity with its inner freedom escapes his gaze. Hence his tendency is always to convert me into the object he sees. The gaze of the Other penetrates to the depths of my existence, freezes and congeals it. It is this, according to Sartre, that turns love and particularly sexual love into a perpetual tension and indeed warfare. The lover wishes to possess the beloved, but the freedom of the beloved (which is his or her human essence) cannot be possessed; hence, the lover tends to reduce the beloved to an object for the sake of possessing it. Love is menaced always by a perpetual oscillation between sadism and masochism: In sadism I reduce the other to a mere lump, to be beaten and manipulated as I choose, while in masochism I offer myself as an object, but in an attempt to entrap the other and undermine his freedom. With a dialectical ingenuity that is almost fiendish Sartre exposes the interplay between the two tendencies. There is no doubt that he sheds light on a tension that must be perpetually present when two persons love each other; but there does seem to be doubt, after we have got through all his pulverizing analysis, that the very excess of his dialectic may not actually make disappear the very possibility of love, as love sometimes (despite him) does really occur in our day-to-day life. What has happened here is simply that Sartre has fallen victim to his own philosophic principles: as he can find in his philosophy no field or region of Being in which the subject, Being-for-itself, and the object, Being-in-itself, really meet, so when he comes to psychology the self must remain irremediably opposed to the Other, and there is no area between in which I may genuinely say Thou to the Other. A Cartesian subjectivity, which Sartre's fundamentally is, must work itself out into just such a psychological theory of the emotions as Sartre has given us.

What he is describing is at bottom the eternal war between the sexes, of which Adler spoke. In fact, if we strip Sartre's psychology of its particular philosophical terminology, it turns out to be fundamentally an Adlerian psychology. Adler, following Nietzsche, based his psychology on the Will to Power, and this, as we see from the endless cycle of sadism-masochism to which he condemns love, is true of Sartre too. Eros disappears before the Will to

Power. Sartre is driven once again into the Nietzschean camp: where Being is lost—the Being that would unite the For-itself, the subject, with the In-itself, the object— man is left to find his meaning only in his mastery over objects. What is the Sartrian project that makes up our very being but a confirmation of the Adlerian notion of a "guiding thread or motive" by which we try to unify and give meaning to our whole life? Like Adler's, Sartre's is fundamentally a masculine psychology; it misunderstands or disparages the psychology of woman. The humanity of man consists in the For-itself, the masculine component by which we choose, make projects, and generally commit ourselves to the life of action. The element of masculine protest, to use Adler's term, is strong throughout Sartre's writings—whether it be the disgust of Mathieu (in *Roads to Liberty*) at his pregnant mistress, or the disgust (it is fundamentally the same disgust) of Roquentin, in *Nausea,* at the bloated roots of the chestnut tree; or Sartre's philosophical analysis (in *Being and Nothingness*) of the viscous, the thick, sticky substance that would entrap his liberty like the soft threat of the body of a woman. And the woman is a threat, for the woman is nature and Sartrian man exists in the liberty of his project, which, since it is ultimately unjustified and unjustifiable, in effect sunders him totally from nature. The whole of Sartre's psychology is thus the Cartesian dualism given a new and startling modern content.

We are now in a better position to assess Sartre's fundamental notion of liberty. He is right to make the liberty of choice, which is the liberty of a conscious action, total and absolute, no matter how small the area of our power: in choosing, I have to say No somewhere, and this No, which is total and totally exclusive of other alternatives, is dreadful; but only by shutting myself up in it is any resoluteness of action possible. A friend of mine, a very intelligent and sensitive man, was over a long period in the grip of a neurosis that took the form of indecision in the face of almost every occasion of life; sitting in a restaurant, he could not look at the printed menu to choose his lunch without seeing the abyss of the negative open before his eyes, on the page, and so falling into a sweat. (He was not a Sartrian, and had not even read Sartre; but his description of his own experience was exactly in terms of this abyss of Nothing opening before his eyes on the page.) Critics may make the superficial observation that this only shows how silly and neurotic Sartre's view of freedom is. But, on the contrary, it confirms Sartre's analysis of freedom, for only because freedom is what he says it is could this man have been frightened by it and have retreated into the anxiety of indecision. The neurosis consisted in the fact that freedom, that total and absolute thing, could cause the abyss to open on such trifling occasions. But the example points up also where Sartre's theory is decidedly lacking: it does not show us the kind of *objects* in relation to which our human subjectivity can define itself in a free choice that is meaningful and not neurotic. This is so because Sartre's doctrine of liberty was developed out of the experience of extreme situations: the victim says to his totalitarian oppressor, No, even if you kill me; and he shuts himself up in this No and will not be shaken from it. Our resoluteness in any choice exacts from us something as total as this, although it need not be exacted from us in so violent and extreme a situation. But he who shuts himself up in the No can be demoniacal, as Kierkegaard pointed out; he can say No against himself, against his own nature. Sartre's doctrine of freedom does not really comprehend the concrete man who is an undivided totality of body and mind, at once, and without division, both In-itself and For-itself; but rather an isolated aspect of this total condition, the aspect of man always at the margin of his existence.

Thus the crucial question, Sartre tells us, is this: Under what *exceptional* conditions does a man really experience his freedom? Notice the word "exceptional" here. Why not ask instead: Under what ordinary, average, everyday conditions does a man experience his freedom? An artist—and particularly not an intellectual artist like Sartre—when the work is going well experiences his freedom as just that effortless burgeoning, swelling, flowing, which has for him the quality of the inevitable flow of nature. It is like that pear tree blooming there in the yard—very different from the nauseating chestnut tree of Roquentin—effortlessly and beautifully bringing forth its fruit into the sunlight. Because Sartre's psychology recognizes only the conscious, it cannot comprehend a form of freedom that operates in

that zone of the human personality where conscious and unconscious flow into each other. Being limited to the conscious, it inevitably becomes an ego psychology; hence
freedom is understood only as the resolute project of the
conscious ego.

Under what day-to-day conditions does the religious man
—to take another example—experience his freedom? That,
from Sartre's thoroughly secular point of view, the beliefs
of religion are absurd does not enter into this question;
for the religious psychology does in fact exist, and any
psychological theory that failed to cover it would be inadequate. How does a St. Paul experience his freedom? He
has died the death, cast off the bondage of an old self, and
now he lives and energetically organizes a church: "And
yet not *I* live, but Christ liveth in me." His freedom is the
surrender to the redeeming image of something greater
than himself. This is the freedom of spiritual man, not
Cartesian man. The project that is the life of a St. Paul is
not primarily a conscious choice of himself, but is the result
of a conversion that arose out of the depths of his unconscious. Cartesian man knows neither the freedom of
spirit nor of nature, for in both of these the dualism of the
In-itself and the For-itself breaks down.

Or, to take a third example, consider the psychology of
the ordinary woman. Not of the women one meets in
Sartre's novels or plays; nor of that woman, his friend,
who wrote a book of feminine protest, *The Second Sex,*
which is in reality the protest against being feminine. No,
take a totally ordinary woman, one of that great number
whose being is the involvement with family and children,
and some of whom are happy at it, or at least as humanly
fulfilled by it as the male by his own essentially masculine
projects. What sense does it make to say that such a woman's identity is constituted by her project? Her project is
family and children, and these do in fact make up a total
human commitment; but it is hardly a project that has issued out of the conscious ego. Her whole life, with whatever freedom it reveals, is rather the unfolding of nature
through her. As soon as we begin to think about the psychology of women, Sartre's psychology shows itself indeed
to be exclusively a masculine affair; but the masculine that

—alone, unjustified, and on the very margins of existence —has sundered itself from nature.

No doubt all of Sartre's theory is, as perhaps every psychological theory must be, a projection of his own personal psychology; there are plenty of signs of this in the novels and plays, where he reveals himself copiously. But he is also a thinker passionately identified with his ideas; and for us the significance of his complicated and often brilliant exploration of human psychology lies in the fact that it stems ultimately from Cartesian dualism, and brings to completion that sundering of man from nature with which Descartes initiated the modern epoch. Sartre is certainly right in insisting that man comes to exist only by sundering himself from nature—that this is his human fate in a universe that knows him not; but it is a question of how far this sundering can go without the human project becoming demoniacal, insane, or simply too brittle to have any human substance. In our own lives, when they are going at their best, the In-itself, the unconscious—or nature—is perpetually flowing through and sustaining the For-itself of our consciousness.

Sartre's freedom *is* demoniacal. It is rootless freedom. This doctrine happens, of course, to be maintained by a man of great good will, generosity, and courage; and the project he has chosen as his own, in which he has chosen himself, is the humanitarian and liberal one of revolutionary action. Sartre's long and checkered relations with the Communists would be a matter of high comedy if they were not so clearly a part of the general contemporary tragedy. Sartre believed that the Communist Party was truly the party of the working class, and he was willing therefore to cast his lot with that party in the field of practical politics. Meanwhile, in philosophy, he intended to retain his own freedom, including his doctrine of freedom. He came to the Communists, offering them all his talents and energy—and was rebuffed. In practical politics Sartre has shown himself very naïve, but in the course of his philosophical quarrels with the Communists he has produced some of the best intellectual polemic of our time. It was a case, in these polemics, of Cartesian man against the Communist robot; and whatever reservations we may have about Cartesian man, he is in part human and dwarfs the party robot. Besides, Sartre is a man of surpassing intelligence, which his opponents among the Communist intellectuals certainly were not. What lay behind the entire controversy was the shadow that Marxist man does not face: Sartre based his revolutionary activity upon a free choice, the Marxist upon an objective historic process, the former recognizing the inalienable subjectivity of man, the latter reducing man to an object in a process. Moreover, Sartre's atheism states candidly what the Philistine atheism of Communism (and all other Philistine forms of atheism) does not have enough imagination or courage to say: that man is an alien in the universe, unjustified and unjustifiable, absurd in the simple sense that there is no Leibnitzian reason sufficient to explain why he or his universe exists. Sartre's atheism—the way in which he exists in it—does not lose its grasp of the essentially problematic nature of man. And therein Sartre points the way to the question Marxist man will have to ask, the devil he will have to face, if and when the classless society should ever be achieved.

It has been remarked that Kierkegaard's statement of the religious position is so severe that it has turned many people who thought themselves religious to atheism. Analogously, Sartre's view of atheism is so stark and bleak that it seems to turn many people toward religion. This is exactly as it should be. The choice must be hard either way; for man, a problematic being to his depths, cannot lay hold of his ultimate commitments with a smug and easy security.

It may be that, as the modern world moves on, the Sartrian kind of freedom will be more and more the only kind man can experience. As society becomes more totalitarian, the islands of freedom get smaller and more cut off from the mainland and from each other—which is to say from any spontaneous interchange with nature or the community of other human beings. Sartre's Orestes says to his celestial oppressor, "I am a man, Jupiter." One imagines the last Resistant of the last Resistance saying No in a prison cell in the Lubianka; saying No without any motive of self-advantage and without any hope that future humans will take up his cause, but saying No nonetheless simply because he is a man and his liberty cannot be taken from him. This last man would exist in a night darker than that into which the great Descartes cast himself, in that historic inn in Holland, when he paused to think and said No to the demon. It cannot be said that Sartre has not given us good warning.

Demonic Fiction of a Yiddish "Modernist"
BY IRVING HOWE

Isaac Bashevis Singer is the only living Yiddish writer whose translated work has caught the imagination of the American literary public. Though his brilliant stories and novels are crowded with grotesque happenings, though they often seem to comprise an alien sub-world of imps, devils, whores, spirits in seizure, charlatans, and false messiahs, the contemporary reader—for whom the determination not to be shocked has become a point of honor—is likely to feel closer to Singer than to any, or most, of the other Yiddish writers. Offhand this may be surprising, for Singer's subjects are decidedly remote: in *Satan in Goray,* the orgiastic consequences of the false messianism of 17th-century East European Jews; in his book of stories *Gimpel the Fool,* a range of demonic, apocalyptic, and perversely sacred moments of *shtetl* life; and now in his new novel *The Magician of Lublin,* a portrait of a Jewish acrobat-magician—Don Juan in late 19th-century Poland who exhausts himself in sensuality and ends his life as a penitent ascetic. Yet one feels that, unlike many of the Yiddish writers who treat more familiar and up-to-date subjects, Singer commands a distinctively "modern" sensibility.

Now this is partly true—in the sense that Singer, though a master of Yiddish prose, has cut himself off from some of the traditional assumptions of Yiddish literature. But it is also not true—in the sense that any effort to assimilate Singer to literary "modernism" without registering how deeply involved he is with Jewish history and faith, is certain to distort the meanings of his work.

Those meanings, one might as well admit, are often enigmatic and hard to come by. It must be a common experience among Singer's readers to find a quick pleasure in the caustic surfaces of his prose, the nervous tokens of his virtuosity—for simply as a literary *performer* he has few peers among living writers—but then to acknowledge themselves baffled when they inquire into the point or purpose of his fictions. That these do have an insistent point and stringent purpose no one can doubt; Singer is too ruthlessly single-minded a writer to content himself with mere slices of representation or displays of the bizarre. His grotesquerie must be taken seriously, perhaps as a recoil from his perception of how ugly—how gratuitously ugly—human life can be. He is a writer completely absorbed by the demands of his vision, a vision gnomic and compulsive but with moments of high exaltation; so that while reading his stories one feels as if one were overhearing bits and snatches of a monologue, the impact of which is both notable and disturbing, but the meaning withheld.

Now these are precisely the qualities that the sophisticated reader, trained to docility before the exactions of "modernism," has come to applaud. Singer's stories work, or prey, upon the nerves. They leave one unsettled and anxious, the way a rationalist might feel if, walking at night in the woods, he suddenly found himself afraid of bats. Unlike most Yiddish fiction, Singer's stories neither round out the cycle of their intentions nor posit a coherent and ordered universe. They can be seen as paradigms of the arbitrariness, the grating injustice, at the heart of life. They offer instances of pointless suffering, dead-end exhaustion, inexplicable grace. And sometimes, as in Singer's masterpiece "Gimpel the Fool," they turn about, refusing to rest with the familiar discomforts of the problematic, and drive toward a prospect of salvation on the other side of despair. But this prospect does not depend on any belief in the comeliness or lawfulness of the universe: whether or not God is there, surely He is no protector. Things happen, the probable bad and improbable good, both of them subject to the whim of the fortuitous—and the sacred fools, like Gimpel, learn to roll with the punch, finding the value of their life in a total passivity and openness to suffering.

It is hardly a secret that in the Yiddish literary world Singer is regarded with a certain suspicion or at least reserve. His powers of evocation, his resources as a stylist are acknowledged, yet many Yiddish literary people, including serious ones, seem to be uneasy about him. One reason is that "modernism"—which, as these people regard Singer, means a heavy stress upon sexuality, a concern for the irrational, expressionist distortions of character, and an apparent indifference to the more conventional aspects of Jewish life—has never won so strong a hold in Yiddish writing as it has in most Western literatures. For the Yiddish writers, "modernism" has often been a mere adornment of manner upon a subject inescapably traditional, or a means of intensifying a sense of estrangement from collective values to which they nevertheless remain bound.

The truly "modern" writer, however, is not quite trustworthy in his relation to his culture; he is a shifty character by choice and need, unable to settle into that representative solidity which would permit him to serve as a cultural "spokesman." And to the extent that Singer shares in the modernist outlook he will be regarded with distrust by Yiddish readers brought up on such "spokesmen" as Peretz, Abraham Reisen, and H. Leivick. There is, to be sure, no lack of admiration among Yiddish readers for Singer's work: anyone with half an ear must respond to the marvelously taut and subtle rhythms of his prose. Still, it is a qualified admiration. Singer's moral outlook, which seems to move equally toward the sensational and the ascetic, and his assumption that in fiction grotesquerie can be made to serve almost as a mode of knowledge, are hardly traits calculated to put Yiddish readers at their ease.

I must confess that my first response to *The Magician of Lublin* was somewhat like the one I have been attributing here to Yiddish readers. The book is not quite so dazzling as *Satan in Goray*, but it does represent Singer at fairly close to his best, particularly in his gifts for evoking the textures of sensuous life and for driving straight to those moments of tension and inner division which reveal the souls of his characters. But while there is no difficulty in making out what happens in the book, there is a real question as to what it all signifies.

The Magician of Lublin centers on the figure of Yasha Mazur, a Jewish acrobat-magician who travels through the towns of Poland, giving performances and entangling him-

self with women. Like other figures in Singer's work, Yasha is "half Jew, half Gentile—neither Jew nor Gentile.
He had worked out his own religion. There was a Creator,
but He revealed Himself to no one, gave no indications of
what was permitted or forbidden." The theme is recurrent in Singer: even the acknowledgment of God yields no
moral assurance, and with or without Him men lose their
way.

At the beginning, Yasha is seen during one of his rare
visits home, basking in his prosperity and enjoying a good
and faithful wife. But he is a restless creature, always driv-
en to test his powers of performance and persuasion, to
try out his gifts in still another place, with still another
woman. These gifts constitute his curse, and his pleasure
in observing his impact upon other people, his undoing.

Yasha moves on, leaving home, visiting his Gentile assistant, who is also a worshipful mistress, having a lively
time with a Jewish whore, skirting the life of a gang of
Jewish thieves, savoring an encounter with some Jewish
white slavers, and finally ending in Warsaw with the biggest risk of his life: a scheme to run off, as he pretends
to be unmarried, with a middle-class Gentile widow. This
woman represents for him—the symbolism is clear but not
insistent—the attractions of the outer cultivated world he
had never been able to reach or conquer. Yasha undertakes
a robbery to get money for his elopement, fails because of
the residual power of his Jewish conscience, and then
rapidly falls into flight, pain, collapse. "He had looked
on the face of death and lechery and had seen that they
were the same. . . . He had seen the hand of God. He had
reached the end of the road." In an epilogue Yasha is
seen at home again, now living as an ascetic who has
locked himself in a hut behind his house, suffering cold,
hunger, and sexual fantasies, worshipped by the credulous
as a new miracle-worker, but still struggling to find his
way to God.

From page to page the story, like anything Singer writes, is
remarkably vivid. Everything springs to life, everything
trembles with the breath of actuality. Yet, as one reads,
one grows uneasy and begins to consider the kind of
criticism to which Singer is sometimes subjected by Yiddish
literary people. Why is this juicy description here, that

sensual evocation there? Isn't there an indulgence in sensation for its own sake, a surrender to rather than a use of the grotesque? Does not Singer sometimes come close to the self-imitation which is the writer's greatest curse, that self-imitation which consists in falling back upon familiar devices and inflections?

It would be idle to say that these things never happen, yet once we bring to bear the perspectives of "modernism," it becomes a bit easier to grasp and thereby "justify" *The Magician of Lublin.* The very incongruity in the conception of a Jewish Don Juan has its obvious ironic appeal and significance—particularly a Jewish Don Juan with a record of success who fails at precisely the point where conventional Jewish wisdom would predict that he would: his encounter with Christian gentility. The ending of the novel also allows us to see that Singer is working out a complex pattern of suggestion, and not merely indulging in his repertoire of tricks. Yasha becomes a penitent, but so weak in body and faith that he cannot trust himself except under lock and key. Nothing is settled, nothing solved. At the end Yasha retains, embarrassingly, the charismatic powers he had enjoyed as a worldling: life is not so different even after the blessed revelation: the flesh continues to lust, the world remains full of temptations, and the fools who populate it still yearn for easy assuagements.

Between the epilogue and the bulk of the book there is, then, an ironic balance: each cancels out the implications of the other, so that finally, as at the beginning, what Singer offers are questions beyond answer. His particular power rests on this ability to hold such contrary elements as the miraculous and the skeptical, the moral and the exotic in a delicate tension. At times, his style seems almost *as if* it were the style of a man possessed, so thoroughly does he give himself to the subject; yet Singer also maintains a rigorous distance, one is always aware of the *conditional* nature of his involvement.

Having gone this far, we must now turn again. If Singer's work can be understood only on the assumption that in some crucial respects he is a "modernist" writer, one must add that in other ways he is profoundly related to the Jewish tradition. And if the Yiddish reader is inclined to slight the first side of his work, so the American reader is likely to underestimate the strength and persistence of the second.

Singer is related to the Jewish tradition not only in the obvious sense that he enjoys a close knowledge of the Jewish past. More importantly, he is one of the few Yiddish writers whose relation to the Jewish past does not depend on that body of attitudes and values we call Yiddishism. He writes *in* Yiddish, but is often quite apart from the Yiddish tradition. He is, so to say, a writer of the pre-Enlightenment and post-Enlightenment; he would be equally at home with a congregation of medieval Jews and a gathering of modern intellectuals, perhaps more so than at a meeting of the Yiddish PEN Club; he has a strong sense of the mystical and antique, but also a stern awareness of psychoanalytic disenchantment; he has evaded both the religious pieties and the humane rationalism of 19th-century East European Judaism. In his fiction Singer has "skipped over" the ideas of the historical epoch which gave birth to Yiddishism, for the truth is, I suppose, that Yiddish literature, in both its acceptance and denials, its writers of faith and its writers of skepticism, is thoroughly caught up with the Enlightenment. Singer shares very little in the collective aspirations or the *folkshtimmlichkeit* of the Yiddish masters; he does not celebrate *dos klaine menshele* as a paragon of sweetness and goodness; he is impatient with the sensual deprivations involved in the values of *edelkeit;* and above all, he breaks away from a central assumption of both the 19th century and Yiddish literature, the assumption of *tachlis,* an immanent fate or end in human existence.

What remains? The Yiddish critic Shlomo Bickel has perceptively remarked that Singer's dominating principle is "anti-Prometheanism," a disbelief in the efficacy of defiance, striving, and pride, a doubt as to the sufficiency of knowledge or even wisdom. This seems true, but only if one remembers that in a good many of Singer's fictions, particularly in *The Magician of Lublin,* the central action does constitute a sort of Promethean ordeal or straining. Singer makes it abundantly clear that his characters have no choice: they must live out their hungers, their orgiastic yearnings and apocalyptic expectations. "Anti-Prometheanism" thus comes to rest upon a belief in the unavoidable recurrence of the Promethean urge—an urge which, in Singer's view of things, is reduced from ideal to obsession or, perhaps more accurately, makes it impossible to separate ideal from obsession.

In the end, what concerns Singer most of all is the possibilities for life that remain after the exhaustion of human effort, after failure and despair have come and gone. Singer watches his stricken figures from a certain distance, with enigmatic moral intent and no great outpouring of sympathy, almost as if to say that before their collapse neither judgment nor sympathy matters very much. Yet in all of his books the Promethean effort recurs, obsessional, churning with new energy and delusion. In the knowledge of its recurrence there may also lie hidden a kind of pity, for that too we would expect, and can learn to find, in the writer who created Gimpel.

The Yiddish Hawthorne
BY STANLEY EDGAR HYMAN

If Sholom Aleichem is the Yiddish Mark Twain, Isaac Bashevis Singer is the Yiddish Hawthorne. I do not know how many reviewers have made that comparison before, since my sins are not great enough to require me to keep up with the reviewers, but the comparison is inevitable. Singer writes what Hawthorne called "romances" rather than novels, and moral fables and allegories rather than short stories. I cannot imagine anyone since Hawthorne writing such a tale as "The Gentleman from Cracow" in *Gimpel the Fool*, in which a generous stranger who corrupts and destroys the little town of Frampol is revealed to be Ketev Mriri, Chief of the Devils. Now Singer has published his third and most Hawthornian romance, *The Slave*.

I do not read Yiddish, I am not familiar with much Yiddish literature, and I have not read Singer's first novel, *The Family Moskat*. The books that I know—*Satan in Goray, Gimpel the Fool and Other Stories, The Magician of Lublin, The Spinoza of Market Street,* and *The Slave* —seem to me incredible in mid-20th century America. Singer has been in this country since 1935, on the staff of the Jewish *Daily Forward,* but America and the 20th century do not exist in his work, except once as a fantastic vision in "The Little Shoemakers" in *Gimpel the Fool,* when a half-crazed old Jew arrives in New York and takes it to be the pyramids of Egypt. Singer's subject is *shtetl* (Jewish village) life in Poland, sometimes in the 17th and sometimes in the late 19th century, and he brings it into being so powerfully that reading his books one soon comes to believe that our world *is* a fantastic vision.

Singer's style, like that of Hawthorne and Melville, is often rhetorical and flamboyant, but there is not an ounce of fat on his prose. His characters sometimes bandy proverbs wittily, like West Africans, and like them he is sometimes folksy and proverbial. Singer's most characteristic style is one of sophisticated ironic juxtaposition, as in a sentence from *Satan in Goray:* "To divert the bride and raise her spirits, the women enthusiastically praised her beauty, stroked her hair, and quickened her with spoonfuls of moldy citrus preserve."

Except for a lady who lives in my house, Singer seems to be the only writer in America who believes in the real existence of Satan. Or perhaps he doesn't. Three stories in *Gimpel the Fool* and two in *The Spinoza of Market Street* are narrated by demons, and the satanic forces are everywhere in the other stories and in the novels. In a few of the stories, particularly the finest of them all, "The Black Wedding" in *The Spinoza of Market Street,* the Evil One is obviously a metaphor for repressed sexuality, and Singer uses his mythology as a psychopathology with the insight of Euripides. At other times Satan and his forces seem as tangible as Moshe the Chimney Sweep.

The Slave is best seen against a background of the other two romances. *Satan in Goray* is an account of the Sabbatai Zevi messianic hallucination as it overwhelms the little *shtetl* of Goray in the 17th century. It is a work of power and brilliance, creating its almost-entirely-Jewish world with easy mastery, from the coarse jokes of the women's bathhouse to the mad messianic rhetoric of the missionary who comes to spread darkness in Goray.

Goray is a "town that lay in the midst of the hills at the end of the world," a town that "had always been isolated from the world." This is Singer's joke. Goray *is* the world, and his parable is of its vulnerability to sin, the devil in the flesh. From the time of the Cossack pogroms in 1648 until 1666, Goray had been without a *shochet* (ritual slaughterer), and thus no Jew in it had tasted meat for 18 years. When Reb Gedaliya settles down to be the new *shochet,* the Goray Jews feast on meat, and soon other pleasures of the flesh follow. Gedaliya preaches a religion of serving God through joy, and argues that since it is the end of days all the prohibitions of the Law have been repealed. The consequent excesses range from simple adultery to sodomy with goats, and one diabolist even goes so far as to shave off his beard and earlocks with a razor. Eventually Goray becomes "an accursed town," Gedaliya turns apostate like his master Sabbatai Zevi, and the end of the novel is the pious moral of the pamphlet on which it concludes: "Let none attempt to force the Lord."

The Magician of Lublin, which I think Singer's finest work, is not about the closed *shtetl* world, but about an infidel Jew, Yasha Mazur, out among the nations in 19th century Poland. He is a performer: a magician, hypnotist and acrobat. Yasha lives his whole life "as if walking the tightrope": married to a pious Jewish wife, Esther; having simultaneous affairs with Zeftel, the Jewish wife of a thief, and Magda, the Polish girl who assists in his act, both of whom are in love with him; meanwhile himself in love with Emilia, a highborn Polish lady. Like Don Juan, "he lusted after women, yet hated them as a drunkard hates alcohol."

In one terrible day, all of Yasha's life goes to pieces. He tries an easy robbery and fails at it, damaging his foot so that he cannot perform; Emilia tells him "You stem from offal and you are offal" and turns him away; Magda calls him a "dirty Jew" and says she is leaving; he finds Zeftel in bed with a man; finally he returns home to discover that Magda has strangled his trained animals and hanged herself. Yasha has tasted the bitterness of the world and "seen the hand of God."

As a result, he becomes Reb Jacob the Penitent, an anchorite saint who bricks himself up in a cell, where he fasts, prays and gives audiences through the window. "You must have some sort of covenant with God since he punished you directly on the spot," Emilia told Yasha when she heard the story of his unsuccessful burglary. His inflamed and swollen foot, risen like dough, is the punishment, and the yeast working in it is God's grace. Yasha, who can "walk a tightrope, skate on a wire, climb walls, open any lock," who can sign his name and shell peas with his toes, is a Jewish Faust, and the book is a parable of the Enlightenment. Yasha's covenant is the covenant of the Law, and when he is knocked off his tightrope he flees to its security and reinforces it with bricks.

Now we have *The Slave,* the most ambitious of Singer's romances so far. It is the story of Jacob, a pious scholar of Josefov in the 17th century, sold as a slave to a Polish peasant, and of his love for the peasant's daughter Wanda, who passes as a mute to live with him as a Jewish wife, "Dumb Sarah." Its theme is universalism, the discovery by Jacob that even the most debased of the Polish peasants are fellow humans, created in God's image, and the humbling of his stiffnecked Jewish pride. Jacob first sees the peasants as subhuman, eaters of field mice, indulgers in abominations, shameless in debauchery and soulless. A description of a cowherds' drunken party as Jacob sees it is truly Swiftian in its bestiality. Yet through Wanda he discovers universal humanity and feels compassion for the cowherds.

Beyond that, Jacob discovers his fellowship with "all living things: Jews, gentiles, animals, even the flies and gnats." He becomes un-Jewishly fond of the cows he tends for the peasant and of his dog. "The idea of feeding on God's creatures now repelled him," and he decides that "Jews treated animals as Cossacks treated Jews." Eventually Jacob eats no flesh, "neither meat nor fish nor anything else from a living creature, not even cheese or eggs." Like the universalizing tracts of the Old Testament, Jonah and Ruth, *The Slave* announces a widening of the limited covenant of the Law; *all* are God's chosen.

This universalist theme is implied rather than stated, but the other Old Testament revolution, the prophetic emphasis on ethics rather than ritual, is openly preached in *The Slave*. In his captivity, Jacob occupied himself with trying to recollect the 248 commandments and 365 prohibitions of the Law and incise them on a rock. After he is ransomed, Law and commentary come to seem hairsplitting and sterile, and Jacob sees the Jews around him as devoutly obeying every ritual injunction but mistreating their fellow men. He discovers "his religion: its essence was the relation between man and his fellows."

Singer's latest parable, then, is the transcendence of law by love. The body was sin in *Satan in Goray;* in *The Slave* it comes close to being salvation. Culture and nature are both necessary. The peasant Wanda lusts for sacred learning; the pious scholar Jacob hungers for the fresh air of the fields. They complete each other, and in a miracle at the end, Jacob and Sarah are buried in a common grave with a common tombstone reading "In their death they were not divided." Jacob fell into slavery, having been rich and lucky before the pogroms, a scholar supported by his wife's family; then he fell into sin with Wanda, convinced that "I am forfeiting the world to come." The rise at the end is comparable. Their son becomes a prodigy and a teacher in Jerusalem; Jacob becomes a saint from whom venomous serpents turn away, and he is believed to be one of the Thirty-Six Righteous who sustain the world.

As it denies *Satan in Goray*, *The Slave* reverses *The Magician of Lublin*. Conversion now is *into* the world, *into* the embrace of the nations. The highest value is human attachment rather than asceticism, ethics rather than observance. Jacob is Yasha reborn, but where Yasha suffered like Job, to glorify God, Jacob suffers like Moses, to prepare him to free those held in bondage.

The second half of *The Slave*, Jacob living in Pilitz with Dumb Sarah, is less effective than the first, Jacob in slavery, which is as great as anything Singer ever wrote. The miraculous end is hard to take, and some of the characters are unconvincing. Nevertheless, *The Slave* towers over everything else being written today. Writing old-fashioned romances in an obsolescent tongue, Singer redeems the time.

Muriel Spark
BY RENATA ADLER

In her early work, Muriel Spark seemed to temporize, to toy imaginatively with light fiction, and to devote only flickering attention to what were apparently her more serious concerns. Her first novel, *The Comforters*, was in part a detective story, in part the familiar trick novel which writes itself in the mind of its major character. Of her collection of short stories entitled *The Go-Away Bird*, "The Portobello Road" was a conventional ghost story; "Miss Pinkerton's Apocalypse" was science fiction combined with a variant of "The Unicorn in the Garden"; and "The Black Madonna" superimposed an old fairy-tale motif (the granted wish which backfires) upon an atavistic theme dear to students of Creative Writing (the birth of a Negro baby to white parents ignorant of their Negro ancestry). None of these stories was trite or pat or trivial; each involved some kind of tinkering with an essentially minor form, its timing, balance, or logical sequence. The detective story was so accelerated that the reader learned what was done and who did it long before the end; the ghost story was so fragile as to be nearly toppled by the brutality of the murder revealed in its final pages; the fairy tale veered abruptly into social satire, and proceeded with deliberate inconsequence.

Certain preoccupations, however, recurred with such striking regularity that they threatened (in minor fiction) to become tedious, and seemed to require that Miss Spark either subdue them, and confine herself to expert entertainment, or find a form to give them serious support. Throughout her work there was, for example, a fascination with the uncanny: a phantom typewriter and a witch in *The Comforters;* a devil in *The Ballad of Peckham Rye;*

a ghost, a flying saucer, a miracle working statue, and an archangel in *The Go-Away Bird;* communication with the dead in *The Bachelors;* and a kind of demonic *possession* (by madness, epilepsy, deformity, or religious fanaticism) of the characters in nearly all of them. Another recurrent theme was violence: murder by drowning, stabbing with a corkscrew, shooting, smothering in hay, or poisoning with insulin in the successive works. There seemed always to be an embodiment of benign and ineffectual authority: nurses, policemen, clergymen, and curious oracular figures (a baron, a streetwalker, an alcoholic, a detective, a graphologist), guardians and interpreters of some principle of secular, divine, or moral law. Finally, there was retreat: withdrawal into a hospital, a village, a sanitarium, a religious order, or, as in *The Bachelors*, a state of celibacy.

What led one to assume that these themes had serious importance in Miss Spark's imagination was not only their persistence in her work but also their obstinate refusal to yield to her style. She could write cleverly over and around them, but something was usually left provisional, artificial, unaccounted for (the uncanny, for example, was often a mere device to trigger diverting action, the violent an explosion, as sudden and uncharted as a land mine); the author's humor and technical facility could neither accommodate nor quite conceal the trick, the sleight of hand. In only two novels did Miss Spark attempt, not merely to spring her preoccupations, but to explore and reconcile them; these were *Memento Mori* and *The Prime of Miss Jean Brodie*. One was an experiment in the abstract— supernatural telephone calls announcing the universal proposition that all men must die to old people, one of whom was eventually beaten to death, and another of whom retreated to a geriatrics ward—*Memento Mori* was remote from any possible immediate experience of the author's. The other novel was more personal, less speculative—the natural magnetism of a teacher, exerting its particular (though nonetheless uncanny) influence upon young pupils, one of whom died accidentally in a hotel fire (the first major non-homicidal death in Miss Spark's writings), and another of whom sought refuge in a convent —the themes of *Jean Brodie* were drawn together in the familiar and the real. The violent issue of both novels had an oblique dramatic fitness (its victims were the *sister* of one major character, the *classmate* of another); like a knight on a chessboard, death struck at one remove from its apparent object, but it was not arbitrary or incongruous. In both novels, however, there remained a trace of the unexplained and unfathomable: the resolution of *Memento Mori* was *too* abstract (the supernatural seemed, in the end, only a glib evasion); the outcome of *Jean Brodie* was too particular and private (the conversion of Jean Brodie's disciple had meaning, in the end, only for Miss Spark).

In her most recent and ambitious novel, *The Girls of Slender Means,* Miss Spark begins with a group within an institution (not a class in a school this time, but a floor in a dormitory for indigent working girls in London) and constructs an intricate personal metaphor for a global concern. The May of Teck Club, which was founded for girls of slender means by Queen Mary while she was still the Princess May of Teck, survived the Second World War, incurring only minor damage from three bombs which fell upon the neighborhood. Although the club has returned, in the early days of 1945, to a semblance of peacetime order and normality, an aging spinster (one of Miss Spark's strange oracles) insists that a bomb has remained undiscovered and unexploded in the garden. Because several years have passed since this bomb may or may not have fallen, even the spinster begins to doubt her story and to treat it as only an amusing anecdote with no conceivably violent consequences. The girls in the club lead their separate lives, working, dieting, trading coupons for clothes, falling in and out of love, and (the slimmer ones) slipping in and out of a bathroom window which has become the fifth floor's only secret exit since the sealing of a skylight in a time no one remembers.

Days at the May of Teck have an almost musical quality, to which each inhabitant and guest of the club repeatedly contributes his identifying chord or refrain: Greggie, the spinster, tells and retells her story of the bombing; Pauline Fox, a mad girl, delivers weekly accounts of imaginary dinners with a famous actor of the age; Jane Wright, considered an intellectual by virtue of her ugliness and her position as a publisher's assistant, tells as if by rote the calorie counts of foods, and types innumerable letters (refrain: Dear Mr. Maugham, Dear Mr. Shaw, Dear Mr. Hemingway) to figures "in the world of books," in hopes of receiving holograph replies; Rudi Bittesch, a young foreign poet, reiterates his fear of wire-tapping, and regularly misuses the expression "By the way"; the radio blares its note of the era with renderings of "There were angels dancing at the Ritz/ And nightingales sang in Berkeley Square"; Selina Redwood, the club's presiding beauty, who conducts a love affair on the adjoining roof, announces her presence with a Poise Speech ("Poise is perfect balance, an equanimity of body and mind . . .") which requires repetition twice each day; Nicholas Farringdon, her lover, contributes slogans from his anarchical work *The Sabbath Notebooks;* and Joanna Childe, a rector's daughter who has sublimated her love for a young curate in the passionate delivery of elocution lessons, adds to the din of personalities with prophetic recitations of "The Wreck of the Deutschland." The days pass, and by the time the bomb in the garden actually explodes, and Joanna Childe, unable to escape through the window, dies praying in the flames, Muriel Spark has created a splendid period piece, and an extraordinarily subtle parable of a larger Society which lives with the unacknowledged threat of a larger, more ominous Bomb concealed in its garden.

The author introduces all her major themes at once, in an overture: an intimation of the return of normal law and authority to London and the May of Teck on VE Day; a brief account of the retreat, years later, of Nicholas Farringdon into a Jesuit order, and his subsequent violent martyrdom in Haiti; and a delicate allusion to a dormant but inexorable evil, the real uncanny, out of doors. Then the narrative broadens, permitting all the characters to sound their identifying chords. Just before the explosion, these reach a kind of crescendo (Selina, Joanna, Greggie, and the radio reciting all at once), the note of death is struck casually, metaphorically, twice ("Jan—*ee!*" says a girl in the corridor, "Don't be so bloody rude, you

nearly pushed me over the banister to my *death*." "Oh,
I'm *dying*," says a girl who is stuck in the window, "Fetch
George, I want George"), then the bomb without warning
explodes, bringing death literally and in earnest. Finally,
the story narrows again, to an end much like its beginning:
another, far less certain, intimation of the return of order,
this one on VJ Day; another reference to Nicholas Farringdon's mysterious retreat and violent martyrdom; and a
delicate allusion to another hypothetical bomb, this one
rumored to have dropped on Hiroshima.

Within the self-imposed limits of her own elaborate parallelism (VE Day, VJ Day; little bomb, big Bomb; girl's
club, Society at large; "Wreck of the Deutschland,"
burning of the May of Teck; death of Joanna, death
of Nicholas), and within the prescribed repetition through
time of each character's identifying speech or mannerism,
Miss Spark allows her narrative to skip from place to
place, in flashbacks and in that curious knight-on-a-chess-
board move which might be characterized as her peculiar
Logic of Deflection. The oblique course of violence, the
vicarious satisfactions of Jean Brodie, the sublimation of
Joanna's love, the conversion (through his vision of evil
and destruction) of Nicholas, even the fact that the
eventful roof (which eventually becomes the only avenue
of escape) should be *adjoining*—each involves a displacement, a step to the side of guilt or danger. The same
sidestep occurs in her style, as the tactful modulation
out of crisis; Miss Spark never insists or intrudes, but
follows each crash with a diminuendo. ("We have buck
for dinner, man," says senile Tuys, having mistakenly shot
the heroine of "The Go-Away Bird" for a buck, and the
next line reveals the error obliquely: "Burial follows quickly after death in the Colony, for the temperature does not
allow of delay." And as the flames near Joanna, the author
chooses to remark, "She wore a dark green jersey and a
grey wool skirt." This essentially comic technique of
dead-pan irrelevance detracts nothing from the dramatic
climax, but rather underscores its seriousness.) "Is it
safe out here?" Selina asks, having escaped from the fire
through a window. "Nowhere's safe," Nicholas replies, and
thereby defines, although Miss Spark does not stress it, the
cause of his ultimate retreat, and the beautifully taken

point of *The Girls of Slender Means:* Nowhere is safe. With her style, her wit, and also her reticence and indirection, Muriel Spark has achieved in this novel that unstressed reflection of the general in the particular, which constitutes an intelligent and moving work of fiction.

Encounter With Necessity
BY IHAB H. HASSAN

> . . . we lie down in darkness, and have our light in ashes.—SIR THOMAS BROWNE, *Urn Burial*

William Styron's first novel, *Lie Down in Darkness,* 1951, remains one of the outstanding works of postwar fiction. This is not sly praise. *The Long March,* 1952, and *Set This House on Fire,* 1960, are in no way shoddy, and indeed the latest of Styron's novels is an exceptional work, as ambitious in meaning as his first may be deft in execution. The three books project very different types of heroes though each is preeminently a hero of our time. Captain Mannix, the protagonist of *The Long March,* is an awkward and unwilling rebel, a soft, scarred, bearlike man who defies the authority of his Marine commander. "Born into a generation of conformists, even Mannix . . . was aware that his gestures were not symbolic, but individual, therefore hopeless, maybe even absurd. . . ." *Set This House on Fire* is a torrid, complex story of crime and punishment, the terror of guilt and the horror of freedom. Its hero, Cass Kinsolving, finally chooses being rather than nothingness because for him, "to choose between them was simply to choose being, not for the sake of being, or even for the love of being, much less the desire to be forever—but in the hope of being what I could be for a time." In all three novels, Styron reveals a brooding imagination, sometimes obsessive, and a dark gift of poetry. The legacy of Faulkner is perhaps apparent in his earliest work; but it is a legacy that Styron has learned to put to his own service—one does not feel quite the same way about other talented writers, such as William Humphrey—and it is mainly recognizable in the intensity of the author's relation to a certain kind of material. For though Styron is a Virginian by birth, he has tried to shake loose from the local colorist's view of things without foregoing the advantages the Southern tradition provides. Thus, for instance, does he say of *Lie Down in Darkness:* "Only certain things in the book are particularly Southern. I used leit-motifs—the Negroes, for example—that run throughout the book, but I would like to believe that my people would have behaved the way they did anywhere." Other motifs which we like to identify as Southern occur in his fiction: the Biblical rhetoric of story telling, the conflict between a tradition of religious fundamentalism and modern skepticism, racial contrasts, the industrialization of an agrarian society, etc. But his concern with some of these motifs, particularly the demonic power of guilt, the black oppressiveness of death or decay, the lurid ironies of Protestantism in the South—"a crazy colored preacher howling those tremendously moving verses from Isaiah 40, while riding around in a maroon Packard"—betrays an imagination nearly religious in intensity, a sensibility closer to the baroque tradition of John Donne and Sir Thomas Browne than to the gothic school of Poe and Company.

The epigraph to *Lie Down in Darkness* contains the following statement from Sir Thomas Browne's *Urn Burial:* ". . . since our longest sun sets at right descencions, and makes but winter arches, and therefore it cannot be long before we lie down in darkness, and have our light in ashes." There is no single hero-victim in the novel. Milton Loftis, his wife Helen, and their daughter Peyton are all locked in a domestic tragedy in which love must wear the face of guilt, and the search for childhood innocence must acquaint the seeker with death. All lie down in darkness. But there is one character whose light is found in ashes: Peyton.

I pray but my prayer climbs up like a broken wisp of smoke: Oh my Lord, I am dying, is all I know, and *oh my father, oh my darling,* longingly, lonesomely, I fly into your arms! . . . Myself all shattered, this lovely shell? Perhaps I shall rise at another time, though I lie down in darkness and have my light in ashes.

This is the stream of Peyton's doomed consciousness before she jumps from a washroom to her death. The two passages quoted, one lying at the outset of the novel, the other very near its close, form a kind of frame, a frame of two mirrors reflecting the darkness and the light of a single life, Peyton's, which in turn refracts the fate of all the others. For Peyton's darkness, however "clinical" it may seem—and there is no doubt that it is more dramatic than clinical—must still illumine the universal urge of human beings to clutch some impossible idea of eternal childhood or innocence, must illumine and expiate that urge. "The real point of *Lie Down in Darkness*," Geismar rightly perceives, "is that, dealing with the Electra complex itself, it has not only made it human and domestic but has returned it, so to speak, to its natural home of childhood feeling itself." This is one aspect of a radical innocence to which Peyton, no simple innocent, is a perverse victim.

The drama of Peyton, however, is enacted within at least three circles of meaning: social, domestic, and private. First, there is the South of the tidewaters in Virginia. The scene conveys, from the beginning, a feeling of something recently denatured and agelessly dissolute:

Riding down to Port Warwick from Richmond, the train begins to pick up speed on the outskirts of the city, past the tobacco factories with their ever-present haze of acrid, sweetish dust. . . .

. . . instead, you look out once more at the late summer landscape and the low, sorrowful beauty of tideland streams winding through marshes full of small, darting frightened noises and glistening and dead silent at noon. . . .

Halfway between the railroad station and Port Warwick proper . . . the marshland, petering out into disconsolate, solitary clumps of cattails, yields gradually to higher ground. Here, bordering the road, an unsightly growth of weeds takes over, brambles and

briars of an uncertain dirty hue. . . . The area
adjacent to this stretch of weeds is bleakly municipal
in appearance. . . . Here there are great mounds
of garbage; a sweet, vegetable odor rises perpetually
on the air and one can see—from the distance fairly
iridescent—whole swarms of carnivorous flies black-
ening the garbage and maybe a couple of proprietary
rats, propped erect like squirrels, and blinking slug-
gishly, with mild, infected eyes, at some horror-
stricken Northern tourist.

Nature may be deformed by factories and gas tanks
squatting on the landscape, but nature also knows its own
forms of corruption. In this, nature reflects Southern society—"The ground is bloody and full of guilt where you
were born and you must tread a long narrow path towards
your destiny," Milton's father says to him before sending
him off to the university. There are scenes—the engagement dance of Loftis, the wedding party for his daughter,
the country club meetings with Dolly, or the descriptions
of the Cartwrights—which reveal the manners of a society
resistant to incursions and still operant. But these ceremonial scenes should be balanced against the glib wisdom
of Berger, the New York invert who says to Peyton,
"It is symptomatic of that society from which you
emanate that it should produce the dissolving family:
ah, ah, patience, my pretty, I know you say symptomatic
not of that society, but of *our* society, the machine culture,
yet so archetypal is this South with its cancerous religiosity,
its exhausting need to put manners before morals, to
negate all *ethos*—call it a *husk* of a culture."
Negation becomes gradually more emphatic in the three
generations which the novel encompasses: Milton's father
with his grandiloquent wisdom; the Loftises themselves,
and the minister, Carey Carr, still genteel in their impotence; and Peyton or Berger for whom cynicism or self-
destruction is the measure of salvation. Milton's father says
to Loftis, "My son . . . we stand at the back door of
glory. Now in this setting part of time we are only relics
of vanquished grandeur more sweet than God himself might
have imagined: we are the driblet turds of angels, not
men but a race of toads, vile mutations who have lost
our lovewords. . ."; and Peyton says to Dick Cartwright,

her contemporary, "Those people back in the Lost Generation. Daddy I guess. . . . They thought they were lost. They were crazy. They weren't lost. What they were doing was losing us." And so the progress of negation leads to the historical event which casts a sinister shadow on the last pages of the novel: the explosion of the Bomb. For it is just as the war ends that Peyton commits suicide; and it is as she reaches out for the last time, reaches out in selfish desperation for her husband, Harry, that he retorts, "Do you realize what the world's come to? Do you realize that the great American commonwealth just snuffed out one hundred thousand innocent lives this week? There was a time, you know, when I thought for some reason . . . I could spend my life catering to your needs. . . ." But does the insanity of the world overshadow Peyton's need or become merely the ghastly correlative of her disease?

Nor does the novel show religion to be a means of genuine social or spiritual salvation. The religiosity of Helen is an extension of her egoism, an inversion of her feminine possessiveness, a token of her revulsion against instinct and life. The gracious dialogues, so redolent with self-pity and theatrical despair, she conducts with Carey Carr are almost the perfect parody of a courtship. Yet Carr, though earnestly devoted to his Episcopal church, cannot raise his faith above the level of poetic compassion. He is good as chorus and preceptor, useless as comforter or savior. When in the final scene of Peyton's funeral Milton goes for Helen's throat in a rage, Carr can only stand by terrified and exclaim, "People! People." Carr is indeed more impotent than Daddy Faith, the Negro revivalist whose baptismal rites fill the strange epilogue of the book. There is power and frenzy in this scene of Negroes ducked in the waters of life, cleansed and purified; there is also awe and joy and simplicity of faith, qualities that are absent from the lives of white people. Drowning is the controlling image of Peyton's last moments, but it is the element of rebirth for Ella and La Ruth. The white girl does not find the father and lover she so desperately needs, but the black congregation finds both: "You, Daddy! Daddy Faith! You loves us! You, Daddy!" Yet what can the contrast do but sharpen our sense of incongruity? How can the tormenting events of the novel be explained in a scene of primitive religious fervor except ironically? The tragic tensions of civilized life, as Styron knows, are not so easily resolved; nor can we all worship at the altar erected on a raft which Styron thus describes: "On it had been erected a sort of stage, surrounded on four sides by a golden damask curtain; embroidered designs—dragons and crosses and crowns, Masonic emblems, shields, bizarre and unheard-of animals, an amalgam of myth and pagan ritual and Christian symbology—all these glowed against the curtain in green and red phosphorescent fabrics, literally hurting the eyes." The depletion of religious symbols from their meaning parallels the depletion of manners from their content.

Domestic life in *Lie Down in Darkness* is equally corrupt. For this is a story of infidelity, of vengeful love, blocked, hurt, and perverted, of adults who can never escape their childhood. It is a story of a husband unfaithful to his wife, a mistress unfaithful to her husband, a girl unfaithful to the man she marries. It is the story of a woman, Helen, who can love only what she can control—her crippled daughter, Maudie, or the childish part of her husband, Milton; of a man whose sensuality is merely a form of dependence on Dolly, and whose love, for Peyton, can never become sensual; of a girl who frantically needs a husband, Harry, precisely because she loves her father, and who hates the mother who is viciously jealous of her. These ambivalences of love are created by a man-child, girl-woman, and mother-neuter—the images of reversion in the novel are legion—who bind the family in a circle of guilt. Something, truly, is rotten in Denmark, as not Hamlet but the mortician, Mr. Casper, reflects, for it is the custodians of death who also hold, it seems, our conscience in custody. Yet the root of corruption may be a kind of innocence, an excess of love which, as Milton understands, always requires forgiveness. Where there is no forgiveness, vengeance takes over—and death. For the living, death is nothingness. It is what Milton feels when his efforts, after Peyton's suicide and Maudie's earlier death, fail to conciliate Helen: "With nothing left! Nothing! Nothing! Nothing!" It is also what Helen feels too late: "Peyton," she said, "Oh, God, Peyton. My child. Nothing! Nothing! Nothing! Nothing!" Strangely enough, it is only Dolly, the outsider, the interloper, who is simple or stupid or forgiving enough to escape the final seal of negation.

And of course there is no surcease of terror as we move from the domestic to private experience where all terror begins, where it must end. The hell of love, the hell of purchasing one's happiness with another's pain, the hell, even, of failing to know the love one is supposed to know—these are dramatized in scene after scene. The gist of it all is that no one has a chance: "Oh Christ, have mercy on your Peyton this evening not because she hasn't believed but because she, no one, had a chance to ever." Peyton must be locked in her destiny; locked in an interior monologue, the formal equivalent of her absolute isolation; locked in a nightmare of strutting pigeons and screeching katydids, those birds that haunt Peyton through-out the novel, symbolizing her sexual guilt and her child-ish yearnings for freedom, and rustling with their wings over her death; locked, again, in a stream of memories from which the sole escape is drowning in the airless void of time, so that at last her flightless birds may ascend, one by one, "through the suffocating night, toward paradise." What paradise? That of a stricken mind, a heart dazed by its strange necessities? A paradise of child-hood, never lost and yet never to be regained? A fool's or saint's paradise?

Obviously this is not the vision of an ancestral South which Styron described as "a land of prim pastoral fences, virgin lumber, grazing sheep and Anglo-Saxons: these, the last, spoke in slumbrous Elizabethan accents, rose at dawn, went to bed at dusk, and maintained, with Calvinist passion, their traditional intolerance of evil." It is rather a vision of tragic ambiguities and ironic neces-sities, of human experience spanning the abyss. It is a vision which must create its own distinctive form.

Lie Down in Darkness is a brilliant formal accomplish-ment. Its focus is narrow in space and diffuse in time. Peyton's hearse is constantly in our view, and the story is quite literally its halting progress, from the Port War-wick railway station, where the remains of Peyton arrive, to the cemetery, where she is laid to rest. The physical fact of death is simple and immitigable. The complexity is temporal, for time, after all, is a function of man's urge to experience and to understand. Time is conscious-

ness—and consciousness in our time has cracked and
splintered. Time in the novel, consequently, is cracked,
too; the story is revealed in flashbacks, and flashbacks
within flashbacks. The fate of the Loftis family cannot
be related by following the Aristotelian precepts of plot.
The fate of the Loftises is, to be sure, settled before
time began and, as Freudians know, time begins when
we fall from childhood. This seems in accordance with
the Aristotelian notion of a tragic necessity. But the
dramatic emphasis of the novel is not on the end; it is
rather on the beginning in which middle and end are
swallowed. Nor is the logic of necessity clear; it is rather
inscrutable as experience itself and demonic as guilt,
the ruling principle of the book. Time, therefore, does not
become merely the passive medium through which guilt is
inherited and expiated. It is an active agent, not erosive
in any predictable way—Dolly, Milton, Helen, and Peyton
come together and fall asunder several times in the course
of the novel—but destructive in a mysterious fashion.
None of the characters can fully penetrate his situation.
Remembrance of things past guarantees no wisdom or
control.

Fractured time makes for a fractured consciousness.
Each of the seven sections of the novel is dominated by
the point of view of one of the characters, though there
are shifts within each section too. Together, these points
of view constitute an ironic commentary on the limitations
of each. Reality is larger than any of the characters can
assess, and the novelist himself can assess it only by
suspending his judgment in compassion for the helpless
isolation of all. Or he can assess it, again, by deliberately
creating various levels of narration in the same episode,
creating, that is, an ambiguity which must stay unresolved.
The crucial incident of Peyton, dressed in tight shorts,
nuzzling up to her father is an example. We see the scene
itself, as it must have occurred, through the jealous eyes
of Helen who narrates the incident to Carey Carr and
at the same time indulges her own vicious stream of
secret thoughts; and we see it again, almost simultaneously, through the eyes of the novelist looking over
Helen's shoulder. The incestuous interchange of feeling
or gesture, whatever it was, thus appears in a haze of
refracted light;   reality is sicklied over with the cast of

illusion; for the only power to assess facts may rest with fancy.

Retrospection in time leads to introspection in the stream of an isolated consciousness—thence the charged images welling up from the past, shards and splinters of experiences forgotten, repeated with hopeless urgency. Hence the involuted sentences, pressing and crowding the meaning of a whole life into one tortured, inexorable, poetic fragment: *"Helen, Helen,* he thought drowsily, *my lost, my lovely, why have I forsaken you?* Visions white as sunlight, perfect as one flower, a gardenia, once remembered from a dance that never stopped till dawn, they came to him briefly, vanished, and he believed he slipped off for a spell, thinking of Helen dressed like a cat, bearing down on him with a knife: only it wasn't a knife, it was something else, a flower or something, and they were in Charlottesville, and there was Peyton too, her lips pressed to his, saying Daddy Daddy Bunny dear, the globe revolving monstrously out of night into day again, turning and turning. . . ."

Day merges into night, reality into dream. The counters of dreams are symbols, which seek, in their obscure way, to make the inalienable privacy of the soul public. These Styron uses with tact, though his obvious and awkward handling of Peyton's "birds" may be a greater concession to pathology than he usually permits himself. But the syntax of dreams is that of free associations, and it is these Styron employs to make vital connections between his characters. Thus, for instance, does Peyton begin by thinking of Harry and end, in the same movement of feeling, thinking of Milton: "How many times have I lain down to sin out of vengeance, to say *so he* [Harry] *doesn't love me, then there is one that will,* to sleep then and dream about the birds, and then to wake with one eye open to the sweltering, joyless dawn and think *my life has known no father, any road to any end may run,* to think of home. I would not pray to a polyp or a jellyfish, nor to Jesus Christ, but only to that part of me that was pure and lost now, when he [Milton] and I used to walk along the beach, toward Hampton, and pick up shells."

This is deft transition. But no transition can establish the real connections in Peyton's life. Her "initiation" to adult recognitions ends in suicide. The pattern of her encounter with experience is finally a closed one, but it is not, for all its external neatness, intelligible. And in a strange way, a way undefinable by any dogma or creed but perhaps simply by the compassion art bestows, her ashes do give forth light. This is what *Lie Down in Darkness*, however overwritten it may be in parts, however elusive its resolution may seem, manages to dramatize for our minds. Stunned and horrified, the reader's mind is purified without recourse to a genuinely tragic catharsis.

The Poetry of Dylan Thomas
BY WILLIAM YORK TINDALL

Dylan Thomas is little known in this country.* By those who have read him, however, he is commonly regarded as the best of the younger poets. In my opinion he is not only the best of these, but the best and most magical English-speaking poet to have appeared since Yeats began to write. Thomas is surprisingly different from Yeats and the other poets of our time. In place of Yeats's grandeur, Eliot's austerity, and Auden's chumminess, Thomas offers a more than Elizabethan abundance.

One might expect a druidical and almost surrealist Welshman to be obscure. But it may seem a pity that a poet as important as Thomas is so puzzling that sometimes a second reading—or even a third—does little to help.

Since the Eliot period readers have become more or less accustomed to poetic obscurity. Some trace it to the separation of the poet from society, others to the lack of traditions. Our age, they say, provides few universally accepted ideas, myths or symbols, for the use of poets, who, like Yeats or Auden, are driven by their need of a central idea to arrange synthetic systems of their own. While Thomas may owe some of his obscurity to his separation from the reader, and to the consequent conviction that he need take no pains to communicate with him, he is free on the whole from privacy. His central ideas and symbols come from our most public stock, from Freud on the one hand and from the Bible on the other. If these familiar clues are kept in mind, Thomas becomes almost readable at fourth or fifth reading, clearer in fact to most readers of our time than Mr. Eliot, who takes what he needs from the *Upanishads* or Milton.

*This essay was written in 1948.

From Freud, Thomas learned about dreams. What he learned accounts in part for the images, the syntax and the themes of his poems, and for their hallucinatory brilliance. A dream, says Freud, as if describing a poem by Thomas, is a series of images, apparently contradictory and nonsensical, but arising from hidden material that yields a clear meaning. On the manifest level of the dream occur those symbols of garden, apple or serpent, that appear so conspicuously in the myths of our ancestors. These symbols are there, says Freud (again as if describing a poem by Thomas), so that they cannot be understood. The conscious mind, beguiled by manifest wonders, is kept by them from awareness of the latent meaning, which is generally sexual. Accepting this theory as a theory of poetic composition, Thomas makes artificial dreams. The rich, attractive confusion of his surface is the manifest level which at once conceals and reveals the latent meaning. When analyzed, or rather psychoanalyzed, the surface disorder yields the hidden sense.

Every reader of Freud knows that hollow objects generally symbolize the female, while long, mobile or fierce objects generally symbolize the male. Thomas' bewildering turtles and asylums are female symbols; his blades, octopuses and thumbs are male. Sometimes by punning condensations, like those used by Lewis Carroll in "Jabberwocky" or James Joyce in *Finnegans Wake*, Thomas combines the relations of the sexes into one figure —for example, "the kissproof world." Kissproof is the name of a lipstick. Therefore this word resolves itself into lip (female), stick (male), and, by its literal sense, frustration. Around these primary meanings, in their context, cluster innumerable associations.

"A face of hands," another image, seems surrealistic. This is not surprising because the surrealists, also exploiting the unconscious, use images of madness, infancy and dream. But there is a difference between Thomas and the surrealists. While they pretend to avoid conscious interference with the unconscious, Thomas is always in apparent control of his materials. In its context, "a face of hands" refers to clocks; on another level, it acts as an image of grief. To Freud, clocks—and presumably their faces—are feminine, hands masculine. Beyond these meanings, however, is the lunatic picture of a face composed of hands.

All these meanings are cunningly contrived, but if nothing other than rational control were operating, the image would be sterile. As it stands, the image appears to be spontaneous. For this effect there must be constant cooperation, during the writing of the poem, between the poet's conscious and unconscious minds—as, for instance, during a day dream in which the conscious employs what the unconscious suggests.

Two stanzas from the first poem of Thomas' *Selected Writings* will serve to show his images in their context and their arrangement. He is speaking of "the boys of summer in their ruin":

> These boys of light are curdlers in their folly,
> Sour the boiling honey;
> The jacks of frost they finger in the hives;
> There in the sun the frigid threads
> Of doubt and dark they feed their nerves;
> The signal moon is zero in their voids.

A few stanzas later the boys reply:

> We are the dark deniers, let us summon
> Death from a summer woman,
> A muscling life from lovers in their cramp,
> From the fair dead who flush the sea
> The bright-eyed worm on Davy's lamp,
> And from the planted womb the man of straw.

Even if we keep Freud in mind, this is difficult. But there is a mad intensity about it that is deeply moving. It is as if, while our intellects were occupied in hunting the sense, the poet's unconscious were addressing levels within us far below the rational. After several readings, however, something comes clear. The principal theme of the poem is the life cycle from conception to maturity. The ruined boys are successively cells, embryos and adults, and their development is parallel to that of the four seasons. In the first stanza quoted above, the climate is wintry; the embryos are in their wombs, awaiting the signal of the ninth moon for birth. The honey images, undoubtedly masculine, are matched by dark feminine hives and voids.

The violent and careful antitheses of boiling and frost, light and dark, death and life, point to Thomas' central obsession: the identity of birth, love and death; of womb and tomb. The boys of summer are ruined because conception is the beginning of death. There is a more complicated expression of the same idea in "Davy's lamp." The meaning of this apparatus is qualified by the fact that it is used in mines (an image of the grave), and by the fact that Davy Jones's locker lies under the maternal sea.

Davy's lamp seems to have little in common with the "man of straw" that follows it. Part of our trouble may come from the apparent lack of connection among the symbols. And, although the syntax of these stanzas is plain, part of our trouble with other poems may come from doubts about the function of the words, and about their relationships.

> After the funeral, mule praises, brays,
> Windshake of sailshaped ears . . .

In the first of these lines is "brays" a noun or a verb? Is "mule" a noun or an adjective? Nothing in the sentence immediately resolves this ambiguity. But Freud's theory of dreams explains both incoherence and grammatical confusion. Dreaming is an archaic process. Incapable of grammar and logic, the dream presents visual images without their connections. However annoying to logicians, such freedom has its aesthetic advantages; for syntax is limiting, and, without it, associations, like that famous horseman, can gallop off in several directions.

Yet beneath this manifest disorder, the poems of Dylan Thomas have great elegance of shape. The song of the boys of summer is tightly constructed. Lines of one stanza echo those of another; the interconnections are firm, and the quarrels among ideas and images are finally resolved. The skeleton of the poem is the latent meaning —which, like that of a dream, may be expressed in statements.

When we have arrived at the shaping statements that compose the latent level, we must not think that we have mastered the poem. The value of the poem is partly a matter of surface tensions and partly the interplay of surface and interior, of fixed meaning and endless variety. Each symbol is connected with the latent meaning, yet each maintains a subtler and almost ineffable relationship with its incongruous neighbors. The demands of this relationship explain why, from the variety that dreams permit, Thomas chose one symbol rather than another —why, for example, he chose a crocodile and a hearse, rather than a steam roller and a pot of pinks.

To a Freudian these pairs of symbols might be almost identical. But Thomas, being a poet, is more than a Freudian—even in his themes. Many of his poems concern poetic creation, in which he finds a parallel to conception and embryonic development. "I, in my intricate image," he says, "stride on two levels." One of these is usually sexual, the other literary. And the same symbols, by a triumph of economy, serve both the levels:

> Especially when the October wind
> (Some let me make you of autumnal spells,
> The spider-tongued, and the loud hill of Wales)
> With fist of turnips punishes the land,
> Some let me make you of the heartless words.
> The heart is drained that, spelling in the scurry
> Of chemic blood, warned of the coming fury.
> By the sea's side hear the dark-vowelled birds.

These lines reveal the poet as a druid casting spells. When the druid speaks of striding on two levels, he is understating his case. Usually he strides on three. The third of these is religious. Reared in the tradition of Welsh protestantism, Thomas is saturated with the Bible, upon which he calls for almost half his images. He is as much at home on Jacob's ladder as on Freud's sofa. If we hold with Freud and Jung that myth is dream, and if we admit the Bible to be myth, then the connection between Thomas' Freudian and Biblical images becomes plain. As his symbols "outelbow" space and time, they serve again with the same economy. "Tree," which is phallic or maternal on the Freudian level, means the cross or the tree of life on the Biblical, and on still another level it means tree.

One of the happiest examples of this double, or rather, triple talk, is the poem that begins "To-day, this insect, and the world I breathe." Cutting his symbolic insect in two, the poet makes head and tail witness to this "murder of Eden and green genesis."

> This story's monster has a serpent caul,
> Blind in the coil scrams round the blazing outline,
> Measures his own length on the garden wall
> And breaks his shell in the last shocked beginning;
> A crocodile before the chrysalis,
> Before the fall from love the flying heartbone,
> Winged like a sabbath ass this children's piece
> Uncredited blows Jericho on Eden.
>
> . . . .
>
> Death: death of Hamlet and the nightmare madmen,
> An air-drawn windmill on a wooden horse,
> John's beast, Job's patience, and the fibs of vision,
> Greek in the Irish sea the ageless voice:
> "Adam I love, my madmen's love is endless,
> No tell-tale lover has an end more certain,
> All legends' sweethearts on a tree of stories,
> My cross of tales behind the fabulous curtain."

The main themes of this poem seem to be the nature of myth, the fall and regeneration of man, and the writing of a poem. The scene in the Garden of Eden is presented in Freudian terms as conception, gestation and birth. References to Don Quixote's windmill and the wooden horse of Troy support the mythical framework. Speaking at the end, Christ or Death, made one by Thomas' passion for opposites, hangs all myths upon the central tree. Why his voice should be "Greek in the Irish sea" I do not know. But what of the insect? "The insect," says Thomas, "is the plague of fables." In at least one of his roles, this doubtful creature represents the multiplicity of fables, eventually made one upon the cross.

This poem is more or less typical of Thomas' early work. In what he published in 1934 and 1936, the climate is that of "the brawned womb's weathers"; the scenery, when not that of womb, is that of tomb or, sometimes, of the Garden. The rhythms are monotonous and hypnotic;

the rhymes, though carefully arranged, are often dissonant. In *The Map of Love* (1939) the poet emerges
occasionally from his obstetrical retreat into the light of
common day. But even the famous elegy for Ann Jones
concerns a funeral. While other poets of the thirties were
trying to come to terms with society, Thomas was gloomily accepting the fundamentals. His only joy appears to
have been the craftsman's joy in technical accomplishment.

After 1939, the air raids elevated Thomas' preoccupation
with what he now called "deaths and entrances" into compassion for mankind. He had been fascinated with horrors of life, but now his concern became what Baudelaire
called the horror and ecstasy of life. He had traced the cycle
of birth, death and birth again within a sexual-religious
frame, but now his concern became the resurrection. In
"Ceremony After a Fire Raid" he grieves over

> A child of a few hours
> With its kneading mouth
> Charred on the black breast of the grave
> The mother dug, and its arms full of fires.

"Grave," "dug" and "fires," as we might now expect,
are ambiguous. The fires—not only those of London—
are vital fires connecting the child with past and future,
with Adam and Eve and the Savior. By Thomas' ritual of
grief, the religion that had seemed almost ornamental is
now alive, and the child, becoming everyman, repeats in
his death man's fall and regeneration:

> Into the organpipes and steeples
> Of the luminous cathedrals,
> Into the weathercocks' molten mouths
> Rippling in twelve-winded circles,
> Into the dead clock burning the hour
> Over the urn of sabbaths
> Over the whirling ditch of daybreak
> Over the sun's hovel and the slum of fire
> And the golden pavements laid in requiems,
> Into the bread in a wheatfield of flames,
> Into the wine burning like brandy,
> The masses of the sea
> The masses of the sea under

The masses of the infant-bearing sea
Erupt, fountain, and enter to utter for ever
Glory glory glory
The sundering ultimate kingdom of genesis' thunder.

In these magnificent lines, the particulars of burning
London are made universal by myth. Freud's imagery of
sex (clocks, urns, steeples and the sea) is raised to the
service of eternal life. Imagery of worship (steeples, bread,
wine and masses) conspires with Freud's to summon glory.

The post-war poems are quieter, but no less magical. Innocent of Freud and the Bible, "Fern Hill" is the recovery
in all its morning freshness of the poet's youth, and,
beyond this, of youth itself:

Now as I was young and easy under the apple boughs
About the lilting house and happy as the grass was green,
    The night above the dingle starry,
        Time let me hail and climb
    Golden in the heydays of his eyes,
And honoured among wagons I was prince of the apple
    towns
And once below a time I lordly had the trees and leaves
        Trail with daisies and barley
    Down the rivers of the windfall light.

Easier than most of its predecessors and much more
tender, "In Country Sleep" is another celebration of childhood—not his own this time, but that of Caitlin, his
daughter:

Never and never, my girl riding far and near
In the land of the hearthstone tales, and spelled asleep,
Fear or believe that the wolf in a sheepwhite hood
Loping and bleating roughly and blithely shall leap,
                    My dear, my dear,
Out of a lair in the flocked leaves in the dew dipped year
To eat your heart in the house in the rosy wood.

The images are less tightly concentrated than usual; the
tensions have been relaxed. That this is fitting in a lullaby
is evident; for if the tensions were maintained, the child
would stay awake. As the poet tires his sleepy girl with

fairy tales (*Little Red Riding Hood* among them), he calms her consequent fear of wolves by the assurance that nature is holy. This conviction is made richly sensuous by reminiscences of Gerard Manley Hopkins:

> Through haygold stalls, as the dew falls on the wind-
> Milled dust of the apple tree . . .

The rhythm too is that of Hopkins, who, along with Donne and Herbert, presides over these later poems. As one might suppose, the machinery of worship is Catholic now, or Anglo-Catholic, and although in the wound and apples some Freudian relics remain, they are sublimated by reverence. The effect of this poem, as of all his later poems, is a tranquillity uncommon in our time.

The Meaning of
Robert Penn Warren's Novels
BY ERIC BENTLEY

If an author makes a deep impression, there comes a time when you are no longer content merely to read his books as they come out. You want to re-read him. You want to know what the body of his writings amounts to. Today for instance, many people must be feeling an interest in the whole body of Robert Penn Warren's writings—not, I hope, because Warren has recently become famous but because one increasingly has the impression that he is the most considerable American writer to emerge since the twenties. As far as recent discussion of Warren is concerned, one's inquisitiveness is sharpened, not by the hullabaloo, but by the strange lack of accord as to the ideas he presents. What has Warren been saying to us? In this sketch of Warren's achievement as a novelist, I shall have that question chiefly in mind. Which is not in the least to imply that it is the most important question that could be asked about him.

I

A convenient point of departure is a meditation on Shakespeare that Warren puts in the mouth of one of his characters. The tragedies, this character says, have all one theme, "the necessity for self-knowledge":

> The tragic flaw in the Shakespearean hero is a defect in self-knowledge. Macbeth comes to ruin, not because he kills (Shakespeare could scarcely have been so naive as to believe that men have not killed and then ruled in prosperity and dreamless sleep—he had, we know, read Holinshed), but because he does not realize

616

upon what grounds it is possible for him, Macbeth, to kill. Bacon wrote: Knowledge is power. Bacon was thinking of knowledge of the mechanisms of the external world. Shakespeare wrote: Self-knowledge is power. Shakespeare was thinking of the mechanisms of the spirit, to which the mechanisms of the external world, including other persons, are instruments. In other words, Shakespeare was interested in success. By success, he meant: Self-fulfillment. But his tragedy is concerned with failure. Naturally. The successful man . . . offers only the smooth surface, like an egg. Insofar as he is truly successful, he has no story. He is pure. But poetry is concerned with failure, distortion, imbalance . . .

This passage, like many things Warren has said about other writers, fits Warren himself like a glove. That we need self-knowledge is, to date, the alpha and omega of his teaching. Like all moral teachings it sounds simple when reduced to a single statement. Like all profound teachings it turns out to be complex as soon as we try to explain it.

Warren's first novel, *Night Rider* (1939), was also his first large-scale treatment of the theme. It tells the story of a Kentucky lawyer of some forty years ago. Mr. Munn joined the "night riders," a band of men who wrecked the tobacco crop of those of their neighbors who refused to join a would-be monopolistic association of tobacco wholesalers. Beginning with sporadic raids, the riders later organize a kind of army and march on a couple of towns. They are put down by National Guards. Mr. Munn is one of the casualties.

Externally, the book is a splendid adventure story which, in the right hands, would make a first-rate movie. Internally, from beginning to end, it is the story of Mr. Munn's search—unsuccessful as it turns out—for himself. He tries to find himself in other people. It is the impression made on him by the local senator, one Tolliver, that sends him into public life. Tolliver appears to have the confidence, the mastery, the suavity and poise that Mr. Munn lacks. Only later does it transpire that the appearance was deceptive. As one of the characters puts it:

618 *Robert Penn Warren*

Tolliver, talking to people all his life, crowds, never being anything except when his voice was talking to crowds; if he had anything in him, any life, sucking it out of crowds, talking. Crowds and women. Never being anything except when he thought somebody else thought he was something. Just that . . . like sucking blood, living off something else.

Mr. Munn's awe before the public man—which drags him into the association and thus into all the catastrophes that ensue—turns to hate. He resolves to kill Tolliver but, characteristically, proves unequal to the job. "I thought I could do it," he whispers brokenly, before going off to let himself be killed by pursuing troops. In a way the remark is the crowning irony of the book. For Mr. Munn is not, in general, afraid of killing. He *has* killed a man. The man he killed (on behalf of the night riders) was someone he had earlier, as defense lawyer, got acquitted, on dubious evidence, of a murder charge. Certainly, the fellow had *wished* the murder: but was that relevant? Wishing a murder you have not committed—the crime of Dmitri Karamazov—is something Mr. Munn can think about later. The murder he is being hunted for at the end is one he did not commit.

A more perceptive man might have learned something from all this about human responsibility. Mr. Munn dies unenlightened—bewildered, unfulfilled, not knowing himself, and therefore unrepentant. We cannot, therefore, learn through his consciousness what Warren has to say. Though the book is Mr. Munn's story, Warren does not have him tell it. We see him from the outside: Warren calls him *Mr.* Munn throughout. And the view of life which the book as a whole enforces is inferred from a whole complex of situations and relationships. We learn a good deal, for example, from other characters. There are three in particular who are further along the road to self-knowledge, self-definition. There is Dr. MacDonald who has in him something of the pioneer generations: since the South threatens to stifle him he will push on west, thus "defining" himself as an intact American. There is Captain Todd, Southern squire and veteran of the Civil War, whose evident "certainty of self" Mr. Munn envies. And there is Willie Proudfit, an unlettered peasant who, in his pioneering adventures and religious thinking, has lived out a pattern of rebirth which Mr. Munn conspicuously fails to match.

These characters bring home the point about Mr. Munn by contrast. Others—two in particular—reinforce it by parallelism. One is Senator Tolliver: is not Mr. Munn just as hollow as this hollow man? Is not the fact that he cannot kill him symbolic? The other is a spinster cousin of Mr. Munn's, Miss Ianthe Sprague, who is only interested in "the fragmentary, the irrelevant, the meaningless":

> And she did not like to talk of the past, and avoided his questions. Indeed, she had little memory of the past. That, too, she had rejected, for out of memory rises the notion of a positive and purposive future, the revision of the past.

Finally, Mr. Munn is "placed" for us by his relation to women. His relation to both wife and mistress reaches a climax and an end in a loveless copulation. Mr. Munn tries to find himself by violently merging with another. (In Warren's poem *Revelation* we find the line: "In separateness only does love learn definition.")

Munn is a failure. We need warmth, but he is cold, and the only half-satisfactory love he can find is with a cold woman. We need wholeness, but he is fragmentary, a helpless prey to conflicting impulses and moods, queer exaltations and prostrating nauseas. The prerequisite of wholeness is continuity with the past and faith in the future, but

> because the future was dead and rotten in his breast, the past, too, which once had seemed to him to have its meanings and its patterns, began to fall apart. . . .

He is as discontinuous as Miss Sprague, and, like Tolliver, tries to have others do for him what he must do for himself. The man with no center is a rider in the night of the spirit.

II

Warren's second novel, *At Heaven's Gate* (1943), is a more ambitious treatment of the same theme. Here Warren tries to give us a whole group of people of roughly equal importance. He tries to achieve unity, not by the relatively easy device of a protagonist, but by the skillfully patterned interweaving of scenes and by the common theme. There is no romance in this book. These people are not removed from us by time. They are ourselves. *At Heaven's Gate* would be remarkable if it were merely a picture of life in America.

But what we are concerned with here is Warren's *interpretation* of this life. In an admirable study of Warren's first two novels in *Sewanee Review* (Winter 1945), Miss Irene Hendry has suggested that, while Mr. Munn in *Night Rider* turns outward to other people in his search for meaning, Slim Sarrett in *At Heaven's Gate* turns inward and fails just as miserably. Mr. Munn, Miss Hendry says, tries to define himself by proxy, Sarrett, though always self-regarding, fails to define himself at all. Thus Warren's argument is by no means a simple case for the inner life and against the outer. The intellectual life is as fraught with perils as the life of action. It can be quite as deadly. Sarrett ends as a murderer.

Although the second novel is not so much the twin or complement of the first as all this suggests (Sarrett being no protagonist), Miss Hendry's point is valuable, for *At Heaven's Gate* does take up the discussion where *Night Rider* left off. Mr. Munn is replaced by Sarrett. Senator Tolliver reappears—with differences, with much more blood in his veins—as the businessman Bogan Murdock. Willie Proudfit has a sort of counterpart in the religious down-and-out, Ashby Wyndham: both represent a consciousness that is cruder yet more genuine than that of the more educated, modern, and secular main characters.

Again Warren's main concern is whether the various characters are moving toward self-knowledge or not. Some are not moving; some move but do not arrive. Already in *Night Rider,* the discontinuity of past and present had been symbolized by father-rejection—as for example in the "heroine" of the book who shouts at her father: "No, I'm not yours! I don't belong to you! Or to anybody!" The lines just about sum up the "heroine" of *At Heaven's Gate,* Sue Murdock. As Miss Hendry indicates, nearly all the people in this novel have rejected their fathers and, thereby, themselves. Sue Murdock's living through others is worse than Mr. Munn's, for she is hardly even pretending to seek her salvation in them. If she likes a man, it is because, like herself, he is "a mess." Even worse: when Sarrett becomes "a part of her," he is "the part of her she wanted to kill."

Though the novel is called *At Heaven's Gate,* the America it depicts is pretty much of a hell. If night is the pervading image and symbol in *Night Rider,* a characteristic image in the later novel—used at least three times—is that of *pus.* Yet Warren is entitled to say, as Ibsen did, that he goes down into the sewer to cleanse it, not to wallow. "There's something horrible in everybody," says the union leader Sweetie Sweetwater, "till they work it out. It looks like a man's got to boil the pus out." Yet, though none of Warren's characters has passed through heaven's gate, thus leaving his mere humanity behind, some approach it. Sweetwater, for instance, has defined himself, even if the definition is a rather narrow one. If Sue meets with the death which she had, in a sense, asked for, and Sarrett survives in a kind of living damnation, at least two of the people in this novel find something in their long search. In a crisis even the hardboiled Duckfoot Blake realizes that there are things that matter. The previously bewildered Jerry Calhoun, who had slept with Sue as joylessly as Mr. Munn with his two women, achieves fulfillment. In *Night Rider,* the fulfillment of Willie Proudfit had been symbolized by one of Warren's favorite archetypal patterns, the homeward journey. Here in *At Heaven's Gate* the fulfillment of Jerry Calhoun is symbolized by a similar pattern, and an even greater favorite of Warren's, the return to the father. (*The Ballad of Billie Potts* has it: "And the father waits for the son./The hour is late,/The scene familiar even in Shadow,/The transaction brief,/And you, wanderer, back,/After the striving and the wind's word,/To kneel/ . . . At the feet of the old man . . .)

III

Warren's third and most recent novel, *All the King's Men* (1946), is an expansion of a play he had written about six years earlier, entitled *Proud Flesh.* The play is possibly the clearest and most concise statement of Warren's main theme.

The hollow man of action—Senator Tolliver, Bogan Murdock—is now the protagonist, Governor Willie Stark. He exemplifies what Sarrett had found in Murdock:

> . . . the special disease of our time, the abstract passion for power, a vanity springing from an awareness of the emptiness and unreality of the self which can only become real and human by the oppression of people who manage to retain some shreds of reality and humanity.

Like Tolliver he seems very much the free and confident man. He can face and manage everybody and everything —except himself. His son's death brings him to the realization that his own life has been dedicated to an abstraction, power. (In his poem *Variation: Ode to Fear,* Warren speaks of politicians who "would skin a pig for the pig's squeal.") He hastily tries to patch up his marriage and purify his politics. But his henchmen will not take it. Now that he has confronted the *idea* of death, the thing itself is conferred upon him.

Before dying, Willie gains an insight into the tragic nature of life. He sees that the "deed in time" is not all, but that "the deed out of time takes the crystalline form at last"—that is, the mere flux of events in history is in itself meaningless: meaning comes from man. But the full significance of the play does not come from the protagonist alone, but from the interplay of several points of view. In politics, the Boss stands midway between "the boys"— the routine politicians headed by Tiny Duffy—and Adam Stanton, the idealist. The former play a game of pure power. The latter will tolerate only pure idea. The Boss has persuaded himself that his natural gifts as a wielder of power are at the service of an idea—in fact, the liberal, humanitarian idea of Adam Stanton's. Thus the Boss is fighting in three directions—with Duffy, with Stanton, and with himself.

In private life, he has also three partner-antagonists: his wife Lucy and his two mistresses, one a carnal affair, the other "idealistic." The carnal affair is simple enough. The "idealistic" mistress, Anne Stanton, is the victim of Willie's illusion that goodness is the root motive of his career. The wife is an almost allegorical—too allegorical

—figure, wife and mother, who is practically Warren's mouthpiece, a spokesman for "purgatorical knowledge," self-definition. All these points of view are framed by the point of view of popular scientism, represented by a chorus of surgeons, always on stage.

Warren seems to have realized that the story of Willie Stark, more fully articulated, could be made to convey nearly everything he had tried to say in all his previous verse and prose. Hence (I conjecture) the novel *All the King's Men.*

Thematically, the novel contains everything that is in the play. The few scenes and encounters of the play give place to a carefully articulated and elaborately counter-pointed piece of fiction. What previously happened all in a few minutes without much show of realism is now spread over a period of time with full explanations supplied. Beyond this sort of adaptation—which is much what one would expect when *any* play is transformed into a novel—there are two crucial changes. A single narrator, Jack Burden, replaces the chorus. And an apparent digression—the story of Cass Mastern—is added.

Jack Burden may at first seem a pretty exact equivalent of the stage chorus; both make us see the tragic story of Willie through the nontragic eyes of a sophisticated modern cynicism. Jack's floridly figurative prose is a fair translation of the chorus's doggerel. But Warren chose to make much fuller use of his narrator than this. He involved him in the main story, gave him, in fact, his own story, until Willie's career was a play within a play. (In an important article in *Accent* [Summer 1947], Mr. Norton Girault has described the many-sided significance of Warren's narrator. I must keep to the single thread of my own argument.)

Jack Burden is another of Warren's disoriented young moderns. We have seen how, in *At Heaven's Gate,* one of them is led back from his father-substitute (Bogan Murdock) to his actual father and thus "saved." This happens incidentally, by no means as the main story of the book. In *All the King's Men,* the saving of Jack Burden, after a somewhat similar fashion, is the culmination of the action. Jack had had two pseudo fathers—his supposed father the Scholarly Attorney and his chosen father-substitute Willie Stark. His true father turns out to be

Judge Irwin, whose death he has caused. On this last event, *All the King's Men* contains several comments, of which the chief are

> Maybe that is the only way you can tell that a certain piece of knowledge is worth anything: it has cost some blood.

And:

> I had dug up the truth and the truth always kills the father . . . and you are left alone with yourself and the truth, and can never ask Dad, who didn't know anyway and who is deader than mackerel.

(*The Ballad of Billie Potts:* "The answer is in the back of the book but the page is gone./ And grandma told you to tell the truth but she is dead.")

What of the Cass Mastern story (the interlude that constitutes Warren's fourth chapter)? It has frivolously been suggested that Warren put it in because it was too good to be left out; and I gather that the London publisher will omit it on grounds of irrelevance. Thematically, however, it is central. Even structurally it seems to me very daring and largely successful—Warren had perhaps learned from Shakespeare that one could put the whole theme of a work into one short and strongly symbolic interlude. Those who cannot read the symbols directly are helped out by some very explicit phrases like "the common guilt of man," statements like "nothing is ever lost" and "only by the suffering of the innocent does God affirm that men are brothers." Above all there is the figure of the spider that is our moral life—wherever you touch its web the vibration shudders through the whole.

This last point is applied to Jack's own story quite overtly. His refraining from the sexual act for fear of breaking his image of Anne is equated with Cass Mastern's evilly performing the act in despite of friendship:

> So, I observed, my nobility (or whatever it was) had had in my world almost as dire a consequence as Cass Mastern's sin had had in his.

A less overt link is between Cass Mastern's religious conclusions and Jack's. Cass states a Christian view of the
problem of evil: "only by the suffering of the innocent . . ."
It is restated in the last chapter of the book by Jack's
father, the Scholarly Attorney:

> Separateness is identity and the only way for God to
> create, truly create, man was to make him separate
> from God Himself, and to be separate from God is
> to be sinful. The creation of evil is therefore the
> index of God's glory and His power. That had to
> be so that the creation of good might be the index
> of man's glory and power. But by God's help.

Jack does not precisely identify himself with either Cass
or the Scholarly Attorney, but he hopes to "understand"
the former, and he says of the latter: "I was not certain
but that in my own way I did believe what he said."

Jack has achieved fulfillment, identification, definition,
self-knowledge. He has been reborn though "the winter
had been long."

IV

What does the conclusion of Warren's book amount to
philosophically and morally? The philosophy, one might
at first be inclined to say, is pure Christian orthodoxy.
Undoubtedly Warren finds the Christian scheme of things
close to the facts of experience, and it is the directly anti-
Christian philosophy of scientism or popular materialism
that he is attacking throughout. (The idea "that all life
is but the dark heave of blood and the twitch of the
nerve" he—Jack, at least—calls "the dream of our age.")
Yet the facts of experience seem to be Warren's sole
criterion. He is utterly empirical. Or noncommittal. "I was
not certain but that *in my own way* I did believe what
he said." An orthodox believer might find confirmation in
these words. A naturalist might place the italics where I
have placed them and feel that Warren helps him to
broaden the basis of, and so strengthen, his naturalism.

What of the book's political morality? It was a pity
that the reviewers regarded *All the King's Men* as primarily another life of Huey Long to be compared with

the other lives of Long and not with the other works of Warren. It must be obvious by now, if my account of the book is halfway accurate, that it is not a political treatise about Long or anything else. Like *Proud Flesh*, it is another study of Warren's constant theme: self-knowledge. Nevertheless, it has political implications—and we may understand them correctly if we see them within the broader frame. Indeed to say that we must see politics within a broader frame—the frame being morality and human life in general—is precisely Warren's thesis. Willie Stark, Adam Stanton, and Tiny Duffy are wrong politically because they are wrong humanly.

This line of thought will be uncongenial to readers influenced by Marxism. Yet to say that it is counter to Marxism—in its insistence that motives *do* matter and that one cannot confine one's attention to the "objective trend" —is to say that it is counter to the political morality of today, Marxist and anti-Marxist, left and right. For the Hollywood war movie, just as much as the Moscow edict, takes politics to be a battle between the Wrong People and the Right People. One judges the man not by his nature but by his affiliation. The same action is good performed by Us and bad performed by Them. All war propaganda depends on this morality, and today we live in a perpetual state of war.

Now if there is anything Warren hates it is this morality. Which is why it was a very sad irony when Mrs. Diana Trilling, in the *Nation*, maintained that the philosophy of *All the King's Men* was a surrender to history and thus an acquiescence in *realpolitik*. To be sure, the war moralist (let the term include Marxists and their opponents) preaches that history is on our side and that the objective trend is more important than the personal motive. But the final conclusion of Jack Burden is: "History is blind, but man is not." The "objective trend" is blind; the "personal motive" is all we have to work with; the person is all we have to see with. This idea is to be found somewhere in the background of all Warren's considerations of history. In *Night Rider,* for instance, where Captain Todd's superior poise is attributed to the fact that he does not look to historical process for moral solace: "he knew things and events were blind." Here again Warren's philosophy is that of the poet with his loyalty to the concrete and the particular and the human, his reluctance to enter the realm of the abstract and the general and the mechanical. Even Mr. Munn saw something of the point when wondering what "the truth" of any historical event is like:

> The truth: it devoured and blotted out each particular truth, each individual man's truth, it crushed truths as under a blundering tread, it was blind.

Thus, also, in *At Heaven's Gate,* a distinction is drawn between the sinister, subhuman mob which prepares for a lynching and the human beings which it later breaks up into. The mob, like history, is blind.

But man is not. Whether or not Warren shares orthodox belief in an order of beings superior to man, he certainly insists on the superiority of man to nonhuman nature. For him man is himself a supernatural being. Superior to nature, that is, but not aloof from it, as Adam Stanton tries to be. Tiny Duffy is of course his polar opposite. Unlike Duffy, who really is the surrenderer to history, to what is, to nature, Willie Stark has a marvelous and truly human gift for dominating nature. That is his greatness— which only abject believers in the sufficiency of the "common man" will dispute or regret. Yet, though Willie starts out as a lover of men, he is soon going to work on some of his fellows as if they were brute nature. "My God, you talk like Byram was human!" he shouts about someone he is "fixing," "he's a thing!" This is blasphemy against the divine in man, and Warren appropriately makes it the beginning of Stark's isolation and downfall. One recalls also how Jack Burden reached his lowest point. It was in his first marriage, not when it broke up ("as soon as I began to regard her as a person, trouble began") but earlier:

> as long as she was really a part of innocent non-human nature, as long as I hadn't begun to notice that the sounds she made were words, there was no harm in her . . .

"As long as I hadn't begun to notice . . ." Jack was a great one for not noticing. He had heard of Berkeley's philosophy while in college, decided that nothing was real if you didn't notice it, and called this decision his Idealism. It enabled him to stay outside of everything. His rebirth means, as much as anything, a willingness to step inside —to accept responsibility or (since Warren has a predilection for theological language) guilt. The book ends therefore when Jack gives up his narrator's, spectator's, role and resolves to go "into the convulsion of the world, out of history into history and the awful responsibility of Time."

These words are not pious verbiage. If Warren criticizes the mere politician and the master *realpolitiker*, he is equally critical of the idealist who wants to keep a corner of the world clean and is "above politics." Adam Stanton thinks of himself as a genuine champion of the ideal but he is really an idealist pretty much in Jack's sense—minus Jack's awareness of the implications and therefore minus Jack's cynicism. That certain unpleasant things have to be done doesn't matter to Adam as long as he doesn't have to know about them. Thus his sister, in the stage version, can quite rightly denounce him:

> Not *his* [Willie Stark's] vanity. But yours, yours now!
> Yours, for you'd make the world one thing and the
>   one
> Thing you, only the mirror's icy dream, and in dark-
>   ness;
> But the world is warm, and you in your ice-ease. . . .

Adam makes an exception of himself as much as Willie or the unregenerate Jack. He refuses to accept the common guilt, and is therefore doubly guilty. He is thus, in a way, a worse man than Willie Stark, a fact which some idealistic readers cannot be expected to relish.

Action is not something which will be *permitted* to Jack after his regeneration. It is something obligatory. It is dictated by his acceptance of responsibility. Politically, it seems, he will be a moderate liberal, for, speaking at the end of a rather practical reformer who had left Willie when Willie started "fixing" people, Jack declares: "It looks as though Hugh will get back into politics, and when he does I'll be along . . ." Jack is not *returning* to active life. He is taking it up for the first time. He *exists* for the first time. Previously he had lived through others—

especially through Willie. But now he is learning to understand Cass Mastern, who said: "It is human defect—to try to know oneself by the self of another." Interpreted politically, Jack's living by proxy puts him precisely in the position of the mobs who gladly let Willie do their living for them.

Not to live by proxy—this surely is a fundamental ideal of democracy; though Warren has been called fascistic. It may indeed be true that Warren is not as sanguine about democracy as some people are. Not that he is against it, but that as a student of human nature he is impressed with the fact that people still *want* to live by proxy. Defending demagogy after his fashion, Willie Stark, in the play, cries: "The *peepul!* The *peepul* is like a girl in her first hot—she may squeal but she loves it!" Warren is not taken in by big talk. But neither is he asking us or "the peepul" to accept the present situation. It is simply that one must not hope for automatic change or for total change. Like Gilbert Mastern, Cass' statesmanlike brother, one should only hope "to do a little justice in terms of the great injustice." One should remember always that no social conflict is ever a crusade—good cause and good men versus bad cause and bad men—because good and bad are always very mixed. "A man's virtue may be but the defect of his desire as his crime may be but a function of his virtue." This is not of course a complete political philosophy, let alone a program. But it is a poet's preface to politics. And today, when many are prepared to reconsider their basic attitudes—"our courage needs, perhaps, new definition"—Warren's books cannot but be pertinent.

v

At any rate, since they have to be taken as serious moral documents, they discredit the current academic view of "tough" American fiction. In a lecture attacking modern novelists *en masse,* Professor Douglas Bush of Harvard not long ago declared that

> the conflict within the individual, between his conscience and his natural self, has been often replaced by a conflict between the individual and social forces.

This may involve a struggle between good and evil, but it is more likely to show a poor creature destroyed by the environment that created him. Moral responsibility is more or less shifted from the individual to society.

What is there here that Warren does not know? Yet Warren, I am told, was included in Mr. Bush's spoken indictment. (His name does not appear in the published version, though Faulkner's does.) Mr. Bush finds modern novels to be "clinical reports on the crude or vicious lives lived by crude or vicious people." He adds: "Indeed we may ask if, in their preoccupation with the submoral, they [the modern novelists] are not cutting the ground from under their own feet, since the submoral level of experience cannot be the tragic level." He finds a formula for the modern novelist: "toughness plus sentimentality." And he expresses a strong preference for Shakespeare.

Well, Warren writes "tough" dialogue, and is capable of sentimentality. His five principal works to date—*Night Rider, At Heaven's Gate, The Ballad of Billie Potts, Proud Flesh*, and *All the King's Men*—are all murder stories in which neither the murderer nor the murdered are exactly —to use Mr. Bush's words—"noble characters, heroic examples." One might ask Mr. Bush how an artist should be inspired by our sordid world—our century of the all too common man—to portray nobility and heroism. How should he avoid that abstraction from the actual situation which is fatal to literature? After all we have the "noble characters, heroic examples" of socialist realism to warn us.

Mr. Bush's account of modern fiction is the familiar academic rejection of the whole naturalistic tendency in modern literature. (I refer now, not to philosophical naturalism, but to the literary naturalism which we associate with Zola.) Two false assumptions, I believe, are involved. The first is that literature can be moral only through the agency of heroic characters, edifying surroundings, elevated tone, and the like. The second is that naturalism— the naturalistic method, not only of Zola and his disciples, but of most modern fiction—implies amorality, not to say prosaic dullness, excessive and mere factuality. It is true that something like the second assumption—without the pejorative implications—underlies Zola's theoretical writings. It does not, however, underly his fiction or that of any modern novelist of rank. On the contrary, modern fiction, influenced as all of it is by naturalism, has found what Mr. Bush, if he chose, could regard as a moral equivalent of nobility, namely, a rich poetic symbolism. It is not that James or Lawrence or Proust or Faulkner "combine" naturalism with symbolism. It is that a naturalistic picture of things *becomes* symbolic if it is well enough done.

When Robert Penn Warren fails, as he sometimes does, it is not, as Mr. Bush's analysis suggests, because he is too naturalistic, but because he is not naturalistic enough. His symbolism is too often something superimposed. The vehicle which Warren devises to carry his meaning is not always as "natural," as "real," as it should be. The worst thing you can truthfully say about *All the King's Men* is that the almost Hollywoodian thriller which is Warren's vehicle is all too easily separable from his theme. That of course is why the book could be a best seller: the public read it *simply* as a thriller.

All the King's Men, the rumor now is, will be a Humphrey Bogart movie. A novel in which so much is derived from Hollywood is given back to Hollywood as to a mother. Consider Warren's characters. *Theatrical,* someone has called them. But Warren's brand of theatricality obviously owes more to the screen than to the stage. Adam Stanton is very much the nice but futile Hollywood professor, Sadie Burke the hard-boiled type, and so on. Stanton embodies an idea, a theme; he has a good deal of the "nobility" that Mr. Bush is after; what he lacks is the naturalness, the psychological reality, that the modern novelist is after.

If the symbolist in Warren seems not to submerge himself in the naturalist, the thinker in him seems not to submerge himself in the artist. Trite as it is nowadays to stigmatize an author as a dual personality, I cannot help pointing to a duality in Warren that may well constitute his major problem: it is his combination of critical and creative power. I am far from suggesting that the critical and the creative are of their nature antithetic and I am fully ready to grant that what makes Warren remarkable among American writers is his double endowment. The problem lies precisely in his being so two-sidedly gifted; he evidently finds it endlessly difficult to combine his two sorts of awareness. There is Warren the critic, the cosmopolitan, the scholar, the philosopher; and there is Warren the raconteur, the Kentuckyan, the humorist, the ballad maker. Sometimes the division becomes an overt formal separation within a work—*The Ballad of Billie Potts* is the obvious example. *Proud Flesh*, at its worst, wobbles awkwardly from one level to the other. *All the King's Men*, as I have suggested, suffers a good deal from incomplete fusion of theme and vehicle. The choice of such a smart aleck as Jack Burden for narrator may have unlocked Warren's marvelous store of humor, but it sadly limited his chances of rendering (without reporting, without too much explicit comment) his theme. And we cannot forgive all the fancy writing, as some critics do, merely on the grounds that the writer is supposed to be Burden and not Warren. Burden was chosen and created by Warren. Critics who write the exegesis of a great symbolic masterpiece with every detail in place are writing of the book Warren *ought* to have written, not of the one he wrote.

Warren is a faulty writer; but he is worth a dozen petty perfectionists. Though commonly associated with "formalists" and "classicists" in criticism, he is close to the type of romantic genius: robust, fluent, versatile, at his worst clever and clumsy, at his best brilliant and profound. On the other hand, he is remarkable for self-discipline. The pattern for the American novelist—Sinclair Lewis is the great example—is that he makes the best-seller lists with a youthful tour de force and spends the rest of his life trying to live up to his reputation. Warren did not write a full-length book between 1929 and 1939. He did not meet with the blandishments of the publicity racket till 1946; too late, I trust, for him to suffer from it. He reminds us of the possibility of a better sort of "American" writing than, say, Howard Fast's, a better sort of "Southern" writing than, say, Margaret Mitchell's. At a time when Americanism in writing suggests the ugly cultural nationalism of Van Wyck Brooks and regionalism suggests the ugly cultural provinciality that allows Dante and Shakespeare to be replaced on college curriculums by the poets of eastern South Dakota, it is very refreshing to find a good writer whom one may meaningfully call deeply American and genuinely regionalist. This means, paradoxically enough, that Warren is not *too* American and not *too* regionalist. He has room for the rest of the world, and I think the rest of world will have room for him. For if you start somewhere you may end everywhere, but if you start nowhere that is also where you will end.

CONTRIBUTORS

RENATA ADLER, a graduate of Bryn Mawr and the Sorbonne, is a staff writer for *The New Yorker*. Her essays and translations also have appeared in *Commentary, The Village Voice, Odyssey Review* and *Lebende Sprachen*.

WALTER ALLEN, the author of two major critical books, *The English Novel* (1954), and *The Modern Novel* (1964), has also written several novels. He was for many years a regular critic for *The New Statesman*.

A. ALVAREZ, a prolific young English essayist, has been poetry critic for *The Observer* (London). He has taught at American universities, and his books include *Stewards of Excellence* (1958) and *The School of Donne* (1961).

DONALD BARR, formerly on the faculty of Columbia University, is headmaster of the Dalton School in New York. He has written many articles on literature and education and two children's books on science.

WILLIAM BARRETT, Professor of Philosophy at New York University, was formerly an editor of *Partisan Review*. He is the author of *What Is Existentialism* (1947; revised, 1964), *Irrational Man* (1958) and numerous articles on philosophy and literature.

ROLAND BARTHES, an eminent French critic, has published several books, including *Mythologies* and *Le degré zero de l'écriture* (1953).

JOSEPH P. BAUKE, professor of German Literature at Columbia University, has written a biography of Christian Gottfried Kerner to be published in Germany in 1965. He contributes regularly to *Saturday Review* and *Germanic Review*.

ERIC BENTLEY, Brander Matthews Professor of Dramatic Literature at Columbia, has published *A Century of Hero Worship* (1944), *The Playwright as Thinker* (1946), *Bernard Shaw* (1947, revised 1957), *In Search of Theatre* (1953), *The Dramatic Event* (1954), and *What is Theatre?* (1956) and has edited numerous collections of classic and modern plays.

MAURICE BLANCHOT is primarily known for his critical works, which include *Faux-Pas* (1943), *La part du feu* (1949), *Lautréamont et Sade* (1949), *L'espace litteraire* (1955), and *Le livre à venir* (1959). Among his novels, all yet untranslated, are *Aminadab* (1942), *Thomas l'Obscur* (1950), and *L'attente, l'oubli* (1962).

JONATHAN COTT, a poet and critic, is a graduate of Columbia College, where he edited the *Columbia Review* and the *Spectator Literary Supplement*. He contributed "The New American Poetry" to *The New American Arts* (1964).

HARRIS DIENSTFREY has written on cinema and literature for *Commentary, Contact, Book Week, Film Culture* and other magazines. He wrote the essay on film in *The New American Arts*.

MANUEL DURAN, professor of Spanish at Yale, is the author of several books of Spanish poetry, including *Puente* and *Ciudad asediada*. He also edited and translated into Spanish an anthology of Italian poetry.

MARTIN ESSLIN, Assistant Head of the radio drama department of the British Broadcasting Corporation, has written *Brecht: The Man and His Work* (1960), *The Theatre of the Absurd* (1961), the sections on Raymond Queneau and Beckett for *The Novelist as Philosopher* (1962), and numerous articles.

RAYMOND FEDERMAN, professor of Foreign Languages at the University of California, Santa Barbara, has written *Samuel Beckett* (1964).

LESLIE A. FIEDLER, the eminent American critic, is Professor of English at Montana State University. His critical books include *An End to Innocence* (1955), *The Jew in American Fiction* (1959), *No! in Thunder* (1960), *Love and Death in the American Novel* (1960), *Waiting for the End* (1964); his fiction is *Pull Down Vanity* (1962) and *The Second Stone* (1963).

ANDREW FIELD, once an exchange scholar at Moscow University, has translated Fyodor Sologub's *The Petty Demon* (1962) and edited an anthology of contemporary Russian literature, *Pages form Tarusa* (1964). His reviews appear regularly in *The New Leader*.

JOHN GASSNER, Sterling Professor and Chairman of Playwrighting and Dramatic Literature at Yale University, has published *The Theatre in Our Times* (1954), other critical books and numerous anthologies of plays.

JACQUES GUICHARNAUD, Professor of French at Yale University, has written, with June Beckelman, *Modern French Theatre* (1961) and numerous articles and translations for French magazines.

IHAB H. HASSAN, Chairman of the Department of English at Wesleyan University, has written a critical study of contemporary American fiction, *Radical Innocence* (1961).

JOHN HOLLANDER, who teaches at Yale, is Poetry Associate for *Partisan Review*. His books include *The Untuning of the Sky* (1961), criticism; and *A Crackling of Thorns* (1958) and *Movie-Going* (1962), both poetry.

FRANCIS HOPE, formerly a Fellow in Modern History at All Souls College, Oxford, is Assistant Literary Editor of

The New Statesman. He writes regularly for several British magazines.

ELLIN HOROWITZ wrote an earlier essay on Ellison as a chapter of her senior thesis at Bennington College. The mother of three children, she has published in *Criticism, Carolina Quarterly* and other magazines.

IRVING HOWE, Professor of English at Hunter College, has published *The UAW and Walter Reuther,* with B. J. Widick (1949), *William Faulkner* (1952; revised, 1962), *Sherwood Anderson* (1953), *Politics and the Novel* (1957), *The American Communist Party,* with Lewis Coser (1958) and *A World More Attractive* (1963). He is the founder and editor of *Dissent.*

STANLEY EDGAR HYMAN, staff writer for *The New Yorker* and literary critic for *The New Leader,* has produced *The Armed Vision* (1948); *Poetry and Criticism* (1961); *The Tangled Bank* (1962), a study of Marx, Darwin, Fraser and Freud as imaginative writers; *Nathanael West* (1962); *The Promised End* (1963) and *Darwin for Today* (1963). A teacher at Bennington College, he is married to the novelist Shirley Jackson.

RANDALL JARRELL, who teaches at the Woman's College of the University of North Carolina, has published fiction, *Pictures from an Institution* (1954); poetry, *Losses* (1948), *Seven League Crutches* (1951), *Selected Poems* (1955), *The Woman at the Washington Zoo* (1960); and essays, *Poetry and the Age* (1953) and *A Sad Heart at the Supermarket* (1962).

S. BEYNON JOHN, who teaches French at The University of Sussex, Brighton, England, wrote *Sartre and the Moral Imagination* (1962).

ALFRED KAZIN, a prolific critic of American and contemporary literature, has written introductions to many books as well as *On Native Grounds* (1942), *The Inmost Leaf* (1955), *Contemporaries* (1962) and an autobiographical memoir, *A Walker in the City* (1951).

FRANK KERMODE, John Edward Taylor Professor of English at Manchester University (England), has written *Romantic Image* (1957; revised, 1963), *John Donne* (1957), *Wallace Stevens* (1960), and *Puzzles and Epiphanies* (1963).

ANNE KOSTELANETZ has written for *Arts, Book Week, Commonweal, Massachusetts Review* and other magazines. She holds degrees from Brown and Columbia Universities.

RICHARD KOSTELANETZ regularly contributes articles on contemporary literature to a variety of magazines, including *Contact, Progressive, Book Week, New York Times Book Review* and *Minnesota Review.* He edited *The New American Arts* (1964), contributing the essays on fiction and theatre.

RICHARD W. B. LEWIS, Professor of English at Yale University, is the author of *The American Adam* (1955) and *The Picaresque Saint* (1958). His reviews and essays appear frequently in several journals.

JACK LUDWIG, who teaches at State University of New York, Stony Brook, has written *Recent American Novelists* (1962), a pamphlet-length critical study; and *Confusions* (1963), a novel. He was co-founder and co-editor of *Noble Savage*.

FRANK O'HARA, on the staff of the Museum of Modern Art, has written numerous books on art, including *Jackson Pollack* (1959), and of poetry, *Meditations in an Emergency* (1957). *Try! Try!* and *Love's Labor: An Eclogue* are two of his plays.

SERGIO PACIFICI, a prolific critic of the literature of his native Italy, teaches at City University of New York. His books are *A Guide to Contemporary Italian Literature* (1962); *The Promised Land* (1957), an anthology of modern Italian poetry; and a projected critical history of the Italian novel.

JEAN PARIS, who has taught at Smith and other American universities, has published in French five critical studies— *Hamlet* (1952), *Shakespeare par lui-même* (1954), *Goethe dramaturge* (1955) *Joyce par lui-même* (1957) and a history of seeing, *L'espace et le regard* (1964). He also edited *Anthologie de la poesie nouvelle* (1957).

HENRI PEYRE, Chairman of the Department of French at Yale, has written scores of articles and several books. Among the latter are *Shelley et la France* (1935), *Le Classicisme Français* (1942), *Writers and Their Critics* (1944), *Les generations litteraires* (1948), *The Contemporary French Novel* (1955), and *Literature and Sincerity* (1963).

NORMAN PODHORETZ, the editor of *Commentary*, regularly writes book reviews for *Show*. Many of his pieces on the American scene are collected in *Doings and Undoings* (1964).

KENNETH REXROTH, the dean of bohemian men-of-letters, has published many books of poetry, plays, criticism, and he is finishing his autobiography. He also has translated the poetry of many oriental, classical and European languages, and more recently he has become a columnist for the *San Francisco Chronicle*.

RICHARD SCHECHNER, author of a forthcoming book on Ionesco, is editor of the *Tulane Drama Review*. Also a director, he has worked in many theatres across the nation.

ROBERT TAUBMAN, a Londoner presently living in France, is on the staff of the Division for Higher Education and Research of the Council of Europe. His reviews of current European literature appear frequently in *The New Statesman*.

JOHN RUSSELL TAYLOR, film critic for *The London Times,* writes on drama, film and television for many magazines. His books include *Anger and After* (1963), a guide to the new British drama; and *Cinema Ear, Cinema Eye* (1964).

WILLIAM YORK TINDALL, Professor of English, Graduate Faculties of Columbia University, has written *Forces in Modern British Literature* (1947; revised, 1956), *A Reader's Guide to Dylan Thomas* (1962), and several other books on English literature.

JOHN UNTERECKER, author of *A Reader's Guide to William Butler Yeats* (1959) and *Lawrence Durrell* (1964), teaches in the Graduate Faculties of Columbia University. He is finishing a critical biography of Hart Crane.

GORE VIDAL finished his first novel before he turned twenty and has written several more since, along with three plays and a book of essays, *Rocking the Boat* (1962).

SHIMON WINCELBERG devotes himself largely to imaginative writing. His fiction has appeared in *The New Yorker, Commentary* and *Best American Short Stories* (1953). His first play, *Kataki,* was included in *The Best Plays, 1958–9;* his second is *The Windows of Heaven* (1963).

GEORGE WOODCOCK, who founded and edited the journal *Canadian Literature,* has written books on *The Writer in Politics* (1950), *Anarchism* (1962), Oscar Wilde, Aphra Benn, Peter Kropotkin, India, Mexico, Western Canada and numerous other subjects. Also an active lecturer, he has taught at the University of British Columbia.

AVON ◆ For Important fiction

John Barth
END OF THE ROAD   GS2   **50c**
THE FLOATING
    OPERA   VS5   **75c**

James Purdy
MALCOLM   GC465   **50c**
THE NEPHEW   G1147   **50c**

Muriel Spark
ROBINSON   V2083   **75c**
THE GIRLS OF
    SLENDER MEANS V2095   **75c**

Isaac B. Singer
THE SLAVE   S140   **60c**
SATAN IN GORAY   G1171   **50c**
THE SPINOZA OF
    MARKET STREET G1152   **50c**